OTHER WORKS BY FITZHUGH DODSON, PH.D.

How to Parent

How to Father

The You That Could Be

How to Discipline with Love

I Wish I Had a Computer That Makes Waffles

How to Grandparent

The Carnival Kidnap Caper

Give Your Child a Head Start in Reading

FITZHUGH DODSON, Ph.D. & ANN ALEXANDER, M.D.

A FIRESIDE BOOK

YOUR CHILD

BIRTH TO AGE 6

SIMON & SCHUSTER, INC.
NEW YORK

A FIRESIDE BOOK
PUBLISHED BY SIMON & SCHUSTER, INC.
SIMON & SCHUSTER BUILDING
ROCKEFELLER CENTER
1230 AVENUE OF THE AMERICAS
NEW YORK, NEW YORK 10020
FIRESIDE AND COLOPHON ARE REGISTERED TRADEMARKS
OF SIMON & SCHUSTER, INC.
DESIGNED BY BONNI LEON
MANUFACTURED IN THE UNITED STATES OF AMERICA
10 9 8 7 6 5 4 3 2 1
LIBRARY OF CONGRESS CATALOGING IN PUBLICATION DATA
DODSON, FITZHUGH, DATE.
    YOUR CHILD.
    "A FIRESIDE BOOK."
    INCLUDES INDEX.
    1. INFANTS—CARE AND HYGIENE. 2. CHILDREN—CARE AND
HYGIENE. 3. CHILD REARING. I. ALEXANDER, ANN.
II. TITLE.
RJ61.D62 1986   649′.1   86-9903
ISBN 0-671-45894-9

ACKNOWLEDGMENTS

When it comes to writing a book, we have always believed that "No writer is an island."

This aphorism is most emphatically true for this book. This book would have been impossible to write without the research and clinical work of physicians, pediatricians, psychologists, psychiatrists, sociologists, anthropologists, and child development specialists. We have drawn liberally from whatever resources seemed helpful in understanding the physical, psychological, and intellectual development of the child from birth to the age of six. However, we have not cluttered this book up with endless footnotes because we feel that the more footnotes, the higher the level of reader boredom.

We would also like to thank the parents and children we have worked with over the years. They have taught us so much by sharing their experiences and insights with us.

We want to acknowledge some of the professionals whose contributions to the understanding of child development have greatly influenced us. We would especially like to mention Donald Stedman, Jim Sidbury, Arnold Gesell, Frances Ilg, Louise Bates Ames, Mary Ainsworth, Stella Chess, William Carey, T. Berry Brazelton, Jean Piaget, Erik Erikson, and Jerome Kagan. We are indebted to many colleagues for their suggestions and advice during the writing of this book: Charlie Mahan, Tonyo Bodo, David Smith, Lynette Lochausen, Jan Rodgers, Phoebe Williams, Amanda Baker, Polly Barton, Fonda Eyler, Helen and Torsten Andersen, Lois and Tim Oliver, Richard and Martha Andres, Sam Katz, and Cathy Wilfert.

Among the friends and colleagues we are most indebted to are our editors at Simon & Schuster, Angela Miller, Sona Vogel, and Barbara Gess, especially for their patience when the book suffered from growing pains; Jenny Gumpertz, our free-lance editor, who is superb and a delight to work with; and Dianne King, our wise and ever-helpful secretary. Our special thanks also to these people who so patiently assisted in the preparation of the manuscript: Dott Tyson, Lynda Kaiser, Collette Ralston, Kelly Alexander, and Connie Barnhill. Our thanks also to the readers of the original rough draft, Jerry and Joan Lachapelle and Robert Du Brow.

Without the help of all these wonderful people we could not have written this book.

Fitzhugh Dodson, Ph.D.
Ann Alexander, M.D.

To Mickey Marich, who many years ago directed her own nursery school when I was her pastor, and who first awakened my interest in child psychology and parent-child relationships.

Fitzhugh Dodson, Ph.D.

To Jim, my partner in parenting, for his continued love, support, and wisdom.

To Kelly, Katie, and Kimberly, our children, who continue to teach me the marvels of children and who have endured the writing of this book with patience, love, and support.

Ann Alexander, M.D.

C O N T E N T S

PART ONE
INTRODUCTION   15
   1 · What This Book Is All About   17
   2 · Yesterday's Child and Today's Child   22
   3 · Good News for Parents   24

PART TWO
INFANCY   33
   4 · Your Newborn Baby   35
   5 · An Overview of Infancy   51
   6 · The Technique of Breast Feeding   64
   7 · The Technique of Bottle Feeding   91
   8 · The Daily Care of Your Infant   102
   9 · Nutrition in Infancy   132
  10 · Discipline in Infancy   144
  11 · Intellectual Stimulation in Infancy   147
  12 · Special Situations in Infancy   158

PART THREE
TODDLERHOOD   177
  13 · Overview of Toddlerhood   179
  14 · Nutrition in Toddlerhood   194
  15 · Discipline in Toddlerhood   202
  16 · Intellectual Stimulation in Toddlerhood   209
  17 · Special Situations in Toddlerhood   215

PART FOUR
FIRST ADOLESCENCE   231
  18 · Overview of First Adolescence   233
  19 · Nutrition in First Adolescence   241
  20 · Discipline in First Adolescence   246
  21 · Intellectual Stimulation in First Adolescence   253
  22 · Special Situations in First Adolescence   257

PART FIVE
PRESCHOOL STAGE   271
    23 · Overview of the Preschool Stage   273
    24 · Nutrition in Preschool   293
    25 · Discipline in Preschool   296
    26 · Intellectual Stimulation in Preschool   308
    27 · Special Situations of the Preschool Stage   313

PART SIX
SPECIAL PARENTING SITUATIONS   327
    28 · The Mother Working Outside the Home   329
    29 · The Single Parent   339
    30 · Stepparents   346

PART SEVEN
TEN COMMANDMENTS FOR PARENTS   353
    31 · Ten Commandments for Parents   355

PART EIGHT
HEALTH CARE   359
    32 · The Well Child: Routine Health Care from Birth to Six Years   361
    33 · Health Problems in Early Childhood   375
    34 · First Aid   459

APPENDICES   471
    A · A Parent's Guide to Children's Toys   473
    B · A Parent's Guide to Children's Books   481
    C · A Parent's Guide to Children's Records   497
    D · A Parent's Guide to Books on Parenting   502
    E · A Parent's Toy Factory   507
    F · Medical Appendix   515

INDEX   521

TO OUR CHILDREN

May our children develop a sense of their own worth.

May they have the courage to be their true selves, as well as the wisdom to listen to the opinions of others.

May they recognize that the flowering of their feelings and affections is as important as the development of their intellect.

May they be strong enough to know when they are weak.

May they have the courage to win not only the victories of life, but also the defeats.

And give them a sense of humor so they can enjoy the foolishness and the foibles of human beings, including themselves.

Above all, let them be true to their own thoughts and feelings, for these are their most reliable guides.

PART 1

INTRODUCTION

1

WHAT THIS BOOK IS ALL ABOUT

This is a true story about a missing piece of information.

One summer the Dodson family decided to spend a two-week vacation back-packing in the high country of Yosemite National Park in mid-July. Our family has always had a love of backpacking and camping, but we had never been to the Yosemite high country. So in order to make sure our trip was a success, we spent a lot of time planning. We read several books to get information on the different trails we wanted to take, what kind of gear to bring, and so forth.

Unfortunately, we were missing one piece of information. None of the books we read informed us that the month of July is the height of the mosquito-breeding season in upper Yosemite!

The lack of this vital information put a huge dent in our vacation. After three days of being munched on by mosquitoes, we decided enough was enough. We packed up our gear and headed for the coast route to Oregon.

Raising children is a lot like that trip. You might start out thinking that all you need to be a good parent is to love your child. Then you quickly discover that besides love you also need information—and *enough* information to handle the job.

Just to take one example: You may have an enormous amount of love for your three-year-old child, and you may even know all sorts of things about nutrition. But if your child is choking on a piece of meat, all your love and knowledge aren't going to do a bit of good unless you know how to dislodge that meat from her throat.

So love alone is not enough. Love must be backed up by a sound knowledge of child care, child development, and child discipline in order for you to raise your youngster successfully.

There are four main kinds of information you will need to do a good job of parenting, and to help your child attain her maximum physical, psychological, and intellectual growth.

1. You will need medical information, so that you can safeguard your child's health and promote her maximum physical well-being.

For example, you should learn how to choose a doctor, and how best to communicate with him. Your brain does not have to be stocked with the same knowledge he has, but you must have enough medical information at your command to know when to call a doctor and what to do until help arrives. For example, it's important to be able to distinguish between a common garden-variety cold in a baby or small child and a more serious ailment that requires immediate medical attention. You should also know when a child's temperature is dangerously high and when prompt medical intervention is required.

2. You will need psychological and educational information, particularly about the five stages of psychological development from your child's birth to her sixth birthday. With this information you can help her successfully master the developmental tasks of each stage. For example, it is vital for you to know how to provide intellectual stimulation to your child in the first five years. You should be aware of the vast psychological differences between a two-year-old, a three-year-old, a four-year-old, and a five-year-old. You should be prepared to encourage the language development of your child in these crucial early years, and thus ensure that she has a head start not only in learning to read but in her intellectual development in general. It is helpful to know how to select for your child the kinds of toys, books, and records that will further her emotional and intellectual growth.

3. You will need to learn methods of discipline by which you can teach your youngster *desirable* behavior. Most parents are unaware that there are methods that not only teach good behavior but also help build the child's self-esteem and self-confidence. Examples of these methods are the positive reward system (Chapter 15), contracting (Chapter 25), the feedback technique (Chapter 20), and the Time Out (Chapter 15).

4. You will need to know another kind of discipline—the kind that teaches your child to avoid *undesirable* behavior. (Unfortunately the same techniques don't work for both types of behavior.) Too many parents rely exclusively on the yell-and-swat method. The best you can say about this approach is that it is woefully ineffective. The worst you can say is that it is badly damaging to a child's self-esteem. Also, do you really want to teach your child that yelling and hitting are the right way to treat others?

We doubt that any one professional person is qualified to guide parents in all aspects of childhood development. That's why this book is a team effort by two specialists: Ann Alexander, M.D., a physician who specializes in pediatrics and child development; and Fitzhugh Dodson, Ph.D., a psychologist who specializes in child psychology and parent-child relationships. Both of us are parents, so we speak to you "from the trenches" about raising children! Dr. Alexander is the mother of three girls, and Dr. Dodson is the father of a girl and two boys.

Throughout the book we give examples from our own families to illustrate various points. When we do this we use our initials (AA or FD) so you will know which of us is speaking.

We think it's important that this book has been written by a woman and a man, rather than by two men or two women. Mothers and fathers see things from somewhat different points of view. We think this difference in perspective is good for their children, and we feel it is valuable to incorporate both in a book such as this.

We have now quickly sketched a picture of what our book *is*. Let us also tell you what it is *not*.

1. It is *not* a book that tells you *the* one and only right way to bring up children. We are very suspicious of anybody who claims to have the only right way. The old maxim tells us that there's more than one way to skin a cat. And believe us, there's more than one way to raise a child.

There are two main reasons why this is true. First, no two children are the same, even in the same family. The child-raising methods that worked well with Martha may fail miserably with Roger. So the methods must be adjusted to the uniqueness of each child. Second, parents are as individual and different as their children, so there is probably no such thing as an ideal set of techniques that will fit all parents comfortably. We urge you to try our many different suggestions about child raising, even if some of them seem new and strange to you. If you find that a new method is helpful, by all means continue using it. But if it just does not feel comfortable and goes against your grain, drop it. A way of raising a child that does not fit your individual personality cannot be of any help to you.

2. It is not a book that underestimates the things you need to know in order to be a good parent. Good parenting is not just being a kind, loving person. If that were all that parenting is, you could rent a kind, loving baby-sitter at a low wage to do the job. No, good parenting is knowing about such things as the Cuisenaire Rods, the Indoor Gym House, the Dome Climber, syrup of ipecac, Children's Book and Music Center, Scholastic Books, what kind of toys are good and what kind are terrible (Appendix A), how to make your own toys for your child (Appendix E), the positive reward system (Discipline in Toddlerhood), the Time Out (Discipline in Toddlerhood), what you can expect of a typical two-year-old (Overview of First Adolescence) or a five-year-old (Overview of the Preschool Stage), how to get your child to pick up his toys (Discipline in First Adolescence), how to keep your child from getting caught in sex-role stereotypes, and how to handle the feelings of anger that you may experience from time to time when dealing with your child (Discipline in Toddlerhood).

3. It is not a book that is concerned only with your child now, when he is little. We also take a look at him as a future adult.

Most parents are like fire fighters running around putting out small fires—dealing with immediate and urgent events in their child's everyday life. They seldom take the time to look ahead to the future and the kind of adult that they hope their youngster will become. We want you to keep in mind the *big picture* of what you want your child to be. You want him to be psychologically healthy; you want him to be capable of caring deeply about others; you want him to be interesting and fun to be with; you want him to be successful and able to relate well to others; you want him to be honest and ethical; you want him not to get too discouraged when things don't turn out as he would like.

Well, he's going to be that kind of an adult only if he starts learning positive personality traits in his first five years of life. And you can help him learn.

4. It is not a theoretical book written in an ivory tower far away from the daily lives of parents and children. We didn't learn what we know solely from

our professional training in universities and medical schools. We learned much of it by raising our own children. We have written these pages, to paraphrase Winston Churchill, in parental blood, sweat, and tears.

We both wish we had had a book like this to read *before* we became parents. So we're giving you a chance to learn by our mistakes, as well as to profit from the smart things we did while we were raising our own kids.

A B O U T   T H E   A U T H O R S

Readers always want to know something about the author of a book they are reading, so let us tell you about ourselves.

Dr. Dodson: I am a psychologist with an A.B. from Johns Hopkins University, a B.D. from Yale University, and a Ph.D. from the University of Southern California. I have been in private practice as a psychologist for twenty-three years.

Before I became a parent, I used to be appalled and horrified at the terrible things parents did with their children. When I became a parent myself, I quickly ceased to be horrified. I remind myself of the story of the psychologist who started out with six theories and no children and ended up with six children and no theories. Since I have only three children, you can easily see that I have three theories left.

At the time of the writing of this book, my daughter is thirty, my older son is twenty-three, and my younger son is seventeen. All of them have taught me a great deal about what I will be talking about in this book.

Dr. Alexander: I have been a pediatrician for seventeen years. I want to underline what Dr. Dodson has said: Having children of my own has been one of the greatest learning experiences of my life. And it continues to be.

Growing up in a small oil-company camp in the jungles of Colombia, South America, as the oldest of six children, I knew at an early age that I wanted to work with children. By the time I was a teenager I had decided that I wanted to be a pediatrician. I have never been sorry about that decision. I thoroughly enjoy working with children and their parents.

My three daughters at the time of writing this book are thirteen, three, and one. They have supplied me with varied experiences in mothering.

I have both breast-fed and bottle-fed my babies. I've had two "easy-to-raise" girls and one who has been a challenge to me from the very beginning. I have both worked outside the home and stayed at home as a mother.

I spend my most enjoyable time with my kids, but they certainly leave me frazzled on many days! When I daydream of leisure it is of playing tennis or golf, swimming, or reading. Who knows—maybe I'll even get to take a cruise someday. Isn't that every mother's dream? No carpools, dentist appointments, dancing classes, laundry, or dirty dishes!

It's unfortunate that society does so little to give parents the vital information they need, particularly when they are becoming parents for the first time. We believe that someday high school courses in parenting will be as commonplace as courses in driver education. At this writing, only Utah has a law requiring every high school in the state to offer such a course. We also believe that sometime in the future evening courses in child raising will be available in college and adult-education classes throughout the entire country instead of in only a relatively small number of cities.

Until that day comes, we offer you this book. We sincerely believe that you will find in it everything you will need to raise your child to be healthy, happy, nonsexist, and capable.

2

YESTERDAY'S CHILD AND TODAY'S CHILD

THE CHANGING AMERICAN FAMILY

Many child-raising books seem to assume that the typical American family today consists of a breadwinner father, a homemaker mother, and their children. They give the impression that parents raise children in a house enclosed by a giant plastic bubble that seals them off from the rest of society.

Unfortunately these books tell parents how to raise *yesterday's* child, and have little to do with the actual American family today. What parents really need is a book that tells them how to raise *today's* child!

The number of mothers in the work force is increasing every year, so that today, half of all women with children under three and 70 percent of women whose youngest child is six to thirteen years old are working outside the home. And the percentage is increasing each year.

Mothers are no longer the only adults who take care of children. Now grandparents or other relatives, paid individual caretakers, day-care centers, and nursery schools are often the "mothers" of children during the day.

The divorce rate continues to soar, and with it the number of single-parent homes. One out of every eight children in the United States now lives in a single-parent home. Demographers predict that one-half of the couples married during the 1970s will eventually divorce, and estimate that four out of ten children born in the 1970s will live in a single-parent home during part of their childhood. With remarriage, it has been estimated that soon one out of every six children in the United States will be a stepchild.

In fact, only about 7 percent of the American population comes from what is perceived to be the typical American family: a breadwinner father, a homemaker mother, and children.

THE CHANGING ROLES OF MEN AND WOMEN

Moreover, the roles of men and women, fathers and mothers, are changing rapidly. The women's movement is opening up many more job options for women already in the work force, and young women today are being presented with a much wider spectrum of vocational choices. More and more people are demanding that sexism be stamped out of everything in our society from hiring practices to school textbooks.

Men's roles are changing almost as rapidly as women's. Men are increasingly liberating themselves from confining sexual stereotypes in which they are not free to be nurturant of babies and small children, to cry, or to show "weakness." Fathers are taking on child-care roles that formerly belonged only to mothers.

It is highly unfortunate that so many child-raising books do not acknowledge the diverse shapes of today's American family.

For example, although some child-care books pay lip service to nonsexism, hardly any offer specific guidelines to tell you how to raise a son or daughter to be free and nonsexist. You won't even find the words "sexist" or "nonsexist" in the index.

Even though some books mention divorced parents, hardly any mention stepparents. In most books stepchildren and stepparents simply do not exist.

The great psychologist William James used to characterize books that he felt were divorced from real life as having "the smell of the library" about them. Our book emphatically does not have the smell of the library about it. It deals with real life: a young mother who is worried because her baby's breathing sounds "funny"; a parent who has lost his temper and thrown a book across the room because his two-year-old is unmanageable; fathers and mothers who quarrel about how to get the baby to stop crying; parents who discover that children sometimes get in the way of sex; wonderful moments watching the antics of a toddler; that awful time when your child first encounters prejudice; separations, divorces, affairs; special times of closeness with your child; the desperate loneliness of the single parent; trying to put a blended family together and discovering all the underground networks of sibling rivalry among children, stepchildren, natural parents, and stepparents.

All these are part of family life in America today. We may wish that they were not, but because they are, the family must learn to cope with them in some way. The aim of our book is to help you. We write about real American families, in all of their dimensions. We "tell it like it is," to help you and your children cope with the real world. And where the real world is deficient, we want to help you try to make it better.

3

GOOD NEWS FOR PARENTS

A lot of people tend to pan parenthood. They say that being a parent is not all it's cracked up to be, that children run you ragged, ruin your marriage, and in general aren't worth the trouble it takes to raise them.

Well, parenting *is* difficult for some people. Why? It's nearly always because they just aren't trained for the job. There are too many things that they don't know—things that would help them be happy and successful as parents.

So before we get into the nitty-gritty of daily care of your baby, we want to give you a set of facts and a philosophy of child raising that are truly good news for parents.

1. All parents make mistakes! How do you think people like auto mechanics, lawyers, CPAs, and chemists learned the complex skills of their trades? By making mistakes! How does anybody learn the skills required for golf, tennis, or bridge? By making mistakes! It is obvious that no one changes his status from amateur to pro without going through a process in which he makes many mistakes. For example, ask any lawyer what his first two years in practice were like. As one remarked, "Boy, if my colleagues knew how many mistakes I made in my first two years I would probably have been disbarred!"

Unfortunately, many parents don't allow for making mistakes in their child raising. There are many reasons for this. For one thing, they often underestimate the complex skills required to be an effective and happy parent. They think that all they need is love and common sense. Then when they don't know how to stop their six-month-old baby from crying or get their two-year-old to go to bed, they panic and feel like failures.

Other parents, who are perfectionists, find it's not as easy to be a perfect parent as it is to be perfect in their job or their housekeeping. It's a lot easier to manage other adults or inert objects than to manage very young, lively children who do not always behave rationally or respond to commands.

Any baseball player who is a consistent .300 hitter will have no trouble landing a job on a major league team. What this means is that he makes a hit three out of ten trips to the plate. No baseball player has ever batted 1.000. That would be perfection. Baseball players are realistic about this. They know that three out of ten is excellent.

Many parents are not as wise as baseball players. They too should give themselves credit for batting three out of ten, instead of berating themselves for making mistakes.

By the way, it is such high expectations that can make the life of a single parent so difficult. A parent in an intact family may be no more skilled than a single parent, but she has a spouse to talk over her mistakes with. The single parent may have a good friend to talk to, but she doesn't have a live-in sounding board. This is one of the reasons we advocate that single parents organize into groups of five or six and meet once a week to talk over the special problems of single parenting. (We will discuss this further.)

At any rate, we suggest that you make allowance for mistakes as you grow and mature in your parenting skills. Each stage of child development will afford you a chance to make new mistakes! But we will help you to avoid some of the pitfalls and to learn and grow through your mistakes.

2. *One mistake won't traumatize your child for life.* Both of us encounter parents who are worried about something they have done, and ask "Do you think that's going to affect Jerry for life?" Our answer is always the same: A single action is not going to cause a child to be traumatized for life. We don't know where people get this mistaken notion, but many seem to have it. Perhaps it comes from watching TV shows based on the kind of erroneous pop psychology in which a psychoanalyst unearths a single traumatic incident which the patient has repressed from childhood, and thus cures his neurosis. In actuality, a neurosis is hardly ever caused by a single traumatic scene but by a number of such incidents and parental mishandlings.

So please relax. It takes time and effort to traumatize your child for life. Chances are that you have not yet invested either enough time or enough effort to do the job. All you have done is commit an N.P.B. (Normal Parental Blooper). Welcome to the club!

3. *You are not 100 percent responsible for the way your child turns out as an adult.*

Many parents seem to believe that their newborn child is like a completely clean blackboard, on which his environment, mainly the parents, writes. Therefore they feel a heavy burden of responsibility. They believe that when he is an adult that blackboard will be covered with what they have written on it.

A doleful picture and, fortunately, one that is false.

The truth is that each child is *not* born as a clean blackboard. Each child comes into the world already equipped with a primitive sort of personality—his basic biological temperament or behavior style. Drs. Stella Chess, Alexander Thomas, and Herbert Birch have shown that babies can be classified according to nine different aspects of behavioral style, such as activity level, intensity of reaction, distractibility, and persistence.

My two sons (FD) are classic examples of the way children in the same family are different from birth. Both have the same genetic background, both were boys, both were bottle-fed. And yet their personalities were quite different from the day they were born.

This was easy to see, for example, when they woke up in the morning to be fed.

Randy, my older, would wake up at 5:00 or 5:30 A.M. and let out a piercing cry that could be heard for blocks. And he would continue to cry at this volume until he got his bottle.

Rusty, my younger, woke up like one of those alarm clocks that purrs softly and then gets louder and louder, until finally you have to get up and shut it off.

First he'd wake up and move around in his crib a little. Then after about ten minutes he would begin a very soft, gentle cry. He would cry that way for about forty or forty-five minutes, and then he'd begin to bellow lustily. Now you knew he really wanted his bottle. But from the time he first woke up to the time he yelled for his bottle nearly an hour had elapsed.

Since these quite different patterns occurred in their first weeks of life, they obviously were not caused by their environment, but were due to two different biological temperaments.

What does the existence of a biological temperament mean to you as parents? For one thing, it means that not all children are equally easy to raise.

My (FD) daughter was a very easy-to-raise child. She was fun to be with, cooperative, and a born diplomat even at an early age. I remember an incident when she was five. We were driving out toward the small town of Hemet, California, in the spring and it was hot and dusty. Robin said to me, "Daddy, if you're hot and thirsty you could get a cool, refreshing milk shake at that Frostee Freeze down the road!"

Who needs a lot of brains to raise a sweet, easy-to-get-along-with child like that? If Robin had been my only child I would probably not be writing this book today. But my two boys taught me that not all children are as easy to get along with and as eager to please as Robin.

When we speak of a more difficult temperament in a child, we don't mean a child who is malicious or evil. We simply mean one who is so exuberant and dynamic and fast moving that it's hard for the average parent to keep up with him.

Kevin is a nine-year-old I (FD) gave a Rorschach inkblot test to not long ago. I had gotten to the very end of the test, where I hand him the inkblot cards and ask him to make up a title for each. He looked up at me and said, "I refuse to do that."

"What do you mean, 'refuse to do that'?"

"Just what I said. I'm not going to do it."

"Do you mind telling me why?"

"Sure. It's stupid, and I'm not going to do it."

In twenty years of testing children, I had become accustomed to their doing what I asked them to do. If they didn't like some part of a test they would usually say things like, "I've got a headache," or "I just can't figure out that one," or "My stomach hurts."

Not a single child had ever come out flat-footed and said, "I refuse to do that." I took this as a challenge and tried my best to coax Kevin into giving the titles. It was soon clear that he was not a child who would let himself be coaxed.

The next thing I knew he had gotten up from his chair, darted around my desk, and was confronting me. "Listen, Dr. Dodson," he said, "I need to sit in your chair and you need to sit in my chair, because I'm the president here and you're the vice president and that makes me the boss!" I decided to forget about getting him to give up the titles and devoted myself instead to getting him to sit back down in his chair.

Now Kevin was not a mean or hostile child. He was just a child who liked to have his own way at certain times. And I could now empathize much more with his mother, who had told me, "There are times when I could kill that kid!"

And yet there was something enormously likable about Kevin. Somehow you just had to admire his determination and derring-do. Of course it was easier for me to admire these qualities during an hour's interaction with him in testing than it was for his mother and father, who had to interact with him six hours a day during the week and fourteen hours a day on weekends. I ended up summarizing my psychological evaluation of Kevin to his parents as follows: "I predict he will either end up president of the United States or be hanged as a horse thief! He's a child with great talents and a compelling, dynamic personality. Most discipline techniques don't work easily with an unusual child like Kevin at this age. Just grit your teeth and hold on!"

So if you have a child who is like Kevin you will need to be very easy on yourself as a parent. If you can shape him into a reasonable facsimile of a co-operative human being, give yourself an A as a parent!

4. It's OK to take vacations from being a parent. In fact, it's more than OK; it's definitely prescribed!

It's a simple psychological law of life that if we don't take regular vacations from our jobs we grow stale, and end up spending a lot of unproductive time on the job, feeling grouchy and irritable.

It's amazing that many parents take regular vacations from their jobs but don't take holidays from parenting. This is especially true of mothers who have no outlets. Just an afternoon or evening away can help you come back with a fresh outlook.

It's OK to attend to your needs as a couple. It's important to relate to each other as husband and wife or as lovers, not just as mother and father.

If you can arrange it, get a baby-sitter and have evenings out, weekends away, or even longer vacations when possible. How often and how long you can take are individual matters depending on your family situation, economic circumstances, and life-style.

Your parents-only vacations should have a good effect on your parenting when you get back. They should also have a good effect on your marriage. And they are good for your kids, too, because they get practice in interacting with someone besides their parents.

5. It's normal for a parent from time to time to feel incredible depths of anger toward a child. Unfortunately, books on child raising typically do not tell parents this. So when parents discover these feelings of rage within themselves, they feel terribly guilty.

We want to say two things about the anger parents feel toward their children. First, it is real; it happens to many parents. One book on child raising speaks of it being normal for parents to feel "annoyed" with their children from time to time. *Annoyed,* my foot! *Enraged* is more like it. So when you find yourself feeling hatred toward your own flesh and blood, don't think you are an awful parent. You're only being normal.

Second, these feelings of rage are typically experienced when your children are frustrating you in some way. But if you have learned a full repertoire of parenting skills, you are much less likely to react negatively. The less you know about parenting skills, the more frequently you are going to find yourself painfully stymied by your child.

6. *It's normal for you to be inconsistent and irrational in your parenting.* We often hear parents criticize themselves for being "inconsistent." But we point out that there is no parent alive who is 100 percent consistent. Consistency is an ideal for us to strive for, not an absolute goal we must reach every day.

There's a very simple reason why all of us are sometimes erratic or irrational or contradictory. Our feelings and moods change from day to day, and even within the same day. And when moods and feelings change, consistency goes out the window. The true consistency that is vital to success in handling children depends upon being reasonably "up front" with our true feelings. For example, if we put on a facade of being loving when we are in fact feeling angry, we will be doing our children a disservice—for our actions will not match our feelings. But if we act angry when we feel angry, then we are being emotionally consistent, and our children will know exactly where they stand with us.

7. *You parents have the unique opportunity of raising the level of your child's intelligence in the first five years of her life.* This may sound like nonsense, but we assure you it is true.

Each child is born with a different intellectual potential. To oversimplify things, we can say that some children are born with average intelligence, some with above-average intelligence, and some with below-average intelligence. Remember, we are speaking about the *potential* intelligence of the child—the intellectual level it is *possible* for her to reach. This potential is determined by her genes.

The intellectual level that she actually does reach is called her *operating* intelligence. And the more stimulation a child's mind receives in the first five years of her life, the closer she will come to operating at her full intellectual potential.

Take an imaginary case. A child is born with an above-average intellectual potential, but her environment does nothing to stimulate and develop her intellect. Another child is born with average intelligence, and her environment is stimulating and rich. Her intellectual potential is still average, but she may function at a higher level than the first child—because the first child's environment did little to help her develop her high potential.

Too many children do grow into adulthood operating on only part of their intellectual power. Dr. Benjamin Bloom of the University of Chicago has amassed an overwhelming body of evidence to show that a child develops approximately 50 percent of her adult intelligence by the age of four, another 30 percent between four and eight, and the final 20 percent between eight and seventeen.

Please don't confuse intelligence with information. Obviously a four-year-old does not possess 50 percent of the information she will have as an adult. Her *intelligence* is the ability of her computer brain to process information coming into it, and to use it to solve problems in the environment. And that's what the child develops 50 percent of by the age of four.

Consider the following facts, which dramatically demonstrate how bright young children are.

When babies all over the world are babbling at about six months, the babbles sound pretty much the same. *Goo-goo* and *nyah-nyah* and stuff like that. Six-month-old German babies and Chinese babies and Russian and English and Italian and Spanish and Japanese babies all sound pretty much the same when they babble.

Here is the proof of the incredible intelligence of young children. By the time these babies, from all over the world, are two or two and a half, they have learned to talk the language of the country in which they are living. This is really an incredible feat, which parents may not notice.

And when you think about how babies learn languages, what is even more extraordinary is that *nobody taught them.* They taught themselves. They listened to the adults and older children around them, and they figured out the logical structure of the language and began to speak it. That's an amazing intellectual feat! Mankind has not yet been able to invent a computer that can do what little babies all over the world do easily and naturally. Fantastic!

Now does it seem more believable that children between birth and six are as smart as we say they are?

Who is going to stimulate your child's marvelous computer brain, with its great potential, during the first five years of her life? You can. Her very first school is called Home University, and you are her most influential teacher.

So one of the best bits of good news we bring you is the great and glorious fact that by wise intellectual stimulation of your child in the first five years of her life, *you* can raise her intelligence level closer to her potential. And you can have a wonderful time doing it, too!

In this book we teach you step by step exactly how to stimulate your child's developing mind. We tell you which educational toys will improve her intellect, and which kinds of toys are shoddy and worthless. We also give you guidance about books, records, and tapes that will help you with your child in Home University. We don't offer you vague ideas; we give you specific, down-to-earth suggestions.

Let us close this section by telling you about some mothers who were outstandingly successful at teaching their children at home in their first five years. This example comes from the research of Dr. Dolores Durkin, a renowned specialist in the field of early reading.

Dr. Durkin was curious about which factors were responsible for children learning to read early, before being exposed to any formal instruction in school. She scientifically designed two research studies, one in California and the other in New York, in which she studied children who had learned to read at least eighteen basic words before they entered first grade, compared with children who had not.

In both studies she tested the reading achievement of the children through several grades. She found that, for the most part, the early readers *stayed ahead* of the other children, grade by grade.

But that wasn't the main thing Dr. Durkin wanted to find out. She wanted to know what was different about the early readers that enabled them to read before they entered school. Her findings were astounding. Dr. Durkin found that there was essentially *no difference* between the early-reading children and the nonearly readers. The difference was not in the children themselves, but in their parents—specifically their mothers. *The mothers of the early readers had provided a more intellectually stimulating environment for their children than the mothers of the other children.*

And what did the mothers of the early readers do that stimulated their children's minds? They didn't use a curriculum, buy reading programs, or give formal lessons. Here are just a few examples.

- They read to their children a great deal, beginning very early.
- They had many materials around the house that stimulated their children's interest in writing: books, a blackboard, paper and pencils, and felt pens. These were "paper and pencil" kids.
- They stimulated their children's curiosity about the meaning of words—on trips to stores, at playgrounds or zoos, watching TV at home, and at other everyday places.
- They took the time to explain the meaning of words to their children. And they "taught" their children when their children expressed an interest, not at some predetermined time.

And there were other differences between the two groups, which could even be called differences in the life-styles of the mothers.

For example, both groups of mothers might take their preschool children shopping with them to the supermarket. But the mother of a child who did not read early might concentrate entirely on buying groceries. She tended to perceive her child as a nuisance who was interfering with getting the shopping done fast and efficiently. But the mother of an early reader had an entirely different attitude. She had fun with her child. She would make shopping into an adventure for her preschooler. She would say things like, "Look here. Let's see what these words say on the cereal boxes. This one says Oatmeal, and that one says Corn Flakes, and that one says Cheerios." Everywhere she and the child went she would call her attention to words connected with where they were and what they were doing.

Dr. Durkin's research clearly shows the power of early intellectual stimulation in helping your child become successful in school. This is thrilling because it means *you* can make a tremendous difference in your child's success in school and later life.

A note of caution: There are many mothers who exert enormous pressure on their preschoolers to achieve intellectual goals that are far beyond them. You might hear one, for example, in a bookstore, saying things like, "I heard there's a book that tells you how to start teaching your child to read at the age of eleven months. Do you have that book? Because my child's a year old already and I want to get her started!" Ridiculous! Teach an eleven-month-old baby to read? Why not teach her trigonometry at age three?

So we hope you won't join the ranks of these pushy mothers. They are doing neither themselves nor their children any good by exerting enormous pressure to achieve impossible intellectual feats at an early age. Instead, adopt an attitude and family life-style that will stimulate your child's developing intellect in a way that is low key, leisurely, and fun for her.

8. It is good news for parents that they can mold a happy and self-confident personality for their child during the first five years of life. Perhaps we should be more precise and say that parents can mold their child's personality *within limits.*

The limits are those set by the biological temperament with which your child is born. If, for example, she is an assertive, strong-willed youngster, you can teach her to be courteous and self-disciplined—you can shape and mold certain aspects of her personality. But you cannot change her basically strong will and her need to assert herself. On the other hand, if your child is rather shy and quiet, you can mold her to be more gregarious and outspoken, but her basic temperament will still be there, and she may always be somewhat on the shy side.

Most personality traits of adults are learned in childhood. Furthermore, most of them are learned in the first five years of life! By personality traits we mean such things as self-esteem, assertiveness, warmth, self-confidence, ability to be open and genuine in one's feelings, thoughtfulness, and perceptiveness as far as other people are concerned.

These facts are particularly important to fathers. Fathers want to be proud of their children when they are grown. They want them to be self-confident, assertive, warm persons with good self-esteem. Yet oddly enough, most fathers unwittingly arrange not to be around at the crucial times when their sons and daughters are learning these personality traits! Many fathers have little to do with their children when they are very young. As one father put it, "I'll be glad when my boy gets to be six. He's only three now, and I don't know what to do with him except put him on my knee and play horsie. But when he gets to be six I can teach him to play baseball and go fishing and do lots of things with him."

Poor deluded father! Like so many other fathers, he doesn't realize that by the time his child is six, he will have had no part in teaching his youngster the personality traits he would like him to have when he is an adult. The sad fact is that in many homes throughout the United States it is only the mother who teaches children the personality traits they will bear throughout their lives.

But if the father is AWOL as a teacher in his child's first five years, the mother is not in a much better position, because she may not have had training in how to help shape her child's personality.

So we are going to give both of you parents a crash course in how to teach desirable personality traits to your youngster before she is six. These are the kinds of things you will want her to learn:

- To be persistent instead of giving up easily.
- To have high self-esteem instead of low self-esteem.
- To be thoughtful instead of selfish.
- To be able to express her feelings instead of keeping them locked up inside.
- To be self-assertive instead of shy.
- To be hard-working instead of lazy.
- To be honest instead of deceitful.

You can start teaching your child these things beginning at birth, and we will tell you **how.**

PART 2

I N F A N C Y

4

YOUR NEWBORN BABY

If you have never seen pictures or movies of newborn babies, or if you have a vision of the Gerber baby, you may be in for a shock when you first behold your own new baby. When she is born she will be covered with a greasy white coating called *vernix*. Remember that she has been swimming around in fluid for nine months, and her skin has needed protection (very much like that of swimmers who try the English Channel). Her face may be puffy, and her head may be somewhat misshapen. Her coloring may be red, with bluish hands and feet. Some parents think their newborn baby is beautiful, but others are disappointed. This is not an uncommon reaction. Sometimes it takes days for parents to feel that their child is beautiful. So don't feel guilty if you aren't elated when you first see your baby.

Some mothers have said that they were disappointed because they did not have a great surge of maternal love when they first saw their babies. This too is normal.

CHARACTERISTICS OF THE NEWBORN

SKIN

A newborn baby's skin is normally pink to red in color, but the feet and hands are usually bluish for the first two or three days. This is due to sluggish circulation and is nothing to worry about. The skin is covered with the vernix, which comes off in the bath but may still be present in the folds around the ears and buttocks. If the baby has been delivered by forceps, there are usually red marks on the face just in front of the ears. These may range from very mild coloring to slight scratches or even black-and-blue marks. They usually resolve within two or three days and are nothing to be concerned about. Over the nose and cheeks you might see some tiny yellow or white spots very much like whiteheads, which are the collection of oil from the sebaceous glands. They too will disappear in time.

There are many types of blotches or marks on the skin of a new baby that might alarm a new mother, even though they are nothing to worry about. For example, the newborn baby has a very reactive skin, and she will develop large red blotches in areas where she is handled. She may also mottle when she cries or becomes chilled. This effect disappears after several months. There is a rash (of unknown cause) commonly seen in newborns, which lasts for several weeks and disappears. It consists of red blotches with small, white, raised centers. The rash appears generally on the face, neck, and trunk and may look scary, but is nothing to worry about. Some babies also develop a sort of acne of the new-born. In fact they may have what looks like pimples all over their faces. These blemishes are probably caused by the mother's hormones during pregnancy. They will disappear with time. Some babies are born with slate blue, well-demarcated areas of pigmentation over the back and buttocks. These will disappear during the first year of life.

Prickly heat is common in both newborn and older babies. It is caused by trapped sweat, which creates a mild inflammation. It looks like small pinpoint pink blotches, with slightly raised, whitish centers, which may even have tiny blisters on them. Prickly heat comes and goes but is usually seen in the areas around the neck where most sweating occurs. It doesn't really bother the baby, and the best treatment is to keep her cool. A cornstarch powder can help in very hot or humid climates.

H A I R

The baby may be covered with a soft fuzz, especially on the lower back and sometimes over the forehead. This will disappear during the first few weeks. It is more marked in the premature baby and almost never seen in the post-mature baby. An infant may be born with almost no hair or lots of hair. Baby hair is seldom curly but may be wavy. It usually falls out gradually, and the new hair growing in may bear no resemblance to the original.

H E A D

A baby's head is always large in comparison with the rest of her body. If a baby is delivered by Cesarean-section or is a breech delivery her head may be beautifully shaped. Most babies, however, are born in the headfirst position and their heads show it. The head and face may be quite puffy from the baby's having been upside-down for some time, which causes edema (accumulation of water in the tissues). There may also be some molding (misshaping of the skull and face), because the baby's head is softer and more pliable now than later in life. The skull bones are not joined together, so they can be moved. Depending on where in the pelvis the baby's head has been, and for how long, she may be born with an asymmetrical skull and face. These features will straighten out after a few days. Even if the jaw and the nose are skewed off to one side and the skull seems pointed in the back, don't worry. All will shape up.

When you touch the head you will feel a soft spot right in the middle of the skull, where the bones of the head have not yet met. This spot is covered with a fibrous tissue and it is perfectly safe for anyone, including siblings, to touch it. The bones will gradually come together in that spot, and it will become hard sometime between six to eighteen months. In most babies there is also a much smaller soft spot in the midline toward the back of the head. It closes in the first few months. These spots are called *fontanelles*. When the baby is quiet the fontanelle may seem sunken, but when she cries the spot may seem to bulge slightly. The pulsation of the heart may also be observed in the fontanelle. The veins on the head appear quite prominent, because of the thinness of the baby's skin.

Some babies are born with a temporary palsy of the nerve to the facial muscles because of a difficult delivery. This will result in the baby's appearing to have a rather crooked smile and in not being able to open one eye on the affected side. This condition is almost always temporary, but we suggest you ask your doctor about it.

A more common type of minor injury is a rounded bulge on the scalp known as a cephalohematoma, which is due to bruising of the head in its passage through the birth canal. Soft and usually an inch or more in diameter, the cephalohematoma is similar to a bruise and is the result of a small torn scalp vein, which caused blood to collect between the scalp and the skull bone. It is gradually absorbed in two to three weeks and leaves no permanent problems.

E Y E S

During the first hour after delivery the baby's eyes will be wide open, looking around at her new environment (an important reason to withhold eye medication for the first few hours—you can request this). Her favorite target will be your face. It is one of the most fantastic feelings in the world when the two of you have your first eye contact! Your baby can see you and will follow you with her eyes. You will immediately become aware of what a real person this little individual is. After the first hour, however, babies usually become rather sleepy, probably because of exhaustion after their difficult journey. If you have had medication during labor and delivery, the sleepiness may be more marked because the baby feels the effects of the drug.

Once the eye medications have been given (most states require eye medication in order to prevent a certain type of infection), your baby's eyelids may swell and there may be a yellowish discharge. This will disappear in four to five days.

Dark-skinned babies may have dark eyes, but almost all light-skinned babies have blue eyes at birth, and six months may pass before the true eye color is established. Some babies (30 to 50 percent) have tiny hemorrhages in the whites of the eyes, and the pupils may appear unequal for a few weeks. Many infants are born with what seems to be little extra pieces of skin in the inner corner of each eye. Because these come over the eye somewhat, you may get the impression that your baby has crossed eyes. If you are concerned, just check with your doctor.

As we have said, your newborn baby can definitely see and may choose different images to look at. She can see best when things are about nine to fifteen inches from her eyes, and she is especially interested in the human face and bright colors. She can follow a bright red object from side to side even in the newborn nursery. She reacts to light and seems to dislike bright lights, especially in the first few days of life. Often babies like to keep their eyes closed. If you particularly want your baby to look at you, as most parents do, you can get her to open her eyes by holding her in an upright position and tipping her slightly backward or forward. She will open her eyes because of a reflex action that nearly all babies have.

E A R S

The newborn baby's ears may be folded because of positioning in the uterus. They will straighten out in a month or two. The baby can hear and will turn her head from side to side when she is aware of a sound. A newborn prefers relatively high-pitched and complex tones, such as those of the human voice. A mother almost instinctively speaks to her newborn in a rather high-pitched voice though she may not even be aware she is doing it.

N O S E

As we mentioned previously, the nose may be pushed off to one side because of the position of the baby in utero, but it will straighten out with time. A baby breathes through her nose rather than her mouth, for the obvious reason that while she is sucking she needs to continue to breathe. Some babies are born with a blockage in the nasal passage. This can result in breathing difficulties but is usually easily corrected. If you are concerned about your baby's breathing, be sure to contact your doctor.

M O U T H

Some babies are born with teeth. These are extra teeth, which are shed before the deciduous, or "baby," teeth come in. If the extra teeth are loose or interfere with nursing, they can be removed.

The baby's tongue appears large and may stick out slightly. She will grow into her tongue with time—don't worry. A baby may also have a short cord under the tongue that seems to hold the tongue down (tongue-tied) and may make the tip of the tongue appear to be slightly heart shaped. The cord will usually stretch with time and does not require clipping.

N E C K

A baby's neck is always short. In fact, it seems to be almost nonexistent, making her look somewhat like a football player. Sometimes one of the muscles along the side of the neck becomes bruised in delivery, or in the uterus before birth or during labor, resulting in the baby's having a wry neck, with the head pulled off to one side. This condition does require some treatment, usually a form of physical therapy to loosen the muscle and allow her head to turn freely from side to side.

C H E S T

The newborn baby often has breast enlargement, which is due to the mother's hormones. The breasts may even secrete a little milk. This phenomenon usually disappears over the first month, but may persist for up to a year. It is important that you do not squeeze or push on the baby's breasts when they are like this, because you might cause an infection.

When looking at the chest you may notice a small bone that seems to stick out at the bottom of the breastbone. It is called the *xiphoid* and is a separate, distinct little bone. This is a normal condition and will become less noticeable as the baby grows.

The baby's abdomen nearly always protrudes slightly. There may be a space between the two middle muscles that run from the breastbone to the navel. It is especially common in prematures. Usually as the baby grows these muscles come together and there will be no problem, but sometimes an umbilical (navel) hernia develops later in life.

The umbilical cord is the most predominant part of the newborn's abdomen. It is shiny and moist at birth and will have a clamp or tie around it. The cord gradually shrivels, dries, and falls off—usually from ten to twenty days after birth. It is important that the umbilical cord be kept dry and that the diapers do not cover it.

A B D O M E N

If your new baby is a boy his scrotum may seem huge, especially if he has been born in breech position. Just as the baby's head is swollen if he is born headfirst, his bottom is swollen if he is born bottom first. The penis is covered with a thin shaft of skin called the foreskin, which cannot be retracted in the newborn. It is not very retractable until around six months of age. You have a choice about whether or not to have your little boy circumcised. There are good reasons for and against circumcision. (See pp. 44–45.) Before you make your decision, the doctor will check to make sure that the opening of the urethra is in the proper position at the end of the penis. Sometimes the opening of the urethra is in an odd position. If so, circumcision would definitely be out of the question at this time, because the foreskin will be needed for corrective surgery later on.

The penis is very capable of an erection and it is not uncommon for your son to have one, especially when the bladder is full or during urination.

If your baby is a girl you will notice that her labia appear swollen. Often there will be a great deal of vaginal mucus, which may be blood tinged. This is a result of the mother's hormones, and the mucus may continue for four to five days after delivery. It's almost as if she were having a menstrual period. Not all babies have this discharge, and there is no explanation as to why it is seen in one and not another.

G E N I T A L S

Because of their position in the uterus and the softness of their bones, babies may appear to have bowlegs and/or turned-in feet. The legs and feet straighten out once the child begins to walk. If your baby was born in a breech position, her legs and feet may be turned outward because of positioning in the uterus. You should easily be able to spread her legs apart at the hips (as you do when diapering her). If you have some difficulty separating her legs check with your doctor. Sometimes babies are born with their hips slightly dislocated, and early intervention is most important. Your doctor will check her legs when he examines your baby, but your observations are equally important.

L E G S

REFLEXES

Your baby is born with many reflexes. (A reflex is a behavior that is elicited automatically or involuntarily by a certain stimulus. For example, when the doctor taps your knee, your leg jerks.) One kind of automatic behavior seen in the newborn is the *rooting response.* This means that when the baby is stroked on the cheek or the side of the mouth, she will turn her face in the direction of the stimulus. This response is obviously an important one for the baby's feeding. When she is held against her mother's breast, she will turn her head in the direction of the nipple. Because of this response it is important that while the baby is nursing, her cheek on the opposite side be left alone or she will turn her head away from the nipple.

Another extremely important reflex for the newborn is the *sucking reflex.* When the lips, the mucous membranes of the mouth, or the soft palate are stimulated, the baby will suck. This is obviously a very important response. It is also one that the baby enjoys immensely, whether she is feeding or simply sucking on her thumb or a pacifier.

Another common reflex in the newborn is the *startle reflex,* or the *Moro reflex,* which occurs when the baby hears a loud noise or is jiggled or dropped slightly. The baby's arms and legs move symmetrically outward, upward, and then inward, almost as if she were trying to reach out and grab onto something with her hands and feet. Some babies exhibit this reflex rather frequently and easily, whereas others who are more placid may exhibit it rarely. It is not an important reflex for the baby's survival.

The baby often has a *grasp reflex,* which occurs when the palm of the hand or sole of the foot is pressed. The fingers and toes automatically curl and hold onto whatever is there. The grasp reflex of the hand is strong enough to lift the infant off the bed if she is holding your finger!

Another reflex seen in infancy is the *supporting response.* When the baby is held upright and her feet are placed on a firm surface, she will extend her legs and seem to bear her weight on her feet. If she is held in an upright position and the upper part of her feet touch the edge of a table, she will lift her feet almost as if trying to step over the table. This is called the *stepping reflex.*

When a baby is moved from a horizontal position to an upright position, she senses the change in position. Unless she is sound asleep she will become alert and open her eyes wide. This is called the *doll's eye reflex* and can be used when you want your baby to look at you!

All these reflexes are involuntary movements. They gradually disappear during the first six months of life as your baby develops her ability for voluntary movements.

BREATHING

Your baby's breathing pattern is quite different from that of an older child or adult. She may breathe very erratically, sometimes sixty to seventy times a minute. Then after a few minutes she may slow down to twenty or thirty times a minute. The premature baby's breathing pattern is even more erratic. Often the preemie will stop breathing entirely and will need to be stimulated to resume. This is seldom a problem in the full-term baby, however.

Your baby may make some noise while breathing. Babies' nasal passageways are small and they tend to have some mucus in them during the newborn period. This mucus can cause a snoring noise while breathing. Some babies also have what is called the *floppy epiglottis syndrome.* The epiglottis is a small piece of relatively firm cartilage over the vocal cords. Babies can be born with less firmness in the cartilage, and when they breathe the epiglottis may flop about, making a wheezing or flopping sound. This should be brought to the attention of your doctor. It usually disappears with the gradual strengthening of the cartilage.

In the first few days of life your baby may have mucus in her throat and seem to be choking on it. If left alone she will usually be all right, although the wait can be frightening to a new parent. If you feel you need to do something, turn her over on her stomach and hold her in a head-down position.

The main thing to remember about your newborn's breathing is that although it may be erratic it should not seem like hard work. And your baby should always maintain a pink color around the mouth.

CRYING

Although newborn babies do cry, especially from about the third day on, they usually don't cry real tears until around four to five weeks. Almost from the beginning you can detect a difference in the cries of babies. Some babies whimper and mew like a kitten, whereas others let out loud bellows. As you become more acquainted with your baby, you will notice that her crying may vary in pitch, intensity, and duration according to the cause. Of course, we don't know whether the baby consciously intends this or whether it is just nature's way of responding to different stimuli. No matter what, your baby's cry will always evoke a very marked response in you. You will be so attuned to it that sometimes you even imagine you can hear it when she is sound asleep!

TEMPERAMENT

Every baby has an individual temperament or behavioral style, which is the product both of genetics and of her intrauterine environment. We are becoming more and more aware, in the study of the newborn, of the differences among babies. You can sometimes tell immediately after birth what kind of temperament a baby has, although many babies are so sleepy for the first day or two that it is difficult to evaluate them until the third day of life.

Your baby may be a very quiet, placid person who cries only when she is hungry and who is content to look around and take in the world. Noise doesn't startle her easily. She doesn't seem to react to pain or to sudden changes in her environment such as a bath. On the other hand, you may have a baby who is extremely sensitive to everything. She cries with any change, is startled at what seems to be almost the drop of a pin, and seems to crave constant attention. These present the extremes; most babies fit somewhere in between. As you learn about your baby's temperament, you will realize what a unique individual she is. Her temperament may not be ideally suited to mesh with yours, and you may have to show extra understanding and flexibility to make a good pairing. Don't throw your hands up in despair if you and your baby don't seem to mesh well at first. The pairing will occur, and you will love your baby no matter what her temperament is. But the sooner you begin to understand her individuality, and the better you understand it, the easier it will be to live together.

ABILITIES

As we have been saying, your baby is not a passive blob of clay, waiting to be molded into an individual. She is a well-structured being with her own timetable of development and her own style of acquiring knowledge about the world. She can cry, cough, yawn, hiccup, and sneeze. She can hear and select those things that she prefers to hear (such as your voice). She has been conditioned prior to birth by different sounds.

Experiments have shown that babies can be quieted after birth by exposure to the sounds of the uterus. You can buy a Rock-a-Bye Teddy with a recording of uterine sounds (souffle), which will soothe a newborn almost immediately. She has learned and remembered the sound from her time in the uterus.

Not only does your baby prefer certain sounds such as the uterine souffle, a maternal heartbeat, and her mother's voice. She can also discriminate among similar sounds. As early as twenty-four hours of age, she can even pick out her own cry from that of other babies. Her own cry soothes her and another baby's will make her cry.

Your baby can see and has visual patterns that she prefers. She is very attentive to faces. It has even been shown in experiments that a baby is capable of imitating her mother's movements, such as sticking out her tongue. Mothers have reported behavior such as this for some time but have been pooh-poohed by the scientific world. I (AA) am glad that now our observations are being borne out.

The newborn can differentiate among smells. The fifth day of life, a breastfeeding baby can distinguish her mother's breast pad from the breast pads of other mothers. She can taste, and she reacts differently to salt and sugar. The baby can also feel, and she prefers soft, smooth, warm surfaces such as her mother's skin or a warm satin blanket.

Your baby can also smile, although smiling usually occurs during sleep and is not in response to any particular stimulus from you. That will come later.

The baby's sleep patterns are not established right away. She sleeps a great deal more in the first three days, gradually decreasing the length of each period of sleep until the third day, when she cries more and sleeps less. Don't attribute the crying and sleeplessness to something you have done wrong. It is a natural development.

Infant sleep is a much more active type of sleep than that of the older child and the adult. Squirming, rooting about, and making funny noises are not at all uncommon. During the first few days, if she is in your room, it does take some getting used to; at night, her noises may constantly wake you. Gradually you'll become accustomed to them, though, and the two of you will be able to sleep well together.

G E T   C L O S E   T O   Y O U R   B A B Y

It is important to give your baby lots of physical contact, nourishment, and love. Talk to her as though she were an understanding individual, and respect her as such. We will talk later about specific activities for stimulating your baby's learning; but right now, picking her up and handling her are the kind of stimulation she needs. In the hospital nursery, premature babies who are handled and receive physical contact become more active and gain weight much more quickly than premature infants who are not.

A baby needs close human contact in order to thrive, but the mother does not necessarily have to be the only one who gives it. The baby's father, siblings, grandparents, friends, or even baby-sitter can give her loving attention. It's very important, however, that the mother and father have a great deal of physical and emotional contact with the baby because it is through this contact that close bonding is achieved.

H O S P I T A L   P R O C E D U R E S

The procedures that will be followed immediately after your baby is born depend on your birthing place, his condition at the time of delivery, and your condition. His mouth and nose may be suctioned gently with a syringe to remove any mucous secretions. The cord is usually clamped and cut after it has stopped pulsating. You may hold your baby in your arms after the cord has been cut and breast-feed if you wish.

Some medical personnel feel that a newly delivered baby needs to be put under a warmer. But it's perfectly safe for a full-term baby to be held by his mother under a blanket; the mother is one of the best possible sources of radiant heat in the room.

The baby's physical condition is assessed by the medical professionals at one minute after birth. His condition is given a rating called the *Apgar score*. This score is based on the baby's color, muscle tone, activity, respiratory rate, and heartbeat. The score is on a scale of zero to ten, ten being "perfect." Most babies have a score of seven to nine. This Apgar score is not a predictor of either the baby's intelligence or his health. But if a baby has a score in the four-to-six range, he will be watched for a few minutes to see if he needs help with his breathing. If the Apgar score is less than four the baby will be limp and pale and will definitely receive resuscitation.

The Apgar assessment is repeated at five minutes after birth. If the baby has not picked up into the seven-to-nine range by then, it is an indication that he is at risk for neurological or respiratory problems. Having a low Apgar does not necessarily mean that the baby's well-being will be affected. It is purely a signal that medical alertness is required.

A procedure that will take place after the baby has been born, but can be withheld until you have had him with you for at least an hour, is the prophylactic eye treatment. Eye medication is given to prevent a gonococcal infection of the eye, which the baby can contract while passing through the vaginal canal.

It is quite possible for a mother to have a gonococcal infection that she is not aware of. This was once the leading cause of blindness in children so you can see why the medication is definitely needed.

Another procedure carried out after the baby is born is an injection of vitamin K. Many babies, because of the immaturity of their livers, do not produce enough vitamin K for blood clotting. This simple injection has greatly reduced the complications of bleeding in babies.

M E D I C A L   C A R E

Your baby should be checked by a physician in the first twenty-four hours of life and daily while you are in the hospital. If you choose to go home early, you must contact your doctor if you have any concerns about your baby's health. Causes for concern might be feeding problems, vomiting, bluish skin color (cyanosis), yellowish skin color (jaundice), no urination, no bowel movements, seizures, or breathing problems. Although very few newborns develop any of these symptoms, a baby who does so can become ill very rapidly. Call your doctor immediately if your baby seems to have any of these problems.

C I R C U M C I S I O N

If your baby is a boy, you and the father may be considering circumcision, which involves the surgical removal of the foreskin of the penis. Circumcision has been practiced traditionally as a religious ritual and also as a social custom, because it was thought that the penis could be kept cleaner afterwards. If you choose to have your boy circumcised, we advise that you have it done in the newborn period, before you take him home from the hospital. If you wait until later in life, the operation will be more complicated and traumatic for him.

After the circumcision a petroleum jelly or boric-acid-soaked gauze pad about the size of a postage stamp will be wrapped around the end of the penis. It will stick on the penis and may have a pink stain or a few drops of blood on it for a few days. Circumcisions are sometimes done using a plastic ring. It will usually fall off after several days. Be sure to ask your doctor or nurse about it before you go home.

Pediatricians now believe that circumcision is not necessary for a child's health. It is true that if an uncircumcised child has not had his penis washed adequately, he could develop an infection beneath the foreskin which could cause swelling, scarring, and obstruction of the urinary stream. Only rarely do such complications arise, however, because cleaning the area is not difficult. (Remember that the foreskin cannot be retracted in the newborn, and no forceable retraction should ever be tried. The foreskin becomes more retractable at several months of age and is totally free by two to four years of age.)

Although they are rare, complications can arise from circumcision. One is excessive bleeding, usually due to some bleeding disorder in the baby. There might also be damage to the penis by surgical error. And in the case of incomplete development of the penis, removing the foreskin rules out any future surgical repairs.

Parents sometimes choose circumcision because they imagine that most boys are circumcised, and they want their son to be like everyone else. Rest assured: There are plenty of men and boys out there who are uncircumcised.

B L O O D   T E S T S

It is the law in all states that after the third day of life, a baby must have a blood test to rule out a genetic disorder called *phenylketonuria*. This disorder, which can result in mental retardation, can be prevented with a proper diet. After your child has been on milk for three days, the test can be administered by pricking his heel and placing drops of blood on special paper. This disease is extremely rare, but because it is preventable, the test is definitely necessary. In many states this blood test also includes an evaluation of *thyroid function*. Low thyroid hormone is another cause of mental retardation in children that can be prevented with early treatment. Some states screen for other metabolic defects as well. Just ask your doctor what is covered. If you take your baby home before the third day of life you will need to bring him back for these tests.

R O O M I N G - I N

Some hospitals offer rooming-in for new mothers. This is an arrangement that allows you to have your baby in the room with you during your stay. The rooming-in can be complete, where the baby stays around-the-clock, or partial, which means that your baby stays with you during the day, is taken to the nursery at night, and is then brought back to you for the 1:00 A.M. feeding. If rooming-in is not available, your baby will be kept in the nursery and brought to you at four-hour intervals each day for feeding.

Whether you are breast or bottle feeding, rooming-in is much more advisable. If he is with you all the time, you can feed your baby on a demand schedule when he is hungry, rather than when the hospital has decided that he needs to eat. Most newborn babies are not on a four-hour schedule, and some awaken and cry for long periods of time in the nursery. They then arrive at the mother's bedside too exhausted to eat.

The other benefit of rooming-in (whether your baby is breast-fed or bottle-fed) is that you have some time in a private setting to get to know your baby and his needs. There is evidence that mothers who have their babies with them in the hospital make fewer anxious phone calls to the pediatrician after they come home from the hospital. They feel more confident and competent about taking care of their babies.

Some hospitals don't allow any visitors except the father when the mother is rooming-in. This is a rather outdated policy, supposedly necessary to decrease the exposure of the baby to germs. We find it difficult to understand why the baby needs to be so protected during the first three days of life if he is going to be sent home so soon thereafter to be exposed to everybody. Some hospitals still require that the father wear a gown and sometimes a mask when he comes in the room to see the mother and baby. We think that this too is an unnecessary and archaic rule. We hope it will disappear in the next couple of years.

V I S I T S　B Y　S I B L I N G S

If your baby is born at home or at a birthing center, you and the father will have the option of having your other children present at the birth. Many families are deciding to do this. It is a personal decision and depends upon the maturity of your children. Obviously, if you have a difficult labor or it is the middle of the night, your two-year-old may not be fully able to appreciate the new arrival.

You should at least be able to let your children in to see you and the new member of the family as soon as possible. In hospitals this has been somewhat of a problem in the past, but visiting rules are beginning to be changed. If enough parents complain about the lack of this option, hospitals will eventually change their rules.

E A R L Y　D I S C H A R G E　F R O M　T H E　H O S P I T A L

Early discharge of the mother is increasing around the country, perhaps as a result of the scarcity of rooming-in facilities, the lack of sibling visiting rights, and the high cost of medical care. If you are having your first baby and do not have anyone to care for you or assist you at home, you should probably stay in the hospital as long as possible. You really need rest and will benefit from having experienced people around to help you learn to take care of your baby.

When you do get home, learn to give up worrying about such things as a clean house and gourmet meals. It is totally unproductive. Your goal is to take care of the baby and get as much rest and sleep as you can beg, borrow, or steal.

If this is your second, third, or fourth baby and you have other young children at home, you may feel quite confident about your ability to care for your baby and be anxious to get home to your other children. There is no reason that you cannot go home after the baby is born, or at least during the first twenty-four hours. You will need to bring your baby back for blood tests after three days. And it is certainly advisable to have some help waiting at home, so you can get your much-needed rest.

I (AA) have found that nearly every mother needs help for those first few weeks after the baby comes. You will be tired and will need to reserve your energy to care for the baby. Make sure that the help you arrange is someone who will not try to take over the baby. Make it clear that you are looking for someone who will take over the household duties while you care for the baby.

Grandparents can often be a big help. But because this is a time when both sets of grandparents may be vying with each other for a chance to come, be diplomatic about how you handle the arrangements, so that feelings won't be hurt. If you have one grandmother who would be better at taking over the house, arrange for her to come first. Then arrange for the other grandmother to come when you are on your feet and feeling more comfortable about yourself and your baby.

If you have no relatives who can help you, contact employment agencies or a reliable bonded maid service, or ask your friends about someone they would recommend. Perhaps it is possible for your husband to take time off from work. If he has been prepared to take over the household ahead of time, this would be a wonderful alternative.

S P E C I A L   S I T U A T I O N S

Some 5 to 15 percent of pregnancies result in premature deliveries—a very upsetting experience for parents. The new baby is usually unlike anything they have ever seen before: A premature baby is tiny, has no subcutaneous fat, and has very translucent, reddish skin; the skin may also be wrinkled and covered with hair; the hair on the baby's head is usually short and fuzzy; there is no cartilage in his ears; the testes may not be descended; and the nails are short.

PREMATURE BABIES

A premature baby is more likely to have respiratory difficulties, jaundice, and infections. He often needs to be in a special unit called the neonatal intensive care unit. If the hospital does not have one, the baby must be taken to a regional neonatal intensive care unit via a special transport system. Regional ICUs are located throughout the states; as a result of these very fine facilities, more and more premature babies at lower and lower birth weights are surviving.

Seeing their baby in one of these units can be scary and mind-boggling for the parents. He is usually hooked up to many kinds of apparatus, with tubes attached to his body. Mothers and fathers are often afraid to touch their baby, and they need special encouragement to do so. More and more support units are now being set up to work with the parents of the premature.

It is perfectly normal and healthy for parents to grieve when a premature baby is born, or to blame themselves even though there may be no reason for guilt. Or they may feel depressed. If the baby is damaged, they may feel that he would be better off dead. At the same time, they also want to fight along with the baby for survival. Because the mother has gone through the labor and delivery process and may be very tired, the father may take over and become involved in following the child's care. It is not uncommon for the mother to hold back and seem to avoid emotional bonding with the baby so that she won't experience such extreme pain if he should die.

In the neonatal ICU parental contact with the baby is encouraged, because the bonding is so important for both the parents and the baby. It has also been determined that if the mother and father have early contact with their baby, their feelings of grief and depression are less profound. It is easy for the parents to feel like a fifth wheel in such a complex medical facility, but they are definitely an integral part of their child's care. They have a great deal to offer their baby, because it is affection and physical contact that will help him to grow and thrive.

Not all preemies are very small, but all preemies are immature. Because of this immaturity their respiratory function may be affected. They have poor temperature control. Their livers are less mature than that of full-term babies; therefore they cannot handle the normal breakdown products of the blood, and jaundice results. Many times they have a poor sucking reflex and require tube feeding. Preemies also have much more prolonged sleep periods, with only short intervals of wakefulness.

Obviously, prematurity can range from mild to extreme. The smaller and less mature the baby, the more problems there will be. There is a slightly higher risk of neurological, vision, or hearing handicaps with prematurity.

The premature baby must be handled normally when he is taken home. The parents also should remember to allow for the age difference between the premature and the full-term baby when comparing their baby with others. The premature baby usually catches up in ability with the full-term baby within two years.

Parents will need a great deal of support from each other and from their doctors, nurses, relatives, and friends during this extremely trying and difficult time. Hospital personnel usually will discuss the premature baby's characteristics with the parents, but if they don't you should remember that no question is a stupid question as far as your baby is concerned. Just remember: Many talented people—including Pierre Auguste Renoir, Charles Darwin, and Winston Churchill—were premature babies.

POSTMATURE BABIES

Postmature babies are those born after forty-two weeks of gestation. These delayed births occur in 12 percent of pregnancies. The postmature baby has decreased body fat, a hairless body, dry and cracked skin, and long nails. Because stools were passed in the uterus and discolored the amniotic fluid, the nails and umbilical cord may be stained greenish-yellow. The striking feature of postmature babies is that they are extremely alert and wide eyed.

The exact cause of postmaturity is not known. But it is believed that any complications that occur from it are due to decreased placental function. If the condition is severe the baby may have respiratory or neurological problems, or low blood sugar. These babies may require treatment in the intensive-care unit. The great majority, however, have no difficulties, and parents have no cause for concern.

INTRAUTERINE GROWTH RETARDATION

Intrauterine growth retardation, which occurs in approximately 1.2 percent of newborn babies, means that the baby is born with a low weight and low height for his gestational age. This condition can stem from fetal problems such as infection, chromosome abnormalities, or multiple births and can result in malnutrition in the fetus. The maternal factors that can cause growth retardation are poor placental function, hypertension, renal disease, low oxygen, malnutrition, anemia, and excessive smoking or alcohol intake. These babies are at a higher risk for respiratory and central nervous system problems. When a growth-retarded baby is born, the causes should be investigated, and parents need to be counseled appropriately by their doctors.

J A U N D I C E

Most newborns experience some jaundice, which causes a yellowish discoloration of the whites of the eyes and skin. A newborn liver is not as capable as an adult liver of handling the normal breakdown products of human blood cells. Jaundice usually peaks on the second to third day of life and gradually diminishes after that. Sunlight speeds up the liver-maturation process, and babies are often treated with special ultraviolet light in the newborn period if their jaundice is severe.

If the jaundice is caused by an underlying difficulty such as blood incompatibility with the mother (Rh factor), which results in excessive breakdown of red blood cells and excessive buildup of waste products, special medical procedures will be used to treat it.

W H A T   A B O U T   Y O U ?

After your baby is born you will be undergoing both physical and psychological changes. Sometimes they are not what you had expected, so be prepared ahead of time. For example, many new mothers think that they will regain their prepregnancy figures right away and feel depressed when they have to wear a maternity outfit home.

P H Y S I C A L C H A N G E S

You will probably lose twelve to fifteen pounds at delivery, although you may lose less, since your body still retains a great deal of fluid for the first two weeks. The swelling of your face goes down rapidly, however, and that is encouraging. Your uterus begins to shrink by about half an inch a day, and ten days after birth it can no longer be felt when you press on your abdomen. You will have a discharge similar to menstrual flow, called *lochia*, which usually lasts about three weeks. It is reddish-brown at first, then it gradually becomes clear. If it becomes bright red or recurs, make sure to call your doctor. You usually will have no menstrual period for six to eight weeks. If you are nursing your baby you may not have a period until you stop nursing. Most mothers who are nursing do not ovulate, but don't count on it! You definitely need to consider birth control if you do not want to become pregnant again right away.

For the first two weeks after the birth you will have increased urination, sweating, and thirst because your body is gradually getting rid of all the extra fluid you needed while the baby was on board. You will also become thirsty as your milk production increases and takes additional fluids from your system. Your breasts will become very full, heavy, warm, and tender. If you choose not to breast-feed you will be given medication to help dry up the milk in your breasts.

If you have had an episiotomy, the episiotomy site will be sore and itchy. If you have had hemorrhoids, you may need to sit on an inner tube contraption to decrease your discomfort. This is a good time to begin doing your Kegels (perineal exercises learned in pregnancy). Any tenderness can be alleviated by sitz baths, anesthetic sprays, and heat lamp treatments.

EMOTIONAL CHANGES

After the baby is born, almost all mothers are emotionally "trigger-happy." Your hormonal changes cause emotional lability, and you will often overreact to situations. You may also find, however, that you are worrying a lot and feeling slightly blue. These moods, which can come on a few days after the baby is born or even several weeks later, are usually due to the fact that all of a sudden you have so much responsibility—but at the same time you need support and comfort. With some women the blues become much more severe and last for a longer time, resulting in postpartum depression. This condition is more common if the mother has been psychologically unprepared for the baby or if the birth itself has been a bad one. If you are experiencing more than ordinary, run-of-the-mill blues, you must discuss your feelings with your husband and your doctor. Be sure to seek psychological help if the problem becomes severe. There is nothing to be ashamed of, and you will get over it. A word of encouragement: If you have postpartum depression with one child you will not necessarily have it with subsequent children.

GOING HOME

An important piece of equipment to remember when you are going home is a car seat for the baby. You may find it difficult to let go of your new baby and put him into the seat, but try to remind yourself that he will be safer that way and you can hold him all you like when you get home.

Some mothers worry about picking up their other children after they get home, because they worry that lifting heavy things may harm them. It is safe to pick up your children, and it is very important to do so. They will be excited to have you and the baby at home, and they most especially need to know that you still love them and care about them as much as you did before this new arrival. And it is important that the person helping you does enough of the household work to allow you to spend time with your older children as well as with your baby.

You can certainly drive a car after you go home. You do not need to restrict your activities in any way; just make sure to rest whenever you feel tired (as difficult as that may be with other young children at home), follow a good diet, and enjoy your baby. Your doctor will probably want to see you in six weeks for a postpartum exam. And your pediatrician will want to see your baby anywhere from two to six weeks after birth.

5

AN OVERVIEW
OF INFANCY

Before we present you, the mother of the new baby, with the material of utmost interest to you now—breast and bottle feeding and daily care—we want to give you an overview of infancy, that stage of development which extends from birth to the beginning of walking (anywhere from nine to fifteen months).

THE "TWIN PEAKS" VIEW OF INFANCY

If you hadn't ever been to San Francisco before, you could learn something about it by riding a cable car and walking around Fisherman's Wharf or Union Square. But this would certainly not give you a view of the city as a whole. If, however, you drove up high in the Twin Peaks area, where you could overlook the city, you would get an idea of what the whole place is like: how the different districts merge into one another and how the city relates to the bay.

That's what we want to do in this chapter: give you a Twin Peaks view of infancy, so that you will not get bogged down in details but will be able to see the whole—wide and clear.

HOW THE INFANT DEVELOPS A PHILOSOPHY OF LIFE

Remember: At each developmental stage your child has a basic task to master. The developmental task for the stage of infancy is that of forming a basic philosophy of life. This philosophy can range from trust and optimism on one extreme, to distrust and pessimism on the other.

There are four main factors that will determine your baby's basic attitude toward his world and himself.

1. Feeding. Is he fed when he is hungry? Many years ago, doctors believed that it was very important to start children as early as possible on habits of orderliness and punctuality. So they wanted to get the little baby on schedule as soon as they could. They even wanted him to have his bowel movements on schedule! His feedings also became a part of this schedule-mania. Whether breast-fed or bottle-fed, babies were put on a three-hour schedule or a four-hour schedule, and supposed to like it. But a baby who wakes up hungry after three hours isn't very happy if he cries and cries to tell the world he's hungry, but doesn't get fed for an hour.

A schedule is always bound to be wrong. Your baby has no clock built into his tummy, and his hunger pangs vary from day to day and week to week.

Fortunately for you and your baby, there is an alternative to the scheduling system. It usually goes by the name "self-demand." We think of it as the natural way to feed a baby. When your baby wakes up crying it is usually because he is hungry and wants to be fed. So you feed him. You don't try to feed him when he obviously doesn't want it, as he will indicate by turning his head away from the nipple or bottle. And you don't hold back from feeding him because the clock says it isn't time.

Hunger is the most insistent need your baby has in his first year of life. All of his other needs are minor compared with this. So if you satisfy his hunger promptly, and cuddle him while you are doing it, you will be performing the most important service you can in helping him develop his basic trust and optimism about the world. Which brings us to . . .

2. Touching . . . the second ingredient. Babies need plenty of physical cuddling—to be held in your arms and stroked, rocked, talked to, or sung to.

Various lines of evidence underline the importance of cuddling for babies. On the level of animal research, Dr. Harry Harlow studied baby rhesus monkeys who were raised by terry cloth dummies with built-in nursing bottles. Although the monkeys got adequate physical nourishment with this system, they did not get sufficient amounts of what Dr. Harlow calls "contact comfort." These babies grew up to be socially inadequate adult monkeys. They developed strange and bizarre mannerisms similar to those seen in human psychotics, and they were unable to mate with receptive monkeys of the opposite sex.

On the human level, studies of babies raised in institutions show the same kind of results. Babies raised in orphanages may receive adequate feeding, but too often the attendants do not have time to cuddle and "mother" them. And we find that many children raised in this psychologically barren and unstimulating environment tend to be, in varying degrees, emotionally impaired.

It's easy to provide the physical cuddling and contact your childs needs to feel loved and happy. Hug him and kiss him as much as you want. He won't mind! Cuddle him and snuggle with him; he'll love it. Talk to him and sing to him. I (FD) talked to my kids a lot when they were babies. Some people thought I was a little crazy when they found out what I talked to them about. I would explain things to them like Freud's theory of defense mechanisms and the history of mankind from the cave man to the present day.

I also sang to my kids a lot when they were babies. I didn't go much for nursery lullabies. I leaned more toward songs like "Erie Canal," "The Eyes of Texas," and "Red River Valley." Those babies were the most appreciative singing audience I ever had!

It doesn't matter what you say or sing. When you talk and sing to your baby, and cuddle, hug, and kiss him, you are saying, "I love you" in the only language he can understand. And by teaching him that he is deeply loved, you are also teaching him a basic outlook of trust and optimism about life.

3. Bonding. The third way for your baby to develop a positive and trusting relationship to his world is for him to have a deep emotional relationship with his

first caretaker or caretakers (who will usually be mother and father, but might be mother and grandmother or some other relative, or a paid individual care-taker). This primary relationship prepares him for those he will have with all the people in his life later.

4. Stimulation. Fourth, your baby must receive sensory and intellectual stimula-tion, both to aid in his general intellectual development and to give him a sense that his world is an interesting and lively place that he can enjoy and feel positive about.

Suppose you are lying flat on your back in bed in a barren, bleak room twenty-four hours a day. From time to time you are interrupted by a Someone who feeds you and changes your diapers or gives you a bath. Otherwise you just lie there. Sometimes you cry because you are so bored and lonesome. You cry and cry but nothing happens. Finally the Someone comes and you hear her say, "I certainly don't know what in the world he's crying about. I just fed him a while ago, and his diaper is dry. I checked and there's no diaper pin sticking him. I don't see what he's got to cry about." Then the Someone goes away.

Such experiences of life in a lonesome, boring, unstimulating environment will not do much to give your baby a sense of positive trust in the world and are likely to retard his development.

Several orphanage studies by Dr. Wayne Dennis make this point very clearly. In the first orphanage in Teheran that he studied, most of the infants had been admitted before they were a month old. They were confined almost continuously in individual cribs. They lay on their backs on soft mattresses all day and night. They were never propped up or turned over, unless they learned to do it by them-selves. Most feedings were given in propped-up bottles. They were bathed every other day and changed when necessary. They had absolutely no playthings. To sum it up: The world in which they lived, day after day, was a bleak and barren one with little sensory or intellectual stimulation.

Dr. Dennis then studied a second orphanage, which had the same basic en-vironment. He found that fewer than half of these children between one and two could sit up. None of them could walk. The contrast with normal American chil-dren was striking. Almost all normal, noninstitutionalized American children can sit alone by the age of nine months; and they can walk by the age of fifteen months—and many begin earlier. Of the two-year-olds in the first orphanage, fewer than 10 percent could walk alone. Only 15 percent of the three-year-olds in the second orphanage could walk alone.

Dr. Dennis later did a study at an orphanage in Beirut, in order to see what effect sensory and intellectual stimulation could have on babies. He selected a group between the ages of seven months and one year. None of them could sit up. He exposed them to a planned program of sensory stimulation. The babies were taken from their cribs for one hour a day and brought into an adjoining room. They were propped up in low chairs and given a variety of objects to look at and handle: pieces of colored sponge, paper bags, metal box tops, fly swatters, fresh flowers, small plastic bottles, multicolored plastic dishes, jelly molds, and metal ashtrays. No adults worked with the babies to stimulate them or help them play with the objects.

Even with this minimal stimulation of one hour a day, without adults, the babies quickly learned to sit up independently. Some of the babies were hesitant with the materials at first, but finally all delighted in playing with the objects. During the course of the experiment, the babies developed at four times the average rate, because of the sensory stimulation.

The message of these experiments seems very clear:

- Don't raise your baby in an environment that is like a bleak orphanage.
- Have objects for him to play with—inexpensive ones are fine (but be sure they are not small enough for him to put in his mouth and choke on).
- And remember that the absolutely best "toy," the one your baby loves the most, is *you!* Nothing else could be as flexible and sophisticated a plaything for your baby as you.

We have lots of specific advice on what you can do to provide a rich sensory and intellectual environment for your baby in Chapter Eleven, "Intellectual Stimulation in Infancy."

P H Y S I O L O G I C A L   C H A N G E S   I N   I N F A N C Y

Now let's discuss some of the physiological changes that occur as your baby's body develops during this first year of his life.

P H Y S I C A L   G R O W T H

One of the most obvious changes is that of rapid physical growth, particularly during the first six months. Every month your baby gains approximately one to two pounds and grows half an inch. This means he will usually double his birth weight by five months of age.

Rapid growth, though at not quite the same rate, continues during the second six months of the first year. By the time your baby has reached twelve months, he will probably have tripled his birth weight and grown approximately ten inches. Because of this rapid growth, proper nutrition is obviously very important.

Even though your baby is capable at birth of many things, some of his physiological systems are still immature and account for the pattern of some of his behavior. Let's take a look at these.

N E R V O U S   S Y S T E M

The nervous system (the brain, spinal cord, and nerves) is immature at birth and grows rapidly in the first two years (your child's brain reaches 90 percent of adult size by age two). Because his nervous system is not well differentiated at birth, he tends to react in a very generalized fashion to any stimulus. For example, if his foot is stroked, he is likely to withdraw the foot, cry, and generally move his whole body. Later during the first year, he is likely to respond to that kind of stimulation by just withdrawing his foot and looking at it. There will be no generalized body movement.

VISION

Your newborn can certainly see, although his peripheral (side) vision is better than his central (straight ahead) vision, which is not fully mature until about four months. He is unable to coordinate his eye movements well until three to six months; thus he tends to have double vision in the beginning. During the first few months he sees best when things are nine to fifteen inches away. After that he can see well enough at any distance. However, he will remain slightly farsighted for the first three to four years of life.

Your baby begins to develop depth perception at around nine months, but it will not be fully mature until he is about six years old. He usually does not produce any tears during the first two to three months of life, because the tear glands are not fully developed.

OTHER SENSES

At birth your baby's senses of taste, smell, hearing, and touch are fully developed, and he can discriminate between different sensations, such as sweet-tasting and sour-tasting substances. He does not like noxious odors, loud noises, or cold, rough textures.

BEHAVIOR

Your baby comes with the capacity for several different behavioral patterns. He can be in a deep sleep during which he breathes slowly and quietly and shows no sign of motion. He may be in an active or restless sleep during which you see movements of the eyes under the eyelids, or body movements; this is considered a dream sleep. He can be drowsy or be quiet and alert. He may also have active, alert periods, or he may cry. During this first year you will see changes in the amount of time that he spends in each of these different states. He sleeps more at the beginning of his first year, usually twelve to fourteen hours a day. This sleep is much more active, and he seems to be dreaming more than half the time. His sleep usually lasts for three hours at a time, and only about twenty minutes of it is deep sleep. As he matures during the first year he requires less sleep, but more of it is deep sleep. By the time he is eight months old, he is very much like an adult, with 50 percent of his sleep a deep sleep, and only 20 to 30 percent of it active sleep.

The state that is most important for his development is when he is quiet, alert, attending to his environment, and very receptive to any stimulation. In the first few months of life, he spends only about 10 percent of his time (three hours a week) in this state—usually during the first five to ten minutes after each feeding. This state increases markedly during the first year, so that by the end of twelve months he can be quiet and alert for stretches of one to two hours.

As a newborn your baby has only short-term memory. The memory capacity increases during the first year, so that by the time he is one year old he can remember events for a long time.

These changes are all part of the development of his infant nervous system.

RESPIRATORY SYSTEM

Although your baby's respiratory system is fairly well developed at birth, during the first month of life there may be an irregular respiratory rate. Don't worry. By the end of the first month the respiratory system will have matured and the rate will become stable at around thirty breaths a minute.

The tissues of the respiratory tract are small and relatively delicate, and the structure is such that an infant is more susceptible to infection. By one year of age, however, the respiratory tract more closely resembles that of the adult.

GASTRO- INTESTINAL SYSTEM

The gastrointestinal system is immature at birth. The swallow is a reflexive action during the first three months. It isn't until after that time that your baby has voluntary control over what he swallows or spits out. At birth he is unable to secrete saliva, but saliva secretion gradually increases during the first two to three months of life. (The saliva during the first year is not too efficient and does not digest food very well, particularly starches.) Your infant automatically tends to stick his tongue out, which is fine for sucking but inefficient for taking solids (this is why feeding solids early can be *so* messy!).

Food moves very rapidly through the entire gastrointestinal system in infancy. The control of this movement is immature, so that sometimes there is reverse flow, and repeated spitting and vomiting are not uncommon. All infants are different, but some may continue to have difficulty through the eighth month, until the gastrointestinal tract has matured. Because of this rapid movement of food through the tract an infant tends to have loose stools. As with the respiratory system, the gastrointestinal tissues tend to be delicate and somewhat susceptible to infection, making the baby vulnerable to diarrhea and vomiting during the first year of life. By the end of the first year these problems are pretty much under control.

ENDOCRINE SYSTEM

The endocrine system is the most mature of all the systems at the time of birth. But the hormonal responses to stress are still somewhat immature, so your baby is less able to keep his body in a well-controlled state. This is the reason that babies tend to react more severely to illnesses that don't affect an older child so much.

SKIN

A baby's skin has all the structures of adult skin, but the functions are immature. The layers of skin are thinner and more delicate, so your newborn's skin is more likely to be blistered by the same stimulus that would only cause swelling in an older child. The infant is also more likely than an older child to lose fluid through the skin. As the function of the skin matures during infancy this water loss decreases.

Underneath the skin are oil glands that produce oil, especially on the scalp, face, and genitals. During early infancy these are very active and account for the formation of "cradle cap" on the scalp and little pimples on the face. As infancy advances, this condition decreases steadily, and the problem is not so prevalent when the child is one year of age. The sweat glands are not functional during early infancy but begin to work a little bit during the first few months of life. The ability to sweat remains minimal throughout infancy; this is offset by the loss of water from the baby's skin. The ability of the skin to contract and shiver in response to cold is very limited during infancy. This reaction improves during the first year but is not fully developed until later in childhood. Because he does not have the automatic bodily defense mechanisms that you have, it is very important to pay attention to your infant's body temperature and not allow him to overchill and overheat.

CARDIOVASCULAR SYSTEM

The baby's cardiovascular system is well formed but somewhat inefficient, because your newborn's heart must beat 130 times per minute (decreasing to about 110 beats by the time he is a year old) to pump the blood through his body.

IMMUNE SYSTEM

The immune system is the system that defends the body against infection. It is functioning at birth but its capabilities improve gradually throughout infancy; and by the time your child is nine to twelve months of age he can protect himself against infections almost as well as you can.

We have described these physiological changes because we believe it is important for you to understand that your infant has very special needs because of his immature body systems. These are needs that you are very well equipped to meet—and you may do so almost instinctively—but sometimes it just helps to understand why they exist.

G E N E R A L   D E V E L O P M E N T

Although we have organized this discussion into three-month periods, remember that these are arbitrary divisions; there is probably not a baby in the world who fits exactly into three-month units. But a breakdown is a convenient way of structuring the information so that you can not only get a general idea of your child's development but see how each period builds on the one that went before.

Remember always that your baby is a unique person, who because of this uniqueness will do lots of things that are perfectly normal but are not found in the pages of any child psychology book. Remember, too, that the areas of infant development—motor abilities, language, and mental and social maturing—not only overlap each other, but one kind of development can take precedence over another from time to time. For example, the nine-month-old who had previously been interested in imitating sounds becomes so interested in crawling and early walking that she no longer seems to be making any progress with language. This is not at all unusual, and the dominance of a particular interest can last for several months.

Here are the guidelines (not the rules) for following your child's development in her first year.

B I R T H   T O   T H R E E   M O N T H S

Think of this time as the "settling in" period, when you and your baby are becoming used to the changes in your environments. The newborn has many capabilities, as we have already pointed out, and she is not totally helpless. Her reflexes help her deal with her environment in a constructive way. For example, her gag reflex helps her to spit up mucus that has collected in her passages as a result of the delivery process. Her blink reflex protects her from too much light. She can avoid smothering by twisting and turning if something is put over her nose and mouth, and she can even bring her arm over in a rather uncoordinated fashion to try to remove it. When she is on her tummy, she can protect herself from smothering by turning her head to one side. She tries to avoid pain by withdrawing. And if she is surrounded by unpleasant stimuli she can totally block them out, even going off to sleep. This is what she starts with. Let's take a look at what else you'll see developing during the first three months.

MOTOR DEVELOPMENT

Initially your baby has poor head control, although she can occasionally lift her head briefly when she is lying on her tummy, and she can turn her head from side to side. By the time she is three months old she has achieved good head control, and she can lift her head quite well when she is on her tummy and hold her head steady when she is in a sitting position.

In the newborn period she tends to keep her fists in a closed position and has a reflexive grasp, but she cannot really hold things yet. By the time she is three months old she keeps her hands open more and is interested in holding objects for a long time. She is also beginning to reach for things, although her reach is uncoordinated. The newborn is very capable of getting her hands to her mouth and often uses them as a soothing device. By the end of the third month she is moving her hands in a more exploratory fashion, although still very much for soothing as well.

The newborn child's uncoordinated gaze becomes quite coordinated at three months of age. Now she definitely uses visual exploration a great deal. She is able to follow objects smoothly across the entire visual range. During these three months your baby seems to spend a great deal of time just staring at her environment and taking it in.

LANGUAGE DEVELOPMENT

Initially, your baby communicates through crying, although sometimes she makes throaty sounds as well. By the end of three months she is making cooing, gurgling noises, and there is (thank goodness!) much less crying. She listens to voices and can distinguish speech sounds by the end of the third month.

INTELLECTUAL DEVELOPMENT

As we have pointed out, your newborn has the ability to discriminate among different stimuli and has a short-term memory. She has the capacity to become bored and shut out the boring stimuli. She is learning during this period that sometimes she can make other things happen. For example, if she is lying in her bed kicking randomly, the movement may trigger the ringing of the bell on her mobile. Initially this is an accidental event, but she will learn rapidly and will begin to kick purposely. By the end of three months she is also able to manipulate a rattle in the same fashion with her hand.

Your baby knows your face and voice very early in the first month. By the age of three months she is attentive to others and can recognize and differentiate among family members.

The most exciting social event is the appearance of a smile, which is the most rewarding thing your child can give you at this stage. Your newborn is certainly capable of smiling with her lips and lower face, usually when she is asleep but sometimes also in response to the human face. The smile gradually involves all of the face so that by the time she is six weeks old she smiles with her lips, cheeks, and eyes in response to specific stimuli—most particularly the human face and voice. Your child initially smiles at you, her mother. And although she gradually begins to include others in her favor, she still smiles differently in reaction to your presence or voice. During this time (usually at around two to three months) she also cries differently when you leave than when other people leave. She is much more responsive to others during the third month, and social stimulation is becoming more important to her.

Her sleeping and eating have become much less disorganized, and by the end of three months she seems settled and more regular. She may need only one night feeding, will sleep approximately ten hours a night, and requires two naps a day (a couple of hours in the morning and a couple of hours in the afternoon).

S O C I A L   D E V E L O P M E N T

T H R E E   T O   S I X   M O N T H S

Think of this as the "friendly, hands-on" period. Your baby is now becoming an explorer of the world beyond her own body. She is interested in all objects and people. She is really beginning to imitate, and her learning is quite obviously rapid.

During this period you see a speeding up of activities, particularly around five months of age. She has perfected her head control and is working on her trunk control, so that by the end of six months she is probably sitting alone without support for short periods of time. She enjoys rocking on her tummy, looking like an airplane with her arms extended. She also likes extending her legs and is beginning to bear her own weight. By the end of this time she probably enjoys bouncing up and down in a standing position. She begins rolling, usually from her tummy to her back first, followed by rolling from her back to her tummy.

She continues to be interested in her hands and is doing a great deal of finger sucking and face exploring with them. Her mouth is very much an exploratory organ and every object she gets goes into it. It is during this period that she usually finds her feet, and begins sucking on her toes in order to know them better as well.

M O T O R   D E V E L O P M E N T

Now she will begin to develop better control of her oral function. She can keep her tongue in and begin to chew and swallow in a coordinated fashion. Her saliva production increases and drooling occurs at around three to four months. Soon she will begin to cut her teeth, and at the end of this period her lower incisors come in. She has much better hand usage and is beginning to show you that she is ready for solids by trying to reach out and pick up finger foods. Her reach is more developed during this period and she grabs objects very well and quickly, so watch out for that hot coffee!

LANGUAGE DEVELOPMENT

In the beginning of this period she is doing a great deal of cooing and babbling and is usually making vowel sounds. By six months she begins to develop more consonant sounds. She loves imitating, particularly clucking noises. She is also able to vocalize her pleasure and displeasure by the end of six months and is a very communicative little creature.

INTELLECTUAL DEVELOPMENT

By the end of this time she is alert for two hours at a stretch and is visually alert close to 50 percent of the daylight hours. She reaches for objects and inspects them all over. At four months, if an object drops she will stare at the place from which it dropped; by the time she is six months old she will reach to grab and secure the dropped object. During this time she begins to coo or hum when she hears music. You can have a wonderful duet singing a bedtime lullaby together. She is also becoming more aware of strange situations and beginning to be disturbed by strangers. By six months, she really notices her mirror image and is able to differentiate herself from her image.

SOCIAL DEVELOPMENT

Now she is an extremely social being who enjoys herself immensely. She anticipates exciting events and initiates socialization, often by coughing or clicking her tongue. She is so social at this time that she may be hard to feed because she is attending to everything and everyone around her. You may have to feed her in a quiet darkened room in order to finish nursing. She particularly likes music and begins to enjoy games such as peek-a-boo. She loves her bath, and at around six months she can take a bath in the big bathtub, because now she has enough trunk control to be able to sit up alone. By the end of this time she also begins noticeably to prefer children to most adults, even in pictures; she perceives their smaller size.

Now she begins to want to hold her own bottle or to manipulate a cup. And by the end of six months she is probably sleeping through the night and sleeping about twelve hours a day.

S I X   T O   N I N E   M O N T H S

This is the "explorer" period, when your baby becomes more mobile and involved with her environment on a larger scale. This involvement and newfound

freedom may also make her feel a little unsure of herself and seem more dependent on you. This is the time when a fear of strangers and separation anxiety
really come into play. She has matured sufficiently to be aware of which people
and things are not familiar and therefore "strange." So don't rush your baby into
new situations.

Your baby is gaining more control of her body during this period. She not only
has good head control, but she is also gaining control over her lower body. She
may rock back and forth on her knees and creep about on her tummy, often going
backwards. Toward the end of this period she is probably crawling on all fours
and moving faster than the speed of light. She can get herself into the sitting position, may even pull herself up to standing, and cruise along the furniture. She is
teething a great deal and everything goes into her mouth, both to explore and to
relieve the teething pain. She is learning to use her hands and fingers much better
and is beginning to use her thumb and index fingers to pick up small objects like
pellets or raisins from the floor. By the end of this time she is using her index
finger to poke into every hole imaginable. She enjoys banging things together in
her hands, and she plays with her toys with great gusto.

MOTOR DEVELOPMENT

During this time she is developing the ability to utter well-defined syllables
such as "ma" and "da." She imitates sounds and will be saying "ma-ma" and
"da-da," and by nine months may be using these words meaningfully. She notices
voices, tones, and inflections. By nine months she may possibly be able to respond
to her name and realize what "no-no" means. She may be able to carry out a simple command like "Get my shoes."

LANGUAGE DEVELOPMENT

During this stage your baby is attentive to detail and seems very self-contained
and studious when examining objects. She begins developing depth perception.
During this stage she develops the capacity to look for a hidden object and know
that just because it is out of sight it is not gone forever. She also begins to notice
the consequences of her behavior, remembering that certain kinds of behavior
have resulted in disapproval or approval. She is very much an imitator of adult
behavior, and has become a source of great delight to the family. At around nine
months, when she is just getting herself upright, she will, because of her newly
acquired depth perception, begin to fear heights and notice vertical space.

INTELLECTUAL DEVELOPMENT

During this time she is developing a sense of humor and may become a tease.
Now she really enjoys games such as peek-a-boo. She is also becoming a little
more independent and resists doing things when she is pressured. She is sensitive
to others, especially other children, and will cry if they cry. She is also more
fearful even of familiar situations such as vacuuming or flushing the toilet. She is
becoming assertive in her play and will fight for a toy with an older sibling. Remember, this is the time when she really notices that her mom is a separate

SOCIAL DEVELOPMENT

person and becomes extremely anxious with strangers and about any separation from her mother. She does not like having you in another room and she wants to follow you everywhere. It is wise to avoid a prolonged separation at this time if you can.

By the end of nine months she can drink from a cup quite well and can hold a cup and spoon in play. She may still need sucking for comfort, however, and may want to continue on the bottle or the breast even though she is able to drink from a cup. As a result of her new fears, she may have more trouble sleeping and possibly become fearful of her bath toward the end of this period.

N I N E   T O   T W E L V E   M O N T H S

This is a time when we think of the baby as "on the move." She spends much more of her time in the upright position as she practices her standing, cruising, and possibly walking. She also smooths the rough edges from her other motor activities such as sitting, crawling, and standing. She gradually becomes less cautious of heights than she was during the nine-month period, and she may become quite a climber. She is beginning to develop a sense of her own separate identity, which may frighten her a bit.

M O T O R   D E V E L O P M E N T

As we said, between nine and twelve months your baby may become a good stander and cruiser, walking by holding onto the furniture or holding onto your two hands. She can probably get herself to a standing position and may even squat to recover a toy. She is quite an adept climber and enjoys going up and down stairs and getting on and off chairs.

Her fine-muscle coordination has improved and she is now able to hold a crayon and make some marks. By twelve months she may even be able to imitate a scribble. She is so good at using her hands that she is beginning to pull off her socks and untie her shoes. Eventually at about twelve months she is undressing herself, especially when you don't want her to! She is adept at using her thumb and index finger in a pincer grasp to recover small items.

L A N G U A G E   D E V E L O P M E N T

During this time she begins to say a few words, "no" being the most common one besides "ma-ma" or "da-da." She enjoys waving bye-bye and can understand simple commands. Her main expressive language is jargon or "word salad," which has the inflection of speech but makes no sense except for a few intelligible words or sounds. But she is beginning to recognize words as symbols and will look up into the sky when someone says "airplane," for example. By one year she may have ten words; but don't worry if your twelve-month-old does *not* have ten words. Babies definitely progress at very different rates. I (AA) remember being so concerned because our second child, Katie, knew nothing but "no" and "hot" until she was eighteen months old—in comparison with her older sister, Kelly, who had a large vocabulary at twelve months. But then at about eighteen months Katie began talking in sentences and hasn't been quiet since.

The love for imitation that began earlier really comes into play during the nine-to-twelve-month period, and your baby enjoys imitating anything that her parents do. She can point to body parts as you say them. She can also scribble quite well, much to your dismay if she uses her crayons unsupervised. She enjoys matching objects for color or shape and begins stacking and nesting. This is the time when she particularly enjoys putting things into containers and taking them out again. She enjoys looking at a book and can turn pages, although not one at a time. You will also observe her experimenting with different ways to attain goals by manipulating objects, for example using a stick to get a toy out from under a sofa or pushing a chair as a walker. It actually begins to seem that she is thinking before she acts. Her memory for past events is longer and she really does begin to understand the consequences of her actions.

During this period your child becomes quite adept at showing her different moods and may become very astute at judging others' moods. She imitates facial gestures quite a bit now and is very aware of nonverbal communication. She is also aware of social approval and disapproval and is developing her own identity. The word "no" begins to come into play as she becomes more assertive. Toward the end of this time tantrums may begin. She is even more fearful of strangers than she was before and feels increased separation anxiety. Your baby's growing assertiveness and independence are also scary for her, and she feels more dependent on you. Basically hers is a process now of taking off on her own and coming back to home base for reassurance.

She is affectionate with her toys and with familiar people and enjoys playing with other children, although most of the time she plays *alongside* them rather than actually *with* them in a social sense.

She is now quite good at feeding herself with a spoon and may even be attempting to use a fork. She not only can undress herself, but she also can help with dressing by positioning her body in a cooperative way. She now probably needs only one nap, usually in the afternoon. She may continue to have trouble sleeping, probably because she is fearful of being separated from you.

So much will happen during the first year of life that we cannot possibly cover it completely, so this has been only a summary of what you might expect. If you would like to read in greater detail about this stage, we can recommend an excellent book, *The First Twelve Months of Life,* edited by Frank Caplan. The book, enhanced by some wonderful photographs, goes into great detail about all the developmental changes that you can expect during the first twelve months of your child's life.

6

THE TECHNIQUE OF BREAST FEEDING

You should decide before your baby is born whether you want to breast-feed or bottle-feed her. There are advantages and disadvantages to both methods, and in this chapter and the next, we will discuss them in detail so that you may make an informed decision. Whatever you decide, remember that the most important elements—love and good nutrition—can be provided by either method.

THE ADVANTAGES OF BREAST FEEDING

Human milk is the ideal nutritional substance for human babies. In addition to providing superb nourishment, breast milk may protect a baby against allergies and illness. Even if a baby is breast-fed for only the first week or two, she receives valuable antibodies against infection.

Breast feeding is a very intimate experience for both mother and baby. The nursing mother feels extremely special and irreplaceable. Breast feeding is also emotionally soothing and physically relaxing, and it helps speed the shrinking of the uterus back to its normal size. In addition, it is very convenient and extremely economical.

These advantages and more would certainly make it worth your while to try breast feeding, if only for a few weeks. If you don't like it, you can always stop; it is much easier to switch from breast feeding to bottle feeding than vice versa. So if you are undecided, consider trying breast feeding at least in the beginning.

You may have heard that if you have any negative feelings at all about nursing you should forget about trying, because you will be doomed to fail. That is simply not true. There is a wide range of physical, psychological, and sociological factors that determines the success of breast feeding. For example, it has been shown that if a woman has a higher education, she is more likely to breast-feed. If she has a supportive husband and close family and friends, she is more likely to succeed. And if she has a physician or pediatrician whose own children were breast-fed, and who is likely to recommend starting solid foods at no earlier than four to six months, she is also more likely to succeed. If she lives in a small community, she will probably nurse for a longer time.

ATTITUDE

One of the biggest blocks to successful breast feeding is attitude: Thinking of the breast as having to do with sex rather than with nourishment. If you have any feelings of shame about nursing, you may prefer to bottle-feed your baby. This is a perfectly sound decision. Remember, your aim should always be to feel happy and comfortable so that you and your baby can share the most satisfying feeding experience possible. Rest assured that your baby will grow and develop perfectly well without breast milk.

THE ROLE OF THE FATHER

When we talked about the ingredients of success, we mentioned the baby's father. He is most definitely a key person in this regard. His feelings as well as yours must be taken into account in making the decision to breast-feed. Most men are proud of their wives' decision to nurse and are very supportive. Before delivery your partner can assist in the preparation of the breast (see p. 66), and after delivery he can help care for both you and the baby.

FACTS VS. MYTHS

Let's now dispel some of the myths about breast feeding and give you some facts:

- Almost all breasts can feed.
- The inability to breast-feed is not inherited.
- Even if you have a nervous disposition you can become a successful breast feeder.
- Your milk is almost always rich enough.
- You will always have enough milk if you nurse frequently enough.
- Your baby will not become allergic to your breast milk.
- Breast feeding will not cause you to lose teeth. (Some people believe that because making milk requires a great deal of calcium, your teeth will lose their calcium and fall out!)
- Breast feeding will not ruin the shape of your breasts.

(There are many factors that affect the shape of the breast, and they are, in order of importance: heredity, age, pregnancy, and, minimally, nursing.) There are mothers who have nursed five children and whose breasts are in much better shape than mothers who have had two pregnancies without nursing. Many mothers who are less well endowed than others truly enjoy pregnancy and the nursing period, because during those times they do not feel so self-conscious and are actually quite proud of their new breast size.

Finally, there is the myth that breast feeding is instinctive and there is no need for education, counseling, or support. This may well be true in societies where girls have grown up surrounded by breast feeding and have had ample opportunities for observation. In our society, however, it is very common for a young mother never to have seen a baby nurse at the breast. The inexperienced mother will certainly be capable of putting her baby to the breast, but she will be less anxious and more likely to nurse for a longer time if she is aware of some of the possible problems and pitfalls along the way.

S U P P O R T   F R O M   O T H E R   M O T H E R S

Mothers who are experienced breast feeders can offer lots of helpful advice and support to the first-time nursing mother. The most well-known support group of mothers is La Leche League International. The league has counselors to assist mothers with all kinds of problems. There are other support groups too that offer similar services. If you do not have any friends to form a support group with, get acquainted with the nursing support group in your area, preferably before delivery. A list of some of these groups is provided at the end of this chapter.

Although you will find your support group extremely helpful, you should also try to acquire some basic information on your own. In the following sections we will give you the information that you will need to successfully nurse your baby.

P R E P A R I N G   T H E   B R E A S T

It is not uncommon for women who are breast feeding for the first time to develop sore nipples. Fair-skinned women, especially blondes and redheads, are especially susceptible. You can prevent or decrease soreness by following some simple steps during the latter part of your pregnancy.

In the last two months before birth, the nipples and areolae should not be washed with soap, benzoin, or alcohol; the breast has its own secretions at this time which protect the area. Your goal now is to toughen the nipples. Expose them to sunlight or air. If you wear a nursing bra, let the flap down as much as you can during the day. The rubbing of your loose clothing against the nipples will serve as friction and toughen the area. If you don't have a nursing bra you might cut out your own bra so that the nipples and areolae are exposed. Sunbathing without your bra on will also help. So will a sunlamp—but be careful! Follow the instructions and don't stay under too long.

Some people advocate the hand expression of colostrum (the clear yellowish liquid that precedes milk production); however, sometimes this stimulates the production of the hormone oxytocin, which causes uterine contractions and can trigger early labor. You should definitely ask your doctor whether or not he recommends expression by hand.

Many women worry that their nipples may not be large enough for breast feeding. You can easily find out by placing your fingers on the outer edge of the areola on opposite sides of the nipple and pushing the areola in toward the chest. This should cause the nipple to emerge. If instead the nipple becomes less prominent, then you have what is commonly known as inverted nipples, which means that they need a little more work to make them come out. Among the most effective aids that you can use are the Woolwich or Eschmann breast shields, which can be obtained through a nursing support group. Wearing the shields inside a well-fitting bra creates a constant, even pressure that will make the nipples gradually emerge. The shields should be worn daily in the last months of pregnancy. You can use shields from the drugstore, but be sure to buy only plastic or glass shields and cut off the rubber nipple, because rubber will result in a buildup of moisture that can lead to more irritation.

It is also important to examine your breasts to see if they are at all inelastic (that is, if the skin on the breasts cannot be pinched without difficulty). Women with inelastic breasts are more likely to experience engorgement in the initial nursing period. Some specialists believe that massaging the breasts with lanolin or cocoa butter in the months before delivery will help prevent engorgement later on.

Many women find that their partners are only too happy to cooperate in toughening the nipple and areola area through stimulation in sex play. Another recommended exercise is light rubbing or buffing of the nipple and areolar areas with a towel for five minutes after a shower or bath. The hard spray of the shower or shower massager on the nipple and areolar areas may also be helpful. While you are taking your shower or bath (or at any other time), pull your nipple out firmly with your fingers until you feel a slight discomfort, and then release it. Repeat the procedure two or three times a day.

G E T T I N G   S T A R T E D

Unless you have been heavily medicated during delivery or your baby is very premature or in some type of distress, you may nurse her immediately. In the hour after delivery your baby is more likely to be alert and active than she is later, and it is wonderful to be able to hold her during this time. We suggest that eye medications be withheld for a while so that the baby can maintain eye contact with you.

The situation may be such in the delivery room that you don't feel comfortable nursing her there. Delivery tables are typically too narrow for comfortable nursing, the room may be too cold, or there may be too much activity, with very little privacy. In this case, relax with the baby in your arms, and wait to nurse until you are in the recovery room, where you and your husband can be left alone to enjoy your baby.

N U R S I N G   P O S I T I O N S

You may nurse in any position that is comfortable for you. But if you have just delivered, you will probably be rather tired and will prefer to be lying down. We recommend that you lie on your side with the baby next to you. You can put your lower arm up over the baby's head or under it (see Fig. A). Positioning your baby properly is the key to successful nursing. Pull her toward you until her chin is in contact with your breast just below the areola. This contact arouses the baby's natural rooting reflex. She will nuzzle in, open her mouth wide, and stick out her tongue to feel for the nipple. At this time you can pull her in closer and guide your nipple and areola into her mouth, stimulating automatic sucking on her part.

She will need to take in not only the nipple but a good portion of the areola in order to suck properly, thus avoiding nipple irritation and ensuring breast emptying. If your breast is too full, compress the areola between your second and third fingers to make it smaller and allow the baby to get more in her mouth (see Fig. B). If you pull her legs closer to you at an angle, you will notice that her head tilts back. This will tend to keep her nose free for breathing. If your baby seems to be having difficulty breathing, you may need to press the upper part of the breast down with your fingers to create an air space (see Fig. C).

Fig. A

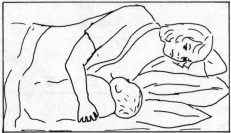

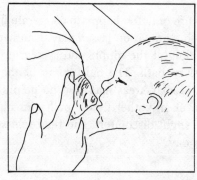

Fig. B

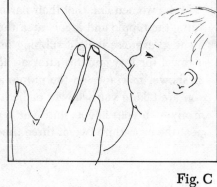

Fig. C

Another position is either sitting up in a comfortable chair or with the head of your bed raised, so you can hold your baby in the crook of your arm. It's important to get very comfortable. Have pillows placed under your elbow so that your arm does not tire. Don't be afraid to ask someone for help.

During this first nursing period it's not necessary to be concerned about how long your baby nurses or whether she nurses on both sides. Just relax and enjoy this very special moment.

WHEN SHOULD THE BABY NURSE?

Your breast-feeding experience in the immediate postpartum period will be somewhat affected by the hospital and birth situation you have chosen. The ideal situation is one that permits you to feed your baby whenever she cries or seems hungry. She will probably want to eat approximately every one and a half to three hours, because it takes about one and a half hours for the stomach to empty after a breast feeding. If you feed your baby every time she seems hungry, with no rules or limitations as to how long she can eat, or how often, then you are practicing what is called unrestricted breast feeding. But you may be in a hospital in which the babies are typically brought to the mothers from the nursery every four hours for feeding, whether they are hungry or not. This is token breast feeding. The baby is fed on a schedule and the time and duration are restricted. With token breast feeding, the baby may also be given water or formula from a bottle.

It has been shown that if breast feeding can be done in an unrestricted way it is much more likely to be successful. But even if restrictions are imposed during the first few days because of the hospital situation, do not despair. You can do whatever you want when you get home. Meanwhile, if you are in a rather restricted environment you may certainly ask that your baby not be given water or formula in the nursery and that she be brought to you throughout the night for feeding. You may also ask that she be brought to you every three hours or whenever she is crying in the nursery. It would certainly take a nurse no longer to bring the baby to you than to go over and prepare a bottle for her when she cries. If you have early and frequent feedings your breasts will be less likely to become engorged, and your milk will tend to come in earlier. If the baby can be fed frequently, there will be no difference in weight loss between the breast-fed baby and the bottle-fed baby in the first five days of life.

FEED WITH BOTH BREASTS

You will want to get into the routine right away of feeding from both breasts. Until your milk supply is well established, try feeding your baby for five to ten minutes on the first breast. She may fall asleep, want to burp, or need a diaper change by that time. Then you can finish on the other side, and the baby can nurse as long as she likes. When it is time for the next feeding, simply reverse the order. To keep track, you may wish to place a safety pin in your bra indicating which side you ended with.

How can you tell whether your baby is full? Babies often nurse with clenched fists, which characteristically relax and open as they begin to feel full. She may make a grimace or arch her back and stretch, or she may simply fall asleep. If she has only nursed on one side and falls asleep, do not try to wake her by jiggling her, snapping her feet, working her jaw, or pinching her. This can be too upsetting for a baby. You might try burping her, changing her diapers, or just letting her rest a while before you try the other side. Many breast-fed babies do not need to be burped, but you might try if she stops nursing and seems uncomfortable.

NURSING PATTERNS

In the first few days after delivery your baby may be quite sleeply and uninterested in nursing. Don't worry about this. She will eat in good time. Some babies are slow to take hold initially, and if you express some colostrum from the nipple and put it on her lips, she will sometimes be encouraged to take some more. Dabbing a little cool water on her forehead may also help rouse her enough to try to take the nipple again. If it doesn't, let her sleep. She'll soon wake again. Most babies can let you know they are hungry by making mouthing movements or sucking vigorously on their hands. If you don't feed them they'll start to fuss and finally, cry. Learn your baby's signals and feed her before she has to cry, if you can.

Dr. George Barnes, of the Yale Medical Center, described many years ago some characteristic nursing patterns that you might see in your baby. He divided nursing styles into five different categories:

1. *"The barracudas"*—These babies are extremely vigorous and long-winded nursers, often going for ten to twenty minutes even from the beginning. They can wreak havoc with a tender nipple, but they certainly make you feel wanted!
2. *"The excited ineffectives"*—These babies tend to become overexcited and cry when beginning breast feeding, alternately grasping and losing the breast. They need to be calmed down and soothed by being held closely and talked to softly. After a few days they will do quite well.
3. *"The procrastinators"*—Until the milk comes in, these babies have absolutely no interest in the breast no matter what you do. Then they settle in very nicely.
4. *"The gourmets, or mouthers"*—These babies will mouth the nipple, smack their lips, taste a little bit, and then repeat the performance before really starting to nurse. It is important not to hurry them.
5. *"The resters"*—These little ones will nurse a few minutes, rest a few minutes, and then nurse a few minutes more. They too do not need to be rushed. Their pace will gradually pick up.

Instead of fitting exactly into any of these categories, your baby may fall in between. But you will certainly recognize a pattern within the first week of life, and discovering it is fun.

COLOSTRUM

During the first few days of breast feeding the baby will be receiving colostrum, which is a clear yellowish liquid. It is high in protein, low in fat, and rich in vitamins A and E, and so fits perfectly the needs of the newborn. Because it is also extremely rich in antibodies, the colostrum adds to the protection provided by the antibodies given through the placenta. Colostrum is known to facilitate good bacterial growth in the intestinal tract and to improve the passage of the meconium (dark green, sticky newborn stool). Colostrum looks thin and watery and certainly doesn't have the appearance of anything very nourishing, but it is just what your baby needs at this time.

Your milk will come in within two to four days after delivery, although one to two weeks will go by before the milk is completely mature. Mature milk is a bluish-white color and rather watery, like colostrum less nourishing-looking than bottled formula. Just remember that your milk is the perfect nourishment for your baby.

THE LET-DOWN REFLEX

Your milk comes in through a mechanism called *let-down*. It can be felt in the breast as a tingling or a sudden tense fullness that mothers describe as "the milk-coming-in" sensation. Some women start feeling it as soon as their milk comes in. Others will not notice the feeling until the third to eighth week even though their milk has come in.

The let-down reflex can be brought on by the thought of the baby, by hearing babies cry, by hand-expressing milk, or by massaging the breast. But the most efficient stimulus is the baby's sucking, which will cause let-down within one minute. The reflex can be inhibited by cold, pain, or emotional stress. Sometimes nicotine interferes with let-down, so the mother should wait until let-down occurs before lighting a cigarette—if she must smoke during nursing. Excessive alcohol (not just one drink) can also interfere with let-down. The volume of milk that a baby receives is definitely affected by the let-down reflex. If there is no let-down, the baby receives much less milk with a feeding and can become frustrated.

Since let-down can sometimes be stimulated by manual expression of the breast before feeding, it may become necessary to do so if your baby is weak or reluctant to nurse and does not stimulate the nipples enough. Hand expression is also helpful if your nipples are sore, for the baby will not have to suck so hard for milk.

The let-down reflex may not become well established right away, and you may need to encourage it. If your breasts begin leaking, pick your baby up and feed her even though she doesn't seem to be hungry. She will nurse a little bit. Try to feed her as often as every two to three hours; and if you know approximately when she is going to eat, about five minutes ahead of time try relaxing in the chair in which you are going to nurse. Have a snack or a drink and just rest and close your eyes. If you are feeling tense, sometimes a glass of wine or beer can serve as a sedative or relaxant. Remove distractions if you can. Once your let-down is well established it will be more secure, as many an experienced nursing mother can tell you. Even a big emotional shock or staying up all night with a sick child will not stop the flow of milk.

But sometimes, in spite of all these efforts, let-down does not occur, and your baby remains hungry even though your breasts are full. Don't give up! You must get in touch with your physician, who can prescribe a nasal spray of oxytocin, which will cause let-down. Usually one spray into one or both of your nostrils two to three minutes before putting the baby to the breast will do the trick. You do not have to continue the treatment for long, because the let-down reflex will be conditioned in this way.

Once your let-down is well established, you may find leaking can be a nuisance. Because the let-down reflex occurs in both breasts at the same time, during feeding you will often have a fair amount of leaking from the breast that is not being nursed. This can be stopped by pressing your finger or the heel of your hand against the nipple. If you are storing or freezing your milk you can also make sure to have a sterile jar nearby to collect any milk that leaks out.

If you are worried about leaking in public, tuck a hankie or gauze pad into your bra. Stop the flow by folding your arms and pressing the heels of your hands against your breasts.

MANUAL (HAND) EXPRESSION

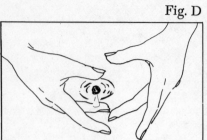

Fig. D

Hand expression is useful in many situations. To hand-express your milk, rest your breast in the palm of your hand, with your thumb on top and your middle finger on the bottom. Gently squeeze your thumb and finger together and move gradually toward the edge of the areola. Do not squeeze the areola or the nipple. Let your fingers go loose and glide back toward the chest, then repeat the procedure (see Fig. D). At first you may not get anything except a few drops, but if you continue for a few minutes you will gradually stimulate a spray of milk. If you have trouble starting the flow, use hot compresses on the breast or do your hand expression while in a warm shower or bath.

MANAGING THE HOME FRONT

One of the keys to successful breast feeding is to get plenty of rest. Try to stay in bed during your first three days at home. And we mean really in bed! Have the baby in a bassinet or crib right next to your bed, where you can reach her easily. If you have other small children at home, keep them in the room with you as much as possible. You will find that if you stay in bed, visitors don't linger. And you won't feel that you should wait on them.

It's very important to take naps as often as possible. Some people recommend three one-hour naps a day. That's fine, if you have a baby who sleeps that long. When your baby is asleep take that opportunity to rest and sleep yourself. Take the phone off the hook and put a "Please Come Back" sign on the door while you are nursing or sleeping.

Many mothers find that on the day when they get home from the hospital they feel frazzled and tired, and their babies seem to be more irritable and need to be fed more frequently. Take heart. Your baby will eventually settle down and you will have plenty of milk.

It is very important to remember to eat. So again, try to arrange for some help for the first few weeks when you are home. Find someone who can do the housework, prepare the meals, chauffeur the other children where they need to go, do the laundry, and basically take care of you—not your baby.

A mother with no one to help her during these hectic days may feel that she doesn't even have time to take a bath. Once the baby's umbilical cord has fallen off, however, you can solve that problem quite easily: Nurse your baby in the bathtub. Bathing together is a good way to get her used to the water. You can relax and feed her at the same time. Be sure to have a rubber mat on the bottom of the tub so that you won't slip. And have a place prepared at the side of the tub where you can lay the baby after she has finished feeding. You can cover her up warmly and complete your bath with her beside you.

No doubt your friends will give you other tips about ways to find rest time for yourself. Use the ones that fit your own style and personality. Before you know it, you will be finding your own ingenious ways to get the rest you need—and soon you'll be giving advice to other new mothers.

C L O T H I N G

Make sure that you have comfortable clothes that also provide easy access to the breast. During the first few weeks you may feel more comfortable in your nightgown than in your street clothes. A nursing bra that covers too much of the breast can prevent good mouth attachment to the areola. Bras with two straps on both sides of each breast work best. You will probably be more comfortable if you wear your nursing bra twenty-four hours a day, to give support to your full breasts.

Later, two-piece outfits are the most practical. You may want to invest in some drip-dry shirts or overblouses. If you want to nurse discreetly you can unbutton the buttons of your blouse and put your baby on your breast, possibly covering her with a lightweight blanket or a diaper.

Y O U R   N U T R I T I O N   A S   A   M O T H E R

All over the world women produce adequate and abundant milk on inadequate diets, although well-fed mothers tend to have healthier infants. If the mother's diet is very inadequate it tends to affect the volume of milk rather than the composition, because milk production uses the essential nutrients from the mother's body before she can use them herself.

During pregnancy, your body builds up approximately two to four kilograms of extra tissue, essentially for the lactation period. Lactation, or the production of milk, requires anywhere from 500 to 1,000 extra calories of energy a day. If you have been well nourished through pregnancy and have this extra weight on board, you will need to eat only about 500 to 600 extra calories, unless you want to gain weight. The better nourished you are and the more fat there is in your diet, the higher the caloric content of your milk, thus the bigger and healthier your baby will be. If you have good eating habits, don't change now. Be sure you eat from the four basic groups—dairy, meat and eggs, fruit and vegetables, bread and cereals—and stay away from empty calories such as sweets. On days when you don't feel that you've eaten adequately, take an iron and vitamin supplement.

L I Q U I D S

You will naturally feel the need for more liquids. Water is the largest component of human milk, and the water in your body will go preferentially to the production of milk, over such things as urine and sweat. Don't force yourself to drink, but pay attention to when you are thirsty. A good time for taking a drink is before or during nursing. Constipation and very dark urine are signs of a need to increase your fluids.

You do not necessarily have to drink milk. You can get your calcium from cheese, yogurt, or ice cream. If you are allergic to milk, ask your doctor about other sources of calcium or the possibility of taking a calcium supplement.

VITAMIN SUPPLEMENTS

If you are a strict vegetarian you will most definitely need a supplement of vitamin B_{12} for your baby's health, because this vitamin is simply not present in a strict vegetarian diet.

It has been shown that the body increases its need for vitamin C with stress. So it is appropriate for pregnant women and nursing mothers to increase their intake of vitamin C, which is rapidly excreted in milk. I (AA) noted in my pregnancies that I had a marked craving for oranges above all other fruit. I had always wondered why until this information came to light. It is interesting to see how the body gets what it needs if you only follow its signals.

TO BE AVOIDED

Some foods can cause your baby to have indigestion, particularly the ones with strong flavors such as garlic, onions, cabbage, turnips, broccoli, beans, rhubarb, apricots, and prunes. If your baby has been nursing quite comfortably and has had no intestinal upsets, and you suddenly notice that she is irritable or has excessive gas or diarrhea, you might review what you have eaten that day; one of the above-mentioned foods may be the culprit. Also if you eat a lot of fresh fruits, such as melons or peaches, the baby may experience some diarrhea. Distress will usually appear approximately six to eight hours after your intake of the offending food and will last about twenty-four hours for the baby.

Excessive use of drinks containing caffeine, such as coffee, tea, cola, and even some of the "uncola" drinks such as Mountain Dew, may build up caffeine in the baby's system and make her rather nervous, fretful, and wakeful. Six to eight cups of these beverages a day should be the *maximum* intake. Less would be better.

Nicotine is excreted in breast milk. If you smoke one pack a day, your baby may show signs of restlessness, vomiting, diarrhea, and rapid heartbeat. Avoid smoking at all while your baby is at the breast—it interferes with let-down, the hot ashes may burn her, and the smoke she inhales can cause respiratory infections and allergies.

One glass of wine or beer causes a very small amount of alcohol to appear in the milk and has not been found to be harmful to babies. However, higher concentrations of alcohol in the milk may cause your baby to develop low blood sugar and fail to grow well, and may possibly affect brain development.

DRUG INTAKE

Any medication or drug that you take can be excreted in the breast milk. We will mention a few here, but it is important that you discuss with your physician the effects of any medicine that you are taking or that he might prescribe for you while you are breast-feeding. We are not saying that you should go without necessary medications; something can usually be found that is safe for the baby, and a schedule of medication (i.e., taking the drug immediately after nursing) can be devised so that the baby receives the least amount possible.

Antibiotics are among the most common drugs prescribed. With the exception of sulpha (in the first month of life), tetracycline, and chloramphenicol, most antibiotics should be quite safe for your baby. Analgesics such as Tylenol are not absorbed as readily as aspirin and can be used safely. Aspirin is absorbed rapidly and can build up in the baby's body because she does not excrete it as rapidly as an adult. If you need to take aspirin, try to do so immediately after nursing so that its effects can peak and ebb before the next feeding.

Anticonvulsants (seizure medications) can create problems and should definitely be checked on. Phenobarbital, which is an anticonvulsant, has not been linked with any difficulties; but if you take it, you should watch your baby for signs of drowsiness.

Many doctors feel that oral contraceptives are best avoided, because we do not yet know the long-term effects on babies who have ingested breast milk containing hormones from the contraceptives. It has been shown that oral contraceptives can interfere with the production of milk at the very beginning of breast feeding. Once lactation is well established, however, they have no further effect.

Antihistamines present no problem. Cough medicines and some medicines for nasal stuffiness contain ephedrine, which can sometimes make the baby irritable. Asthma medication such as theophylline has been shown to be safe.

If a mother must undergo diagnostic tests using radioactive material, it is essential that she stop breast feeding for at least twenty-four hours and sometimes for as long as seventy-two hours after the intake of the radioactive materials. Again, she should always check with her doctor.

We know definitely that heroin is excreted in breast milk, and the baby can become addicted. Methadone and Darvon are also excreted abundantly into breast milk and should be used carefully.

COMPONENTS OF HUMAN MILK

As we mentioned above, water is the largest component of human milk. And studies done in hot, humid climates show that the mother's milk provides the baby with adequate fluid intake without the need for supplemental water.

Fat is the second largest component and is essential for proper brain maturation and development. The amount of fat in breast milk varies with the stage of feeding and the time of day. For example, there is increasingly more fat in the milk as it is produced from early morning until noon. And there is much more fat in the milk produced at the end of the feeding; therefore the baby who nurses for a longer time, at least more than five minutes, will receive many more calories and be more satisfied. The amount of fat also varies with the stage of lactation, and there is less fat in the milk after the baby is six months of age.

The breast milk of a mother with an adequate diet contains all the vitamins a baby needs with the possible exception of one, vitamin D. Because breast milk is low in vitamin D, many physicians believe in giving a vitamin D supplement to nursing babies. This supplement is especially important in areas of the world where there is not much sunshine or where the baby is not exposed to outside air and sunshine, or if the mother has a poor diet. Vitamin D deficiency in babies can result in a bone affliction called rickets. If there is any question about sufficiency, it is much simpler to go ahead and give the vitamin D drops.

Physicians used to believe that breast-fed babies did not get enough iron and that they needed an iron supplement. But now it has been shown that iron absorption from breast milk is very efficient and that there is no need for supplements in the first six months of life. After six months the baby definitely needs more iron than can be obtained from breast milk; but as the baby usually begins eating solids about this time, she can get her iron from these sources.

Fluoride levels are low in breast milk, even if the mother is drinking fluoridated water. Therefore many physicians recommend a fluoride supplement during infancy; however, studies in which breast-fed babies and bottle-fed babies have been compared in terms of dental health show that the breast-fed babies have fewer caries and better dental health, even though fluoride was not given. If your family has a history of tooth decay, a fluoride supplement should be considered for extra protection.

The fine curd of breast milk makes it easy to digest, and its white blood cells, antibodies, and immunoglobulins seem to protect the gut against the invasion of viruses and bacteria. That is why breast-fed babies have a lower incidence of gastrointestinal and respiratory infections, both bacterial and viral.

Breast milk also seems to have qualities that protect babies from allergies. Twenty percent of all infant allergies are to cow's milk. Food allergies can result in colic, excessive vomiting, diarrhea, blood in the stools, blood in the vomitus, weight loss, failure to thrive, eczema, runnny nose, or asthma. If your family has a strong history of allergies, the chances of your baby's developing allergies will be lessened by breast feeding for the first six months of life. We will deal in more detail with the subject of allergies.

DEVELOPING A SCHEDULE

During the first month of life the newborn baby usually needs to eat about ten times a day. There may be one period of the day when she will go for five to six hours without waking. But she will make up for that time with more frequent feedings in between. Other babies like to eat every two to three hours. Some less fortunate mothers have voracious little nursers who want to eat every one to one and a half hours. A mother with such a child once complained to me (AA) in one of her exhausted moments that she felt as though she had given birth to a leech! If you are really lucky, you may have a baby who tends to be at the other extreme: hungry only about every three to four hours.

Breast milk empties from the baby's stomach in one and a half hours—certainly much more rapidly than formula, which stays in the stomach for approximately three hours. Some babies can tolerate an empty stomach longer than others; the active, alert baby is less able to do so than the placid, sleepy baby.

For example, in the beginning there will be days when the times between feedings seem to be lengthening, and you will give a big sigh of relief—thinking the hardest part is over. But then the very next day all your hopes may be shattered when the baby wants to eat even *more* frequently! This usually means that it is time for your milk production to increase to satisfy her growth needs. We call these days *frequency days*. They typically occur around the sixth day, the fourteenth day, and during the third to fourth months of life. Your baby will want to nurse more frequently for several days and will probably want to stay at the breast for a longer time. I (AA) have had many mothers call me in a panic because they were sure their milk was not rich enough and they thought maybe they should give a supplement. I definitely do not advise giving a supplement on a frequency day, because the baby—being satisfied with the supplemental feedings—would not stimulate the breast to produce more milk.

The production of milk is a beautiful example of the theory of supply and demand. The more milk the baby needs, as signaled by her sucking, the more milk the breast will produce. When the baby suckles less, the breast produces less milk.

After the first month a schedule will gradually begin to emerge. Your baby will probably need to eat about eight times a day during the second and third months. This pattern will decrease to seven times a day in the fourth and fifth months, and by the sixth month she will need to eat about five to six times a day. Some babies will begin to drop their night feeding (the one between twelve at night and six in the morning) as early as six weeks to two months. But it is certainly not unusual to see this night feeding continue on into the fifth month, and is one of those situations when breast feeding seems so much more convenient. You can take the baby into bed with you and nurse her while you doze.

If you don't see a schedule emerging for your baby, don't assume that something is going wrong. Start keeping a daily diary of the times of feeding and their duration, the sleep periods and their duration, and the wakeful periods and their duration. Many times by simply keeping such a diary you yourself will begin to see that your baby is truly developing a schedule, and you can relax. Otherwise, take the diary to your pediatrician. He will probably find a pattern.

To establish a schedule for breast feeding, milk production must be adequate. And there are three keys to assure effective milk production.

1. *Suckling at the breast must occur.*
2. *The breast must be emptied at every feeding.* Otherwise, less milk will be produced for the next feeding. Studies have shown that almost all the milk is taken in by the baby in the first seven minutes of nursing. If she continues to nurse after that time, the smaller quantity of milk that she receives is of higher caloric content, for it contains more fat than the milk at the beginning of the feeding. The extra suckling will stimulate more milk supply and also give the baby the comfort she needs. The baby will stop nursing when she has had enough nutrition and comfort. Don't worry if she stops after five minutes or needs to continue for twenty or thirty minutes. She is merely doing what she needs to do.
3. *The mother must take in the proper nutrients herself.*

THE REWARDS OF GIVING

The hormonal release that occurs during breast feeding has a very calming effect on the nursing mother. It lessens her response to stress, gives her a more even mood cycle, and is physically relaxing. In the early stages there is also great physical need to have the breasts emptied if they are overfull. Sometimes I (AA) just couldn't wait for my baby to get down to business! This helped to show me that I needed my baby as much as she needed me, and I felt very grateful to her for helping me out.

Breast feeding is a psychologically satisfying experience. You feel very proud that you can produce something that makes your baby grow so strong and healthy. If you are advised to stop nursing suddenly, a marked grief reaction will occur. You may go to extremes to avoid stopping, even denying yourself medical care. This reaction is a very normal one, though many physicians and others find it hard to understand and may make you feel like a neurotic, hysterical mother. But don't you believe it! You're only following a natural instinct to preserve something that is very special between you and your child.

GROWTH OF THE BREAST-FED BABY

Bottle feeding has been in vogue for so long that the standards of growth and development in the first months of life are based on those of bottle-fed babies. Because bottle-fed babies are more likely to take in extra calories (especially from the earlier onset of solid foods), their weight gain is usually more rapid. Thus breast-feeding mothers may fear that their milk is not rich enough, whereas in fact the bottle-fed babies may be overfed. The average breast-fed baby gains four to seven ounces a week, or one to two pounds a month. It usually takes one hundred days for him to double his birth weight.

One of the periods in breast feeding when some physicians are concerned about weight loss and may try to intervene is the first few days of life. Typically the bottle-fed baby is given feedings of sugar water and formula. It has been the custom in many hospitals to give the breast-fed babies bottles of sugar water and/or formula also, under the hypothesis that because the breast milk does not come in for several days, the baby cannot be receiving any nourishment. All bottles tend to confuse the baby because of the difference between the rubber nipple and his mother's nipple. In fact, studies show that such supplemental feedings usually have a reverse effect from that expected: Breast-fed infants who are given added water or formula in the first few days of life lose more weight and are less likely to start gaining prior to discharge than those who are entirely breast- or bottle-fed. All babies lose weight in the first few days of life, but they usually regain it within five to ten days.

There are rare instances, of course, of the breast-fed baby failing to thrive because of health problems or a problem with his mother's milk. In these cases the baby will need supplemental feedings.

BREAST PROBLEMS

Some mothers experience problems with their breasts, most often in the initial nursing period, that can cause anxiety and concern as well as occasional discomfort.

ENGORGEMENT

One of the first concerns of the mother, particularly the first-time breast-feeder, is that of engorgement. There are two types of engorgement. The first is areolar, when excessive milk causes swelling in the areolar area, making it hard and full, so that the baby has difficulty getting a good hold for sucking. Consequently, he sucks only on the nipple, which does not result in good milk flow and also bruises the nipple.

When areolar engorgement occurs it is important to lightly massage the area with your fingertips and hand-express milk until your areolar area is soft (see p. 68). Even if no milk is expressed, doing this rhythmically for five minutes on each side will soften the areolar area enough for the baby to get a better hold.

The second type of engorgement involves the peripheral area of the breast as well as the areola. The whole breast becomes full, quite hard, tender, red, and shiny. The breast aches and throbs and feels warm to the touch. It hurts to move, and the mother may have difficulty sleeping. Breast massage or hand expression of milk is nearly impossible because the breasts are so full and hard. In this situation, soaking in a warm bathtub or standing under a hot shower will assist in softening the breast and starting the milk flow.

While taking the bath or shower you can begin gently massaging the breast from the periphery to the areola, followed by hand expression. If you can hand-express enough to make the areolar area soft, your baby will do the rest for you. It is important to nurse frequently and for long periods of time so that the breast is emptied completely. If your baby is unable to nurse because of illness, you might check with your physician about the possibility of using a breast pump. The best is the Egnell Pump, which simulates the milking action of the baby. The traditional electric pump and the hand pumps can be sheer torture in this situation.

It is important when your breasts are engorged to have very good support from your bra. Aspirin or Tylenol, and, if necessary, codeine, can help get you through this difficult but brief period. The situation rarely lasts longer than two to three days and need not last more than one day if your baby is a good nurser.

PLUGGED DUCT

Another complication that can develop at any stage of nursing, but more frequently in the first few weeks, is a plugged duct. This happens when some of the milk has caked and hardened inside the duct in one section, causing a hard, tender, reddened area on the breast near the nipple or in the peripheral area. Because the condition is usually due to inadequate emptying of a given section, try changing your position for nursing. For instance, if you always nurse lying down on your side, the area least likely to be emptied is that under your armpit. To avoid developing a plugged duct in that area, alternate between lying down and sitting up while you feed your baby.

Sometimes dry milk secretions can cover some of the nipple openings (there are many—approximately fifteen to twenty-five), preventing good milk drainage. Simply soaking the nipple area in warm compresses and gently rubbing will remove these secretions. Do not use soap or alcohol, for they irritate the nipple. Another possible cause of this condition is a bra that is too tight in one area so that the ducts are compressed and the milk cannot be obtained.

A warm bath or hot compresses can also be very effective in relieving the discomfort of a plugged duct. Nursing frequently and for longer periods is helpful too. And while nursing or while in the bathtub, try gently massaging and compressing the hardened area toward the nipple. If one breast is very tender and initial nursing is painful, nurse on the opposite side first in order to allow the let-down reflex to occur.

BREAST INFECTION

Sometimes a breast problem develops into an infection, which is called *mastitis*. Mastitis consists of breast tenderness as well as a flu-like syndrome with fever and malaise. The treatment for this condition is antibiotics for at least ten days, plenty of rest, a good support bra, heat to the area (if you need to be up and around, a small baby's hot-water bottle wrapped in a washcloth and tucked into your bra can be very helpful), and pain relievers such as aspirin or Tylenol, or if necessary, codeine. Doctors used to believe that if a breast infection developed, the mother should stop nursing on that breast; however, we now believe that this approach is definitely wrong. It is important to keep nursing on the affected side in order to keep the breast empty and to prevent development of breast abscess. Nursing frequently and for long periods is definitely recommended. The breast milk of mothers with mastitis may have increased levels of salt, which can be harmful to infants. Taste your milk. If it tastes salty, tell your doctor.

If a breast abscess does develop, it must be opened and drained. In that event, the mother should nurse on the good side and hand-express on the abscessed side until the breast is adequately healed (usually just a few days). Fortunately, abscesses are extremely rare.

After antibiotic treatment, secondary fungal infections of the nipple may occur. This can be painful, and nursing causes stabbing pains. Treatment will be required for both mother and baby. Anything the baby has sucked on, such as a pacifier, should be thrown away to avoid reinfection.

SORE NIPPLES

Another source of discomfort in the early period is sore nipples. In the first few days it is common to experience sudden twinges of pain when the baby first grasps and sucks on the breast. As the feeding progresses, this pain disappears. The twinges should no longer occur once your let-down reflex is well established.

It is important to continue to expose your areolae and nipples to air from the very beginning. Leave the flaps of your bra down after nursing or cut holes in your bra if you do not have flaps. When nipples are particularly tender and clothing irritates them, some mothers have found it helpful to insert old-fashioned tea strainers (which you might find in a dime store) inside their bra cups, which protect the nipples while allowing air to circulate. You can also try a heat lamp or an electric lamp with a 60-watt bulb—for twenty minutes two to three times a day.

We also recommend the careful use of a sunlamp at a distance of four feet, but make sure that your eyes are covered. On day one, allow your exposure to be half a minute; on days two and three, one minute; and from then on, two minutes per day.

Sucking or licking the nipple irritates it. Your baby will do this if you try to feed him when he is too sleepy or not hungry. This also happens if he is hungry, but not positioned properly at the breast. Gently pull back on his forehead and look at him while he sucks. Is most of the areola showing? Are his cheeks dimpled? Are his lips puckered? If any of these are true, he is not sucking properly. Remove him gently and reposition him so that he has good suction on the areola (p. 68).

If your nipples are so tender that you feel apprehensive about the initial suck, try to relax by drinking a glass of beer or wine. Take some aspirin or Tylenol and hand-express some milk before the feeding, so that let-down can occur. Alternating feeding positions may also help.

CRACKED NIPPLES

If pain persists through nursing, your nipples should be examined in a good light to check for the possibility of cracks. When there are true cracks in the breast, some people recommend that the infant be taken off the affected breast for twenty-four to forty-eight hours, with nursing continuing only on the other side. We do not agree; for when nursing is stopped on a breast, engorgement and possible plugging of the ducts tend to result.

We believe that the best method for dealing with cracked nipples is that recommended by Dr. Ruth Lawrence at the University of Rochester, a pediatrician who is an expert in the area of breast feeding. She recommends both hand expression of some milk before feeding and careful positioning of the baby on the breast to avoid aggravating the cracked condition. The baby should nurse on the unaffected breast first, and the affected side should be left exposed to the air. Dr. Lawrence also recommends applying some of the expressed breast milk directly on the nipples and letting it dry there between feedings. In addition, she advocates exposure to dry heat four times a day for fifteen to twenty minutes with a 60-watt bulb, or a heat lamp placed eighteen inches away. If necessary, a nipple shield can be used while nursing, but she does not recommend these unless all else has failed. She cautions against the use of shields made entirely of rubber, because they draw and pull the skin. Glass or plastic with a rubber nursing nipple works well and has the advantage that the mother can see the milk through the shield.

If these remedies are not successful, you will temporarily have to stop nursing on the affected side and turn to hand expressing or pumping. You may also need to take aspirin or codeine just after nursing. The encouraging part is that once the cracked nipples have healed, it is very unlikely that the condition will occur again because the nipples and the areolae will now have been adequately toughened.

FLAT NIPPLES

The other difficulties that can arise are all related to flat or small nipples. In these cases, it is helpful to compress and flatten the areolar area and breast between thumb and middle finger, to provide as much of the nipple area as possible for the baby to get a good hold. Sometimes a nipple shield is necessary for the first few minutes of the feeding, to draw the nipple out. Then it should be removed and the infant put right on the breast to finish the feeding. Once nursing is well established, flat or small nipples do not continue to be a problem.

FLABBY BREASTS

Often a mother becomes concerned after she comes home from the hospital because her breasts, which were so engorged and full, suddenly seem soft and flabby. This is a very natural condition which has nothing to do with milk production. Don't worry: There is plenty of milk for the baby.

INFANT PROBLEMS

CHOKING

Sometimes infants develop problems that create anxiety during the nursing period. For example, occasionally if a mother has a very strong let-down reflex, the milk will come out in a spray while the baby is nursing, causing him to choke or cough and scaring the mother. If this happens with your baby, don't worry. He will soon be able to adjust. In the meantime, just hand-express your milk to decrease some of the pressure before putting him to the breast. You only have to do it on the first breast, as the second one will already have leaked somewhat before he begins.

PHYSICAL ABNORMALITIES

Some babies are born with an abnormality of the jaw, nose, or mouth that interferes with nursing, by either breast or bottle. If your baby has a receding chin, or small jaw, you can help by holding his jaw forward while he nurses. To do this, hook the angles of your baby's jaw with your finger and thumb and gently pull forward while his chin rests on your hand. If this is difficult, call your doctor, nurse or nursing support group for some help. The child born with a cleft lip or palate may require a special device that fits into the mouth to promote good sucking. The physician will put this in; he realizes that it is important to encourage the suck in order to strengthen the tongue and jaw muscles and to encourage proper development before corrective surgery is performed. If you feel you need it, be sure to ask for help from someone with experience in these types of feeding problems. It sometimes takes only a few suggestions to get you over the hump.

POOR SUCKING

A baby with normal jaw development may initially have poor sucking and not be able to hold onto the nipple area. If this happens you can compress the areolar area between your thumb and index finger and hold it in the baby's mouth throughout the feeding. As he becomes older and stronger, his sucking should improve and this problem should disappear.

Sometimes a baby who has been exposed to rubber nipples on a bottle may become upset or frustrated when he tries to nurse at the breast. In this situation you will need to soothe the baby and keep trying. It helps to express some milk and let him taste it, so that he knows he will get something for his efforts. Some mothers even put corn syrup on their nipples in order to entice the baby to stay there. Take heart! Your baby will learn to nurse at the breast in no time at all if you just relax and take it easy.

You may have a very fussy, active baby who cries shortly after feeding and seems to want to nurse again, only to spit up and cry some more. Wrap the baby snugly and warmly, and hold and cuddle him closely. While you are doing this, try to give him a pacifier to satisfy his extra sucking needs without offering him any more milk. If you are lucky he will learn to take the pacifier, but don't count on it! Some mothers with babies like this have found it helpful to nurse frequently, using only one breast at a feeding. The baby can then suck on the breast after it has emptied. **F U S S Y   B A B Y**

Sometimes a mother becomes concerned about the bowel movements of her nursing baby, especially because they are different from the bowel movements of a bottle-fed baby. They tend to be the consistency of pea soup—rather loose and unformed, with a very mild odor. They can vary in frequency anywhere from six to ten a day or sometimes, as the baby gets older, once every four to five days. Don't worry. This is a normal condition. **B O W E L   M O V E M E N T S**

Although breast-fed babies have less chance of being colicky, colic can certainly develop. **C O L I C**

S P E C I A L   S I T U A T I O N S

There are several special situations that can cause concerns about breast feeding.

There is no reason why the mother who has had a Cesarean section should not breast-feed. She may feel alert enough to be able to put the infant to the breast within the first twelve hours. Sometimes a mother who has had regional anesthesia can nurse within the first hour after surgery. **C E S A R E A N   S E C T I O N**

The mother wanting to breast-feed after a C-section will need a great deal of help from the nursing staff—especially if she has had a spinal anesthetic and must lie flat on her back for the first twenty-four hours in order to prevent headaches. If she has someone to pick up the infant for her, there is no reason that she cannot nurse.

She will probably need pain medication for the first seventy-two hours, and in the first forty-eight hours this should not affect the infant at all. In the next twenty-four hours, however, the medication should be given immediately after breast feeding, and should be limited to short-acting drugs, so as to affect the baby as little as possible.

It is especially important when a mother has had a C-section that she get sufficient rest in the hospital and at home.

TOXEMIA IN THE MOTHER

During pregnancy, a mother's health can be jeopardized by toxemia, a condition causing high blood pressure and sometimes convulsions. The condition usually begins to improve twenty-four to forty-eight hours after the baby is born but may continue for a longer time. The mother requires sedation during this time, but when the sedative intake has been decreased she can begin to breast-feed her baby. The baby should be observed carefully for any side effects, such as drowsiness.

ILLNESS IN THE MOTHER

Any minor infections, such as a cold, the flu, or gastrointestinal upsets, present no problem for breast feeding. The baby has already been exposed to your germs before the symptoms appeared, and many times he does not contract the illness. You have provided him some protection through the immunity in the breast milk.

If your illness is more serious, you must discuss your breast-feeding plans with your doctor. If you are hospitalized, you may pump your breasts in order to maintain your milk supply while your baby is fed at home. In some cases, if your illness is not that serious (for example, an appendectomy), the baby can be brought to you in the hospital for feeding.

In some hospitals, if it is safe for the baby and for you, you may have rooming-in while you are sick. If rooming-in isn't permitted, you should explore all the other available options. At times like these, consulting with one of the nursing support groups can be very helpful.

PREMATURE BABY

There are many degrees of prematurity, and if your baby is healthy and vigorous enough you may be able to put him to the breast immediately. Many prematures are unable to suck vigorously enough to nurse, however, and need to be fed for a while by tube or with a special premature nipple. If you wish to breast-feed, be sure to let your pediatrician know. In most neonatal intensive-care units there are people around who can assist you.

Fig. E   Make sure to hand-express your milk every two to three hours if there are no electric breast pumps available. Usually the hospital will have one, or you can rent one. You can contribute your colostrum to the baby's feeding and give him extra protection in his newborn period. Don't be discouraged if you express very little milk at first. You will produce more milk when your baby is able to suck at your breast.

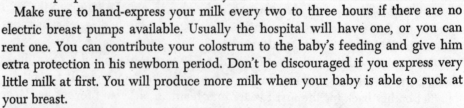

Remember that when the baby comes home from the hospital you may not yet have enough milk to satisfy his nutritional needs. Some doctors recommend giving a supplement during this period. But the University of Rochester reports that they have had excellent success with maintaining the nutrition of the breast-fed premature baby by using a special device called the Lact-Aid Nursing Supplementer (see Fig. E). It is available from Resources in Human Nurturing International, Denver, Colorado 80206, telephone 303-338-4608. With this nursing aid the baby receives the supplemental formula from a bag taped to the mother's breast. A tube carries the formula from the bag down to the mother's nipple, where the baby sucks. Less formula is needed in the bag each day, as the infant obtains more milk from the breast because of the increased nipple stimulation. The nourishment provided in the Lact-Aid Nursing Supplementer should be regular-strength formula. It is important to avoid even a day of underfeeding with a premature baby, especially one who has been in the intensive-care unit.

THE DELAYED OR RETARDED BABY

Sometimes babies are born with obvious developmental problems such as Down's syndrome. Such a baby can still be breast-fed, and he will certainly benefit from it. Some babies like this are rather placid and weak, so nursing takes a longer time and requires more effort. Others are fussy and rigid. They may startle easily or have muscle movements that tend to make them push away from the breast when they are turned to it. You can control these movements by wrapping the baby snugly in a blanket with his arms held to his chest in a flexed position. At first, he may not have good sucking or rooting reflexes and may choke easily, but do not give up.

There are professionals who are experts at feeding infants with developmental problems—occupational therapists, physical therapists, special pathologists—and you could consult one of them if you wish to continue breast feeding.

A SICK BABY

Breast milk is likely to keep your baby more healthy, but illnesses do occur. If your baby develops diarrhea, keep on nursing him. Doctors often want to put a bottle-fed baby on clear liquids when he has diarrhea, but breast milk is easily digestible and there is no need to stop nursing. In fact, you will probably nurse more frequently because it is comforting for the baby, and if he has a temperature he will be thirsty. If your baby has a respiratory infection with a stopped-up nose that makes nursing difficult, your physician can prescribe nose drops for him.

Should your baby require hospitalization, you would probably want to stay with him if possible. You can certainly breast-feed him if he can be held. If not, you can pump your milk and have it given to him by other means.

My (AA) husband, who operates on tiny infants with heart defects, often comes home marveling at the dedication of the nursing mothers of these infants. The babies are in the intensive-care unit, hooked up to so many tubes and monitors that breast feeding is impossible. Yet their mothers continue to pump their breasts and express their milk every 2 to 3 hours, freezing what they have and bringing it to the hospital.

IMMUNIZATIONS

Breast feeding does not alter your baby's need for his regular DPT (diphtheria, whooping cough, and tetanus) shots and boosters. Doctors used to believe that breast milk might interfere with polio immunizations. But now this has been disproved, so no special arrangements need be made with polio immunizations. Measles, mumps, and rubella vaccines can be given on a regular schedule.

If you need to be vaccinated, check with your doctor or the health department first. You should not have a smallpox vaccination if your child is under one year of age. This prohibition has nothing to do with breast feeding or bottle feeding. It is the infant's contact with the vaccination site that causes the risk.

PREGNANCY What if you become pregnant while you are nursing your baby? There should not be any physical problems as long as you make sure to increase your dietary intake to meet both the needs of the baby at the breast and the baby growing in your womb. You will also need plenty of rest. After the second birth you can continue to nurse both your older child and your baby if you wish to do so. Again, be aware of the need for rest and more food. If you plan to stop nursing your older child after the new one is born, you should probably do so before delivery so that he doesn't have too many adjustments to make afterward.

MULTIPLE BIRTHS You can certainly nurse twins and even triplets, as many mothers have done. Twins can be nursed simultaneously, thus saving you some feeding time. They can be put to the breast in crisscross fashion (see Fig. F) or be held in the football fashion, propped up on pillows (see Fig. G). If they don't wake up at the same time at night you can breast-feed the first baby and then awaken the other to feed. You can also burp one by laying him on his tummy across your lap and patting him while you nurse the other. Obviously feeding triplets becomes more complicated; and if you get too fatigued you may need to give some supplements. We urge you to contact a nursing support group for advice about feeding more than one baby.

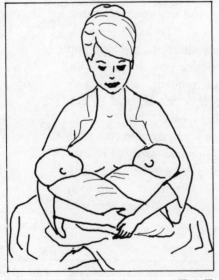 

Fig. F   Fig. G

OTHER YOUNG CHILD AT HOME Sometimes older siblings are jealous not only of the new baby but also especially of the breast feeding. And you'll discover it's certainly not easy to nurse your baby with your toddler crawling all over your lap or choosing that particular time to flush his diaper down the toilet. You can help ease the initial time of jealousy by explaining to your older child that you fed him in this way too and gave him the same special time and attention. You can include him in the feeding process by reading to him or rocking him while you nurse the baby. If you are nursing the baby in bed and it is time for your older child's nap, just bring him into the bed with you and make it fun so that you all can take a nap together. Don't be shocked if your toddler, or even an older child, wants to take a sip of what the baby is drinking. It may seem a bit odd to you but try simply to allow it to take place. He will usually figure out that it is not anything special and go on about his business.

Nursing in public can be done quite easily without attracting attention if you wear suitable clothes. It is possible to nurse so discreetly that others are unaware of what is happening. If you are nursing in public and do not wish to be disturbed, pick up a book or magazine and people will be less likely to approach you. If you are out on a shopping spree and the baby suddenly decides to be hungry, you can use the ladies' room or dressing rooms in the store. I (AA) have often returned to my car to nurse if no suitable facility was available.

Traveling is certainly easier with the breast-fed baby, because you don't have to carry all the feeding paraphernalia.

NURSING IN PUBLIC

There is absolutely no reason why a nursing mother cannot enjoy sex. In fact, some women say they feel more sexual desire while they are nursing. (Others, however, say that they become less interested in sex.)

There is no reason to avoid contact with the breast during intercourse, but you and your husband should know that sexual stimulation will trigger let-down—so be prepared for the possibility of a sudden spray of milk. Some nursing mothers experience pain during intercourse because of dryness of the vaginal mucosa; this is due to the hormonal changes related to breast feeding. The situation is easily remedied, however, by applying an estrogen cream or any lubricating agent at the time of intercourse.

SEX AND BREAST FEEDING

Many, many working mothers nurse their babies, but if you do not work at home some juggling is involved. Some mothers work part-time with flexible hours so that they can breast-feed their babies for most of the feedings, perhaps having one bottle supplement (either stored breast milk or regular formula) a day. I (AA) have known mothers who have handled the situation by arranging for a cooperative and understanding baby-sitter who lives near their place of work, so that they can take their lunch hour or break period and walk over to nurse their babies. Obviously nursing on the job is easier once your milk is well established and you have some schedule—usually by around three months.

If you must be gone all day you can nurse your baby in the morning and hand-express any leftover milk to be saved for supplements later on. At lunchtime you can express milk to make yourself more comfortable, and save it, if there is a refrigerator on hand. When you get home from work you can nurse the baby, then nurse him at bedtime and again during the night. If you don't wish to go through

WORK AND BREAST FEEDING

the trouble of hand expressing or using a commercial breast pump to collect your milk, you can certainly supplement any missed feedings with the bottle. Your breasts will adjust to such a schedule, and after a week or so you should not need to hand-express milk for your own comfort if you have missed any feedings.

Obviously if you intend to combine a job with breast feeding, you will need the support and cooperation of your husband, family, and any child-care people.

BREAST REJECTION

It is not at all uncommon for a baby to reject the breast. This may occur at around three to four months of age. He may skip several feedings and then go right back to nursing. Don't worry about it. If your milk supply is well established, as it should be, you can certainly give a supplemental bottle if you have to. Some mothers report that when they start menstruating, their babies reject the breast on the first day, so that bottle supplements and hand expression are necessary. After that one day the babies go right back to nursing. A baby may also reject the breast eight to twelve hours after you have eaten strong foods such as garlic or onions.

Just because the baby rejects the breast does not mean that the time has come to wean; the rejection is usually just temporary. Sometimes a baby will turn away from only one breast, and prefer to nurse totally on the other side. If you wish to entice your baby back to the rejected side, here are some suggestions. First, the breast that the baby doesn't like may be slightly harder or fuller than the other one, so that it is more difficult for him to grasp the areola. If so, you can hand-express the milk to make the areolar and nipple area softer. You can also place a little corn syrup on that nipple, as we have recommended previously. Sometimes you can fool the baby by holding him in the same position for the rejected breast as for the other breast. Tuck his legs under your arm toward your back in the football hold, rather than resting them on your abdomen.

USING A SUPPLEMENT

Supplemental bottles can certainly be used while you are breast feeding, especially after your breast milk is well established. One bottle a day is not going to interfere with your breast feeding. It is only when bottles begin to show up more and more frequently during a twenty-four-hour period that your breast-milk production will decrease.

WEANING

Weaning is the beginning of a transfer from dependence on mother's milk to other forms of nourishment. This can occur at any time. If there is no reason for weaning early, the baby will gradually wean himself. At around nine to twelve months the baby will need more protein than the breast milk can provide. There is no reason to discontinue breast feeding when solids are begun; breast milk is beneficial to the baby through the entire first year of life.

Some babies, whether breast-fed or bottle-fed, will no longer feel the need for suckling as early as nine months of age. If they are breast-fed they will not want to be held for a feeding and will not come to the mother seeking it.

Sometimes babies who are teething, at around five to six months, will begin biting the breast. This is not a sign that the baby wishes to be weaned; it is merely a reflex for stimulating his gums. He can be quickly taught that this is not a suitable time for teething; simply remove him with a firm "no" the first two or three times he does this. Your baby may also bite because he is not interested in nursing at a particular time, even though you, because of your other demands, want him to do so. This is his way of showing you that he is going to become independent!

Most babies will continue nursing through the end of the first year, and some will nurse for several years. The breast becomes not so much their primary source of nutrition as a comfort station. You don't really need a plan for weaning if you are available to your baby or toddler and can respond to his needs. At some point he will gradually become less interested in the breast, and before you know it you may be left with just an early-morning or bedtime feeding—without really realizing how or when it happened.

If you should want or need to discontinue nursing, you can plan a gradual weaning. Simply replace one feeding at a time with solids, a bottle, or a cup. You and your baby need about a week to adjust to each such change. So after replacing the first feeding, wait a week and then replace another feeding, preferably at the opposite time of day. Continue this until only the early-morning and late-evening feedings are left. If your reason for weaning is that you are going back to work, these two feedings could certainly be maintained as long as you both wish. Or you can continue weaning until no breast feeding is necessary.

Weaning must sometimes be done very suddenly because of a mother's serious illness or an unexpected separation of mother and child, and a surrogate mother may need to be found for a feeding or two so that the baby can switch comfortably to a bottle. If the baby is already used to taking some bottles, sudden weaning is less of a problem. The mother may experience a great deal of discomfort, particularly if the weaning occurs during the first few months of breast feeding. There may be excessive engorgement and a flu-like syndrome with fever, which will last from three to four days and then disappear on its own.

We have mentioned that emergency weaning can be depressing for a mother who wishes to continue. She needs a lot of support to help her deal with her feelings. Even the mother who weans gradually, whether because of her own needs or because of her infant's lack of interest, may experience some sadness at the thought that this special time has come to an end.

NURSING SUPPORT GROUPS

Here are the names of some nursing support groups you may wish to contact.

La Leche League International, Inc.
　9616 Minneapolis Avenue
　Franklin Park, Illinois 60131

International Childbirth Education Association
   2763 N.W. 70th Street
   Seattle, Washington 98167

Resources in Human Nurturing International
   P.O. Box 6861
   3885 Forest Street
   Denver, Colorado 80206

7

THE TECHNIQUE OF BOTTLE FEEDING

As we have said, it is important to make a decision before your due date about whether you intend to breast-feed or bottle-feed your baby. If you plan to bottle-feed, you must also decide on the type of bottle and type of formula to use, so that you can have them on hand before the baby arrives.

CHOOSING THE BOTTLES

There are several types of bottles to choose from. See what's available, and talk to your friends who are bottle feeding, to see which kinds they prefer.

Glass bottles are easy to sterilize, but they can also be broken. Plastic bottles tend to lose their shape when sterilized, but they are very light and your baby will be able to hold them by herself when she gets bigger. A bottle that is also very light and very convenient is the kind that holds a sterilized plastic liner. These save you the trouble of sterilizing but are slightly more expensive than the other types of bottles.

If you plan to make up twenty-four hours of formula in advance each day, you should buy from eight to ten bottles and caps and twelve to sixteen nipples. If you are using the bottle with the disposable liner, you will need only six to eight bottle holders and twelve to sixteen nipples. If you plan to prepare an individual bottle at each feeding, you will need only two or three bottles and four to six nipples.

Among nipples, we recommend the one that most approximates the human nipple; it is shorter in length than many of the others on the market. Remember, however, that every baby is unique, and yours may in fact do better with a longer nipple.

We suggest also that you buy eight-ounce bottles rather than smaller ones, as your baby will eventually be taking eight ounces at a feeding.

CHOOSING THE FORMULA

Prepared formulas are usually made from cow's milk, which contains more protein, more butterfat, and less sugar than maternal milk. In order to make the cow's milk more suitable to the baby's digestive and nutritional needs, prepared formulas also contain added sugar, water to dilute the concentration of protein, and vegetable oils to replace butterfat. You can learn to make your own carefully measured formula with evaporated milk, water, and sugar, if you wish, and it may be every bit as good as the formula you buy from the store. But it's a lot more trouble. A word of caution: Babies do not tolerate regular cow's milk well until at least six months of age, so do not fill your baby's bottle with just plain milk.

Commercially prepared formulas also have added vitamins and sometimes extra iron as well. Many experts feel that these additions are necessary for good nutrition through twelve months of age. Your own home-prepared formula will not have these extra ingredients, so you should discuss this point with your doctor before deciding to make your own formula.

In addition to proper nutrition for your baby, you will also want to consider the factors of economy and convenience.

The least expensive formula is that which you prepare yourself using evaporated milk. It is convenient because the ingredients are readily available, but it requires more work and time to prepare. If you are interested ask your doctor about it. The next most economical formula is the powdered prepared commercial type, which you dilute with water. It requires more shaking than the other preparations, but the powder is easy to store on the shelf (always covered) and there is less wastage. It is also lighter and so easier to take with you when you are traveling. The next formula in order of expense is commercially prepared concentrated formula, which is available in thirty-two-ounce cans. You dilute it with water, one to one. The unused portions may be stored in the refrigerator (always covered) for as long as forty-eight hours after opening. The unopened can may of course be kept in your pantry. Next is the canned formula that does not have to be diluted and is ready to use. It has already been sterilized, and you simply wash the top of the can before opening it. This formula is obviously very convenient, but the cans are bulky if you are traveling.

The most convenient and most expensive type of prepared commercial formula is that which comes ready to use in disposable bottles. These are useful to an inexperienced mother in the beginning, for she does not have to worry about making formula when she is just getting used to taking care of her baby. It is also extremely convenient for traveling.

You may want to use a formula that does not contain cow's milk. Cow's milk is one of the chief causes of allergies in young children. If your family has a history of allergy, you should ask your doctor about using goat's milk or a milk substitute. To ensure that a milk substitute supplies the appropriate nutrients for your baby, ask your doctor to look up the particular formula that you are using in the literature at his disposal, to make sure that everything in the formula is as it should be.

PREPARING THE FORMULA

One of the most important steps in preparing your baby's formula is good hygiene. Because a newborn baby is more susceptible than an adult to infection, extra care should be taken to keep the bottles and milk germ-free. Wash your hands before preparing the formula or handling sterilized bottles. And remember that bacteria love warm milk; they will multiply rapidly if the formula is left to stand. Try to keep the milk you prepare as germ-free as possible, but don't get "crazy" about it!

Obviously all the equipment you use needs to be clean. Scrub the bottles with a bottle brush. Turn nipples inside out and clean them with a nipple brush or toothbrush to get into the cracks along the edges. Run a toothpick through the holes to make sure any buildup of scum is removed. Before opening a can of liquid concentrate, wash the top with hot, soapy water, rinse and dry well.

Before you use any formula check the expiration date on the container. Do not use it if it has expired. In preparing the formula remember to add *exactly* the amount of water called for in the directions on the box or can. The concentrations of these formulas are exactly suited to your baby. When you use powdered formula, measure with the scoop and level it with a knife. Measure the water level correctly by holding the measuring cup or bottle up to eye level. One caution when using the disposable plastic liners: The markings on the outside holder do not always correspond with the amount of liquid in the plastic liner, so always use a measuring cup. Be sure to cover the can of any unused liquid concentrate and refrigerate. Use within forty-eight hours.

Most parents feel that babies prefer warm milk. Surprisingly enough, studies have shown that a baby will take it cold or warm. If you wish to warm it, sit the bottle in a pan of hot water for several minutes or in a microwave oven for several seconds. To avoid scalding your baby be sure to test the temperature by letting some of the formula drip out onto the underside of your wrist.

There are several methods of preparing formula, all of them resulting in a germ-free food supply for your baby. Pick the way that best suits you and your life-style. Just try to keep it simple. Remember that the time you spend scurrying around performing unnecessary tasks is time that you could be spending enjoying your baby.

THE TERMINAL HEATING METHOD

This method allows you to prepare enough formula to last twenty-four to forty-eight hours. Both bottles and formula are sterilized together.

1. If using a liquid concentrate, open the can by punching holes with a clean can opener.
2. In a clean bowl, mix the formula with tap water as directed.
3. Pour the needed amount of mixed formula into the clean nursing bottles. Put nipples, caps, and collars on the nursing bottles loosely. The nipples should be upside down. Don't touch the sterile nipple tops when you are putting them on.
4. Put the bottles right side up, on a wire rack or clean towel in the sterilizer (or any deep pot) and add about three inches of water and bring to a boil.
5. Cover and let boil for twenty-five minutes.
6. Remove from the heat. When the bottles are cool to the touch, tighten the caps and refrigerate the bottles. Use within forty-eight hours.

THE ASEPTIC METHOD

This procedure involves sterilizing bottles and formula separately.

1. Put bottles, nipples, caps, collars, spoon, can opener, measuring pitcher, and tongs (with handles up) in a rack or clean cloth in a sterilizer (or deep pot). Fill with water, cover, and place over heat, bringing to a boil.
2. In another pan bring to boil the correct amount of water needed for mixing the formula plus two extra ounces to allow for evaporation. Cover. Remove both containers after five minutes. Allow them to cool.
3. Wash the top of the formula can with soap and hot water. Rinse, using a little of the boiled water, and dry. Shake well and punch two holes in the top with the sterile can opener.
4. Use the sterile measuring pitcher to measure water and add the correct amount of formula. Stir with sterile spoon.
5. Pour appropriate amount of mixed formula into the nursing bottles. Using clean tongs, put the nipples, collars, and caps in the bottles. The nipples should be upside down. Don't touch the sterile nipple tops when you are putting them on.
6. Refrigerate and use within forty-eight hours.

A variation of this method can be used with a liquid concentrate. Pour the concentrate into presterilized bottles or bottles with disposable plastic liners. Dilute with water that has been boiled in a teakettle for five minutes. Put the nipples, collars, and caps on as described above.

THE SINGLE-BOTTLE METHOD

With this procedure one bottle may be prepared at a time, avoiding the need to sterilize the bottles and nipples.

1. Boil thirty-two ounces of water in a pan for five minutes.
2. At the same time, place a quart jar or bottle upside down in a deep pot with several inches of water. Include the lid and a can opener. Cover and boil for five minutes.
3. Remove both pans from heat and allow to cool. Refrigerate the water in the sterile container.
4. When it is time for a feeding, pour the correct amount into a clean nursing bottle.
5. Rinse the top of the formula concentrate can with some boiled water and open, using the sterile can opener. Add the correct amount to the water in the bottle. Attach a clean nipple and shake gently to mix.
6. Cover the concentrate and refrigerate for no longer than forty-eight hours.

OR

1. Using the procedures noted in the Aseptic Method above, mix boiled water and formula concentrate in desired proportions.
2. Pour into a sterile quart jar or bottle and refrigerate for no more than forty-eight hours.
3. When it is time for a feeding pour the desired amount into a clean bottle and attach a clean nipple.

GIVING THE BOTTLE

Giving a baby a bottle is not difficult to learn. The hospital or birth center staff can help you get started, but your best helper will be your baby herself, who has all the natural reflexes that make her want to eat.

Feeding time is very special for both you and your child. It is the natural time for physical closeness, eye contact, and even some "conversations." It is a time when your baby will appreciate you for alleviating her discomfort.

Make yourself comfortable, and have some support for the arm that will be holding the baby, because that head gets awfully heavy after a few minutes. If you are at home, take your phone off the hook and put a sign on the door asking people to please come back later. If you have other young children, have a book or some little games available so that they can be entertained while you feed the baby. A doll with a bottle is a big hit. You'll need a table to put the bottle on while you're burping her. You'll also need a diaper over your shoulder for burping, which can also be used under the baby's chin for dribbles.

Don't try to feed your baby while she is crying. Take some time to rock and comfort her until she has settled down. Then support her in the crook of your arm with her head higher than her stomach, and you are ready to go. Stroke her cheek that's next to you, and she will turn with her little mouth open. Touch the nipple to her mouth and she will start to suck. Keep the bottle tilted so that she is sucking only milk through the nipple, not milk and air. If you are using a disposable bottle this is not a problem, because the liner collapses and creates a vacuum. Sometimes a baby will just move the bottle around instead of getting milk out, so hold the bottle firmly.

Don't be surprised if your baby doesn't want much the first three to four days. She is not very hungry then and usually would just rather sleep. She'll take it much better when she is really hungry. You'll know she has had enough when she turns her head away, sometimes with a little smile, and falls asleep with milk dribbling out of her mouth. Or she may just stop sucking. Pick her up then and try burping her (see p. 244). If she hasn't taken much and falls asleep, don't try to wake her by shaking, pinching or prodding. This can be too upsetting for a baby. Dabbing a little cool water on her forehead sometimes helps to rouse her enough to try to take the nipple again. If it doesn't, let her sleep. She'll soon wake again.

Some babies work and nurse until all the milk is gone. Others need burping two or three times during the feeding, because an air bubble will sometimes give them the false feeling that they are full. If she gives a good burp you might try and see if she wants any more. Don't expect her to eat the same amount at every feeding. The food intake of bottle-fed babies may vary greatly—from perhaps two to three ounces at one feeding, to up to eight or ten ounces at another.

If your baby does not drink the whole bottle, you can return the partly full bottle to the refrigerator promptly, to be used one more time (do not add any new formula to it). But if the feeding has lasted a long time (longer than thirty minutes) and you have some concern about how fresh the milk is, just throw it away.

After each feeding, rinse the bottle and the nipple and leave them in water. You should do this to avoid drying and caking of the milk, which make cleaning more difficult later on.

Remember that your baby will express her own personality and style in the way she feeds. This is a good time to get to know more about her. (See our discussion of feeding styles, p. 70.)

Y O U R   B A B Y ' S   F E E D I N G   S C H E D U L E

Some mothers worry that if they feed their baby whenever she is hungry, she will get into the habit of eating frequently. This is simply not true. The bottle-fed baby should be treated exactly as if she were breast-fed and be offered milk whenever she seems hungry. She'll let you know by making mouthing movements or sucking vigorously on her hand. If you don't respond, she'll start to fuss and, finally, cry. You don't have to wait until she cries to feed her. Watch for her signals, if you can. Feed her before she is upset. The feeding should stop when the baby is no longer interested. Although the bottle-fed baby is often hungry less frequently than the breast-fed baby, because it takes longer to digest cow's milk, in the first few weeks of life her digestive system is immature, and she may get the wrong message about whether she is hungry or not. She may even wish to eat every hour for a while. But take heart—a rough-and-ready type of schedule will evolve.

If you choose to put your baby on a four-hour schedule you certainly can do so, but you can also expect to hear more crying and to spend more of your time trying to comfort a hungry baby. Oftentimes a baby will fall asleep from the exhaustion of crying and then will take only a small amount at her next feeding. And then she may wake up before her next feeding time, hungry again.

Begin your feeding with three to four ounces in the bottle. If your baby drinks all of this and seems satisfied, fine. If she still seems hungry, add one or two ounces more to that bottle or simply take another bottle from the refrigerator. At the next feeding be sure that the bottle has a little bit more than the baby took the previous time. She will gradually increase her needs until she is taking eight ounces at a feeding.

Your baby does not need anything else to eat or drink in the first four to six months of life. You may certainly give her foods or fruit juices, but this is not necessary. Why not make it easier on yourself?

PROBLEMS WITH NIPPLES

Sometimes the holes in nipples are too small and the baby will get too little milk for an awful lot of work. This results in fussing, tiring, and sleeping before finishing. If the nipple holes are too large, she will choke or else consume all she needs without getting enough sucking, and she will not be satisfied. You can check by holding the bottle upside down and observing how the milk comes out. It should come out in a spray and then in drops, several drops per second. The best way to decide if the nipple hole is the right size is by observing your baby to see if she is satisfied.

But suppose you do have a problem with the nipple. Perhaps the milk is coming out too fast. If you know the holes are the right size, then perhaps too much air is getting into the bottle, causing the milk to flow faster. On a regular bottle, the cap can be screwed down more tightly, creating a partial vacuum so that the milk will flow less easily. (Usually there is no problem with a disposable bottle, because it already has a vacuum.) Suppose the nipple holes are too small. You must either enlarge the holes or make some new ones. Heat a needle to red-hot and stick the point into the old hole to enlarge it, or make a new hole next to it. (To avoid burns, stick the dull end of the needle into a cork, wrap it in cloth, or use pliers.) Another method is to make a crosscut (X) in the nipple with a razor blade. Be sure you make this very small in the beginning and work your way up as your baby needs it.

KEEPING THE BOTTLE OUT OF THE REFRIGERATOR

As we said, it is not wise to save the bottle after it has been outside the refrigerator for more than twenty to thirty minutes. Certainly do not allow the bottle to lie around in the baby's bed, buggy, or stroller for an extended period of time and use it again.

If you are taking the baby out and will need to feed her while you are gone, you may want to use the prepared disposable bottles even though they are more expensive. Or you can safely take the regular bottles you have prepared, by putting them into an insulated bag or picnic cooler (this will be good for about six hours), or by burying the bottles in a plastic bag filled with ice cubes (good for about four hours).

PROPPING THE BOTTLE

Propping the bottle is a necessity at times. It has been done for years by many good mothers. But babies who have their bottles propped on a continuous basis do not get the cuddling and holding they need. They also have an increased incidence of ear infection. This is thought to be due to the fact that when the baby is lying flat there is more chance that milk will be forced back into the eustachian tubes, which connect with the ear.

If you must prop the baby's bottle for an occasional feeding while you tend to other children, just be sure to cuddle and hold her at other times, so that she can get the loving she needs from you. Bottles can be propped on pillows, but an inexpensive store-bought holder works much better.

WHEN THE BABY WANTS TO HOLD HER OWN BOTTLE

At around six to nine months babies begin to sit up and grab and hold on to things. This is the time when you may find that your baby would rather sit up for her feeding and hold her bottle herself. If you do not use disposable liners, you can buy a tubelike device for her bottle that sticks down into the milk even when she holds the bottle while sitting up, so that she sucks in only formula, not air.

If you don't want your toddler walking around with her bottle, then don't let her get the idea that she can drink from her bottle anywhere but on your lap. If you don't mind seeing your toddler with a bottle and she wants to get down, allowing you some free time for other things, let her. Just make sure that the bottle is removed after twenty to twenty-five minutes, because milk or juice is a breeding ground for bacteria. Also, prolonged contact with milk or sweet liquids will result in tooth decay.

Your baby may simply not tolerate being held on your lap after she is more mobile. She may, in fact, also be telling you that she is no longer interested in nursing. This happens with many bottle-fed and breast-fed babies around nine months of age. If she acts as if she wants to get down, put her bottle in the refrigerator and offer her some formula in a cup. She may be perfectly happy to take her meal this way. And what an easy way to wean her.

THE BOTTLE-IN-BED HABIT

This is also the time when you can get into the bottle-in-bed habit. Some babies who reject holding still need the comfort of sucking at bedtime to settle themselves. I (AA) have had two of these! This, like propping, has received a lot of negative publicity. I (AA) have certainly felt embarrassed myself about admitting that I was allowing my baby to take a bottle to bed.

There are two reasons for trying to avoid the bottle-in-bed habit. One is to prevent the *nursing bottle syndrome*, a condition of tooth decay caused by prolonged contact of the front teeth with a sugar-containing liquid—milk, juice, cola. This occurs in children who suck on their bottle for a long period of time, perhaps throughout the night. If your child likes to take her bottle while she lies in her bed at bedtime, take some precautions. Remove the bottle as soon as she has finished it or has gone to sleep. Fill the bedtime bottle with a less sugary liquid—water or diluted fruit juice or formula.

The second pitfall of this habit is that it may foster night waking in your baby. It works this way. All people, including children, learn to associate certain conditions with falling asleep. Some have favorite pillows, for example. When those conditions are not there the easy-going and adaptable souls can adjust. Those who do not like change and are more intense in their reactions to it, cannot. It is normal to awaken briefly several times during the night and fall right back to sleep. The children who fall into the latter category and who have learned to associate having a bottle in bed with falling asleep may not be able to go back to sleep without that bottle. Others have no difficulty at all and never cry for a bottle during the night.

So if you have a child who resists any change in her life you might remember the adage: An ounce of prevention is worth a pound of cure. Try not to allow a situation to develop which you will regret later. Give your baby her nighttime bottle before bedtime. Allow her to learn to fall asleep without it.

WHEN TO WEAN

Some babies will give up the bottle very early—perhaps as early as six to nine months—since they have other means of soothing and sucking, such as a thumb or pacifier. Some babies who use neither thumb nor pacifier will give up their bottle as early as nine months. Other babies have a need to suck on a bottle as late as two or more years of age.

The weaning process can be a very gradual one and doesn't have to be traumatic. There are advantages to leaving the weaning process to the baby: Sucking is the baby's way of soothing or relaxing herself. It often helps her settle down for sleep.

But beware! At about nine to twelve months of age, a baby can become more and more attached to her bottle, turning to it for comfort whenever she is upset or tired. This is more likely to occur if the bottle has an appealing beverage in it—milk, juice, soda, sweetened tea. This invites tooth decay and excess calories.

Your goal therefore in weaning is to avoid the pitfalls and still fulfill your baby's needs for comfort sucking.

BEGINNING CUP DRINKING

At around five to six months of age your baby will be ready to begin cup drinking. Using a cup with a lid and a spout such as the Tommee Tippee is very helpful for the transition between sucking and regular drinking. You can offer her cold or warm formula, juices, or water in it. At first, she'll drink only a little. But after she is taking three meals of solids a day (around eight or nine months) and as she becomes more adept at drinking from the cup, you can gradually drop the bottle feedings, one at a time, if she doesn't drop them herself.

The first to be dropped should be the meal at which she is least tired and is likely to eat and drink well—usually breakfast or lunch. Begin by offering one to two ounces of her formula in the cup, giving the rest by bottle if she wants it. Gradually increase the amount given in the cup until she is able to take four to eight ounces at a meal. She really won't need eight ounces of milk at every meal once she is taking solids. Once she can drink this amount, don't offer the bottle at that meal. It helps to keep bottles out of sight at this time. If she is unhappy without it, go ahead and give her one to two ounces in the bottle. Wait a few days and try again. Or consider trying at a different time of day.

After she has gone without a bottle at one meal for about a week, try dropping another one at a different meal. If your baby is accustomed to taking a bottle just before nap and bedtimes, these will usually be the last to go. She may want both or one of these through the second year of life or longer.

Once she is twelve months old she will probably be drinking four to eight ounces of liquid from a cup at each meal and will no longer need formula. She may still need the pleasure of sucking though. In order to avoid tooth decay and excess calories we advise giving water in the bottle. This can be done gradually. First switch to juice in the bottle, with an equal amount of water. Over two to three weeks, increase the dilution until there is nothing but water in it. If she wants something better to drink, offer it in her cup and give her the bottle with the water. Most babies will eventually choose the cup and gradually wean themselves. You will have given them the chance to retain their comfort sucking, but have removed the pitfalls of tooth decay and excess calories.

The time it takes to make the transition depends very much on your baby's temperament and needs. The "easy to manage," placid child will be able to handle the change more rapidly than the tenacious, more difficult child. Stresses such as leaving on a trip, the birth of a new baby, or an illness will delay the weaning process. If you know these are going to occur hold off weaning at that time.

A very few children, when left to wean themselves, continue taking the bottle until they begin to interact with peers in school. The peer pressure is definitely and rapidly effective and the parents didn't have to do a thing!

HOW DO YOU FEEL ABOUT WEANING?

What if you feel irritated at seeing your daughter still needing a bottle and you are gritting your teeth every time you fix one? It's time to examine your reasons for feeling like this. Sometimes you may be receiving pressure to "cut out this bottle bit" from others whom you respect, or maybe Susie isn't as fast at giving up the bottle as Johnny next door and it is making you feel inadequate as a mother. Explore your feelings with your mate or a close friend. By understanding the reasons for them, you may be able to relax. But if your irritation continues and interferes with your other interactions with your child, total weaning may need to be accomplished in a more rapid, but still gentle, fashion. Use the positive reward system we discuss below.

WEANING AND THE POSITIVE REWARD TECHNIQUE

In this situation the positive reward techniques (discussed in Chapter 15) can be useful. Talk with your child first about what you plan. Tell her she is growing up, becoming a big girl. Tell her big girls don't use bottles anymore. Acknowledge that she likes the bottle and that it may be hard to give it up all at once. Tell her you are going to help her all you can. Let her pick the time she thinks she can give up first. Tell her that there will only be water in the bottle then. Her preferred drink will be in her cup. When she chooses the cup over the bottle, reward her. Give her something she really likes—raisins, gum, crayons, stickers, happy faces, or stars. Couple it with lots of praise, pats, or hugs. She may choose the bottle with water at first and scream for something else in it. Do not give in. If she needs sucking, she can get it with water. When she sees that you mean it, she'll soon opt for the cup.

Do this until all bottle feedings are eliminated. The bedtime bottle is usually the hardest to give up. She may need extra rocking, stories, or patting to help her settle down to sleep at this time. But she *will* learn. Some children may give it up immediately with no regrets or need for extra solace—almost just with the idea of being "a big kid." Others may require extra work but will get there eventually.

PLAYING "BABY"

Sometimes long after weaning, your child may want a bottle if she is around another child with a bottle. My (AA) Katie and Kimberly both did this as late as three years of age. It's fun to play "baby." Don't panic. They will play, get it out of their systems, and give it up—too much work, that sucking!

As an overall approach to your baby's giving up her bottle, we think you need to read your baby's cues. Don't rush her—you'll avoid a lot of needless strife. Your job is to create a setting which helps her make the transition smoothly.

8

The Daily Care of Your Infant

If this is your first baby, in the first few weeks or months after he is born, your family unit will be experiencing a lot of stress. "Two's company, three's a crowd" may really hold true. So far, you've probably worked well together as a couple; but adding that extra little ingredient—*an unknown*—may threaten to upset the applecart. Be patient with each other and remember that you will need time to adjust. If you try your best to simplify your lives and the daily care of your infant, you will find the time you need to get used to your new roles in a threesome rather than a twosome.

To begin with: Try to remember a few things about new mothers and fathers.

- Mothers typically feel physically drained and exhausted after the labor and delivery.
- Fathers may feel mentally drained and not quite sure where they fit in anymore.
- There are unending nights of interrupted sleep, which add to the anxiety and tension.
- There may be no one to help at home once the dust has settled.
- You may have some unrealistic expectations of one another and yourselves in your new roles as parents.

BOTH PARENTS ARE CARETAKERS

Some people feel that there is only one "right" way to interact with a baby, and the mother's way is the one. But both parents each have a special and unique way of interacting with their baby. He will enjoy the differences and respond to both with pleasure.

Mothers tend to be very sensitive to their babies and to interact at the baby's pace. They operate in a gentle, low-key fashion and the baby is quietly alert and happy. Fathers, on the other hand, often set a different pace with the baby: They may behave in a more forceful, playful, and slightly rougher way. This usually jazzes the baby up and delights him. To sum it up, mothers stroke, fathers poke. The two styles are complementary, and they increase the baby's experiences. So each has a special role, and your baby will become equally attached to both of you.

In the beginning the mother is usually the primary caretaker, especially if she is breast-feeding. But involving the father in the baby's care from the beginning is essential too because it speeds his attachment or bonding to the baby and provides the mother with much-needed help as well. Remember, every time the father gives the baby a bath, changes his diaper, or does other ordinary everyday things with him, he is increasing his emotional bonding with the baby.

It is very evident, also, that just having the father around is a tremendous support for the mother. He is a great help in dealing with relatives and well-meaning friends who may unintentionally hurt the mother's feelings or intrude and create additional work for her at this difficult time. He can be there as a sounding board for the mother after a particularly tough day.

We hope that society will someday recognize the fact that the father has a large role to play in nurturing and giving care to the young infant—that he will be able to get paternity leave from work and become an active helper when he is most needed. With the demise of the extended family in our society, mothers are often left alone to care for their babies at a time when they may be neither physically nor emotionally equipped to deal with this trying task.

SURVIVING THE FIRST FEW WEEKS

In the first month particularly, the behavior of the baby seems very erratic: He sleeps, he eats, he frets and cries—unpredictably. It is during this time that parents realize they may have had unrealistic expectations about what having a baby is all about. They may unconsciously have thought that a baby is like a toy, but now they must face the stark reality that they have the care of this new little person in their hands for twenty-four hours a day—and that, in many respects, their needs must come after his.

You may be absolutely amazed at how much time it takes to care for an infant and how little time you have left over for yourselves or each other. Even if you are blessed with a remarkably easy baby, who only eats and sleeps and requires little effort, he will still keep you tied to the home front.

It's important to remember that your feelings about this baby, particularly in the first months, will be ambivalent: You may feel very tender and loving one minute when he is feeding or sleeping, and very frustrated and angry the next when he cannot be consoled. It sometimes takes time to learn to love your baby and to understand him. Just remember this: most parents report that by the time their baby smiles at six weeks of age and gives them more tangible positive feedback, they are absolute putty in his hands.

One way to learn to enjoy and appreciate your baby is simply to allow yourself to feel the physical pleasure that a new baby gives. The way he nestles into your neck and into the crook of your arm, the fell of the soft fuzz of his head against your cheek, and the grip of his fingers on yours seems to bring forth all the pleasurable feelings and protective instincts necessary to ensure his survival. Strive to enjoy those moments and make them last, and the harder times will be easier to take.

The key to surviving the first few weeks is to keep the care as simple as possible so that you can have more time to enjoy the cuddling. With your first baby you tend to be more anxious, and you may wonder if your baby will survive your mistakes. By the second or third you will have learned Grandmother's First Law: Your mistakes usually upset you more than they upset your baby.

Your baby knows what he needs, if you can simply learn to read his signals.

Y O U R   B A B Y   I S   A   P E R S O N

Remember, your baby is a one-of-a-kind person. He is the product of your genes and his intrauterine environment. His responses to his environment are unique to him. He has his own special temperament or behavioral style. You'll be learning all this in the first few months, just as you would with any new acquaintance—only with much more intensity. The more you can appreciate and learn about infant behavior, the easier your job will be.

To understand behavior and temperament in childhood, the work of Drs. Alexander Thomas, Stella Chess, and Herbert Birch is helpful. Studying the temperament of over two hundred children, they have identified nine characteristics of behavior:

1. *Activity level* refers to the general motor behavior of the child. Is he a very active child, a consistently quiet child, or somewhere in between? Babies differ in their wiggling, vigor and rate of sucking, and sleep movements.
2. *Regularity* describes the predictability of patterns for hunger, sleep, and bowel movements. All young infants are unpredictable in the first few weeks but become more regular and predictable as they mature. Is your baby one whose schedule developed early or is he still unpredictable when other babies seem settled?
3. *Reactions to new situations* refers to the initial reaction to anything new. Does he approach it positively and eagerly, or always withdraw until he is more familiar with it? This could apply to new people, foods, beds, and to new situations such as bath time.
4. *Adaptability over time* refers to the child's ability to adjust to changes over a period of time. If he has an initially negative reaction, such as being unable to sleep in a new environment, how long before he is able to adjust?
5. *Level of sensory threshold* describes his overall response to stimulation. Does he sleep through anything or awaken at the drop of a pin?
6. *Intensity of response* describes the energy content of the child's response, whether positive or negative. When thwarted does he have an intense screaming spell or simply fuss quietly?
7. *General mood* refers to the baby's overall attitude. Does he tend to be irritable and fussy or generally happy?
8. *Distractibility* describes how much it takes to get a child's mind off his present activity. Does he stop sucking as soon as anyone enters the room? When crying and upset, is he easy to quiet by making an interesting sound or changing his environment?
9. *Persistence and attention span* focus on the child's ability to return to a previous activity if interrupted, and how long he will generally attend to a given activity.

These characteristics are not always consistent in the newborn period, but they stabilize during the first two to three months and remain fairly consistent throughout childhood. Thomas, Chess, and Birch found that these characteristics could occur in certain combinations, resulting in three types of temperament.

THE ''DIFFICULT,'' ''EASY,'' AND ''SLOW TO WARM UP'' CHILD

Most children fall into the "easy child" category in varying degrees. They are a parent's delight: predominantly happy; willing to approach new situations; adaptable; having regular patterns of sleep, eating, and bowel movements; and reacting emotionally with low to moderate intensity.

A small percentage of babies display the characteristics of a "slow to warm up child." They react negatively to new situations and are slow to adapt. Because they seem unhappy, parents may feel unhappy around them and even avoid interaction with them.

A small percentage of babies display characteristics of the "difficult child." They are unpredictable and irregular in biologic functions, have withdrawal responses to new situations, are slow to adapt, are very intense, and often have a negative mood. They are a parent's nightmare! You can really lose confidence in yourself in a hurry!

Many children fall somewhere in between these categories. They may have some characteristics that make them a joy to handle, while others tax your patience. Try to understand that behavior that may cause you difficulty is simply your child's way of dealing with the world—not a negative action directed personally at you.

These behavioral patterns are not well established in the newborn period: nevertheless Dr. T. Berry Brazelton has done wonderful work in helping us understand temporary individual differences in babies in the first weeks of life. He has found that there are newborns who are hyperresponsive to external stimuli; they are hyperexcitable and irritable and may be difficult to soothe. At the opposite end of the spectrum is the hyporesponsive baby, who is sluggish and poses a different dilemma for a parent.

Fortunately these difficulties are usually resolved as the baby becomes more mature. In this chapter we shall be presenting methods of care suited to the individual needs of different babies. We are certain that as you become adept at reading signals from your baby you will be able to adapt your responses.

B A S I C   E Q U I P M E N T   N E E D E D   T O   C A R E   F O R   Y O U R   B A B Y

It is good to have a basic wardrobe ready for the first three months. Here are some suggestions if you are able to wash every other day.

L A Y E T T E

- Four terrycloth jump suits
- Six kimonos
- Four to six undershirts (These are optional, as the kimonos are much more practical in the summer months and easier to dress the baby in than an undershirt. During the winter months, however, an undershirt is a good underlayer for the jump suit or the kimono.)
- Four dozen diapers (if using cloth, get prefolded type)

- One or two sweaters
- Three crib sheets
- Three bassinet sheets (Pillowcases may be used on the bassinet mattress just as easily.)
- Twelve rubberized flannel pads—six large ones for the crib, six small ones for the bassinet (You won't have to change sheets so often.)
- If your baby is born during the winter months, you will need a bunting and a heavy carriage blanket.
- One hat (a sun hat for the summer months, or a close-fitting woolen one for the winter months)
- One or two pairs of booties
- Two bibs (optional—usually a diaper will catch any drools while feeding)

Other supplies to have on hand include:

- Two pint jars to hold cotton balls and water for changing the baby
- Baby nail scissors
- A thermometer—ask your doctor about which kind he or she prefers
- Petroleum jelly, baby lotion, or baby powder (not necessary but optional if you enjoy putting it on and the smell of it)

C R I B

A crib is essential. Make sure it meets safety standards:

- The design of the headboard and footboard should not have any spaces in which a standing child could catch his head or neck and become trapped. (See Fig. 1)
- The slats should be at most 2⅜ inches apart so that a baby's head cannot slip through. If you have an old crib with slats wider apart, it can be made safe by using a crib bumper. In order to enclose the space between the bumper and the mattress and prevent the baby's slipping between slats, an old sheet can be attached or sewn to the underside of the crib bumper, just loosely enough to allow the mattress to fit snugly inside the enclosure. (See Fig. 2.) The fabric extends below the bumper and under the mattress and is a barrier to the spaces between the slats. It also keeps the bumper from sliding up.
- A crib bumper protects the baby from hitting his head against the crib sides, too.
- The mattress should fit snugly.

B A S S I N E T

A bassinet is a handy piece of furniture. But if you do not have one, don't worry; hospitals often send the baby home in a cardboard box that will suffice until he is big enough to sleep in a crib all the time.

C H A N G I N G   T A B L E

A changing table is very helpful, and there are combinations in which the bureau is below the table. You must be sure the changing table has a method for strapping the baby down to prevent falls.

Fig. 1

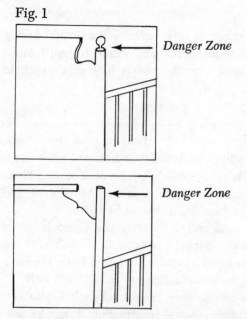

→ *Danger Zone*

→ *Danger Zone*

These illustrate unsafe designs for crib headboard or footboard. A standing child could squeeze his neck into the space and become trapped.

Fig. 2

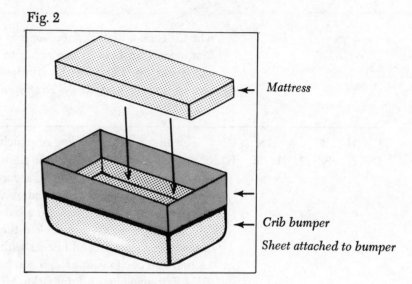

← *Mattress*

← *Crib bumper*
Sheet attached to bumper

A sheet is attached to the crib bumper, creating an enclosure for the mattress. The mattress should fit snugly.

C A R   S E A T

Another necessity is a car seat for the ride home from the hospital and other trips. Make sure that the one you purchase has been tested for safety and meets the federal guidelines. There are car seats for infants that can be converted for older children. These are the most practical, because you would need to buy only one. I (AA) personally have found that a car seat that does not have to be tethered in the back to meet the safety standards is the most practical, because it is easier to use in someone else's car if you need to. More and more communities are offering car-seat rentals through medical auxiliaries or highway patrol offices so you can try different types of seats before buying one.

B A T H T U B

A sink with a towel on the bottom to prevent slipping will do. However, there are so many clever devices on the market that allow you to bathe your baby more easily it is worth the investment. Read our section on bathing (p. 125) to get some ideas on what to buy.

S A N I T Y   P R O T E C T O R S   (Y O U R   O W N ,   T H A T   I S !)

Let's take a look at some equipment on the market that will help you get through the day and keep both you and your baby happy.

I N F A N T   S E A T

We heartily recommend using the infant seat, for in it your baby can be comfortably placed in a sitting position. Pillows and sofas don't give enough support at this age. It can be used anywhere and is very useful for holding your baby when he begins to eat solid food. Caution: Never leave him in the infant seat when it is on a high surface, such as a table, or sofa, unless you are right beside him; once your baby is beginning to be more mobile and strains to pull himself up, it can tip. Look for the sturdiest kind with the widest base of support, to reduce tipping. And always strap him in.

INFANT CARRIER

The infant carrier—a sling or pouch for carrying your baby on your chest, back, or at your side—is a godsend. It allows you to go about your business while keeping your baby close, warm, and secure. It's especially helpful with a more difficult baby who demands a great deal of attention, security, and physical contact. The side sling is not appropriate for a baby without head control, however.

The most common carriers are the Comfi and the Snugli. The Comfi is one of the easiest to put on and fastens with metal hooks. The fabric is washable. If you cannot find one in your area, it can be ordered by writing to Comfi Baby Products, 5754 Fairlawn Shores, Prior Lake, Minnesota 53372. You can call 800-453-2400.

The Snugli is handcrafted and made of corduroy or seersucker. It is also very expensive. It is priced so high because of its unusual construction: It can be used to front-carry an infant as well as to backpack a two-year-old. This type is especially good in the cold weather because it encapsulates all of the baby except most of his head. There is a denim version of the Snugli which is less costly. It can be obtained at your local baby store or by writing Snugli Cottage Industries, 1212 Keergulch, Evergreen, Colorado 80439.

SWING

There are swings that can be wound up and allow the baby to rock for ten to fifteen minutes. They are very helpful, particularly in the first few months of life. Once your baby can sit alone they are not safe, however, because he may make it tip. Borrow one if you can, because you will use it for only a short time. If you do have to buy one, look for the kind that swings on its own for at least ten or fifteen minutes. Make sure you give him extra protection in the swing by putting small rolled blankets or pillows along the sides and in the front—otherwise he might topple over and hit his head on the front bar. But don't overdo the swing; remember that as much as your baby may enjoy the swing, he enjoys and needs *you* more.

PLAYPEN

A playpen is a very practical device when used properly. It can permit your child to be in the room where the action is and protect him at the same time. It must meet safety standards: slats 2⅜ inches or less apart, tightly woven mesh, secure hinges, well-fitting foam pad. Be sure metal latches are on the outside. If your baby is in a pen, siblings or pets are less likely to step on him, and he is less in danger of having a toy dropped on him. Never leave the sides of a mesh playpen down while the baby is inside. Babies can suffocate in the mesh. Place his own toys inside the playpen. When he is learning to stand he can hold on to the playpen and move about without fear of banging into corners of furniture or falling on a hard surface. You can also take the baby outside in his pen. But remember the old adage about "too much of a good thing": don't use the playpen too often. An infant who can't crawl needs to be held and cuddled frequently and should be moved about his environment when he is awake, at least every hour or so. The crawler or toddler, especially, needs the freedom to explore his environment. He should be in a playpen for only short periods, when he needs to be kept out of trouble.

Sometimes the playpen is a good escape place for an older sibling who wishes to play with her toys, unhampered by her nine-month-old brother. Let her play in it. It is also a wonderful place to put your Christmas tree during those first two years!

STROLLERS

Strollers are good for going on outings and for shopping. The type of stroller that you buy basically depends upon your life-style and your needs. There is no such thing as a "perfect for everything" stroller. If you use a stroller constantly—as you would if you don't use a car—you will need one that is very comfortable for the baby. It should be quite heavy with good back support. Unfortunately, these strollers are not easily collapsible or may not be collapsible at all, and thus are not portable.

If you can use a collapsible stroller you don't need to worry so much about back support. The umbrella stroller is very popular for this purpose. Some strollers have swivel front wheels, making the going easier except on rough terrain. If your children are two years or less apart in age, a twin stroller that seats two children is a necessity.

Some mothers have two types of strollers and use them according to the activity. When you consider buying a stroller, look for certain safety items:

- Safety straps that cannot be undone by your child.
- Latches that snap tightly in place so that the stroller will not collapse.
- Brakes.
- Stability: Check for easy tipping. The wheel base should be wide enough to remain on all fours even with the child hanging over one side (as they frequently do). To prevent tipping over backwards, make sure that the bottom baskets end in front of or over the bar between the rear wheels.
- Noninjurious parts: Make sure there are no sharp or pointed surfaces that can hurt your baby.

Something else to remember when you are using a stroller is that you should not leave your baby unattended in it. Strollers have been known to collapse and suffocate the baby. The safety strap should always be fastened. Take the baby out of the stroller to go up and down more than three steps. The umbrella strollers are not particularly good support for babies who do not have good head and trunk control. Blanket rolls on both sides of the baby will help prevent slumping. Until he has a steady head and strong back you can use your baby carrier, such as a Snugli or Comfi. A pram or a carriage is another alternative; or a heavier stroller that can be reclined so that your baby can lie down.

B A B Y
W A L K E R S
Baby walkers are seats that usually have springs for bouncing or wheels for getting about. They are enjoyed by babies who have head and trunk control but are not able to move about yet. These babies relish the independence and the ability to make themselves move by simply using their feet. Children usually use them during their second six months. Although these walkers can be very helpful, there are some things to be careful of.

- Check the walker to make sure it has a wide enough base so that it will not tip if the child leans over.
- Make sure that the walker is used on a flat surface and not near any stairs. Some pretty serious accidents have occurred when children have tried to manipulate their walkers down the stairs. All stairways should be blocked off anyway.
- A baby can also tip over while trying to pilot his walker over carpets or thresholds.
- The type of walker that has an X-frame can collapse, or a child can catch his finger in the latch.
- No child in a walker should be left unattended.
- Do not leave your child in a walker for long periods of time—thirty minutes at the most. He needs to get down on the floor for good motor development.

H A N D L I N G   Y O U R   B A B Y

It has been said that touch is the language of love. And that's what you'll be doing a lot of while you're caring for your baby. Bathing, diapering, feeding, and holding provide opportunities for touching, exactly what he needs to grow and develop well. Through your touch you communicate the caring and love he is eager for. So we recommend lots of physical contact throughout childhood, but most especially during the daily care of your infant.

B I R T H   T O
T H R E E
M O N T H S
PICKING UP AND HOLDING If you haven't had much experience handling newborn babies, trying to pick one up in one piece, without appendages flopping in all directions, can really make you feel like a "fumble fingers." Don't worry; in a day or two you'll be a pro.

Give the baby some warning that you are there; talk to him and touch him before picking him up. Don't swoop him up, because he will be startled and he'll cry, changing suddenly from a floppy bundle to a stiff one. As you talk to him, lean over as closely as possible and slip one hand under his head and the other under his buttocks. If he is on his tummy, gently roll him over onto his back first. Cradle him securely at your shoulder with his face nestled into your neck (see Figs. 3–4). Always keep his head supported when he is in the upright position.

When putting him down, reverse the procedure. Put him down on his back and roll him over on his tummy afterwards.

Fig. 3 *Roll the baby over onto his back. Slip one hand under his head, the other under his buttocks. Lean over very close. Pull the baby close to your body with the buttocks hand while the other supports his head.*

Fig. 4 *Holding his lower body against your torso, lift his head and trunk to rest against your shoulder.*

You may carry your baby in the upright position with his head nestled at your shoulder and supported by your hand, with his buttocks held by your other hand or the crook of your arm. You may also carry him in the more supine position with his back in the crook of your arm.

The more you hold your baby, the more quickly you will learn to interpret how he is feeling and what he needs. The baby uses body movement to communicate—he may squirm when he is preparing for a bowel movement, tense when he is actively studying something, relax as he becomes sleepy. You can feel all this while you are holding him and will soon feel quite competent in understanding what he is trying to tell you. But it takes practice. A study has shown that carrying young infants (up to three months) while they are content or asleep in addition to the standard holding during feeding or in response to crying significantly reduces the amount of time they cry during the day. So practice has an additional payoff!

There is a method of holding your baby that is especially good for communicating and maintaining eye contact. It allows you to face each other directly. Prop your baby against your legs (Fig. 5), with his feet against your abdomen and his body extending out at a 90-degree angle. He should be in a reclining position, but with head and trunk raised at about a 45-degree angle (if you are sitting, prop your feet on a stool or cross one leg over another to support his back). You can do this standing up by putting your arms together with both hands under his head, with his body lying on your arms (Fig. 6). This *en face* position encourages your baby to open his eyes and look at you. Babies love it and so will you.

WRAPPING Tiny babies under three months of age enjoy the feeling of being secure and bundled up. One of the most effective ways to give your baby that feeling is to wrap him up, or swaddle him (see p. 113). This allows him to stay warm, but more importantly, it keeps his own jerky movements from disturbing him. It is especially helpful for inducing sleep, and it can also provide some babies the extra security they seem to crave all the time. Once your baby becomes

Fig. 5   *En face position (sitting)*

Fig. 6   *En face position (standing)*

stronger and more in control of his limbs, he will fight swaddling and it is no longer effective.

HANDLING WHEN CRYING   How should you handle your baby when he cries? He is trying to communicate with you and needs to know you'll respond. A study done by Dr. Mary Ainsworth at the University of Virginia revealed that young babies who are attended to immediately and not left to cry it out are babies who cry less as toddlers. If you respond immediately (within one to two minutes), he'll be learning trust. You are not spoiling him and, in fact, you are saving yourself time in the long run. If you don't respond, he'll cry fiercely and may stop only from exhaustion. If you have an intense child, he may never seem to stop (some mothers have reported two-hour crying sessions!). While he is crying, you'll be upset and accomplish nothing. Your baby, meanwhile, is learning that the world isn't a safe and comfortable place.

The best thing to do when your baby cries is to pick him up and cuddle him. This may be all he needs.

But what if it isn't? Feed him if it's been more than one and a half to two hours since he last nursed or two and a half to three hours since his bottle. He won't take much if he's not hungry. Change him if he's soiled. If he has just eaten, he may need to burp. He may be full but need more sucking time. Try giving him your little finger or a pacifier to soothe him. Some babies need several things at once—swaddling, sucking, holding, rocking, and singing. Some prefer being walked and jiggled gently. The rhythmic motion of the automatic swing, a buggy ride, or sitting on top of a washer or dryer in an infant seat may help. Other fussy babies respond to continuous low-pitched steady noises such as vaporizers, fans, records of winds or oceans or the Rock-a-bye Teddy. Many babies will drop off in a car. I (AA) have been on many a midnight ride to soothe a fussy one. If

Fig. 7   *Swaddling*

Step 1. Fold the blanket into a large triangle. Place the baby on his back. Tuck one side over the baby, securing the arm in a flexed position.

Step 2. Secure the other arm in a flexed position by tucking the other side of the blanket around the baby.

Step 3. Tuck the tip of the blanket up and under the folded sides. You may secure it with a pin, but it is not necessary. Baby is ready to go to sleep on his tummy.

Step 1.   Step 2.   Step 3.

he enjoys a bath, try that. Some babies cry when they're tired. Cuddle and rock him, put him to bed and let him settle himself if he can. Sometimes a change of parent helps. The parent who has been struggling to read a baby's needs can become tense and anxious. The baby may simply be feeding that back and may quiet when a more rested and relaxed "team" comes in.

You may be in the small percentage of parents who have been blessed with a "difficult to manage" child. When I (AA) say blessed, I do not mean it totally tongue in cheek. Having had one of these little imps, our Katie, I realize now that that first year or more of misery, if survived, can produce an absolutely delightful creature—not without problems, but with an incredibly unique way of looking at the world.

Katie was a hyperresponsive baby who startled frequently and who could not be soothed easily. She ate ravenously and loved it, but slept only fifteen minutes at a time and awoke irritable and unhappy.

We tried everything known to man to get Katie to sleep. My husband finally invented his own Rube Goldberg contraption, the Alexander Rocking Bassinet, a mechanized bassinet that sent our friends into gales of laughter. He used a respirator such as those in the intensive-care nurseries and hooked it to Katie's bassinet to rock it. He regulated it so that she would be rocked at a regular twenty-six rocks per minute. If the switch was moved from twenty-six to twenty-four or twenty-eight or any other deviation, she would awaken with a yell and not settle down until we went back to twenty-six—a beautiful example of resistance to change.

This worked nicely until Katie became so heavy that the machine could no longer rock the bassinet. The screaming resumed and I was about to go over the edge. All the rides in the car, all the turning on of the washer and dryer and vacuum cleaner could not do the trick. One day I had decided to dry her diaper rash with the hair dryer. She was screaming bloody murder as always. But as soon as I turned on the dryer she stopped in midscream, gave a yawn, and went to sleep!

I could not believe it. I turned off the hair dryer, and instantly the screaming resumed. I repeated the hair dryer trick and, *Eureka*—quiet! The dryer that I used was a model with the cold air cycle. It was my more expensive hair dryer, and of course no other dryer would do to calm Katie. Because we used the cold air cycle, we ran it for a year before it eventually died. We even taped the sound to take on car trips and never went anywhere without it. That particular sound seemed to help soothe her so that when she was fatigued and tense she could settle down and sleep. After she was sufficiently rested she would awake, even though the hair dryer was running, and be a sunny little baby.

The hair dryer may not work for every baby, but it is certainly worth a try as a last resort. It is important to keep it on the cold cycle and to put it as far away from your baby as possible so that the air doesn't blow on her and the sound is not so intense. If your baby settles down and goes to sleep with the hair dryer, try turning it off once to see if she'll stay asleep. Your hair dryer will last longer. If that doesn't work, leave it on—you need your sleep.

Let's take a look now at the kinds of babies who require special techniques of handling.

THE HYPERRESPONSIVE BABY

Like Katie, some babies are hyperresponsive, so that a very little stimulus will startle them or make them cry. This kind of baby often has an intense personality and cries desperately when hungry. He has difficulty relaxing into sleep, many times being awakened by his own jerks and twitches. He tenses when picked up, and he seems to hear everything.

Your goal in working with this baby is to try to keep the stimulation to a minimum, handling him calmly and soothingly. You should pick him up particularly slowly and gently, with plenty of warning, supporting his head very carefully. This is a baby who needs to be carefully wrapped, or swaddled, and carried against your chest. The Snugli or Comfi is helpful, for he can feel secure in these. You should keep your voice calm and quiet. This is a baby who definitely will not enjoy a bath in the first few weeks. Take heart, he may later become less sensitive to external stimuli.

THE "NEGATIVE" BABY

Another type of baby tends to have a negative view of life: Nothing really seems to please him. He is tired and fussy but can't relax enough to sleep and often sleeps less than other babies. He may not be a good feeder and is not particularly sociable afterwards. He awakens fussy and usually awakens frequently at night. If he is not feeding well, he tends to gain weight more slowly.

Because he is not very responsive to your overtures, you may feel very rejected and want to give up. It is important to remember that his behavior is not a criticism of you! He, more than other babies, needs your continued patience and attention to help him adjust and adapt. Because he is a baby who needs a great deal of contact with you, the carrier that holds the baby next to your body can be very helpful. Carrying him about as you do your daily chores not only gives him physical contact but also lets you talk and sing to him.

He probably also will feel more secure when he sleeps if he is swaddled. If he is a poor feeder, offer milk as often as he will take it in order to encourage weight gain. He probably is a child who will not adapt well in the beginning to new situations, and these ought to be kept to a minimum for now. He may enjoy a nice warm bath if you are in the tub with him, but not alone. We will discuss these options in the section on bathing (p. 125). This child may be in a transient stage and may become a happy little thing by the time he is three months old. On the other hand, he may continue to look at life in a more serious and cautious way. Just remember that he can be helped to enjoy new situations through your patience, love, and attention.

THE VERY WAKEFUL BABY

The very wakeful baby is one who does not sleep as long as you might expect of a newborn. He is not unhappy, but he simply stays awake and is alert, avidly taking in his environment. You will need a lot of energy and ingenuity to keep him free from boredom:

He is at an age when he cannot entertain himself, cannot handle toys, cannot play with siblings, or can't even sit up well. At this time an infant seat that can be moved from room to room comes in handy. The baby sling or carrier can also be a big help. Also, try placing a mattress or pad on the floor so that he can be on his tummy or his back. Remember that you may need to move him around every fifteen minutes or so, because his "entertainment" span is short.

THE SLEEPY BABY

The sleepy baby, on the other hand, is one who is absolutely no trouble. He may even have to be awakened for his feedings and often falls asleep in the middle of one. He does not cry, but on the other hand he is rather unresponsive. This can be disappointing, but it does allow you some time to regain your strength and catch up on sleep. One of the things to watch out for, however, is that he does receive enough food. He is not really ready to sleep through the night for ten to twelve hours and may need to be awakened for his late feedings. When your baby is awake, take every opportunity to talk to him and stimulate him so that he will realize that the awake times can be fun. Putting him in the *en face* position to encourage him to open his eyes is also helpful. If he sleeps a lot when being carried in your arms or a sling, an infant seat is the ticket to encourage wakefulness.

THE TENSE BABY

Some babies resist cuddling. They are tense and stiff, and push you away. They really need the cuddling, however. Swaddling and holding the baby close are helpful with these newborns. John A. B. Allan, a psychologist, has reported success with the following technique for the two-to-three-month-old infant with this behavior. Lift your baby underneath both arms, keeping the head slightly forward. Move him up and down, back and forth in space while you look at each other.

Keep smiling. Most babies will smile and relax even if they were screaming to start with. Do this for about five minutes whenever you want to cuddle your baby and he seems stiff. Follow this with a gentle massage for extra relaxation.

Sometimes a baby may be so tense that the relaxation is only temporary. If so, move his arms and legs by opening them gently and rhythmically like an accordion. He may get angry and cry, but the crying will subside to sobbing and, finally, relaxation. You can then hold him close with his chin tilted to his chest and his elbows and knees flexed. Make sure his hands and feet are crossing over to touch each other. In time and with perseverance, the stiffness will decrease and you'll see more smiling and cuddling. He'll then be more responsive to normal parenting practices. Read our section on sensorimotor stimulation for more suggestions. In the case of a very few children, however, the stiffness and tightness do not improve with these efforts. If this is true of your baby, talk to your doctor; you may need further evaluation to find the cause of his tenseness and a solution.

THREE
TO SIX
MONTHS

HOW TO HOLD YOUR BABY   Your baby is now ready for a lot of give and take. He has head control and is developing trunk and back control and learning to sit alone. You needn't worry that his head will jerk about, and he "helps" you when you pick him up and carry him. He likes being carried in a more upright position, and toward the end of this time he will be fighting the restraint of the infant seat more often than not—sitting on a lap is so much better. He also likes the kind of infant carrier that allows him to sit up and look all around and get a good view of the world.

Because he is developing, he is wiggly and a little more rambunctious at diapering time and when he is being dressed and undressed. But at least he doesn't have that rag-doll feeling when you're trying to get a shirt on him. Just hold on to him or buckle him in on the changing table.

INTERACTION WITH YOUR BABY   This is a time of maximum smiling and eye-to-eye gaze. You'll experience a lot of give and take—either one of you may initiate the interaction. Your baby will adore your attention and approval.

The easy baby is active and happy. He initiates interactions and will practice alone, giving himself a great deal of stimulation. He is fun to be with. The less responsive, slow-to-warm-up, quiet child needs you to do the initiating and to encourage his responses. He needs extra stimulation, but once you get him going, he loves it.

Because the slow-to-warm-up child tends to avoid new situations, a parent may try to keep him out of them. Don't. He needs the experiences. But introduce them to him slowly, in a comfortable and relaxed way. Don't get discouraged if he seems uninterested and turns away. Give him time. You'll need to hold him close and give him physical comfort at the beginning.

The difficult child will tax your patience—still seeming to have no pattern or predictability established, still intense. He *demands* interaction. With his extra maturity at this time, he is easier to interact with now, and when he is happy, his intensity makes the experience a thousand times more enjoyable for you. You will have learned ways to soothe him and he is intensely grateful to you. So hang in there; it's worth it!

PHYSICAL PLAY   Your baby probably enjoys a little more physical play now. His head control is good and he loves movement. He can tolerate gentle rough-housing, such as holding him in the air and gently wiggling him back and forth. Although most babies love this kind of play, some are frightened by it, so don't push it. Babies and young children should never be roughhoused with vigorously, thrown in the air, or jerked or shaken: Their heads are heavier in relation to their necks—a setup for whiplash; and the small veins in the brain are delicate and can (though rarely) rupture and result in hemorrhaging.

SOOTHING   Soothing your baby now may require more action, too. More rapid and vigorous rocking is helpful. Cribs can be equipped with rockers or springs so your baby can soothe himself when he is settling down. Don't be surprised to hear him rocking in the middle of the night.

During this period your baby becomes aware of you as a person. He is beginning to adapt to family schedules and fit in better; however, remember that he is the least adaptable member of the family. He is beginning to try to exert some control and will feel frustrated if thwarted. If he responds with anger, try to figure it out. Are you perhaps being too controlling? Be careful: Too much restraint may result in your baby's becoming too passive. His need to assert himself is a healthy one, so encourage it whenever you can.

SIX TO TWELVE MONTHS

Holding your baby during this period is like holding a wiggleworm at times. He is much more interested in getting down and exploring his universe than staying in your arms. He is still, however, very much focused on you, his mother, and sometimes he'll be your shadow about the house. Your job is to be available, to keep his environment safe, and to set appropriate limits.

This is a good time to remember not to disturb your baby when he is busy learning to manipulate a new toy or exploring a new cupboard or whatever has captured his attention. It is tempting to do things with him because he is such fun, but let him learn to persevere on his own. This also means clearing the environment of as many "no-no's" as possible so that you won't have to interrupt him. He'll learn about breakables soon enough in his lifetime.

At this time the baby with the high activity level can become a problem. He'll probably walk early, climb out of his crib early, climb up on tables—you name it. Keeping him safe is a big goal.

Install gates at the tops and bottoms of stairs, put corner guards on sharp furniture, and lower the crib mattress so that he can't climb out. If he still climbs out, you can put the mattress on the floor and baby-proof his room so he'll be safe when he's in there alone.

This child thrives on outdoor activities and rough play. He is likely to be over-stimulated by bedtime, however. Settling him down with a bath and quiet water play or book time for the last hour of the day is essential.

Most children begin to experience some anxiety in the presence of strangers now. See our discussion of how to deal with the problem on p. 169.

Now let's get down to the nitty-gritty of your baby's daily care.

D I A P E R I N G

For those of you who have opted to use cotton diapers that are not prefolded, because of their economy (the drying time of prefolded diapers is considerably more than that of nonprefolded), we illustrate below two methods of folding and diapering. Choose the method you prefer.

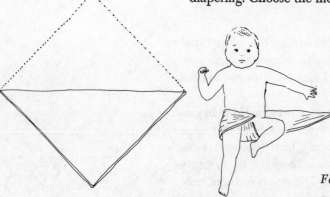

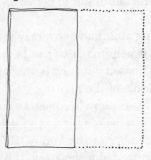

Folding and diapering—Method #2

Step 1. Fold diaper lengthwise.

Step 2. Put baby on diaper. Fold front of diaper over so there is a double thickness to absorb more moisture. Bring the front over the baby's tummy and pin back of diaper to front at sides.

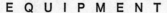

Folding and diapering—Method #1

Fold diaper into a triangle. Place baby on diaper so that bottom point is brought up between the legs. Pin the three points together at the waist.

E Q U I P M E N T

The easiest place to change diapers is on a high, firm surface such as a padded changing table. You can use a regular table, but babies roll more on an unpadded surface and are likely to be frightened by it. You can change your baby on a sofa or a bed, but a changing table is better because it has a strap that can keep the baby on the table if you have to turn your back to get something. Of course you can also change him on the floor, if he is playing there when he needs changing.

It is important to keep your cleaning equipment such as washcloths or cotton balls, soap, and a jar of water or lotion beside the changing table. A roll of masking tape is also a necessity when the tape on the disposable diapers refuses to hold.

H A N D L I N G   W H E N   C H A N G I N G

To change a diaper, place your baby gently on the table. Always keep one hand on him during the process, particularly as he gets older, because you never know when he may decide to turn over. When lifting his legs to clean his bottom, keep a finger between his feet so his ankle bones won't rub together. A tip you will appreciate if you have a little boy is that of keeping a cloth or diaper over the penis while you are cleaning him; boys often urinate just one more time. If you are using cloth diapers and diaper pins, be sure to keep your fingers between the pin and the baby's skin in order to avoid pricking him. Pins slide in better if you stick them in a bar of soap occasionally. Leave the wrapper on.

Babies are often in a wakeful state while or after being changed. This is a good time to give your baby a tummy rub, as you lean over him, smiling and talking gently.

C L E A N I N G   B A B Y

You don't need to wash your baby's bottom after every change of a wet diaper. Once or twice a day is sufficient. Use a wet cotton ball or a wet washcloth—he'd prefer to have it warm—and have a dry washcloth or towel close by so you can pat him dry. If he has sensitive skin, make sure you pat him dry after every diaper change, particularly in the creases and skin folds.

When he has a bowel movement, remove the majority of the BM by wiping him with the dirty diaper. Clean the soiled area with a warm soapy washcloth or cotton ball, followed by rinsing with a clean wet cloth and then drying. Cotton balls with baby lotion can be used for the cleaning process also. It is not necessary to put lotion on your baby's bottom, but you certainly may if you wish. Talcum powder is not necessary and in fact can create problems when inhaled into the lungs. If your baby chafes easily, then use powder of the cornstarch variety. Be sure to put it in your hand first and then spread it thinly on the baby's body.

P L A S T I C   P A N T S

The disposable diapers have waterproofing built in, so there is no need for plastic pants. Plastic pants can be used with cloth diapers, but if your baby has sensitive skin and tends to have diaper rashes we would advise against them. They simply keep the moisture in and encourage a rash. You can still use them for special occasions. If you are using them, try to keep them as loose as possible. If they're the snap type, undo the bottom snaps. This allows some moisture to escape and some air to be let in.

H O W   O F T E N   T O   C H A N G E

Most babies don't mind being wet as long as they are warm, so it is not necessary to change your baby every time the diaper is damp unless he is susceptible to diaper rash. Plan on changing him once at each feeding and, if necessary, in between. New babies often urinate twenty to thirty times a day; you could run yourself ragged if you tried to change him every time he was wet!

L A U N D E R I N G   C L O T H   D I A P E R S

If you are using cloth diapers make sure that they are well laundered, either by a diaper service or by you. Babies can develop a rash from the ammonia in the urine if it isn't completely washed out, as well as from laundry detergent if it isn't rinsed out.

You must have a diaper pail in the room with a chemical diaper sterilant in it. Submerge the diapers in this sterilant until laundry time. Scrape bowel movements off into the toilet before putting the diaper in the pail. Obviously, the diaper pail needs a lid. When you are ready to wash the diapers, empty the pail liquid into the toilet. Rinse the pail well. The diaper sterilant is poisonous and contains bleach, so it is important that you wash it off your hands, and don't put colored clothing in the diaper pail. Wash on the hottest cycle in your washing machine with a very mild detergent, and be sure everything is rinsed well. If your baby develops diaper rash you may have to run the load through the rinse cycle again or use an extra soak cycle to assure proper rinsing. The diapers may be tumble-dried or hung outside to dry, and you may use fabric softeners. If your baby does develop a diaper rash, however, the fabric softener may be the culprit. Try leaving it out and see if the rash clears up. Or try putting one cup of vinegar in the rinse water.

N A V E L   C A R E

The umbilical cord is made of a white, jellylike material with three blood vessels running inside of it. It will have been clamped and cut by the obstetrician or midwife. It has no nerves and is not sore. It gradually dries and withers, turning brown or black. In a week to three weeks it will fall off. Oozing of blood may occur at that time. Call your doctor if there is oozing or bleeding from an area larger than a nickel or if it lasts more than three days. The cord will fall off sooner if you keep it as dry as possible. This means making sure that the diapers are below the cord. Give it some extra drying by dabbing the navel with alcohol with every diaper change. Some doctors recommend not bathing babies during this time, but others feel bathing is not a problem if you dry the cord afterward. It can be dried by dabbing with a sterile cotton ball or by setting your hair dryer on a low warm setting and blowing on it. While it is withering, the cord has a certain smell, which alcohol sometimes combats as well. The smell comes from bacteria that have collected on the cord.

Sometimes when the cord falls off it leaves a raw spot that is reddish and wet. This is called granulation tissue, and if it is kept dry it will scab over. Again, make sure that the diaper is kept well below the area. Alcohol cleaning, four to six times every day, should be continued. Use soft cotton swabs (Q-tips) and clean in all the crevices. If it doesn't seem to be healing, consult your doctor. If the navel and the skin around it become red, then there is probable infection and you should call your doctor immediately.

U M B I L I C A L   H E R N I A

Most babies' navels resemble little flower buds. All babies have an opening in the deeper muscular layer of the abdomen where the blood vessels in the cord went through, and some babies have bigger openings than others. Sometimes when a baby cries a small part of intestine is pushed through this opening and makes the navel puff out more. This is what we call an umbilical hernia, but it does not cause the problems that other hernias sometimes do.

When the opening in the muscular layer is small, it is likely to close over within a few weeks. If it is larger it may take months or years to close, and the protrusion of the intestine may even be the size of a lemon. This protrusion is nothing to worry about, however, because the intestine does not become locked inside the opening and can be pushed back very easily. The hernia will probably take care of itself as the baby grows and his abdominal musculature becomes more developed. If it does persist as late as six or seven years of age and is quite large, then a simple surgical procedure may be necessary.

CIRCUMCISION CARE

If your baby boy has had a circumcision it will take several days to heal. You can protect his circumcision area from the diaper by loosely wrapping the end of the penis with a one-inch-square piece of vaseline petroleum jelly gauze. The hospital can give you some before you leave or you can make your own. Do not be concerned if the diaper is pink stained, for there may be some oozing and tenderness around the site for a few days. Once the oozing has stopped and a scab has formed, you can leave the gauze off. Call your doctor if the end of the penis turns blue, if there is a poor urine stream, if there is pus or drainage, or if there is true bleeding from the incision.

DRESSING AND UNDRESSING TECHNIQUE

This activity is never going to be your baby's favorite. When undressing your child try to keep as much of his body clothed as possible, leaving his shirt on when you are changing his bottom clothing and vice versa. If you do have to have him completely naked, it sometimes helps to put a blanket or towel across his abdomen so he feels less vulnerable. We don't know why very young babies dislike being naked, but perhaps it is the new sensation of cool air against their skin.

When your baby is older and has more control of his body you will find that dressing and undressing are easier because he is not so floppy; however, he may not like lying still for even a few seconds. It is helpful then to have something to entertain him with. A mirror on the wall next to the changing place, a mobile, a toy, or a song from you will help to distract him. When putting on garments such as shirts or long pants it is simpler to have your baby on your lap. There are some children, however, who absolutely have to be dressed on the run. I (AA) became quite adept at diapering our Kimberly while she was standing absorbed in a picture book. I even became able to diaper her while she was walking around—a little lopsided sometimes!

GARMENTS

It is easier to dress and undress your child if you keep his garments simple. Shirts with snaps up the front are far superior to shirts that must be pulled over the head. If you do have a garment that must be pulled over the head, snaps on the shoulder, which make a larger opening, are helpful. When you pull something over the head, always start at the back of the head and then pull down over the face, putting the arms in the sleeves last. At a young age when your baby has less control over his limbs, it is better to pull the sleeve over his arm rather than pull

his arm through the sleeve. One of the easiest ways to put on shirts and upper garments is to prop the baby on your lap with your legs crossed, as shown in the illustration.

Dressing your baby during warm weather is very simple, because he probably needs only a loose cotton kimono or T-shirt with a diaper for most of the day. In cooler weather he needs layers of light clothing rather than one heavy piece. Layering conserves heat more efficiently, and layers are easy to adjust if the temperature changes a bit. A one-piece stretch suit is very helpful to protect your baby from drafts.

F E E D I N G

We have discussed feeding methods in Chapters Six and Seven. We urge you to reread these at this time.

Feeding time is an excellent time for interacting with your baby, but not for excessive stimulation. Obviously you are both in an ideal position to gaze at each other, a wonderful pastime. Remember, however, that your baby's main need is to eat. He will suck in a certain rhythm—usually suck, suck, suck, suck, pause, suck, suck, suck, suck, pause. It is during the pause when he will be interested in interacting with you, ready for stroking, patting, talking. Leave him alone while he is sucking, simply holding him close; you may croon or rock gently, but don't distract him. He will swallow less air, take in more milk and feel comfortable sooner. Take your cues from him; he'll let you know when he wants more than milk.

The hyperresponsive baby who is extra sensitive to any stimulation and very distractible needs more controls at feeding time. You may have to feed her in a darkened room, with a continuous low-intensity background noise (fan, air conditioner), swaddled in a blanket to prevent movement.

B U R P I N G

Both breast-fed and bottle-fed babies may swallow air while feeding, though it is more common in the bottle-fed baby. Swallowing air distends the stomach and may cause discomfort. Your baby will let you know how she feels by stopping in the middle of feeding or by seeming uncomfortable. If she is sucking vigorously, there is no need to stop to burp her until she pauses. If you are breast feeding you can try burping when you change breasts.

TECHNIQUE

Burping is done by holding your baby in an upright position, usually against your shoulder. Put a diaper or cloth over your shoulder to protect you from any spitting up. Rub or pat your baby's back gently. Until she has head control (around three months), you will have to support her head so that it doesn't flop around. Another method is to sit your baby sideways on your lap. Let her lean forward from the hip against your hand, while you gently massage or pat her back with your other hand.

If she hasn't burped after a minute or so there is no need to continue. She may burp later or not need to burp at all. A word of warning about burping: Be gentle. You really should not use much force at all. Remember, you are ten to fifteen times as heavy as your baby. Too-vigorous burping can even result in a whiplash injury and damage to the delicate blood vessels in a baby's brain.

SPITTING UP

Your baby may spit up slightly when she burps. It will simply be undigested milk mixed with mucus and saliva. There are several reasons for spitting up. The baby may have eaten too much, fed too fast, been bounced or jiggled too much before or during feeding, or cried too much and swallowed air before her feeding. Or there may be air in the bottle or the nipple hole may be too small so that the baby must resort to vigorous sucking, which causes her to swallow air.

Some babies are spitters and some are not. Some babies even spit up in their sleep. If you have a chronic spitter, it may help to keep her in an infant seat at a 45-degree angle for about thirty minutes after eating. Even better, keep her on her tummy at a 30-degree angle by raising the mattress of her bed with a wedge. Put a blanket between her legs, diaper fashion. Pin the sides to the sheet, creating a sling to keep the baby from sliding. Or have her lie on your chest while you are resting at a 30-degree angle. If your baby is a spitter it is definitely advisable to have her sleep on her tummy.

HICCUPS

Many babies have hiccups, and some are hiccupers even before they are born. No one really knows what causes the hiccuping, but it may be due to sensitivity of the diaphragm muscle. If your baby has the hiccups, try putting her to suck or offering her water in a bottle. But don't worry too much; hiccups don't really bother her, and the tendency will disappear with time.

FRESH AIR

Barring rain or below-freezing temperatures, an hour or two outdoors each day is good for your baby, and for you too. If you can spend that time walking, you'll fill your own need for physical exercise. When your baby is older she can walk too; a pattern of daily exercise should be instilled early. Of course your baby can also get her fresh air playing in the playpen or sleeping in her carriage out of doors.

DRESSING FOR OUTDOORS

It is important to dress your baby properly for outdoors because babies' temperature-control mechanisms do not operate very well in the first few months. You don't want her to be either chilled or overheated. If the weather is cool, she'll need several layers of clothing. Her head should be covered with a knit cap or bonnet, because she can lose a lot of heat from that large body surface (a baby's head is proportionately much larger than an adult's). A baby who is becoming chilled will start to act restless and fussy and become pale. A baby's hands always tend to be cool, so feel her feet and legs to check for temperature. If they are cool, she should be brought inside. If her abdomen and trunk are cold she is definitely overchilled and should be brought in immediately. Warm her up by holding her against you, with blankets over both of you to trap your body heat.

Guard, too, against overdressing your baby, particularly in hot weather. If she is overheated her face will become flushed and she may sweat. Remove some of her clothes and fan her. If she is dry and flushed she'll need sponging to give her the extra moisture to cool down.

At the beach there is a reflected glare, so make sure to keep a young infant in the shade at all times. An older, more mobile infant should be protected by a hat and a sunscreen. In the early months babies' skin is very delicate and will burn easily. Remember, sunburn doesn't show up for several hours, so you can be fooled.

D E N T A L   H Y G I E N E

As soon as your baby gets her first tooth it is important to try to keep her gums and teeth clean—although she won't especially enjoy the process. Most dentists recommend that you use a two-by-two-inch gauze pad. Put your child in your lap with the crown of her head facing your abdomen and her feet facing away from you. Lean over so that you can see what you're doing, and gently open her mouth with your finger. With the gauze pad, gently rub the gums along the jaw ridges on the tops and bottoms. This helps to keep the gums clean of food matter and stop the buildup of plaque and decay. It also allows you to get your child accustomed to having someone work with her mouth. You will have to help her with her dental hygiene for a good six or seven years. There is no need for toothpaste; but go ahead and use it if your baby likes it, because it does offer some fluoride protection.

G E N E R A L   H Y G I E N E

It is important in infancy to protect your baby from an overdose of bacteria. This is the reason for the care you take in the feeding. The most important thing to remember is that an object is not dangerous if it is dry and free from food. In other words, anything that is simply dusty or grubby is really of no concern. But when an object has been in contact with food—especially dairy products—and left at room temperature, it is unsafe because bacteria will grow rapidly on the food. Bacteria are also found in feces, so it is important that you, or any caretaker, wash your hands after a bowel movement. Also make sure to wash your baby's hands if she has been touching her genital area or soiled diaper while she was being cleaned up. It is equally important to mop up any "accidents" or spit-up milk that have accumulated on rugs or furniture. Your baby's pacifier, unless it has been dipped in Karo or maple syrup, does not need to be sterilized; just rinse it off if she drops it. There is no need to wash off toys unless they have been spit up on or soiled by feces. Finally, be prepared! During later infancy you may be stunned one day when you walk into your baby's room to find that she has decided to paint the walls, her crib, her toys, and herself with fecal material!

If you have an infection, your hands will readily transmit the germs. Careful and frequent handwashing before handling your baby is essential then.

B A T H I N G   A N D   C L E A N I N G

H A N D S   A N D   F A C E

In the first few weeks, bathing your baby should be the *last* thing on your list; she simply doesn't need a lot of baths at this time. There are so many other things that you can be doing together now.

You must clean some areas of her body, however. Wipe her face once a day with a warm, damp washcloth (no soap) to remove any milk or matter from her nose or eyes. Her hands can be wiped off at the same time. If she puts her hands into a dirty diaper, wash them with a soapy washcloth and rinse with a clean, wet one. Babies sweat on their heads and behind their ears and necks, so wipe these areas at the same time you clean her face. To dry your baby, blot her with a soft towel, because her skin is tender. The cleaning can be done in your lap or on the changing table or a bed. She appreciates your leaving her clothes on and being in a warm room. Babies hate feeling chilled.

Do not put anything into your baby's ears or nose; the mucus and wax are there for a protective purpose. Sometimes you may see a piece of dried mucus blocking one of your baby's nostrils. This can be removed gently with a damp Q-tip (soft cotton swab).

B A T H

Some babies love it; others fear and hate it. Parents may have anxious feelings about bathing too, because there is nothing scarier than trying to hold on to a slippery, soapy, floppy new baby. To make both you and your baby more comfortable at bathtime, try using some of the bath-aid devices on the market. One of these is a foam insert which can be put into a small tub, a sink, or even the bathtub. It sits on the floor of the tub and holds the baby, leaving both your hands free.

The Tubby is another helpful device. It is a plastic, inflatable tub resembling a life raft. It can be placed on a counter and filled with a few inches of water, and your baby can lie in it with her head resting on the side. Again, your hands are free. I (AA) used a Tubby with both Katie and Kimberly, and put it in the bathtub with me. The baby could float around, we could play water games, the water remained warm, and I could readily hold her and calm her when she became fussy. This is a useful technique for babies who are frightened by bathing. They can become accustomed to the water while being closely held by Mother.

The infant seat, if any holes in the pad are sealed (masking tape will do nicely), can also be placed in a tub or sinkful of water. It comes in handy if an older brother or sister just can't wait to take a bath with the new baby. It also can be handy if you only need to do some hair washing; if you incline the seat as far back as it can go, water won't run into the baby's eyes.

Even if something goes wrong and your baby's head slips under water, don't panic. She comes equipped with an automatic reflex to protect herself, and she will hold her breath—something she learned in utero, we guess.

Another key to a successful bath is planning ahead. Take the telephone off the hook. Warm the room. And make sure that all the equipment—soap, washcloth, towel, lotion, powder, clothes, and blankets—is at your side.

Wash the face without soap—soap stings, and she doesn't really need it. Wash the head with a soapy washcloth and avoid drips down the face by wringing the washcloth out thoroughly. Rinse the soap off the head by going over it with a wet washcloth several times. Then soap your hands up and rub the body all over—a soapy massage she'll love.

There is no need to be extra vigorous in the genital area. It can be washed in the same way as the rest of the body. There used to be a great deal of concern that uncircumcised boys needed to have the foreskin retracted in order to wash out all of the smegma that collects between the foreskin and the head of the penis. Don't do this—it hurts the baby unnecessarily, for we now know that the foreskin and the head of the penis are joined at birth and only gradually grow apart. In fact, the foreskin cannot be retracted completely until the baby is about two to three years old. We also used to believe that little girls needed to have their labia separated and their genitals cleaned vigorously. This is not necessary. These areas have their own mucus with some cleaning abilities. Some babies in fact are very sensitive to soap and it can sting, so just use a wet washcloth.

If after the bath you wish to put on lotion or powder, avoid lung-irritating powders containing talc or zinc. Use a cornstarch powder instead.

When your baby has learned to sit alone, playing in the tub is a wonderful pastime for her. There are small seating devices with suction cups that can attach to tub bottoms. They have straps to put around the baby's torso and help support her. If you don't have the seat, you can put a towel on the bottom of the tub to prevent slipping. Also, the baby bathtub with water in it can be put into the large tub. Then your baby can play in it and splash all she wants.

One note of caution: Do not leave your baby in the tub unattended. Also, remember that once your baby can crawl, faucets are very inviting. Her skin is very sensitive and will blister with water over 130 degrees. Cover the hot-water faucet with a washcloth. If you can, turn your hot-water-heater thermostat down to 125 degrees, to be on the safe side. The water will still be hot enough for laundering diapers.

Y O U R   B A B Y ' S   S L E E P

T Y P E S   O F   S L E E P :   Q U I E T   A N D   A C T I V E

The baby's sleep is an area many parents worry about. We think it helps to understand a little bit about the two types of sleep that you will see in your infant. They are the same kinds that older children and adults experience, but in different proportions. First, there is *quiet sleep,* in which there is no evidence of eye or body movements and respiration is slow and regular. Second, there is *active sleep,* or rapid-eye movement (REM) sleep in which it is evident that the eyes are moving under the eyelids. In REM sleep, your body movement and respiration are increased and irregular, you can be easily awakened—and you will usually remember your dreams. During the night your sleep cycles several times between active (REM) sleep and quiet sleep. You usually awaken briefly at the end of each REM cycle and go right back to sleep, often not realizing you had awakened.

The full-term newborn baby spends slightly more time in active sleep than in quiet sleep, and that's why he awakens more frequently. By two months of age a baby has developed a greater proportion of quiet sleep with a decrease in active sleep—an indication of the maturation of the central nervous system. By three months he has developed twice as much quiet sleep as active sleep. Perhaps babies decrease their need for active sleep as they get older because they receive much more external stimulation during their waking periods, so that they need less stimulation while asleep.

A M O U N T   O F   S L E E P

Studies by Dr. Arthur Parmalee of UCLA have shown that the mean amount of sleep for a baby during the first three days of life is 16.6 hours, with a range of 10.5 to 23 hours. The duration of her awake states in these first three days is greater than it will be for the rest of the first month.

According to Dr. Parmalee, by the end of the first month the average sleeping time for a baby has decreased to 15.5 hours a day. She can stay awake for about 3 hours at a time and can sleep for as long as 6.5 hours. These average sleep and wake times gradually change, until by four months she averages 14.5 hours of sleep a day, can stay awake for as long as 3.5 hours, and can sleep about 8.5 hours at a stretch. By one year of age she still requires almost 14 hours of sleep a day, but she has organized herself so that she is sleeping at night for approximately 12 hours and has 2.5 hours of nap time during the day, usually in two nap periods.

See? It will get better! Your goal is to help her establish these patterns as quickly as possible for both of your sakes. But remember that your child is an individual, and these sleep statistics are only averages. Don't be concerned if your child needs more sleep or less sleep than these figures indicate.

THE BABY'S BED

Basically, a baby can sleep anywhere. She can sleep in a dresser drawer that has been pulled out (if the bottom of the dresser has been weighted to keep it from tipping), a bassinet, or a crib. A crib may make a tiny baby uncomfortable, however, because it is a wide open space. In the beginning it helps to have a smaller area in which to put your baby to sleep. The little bassinets with wheels are very helpful because the baby can be moved about the house. It is important, no matter what device you have, that the mattress be firm and that it fit well, with no space between the mattress and the side of the bed that would allow the baby to get wedged in and suffocate. The mattress should either be plastic or be protected with a plastic sheet that can be tucked under the bed and covered with a soft, warm flannel undersheet. Babies appreciate softness and warmth, and since cotton sheets tend to be cool, it is good to cover the mattress instead with a flannel cloth or even a diaper. Also, Snugli Products sells a lambskin wool pad which is a natural insulator as well as fun for your baby to snuggle in at bedtime.

S L E E P I N G P O S I T I O N S

When you put your baby in bed it is preferable to put her on her tummy. Most babies prefer this and it makes sense in the beginning, when they may be spitting up more. If they vomit while on their backs, they may choke. Another problem with putting the baby to sleep on her back is that babies tend to lie with their heads turned always to the same side (usually the right). This can lead to flattening of the head, although the lopsidedness will disappear when she gets older and is on her feet.

If you have a baby who absolutely will not lie on her stomach, then you will just have to make the best of it and let her sleep on her back. Try to keep her head turned to opposite sides each time you put her down. You may be able to do this by hanging something attractive that she enjoys looking at on the side of the crib. Then each time you put her into the crib, put her down in the opposite direction from the time before. Some people recommend that you lay a child on her side; however, we have found this to be very ineffective, for babies inevitably will slump over onto their tummies or backs.

Once you have placed your baby on her tummy very gently, cover her if it is cool with a light acrylic blanket and simply layer more light blankets. Tuck the blankets in under the mattress to secure her in the bed and help her have a feeling of closeness. If she is a restless baby and kicks off blankets, in cold weather you can put her in the little nighties with bottoms that tie off, or a sleeping bag. She does not need a pillow; she prefers the independence of turning her head from side to side without anything in her way.

F A L L I N G A S L E E P

In the first few months your baby will probably fall asleep right after her feeding and you will put her to bed. But around three to four months, when she is able to stay awake after eating, you will need to seriously consider how you put her to bed. She will begin to associate certain conditions with falling asleep. All of us do to a certain extent—a special pillow, a fan noise, music—and we miss them when they're not there.

Suppose your baby continues to fall asleep at night while she is being rocked or nursed. She is learning to associate falling asleep with these activities and will begin to require them consistently. When she has her normal brief night wakings she may not be able to fall back to sleep without those very same conditions—rocking or nursing. Are you willing to provide this for her several times a night?

Beware of any condition needed for sleep which your baby cannot recreate for herself during the night—a pacifier, a bottle, or a warm body beside her. Obviously some babies will not have a problem when they awaken at night. More adaptable and easy-to-manage children can adjust to the difference and fall back to sleep on their own. Their counterparts, who are less adaptable and more intense in their reactions, certainly cannot, and your sleep will be interrupted.

Why take a chance? Develop a bedtime routine you and your baby can live with. After dinner give your baby a nice warm bath to relax her. Play quiet games; snuggle in a chair with a picture book and "read" to her. Feed her a little earlier than her usual bedtime so that she will remain awake after the feeding. While she is sucking let her hold a soft blanket or toy which she can take into the bed with her. Afterward rock her or pat her gently, but just enough to relax her. Put her in bed while she is awake. Let her learn to associate sleep with her own bed and with that special blanket or soft toy. They'll be there when she wakes in the night. If she associates them with falling asleep that's just what she'll do—fall back to sleep.

She may fuss and root around for a bit but let her, she'll usually settle down. If she has trouble settling, pat her bottom, jiggle the bed, or put your hand on her back to help calm her. Read our section on Bedtime Blues to learn how to handle persistent crying. Some children have more difficulty falling asleep on their own, but they can learn.

SLEEPING PATTERNS

Remember that a lot of babies' sleep in the beginning is active sleep. They make noises and fuss but are not really ready to be picked up. Many times new parents are so eager to hold their new baby that they inadvertently awaken her before she is ready. If you hear her fussing or moving about in her room after she has been sleeping, let her be for a few minutes. Wait until she lets you know that she wants you by giving more forceful yells or cries.

NOISE   There is no need to have everyone tiptoe around the house when the baby is asleep. It has in fact been shown in studies that babies sleep much better with a background noise such as the radio or a steady hum rather than absolute quiet. It is the change in noise that awakens the baby. In the beginning months when she is establishing her sleep patterns, it helps to have some continuous noise, either a softly playing radio, a fan, or a Rock-A-Bye Teddy with its uterine sound, while your baby is asleep. These aids are particularly effective with the baby who has a low threshold to external noises, because they help to block them out.

SLEEPING THROUGH THE NIGHT   After the first four weeks your child is more regular in her eating times, and she may be able to sleep for a period of six hours at a time. Aim to get those six hours to occur at night, if they don't already. You can do some manipulating in order to help her. If you fed her at 8 P.M. and it is now 10:30 or 11:00 and you want to go to bed, you can gently try to waken her and feed her before you go to bed. It will be close enough to her feeding time that her stomach will have emptied and she will probably be able to take a fair amount. If she is extremely sleepy and does not wake even after you put a cool wet cloth on her forehead, let it go and try again the next night. Also, you might try to bring this about by treating the nighttime bedtime in a slightly different fashion. During the day she could sleep in a brightly lit room without necessarily being burped after a feeding, so that she might wake up after a short time. At night you should make sure that you get any burps up so that they will not awaken her. Sometimes bathing at night helps relax her, and then swaddling gives her the soothing feeling of cuddling and security—although this type of wrapping is advisable only in the first few months of life, before your baby is ready to move about. A darkened room is also helpful at night to remove external stimuli that she might notice on opening her eyes. A dim night light is essential, however, so that you will be able to find your way in and out of the room.

Your baby will probably wake up in the night for feeding for at least several months. Some babies sleep through the night much sooner than others, sometimes as early as one month. A few babies, however, require a feeding in the middle of the night as late as eight months or more. However, if your baby has slept poorly from the beginning with frequent waking and crying, consider a cow's milk allergy. One study of a group of such children found that within two weeks of switching to a milk substitute their sleep problems subsided.

When she does awaken for a feeding in the night it is important to go to her as soon as she begins to cry (not simply fuss). Make this feeding one in which she is handled warmly and gently, but is not overstimulated with talking or playing. Feed her in the dark and keep it brief. After she has been fed, put her back in the bed and let her settle herself.

Babies rarely awaken because of wet diapers, but if they do it is usually in a cycle of active, or REM, sleep. It is important not to go in to her but to allow her to handle this waking by herself if she can. If it is quiet she can usually go back to sleep. If she's being kept awake by the wet diaper and begins to cry, go in and change her, but don't play with her. Be matter-of-fact.

BEDTIME BLUES

During the last half of her first year your baby begins to develop the ability to keep herself awake longer after feeding and may not want to go to bed. She seems to be having such a good time that she really never wants to go to bed no matter how sleepy she gets. She is also experiencing a normal developmental phase, separation anxiety. She does not want to leave you.

This is when it is important to follow a bedtime routine. Let her kiss two or three favorite toys goodnight and stay in bed with a dim light on. You can keep yourself busy around her room and talk back and forth to her so she knows you are still around. In this way, the transition from being out with everybody to being by herself is a gradual one. Many babies develop other comfort habits at this time, and we will discuss them in the following chapter.

Despite all these rituals and comfort habits, some babies still have difficulty settling down. If your baby is one of these, it will take a little time, but you can help her. Go through her bedtime ritual, kiss her, and put her down, tucking her in. Then matter-of-factly leave the room. If she does cry after you leave, go back to her, kiss her or pat her, but do not take her out of the bed. Do not stay in the room with her. You are trying to let her know that you will come when she needs you, but she will not be able to go out of the room and be with the other people. You also want her to learn to fall asleep alone. You may have to go in repeatedly in response to her crying, but lengthen the time before you return. Try five minutes the first time, ten minutes the second, fifteen minutes the third, and twenty minutes as the maximum interval. She will get the picture that you are not going to give in. After a matter of days she will probably give it up.

The same thing is true with waking in the middle of the night. During this period, babies who have slept all through the night may begin awakening and crying. Look for the reasons. It may be outside voices, or perhaps she is cold or has a diaper rash. If you can eliminate the cause, she may not waken again.

Sometimes babies awaken because of nightmares or night frights. This can happen when a baby has been under stress or is excessively fatigued. It may be her way of letting you know that she needs some extra attention. Go to her when she cries and gently lay her down in the bed, covering her up. Pat her back or her bottom, soothing her for a few minutes before you leave the room. If she cries again you may have to repeat this again. Try to keep these periods brief and without any extra reinforcement. Most children will soon adapt to sleeping through the night again. But letting her cry it out is not meeting her needs, and going in to soothe her will not spoil her. Something fairly important awakened her and she needs a response from you to feel taken care of. Be kind but firm, telling her it is sleeping time and that everything is all right, and letting it be clear that she will not get out and play.

NIGHT WAKERS

Most children (90 percent) sleep through the night without problems by the time they are five months. However, yours may be an exception! Dr. William Carey, a pediatrician expert in infant temperament, has found that children with ongoing night-waking problems have the temperament characteristic of being very sensitive or hyperresponsive to all stimuli. They are more likely to fully awaken at the end of the REM cycle and have difficulty falling back to sleep no matter what. This observation is a psychological boon to parents; people used to think that if a child awakened at night after six to eight months of age, it was the parents' fault. In some cases this may be true, but in most cases it is the child's own temperament. The waking does create problems, since parents need their sleep and can become very resentful when it is interrupted night after night, month after month.

If your baby is a night waker, take a look at her general responsiveness to stimuli. Is she very sensitive to noise? Does she notice everything? If so, then she fits into the hypersensitive or hyperresponsive category. She doesn't wake up intentionally, and it's hard on her, too.

Perhaps some adjustments would help. Of course, keep her evening time quiet and relaxing. Have low background noise such as a radio or fan going in her room to block out other noises. Make sure her room is a good constant temperature, without drafts. Cover her snuggly, put on one-piece pajamas and a double diaper to cut down the damp feeling. Think of anything else that might cause her to wake up, and see if you can change it. Then cross your fingers and pray!

9

N U T R I T I O N
I N I N F A N C Y

As most parents instinctively know, good eating habits and good nutrition are the foundation of good health.

The best time to begin establishing good eating habits is during your baby's first year. You needn't worry too much about nutrition during the first months, because your baby is receiving his nourishment from your breast milk or from formula. Nutrition takes on more importance as he gradually begins to eat solid foods, and one of your main goals at this time is to help him feel happy about eating them.

Beginning solids can be a real adventure. But before we start off, let's talk about some of the tools and some of the information you may need in order to set the stage.

S E T T I N G T H E S T A G E F O R G O O D N U T R I T I O N

First of all, we would like to make a distinction between hunger and appetite. Hunger is a really unpleasant sensation that may make you feel weak and restless and give you pains in your upper abdomen. All healthy babies naturally feel hunger. Appetite, on the other hand, is learned or acquired. Appetite is the pleasurable association of a food with a past experience. Children develop appetites for certain foods because of flavor, color, or texture, or because they associate the food with a pleasant environment. Helping your child develop an appetite for appropriate foods is one of your major missions during his first few years of life. Obviously, you can ensure a pleasant association with food in general by providing it in a pleasant, warm way and by trying to avoid friction at eating time.

B A S I C S O F N U T R I T I O N

In order to decide which foods are appropriate for your child, you need to know some of the basics of nutrition. The fundamental needs of growth and health are met by the intake of proteins, carbohydrates, fats, vitamins, and minerals. Proteins, carbohydrates, and fats all provide energy, which is essential to make your body run. Vitamins and minerals do not provide energy but are essential for the maintenance of normal chemical reactions.

Proteins make up part of the structure of every cell and are important for the production and growth of healthy body cells. They can be found in meat, poultry, fish, dried beans, peas, eggs, cheese, and milk.

Carbohydrates are found in cereals, potatoes, dried beans, corn bread, and sugar. They supply energy for the body and are the major source of energy for the central nervous system. They also provide fiber, or roughage, which is necessary for good digestion and elimination.

Fats supply twice as much energy per gram weight as proteins or carbohydrates. They constitute part of every cell in our bodies. A layer of fat is necessary for maintaining body heat, and it is essential for the development of the central nervous system, particularly in the first few years of life. In babies, a layer of fat is an extremely good protection against sudden loss of intake such as with vomiting and diarrhea. There is a limit, however, to how much fat is needed for health.

T H I N   V S   F A T   B A B I E S

One of the biggest changes in infant nutrition in the last ten to fifteen years has been to throw out the old adage that a fat baby is a healthy baby. This philosophy had promoted overfeeding of infants. Because animal studies showed that overfeeding in infancy causes an increased number of fat cells, doctors began to fear that if the infant developed too many fat cells he would be destined to obesity. Therefore, physicians felt obliged to impose skim-milk reducing diets even in early infancy. More recent studies have shown, however, that infants on skim milk cannot possibly ingest enough energy to meet their nutritional requirements. Fat in the milk is necessary for good absorption of calcium, and fatty acids are important in the development of the central nervous system. Because of the potential risks in putting infants on reducing diets, most doctors now feel that when a baby is fed in a nutritionally sound way, the question of overweight resolves itself.

Obesity in children does not seem to be directly linked to what happens in infancy. In a study of obese preschoolers, for example, only 10 percent had a history of being obese as babies. In fact, the majority of them were children who had had feeding problems and been small as infants. Perhaps they were fed too much nonnutritive food by overly concerned parents. We believe there are strong genetic factors in obesity, because it has been found that children of obese parents are three times as likely to be obese as those whose parents are lean.

P A R E N T A L   I N F L U E N C E

Obviously more than genetics is involved; family influences such as attitudes about food and eating are important in determining whether a child will become obese.

It is important for you as parents to look at your eating habits and decide which ones you would like to pass along to your baby. One interesting study shows that children seem to dislike the vegetables their fathers dislike. Delving deeper into the study, however, we see that these mothers never served anything but the fathers' favorite vegetables, even if that meant only peas and corn! We do pass on our food likes and dislikes to our children.

As we have discussed, the first year of life is one in which the baby is moving from a state of complete dependence to one of progressive independence. There will be an orderly and predictable sequence in his adaptation to eating solid foods and entering the more grown-up world of eating. If you know what this development sequence is, you can avoid starting at too early a stage for him to appreciate it and handle it well, or at too late a stage for him to want it. Let's take a closer look at this developmental sequence.

O V E R V I E W   O F   F E E D I N G   D E V E L O P M E N T S

T O N G U E   A N D   M O U T H   C O N T R O L

Every infant has a reflexive suck and will continue to use it to take in liquids well into the second half of his first year. When he sucks he also tends to stick his tongue out, a very essential part of the sucking mechanism. However, automatically sticking his tongue out when food enters his mouth interferes with taking solid foods in. Hence the very messy picture of babies with food all over their faces and all over their feeders! Around the age of four to six months, however, you will notice that your baby is becoming less interested in sucking, and he may even shun his pacifier. His tongue no longer comes out of his mouth automatically when something is placed in it. He has much better mouth and lip control, and if a spoon is placed in his mouth, he is likely to use his lower lip to help hold the spoon in place. He will also draw his lip in when the spoon is removed in order to keep the food in his mouth. This obviously makes things much more tidy when it comes to feeding.

H E A D   A N D   T R U N K   C O N T R O L

Have you ever tried to eat lying down or even reclining at a 45-degree angle? Not much fun, is it? So the trunk control that your baby acquires during the fourth to the sixth month of life is an extremely important aspect of developing his ability to take in solid foods. With the development of good trunk control and stability, your baby not only can sit well but also can use his arms and hands in a much better fashion. He can reach out and grab objects, including food.

T E E T H

What else happens around six months of age? This is usually when the teeth appear. And the beginning of chewing motions is evident when food is placed in your baby's mouth. He still has no molars so he can't grind his food. And obviously he cannot eat the same foods that we can, but he is definitely ready to chew on things. He is ready for finger feeding, which means chewing or gumming soft strips of food that he can hold for himself.

S E L F   F E E D I N G

Your baby still needs to take the majority of his liquids through sucking, because he is not yet adept at drinking from a cup. By seven months, however, he is quite adept at handling his own bottle. By nine months your child has developed a pretty good pincer grasp (thumb against index finger) and is ready to finger-feed on smaller objects. He definitely needs something to chew by now. If children don't get chewable food by the age of nine months they are less likely to accept solid foods offered later on. In other words, the period from seven to nine months is really a critical period for developing and using chewing skills. By one year your baby will probably have some molars and be able to grind food. This means that he is ready for more of the family's food. And because of his improved finger and hand control, he is also ready to begin to feed himself by twelve to fifteen months.

By the end of the first year your baby understands more about containers and the necessity to hold them upright. (He has had a lot of experience dumping their contents out during these last few months.) He may still want to have his bottle or nurse at the breast at this age, but if he no longer desires sucking he is decidedly capable of obtaining enough fluid from a cup.

F E E D I N G   E Q U I P M E N T

Physical comfort is certainly a key to helping your child enjoy his feeding experiences. At first Mom's lap may be the very best spot. It's comfortable, and Mom's arm can provide the trunk support that he may need. And the extra cuddling is fun. His infant seat in the most upright position is also a good spot, because this way you and your baby can have a face-to-face conversation while he is taking in his food. See which one you both prefer. When he is comfortable sitting alone, a high chair is a good idea.

H I G H   C H A I R

When you look for a high chair, one of the most important features is comfort. Take your baby with you when you shop, so you can put him into different ones and see which one he seems to fit in best. Safety is an important feature. Look for a strong, easy-to-operate safety belt and crotch strap. You really need the crotch strap, because one of baby's favorite games is SUTT—Sliding Under The Tray. To keep the baby from sliding, some mothers have found it helpful to put a piece of foam under the baby so that he is not sitting directly on the slippery seat. Bathtub stickers can provide traction too.

Another feature to consider is how easy the high chair is to clean. Removable trays are essential. If there is a lip on the tray, spillage can be kept to a minimum. Try out the latches in the store, because there is nothing more frustrating than having a high-chair tray that is difficult to undo. Also make sure that there are no parts on the latches that could pinch or scratch your baby. The chair should have a high enough back to support your baby's head, and an adjustable footrest so that he can have his feet planted firmly on it while he is eating, which adds to his stability.

Speaking of stability, many a baby has fallen out of his high chair or pulled it over on top of himself. You want to avoid this at all costs. Be sure that the base of the chair is much wider than the seat. When you shake the chair it should not feel rickety. High chairs are easy to store, because they fold up. But be sure that the locking device is strong and that it cannot fold up by itself. When your child is older, you can remove the tray so that he can sit in his chair at the family table.

FEEDING TABLE

A feeding table is more expensive than a high chair, but it is safer because it can't turn over. It's also a little harder to get the baby in and out of. It provides a lot more table surface around your baby, for him to play on with his food or other objects. When your child becomes a toddler, however, he would rather sit at the table with the rest of the family than in a feeding table by himself, so a high chair is likely to have a longer useful life. If you decide on a feeding table, be sure it has a strong adjustable footrest, crotch belt, seat belt, and an adjustable seat.

CLIP-ON BABY CHAIR

There is a relatively new product on the market—a baby chair that can be clipped onto a table. Some of these do not have high enough backrests, but some do have a high backrest and a good solid footrest. In such a chair the baby can sit at the table with the rest of the family, whether at home or at a restaurant. Sitting at the main table provides more space on which to put the food and less likelihood of things being thrown overboard (usually done over the front of the tray). When your baby is very young, however, it would be difficult to feed him in one of these chairs unless the table was particularly narrow so that you could sit across from him.

UTENSILS

As far as the baby utensils you need are concerned, a demitasse spoon does very nicely in the beginning, for it is exactly the right size. Later you would want to consider buying a spoon that is rubber coated, for your teether, or a spoon with a swivel bowl, for the child who likes to feed himself but is not quite as adept as he needs to be. A blunt-tipped spoon is also very helpful for shoving food around on the plate. Your child will not be ready to use a fork in the first year of life, but if you are buying a spoon you might as well buy a fork at the same time. A fork with short, blunt tips is best for the beginner.

CUP

When looking for an appropriate cup for your baby to begin drinking with, remember that it needs to be unbreakable, sturdy, and not so heavy that it is difficult for him to hold. The Tommy Tippee cup is an extremely good first cup. It is weighted so that if it gets knocked over it will return upright. It also has a lid with a spout on it for the child who is just beginning to learn to take liquids this way and still needs a little bit of sucking. Your child is definitely not ready for straws at this time, so don't bother buying a cup with a straw attachment. That will come later. One trick that was helpful for me (AA) was to put a rubber band around my daughter's cup so that it didn't slide out of her slippery hands when she was trying to drink.

PLASTIC PLATES

Plastic plates are also essential. There are some special baby-food plates which have a suction cup on the bottom, so that your baby is less likely to be able to throw it on the floor. But don't count on it 100 percent, because babies are a lot stronger than you think. In fact, if you use a high chair and you keep the tray very clean, there's no reason you can't just put the food right down on the tray and avoid the nuisance of plates being thrown on the floor.

Speaking of throwing plates on the floor, you now have a wonderful new use for all of your newspapers. Begin the day with several layers of newspapers spread out under the high chair. After each meal you can peel off a layer and throw it in the garbage!

B I B S   A N D   C O V E R A L L S

How about protecting the baby himself from these showers of food? Most mothers use bibs. The plastic variety can be wiped off. The terry-cloth variety absorbs spills more readily but has to be washed in the washing machine. Or you can buy a bib made of a very hard plastic, covering the baby's whole chest, with a lip at the bottom to collect spills (sold by Mother Care). I (AA) have found that many mothers are very happy with this type, because it does effectively collect many of the spills; however, other mothers have said that their baby did not like having the heavy plastic around his neck and chin. One mother suggested putting a rain slicker over the baby for each meal. It certainly keeps your baby clean, but he may not like having to struggle through all that material to get his arms out on the tray. Talk to some of your friends and see what has worked for them.

The next thing you need to know is just *when* should you start?

W H E N

As we have already mentioned, your breast milk or the formula provides all the nutrition your baby will need for at least the first six months of life and on into the second six months. But during the second half of the first year your baby will need some extra sources of iron and protein. This addition to her diet coincides with her developmental ability to take in solid foods. However, there is no guarantee that she will obligingly open her mouth when the spoon approaches—and no guarantee that she will pay the same kind of attention as you do to getting the feeding job done. Patience and good humor will help.

Another reason to wait until about six months is that your baby's intestinal tract is better able to digest and react to foods at that time. If there is a strong family history of allergies, you would definitely be wise to wait at least six months before starting solids. If she has a history of loose and frequent stools on breast milk or formula, it might be best to wait until eight months. There may be a lot of social pressure to start your baby on solids early, but it really pays off if you can wait for the right time for you and your baby.

Your baby may give you some obvious clues when she is ready to start on solids. Around the age of four to six months she may begin to increase her nursing demands, waking up at night when she did not previously wake up, increasing the number of feedings in the day, and still seeming to be hungry after she has had eight ounces in her bottle or thirty minutes at the breast. She may also want to grab and chew on everything. If she doesn't give you any of these signals, you can wait until she is six to seven months old. Some people advise that you can judge the right time for starting solids by the weight of the baby, thinking that babies who weigh twelve pounds (usually around three months) are ready for solids. This has not been my (AA) experience. Two of my own babies weighed between seventeen and nineteen pounds (five to six months) before they indicated they were ready for solids to be added to their breast feeding, by helping themselves to any food that was on my plate.

Just as it is a good idea to wait until your child is developmentally ready for solids, it is also important to offer them to your child when she indicates the need. So keep your eyes open for your baby's signals that she is ready for solids.

Now let's talk about *what* to feed her.

W H A T

You may start your child on any type of solid food you wish. But it is important to add only one food at a time and to wait five days before adding another. Waiting five days lets you spot any sensitivity to the food. A baby who is sensitive to a food may react wtih wheezing, increased vomiting or diarrhea, colic, sore bottom, or a rash. If this happens with your baby, eliminate the food that seems to cause the problem for at least a week and then try again. You can repeat this two to three times, and if the same reaction occurs, wait another six months before you try that food again.

As we have said, there is no magic in the order in which you start foods. I (AA) have found that iron-fortified baby cereal is a very nice starter because it has an increased iron content that your baby is beginning to need at this age. It is also easy to prepare, and babies seem to like it. Rice cereal is the least allergenic of the cereals. If there is any family history of allergies, we would surely advise you start with that. You can then go on to the other cereals if you wish. Oatmeal and wheat are especially nutritious, but wheat is among the most allergenic foods for very young children. Don't try the mixed cereals during the first year of life, because if one of the grains bothers your baby, you won't know which one it is.

If your baby doesn't like cereal even after you have sweetened it with a little bit of sugar, you can go on to try fruits. A little mashed ripe banana creamed with a little breast milk or formula, if necessary, is a real winner with a lot of babies. Some mothers even prefer to start with this before cereal. Meats can be added next, since they are the best protein supplier.

COMMERCIALLY PREPARED FOODS

Many mothers ask whether commercially prepared baby foods are better than baby foods prepared at home. This is really an individual choice, but we can give you some facts on which to base your decision.

Commercially prepared baby foods are very convenient, but obviously they cost more than food prepared at home. Many mothers like to take the commercial variety on trips so that they can have something available for their baby at any time. Commercial preparations have fewer calories and less salt and sugar than most table foods prepared at home. Be sure to read the label, however, for commercial preparations have cornstarch fillers, which are unnecessary calories. If you do use them, buy the plain type; for example, buy meat rather than meat dinners. Baby-food desserts are just pure carbohydrates and calories and are really not necessary.

HOME-PREPARED FOOD

Table foods, on the other hand, are readily available for your baby, since they can be the foods that are prepared for the rest of your family. If you are concerned about too much salt or sugar, remove the baby's portion from the fruits or vegetables before you add the family's seasonings. You can mash, blend, moisten, sieve, or grind the food. You can also freeze it in ice-cube trays or plastic bags to be taken along on trips or to warm up for the baby on nights when the family menu is something like lasagna, which may be too spicy for your baby's taste. It's important to prepare the foods carefully and make sure the counters are clean, particularly after you have mixed raw meat or raw eggs over them.

Be sure *not* to feed your baby honey! Don't use it as a sweetener for her home-prepared foods or formula, or on her pacifier to promote her sucking on it. Honey contains spores of *clostridium botulinum*. They are extremely resistant to heat, and ingestion of these spores in infancy can result in botulism, which can cause serious sickness or possibly death.

Many babies start eating food right from the table with the rest of the family, if it can be mashed and moistened with water, broth, gravy, formula, evaporated milk, or breast milk. Babies like food about the consistency of thick cream.

Fruits can be eaten with the family. If the fruit is canned, pour off that heavily sweetened syrup and then mash or blend the fruit. Fresh fruit can be a bit of a problem because of its firm texture. Scrape off a little fruit with a spoon, if it is of the coarser variety. Raw vegetables can be shredded and given to your baby once she has established a fairly good chewing ability. Baked or sweet potatoes are very good sources of starch, iron, and vitamin C. They have a texture babies usually like, particularly if moistened. Other cooked vegetables, mashed or strained, can also be offered to your baby.

Organ meats such as liver, brain, and kidney are excellent sources of protein and are often very popular with infants. Slice and sauté them (brain and kidney need some preparation first) in hot oil just long enough to brown them without making them too tough. These are excellent for finger food, as are strips of oven-dried whole wheat toast, or bagel strips. Once your baby has begun to acquire a fairly good pincer grasp give her cooked peas, cheese, or Cheerios, which are all-time favorites for the child beginning to relish her independence. Babies also enjoy egg yolk, hard-boiled or poached. Eggs can be cut into pieces for finger food or mashed for breakfast.

DECREASED LIQUID INTAKE

As your baby increases her solid intake she will begin to decrease her milk intake. She will be increasing her calcium intake in solids by eating cheeses and yogurt. As we said earlier, your baby doesn't need skim milk or low-fat milk during the first twelve months of life.

A L L E R G I E S

If your baby has allergies or you have a strong family history of allergies, it is wise not to switch from formula to milk until twelve months of age. If allergies aren't a problem, you can switch to whole vitamin D milk when your child is taking in approximately six ounces of solids a day. Obviously, if you are continuing breast feeding, cow's milk allergy does not concern you.

Certain foods tend to cause more allergies than others, especially during the first six months of life. But avoid them for the entire first year if you have a family history of allergies. These foods are egg whites; milk products such as cheese, yogurt, and ice cream (which is made with egg whites); chocolate; citrus fruits; seafood; and wheat products.

H A R D - T O - DIGEST FOODS

Some foods are hard to digest, such as cabbage, cauliflower, broccoli, Brussels sprouts, berries, and grapes with skins on.

It is not uncommon to see undigested vegetables in the bowel movements of a baby. Don't worry about this. It's not bad unless you see increased looseness of the stool, or mucus or blood in the stool. Some vegetables may give you a bit of a start. I (AA) remember a mother coming to see me, worried that her baby was bleeding because her bowel movements had turned red. As we talked further, we found that her baby had been fed a lot of beets recently! Yellow vegetables, such as carrots or squash, can give a yellowish tinge to a baby's skin and have caused many a mother to believe that her baby has jaundice. Asparagus gives a very strong smell to the urine, and spinach and oranges sometimes chap a baby's lips and anal area.

D A N G E R O U S F O O D S

There are certain kinds of foods that you should avoid even after your baby is a toddler, because they are easy to inhale and choke on. These foods are: hot dog pieces, uncooked peas, cooked or uncooked corn, popcorn, raisins, nuts, raw carrot sticks, celery sticks, raw fruit pieces, berries, grapes, hard candy, gum, and other similar small pieces of food that require chewing. Remember that your child will really not be a very adept chewer until she is two. And until then she can have her nutritional needs met without eating from this potentially endangering list. Nuts—including any foods with nuts in them—are particularly to be avoided. Choking while eating foods is not uncommon up until your child is three to four years of age. Nuts are a special problem because the oils in them cause a severe reaction in the lungs that results in infection. Avoiding nuts can be a bit of a problem when you have older children at home who are eating nuts, as I (AA) have experienced in my own family. However if you stick to it, and your small children understand that nuts are off limits, they will accept this and become quite cautious about nuts being offered by other unknowing adults.

DR. BRAZELTON'S R U L E O F T H U M B

We have talked about all the choices of what to feed your baby, but we really like Dr. Berry Brazelton's way of looking at the child's nutritional needs by the age of twelve months. It is so simple that it helps remove any concern about whether your child is getting the right foods. She basically needs only the following each day:

One pint of milk or milk substitute (a *half* cup of milk is equal to a one-inch cube of cheddar cheese, a half cup of yogurt, a half cup of cottage cheese, two tablespoons of cream cheese, a half cup of ice cream or ice milk, or a half teaspoon of calcium substitute)
A piece of fruit or an ounce of fruit juice
Two ounces of an iron-containing protein (such as one egg, two ounces of meat, a half jar of baby food meat, or a small burger)
A multivitamin preparation

Something that can make this new adventure with your baby in the world of solid foods more fun is knowing *how* to offer these foods in the most pleasant way possible.

H O W

Remember that your baby would much rather receive solid foods in an upright position, and it's not necessary to have food-warmer plates, since your baby really prefers her food at room temperature during this first year.

Since you want her feeding to be a relaxed, peaceful time it is probably best to feed her when you are not too frantically busy. This is probably after her bottle or her nursing period in the midmorning or midafternoon, or at night before she goes to bed—whatever suits you best. In the beginning she will probably want to nurse first, and when she reaches a pause in her nursing you can offer her a minuscule amount, about a quarter of a teaspoon, of the solid that you are going to begin with. Put it on the end of the spoon and place it between her lips so that she can taste it. If she likes it she'll open up her mouth, and then you can place the spoon farther back in her mouth so she can swallow. Obviously, if she seems to want more you can offer more, even at the first feeding. She will show you when she is no longer interested, by closing her mouth, spitting her food out, turning her head away, or shaking her head. (When she is older and in her high chair, one of her clues will be when she stands up in the high chair, indicating that she wants out.) One of the guidelines for quantity is that she needs only one tablespoon of a particular food per one year of age.

B E H A V I O R   P R O B L E M S

There are certain things to remember that will help you avoid getting into behavior problems at feeding times. For example, even though it may seem funny to see your baby spitting out her food, it is important not to laugh, or she will begin to think she is pleasing you and will continue doing it for your reaction. Babies enjoy throwing or dropping their food off the tray, and this is a normal developmental phase. But if you don't particularly enjoy picking food up off the floor, don't react to this in any way that reinforces it. Remember that you don't need to coax or cajole your baby into eating. But it's certainly OK to pat her or engage her in a conversation with a lot of smiling when she is eating appropriately.

E A T I N G   A N D   N U R S I N G

After your child has eaten her solids and indicates she doesn't want any more, you may offer her the bottle or the breast to see if she wants to continue nursing. You will see a gradual change in her interest in nursing before eating, and eventually she may want solids first and nursing after. Lunchtime is usually the first meal at which you'll notice this. Suppertime will probably be the next. The early-morning feeding, when your baby is most ravenous, will be the last to change, and for some time she will still like having her bottle or her breast feeding before beginning her solids. The late evening feeding remains a time for only breast feeding or formula, particularly if your baby uses sucking as a way of settling herself down.

N E W   F O O D S

When you are adding a new food to your baby's diet, do it when she is hungriest. It doesn't matter if you offer your baby vegetables for breakfast, because she doesn't know our adult patterns for eating. If she is not interested in that particular food, forget about it for a week or so and try it again. If she balks at it and chokes, you might want to taste it and see if it is all right. Sometimes we offer babies things that we wouldn't dream of putting in our own mouths! And babies, like the rest of us, have particular likes and dislikes and they will let you know it. Don't try to force a food on her. If your baby has trouble handling a food because of its texture, try moistening and straining it some more.

F I N G E R   F E E D I N G

When your baby is ready to finger-feed, she'll let you know by taking food from your plate or her plate or grabbing the spoon every time you try to get it to her mouth. Just put the finger foods on the tray and let her at it. Remember that babies like to dabble and mess with their food, sometimes smelling it or playing with it before they are ready to eat it. If she grabs the spoon while you are trying to feed her, give her her own spoon to hold. As she becomes more adept at handling it you may want to trade spoons with her after you have filled yours, and let her see if she can put it into her mouth by herself. She will be thrilled with her independence.

I N D E P E N D E N C E

Remember, independence is the goal that you are trying to achieve. Even though it's extremely messy and sometimes you feel like gagging, let her try it on her own. This does not mean that she is not going to need some help from you. At first she will not be terribly good at feeding herself and will tire of doing it. If you think she is still hungry, offer the food to her from the spoon. If she isn't interested, forget about it and clear it away.

C U P

One of the ways for your child to become accustomed to using a cup is to let her play with it when she is able to hold objects well, at around five months of age. Give it to her empty and play a sipping game with her. Gradually add a tiny bit of water or juice and let her try it. Fruit juice or vegetable juice is as good as a fruit or vegetable in the solid form, since they both supply necessary vitamins. Canned vegetable juices are very salty and may need to be diluted with water. There is no need for sodas, Kool-Aid, or other non-nutritive substances. Some babies enjoy strained soup broth, which contains very good nutrients. If you give your baby a cup that doesn't have a lid (such as the Tommy Tippee cup) remember that blowing bubbles is a particularly interesting pastime. You are not going all out at this time to teach your baby Amy Vanderbilt etiquette, so if you can stand it, go ahead and let her blow. It is building up good oral muscle control.

E A T I N G   P A T T E R N S

By the time your child is eight months of age, her menu may look something like this:

Breakfast: Cereal and egg yolk
Lunch: Fruit or vegetable and yogurt
Supper: Meat and a vegetable or fruit with the family

Just because we say this is ordinarily what your child may eat every day by her eighth month, there is no guarantee her menu will continue to look like this. She may, for example, stop eating for several meals and want only milk. This will then be followed by a period when she may eat a tremendous amount, only to drop back again. Don't worry about this. If your baby is being offered a sound diet, she will eat from it what she needs to grow. Remember that the growth spurt is slowing down after six months of life, and your baby's hunger pattern changes appropriately. If she seems healthy in every other respect, relax.

Your goal in this first year of life is to help your baby recognize that food is simply that—food. It is not something to be used as a weapon to manipulate anxious mothers and fathers. I (AA) remember the panic I felt when my daughter, Kelly, at twelve months, decided to consume only Cheerios for breakfast, lunch, and dinner. I held myself together for the first day, acting pleasant and nonchalant. By the end of the second day, I was talking to myself in the bedroom, using all the reassurances I give my patients. I gave her a multivitamin preparation, her formula, and fruit juice. I knew, intellectually, that would be adequate for some time. But I was becoming a basket case as it continued into the third day! Then, miracle of miracles, she refused Cheerios and would eat only hamburger and peas for the next three days! I had been so tempted to coax, cajole, threaten, and even starve her, that I can really empathize with parents who go through this. Just hang in there. Don't let it become an emotional battleground.

10

D I S C I P L I N E
I N   I N F A N C Y

Your immediate reaction to the title of this chapter may be, "Discipline in infancy? That's terrible! Who would want to scold or spank a sweet little baby? Babies are too young to discipline."

Your reaction is very understandable if you think of the word *discipline* the way many people do. To most people, discipline means "getting tough" with a child—spanking him or grounding him or taking away privileges—to force him to "behave."

But you need not define discipline as some kind of punishment. We define discipline as *teaching*. To discipline a child is to make him a "disciple" of yourself, his teacher. We believe that when you teach your child to be more assertive and speak out for himself, to be courteous and to write thank-you notes, to love books and reading, to handle relationships with his playmates, you are disciplining your child. It is not something that just happens occasionally. It is a process of teaching and learning that goes on continuously between you and your child.

This concept of discipline is more conducive to a happy parent-child relationship. Also, once you think of discipline as teaching, there is solid scientific information available on how to do it well.

But in a teacher-student relationship, or a parent-child relationship, before you try to teach the child anything, there is something else you must do. You must establish *emotional rapport* with him.

E M O T I O N A L   R A P P O R T

Emotional rapport means a feeling of closeness and warmth between the two of you, a mutual liking. Without rapport, a child will not be motivated to learn what you want to teach. Emotional rapport is the foundation for discipline.

For example, when I (FD) have a new child patient for therapy or psychological testing, I begin by building rapport.

First I come out and meet the child in my waiting room. Then I ask a simple question, to which I have never had a negative reply in twenty years. I ask, "Ralph, do you like doughnuts?" Then we walk over to a doughnut shop, conveniently located near my office. On the way over and back, and while we are eating doughnuts, I ask the youngster about such things as TV programs he likes, whether he has a pet, what sports he likes, what he likes best in school, what he likes least in school, whether his teacher is nice or mean, what movies he likes to see, whether he has any brothers and sisters and whether they are pests. By the time we have explored all these aspects of his life and what he likes and dislikes, rapport has been established. He has experienced me as a nonjudgmental person who is interested in his life and with whom he can talk about anything. By the time we get back to my office he is ready to begin his testing or therapy.

How does this apply to you, in becoming a teacher for your child? It means you need to spend some time regularly, preferably every day, establishing rapport. You accomplish this by doing things together on a one-to-one basis, things the two of you enjoy: taking a walk, reading a story, watching TV together, having an ice cream treat. If you were to analyze the interactions between many parents and their children, you would find that they often consist of the parent's commanding, urging, lecturing, or chastising the child. No rapport gets built that way.

E S T A B L I S H I N G   R A P P O R T   W I T H   Y O U R   B A B Y

Now let's get back to our baby in the stage of infancy. Every time you do something for your baby you are building rapport with her. When you feed her she loves it, and she associates your body and your face with the good sensations of being fed. In fact, feeding your baby is probably the main thing you do at this stage that builds rapport.

When you cuddle her you are also building rapport. She loves it, and she loves you because you are providing it. When you give her a bath she exults in the feeling of the water on her body and the nice slippery slide of the soap over her skin, and she loves you for giving her this pleasure. When you are talking or singing or cooing to her, she learns to identify and love the sound of your voice. Even when you are changing her diaper, talking and laughing with her while you do it, she loves the attention you're giving her. You are building rapport.

The result of all this is that by the end of the stage of infancy, when she begins to walk (roughly the first birthday), a strong emotional bond has been created between the two of you. In the next stage, toddlerhood, it is this rapport that will make her want to do the things you ask her to do.

Remember also that you are not merely building rapport with your baby: You are teaching her to have a sense of basic trust about herself and life, and an optimistic view of her world.

S P A N K I N G

We would like to mention one particular discipline method we hope you will avoid, because it destroys rapport. As your baby grows bigger and heavier, you may have difficulty changing her diaper if she wriggles and squirms. When this happens, some parents give their baby a few good whacks to get her to lie still. What's wrong with that?

There are several important things wrong with it. It's true that it is easier to change her diaper when she lies still. But what have you taught her? You have taught her that she is a tiny, helpless person confronted by a huge powerful ogre who can hurt her. You have begun to teach her to be afraid of you. Remember, you are her first and most important teacher, not only in the first five years of life, but up to age twenty-one. We don't think it's a good thing to teach a pupil to be afraid of her teacher, for if she is afraid she will avoid you.

So the fast slap on the bottom may seem useful, but it's not worth it when you consider what it begins to teach your child about the parent-child relationship. Instead, if your baby begins to squirm as you are changing her, sing to her or do something to distract her, so that she will settle down of her own accord.

Just remember that rapport is the foundation of all discipline. When it comes to discipline itself, there is really very little you need to teach your infant. Later you will want to teach her to pick up her toys, hang up her clothes, go to bed at a regular hour, follow your directions, and so forth. But right now, she is only a baby.

I N T E L L E C T U A L   S T I M U L A T I O N

We have spent most of this chapter talking about the importance of establishing rapport with your baby. In our next chapter, "Intellectual Stimulation in Infancy," we will dicuss how to stimulate your baby to help her develop her general intelligence.

This type of intellectual stimulation probably doesn't sound like discipline at all. But when you are stimulating her intellectual development you are also disciplining her. For, as we have said, discipline and teaching mean the same thing. And when you take this broad view of the situation, it will give you a completely new way of raising your children, a way that is more fun for them and easier on you.

11

INTELLECTUAL STIMULATION IN INFANCY

As an infant, your baby will be learning a multitude of things about herself and her world.

First, she is learning her basic feelings about herself and her world, and the *feelings* your child learns now about herself and her world are more important than any *facts* she learns. For your child is a *feeling* person long before she is a fact-learning person. Her basic attitudes toward herself and the world will influence her attitudes toward acquiring knowledge and education the rest of her life.

In addition to feelings, of course, your baby is learning innumerable facts about herself and the world, which she files away in what we call the "storehouse" (her computer-brain filing system). Her natural curiosity is a basic drive that enables her to learn about the world. You will want to reward and encourage her curiosity, which helps it to become stronger.

SENSORY AND MOTOR STIMULATION

The famous Swiss psychologist Jean Piaget said, "The more a child sees and hears, the more he wants to see and hear." The more chances you give your baby to be stimulated, the more stimulation she will seek out.

The stimulation your baby needs is not that of abstract mental information. She needs sensory stimulation and motor stimulation. She is constantly reaching out to her environment, absorbing all the information she can, through her senses and bodily motor apparatus. She does this with a degree of concentration that is usually underestimated. A word of caution, however: Your baby has limited ways of telling you when she's been bombarded and had enough stimulation for the moment. Be on the alert for her cues.

If you've been engaging her in some "talk" or play and she begins to look away or turn her head away, she's telling you—enough! Give her a break. If you overdo she'll become irritable, and hard to handle. When she's ready for more, she'll seek you out with her eyes. Remember that even in infancy she needs to take the lead in learning—you're there to help her, not push her.

BIRTH TO THREE MONTHS

Many years ago the renowned psychologist William James said that the baby experiences the world as "one great blooming, buzzing confusion." For many years people believed this to be true. But recent researchers have shown that the baby is far more capable visually and perceptually than James gave her credit for. In the 1970s, Dr. R. L. Fantz conducted an extensive series of studies that

YOUR BABY IS CURIOUS WITH HER EYES

have thrown a great deal of new light on what infants are capable of seeing and what they like to look at.

WHAT BABIES LIKE TO LOOK AT

It was Dr. Fantz who demonstrated to us that apparently babies have an innate preference for looking at human faces. He presented infants as young as ten hours with pictures of "scrambled" human faces, in which the features were rearranged in grotesque and unnatural patterns, and also pictures of normal human faces. The babies spent much more time looking at the normal faces.

Young infants also prefer looking at complex patterns rather than simple ones. In Dr. Fantz's research they spent much more time looking at patterns such as a bull's-eye or a checkerboard than they did at simple stimuli such as plain circles or triangles.

Another experiment reveals some fascinating things about infants, which is that even very young babies prefer to see clear images rather than blurred ones, and they can express this preference through their behavior. A group of thirty babies, only five to twelve weeks old, were shown a silent film of Eskimo family life. The movie was a color film with close-ups of expressive human faces. The experiment was arranged so that the babies could adjust the clarity of the picture by sucking on a uniquely rigged pacifier. The babies *learned to keep the picture clear* by regulating the length of their pauses between bursts of sucking!

The results of all of this new research on babies is to make it clear that from the moment your baby is born, she is capable of seeing and hearing much more than most people think she can. And whatever she hears, feels, and sees, she registers in the storage box of her brain-sized computer. This means that you can begin playing with her much sooner than you probably think you can.

From her earliest days, your baby enjoys having something interesting to look at. You can show her many different objects that are colorful or have interesting patterns. We suggest a few now.

MOBILES AND MIRRORS

By the age of about three weeks, your baby enjoys having a colorful mobile while she is in her crib. But don't buy one of those mobiles that is designed to look cute to you but may not interest your baby. Since babies enjoy human faces so much, find a mobile that will let her see human faces in bright colors. If you can't find one in a store, you can make your own. Cut out or draw crude pictures of faces—babies focus on the top of the face so accentuate eyes. Paste each picture on a piece of cardboard. Using string or ribbon, attach each piece to the side of the crib, hanging them between the slats.

A mobile does not have to be for visual stimulation only. If the mobile has chimes on it your baby will soon learn to make the chimes ring through the motion of her kicking.

You do not need to worry about your baby being able to reach the mobile at this age, because she is too small and immature. But when she can reach and grasp, it is important that the materials of these toys cannot be broken into small pieces. For she will surely put them in her mouth, and she may choke on them. A commercial mobile, meeting safety standards, is needed then.

We recommend hanging mobiles on the side at this age because most young babies, lying on their back, prefer to look to one side, usually the right. Observe your baby to see in which direction she likes to look, and then hang the mobile on that side. Remember, she sees things best nine to fifteen inches away. Incidentally, you should also take this preference into account when you place her in her crib. Make sure that on the side where she looks most, she is facing something more interesting than a wall, unless you decorate the wall for her.

At around two months, your baby begins to get interested in mirrors. The mirror you get for her should not be glass (which might break), but steel, about four or five inches in diameter. You can hold or hang the mirror about nine to fifteen inches from the baby's eyes. You will find that a mirror beside the changing table is a very handy distraction when you are changing diapers, especially if your baby tends to wiggle and squirm.

Childcraft makes a two-sided baby mirror. Its frame has six finger-sized holes, so it's easy for you to hang it on the side of the crib. It will also be easy for the baby to grasp and carry when she is older.

But don't forget, it's her mother's (or father's) face she likes to look at most of all. So give her plenty of opportunity to look at you. Bend down close to her face, and talk to her. Sing to her. Make funny faces for her. She'll be the best audience you've ever had!

INFANT CARRIERS All of the infant carriers offer a very convenient way to carry your baby around, and give her the opportunity to look about and take in a wealth of new visual stimuli. You can pack her around the house with you and take her on shopping expeditions.

Several times during the day you can put your baby in her infant seat, where she can watch you work. All of these things will gratify her craving for a variety of visual stimulation and provide her with a very rich visual environment. This is far better than letting her lie in the comparatively bare environment of a crib all day.

It is particularly important for your child's later development that she have a stimulating auditory environment as an infant.

YOUR CHILD IS CURIOUS WITH HER EARS

TALK TO YOUR BABY! You can start immediately after birth to stimulate your child through her ears, by doing exactly what we suggested earlier for building rapport: Talk to her. Many mothers tend to their babies without saying a word, as if they were living by a vow of silence.

Don't be that way! Talk to your baby! Talk to her from the day she is born. Talk to her when you're feeding her, when you're giving her a bath. Whenever you're around her and she's awake. But don't force yourself to talk to her when you don't feel like it, such as when you're grumpy or ill. Just talk when the spirit moves you and you enjoy it.

Whether or not you are aware of it, through these conversations in earliest infancy your baby is beginning to learn to read. Your speech gives her a head start in oral language development, which is the foundation for later written language and reading.

You can also do silly things for her that enrich her auditory environment, such as making funny noises. I (FD) especially like to make funny noises for babies, and I've developed quite a repertoire over twenty years' time. If you can't make funny noises, you can recite a poem to your baby. Or, if you know it, you can recite the Pledge of Allegiance or the Declaration of Independence. Whatever you do, she will love it.

IMITATE YOUR BABY   Your baby starts playing with sounds early in life. When she begins to coo and gurgle during the first month, it excites and pleases her if you make the same sounds back. She will want to make the sounds some more so that she will get the same response from you again.

Your baby is learning a valuable lesson from this verbal interchange. She is learning she can do things that have an effect on her environment—she is living in an environment in which she can participate. This valuable lesson helps her to learn, even as a tiny baby, that assertiveness pays off.

MUSICAL INSTRUMENTS   There are several simple instruments you can "play" for your baby, such as a toy xylophone or an autoharp or a harmonica. You don't need to be able to play tunes on them; merely make different sounds with them. This teaches her to discriminate between sounds, which will help her when she is learning to read and needs to discriminate the sounds of language. Just be careful not to play too loudly, since babies are frightened by loud noises.

RECORDS AND TAPES   Another excellent way of stimulating your child's auditory environment is to play her the recorded music of different cultures. Play classical music, African music, Hawaiian music, and American jazz. Listen to music played on the Russian balalaika, Greek bouzouki, Indian sitar, and Japanese koto. Your baby cannot help learn to discriminate between the quite different tempos, melodies, and instruments of this music. See Appendix C for lists of interesting music and how you can get the records and tapes. If any of the music causes your baby to cry, stop immediately. You can try it again at a later time and at a softer level.

Remember that in these early months you do not expect your baby to respond in any special way when you play a particular record. She is merely filing all these sounds away in her mental storehouse. Later on she will be able to give you an outward response to different kinds of music.

YOUR CHILD IS CURIOUS ABOUT HER BODY

SENSORIMOTOR STIMULATION   Your baby needs to learn the feel of her whole body and how it moves in space. She'll be uncoordinated in her motor movements but soon she'll pull it all together to accomplish what she wants. You'll be helping her with all of this as you carry her and handle her throughout the day. You can give her different experiences by putting her in varied positions—on her tummy, on her back, in an infant seat. This period is a good time to play some games which can heighten her awareness of her body. We suggest these:

Game One: Undress your baby and lay her on a firm bed or foam-rubber pad on the floor. Put your face down close to hers and talk to her softly. As you are talking, stroke her very gently all over—her hands, arms, torso, legs, feet, face, and head. You should continue with this for no more than five or ten minutes. (Warning: With a boy baby, you may be surprised in the middle of one of these games by a stream of urine whooshing straight up in the air! But it's important for the baby to be naked for this game, so you'll just have to take your chances!)

Game Two: Do the same thing as Game One, only instead of stroking the baby, lightly and gently pat her all over, five to ten minutes.

You can play one or two of these games every day with her if you like, perhaps as part of her daily routine, such as before or after her bath. Here are some books in which you can find other games of this nature: *Baby Learning Through Baby Play,* by Dr. Ira Gordon; *The Baby Exercise Book,* by Dr. Janine Levy; *Games Babies Play,* by Julie Hagstrom and Joan Morrill; and *Learning Games for the First Three Years,* by Joseph Sparling and Isabelle Lewis. They offer suggestions that are helpful throughout the first three years.

THREE TO SIX MONTHS OF AGE

YOUR BABY IS CURIOUS WITH HER HANDS

In her first three months, your baby has been exploring her environment with her eyes and ears. But now she begins to reach out with her hands as well. This action signals transition from a passive, helpless orientation to an active, manipulative, exploratory attitude toward her world. She manifests what has been called "touch hunger." She now loves to grasp, touch, feel, and manipulate objects. Previously she had discovered with her eyes that objects have form and color. Now she begins to discover with her hands that objects have other qualities: hardness, softness, and texture.

No scientist studying the physical world is more fitted with determination in his research than a four-month-old baby exploring the softness, hardness, smoothness, roughness, dryness, or wetness of different objects. So give your baby a hand in her scientific research. Put lots of different kinds of objects within her grasp and let her feel and manipulate them. Just be sure none of the objects are so tiny she could swallow them.

TOUCHING AND FEELING   Rattles now come into the picture. Browse through your local toy store for a variety of rattles, or order them by mail from one of the companies we recommended in Appendix A, "A Parent's Guide to Children's Toys."

Why not be the first one in your neighborhood to browse through your local pet store? Hard-rubber crackle bones, doughnuts, and balls with bells inside are often as much fun for a baby as for a puppy.

You can make a texture pad for her, consisting of swatches of different materials such as burlap, velvet, silk, corduroy, wool, satin, velveteen, cotton, and terrycloth. Sew the patches on a double thickness of heavy cotton. Be careful to stitch each piece on very carefully, so there are no ravelings. Don't leave her alone with it, however, or she might possibly choke on the ravelings.

Also, but again only when you are with her, give her the experience of feeling different textures: wood, foam rubber, hard plastic, rubber, ice cubes.

As soon as your baby can sit up unaided, cloth blocks are a good toy for her because they are easy for her to grasp, interesting to look at, and easy to stack. We recommend the cloth blocks by Childcraft.

CRADLE GYMS A cradle gym, or crib gym, is also a good educational toy, which encourages the development of the baby's eye-hand coordination. It is an assortment of simple objects that the baby can handle, pull, or strike, all attached to a bar that goes across the width of the crib. It is excellent for your baby from about three through seven months, while she is still content to lie on her back.

STUFFED ANIMALS Five to six months is also a good time to get your baby a "lovey," or stuffed animal (which she may carry around with her for years). She will love the soft, squishy feel of it. A good stuffed animal for a baby should be between eight and twelve inches high. It should be sturdy enough to withstand *a lot* of rough handling. The eyes and ears should be firmly anchored to the body and contain no metal connecting wires. The materials of the animal should be washable and flame-resistant. The fur should not shed. The dyes should be nontoxic because the animal will spend a lot of time in your baby's mouth.

YOUR CHILD IS CURIOUS WITH HER MOUTH

Babies and young children love to put everything they can find into their mouths, beginning usually around three or four months. The mouth is a much more important sensory organ for babies than it is for older children. When your baby puts something in her mouth, she is constructing a mental model of the object in her brain and learning more about her environment. And that's very important.

Just because your baby is learning about the world by putting things into her mouth, don't think it's OK for her to put anything she wants into it. She could easily swallow something that would choke her or make her ill. On the other hand, don't be so fearful about this that you don't let her put anything at all in her mouth. This would frustrate her strong drive to learn about the world through her mouth. So follow a middle course and let her chew on things that are perfectly safe to her: teething rings, which come in various kinds and sizes; large rattles that are unbreakable; a big kitchen spoon, and so forth.

YOUR BABY IS CURIOUS ABOUT HER BODY — HOW IT FEELS AND MOVES

SENSORIMOTOR STIMULATION Give your baby the chance for play in the nude. Very few parents think of doing this, but your baby loves it, from about three months on. She feels free and open when she is unhampered by clothes at this age. She has the opportunity to "discover" the parts of herself that are usually covered up. This type of naked and open play helps her build healthy attitudes to her body and sex, which will be important later on. It's important to see that she is warm and safe. In spring and summer, outdoors naked play on a blanket on the grass is ideal. In fall and winter, indoor play can make use of a blanket spread on a warm floor.

She'll provide her own motor stimulation. She can roll over and is learning to sit. The books on exercises and games which we recommended previously offer some excellent motor activities you'll both enjoy.

PLAYPEN   If you're going to use a playpen it's best to put your baby in it by the age of three or four months, before she has learned to sit and crawl and develop the freedom of the floor. If you put her in the playpen at a later age, she may consider it a prison. Set the playpen near where you are working in the kitchen or family room. This gives the baby a chance to enjoy your company and see what is going on.

We suggest you give a lot of thought to the use of a playpen. Ideally, we think it is best for your baby's development *not* to be confined in a playpen for long periods. Your baby will develop a sturdier sense of independence, be able to explore more, and will make greater strides in her development. Use it judiciously, usually only to ensure your baby's safety when you can't be readily available.

RECORDS AND TAPES   She'll still love the music you've already been playing. Now she will also begin to enjoy children's nursery rhymes and simple songs. She'll like to sway with you to the music and it's a wonderful way to relax after a long day.

Around five to six months your infant is increasingly interested in sound. This is a good time to present her with a new kind of stimulation toy. Get a tape recorder and put it near her crib at some time when she is likely to be awake and happy, such as the early morning. Later you can play her own sounds back to her.

YOUR BABY IS STILL CURIOUS WITH HER EARS AND EYES

READING   We suggest you start reading to your baby when she is around three months old. She'll be awake for longer periods of time now. When you start reading to your baby, you are trying to accomplish several things. First you are trying to hook her on book reading before she becomes an active toddler and doesn't want to sit still. Second, you are trying to condition her to settle herself for sleep while you read to her, hoping this will carry over when she is older. And last, by reading to your baby you are giving her a head start on learning to read. Books will become second nature to her and she'll be eager to "crack the code."

When reading to your baby make sure you both are comfortable. Keep it short and simple. When your child looks away or squirms, stop. Try books with large colorful pictures you can point to and label for her, or nursery rhymes you can rock to while you read. The Mother Goose rhymes are old favorites. We suggest you supplement the Mother Goose rhymes with a book of modern nursery rhymes. The only one of these we know is *I Wish I Had a Computer That Makes Waffles*, by Dr. Fitzhugh Dodson. It's the first book of modern nursery rhymes since Mother Goose in 1765. Dr. Dodson thinks it's very good, but he might be biased.

We recommend that you read more on the art of reading to your child. Two books that are very helpful are: *Growing Up Reading*, by Linda Lamme, and *Give Your Child a Head Start in Reading*, by Fitzhugh Dodson.

SIX TO TWELVE MONTHS

During this period your baby is *on the go.* She's learning to sit, crawl, stand, and may even be walking. She has moving on her mind. But there are other things she enjoys, too, and she uses all her senses with gusto.

REPETITION

It is during this period, from six to nine months, that your baby begins to be fascinated by repetition. She delights in repeating things over and over and over again until she feels they are mastered. For instance, she may want to bang and bang and bang again with some object on her high chair or feeding table. It is hard for an adult, who is usually quickly bored by repetition, to realize how much joy the baby gets out of repeating things.

IMITATION

From six months on, your baby begins to discover the joys of imitation. This will quickly become one of her most powerful social motives all the way through childhood. Your six-month-old baby imitates hand gestures you make, such as wiping up food with a sponge. She also imitates the various sounds you make. Long before your baby can talk she finds ways of communicating what she wants to other people. She is like a traveler in a foreign country who does not speak the language, but who is able by gestures to indicate what she desires.

THE BATH

She is now ready to take her bath in the bathtub. It's important that you keep the water shallow and that she not be left alone, for she could still slip and drown. Put in a supply of floating water toys, washcloths, and plastic cups, and a whole new world of delight will be opened up to your baby. Water play is one of your baby's best-loved types of play. Perhaps it is due to memory traces of her life in the amniotic fluid in the womb. But whatever the reason, water play is one of the most soothing and relaxing types of play for babies and young children.

PRETODDLERHOOD—THE CRAWLER

Around eight or nine months, your baby will probably begin to crawl, and this ushers in the period of pretoddlerhood.

We hope you have childproofed your house as discussed in "Accident Prevention" in Chapter 12 because then you can let your crawler freely explore the place to his heart's content. This is probably the most important thing he can do in this pretoddler period to develop his intelligence.

For months your baby has been lying supine, and now suddenly he can crawl. What a thrilling discovery that is for him! He is like an avid explorer who has been looking for an undiscovered country. Suddenly he comes to the top of a mountain ridge and looks out—and there it is! Here are these stairs that he can crawl up and down. Here is this cupboard in the kitchen full of Mother's pots and pans. In fact, as his crawling widens, he becomes aware that he has a whole house to explore—fantastic!

The scientist who makes new discoveries about the nature of man and the universe, the businessman who dreams up new ways to advertise and market his products, the artist or writer who finds new ways to put into paintings or books the meaning of life, all of these people got their creative start in life when they were eight months old and were allowed to explore their world freely.

Unfortunately, many small crawlers are hemmed in by playpens, indoor fences, gates, parents, and grandparents telling them, "No, don't touch that!" A crawling baby and a cluttered house go together like hot dogs and mustard. There is no doubt it would be more convenient for you to use playpens, indoor fences, or other restraints on your crawler's curiosity. But you do pay a price for it. You dampen his curiosity and the growth of his intelligence.

TOYS FOR YOUR PRETODDLER

In addition to simply letting your crawler explore the house as it is, you can furnish him some extra things to use in his scientific studies. Get about thirty or forty objects of various sorts—a ball, a sponge, a sanded piece of wood—and present them to him, along with a sturdy plastic container to put them in and take them out of. It is important for you to recognize that *anything* can be a toy at this age.

Get a box and put into it a number of "worthless" objects which your baby will enjoy examining and playing with, such as: bright-colored pieces of cloth, rocks that are too large to be put in his mouth, old plastic cups, pan lids to bang together, a big spoon, plastic margarine containers, etc. Become aware of all of the little "goodies" that pass through your house and put them in the play box for your baby. Once you get in the habit of accumulating these "everyday" playthings, he will have a never-ending stream of new, inexpensive toys.

Balls of varied sizes and shapes are very good for crawlers. Any ball from eight to twenty-four inches in diameter is fine. This age child also likes footballs, because of their strange and unpredictable paths when pushed.

For your baby's water play in the bathtub the Busy Bath toy by Gabriel is excellent. Unfortunately, your crawler also likes water play in the toilet. Probably the simplest thing to do to prevent this is to put a lock on the bathroom door.

But never forget that your baby's most beloved toy is YOU! By the time he is eight months old and becoming a highly imitative person, he especially likes to imitate your actions. Once you realize this, it opens a whole new world of play possibilities with your baby.

YOUR WORK IS YOUR BABY'S PLAY

This is the key: What is work to you is play to your baby. You are washing the dishes, but to him it's a game. So as you do your regular housework and cooking, let your baby "help" you. It seems a fascinating game to him. Give him an extra dustcloth to use in helping you. Let him follow the vacuum cleaner around, with its intriguing sound.

When you are cooking, put your baby in his high chair and give him odds and ends of food to squeeze together, hammer on, and taste. If you do gardening, your baby will like that also. He will like to dig in the earth with you and snatch handfuls of grass.

Shopping with a young baby is for many mothers a nightmare, but it doesn't need to be that way. Make sure he is rested and fed before you go. Give him a small box of teething biscuits at the beginning and let him munch on them while you talk to him about the things you are buying. Begin by making shopping fun at this early age and your baby will really look forward to it later on.

Instead of wrestling with your baby when you unpack your groceries, make a game out of it and let him participate. Have the clerk put all of the breakable or squashable items such as eggs, tomatoes, bread, and milk into a separate bag. Then let your baby unpack the cans and grapefruits and similar things. He will love to do it!

Naturally, it takes you longer to let your baby help you do your housework, cooking, and shopping. But it is worth it many times over. You will have a happy baby and you will be cementing the strengths of the relationship between you.

LANGUAGE DEVELOPMENT

During this period your baby acquires a great deal of babyhood sophistication. He can begin playing such advanced games as Pat-a-Cake and other traditional imitation games of babyhood. Although he cannot talk well yet his communication skills have improved enormously. He can now understand a great many things that are said to him. He can understand simple commands. He is also able to pick up certain words which act as cues for familiar games or routine activities such as eating and bathing. I (FD) remember my son Randy's primitive but clear communication when he was ten months old. When he was tired and wanted to go to bed he would say, "Botto nigh-night," meaning "Please fix my bottle; I want to go to bed."

LABEL THE ENVIRONMENT

You'll be talking to your baby while you are together. It comes naturally—he'll demand it of you. Remember that he is learning to label his environment now so speak slowly and keep it simple.

At eight or nine months your baby is ready for you to begin playing Label the Environment with him. This is the game in which you start teaching him that everything in the world has a name. Point to an object or, if possible, let your baby handle it. Say its name several times. He'll enjoy hearing it.

You can play the labeling game with your baby anywhere, anytime. At this early stage of development he may only register internally—in his storehouse—what you say to him. At a later stage he will repeat the word after you. This labeling game is one of the most powerful things you can do to stimulate his language development.

BOOKS

Now he'll enjoy handling his books himself. "That's ridiculous!" you may think. "He is only going to put the book in his mouth!" Exactly. That's the way he finds out what everything is like—including books.

His first books should be of cloth or heavy cardboard, preferably with thick cardboard pages. These books basically consist of pictures, along with single words of familiar objects. They are actually a different form of the labeling game.

You show your child the pictures and say the word out loud to him. Then he will probably want to handle the book himself. He may pat and stroke the pages a bit, and then into his mouth it goes! Later, he will look at the pictures and croon a few nonsense syllables over the book. This is his early version of "reading." But don't make the mistake of underestimating the importance of what is happening. He is becoming familiar with books at this early age and laying a foundation for developing a love for reading and books later.

Many parents think that nothing important is going on in their baby's mind during his first year, the stage of infancy. But you know better. You know it is the most important year of his life, because it is the beginning of his intellectual development.

Remember, though, no materials, toys, or equipment—not even a million-dollar computer—could compete with you when it comes to stimulating your baby's development. He prefers you.

If you take extra time out to be with your baby for just five minutes at a time, to talk and sing and croon to him, and if you do those same kinds of things when you feed him and bathe him and change his diapers, that is absolutely the best and most important intellectual stimulation he could ever have.

12

SPECIAL SITUATIONS IN INFANCY

GASTROINTESTINAL FUNCTIONS

BOWEL MOVEMENTS

All new parents are extremely aware of their baby's bowel movements, since changing diapers is one of the most frequent things parents do, particularly during the first few months of life. In the first twenty-four hours, the bowel movements consist of a greenish-black sticky substance called meconium. This is the substance that has been in your baby's gastrointestinal tract during the pregnancy. It will be passed during the next three to four days, as the stools gradually make a transition to greenish-brown and then to a greenish-yellow color, and become less sticky. The stools may also have blood and mucus in them. This is not a cause for alarm in the first few days of life, since your baby may have swallowed some blood and mucus during the delivery process.

The stools of the bottle-fed baby are usually of a pasty consistency and a pale yellow or tan color. They smell rather foul, and your baby will have anywhere from one to six a day. Typically as your baby gets older, the stools will decrease in frequency and may have a tendency to become firmer. The breast-fed baby has stools that are pasty or the consistency of thick cream soup, with little curds in them resembling scrambled eggs. They tend to be yellowish and do not have the bad odor of the bottle-fed baby's stools.

Whether you are breast-feeding or bottle-feeding, you may notice that your baby is straining or trying to have a bowel movement during or right after a feeding. This is because of fullness in the stomach, which stimulates bowel contractions. This is called a *gastrocolic reflex*. If your baby is straining while sucking at the nipple, it helps to stop the feeding for ten to fifteen minutes to allow his intestines to settle down. Then begin again.

As we have mentioned before, stools can change in color as a result of taking in certain nutrients. If your baby is on iron, the stools can turn black; if he is taking in beets, the stools may turn red. When your baby gets older and is on solids, you may also notice that some of the vegetables pass through undigested. This is perfectly normal. Mucus may appear in the stools of babies who have colds, as a result of their swallowing mucus from their nose or respiratory tract.

Occasionally you may see blood in the stools of a baby. Small streaks of bright red blood usually indicate that there is a tear, called a fissure, in the anus, and is usually due to constipation. It is important to let your physician treat this, so your baby does not develop more constipation. The baby will try to withhold stools because the pain of passing them with a fissure is intense. If you notice the small streaks of blood but cannot see your pediatrician right away, put some petroleum jelly around the anus at the time your baby is trying to pass a stool. This will alleviate some of the discomfort. If you see large amounts of blood in your baby's stool, it is important to call your doctor immediately. This is extremely rare and usually indicates a more serious disorder of the gastrointestinal tract.

CONSTIPATION

Constipation is one of the more frustrating problems in infancy. People have different definitions of constipation. And often what a parent interprets as constipation in a baby, such as having a stool once every two to four days, is truly not constipation. Their baby's bowel schedule may simply vary from the typical. The breast-fed baby may go six to seven days and the bottle-fed baby may go three to four days between bowel movements. As long as the stools are soft, the baby is having no problems. When your baby begins having hard-formed bowel movements or small, dry pellets, then constipation is occurring. This can result in an anal fissure.

Some parents are concerned when their baby turns red, grunts, groans, cries, and strains to pass a bowel movement, and yet it still comes out in a loose, pasty form. We do not know the real reason for this type of problem. We speculate that perhaps it is because your baby is immature and has not yet developed the coordination and strength of musculature to eliminate the stools easily. It is also hard to have a bowel movement lying down! Try placing your child in a more upright position, on your lap or in an infant seat, with his feet resting on a surface he can push against. I (AA) experienced this with our third child, Kimberly. I remember how anxious and concerned I felt when she seemed to be suffering so much. I wanted to do something for her, and this seemed to be most effective. However, I learned that she was perfectly able to have her bowel movements without this help from me—I would often find her with dirty diapers when I had not been around to agonize over her struggle.

Constipation is commonly seen during an illness in which the baby has decreased his fluid intake or had fever, which can use up body fluids. This constipation can be expected to improve without any particular treatment once your baby is taking more fluids and feeling better. Another cause of constipation is narrowing of the anus (anal stenosis). This may require some stretching, done by your physician.

When your baby begins solid foods he may have some constipation as a result of the change in diet. You can improve the condition by eliminating whatever food you have just added, to see if that is causing the constipation. You can try the food again after a few months.

It is important not to give your infant suppositories or laxatives without discussing it with your physician, who will want to make specific recommendations. Mineral oil is absolutely a no-no in infancy, since babies may choke on it and get mineral oil into their lungs, which can result in serious pneumonia. If your baby is constipated and you cannot discuss the problem with your doctor right away, try some adjustments in diet. For instance, if you are feeding sugar water to him, stop it or change the sweetening to dark corn syrup (one teaspoon to four ounces of water); or add dark corn syrup to his formula (one tablespoon per bottle).

Stewed prunes, apricots, pears, or diluted juices are another effective alternative. Begin with very small amounts, approximately one to two teaspoons a day, and increase to four teaspoons until effective. Some babies get crampy and have excess gas with prunes, but this is not common. The juices can be diluted one-to-one with water or can be bought already prepared for babies. If your child is on solids, increasing the amounts of unrefined grains, such as using dark bread instead of white bread, and giving bran can also be very effective.

If these changes do not result in any improvement, contact your physician so your child can have a complete checkup. Very rarely, children are born with a disorder of the gastrointestinal tract called *megacolon* (*mega* means large). This results in constipation or bowel problems that show up very early, usually in the first few weeks of life. It causes progressive distension of the abdomen, and your baby may alternate between constipation and diarrhea. The problem is caused by a congenital absence of nerves in a portion of the colon wall. It can be treated medically and surgically—but early diagnosis is important.

D I A R R H E A   When the consistency of the bowel movements changes from a normal stool to a looser or watery consistency with a greenish color and often a bad smell, your baby has diarrhea. Sometimes the stools contain mucus, pus, or blood. The baby's gastrointestinal tract is extremely sensitive and often indicates problems elsewhere in the body, so diarrhea is not necessarily the basic problem.

The rate of passage of stools through the GI tract can be accelerated by increased fluids, fruits, or vegetables; infection in the tract or elsewhere; inflammation in the tract or elsewhere; antibiotics; or the introduction of solid foods before the tract is mature enough to digest them. Sometimes poor digestion of solid foods results when the baby does not have the enzymes necessary to break them down; this is a congenital condition that usually results in a chronic problem, which could be determined by your doctor. Continuing or severe diarrhea requires a physician's attention—when stools are too frequent and too rapid the baby may lose nutrients, salt, and water which the body has not had time to absorb from the colon.

Diarrhea is also frequently caused by an oversupply of bacteria, as we have discussed before. Milk is an excellent growth medium for germs. Infection can be avoided by careful preparation of the baby's formula or food, including refrigeration as promptly as possible. Other sources of germs, once your child is a little older, are the spouts on the lids of training cups, straws that are used over again, and even scoops used to dish out ice cream in the ice cream store. It is therefore helpful to boil the lids and clean out or not reuse straws. And avoid getting ice cream in a store where scoops are reused without cleaning.

A type of diarrhea that may be seen in the first few days of life of the breast-fed baby is one in which he has very frequent watery, almost explosive, stools, particularly around feeding time. This is nothing to be alarmed about. Go right on feeding your baby; he will settle down in a few days. The condition is probably due to immaturity of his gastrointestinal tract and the rapid and easy digestion of breast milk.

If your baby has a gradual onset of diarrhea with looser stools but no increase in frequency, and with no signs of fever, lethargy, or stools with pus or blood, then it is probably due to a dietary problem. If your baby is on sugar water, try taking the sugar out of it. If he is on fruits or fruit juices, you can see if any of them is the culprit by temporarily stopping them. Bananas are usually OK to continue because they do not typically cause diarrhea. Vegetables or vegetable juices may also result in looser stools, but baked potato is probably all right. If you are using unrefined grains or unrefined sugars, try cutting those out of the diet. If you are breast-feeding, check your intake—caffeine, tea, or laxatives could be at fault.

If these things do not work or if the baby has loose watery stools that increase in frequency, contact your doctor.

If your baby experiences sudden diarrhea with any of the following symptoms, it is imperative to *get her to the doctor right away:*

- temperature greater than 99.7° F. rectally, or less than 97° F. rectally
- mucus, pus, or blood in the stool
- lethargy
- signs of dehydration such as decreased urine output, sunken eyes, and dry lips
- stools passed every two hours or less
- diarrhea accompanied by vomiting
- shallow, rapid breathing

Fast medical attention is important, because babies do not have the reserves to handle extreme losses of body fluids. Until you can get your child to the doctor, it is important to stop the solids, stop the formula, and give him small amounts of clear fluid such as Gatorade, Pedialyte, gelatin water, or weak broth (one cube to one quart of water) very frequently. It is all right to continue breast feeding him. He may not feel like sucking, either at the breast or the bottle. In that case you may have to use a small teaspoon to get some kind of fluid into him. Save a dirty diaper and take it in to the doctor for her to examine.

For infants, the use of stool hardeners such as Kaopectate is not recommended in most cases. But your doctor may recommend a medicine such as Donnagel, which relieves the painful cramping of the gastrointestinal tract. Because the anus and surrounding area can become irritated, rinse well with warm water after each stool and protect it with ointment (zinc oxide, petroleum jelly).

INDIGESTION

Babies sometimes have indigestion due to intake of foods not suitable for their gastrointestinal tracts. They may look very much like colicky babies, with drawn-up knees and abdominal discomfort. However, rather than crying for three to four hours at a time, they tend to be fretful for the whole day. They pass gas frequently, spit up frequently, and even vomit frequently. They may also have loose, greenish stools. This usually indicates that the baby's diet is not suitable. It may be that your baby is allergic to cow's milk formula or soy formula or some solids he has been taking. It's important to discuss this with your physician in order to get some relief as soon as possible.

VOMITING

In an earlier chapter we mentioned spitting up, which is a common occurrence in infants. The causes are not known but it possibly indicates some immaturity of the gastrointestinal tract. It disappears at around eight months of age. Spitting up can be quite a nuisance when you are taking your baby out and want him to look and smell his very best. Take a rag soaked in a solution of baking soda and water with you. You can use this to wipe up the spit, since this is an excellent odor absorber. (The odor of spit-up formula is far more pronounced than that of breast milk.) At home, your baby can wear a bib that has been sponged with baking soda and water, so you don't constantly have to wipe up to avoid the smell.

Sometimes the substance ejected is curdled, smells bad, and is in large quantities with enough propelled force to travel at least several inches from the mouth. It can be the result of a delayed burp, a digestive disturbance, or maybe the early sign of an illness.

Vomiting is seen more often in babies who tend to be more irritable and tense than other babies. It may happen only once a day, or it may happen more frequently, but it is ordinarily nothing to worry about.

Vomiting can be of such force that it is projectile in nature and may travel three to four feet. This is seen most frequently in a condition called *pyloric stenosis*, which occurs around six weeks of age and is more frequent in the first-born male. It is caused by an abnormality in the muscle leading from the stomach to the intestines. This can be easily corrected with a small operation. If your baby has projectile vomiting, call your doctor immediately.

If your baby has vomited once but does not seem ill, try holding off feeding for three hours and instead give him clear liquids: Gatorade, diluted (1:1) ginger ale or 7-Up, or Pedialyte at room temperature, in doses of one to two teaspoons every fifteen to twenty minutes. (Cola and tea are often recommended, but they are irritants to the stomach as are aspirin and chocolate, and they should be avoided.) If doing this does not help and the vomiting continues, get in touch with your physician as soon as possible.

TEETHING

Your baby's first tooth is a really exciting occasion. Some babies have mild problems cutting their teeth, and some have smooth sailing. Some babies have difficulty with a few teeth and not with the rest. Other babies have problems with all of them. The time of tooth eruption varies greatly, although it is more constant in girls. The first tooth erupts anywhere from the third to the twelfth month; in a few children it is apparent at birth. Prior to seeing any change in the gums, you may note at around three to four months that your baby is beginning to want to chew on things and may be drooling excessively. The sign that the tooth is about to erupt is the appearance of a small pale bump on the gum. The first teeth to come in are usually the lower incisors. But don't worry about the order in which the teeth appear. It really doesn't make any difference.

With a child who is having discomfort in teething, you will see that his gums are red hot and swollen around the small pale bump. This inflammation may result in a mild diarrhea or stomach upset and even a very low-grade fever (less than 101°). However, if your child has diarrhea or a fever while teething, don't just assume that the teething is the cause. It's possible that an infection that needs treatment is present. It's not unusual for a pediatrician to see a child who is seriously ill with an infection, whose parents have not sought treatment because they believed that all the symptoms were due to the cutting of a new tooth. It's better to be safe than sorry. Call your doctor.

When your baby is having teething problems he may refuse the breast or the bottle and be more wakeful at night. There is no sure cure for this except the eruption of the tooth, but a few tricks of the trade may help. Some babies love to chew on a clean washcloth with crushed ice in it or on the nipple of a bottle with ice-cold water or juice in it. Others prefer rubber teething rings. Make sure that the ring is not brittle and that pieces will not break off. Some, like our Katie (AA), prefer chewing on the wooden railing and headboards around the crib. Katie's crib looked like the squirrels had attacked it. We had to wrap the wood with tape in order to prevent her getting large chunks of wood in her mouth.

Your teething baby may enjoy chewing on a hard bone or a piece of zwieback. This should be done only in the sitting position, so that he will not choke. He may also like to have his gums rubbed, although many babies don't. Numbing medicines to rub on gums, such as Orajel, can be bought at the drugstore. Some of these have benzocaine in them and can be sensitizing, producing an allergy, so we don't recommend them. A fruit brandy will do as nicely. Aspirin or Tylenol will also help relieve the pain (dosage chart 34:36).

Another problem with teething is that with all the drooling, your baby may get very chapped skin around the lips. It is important to keep the lips and the area around the lips dry and lubricated, by using a mild skin cream if necessary. When your baby sleeps on his tummy, all the saliva drools out, leaving his face in a puddle. He can become very chapped. You can prevent this by putting a bath towel under his crib sheet to soak up the moisture. Cream his face at bedtime for extra protection.

G E N I T O U R I N A R Y   P R O B L E M S

A question frequently asked by mothers is "How do I know if my baby is urinating enough?" A baby can never urinate too frequently. The only concern, particularly in the newborn period, is when the baby remains dry for more than three hours even though he has been drinking normally. If your baby seems to be staying too dry, first make sure that he is getting enough fluids. If you feel he is drinking enough, and he remains dry for four to six hours, or he pushes hard to pass urine and the stream of urine is very small, you should call your physician or nurse. The baby may have a urinary tract obstruction that needs to be handled as soon as possible.

Another problem that may be noted in the newborn period is the sign of blood in a wet diaper. If this is not due to the vaginal or penile bleeding discussed in the chapter on the newborn baby then it is important to take the diaper in and show it to your doctor. Sometimes there are chemical products in urine called urates, which may make a reddish ring around the urine stain.

If your baby's urine smells very strong or fishy, and his fluid intake is normal, this may be a sign of infection and you should consult your physician.

S K I N   D I S O R D E R S

D I A P E R
R A S H

Diaper rash is common, because in the groin the skin temperature and humidity are high even without a diaper. This, combined with the friction of the diaper against the skin, makes the area more vulnerable. Babies have individual variations in sensitivity, so not all babies, even under the same conditions, will get diaper rash.

When diaper rash starts out it is a collection of small red pimples with patches of rough, red skin and possibly some whiteheads, very similar to prickly heat. The affected area, by continuing to remain wet and rubbed against, can become raw and give the appearance of very shiny red parchment. This type of diaper rash is seen more frequently when the baby wears cloth diapers that are laundered at home.

If your baby has diaper rash, he should be changed as soon as he wets. If the rash is severe he probably will not be comfortable if washed with soap. Instead, you can clean him up with a lotion such as Cetophil on a cotton ball. Clean him at every changing and pat him dry with a towel, making sure that you get into all the skin folds. I (AA) found it very helpful to dry my girls off with the hair dryer on a warm cycle. Do not use powder.

If you are going someplace where you may not be able to change your baby often enough, you can protect his skin by applying a thick coating of zinc oxide ointment. Some people recommend petroleum jelly, but I (AA) have found that it tends to make the skin more raw and do not recommend it. Zinc oxide sometimes leaves a ring in the washing machine when you launder the diapers, but you can simply wipe out the ring with alcohol. Using a disposable diaper liner to absorb the moisture is also helpful protection if you have to go out. Plastic pants should be avoided when your baby has a diaper rash, since they increase the humidity and moisture in the diaper.

If you don't have to take your baby out, however, leave his bottom bare. Fresh air is the best treatment for diaper rash. Obviously you want to lay your baby on a waterproof pad with diapers over it and would need to cover him with a blanket or diapers if the weather is cold.

At night double-diapering can also help, particularly when your baby is older and putting out a lot more urine. You can double-diaper with the disposable diapers, but be sure to cut a hole in the plastic of the inner one in order to drain out the moisture to the outer diaper.

There are also other types of rashes that can appear on your baby's bottom. If he simply has a raw, red area around the anus, it is more than likely due to irritating bowel movements. This can occur with new foods, or sometimes when the baby has taken citrus fruits. It can also occur when your baby has diarrhea.

Putting zinc oxide ointment on the raw area helps to protect it as well as relieve the discomfort your baby will experience with subsequent bowel movements.

Sometimes babies develop a diaper rash that consists of small pink bumps in the diaper area. This is usually due to perfumes or talcs in disposable diapers, or sometimes to detergents not thoroughly washed out of cloth diapers. If you are using disposables, try changing your brand. If this doesn't work, switch to cloth. If you are already using cloth, then follow the washing suggestions earlier in this section and in our chapter on the daily care of your infant.

Some diaper rashes require a check by your physician. There is one called *seborrheic* diaper rash which is red, greasy-looking, and usually worse in the skin folds. Your baby may also have a similar rash on his head and neck and around his ears. A steroid cream is required to clear up this type of rash.

Diaper rashes can also be caused by a fungus called monilia, the same fungus that can cause thrush in the mouth. It usually appears in the diaper area as a bright red rash with a rather marked border, which appears scalloped. It may have small blisters or pustules on the surrounding skin. This too requires a prescription ointment. If it recurs frequently, which is not uncommon, your doctor may need to prescribe a course of oral antifungal therapy to control it.

If your baby develops pustules or boils in the diaper area, they may be bacterial. It is important to take your baby to your physician as soon as possible, as he may need an antibiotic.

PRICKLY HEAT

When babies get hot and sweaty they develop prickly heat, just as older children and adults do. This happens more frequently in babies, since they cannot tell you when they are too hot and sweaty. Prickly heat appears as clusters of raised pink blotches with white centers. It is usually found around the neck and shoulders, where sweating tends to occur. It occurs in hot weather most frequently, but it is also not uncommon in cold weather when babies are overdressed. The treatment for prickly heat is to dress the baby coolly and apply a light covering of a cornstarch powder. When applying powder to your baby remember to put the powder in your hand and gently pat it on so that your baby will not breathe any of it into her lungs.

CRADLE CAP

Cradle cap, which is an accumulation of sweat and oils on the scalp, is not uncommon in babies. When cradle cap is heavy, it appears as brownish patches that can be flaked off when scratched. It is more common in hot weather and in babies who have tendency to sweat or who have oily skin. Cradle cap is a form of seborrhea, and when it is severe the child may develop a seborrheic rash around the ears, face, neck, and even the diaper area. To avoid its occurrence wash your baby's head every day with a wet washcloth. Don't be afraid to rub the soft spot, for the soft spot is very tough and it's important to wash it. A new baby's head can be shampooed about once a week, using a gentle baby shampoo. If your baby has a tendency to sweat quite a bit, you could shampoo her two to three times a week.

If severe cradle cap should develop, discuss this with your pediatrician. She will probably recommend that you use a dandruff shampoo until it is clear. When washing your baby's hair, particularly in the first six months of life, it is not necessary to pour water over her head. In addition to the suggestions on page 126, headbands can be purchased that help keep the water from running down the face, and some mothers have even found that swimming goggles do the trick. If your baby is frightened by hair washes, it is usually because of water in her face, not the soap.

T H R U S H

You may notice that your baby has developed white patches on her tongue or lips or the inside of her cheeks. It looks like curdled milk that cannot be wiped away easily, and if you do wipe it away the skin is red underneath. The baby may also be uncomfortable when eating. Thrush is caused by the same fungus (*monilia* or *candida*) that causes some diaper rashes. It has nothing to do with poor care. It simply has to do with the fact that your baby's immune system is not very well developed in the first few months. Thrush can also occur as a result of antibiotic therapy. Antibiotics alter the normal bacteria in the gastrointestinal system, and the fungus then has an opportunity to grow. You will need to take your baby to the doctor, who will probably treat her with oral antifungal agents. If you are breast feeding it is also important to discuss this with your doctor, for you may have a similar infection around your nipple, requiring treatment, too.

C E N T R A L   N E R V O U S   S Y S T E M   I M M A T U R I T Y

Newborns and young infants have not yet pulled themselves together, and this is particularly apparent in their nervous system regulation. In "The Newborn Baby" we discussed how your baby will have a startle reflex when she experiences any sudden change in position or environment, such as bright lights or sudden noises. Some babies, particularly those with low sensory thresholds, startle more frequently. Their arms and feet may also tremble when they are crying vigorously. Newborns may have twitching of the fingers, especially when they begin to be upset. These are all normal occurrences in newborns and will improve with time.

Certain twitches and trembles, however, must be checked out by your physician. They may be indicative of mild seizures or epilepsy and need to be treated as soon as possible. If you notice that your baby has rhythmic twitching or jerking of an extremity or extremities at times when she is not startled or upset, and especially if she is sound asleep, it is important to contact your physician. You might notice repetitive blinking of the eyes or twitching of the lips, which would also need to be brought to your doctor's attention. Other signs of seizure activity would be if the baby's eyes roll back in the sockets, especially if accompanied by twitching or jerking. Very sleepy babies will sometimes roll their eyes back and forth. Do not become concerned about this.

C O L I C

The word colic strikes fear into any parent, especially a parent who has had to survive it. Colic can be defined as severe, constant crying for a period of several hours, usually occurring between 5 and 10 P.M. or, if not then, at the same time every day. It usually occurs three or more days a week. The baby seems to be having abdominal pain, may pass gas, may draw up her knees, and has a distended abdomen. She wishes to suck often, but this does not seem to soothe her. Colic typically begins in the second to third week of life and improves by the third month in most cases. Some babies, however, continue the pattern until about six months of age. There are many things we do not know about the causes of colic, but we do know there are many different ones. If your baby has colic symptoms it is important to take her to your physician so that physical problems can be either treated or ruled out.

Here are some of the possible physical problems. Some babies have an intestinal disorder called *anal stenosis* (narrowing of anus) or have an anal fissure (tear) which causes constipation and abdominal distension or some sort of hernia. Your baby may have a genitourinary infection with no symptoms other than colic. Breast-fed babies may have colic because of a sensitivity or allergy to products their mothers are eating or drinking: cow's milk, shellfish, eggs, wheat products, or caffeine. Stopping these may cure the colic. Some colicky babies are sensitive to cow's milk or soybean formulas and need special formulas containing no milk at all, such as Nutramigen or Progestamil. If your baby has this problem, however, it does not mean that she will never be able to drink cow's milk again— it can be reintroduced at three months, six months, nine months, or twelve months; and in most babies, by twelve months any sign of sensitivity is gone.

If your baby has been good-natured for several months and all of a sudden begins to develop a colicky pattern, it is important to look at any dietary changes you may have made, and to stop them temporarily.

Colic is a rather common occurrence in the first six months of life. Anywhere from twelve to thirty percent of babies have colic, and it is more common in the difficult-to-manage child. They are so sensitive to outside stimuli that by the end of the day they are overstimulated and can't handle all the confusion and chaos that occurs around dinner time. Some babies have colic from sucking too much air, because the nipple is either too small or too large. These causes are easily remedied. Some people feel that maternal anxiety can cause colic. Having been the mother of a baby who cried incessantly, I (AA) feel that the crying produces the anxiety and not vice versa. However, a parent's anxiety can increase the baby's tension, setting up a vicious cycle.

HOW TO DEAL WITH COLIC

There are some tricks you can learn for dealing with the colicky baby, which can help alleviate the problem even though they may not cure it. Notice the time of day when your baby begins to cry. If it is around dinner time, then keep down the stimulation in late afternoon. Give your baby a warm bath and a nice relaxed feeding, and swaddle her to prevent startling and jerking. Put on a machine with a steady noise—fan, vaporizer, vacuum, a Rock-a-Bye Teddy with its uterine sounds—and lay her on her tummy on a warm hot-water bottle (make sure that it is just warm to the touch and not hot). Do all of this about an hour before everyone comes home for dinner, and make the baby off-limits to excess noise or attention from the rest of the family. This routine sometimes does the trick.

Some colicky babies respond to rocking, such as in the baby swing; others respond to being held in the Snugli against the chest and walked around. Some will respond only to lying across their mother's knees on their tummy on a warm hot-water bottle and being patted and jiggled gently.

In spite of all these tricks your baby may continue crying. If you have explored all possibilities and your baby is still not satisfied, put her down in her crib and let her cry for fifteen to twenty minutes. Then pick her up again and offer her a little warm sugar water in a bottle, burping her carefully afterward. If she continues crying, and rocking and swaddling don't help, repeat the process. Eventually she will settle down and go into a deep sleep. These babies do in fact sleep better through the night, probably from fatigue caused by all that crying. Parents sleep better through the night too, probably also because of fatigue from all that crying.

You can try medication and sedation for the baby, but in most studies this has proved ineffective.

Colic will eventually pass, and it helps to remind yourself of this. And please don't take the crying personally. It does not reflect on your care of your baby at all. If you can find a friend or relative to sit with the baby and get away for a while, all the better. A change of scenery does everyone a lot of good. Don't be surprised, however, if even when you are out you hear that baby's crying in your mind. You are not hallucinating; it is just hard to wipe it out.

B A T H T I M E   P R O B L E M S   O R   F E A R S

Some babies who take to their bath in the beginning become frightened after having been avid bathers all along. This is particularly true around eight to nine months, when babies become very averse to having water in their faces. It is important not to force your baby into the tub. Stop, take a look at what seems to be bothering her, and make some adjustments.

You can keep her perfectly clean by giving her a sponge bath while she is seated on your lap. If your baby is used to sitting in a tub of water but now resists it, put the tub with a little bit of water in it in front of her while you sit her on the floor and sponge her off. She will probably play with the water with her hands, and she may gradually try to crawl in, forgetting that she had any fear before. If she has developed a fear of the large bathtub, you might try putting a smaller tub of water for her in the empty bathtub. She then may gradually become interested in the larger tub again.

If your baby is happy with her bath, you might think it would be fun to let her take a shower with you. But showers are frightening to young children. As we said, children do not particularly like water in their faces, especially in the latter half of the first year. Hold off until your child indicates a real desire for a shower.

STRANGER ANXIETY AND SEPARATION ANXIETY

We mentioned earlier that around six to eight months of age your previously friendly little baby may become anxious and fearful in the presence of a stranger. You'll see more clinging, head-hiding, or even crying when someone new appears. The slow-to-warm-up child will have the most difficulty. It helps to explain to the other person how the child is feeling. Ask her to hold off actively engaging in contact with the child until he indicates he is ready. When he begins to look at the stranger or hold his arm out to her, he is showing his readiness. It helps to hold him close and to be relaxed. He'll pick up from you that the stranger is a safe new person.

The fact that your baby now has the ability to discriminate a stranger from a familiar person is a sign of maturity occurring in her young brain. Some babies react more vigorously than others to this phase, depending on their temperament. It is obviously a bigger problem for the slow-to-warm-up child and the difficult-to-manage child, who do not adapt to change well.

It is around this same time that your baby will also experience anxiety at separating from you even when left with a familiar baby-sitter. These problems peak at around fifteen months and are usually gone by the third birthday, although the slow-to-warm-up child may have separation difficulties for longer. Many mothers complain that although they have had the same baby-sitter for months, now that their baby is eight months old, she cries every time the sitter appears. This is not because the baby dislikes the baby-sitter. It is because the baby is aware that when the baby-sitter shows up, Mom is about to disappear. Although this can be very anxiety-producing for you, try to think of it as an indication that your baby is maturing. And even though the baby may cry vigorously, once you have left she will probably settle down and be content. However, if your baby is miserable while you are gone, then it is important to look into the quality of the baby-sitter or day-care situation.

RITUALISM

It is at this age that your baby also may begin to have difficulty going to bed at night, as we discussed previously. We have recommended ritualizing bedtime as one solution to this problem. We also suggest that you ritualize your other leave-takings.

Do *not* sneak out. Be matter-of-fact about leaving, but assure your child you will return. Arm your baby-sitter with some familiar games and tasks to do with the child while you are gone, and have them start playing one of the games even before you leave. The ritual might include kissing or waving good-bye at one special spot. Let your child work out the ritual, but beware that she not drag it out, as children quickly learn to do. Our Kimberly (AA) even at three years of age still likes to kiss us good-bye through the car window and watch the car pull away, whereas our Katie, at five, could care less whether we leave or not.

TIMING

If you are planning to return to work after the birth, it is helpful to do so prior to the onset of separation anxiety—eight months of age—or after it peaks around fifteen to eighteen months of age. If you can wait until about age three, the anxiety will have subsided considerably. If you absolutely must return to work during your child's most difficult time with separation anxiety, at least you will know that she is going through a normal phase and is not reacting just because you have suddenly started work. Nothing can make a mother feel guiltier. The same holds true for taking parental vacations without your child. It would be better to avoid at least the onset-to-peak period of anxiety, which is especially difficult for your child.

COMFORT HABITS

It is around the time of separation anxiety, at eight to nine months of age, that your baby may develop comfort habits—having a favorite blanket or stuffed animal or some sucking device for soothing purposes. She will usually need this most when she is tired and settling down to go to sleep. Since she is learning to depend more on herself than on you, she uses a transitional object, or "lovey," for this purpose. If she has a comfort habit that is less firmly attached than her thumb, it is important to remember that if you go anywhere (especially on a trip), you should not leave home without it. Many a frustrated parent has had sleepless nights when that happens.

If your baby is particularly attached to one animal or blanket, it helps to have a second one as a spare. Interchanging them is helpful. For if she uses only one, it develops a characteristic odor that the new one won't have when you need to use it. This odor may not be terribly pleasant to you, especially if it is a blanket that has been frequently wet and soiled. It is also helpful, as a child gets older, to cut the blanket or diaper into strips so that you have several replacements. Your child will require this less and less, and usually by the time she is five or six she no longer needs it when she goes to sleep.

If your child does not develop a particular attachment or comfort habit, don't worry. She is simply able to handle her transitions internally.

BABY-SITTERS

Most parents find that it helps their mental states and their marriages to get away from the baby or children every once in a while. A good baby-sitter is invaluable unless you are fortunate enough to have relatives around who can help you out. The first few weeks you will probably not feel like getting out, and you certainly will not want to go anywhere without your baby. This is a perfectly natural feeling. Do whatever suits you. It is helpful, however, for the baby to get used to being handled by others. In an emergency, you might have to leave your child and not be available to care for her.

PREPARING YOUR BABY-SITTER Here are some cardinal rules in selecting a baby-sitter. You will want one who will put your child's well-being first, with respect to physical safety and emotional needs. Select an experienced caretaker who seems to enjoy children and who has been recommended to you by someone whom you respect and whose values you share. You can usually find a good baby-sitter through friends, your church, your doctor or nurse, or through your local high school or college.

After selecting a baby-sitter, it is important to get acquainted with her before you need to leave her with your child. This way you can judge for yourself whether her personality is the type that would be suitable for your child, and whether the two of you can feel comfortable with each other. Have her come over a few times before you leave her with your baby, so that the baby can become used to her.

Familiarize the sitter with your child's routines, but also leave everything in writing. Make it clear that your baby comes first—not keeping the house neat, watching TV, or talking on the phone. Let her know what food and drink she is allowed to consume. Show her where the lights are, the fuse box, the thermostat, and the alarm system and how to shut it off. Have a flashlight with working batteries handy, also a blanket and pillow if you are staying out late. Review with her what to do in fire and other emergency situations. Make sure that emergency numbers, the number of your doctor, and where you can be reached are readily available. Tell her never to leave your child alone and to lock the doors and windows after you have left.

When leaving your child with the baby-sitter for the first time, it helps to have the baby already prepared for bed and fed, if possible. Especially with an older child (six months or older), it is important that the sitter be told the bedtime ritual and be given a favorite book to read to her. Suggest she start reading before you leave to ease the "good-byes." *Always* tell your child good-bye—avoid the temptation to sneak out or he'll become very fearful every time you leave the room.

In Appendix F is a chart you can photocopy and use to write down all the instructions and information that your baby-sitter needs.

ENVIRONMENTAL CHANGES

Changes in your baby's environment can result in some problems at times. Changes might include company, traveling, visiting other people, and moving. Planning ahead for both the expected and the unexpected will help to make these times passable.

TRAVELING

If you are traveling a long distance and can afford air travel, that is the most convenient. If possible, try to time the flight to coincide with when your baby is likely to be awake and not in need of a nap. The younger baby may be lulled by the sound of the plane engines, but the older baby may be so stimulated by the new surroundings that although she is totally fatigued she cannot go to sleep. When you make your reservations, advise the airlines that you have a baby and see whether they can have a stroller or cart available for you, if the airport is a large one. And ask for a seat with the most leg room, so that you can put the baby down on a blanket on the floor during the flight.

Some airlines will provide a cardboard bassinet, or if you can take your car seat on the plane and there is enough room, it can be strapped into the seat next to you. To carry your supplies, take as lightweight a shoulder bag as possible. If you are breast-feeding, you have nothing to worry about as far as the supply of nutrition. But if you are bottle-feeding, take at least one more feeding than you would expect to need, in case of delay. Take formula that is already prepared in the can and can be poured in the bottle and heated on the plane. Take a supply of premoistened towels, a bib, a light blanket, teething biscuits, toys (two to three), and books, as well as a change of clothes for the baby. And of course disposable diapers are a real boon when traveling. The umbrella stroller is helpful for use in the airport and can be put in the coat rack on the plane. A baby sling or a backpack is also useful. If there is no room for the baby's car seat on the plane, it can be checked with the luggage since it is crash-proof. Air travel with infants can be fun and even relaxing.

When traveling in your car, again make sure that you have more than enough supplies in case of a delay. Try to observe your baby's normal eating and sleeping schedule. When traveling past bedtime, change your baby into pajamas. A baby needs to be taken out of her car seat every two hours or so for a stretch and some fresh air. She will be more comfortable riding for long periods in her car seat if you fold a receiving blanket under her buttocks and thighs so that her knees can be slightly flexed. Then put blanket rolls around the side, so she can lean her head comfortably. Take a selection of familiar toys, books, her "lovey," and some new toys to help pass the time. Remember, however, that you are not going to be able to make the same time you did when traveling by car without children. If your baby sleeps well in the car you might try starting your trip in the afternoon, so she can sleep for most of the trip.

M O V I N G

If you are moving to a new home, don't ship the baby off to Grandmother's during the move. Your child will probably make the adjustment better if she is part of what's going on, especially if she is over six months of age and can discriminate the old and the new. You can get neighbors or sitters to help take care of her while you are busy. As soon as you get into your new surroundings, prepare her room first. If possible, arrange it just like her room in the old house. You may expect some regression, but, if handled gently and understandingly, this will pass in a few weeks.

P E T S

Babies do not need pets. Adding one to your family during your baby's first year, especially a pet that must be trained and housebroken, is not advisable. Your new baby needs as much of your energy and time as you can possibly give. However, you may already have a dog or cat, and if so that pet is very much a part of your family and there is no need to remove him. Remember, dogs and cats can be extremely jealous of the new addition. They may show this jealousy by regressing to soiling the house or by becoming hostile or withdrawn. Some pets become very protective of the new baby and will not leave her side.

It is important to lay some ground rules for the pet before the baby comes. When the baby's room is being set up, teach the dog or cat that he is not allowed into the room even when the baby is not there. Or if you feel that is going too far, teach the pet not to sleep or play under the crib or around the high chair. It is possible for a pet, in a freak accident, to knock a high chair over or to hit a guardrail on the crib and allow an infant to fall out. A cat especially likes to sleep against a warm body and will leap at the opportunity to get into the baby's crib. A net over the crib or bassinet will discourage this. It will also detour any objects that might be thrown in by other young children. **G R O U N D R U L E S**

Don't leave your child alone with a dog for the first five years of life. Train your dog to follow you whenever you leave a room. Even familiar, trusted pets can turn on young children, especially when a crawling baby creeps up on them when they are asleep and pulls on their fur. It is just not worth risking harm.

Avoid confrontations between dog and baby by removing the dog's food and water dish and toys when the baby is awake. Feed the dog when the baby is asleep. Some people have tried to chain or tie their dog up in their home in order to keep the dog away from the baby. Unfortunately this increases aggressiveness in the dog, since he feels the need to protect his limited territory. Some people have had their male dogs neutered in order to cut down on aggressiveness, and this has been helpful. However, if the dog has ever bitten any child or household member it is safer to remove the animal from the home.

If your dog is outdoors a great deal he may be infested with ticks. This should be checked carefully because tick bites can result in illness in children. If your dog has fleas it is important *not* to use a flea collar. These are toxic to a young child, who might reach out and touch the collar and then put her hand in her mouth.

By the way, a dog's mouth is probably more sanitary than a human mouth. So a lick by a dog on your baby's face is not the end of the world. It is obviously necessary, however, to keep your dog or cat as healthy and as clean as possible and free of worms or parasites since their feces will contain these organisms and will contaminate the soil your child is playing in.

A C C I D E N T   P R E V E N T I O N

We stress accident prevention over and over again because it is the leading cause of injury and death in childhood. In the first six months of life, when your baby is not able to get about and get into things, there are still precautions that you should take.

- Obviously she needs to sleep in a safe spot, with crib rails that are not too far apart and headboards in which her head cannot get wedged.
- It is important not to leave her on a high table or other surface unstrapped.
- She should always be strapped into her stroller or infant seat.
- The paint on furniture or toys should be lead-free.

- When you hold your baby you should not have hot liquids in your hand or be eating hot foods or smoking. Make sure that electrical cords, which babies love to pull or chew on, are out of reach.
- Don't leave your baby alone in the house.
- If you need to leave the room and your baby has learned to scoot about on the floor, then put her in the playpen while you are gone.
- This is the time when it is important to lock up all medications, cleaning agents, and gardening agents, and make sure that they are all kept in the original containers. I (AA) have seen many a poisoning occur because the kerosene was kept in a soft-drink bottle in the lower cabinet. The Poison Control phone number should be on your emergency call list. Should your baby get into something, call Poison Control immediately. Know the name of what your baby got into and approximately how much was taken. Have syrup of ipecac on hand to induce vomiting in case the control office advises you to use it.
- Car safety: Your child should always be restrained in an infant or child car seat that has been crash tested. Some states have laws requiring these safety devices for very young children.

For the last half of her first year, your baby is in much more jeopardy because she is mobile. In addition to taking the precautions listed above, get down on the floor and crawl around to see just what your baby could get into. Make sure that:

- there are no small swallowable objects on the floor
- electrical sockets are covered (you can buy devices in the hardware store)
- stairs have stair guards at the top and bottom to prevent falls
- lower bureau drawers contain no harmful objects or that the drawers are locked.

Also:

- Remember that plastic bags can cause suffocation, and make sure there is no pliable plastic in your baby's reach.
- Do not have your baby's crib near a window where she can get caught up in the cord of the venetian blind, drape, or window shade.
- Don't ever tie strings or cords around your baby's neck and don't tie your baby in bed. In fact, clothes with snaps are preferable to those with ties. Do make sure buttons and snaps are secure and recheck periodically to avoid swallowing or choking accidents.
- If your baby is pulling to stand up she is probably using a table, the corners of which need to be covered with foam tape or special rubber devices that you can obtain at the hardware store. Make sure that the table is sturdy and that it will not tip when the baby hangs on to it. Make sure that no tables have heavy objects on them that can be knocked over, or small or sharp items that can be put into the mouth.
- Make sure that lamp or appliance cords are not hanging down waiting for a little hand to pull on them and topple something over.

- When traveling in the car, clear out loose objects that can become missiles should you have to stop short suddenly.
- Wastebaskets are a wonderful hunting ground for a child. Make sure that nothing sharp, swallowable, or sick-making is in there (razor blades, needles, buttons, pencils, ashtray contents). Many a baby has become ill chewing on cigarette butts.
- Make sure that the plants in your house are not poisonous. You can call Poison Control to find out which ones are. We have a list of more common ones in Appendix F.
- Bookshelves are also a wonder for children, who delight in pulling the books out. If you jam the books in tightly they will be unable to get them free.
- When your baby is just beginning to walk put pads under rugs to avoid slipping, or take the rugs up.
- At Christmastime you will need to put the tree up on a high table, or put it in the playpen, to avoid confrontations between Christmas tree and baby.
- It is in the second half of the first year that your baby runs the risk of being burned by hot water in the bathtub, as we have cautioned before.
- When you are cooking be sure that the pots are turned with the handles inward. Fry on the back burner if possible, with only simmering on the front.
- Do not put the soap into the dishwasher until you are ready to shut the door and start it. The dishwasher compound is an extremely lethal poison, and young crawlers and standers love to poke their fingers into the dishwasher soap container.
- If glass gets broken, vacuum up the pieces or wipe them up with wet paper towels to eliminate the possibility of cuts.

Scary as this list sounds, we are not encouraging you to become a basket case about your child's safety. But do use common sense and take these precautions in your own home and in any home you may be visiting in order to avoid a possibly harmful situation.

One last precaution: Do not carry medications in your purse, and make sure that other persons you are with keep their purses out of reach. When you are visiting friends and relatives for any length of time, ask permission to babyproof their house, and then put everything back in its place when you leave.

PART 3

T O D D L E R H O O D

13

O V E R V I E W   O F
T O D D L E R H O O D

S E L F - C O N F I D E N C E

Toddlerhood starts when your child begins to walk. This might be as early as nine months or perhaps later, at twelve or fifteen months. It lasts until roughly his second birthday.

Remember that in each stage your child has a developmental task to master. In infancy his task was to build a sense of basic trust and optimism about himself and his world. In toddlerhood, your youngster's basic task is to develop self-confidence. This is when confidence or lack of it are both learned.

If you wanted to teach your child low self-confidence, you would slap his hand and say "No-no! Don't touch that," every time he reached out to something. You would constantly criticize him. While his self-confidence might have started out at 9, on a scale of 1 to 10, after a year of criticism and constant repression of his drive to explore it would probably be down to around 2 or 3.

I (FD) have my normal quota of faults (and I can itemize them for you if you have three or four hours free) but I have been very fortunate in having had a great deal of self-confidence throughout my life. I connect the beginnings of this self-confidence with the way my mother allowed me great freedom of expression in my toddlerhood play.

I remember very vividly having my own special play space in our backyard. It was right off the back porch, about six feet square, part of it in grass and part of it just bare earth. And it was here in every season but winter that I played in my little earth and mud kingdom. I never had a sandbox, but I delighted in building roads and houses in the earth with my hands and a small toy shovel, and moving my metal cars and trucks around in Earth City. My mother also let me use water in my play, and make things out of mud. The only rule was that I had to wash it off when I came into the house.

I never received criticism or restraint about my play in my little six-by-six earth kingdom. And my mother had that same attitude in raising me as I grew older. She used to say things to me like, "Son, anything you like to do, I know you can do it."

So I just took for granted that whatever I tried would turn out well. It didn't occur to me that I could fail at something. And even though I might be a little scared of something very new, I would always try it.

I've gone into such detail on this point because I want you to see how important the stage of toddlerhood is for the future of your child. And for you to realize that what you do now can help build lifelong self-confidence in your child.

Your baby couldn't develop his self-confidence earlier because he could not walk and explore the world by himself. But now that he can, his self-esteem and confidence will be developed by his successes and by your approval. You can help by giving him an environment in which he can succeed, and by praising him when he does.

One of your major concerns as a parent is to provide a safe environment in which your toddler can explore. He is a baby and yet he is not a baby. He has the limited judgment of a baby and yet the locomotion of an older child. This combination is what poses the major problem for parents.

Our chapter "Special Situations in Toddlerhood" provides an in-depth discussion on childproofing your home for accident prevention. It is extremely important that you read and follow the safety suggestions outlined there. Unless your toddler's environment is a safe one, his drive for independent exploration will be thwarted by a constant stream of "no-no"s and he will lose many opportunities for learning and mastery through his play.

P L A Y   I S   T H E   W O R K   O F   T H E   C H I L D

It's unfortunate that in our adult world many people do not know how to play. Many people, particularly men, are workaholics who feel compelled to spend most of their lives in work, with little time left for play and recreation.

It's a shame that some people live this way. For play is a psychological necessity for adults. Through our play, recreation, and vacations we quite literally re-create ourselves. We are psychologically at our healthiest when we can swing naturally back and forth between work and play, enjoying each in its place.

For your child, however, particularly when he is young, play has a different function. Play is the main way your child learns about his world. Toys and playthings are the textbooks by which he "studies" and understands his world. When he is playing he is learning, and when he is learning, he is playing; it's all the same.

When adults play, they do things they don't ordinarily do in work. They swim, ski, watch TV, play racquetball, or go to the movies. But when young children play, they imitate adult *work*. They pretend they are keeping house, repairing buildings, treating patients, installing phones, flying airplanes, and repairing cars. This is how they learn about the world. That is why we say that play is the work of the young child. It is the most important way by which your youngster educates himself.

Be sure to consult Chapter 20, "Intellectual Stimulation in Toddlerhood"; and the toddlerhood section of Appendix A ("A Parent's Guide to Children's Toys") for comprehensive descriptions of all the wonderful toys and playthings your toddler can use in learning about his world.

P O S I T I V E   G E N D E R   R A I S I N G

Now let's talk about the relationship of play to *positive gender raising*. This is a new term we have coined to replace the term *nonsexist child raising*, which we think is a negative way to describe a positive process, like calling good news non-bad news. Not only that, but the term, nonsexist child raising, is unfortunately loaded with confusion and misunderstanding.

Recently I (FD) asked nearly a hundred people (both men and women, picked at random) this question: "What is your opinion on the meaning of the phrase, 'nonsexist child raising?'" The most accurate answer came, interestingly enough, from a father. He said, "I think it means you are trying to raise a *child*, rather than forcing a boy to fit an outmoded stereotype like boys don't cry, or forcing a girl to fit a different outmoded stereotype, like girls must be pretty and submissive to men." Few others expressed the concept this clearly. About 40 percent gave the general idea in such words as, "You let boys play with dolls if they want to and you let girls play with trucks." However, when I asked them exactly how parents could raise children without stereotypes, they were generally at a loss.

Besides uncertainty, there were also some incredible answers. One woman said, "Well, I think that nonsexist child raising is this: You don't raise the child to be either a boy or a girl, but something sort of in between." This one from a man: "It means that you don't let the child learn anything about sex at all and you stop him from hearing any dirty words." And a mother said, "I guess it means that either the mother or the father could raise the child." Not so bad as a concept, but far off the real meaning.

These answers give you a rough idea of the muddy thinking that exists around the old term "nonsexist child raising." In fact, this kind of confusion surrounds many of the crucial issues in child raising today.

So let's clarify some basic issues:

1. *All* children have a gender, either male or female.
2. Male and female are not the same; there are not only physical but also psychological differences between boys and girls. This does not mean that one gender is superior to the other; it simply means they are different.
3. For centuries in the United States, women have had negative gender raising. They have been raised to have fewer life options and vocational options than men. They have been raised to be subservient to men. All this and much more add up to the fact that women in general have been raised to have low self-esteem, rather than a positive view of themselves as women. The very structure of our language contains thousands of ways in which women are assigned a secondary role to men.
4. We are now in the midst of a revolution in which women are demanding equal treatment by society. For example, women are insisting on equal job opportunities and equal pay. We are in hearty agreement with these goals, and we think that children should be raised to believe that the two genders are equal and should have equal rights in our society.
5. In the past, unfortunately, both boys and girls were taught a whole set of attitudes and beliefs which hung around their necks like an albatross and prevented them from being who they really were as individuals. Boys were taught that they should hide their feelings and be aggressive. Girls were taught that they should be sweet, meek, and noncompetitive.

These sexual stereotypes have been unwittingly taught by parents, have been put into the choice of toys the children are given to play with, and are found in the books they read.

6. We believe it is important for you as parents *not* to perpetuate these gender stereotypes and myths that prevent your children from being their own free and wonderful individual selves. There are many ways you can raise your children to have positive feelings about both genders.

7. Toddlerhood is the stage in which the learning begins which will either aid your children to be free of gender stereotypes or will teach them to grow up to be mere cardboard cutouts of stereotypes that should have been discarded long ago.

What are the ways in which you as a parent can give your children the freedom to be their own positive selves?

1. *Toys.* This is where the subject of play meshes with the subject of positive gender raising. Toys have no gender. That is, no toys are necessarily for girls only or for boys only. Present a wide spectrum of toys to your child, a little at a time, from dolls to blocks to cars and trucks and see how your child responds. Do not "nudge" your child to play with any particular toys. If you have both boys and girls in your family, you will probably find that they will gravitate toward some different toys and some toys will be used with equal gusto by both of them.

2. *Reading to your child.* You will find a list of positive-gender books in Appendix B which you can read to your child at this stage. You will also find books that are sexist but otherwise excellent. Rather than have your child miss these fine books, we suggest you read the book to your child but at the same time explain what is sexist in it and why this is wrong.

3. *Role modeling.* Your children's radar will be finely tuned to the conversation and role modeling of their mother and father. If the children live in a family where women are put down, they will pick that up, believe us. (For example, the family is out driving and Daddy grumbles, "There's another one of those lousy woman drivers!") On the other hand, if Mother and Daddy demonstrate by their actions and speech that women and men are equal and deserve equal and fair treatment in our society, this is the attitude that will be picked up by the children's radar.

4. *Reinforce attributes and achievements of females.* Since women have been cast in the role of second-class citizens for so long, you will need to make special efforts to elevate the status of women in your children's eyes. For example, compliment your daughter whenever you can on her assets or special qualities. And whenever you read about a woman who has had some special accomplishment, or you've seen it on TV, point it out to your daughter.

Follow through on the positive gender raising suggestions we give you here and in the next two stages of development. You will find that your girls and boys will naturally be different from each other, but proud to be what they are. And each will respect the other.

Equal but different. This is the bottom line of successful positive gender raising.

P H Y S I C A L   A N D   P S Y C H O L O G I C A L   G R O W T H

Many times the toddler has intentions that far exceed her abilities. She will so much want to imitate what you do and to try new things, and she may become frustrated when she is not able to do it successfully. It's especially helpful now to have some information about what you can expect of your child. If you understand her capabilities, you will be less likely to allow her to get into a situation in which she is doomed to failure, and less likely to encourage her to do something she is unable to do. So let's go over some of the changes in your child during this period and discuss the types of skill acquisition you can expect to see develop during this year.

P H Y S I C A L   D E V E L O P M E N T

First of all, the toddler is the cute little youngster with the tummy that sticks out and the spine that curves in at the base, with her legs spread wide apart, leaning slightly forward in order to keep her balance in her newfound mobility. Her head still looks rather large for her body, and her legs are short. Her growth spurt of the first year of life has slowed down considerably, a combination of a decreased appetite and more active movement. In the first six months of toddlerhood (from around twelve months to eighteen months) your child should gain two to three pounds, grow two to three inches, and double the number of her teeth from six to twelve. In the latter half of the second year (from eighteen months to twenty-four months) she should gain another three pounds, grow another two inches, and increase her number of teeth to sixteen. Of course this growth pattern varies greatly from individual to individual. If you want to keep an eye on your child's growth, ask your doctor for a copy of her growth chart; she'll be glad to give you one.

S L E E P

Your child sleeps about thirteen hours out of twenty-four now. She is making the transition from two naps a day to one nap right after lunch of approximately one to three hours. During the transition she can be a real grouch as she gradually adjusts to losing some of her daytime sleep. However she may also be fighting sleep and in fact may not sleep during nap time. But put her in her room and in bed, with some toys and books, to give her some time to wind down and rest. She may not sleep for several days, and then one day have a long nap.

As your child becomes more and more aware of herself as a separate person, anxiety about being separated from you increases and manifests itself in a resistance to going to sleep, particularly at night. We discuss ways to handle this in our "Special Situations in Toddlerhood" chapter.

Your child's body systems are continuing to mature during this year. Some of them have immaturities which will affect the way in which you care for her. Let's take a look.

S K I N

Your child's skin matures very slowly and still has not reached the maturity of an older child with more adult-type thickness. Because her skin is sensitive, you will still see diaper rashes and other rashes more commonly now than in later childhood. She might exhibit a skin rash with an infection or with a chemical imbalance of the body system. You will also notice chapping more frequently because she is more often in the outside world and exposed to the environment. Because her skin is thinner and more delicate, she loses body fluid through it, and there is therefore more chance of her skin's becoming dry and chapped. She is also more sensitive than you to heat, with a greater need for drinking fluids to replace her losses.

HEAD AND FACE

It is during this time that the soft spot on top of her head, the fontanelle, will close. This occurs usually around sixteen to eighteen months. The growth of the head has slowed, which indicates that the rapid brain growth of the first year has also slowed.

EYES

Your toddler has normal visual capabilities but still tends to be somewhat far-sighted. She can accommodate very well for near vision, however. Her depth perception is continuing to develop, but it does not completely mature until about six years of age. So she still has difficulty judging distance and will tend to bump into things. She will also hesitate while going down steps, in order to get her bearings as to just how far she has to step. It helps to understand this. Many parents feel that their toddler is just a clumsy little person who knocks things over carelessly. They do not realize that her capabilities are not quite so expert as theirs.

EARS

The eustachian tube, which connects the middle ear to the back of the throat (the pharynx), has a crucial role in equalizing the pressure in the middle ear, and any interference in its function can be extremely uncomfortable (like take-off or landing in an airplane). So you can understand how your toddler feels when she has problems affecting her ears. Since her eustachian tube is still short and soft, it is susceptible to swelling and obstruction from allergies or infections such as colds, and she will probably have a higher number of ear infections during this period than later in childhood.

NOSE, MOUTH, AND TEETH

Your toddler's nose still has its pug appearance but is essentially mature. She will double or triple her number of teeth, now getting her first four molars, her canines, and the remainder of her incisors. She will still have a lot of saliva production with her teething. But you can expect a decrease in drooling during this period, since her swallowing mechanisms have improved and she is now able to swallow well.

IMMUNE SYSTEM

Your child's ability to protect herself from infection is quite good now. She can manufacture all the antibodies that you can. But she will contract many more infections than you, because her system hasn't had previous exposure to these infections, and therefore has not yet produced the antibodies to fight those infections.

The average number of colds during this time is six to nine a year, which means about one every four weeks if she has none during the summer months.

Your child's heart and vascular system are essentially mature now. Her heart rate averages about 110 beats per minute, with a range of 80 to 130.

CARDIOVASCULAR SYSTEM

Your youngster now breathes at the rate of approximately 28 breaths per minute. This changes, obviously, when she is exercising. Her respiratory system is still not that of a mature child, and it continues to grow rapidly, but at a slower rate than it did in the first year. Her windpipe (trachea), which is made of cartilage, is softer than that of an older child and its diameter is smaller. Because of this it is more vulnerable to inflammatory processes and you may see a higher incidence of croup or bronchitis.

RESPIRATORY SYSTEM

Although your toddler's GI system is not fully mature, it is functioning maturely enough to handle and digest a normal diet.

Your toddler's gastric juices are very responsive to the sight and smell of food and to emotional states. She tends to be emotionally labile. It is for this reason we stress in our chapter on nutrition that mealtimes be kept as pleasant as possible, in order to allow the gastric juices to flow normally. If you try to force-feed her, she may vomit, because she is upset and has not produced the normal flow of gastric juices.

Your child's stomach empties much more quickly in toddlerhood and continues to do so throughout childhood. This is why she needs frequent snacks, as we suggest in our nutrition chapter.

Her bowel movements are still somewhat involuntary, but she is gradually developing the ability for voluntary control. She will be able to control them by the age of two to three years.

GASTRO-INTESTINAL SYSTEM

Your toddler's kidneys and bladder are essentially developed. Since her kidneys can now respond more quickly and appropriately to changes and imbalances in the chemistries of the body, she is less susceptible to illness from this cause. Her urine output is affected by how much she drinks, by how active she is, and by temperature changes. (Being cold increases the need to urinate.) She wets her diapers eight to ten times in twenty-four hours. She puts out about two ounces at a time. Urination is still pretty much involuntary for most toddlers until the latter half of this year.

GENITOURINARY SYSTEM

Her system of muscles and bones is really growing during toddlerhood as you might expect, with all her increased motor activity. Muscle growth is responsible for the largest growth and there is steady improvement in her motor control during this time. This is when the toeing-in seen in infancy begins to correct it-

MUSCULOSKELE-TAL SYSTEM

self. Your toddler will also begin to develop an arch in her foot as the fat pad is worn away.

It is during this period that individual differences will be noticed in motor capabilities. For instance, black children are usually more advanced in motor abilities than whites in toddlerhood. And girl toddlers are sometimes more advanced than boys.

NEUROLOGICAL SYSTEM

This is still a rapid period of growth for the nervous system. By two years of age, your toddler's brain will have reached 90 percent of its adult size. Because of this rapid growth, she has high requirements for oxygen and sugar to provide energy for her brain cells. Malnutrition during this period does not affect the number of brain cells, but it does affect the size and maturation of the cells. Your toddler still needs an adequate amount of fat in her diet in order to allow the maturation of the nervous system to take place. Just follow the suggestions in our nutrition chapters, and your child's brain maturation needs will be well met.

DEVELOPMENTAL MILESTONES

As we have mentioned before, your child is a unique individual, with a unique temperament or behavioral style. We discuss this at length in our chapter "The Daily Care of Your Infant" and urge you to read it if you have not already done so. By looking at how your child reacts to and interacts with her environment you will gain the greater understanding necessary to modify her environment for optimal development.

We give here a general overview of the skills your child will be acquiring during toddlerhood. We have grouped them into four categories: motor, language, mental, and social, recognizing that there is overlap between the areas.

MOTOR DEVELOPMENT

In the first half of toddlerhood, mobility is the main thing on your child's mind. When she begins to walk, she walks with her legs wide apart, staggering almost like a drunken sailor. But this gait rapidly becomes much more smooth. By eighteen months she is a climber, able to climb steps one step at a time. Within a few more months she will be able to walk down the steps with her hand held. By twenty-four months she can run quite well. This last half of toddlerhood, when she is able to run around, is a much more dangerous time, as we have mentioned.

In the first half of toddlerhood your youngster loves to play with push-type toys such as a doll carriage or a toy lawn mower, since she needs this for walking stability. But by the last half of toddlerhood she is a real "puller."

Because the toddler's gross motor activity is so obviously changing, sometimes we don't notice the fact that she is also improving her skills in the use of her hands. Your child is beginning to enjoy playing with small blocks and other objects. And by the time she is eighteen months of age, she can build a tower of two cubes. At twenty-four months the tower can be as high as four cubes, as her ability to use her fingers and hands improves dramatically. Remember that she is now feeding herself, which gives her considerable practice in fine motor skills. You can introduce crayons at this time, for she enjoys scribbling. She may even be able to draw straight lines by the time she is a year and a half and make circular motions around two years.

One of your child's major accomplishments during this time is the beginning mastery of a very complex set of motor and mental skills. These are the skills of dressing and undressing herself, as well as doing her own grooming. Later in the chapter we will talk about this aspect of your youngster's move toward independence.

LANGUAGE DEVELOPMENT

We have mentioned before that sometimes when one area is developing very rapidly it seems there is no development at all in another. This is the case with language development in the first part of toddlerhood. It sometimes seems to come to a standstill, with almost no new words being added. This does not mean, however, that language development is absent. While your toddler is busy running around enjoying her new freedom and independence, she is storing up all kinds of words and ideas.

Your child is working on her language through looking, listening, and motor development. She is improving the coordination of the muscles of her mouth, tongue, and throat by eating more and more solid foods. She is increasing her experience and general knowledge through her new motor ability. She is understanding a great deal. But word production usually lags two to four months behind understanding. You will notice that she can point to pictures before she can say the words.

During the first half of toddlerhood, your child may add only ten to twenty words to her vocabulary. She jabbers with adult-type intonations, and with a few words scattered in between. At around eighteen months, language production seems to take off. By the time she is two, she will probably have a vocabulary of two to three hundred words and be combining words into phrases or short sentences. These are very primitive sentences, sometimes lacking all the extra words you and I take for granted. But very obviously they are mental combinations that represent ideas.

Adults are the best models for language learning. This is why the first-born child usually has a better vocabulary and is more articulate than her siblings, who have other children rather than adults as their primary models for learning.

When you are talking to your toddler, use simple, slow speech and repeat a new word several times in different ways. For example, when you see a squirrel in a tree you might say, "Emily, look at the squirrel. The squirrel is in the tree. The squirrel is brown." It also helps your toddler if you talk about what you are doing while you are doing it, even sweeping the floor. This may seem like a boring one-sided conversation, but you are actually helping your child in her language development. You can also talk to her about things that she is doing.

One of the biggest frustrations of toddlerhood, which can lead to temper tantrums or screeching, is your toddler's desire to communicate and be independent when she doesn't have the ability to do so. This can be totally frustrating to you too, when you have been trying hard to understand what it is your toddler wants but can't figure it out. If you have a particularly intense child who is very persistent, this can lead to some difficult moments. The toddler, remember, still feels that you are an extension of herself and should be able to understand her every wish. But her wishes are more complex now than when she was a baby, and more difficult to express. But this is a short-lived period, and when your child's language improves, peace may reign.

MENTAL DEVELOPMENT

You will almost be able to see the wheels turn in your toddler's head. It's truly exciting! In the first half of toddlerhood she is the great experimenter. She is trying to learn how to master and perfect her environment. She needs to repeat actions over and over again, trying to prove to herself that the effect is constant. By the last part of toddlerhood she seems to be able to figure things out more in her head. Her memory is good and she has learned her lessons well. This is when she will begin using her toys in pretend-type games. Earlier, if you had given her a telephone she probably would have looked at it over and over again, looked underneath, banged it, and enjoyed every minute, but not used it as it was meant to be used. But in the latter half of toddlerhood she will have figured out the nuances of the telephone and be able to sit and use it as you do, jabbering away, and even making it a game with you by offering the telephone to you to talk.

It is during this later period that your child has a greatly increased desire to imitate adults. She will want to follow you about the household, doing what you do. She very much needs your approval and will delight in performing for you, her captive audience.

Imitating is a form of learning for your toddler. She will play imitation games with you for long periods of time and will want things repeated over and over again. This can create some problems, because her energy sometimes exceeds yours. If you have a limited amount of time, it helps to let your toddler know ahead of time that you will play with her until the end of a certain game, or to set a buzzer and let your toddler know that when the buzzer rings, the game will be over. You can capitalize on your child's interest in imitating everything you do in the house. She may particularly enjoy putting away groceries. She may also enjoy putting away her own playthings in the latter half of toddlerhood, especially if you have a special place for each thing. Toddlers love the sense of a successfully completed task. And you may be fortunate enough to set a habit that will continue into the preschool state. But don't hold your breath!

Your toddler loves her world and is eager to learn from it. That is exciting for a parent in itself. But, a tired mother can reap additional benefits during this learning process. If your toddler's home environment is both safe and intellectually enriching, she will be able to entertain herself, completely happy, for longer and longer periods of time!

SOCIAL DEVELOPMENT

There is so much happening in the area of social development during this period that we will divide the discussion into several areas: Parent/Child Interaction,

The Drive for Independence and Its Hazards, Peer Interaction, and Learning Self-Care.

During the first months of toddlerhood you may notice that your youngster is much more absorbed in her own activities for a longer period of time. She seems to ignore you for a while. This does not mean she doesn't need you, however. For you will note that she returns to you, her home base, every so often for some warm attention.

This returning to home base is almost like a refueling, giving your child enough psychological energy to continue on with her tasks. If a stranger comes on the scene, she will probably need to come over to you immediately, stay beside you until she has assessed the situation, and then take off on her own endeavors. If you have a child who is slow to warm up, however, she will need to stay at home base longer. There is no need to be embarrassed about this and no need to push her off to her own play. Let her stay beside you as long as she needs; she will handle the situation in her own good time.

After about four to six months of this type of behavior, you will notice that your child now seems to need you to share in every new experience she has. She may call you or follow you around much more than she did in the first half of toddlerhood. She needs to know where you are all the time. And she will use every trick of the trade to get you involved in what she is doing. For example, if you are sitting down, she will pile toys in your lap.

This sudden dependence can be a difficult development for a parent who has enjoyed the last few months of having a little bit more time to herself. But it is a normal and healthy response of your toddler. So don't feel that your child is spoiled, wants your entire attention, and wants to prevent you from doing anything else. What you are seeing is actually the push-pull she feels about becoming independent. From time to time she needs to be very dependent on you. Her increased, temporary, dependence is really a sign of her maturing.

PARENT/CHILD INTERACTION

Your toddler will be showing the signs of beginning self-assertion and a drive for independence. Her self-assertion is part of her developing self-esteem. And with this, the first signs of negativism become apparent. She is learning that she has some control of herself and shows it by closing her mouth firmly when Mother wants her to open it to take that last bite of food. For the same reason, she runs away when Mother asks her to come put her shirt on. She is not being defiant or hostile, she is just flexing her muscles and learning what she can do.

Just as your youngster is learning what she can and cannot do in her drive to control her body and her environment, she is learning what she can and cannot do in her social interactions. She needs consistent limits. They must be given gently and diplomatically, or confrontations will be inevitable. It is best at this stage to avoid confrontation, by using diversion or distraction. Steer her away from situations doomed to failure and into situations where her self-assertion will succeed.

THE DRIVE FOR INDEPENDENCE AND ITS HAZARDS

TEMPER TANTRUMS   Because your toddler often exceeds her capabilities, and is unable to relieve her frustration through verbal communication, we often see in toddlerhood an increase in the use of comfort habits, especially those with motor activity, to relieve tension. Such comfort habits would be thumb sucking, rocking, hair twisting, or even head banging. Sometimes, however, the child's frustration and sense of failure will result in an explosion of rage known as the temper tantrum. Tantrums often begin in the later months of toddlerhood, peaking in first adolescence (two to three years of age). Temper tantrums can be pretty scary for the parent, but they are devastating for the child. We will discuss techniques for handling them in Chapter 17.

Your youngster may also now begin showing some signs of aggression, including hitting or biting. She is not being hostile or destructive. She is trying to master a situation in her very immature way. She is showing you her need to assert herself, but is also demonstrating her lack of self-control. It is important that you or any caretaker not hit or bite her back. In her eyes, this puts the person she thought was in control at her level.

Children often behave aggressively when they are tired, hungry, or overstimulated. If possible, avoid such situations in this stage. *Environmental control*—arranging the environment in such a way as to decrease as many frustrations as possible—will help circumvent some of the problems. Often you can distract your child from a potentially tense situation into one in which she can relieve some of the tension in more acceptable ways such as running, jumping, marching to music, pounding play dough, or even rocking in a chair and looking at a book. Sometimes avoiding confrontation is not possible, and hitting or biting will occur. Your toddler needs to be taught the limits for desirable behavior but at the same time needs to realize that you accept and understand her feelings. To do this you need to label her feelings and at the same time indicate your disapproval of her acting them out in such a way. For example, "Sara is really mad and I understand, but it is not OK to bite." If you cannot distract her from a situation, you may need to remove her from it. And occasionally you may need to use a Time Out in her room or playpen (see "Discipline in Toddlerhood").

Some parents become very concerned about their child at this stage, particularly if she is a very intense, persistent child who tends to be quite aggressive. Take heart, this aggressiveness will peak but then gradually decline by the time she is about three. She will have learned some self-control and some alternatives for getting what she wants. You as a parent can help her begin to learn alternative solutions in toddlerhood.

ANXIETY   With all your youngster's assertion and independence comes anxiety. She needs to learn to be independent, but it can be scary. She has depended on you for so long. We discussed separation anxiety in our overview of infancy. The anxiety of being separated from Mother peaks at the age of fifteen to eighteen months. She does not want to be separated from you in a strange place, clings to you when new people come on the scene, and may develop fears of common everyday things that never bothered her before such as dogs, thunder, and the dark. She is more difficult to settle down at bedtime and at nap time and essentially is uneasy in any novel situation, not wanting change. All of this is more marked with the child who is slower to adapt.

GAME PLAYING   Because of your toddler's resistance to change, she will take twice as long to do things as she did previously. She does not like to be hurried or pushed into changing her activity. Again, diversionary tactics is the name of the game. When it is time for bed you can get her to her room much more quickly by pretending to be birds or airplanes than by saying, "It's time for bed," and trying to get her to walk down the hall. Dressing and undressing can become power struggles, with your toddler often winning unless it can become part of a game such as "skin the cat" or "where's Evie?"

If you can allow enough time to accomplish necessary tasks with your child without confrontation, turning them into games whenever possible, you will have a sunny, happy toddler who delights in herself, you, and her world.

PEER INTERACTION

Your toddler enjoys being with children her age, but in small numbers. She may be as afraid of a strange child as she is of a strange adult. She may even cling to you and avoid the other child. Give her time and don't push. She will gradually warm up to the new child. She will interact with him briefly but on the whole will go about her own business, although often watching the other toddler and imitating him.

She is beginning to show signs of developing empathy and will become very concerned should the other child become upset and cry. She may try to comfort him and may even cry herself. She is not much good at sharing, since she is really beginning the "me" and "mine" stage, which becomes worse in first adolescence. The aggression we talked about will surface in her social interaction and can be avoided by keeping the play periods short and occurring at times when she is neither tired nor hungry. Allow for as much motor activity in the play as possible, preferably outdoors. If your child becomes cross and starts having difficulty with her peers, remove her from the situation before it escalates. Keep the sessions short and sweet and you will both leave with a good feeling.

LEARNING SELF-CARE

At home your child is learning self-care skills in her drive for independence. She is becoming quite adept at undressing herself, often much to Mother's dismay. When our (AA) girls were toddlers, over the years I can remember putting each of them outside, nicely dressed, only to find them stark naked within a matter of minutes. They were *so proud* of their new skills!

GETTING DRESSED   Your child will also be trying to dress herself, although clumsily. You will need to begin the job, allowing her to do the finishing up. For instance, pull her pants up to the knees, and let her pull them up to the waist. And put her socks on up to the heel; she can do the rest.

Dress for success in this stage. This means keeping the clothes easy to manage so that your child can begin to feel competent with them. Use pants with elastic waistbands. If the clothes have zippers, add a ring to the zipper to make pulling up and down easier (however if your child is going outside and you want the clothing kept on, turn the zipper to the back). Rather than buttons, have large snaps that your child can handle. Buy her some stretch socks in large sizes and keep some soft, loose slippers around so that she can experiment with taking them on and off. Remember that a dirty toddler is a normal toddler. So make sure her clothes are durable and practical.

GROOMING   Your youngster will love learning to wash her hands and face so you will need a stool at the basin so she can climb up and down by herself. Let her wash her own hands and face. You can always get the missed spots later. She will want to brush her teeth and hair too. Let her do as much as possible by herself. You can complete the job on her while she is concentrating on doing the same to her doll or a stuffed animal. Another ploy is to let her do it and then allow you to check her over while you praise her for the good job she has done.

Checking your toddler's grooming job and praising her is a particularly good idea with toothbrushing. Use the toothbrush to check her work. Or pretend you are the dentist and check to make sure all the "bad bugs" are out. She may allow you to continue cleaning her teeth with her head in your lap (as described in Chapter 8, "The Daily Care of Your Infant"). However, she is more likely to want to watch the process in the mirror. Let her stand in front of you looking into the mirror, with her chin held by one of your hands while you brush with the other. You can also begin to teach her to brush her own teeth.

Toddlerhood is the stage when it is preferable to use a nonfluoride toothpaste if your water contains a good fluoride supply or if your child is on fluoride medication. A toddler loves the sweet taste of toothpaste and may swallow so much of it that she develops mottling of the enamel from excessive fluoride.

TOILET TEACHING   When discussing self-care during this period, the issue of *toilet teaching* often comes up. We believe that parents should never attempt to toilet-teach a youngster before the age of two. To do so is to cause frustration to the child and exasperation to the parents, because ordinarily a child has not developed the neuromuscular control necessary to control her bowel and bladder until the age of two. However, you can lay the foundation now for toilet teaching, by giving your child word labels to connect with bowel movements and urination. She needs names in order to understand what you are talking about when you are ready to toilet-teach her.

All during toddlerhood you will be giving your child labels for everything, and she will be sopping them up like a sponge. She will quickly learn the new toilet-teaching labels you give her. When she has dirty diapers, you can say, "Sandy has a BM" (or any word that suits you) "in her diaper. See the BM?" When she knows what that is, you can move one step further by teaching her what she is doing when she is in the process of having a bowel movement. "Sandy is making a BM in her diaper. When she's finished we'll clean the BM up." The same technique can be applied to urination (often called "pee-pee" or "wet"). When you are using the toilet and your toddler is observing (they always do!), use the same labels for your own activities.

As for teaching your child to use the toilet herself, leave that until the next stage, that of first adolescence. We will give you clear, step-by-step methods for doing it at that time.

T H E   J O Y S   O F   T O D D L E R H O O D

Toddlerhood should be a wonderful time for every parent. A toddler ordinarily is not defiant or belligerent. If you give your toddler the privilege of growing up in a toddler environment rather than an adult environment, you should have little trouble with her. You will find her happy, well-adjusted, and a joy to have around. It is only when you confront her toddler behavior with adult standards that she will be unhappy and difficult. She lives in only one kind of time: the eternal NOW. She can neither make nor break a promise, for she cannot truly remember the past or plan for the future. She functions only in the enthusiastic present. This is the one time of her life when she is in what we may call a state of naive innocence. She is not yet capable of being sophisticated or sometimes snotty, as she is in later stages. She is having a love affair with the universe, and you are privileged to participate in it.

14

NUTRITION IN TODDLERHOOD

THE TODDLER'S EATING STYLE

Few toddlers are likely to win awards for being great eaters. Your baby who used to love to sit down with you and be fed, eating ravenously, may turn into an impatient little guy who would rather mess with his food than eat it. Why does this happen?

First of all, your toddler is engrossed in his new skill of walking, of being on the move and exploring. So sitting still for any length of time is definitely not his thing. Secondly, this is a time when he experiences less of a growth spurt. During the first year of life your child probably tripled his birth weight, but during his second year he will gain only three to seven pounds. Therefore his food intake decreases; he simply does not need to eat as much as he did before.

Your toddler may also have odd food preferences from time to time, even more than he did in late infancy. But try to stay calm regardless of what your toddler does or does not eat. Your concern about your child's eating can cause a contest of wills at mealtime, which can become a vicious cycle that is very difficult to eradicate later. In this chapter we will be discussing ways to avoid this battle-ground and to keep your sanity as well.

Toddlerhood is the stage in which your child will refine his eating skills so that by the time he is two years old he will be rather adept at handling eating and drinking utensils. This is *not* a time for refining his table manners. That will come later.

At the beginning of toddlerhood your baby may be able to hold his cup and drink liquids adequately. However, the cup still needs a lid because he drops it frequently, throws it on the floor, and definitely has trouble tilting the cup to his mouth at the right time. He often ends up with gigantic spills down his front. By the time he is eighteen to twenty-four months he can hold a cup quite well, even a small glass. He has accomplished the tilt that is needed at the last minute to get the liquid into his mouth without spilling. And he is not ordinarily inclined to throw or drop his cup over the edge of the chair. However, he still has many accidents and knocks his glass over, so a lid is still very helpful.

Your toddler's skill with a spoon will gradually improve. At fifteen months he may still have difficulty scooping the food onto it and getting it into his mouth. A last-minute "dump" is not uncommon. By around seventeen months he can probably handle his wrist well enough to make scooping less difficult. But getting the cargo into his mouth may still create problems. By twenty-four months, however, he has acquired good coordination in his wrist, elbow, and shoulder movements. He should be able to get the spoon to his mouth without much spilling.

If you haven't guessed already, this is definitely messy-eating time. Although he uses a spoon, he will also resort to fingers when he needs to. Surely you've seen pictures of toddlers with food all over the tray, a spoon in one hand, and a glob of pudding in the other. They learn a great deal by handling the food. They like to feel it and sometimes smell it before they put it in their mouths. You may find this rather revolting, but avoid the urge to feed him yourself. He learns by doing it himself.

Your toddler also becomes more adept at chewing at this time. At around twelve months of age he will have a set of molars, so he can grind some foods. By the time he is two and a half, his chewing motions are so refined that he can handle most adult foods.

FEEDING EQUIPMENT

The feeding equipment you used at the end of infancy is still suitable for your toddler. He still needs to be in a high chair with a belt around him. He needs nonbreakable dishes, a cup with a lid, and a small spoon and fork. You still need some protection on the floor, probably even more than you needed in late infancy, but during this period he will gradually begin to adapt himself to more grown-up ways of eating. By the end of the year he may be able to sit nicely at the table, probably in his high chair with the tray removed, and eat with the rest of the family, *for a short period of time*.

These first years are the time when your baby is developing tastes that he will probably carry with him for the rest of his life. So if you don't want to encourage his becoming a heavy sugar or salt eater later in life, don't put them in his food now.

Basically your toddler eats what the rest of the family eats—a mixed diet of the necessary nutrients (proteins, carbohydrates, fats, vitamins, minerals, and water). In Appendix F we have listed suggestions for meeting his dietary requirements. Most foods need to be mashed, pureed, strained, or moistened, to suit his chewing abilities. Harder foods must be cut into small, bite-size pieces. You may offer your toddler a variety of foods in very small quantities, but he probably doesn't like his foods mixed together. He prefers moist foods, because they are easier to chew. This is why a toddler will usually choose moist pieces of chicken or a hot dog over the more delectable pieces of steak or roast.

Your toddler likes soup but is still not able to spoon liquid from a bowl, and he may refuse it for that reason. At this age, it is easier to change the food than change the child. You can strain the soup and offer the solid portion to him in a bowl so he can spoon it up or finger-feed himself. Then give him the broth in a cup so that he can drink it.

Your toddler can eat almost anything you give the rest of the family except the foods he might choke on, which we mentioned in Chapter 12, "Nutrition in

Infancy." If you have been avoiding allergenic foods in infancy, he may begin to eat these at twelve months of age. Discuss this with your doctor.

This is a time when mothers become concerned about whether their child is eating a properly mixed diet, with something from each food group each day. Unfortunately, many toddlers seem to like a limited variety of foods. So it helps to take the longer view and be concerned that your child eats the right nutritional mix over a period of one or two weeks, rather than every day. When he is on one of his eating jags and wants, say, a peanut butter sandwich at every meal, give it to him. But also serve him a *small* portion of other foods. If he refuses the other foods, perhaps only smelling or feeling them, don't worry about it. Remember, too, that if your child refuses to try a new food several times, this does not mean that he will refuse it when it is offered the next time. Wait a few days and try again, but don't coax or try to cajole him into eating what he does not want to eat.

No one food is absolutely more nutritious or better for your child than another food. For instance, milk is a food in which there is a good combination of calcium, protein, carbohydrates, fat, and vitamins. But these same nutrients can be obtained in other foods or in other forms of milk such as ice cream, yogurt, or pudding. Many foods can be presented in a variety of forms. An egg is equally as valuable fried on a plate or in an egg custard or an omelette.

V I T A M I N S   A N D   M I N E R A L S

What about the need for a multivitamin preparation? Vitamins A, D, E, and K are fat-soluble vitamins and can be stored in the body for some periods of time, so your child does not necessarily have to get them on a daily basis. The B vitamins and vitamin C are water-soluble—they cannot be stored and need to be taken at least every few days.

Sources of all of the vitamins are listed in Appendix F. They are very prevalent in common foods and your toddler will usually take in a more than adequate amount. If your child has not taken in anything but peanut butter for a week, you might want to give him a multivitamin preparation; however, it is probably not necessary, for he will eventually broaden his eating horizons.

I R O N

What about the need for an iron supplement? Iron is an important mineral and is found in red meats, baked beans with molasses, prunes, hot dogs, eggs, and fortified infant cereals. Many toddlers are not particularly good meat or egg eaters in the beginning of their second year. In order to assure that your child is getting the proper amount of iron, it is wise to continue until the second half of this year with the iron-fortified cereals. There is no reason why he shouldn't continue eating these cereals on into childhood, as long as he likes them. If you are using the cereals, or if your child is a good eater of foods containing iron, there is no reason to give an iron supplement. In fact, you would probably want to avoid it, since iron tends to constipate. If you are concerned about whether your child is getting enough iron, discuss it with your doctor.

Calcium for growing bones and teeth is important to consider at this time. C A L C I U M
One to one and a half pints (two to three cups) of milk a day is all your toddler
needs. If he doesn't get his calcium this way, other sources of it are listed in
Appendix F.

Now let's talk about two areas that have become sources of great concern
in the past few years. These are *sweets* and *junk foods*. Sweets are foods that
contain natural sugars, such as fruits (fresh, canned, or dried); or products made
with refined sugars or honey, such as cakes, cookies, candies, ice creams, and
sugar-coated cereals; or simply refined sugar or honey alone. Sweets are a source
of carbohydrates and in some forms offer many other nutrients. A list of popular
sweet foods and their sugar content is found in Appendix F. The sweets that
concern people most are those with the highest sugar content and lowest content
of other nutrients, such as candy and soft drinks.

At the other end of the spectrum are fruits, which have sugar in a much lower
concentration and are an excellent source of valuable nutrients. Fresh fruits are
sweets in a very superior form. They haven't too much sugar or too many calories,
and they are not sticky or chewy enough to promote tooth decay. Canned fruits
often have sugar added, increasing calories and the potential for tooth decay.
Dried fruits (raisins, apricots, etc.) are higher in sugar and calories, and are
sticky—so they are actually worse for the teeth than cookies, cakes, ice cream,
and soft drinks. Baked goods, such as pies, cakes, and cookies, while high in
sugar and calories, can be good sources of other nutrients if chosen correctly.
A peanut butter cookie has more to offer than a sugar cookie, for example. Sweets
that may present problems are the high-sugar low-nutrient types as well as the
chewier sources of sugar.

Humans do seem to have a preference for sweets, even in infancy. A newborn
much prefers sugar water to salt water or plain water. The tendency to prefer
sweets is also something that seems to be genetic rather than environmental.
In a family with three children, there may be one with a sweet tooth and two
who really could care less, even though they have all been offered the same
foods and exposed to the same dietary habits since infancy.

Sweets can cause several problems:

- They have a special potential for inappropriate use. Parents sometimes give
  sweets as a source of comfort or withhold them as punishment, which makes
  the sweets seem extra desirable, far beyond their nutritive value.
- The sweeter the food, the higher the calorie count, and overdoing calories
  can lead to obesity.
- When high-sugar-content snacks are eaten just before mealtime, the sugar
  decreases the hunger pangs—and your child's appetite.
- In our discussion of "nursing bottle syndrome" in Chapter 9, we said that
  prolonged contact of tooth enamel with any sugar substance promotes tooth
  decay. This includes fresh fruit (apple peel, for example, can wedge in between teeth) but is worse for sticky, chewier foods such as dried fruits and
  chewy candy. Eating a sweet over a long period of time (like a lollipop) is
  worse than consuming a sweet within a few minutes. Eating sweets with

other food or drink is better, for this will help to wash the sweets away from the teeth. Foods with high fat content (butter, peanut butter, fried foods) will coat the teeth and give some protection also.

LIMITING SWEETS

There are ways to overcome some of these problems with sweets. First of all, if you don't eat sugary foods, and don't have other children around who do, your toddler won't know about them. Feeding him fresh or canned fruits (with the syrup poured off) at meals will satisfy his desire for sweets. However, be prepared for changes when he hits two to three years of age and is introduced to the candies and sodas so prevalent at birthday parties. He'll probably love them!

Don't panic. Incorporate his sweet desires and intakes with his other nutrition needs, and be matter-of-fact about it. If he likes candy and you give it to him at home, buy the type that is not sticky and give it to him with his meals as dessert. A few M & Ms after his hot dog and green beans isn't so terrible. He'll be full so he won't need the whole package (unless he sees it). If he eats the candy beforehand, he won't be spoiling his meal. And his teeth will be protected if he is eating the sweets with other food and drink, more protected if you can rinse his mouth by giving him water, and even more protected by brushing his teeth after he eats.

Family desserts such as cakes, pies, and puddings may be sweet but are also sources of other nutrients. Your toddler may certainly eat small portions of these at mealtimes. Simply consider it part of his daily intake. Let him eat them when you do, and offer fruit at the meals he eats alone.

HYPERACTIVITY

Refined sugar is sometimes blamed for hyperactivity in children. This may in fact be true for a small percentage of children who have some sort of allergy or reaction to sugar or sugar-containing products. Obviously, not all children react this way. If you feel that your child is having this kind of reaction it is wise to keep a daily diary of what he eats and what his behavior is. This way you can begin to see whether there is a pattern associated with his eating sugar or any other food.

JUNK FOOD

Junk food is another pet peeve for many parents, but junk food means different things to different people. It can mean a hamburger and apple turnover from a fast-food restaurant, or a snack food such as potato chips. But in fact, these foods are neither more or less nutritious than some of the foods you serve at home. Eating a hamburger, french fries, and a milk shake at a fast-food restaurant makes for a fairly well-rounded meal. Although high in calories and fat, it provides basic nutrients and lacks only some vitamins that could be provided by fresh fruit or a vegetable at a later meal. Some parents think of foods such as potato chips as junk food because the child picks them out for himself and may also put an undue value on them as a snack. If your child is over-snacking on this kind of food, why not offer it to him at his meals instead? Save that piece of fruit or bread and butter that he didn't eat with his meal, and offer that to him at snack time.

Finally, the main concern of most parents is that junk food will be too high in calorie content (from sugar, flour, or fat) and too low in nutritive content. This can be a legitimate concern with an older child over whose snack time you may have little control. But you can regulate the nutrients a toddler consumes simply by following the guidelines in this chapter. And in doing this, you are giving your child an excellent foundation for good health as well as helping him learn to like a wide variety of highly nutritious foods. Hopefully, later on, this background will stand him in good stead through the school years, when temptation and opportunity for high-calorie foods abound.

There are many ways to skin a cat; and there are many different ways to present a food to your toddler so that he can find a preparation he likes. You will find some wonderful food suggestions and recipes in two books that I (AA) have particularly enjoyed with my children. The books are *Feed Me, I'm Yours* and *Taming the Candy Monster*, both by Vicki Lansky.

FEEDING TECHNIQUES

Now let's talk about how to keep your toddler interested at mealtimes and willing to try new foods. We've already mentioned putting a variety of foods in front of her and leaving her alone to test and try what she wants. Always remember to serve new foods only with familiar and accepted ones. If you don't like waste, serve her very small portions of each food and offer her more when she has finished them. Be prepared for the most ghastly combinations that you can imagine—green beans dumped in ketchup, bananas in mustard, and pickles with ice cream!

Some mothers put the dessert, if it is a nutritious one, on the table along with the main course. That way your toddler does not begin to think of dessert as a special treat at the end of the meal but will eat all of the different foods and value them equally. Other mothers find that it is not a problem to go ahead and offer the main course, and then offer a small portion of dessert at the end. It is when you coax your child to "finish your meal or you won't get dessert" that problems can arise. If your child doesn't want all of her meal and any of it is salvageable, then save it for snack time, as we suggested earlier.

MEALTIME

Most children at this age will need five small meals or three large meals a day. Five small meals are probably better, since nearly all childern need a mid-morning or midafternoon pick-me-up. Remember that snacks should consist of foods that are part of her daily nutritional requirements. Structure your child's mealtimes and snack times so she can develop a sense of hunger between feedings. If she is allowed to eat throughout the day, then no real sense of hunger will develop and you will have a child who only nibbles. Keep mealtimes regular to avoid the problem of a child who comes to the table exhausted, and even though hungry, is too tired to eat, because the family dinner has not been served until eight o'clock.

Observe your child to see at which meal she seems to be hungriest, and offer her more food at that time. Respect her need to sit back and eat little at the other meals. Some children will never be big dinner eaters and some will never be big breakfast eaters. However, if your child seems to be unusually less hungry for a period of a day or more, it's a good idea to look for reasons why. She may be coming down with something or be simply exhausted after a few hectic days of family vacation. Or she may have been rather sedentary (unusual for a toddler!) for a few days, which lowers her energy requirements and therefore her need for food. Or sometimes a not uncommon event has occurred: She has been at Grandmother's for a few days and is still stuffed to the gills. She may even have gained weight she doesn't need, so her body is letting her know; and her hunger is decreased.

CHOICE OF FOODS

As we have mentioned, it is important to put a variety of foods in front of your child, but make sure that some of her favorites are on her plate. Children at this age like a color contrast in their food and enjoy different textures. For example, your youngster might like a crisp green vegetable with yellow squash, soft noodles, and moist chicken. Children seem to prefer raw vegetables to cooked vegetables, and being able to dip them in a dip (made from yogurt, cottage cheese, or sour cream) makes it even more exciting. Grating carrots and celery avoids the problem of choking and also makes the vegetables easier to chew. And your toddler will love feeling the piles of grated food. Sandwiches that have been cut out with a cookie cutter are infinitely more interesting than the usual rectangular shape, and they will serve to interest your child in trying a different type of sandwich.

Remember that each child is different; and each child has a different approach to things in general, including foods. If yours does not adapt quickly to new situations, she may not adapt quickly to new foods.

I (AA) found a very good way to entice my reluctant eater, Kimberly, to try new foods. I did not put the new food on her plate; I treated it as grown-up food and put it on everyone's plate but hers. This immediately stimulated her interest. Then she would be "allowed" to have a bite from my plate and decide for herself whether she liked it or not. She now adores asparagus and broccoli.

EATING WITH THE FAMILY

Parents and siblings are very much the model for your child at this time. If the rest of the family eat their food and don't complain and moan about it, your toddler is likely to do the same. This is the time you can introduce your toddler to the family meal. But we suggest that it be for only a short part of the meal in the beginning (say, five to ten minutes), because toddlers do not like to sit for long periods of time. If she gets down after a few mouthfuls, simply clear her plate away. That way she will soon understand that once she gets down she will get no more food. Obviously you will have fed her some of her meal before she came to the family table.

Another way to encourage good eating and to begin to develop appropriate behavior at the table is to talk to your toddler while she is eating. Just don't discuss how much she has to eat or how much she has eaten. When she is behaving well, smile and pat her to let her know how you feel. If she begins to act silly, drops her food over the edge, or stops eating, you should pay no attention to her. That way she will learn that this behavior does not get the concern and attention that she may want. By paying attention to her good behavior you can avoid the situation that I (AA) encountered with one family. The mother would read the paper while her little boy was eating quietly and appropriately. She would pay attention to him only when he dropped his food over the edge or threw his cup. You guessed it. The cup throwing and food dropping increased, until mealtime became a psychological disaster zone.

When you take your toddler out to eat with the family, we recommend that you frequent fast-food restaurants or else call your order in ahead, such as with pizza (a very nutritious food), so you don't have a long wait. You can bring along some grated carrots or an orange or apple, to round out the nutrients. Something that I (AA) have found to be very helpful, if you do not wish your child to have a high-calorie shake or cola drink, is to ask for a glass of ice water with a straw. Your toddler will be perfectly content with this and not realize that she is drinking something different, especially if other family members are drinking a colorless beverage such as 7-Up or Sprite.

As you can see, toddlerhood is a period which will test your imagination, patience, and diplomacy at mealtimes. You can get through it by remembering that your youngster has an innate hunger drive which is sometimes satisfied by a limited variety of foods.

15

DISCIPLINE IN TODDLERHOOD

A number of years ago the Harvard Preschool Project began a long-term study of the mothers of preschool children. One of their findings was that by and large the mothers were competent in the care and handling of their babies. But when their children began to walk and entered the stage of toddlerhood, things changed drastically. Some mothers were completely flummoxed by their kids.

There is seldom any reason for real conflict between a baby and his parents, even though there may be occasions when the baby wants to do one thing (cry) and his parents want him to do something else (stop crying).

But everything changes in toddlerhood when the child begins to walk. The toddler has a great urge to explore, and he has the energy and the mobility to do it. When his mother takes him to the market, for example, he may want to race up and down the aisles and pull packages off the shelves, due simply to this urge to explore. Naturally his mother will not be too keen about this. The child may want to climb onto the kitchen counter and crawl into the top-most cupboard. His mother will not be wild about this idea either. And so on.

A first-time mother will be astounded by the number of things her toddler can get into before she is even aware of it. Many mothers have the same trouble handling a toddler that they would have if a high-spirited monkey suddenly came to live in their house.

Many parents find it difficult to manage their toddlers simply because they don't understand how to do it. A toddler is actually easy to discipline, *if* you know how.

Consider this: When you take your toddler to a playground and he climbs on the climbing equipment or plays in the sand with his cars and sand toys, you don't have any trouble with him. Why not? Very simple. The environment of the playground is suited to the life-style of the toddler, which is to explore anything he can get his hands (or mouth) on. The dominant passion of his life is exploration. And a playground lends itself admirably to this drive.

But while a playground is perfectly suited to the toddler, your home probably is not. The average home is likely to be full of objects that can be easily damaged by a toddler—floor lamps that can be knocked over and broken; coffee tables filled with brittle knickknacks; breakable vases; unlocked medicine cabinets with all sorts of medicines, some of them lethal for a young child.

The combination of an active, exploring, "into everything" toddler and the adult environment of the average American house can frazzle the nerves of any mother. She must chase after her child from morning to night, yelling, "Leave that alone!" and "No, no, don't touch that—it'll break!"

The solution is very simple, and we wonder why so few parents use it. The answer is to childproof the house, which means two things. First, remove from the house (or lock up) anything that can harm or injure the child, or anything that the child can harm. You will find very explicit directions for this in Chapter 12. Second, provide enticing objects and toys for your child to play with—for example, the Toddler's Gym for indoors and the Cone Climber in the yard. When you do these things, you are using the discipline method of *environmental control*.

E N V I R O N M E N T A L   C O N T R O L

The use of environmental control is preventive discipline. It eliminates at one stroke thousands of no-nos, frazzled parental nerves, and worry about whether your child is safe.

Here's another example of environmental control, which only a very small minority of parents use. When I (FD) travel around the country on TV and radio tours I sometimes encounter an interviewer (usually a man with no children!) who tries to convince me that there are times when you simply *have* to spank children. He will say, "What about a two-year-old child who keeps running into the street?" I answer very quietly. "No, you don't have to spank a two-year-old to keep him from running into the street. I never spanked my two-year-olds for doing it, because none of them ever ran into the street." And then I explain, "When my kids began to walk, I built a big, sturdy, six-foot fence all around the house and yard. I made it of smooth wood, so there would be no splinters, but especially no hand holds or leg holds for climbing up. Once I had done that, there was absolutely no way my toddlers could get into the street."

Think of all the problems that are prevented by that simple six-foot fence! Incidentally, don't use chain link, because it's too easy for an agile toddler to climb, using the links for hand and leg holds.

Here's another example of environmental control. Almost every year I (FD) hear a story or two like this: "Last month was just ghastly for us," a mother says. "We took our preschoolers and went back to visit the folks in Nebraska. The kids were teasing and fighting all the time, and it was awful! We're never going to do that again."

As you ask some questions about this journey, the reasons for the disaster become clear. The environment of the back seat of the car was purely adult; it bore no resemblance to a toddler environment. There were no toys for the two children to play with, except a few picture books. The parents had no special toys stashed away to bring out when the behavior got particularly sticky. They did not stop periodically at a park or grassy area where the children could run off some of their surplus energy. They did not stop from time to time for a snack break.

In other words, the parents expected the kids to behave like little adults—to sit quietly in the back seat and watch Kansas roll by! Very painfully, they learned that toddlers are not capable of that. If they had used environmental control, the children would have behaved very differently.

D I S T R A C T I O N

Another method of discipline is *distraction*. Toddlerhood is really a delightful stage, for toddlers are full of a naive innocence they will never have again. Part of that naive innocence is that they are highly distractible. Each new stimulus they see immediately claims their attention.

You can use this to direct your child's attention away from something you don't want him to get involved with. And don't be afraid to ham it up when you do it.

For example, I (FD) remember when my older son, Randy, was about eighteen months old. We were driving along and suddenly I noticed that a small circus had been set up that morning on the parking lot of a department store. In a minute or two Randy would see it, and I could just picture how he would cry and yell if I did not take him.

So I quickly swung around and pointed out the other window. "Randy, look at the horsie, look, look!"

He turned and looked out the window.

"Where horsie?"

"Right there," I said, pointing.

He looked intently. "No see horsie."

"Maybe it's gone," I said.

By this time we had safely passed the little circus. Distraction had done its work.

Make use of distraction when you need it with your toddlers. Unfortunately, when the next stage—first adolescence—sets in it may no longer work.

The next techniques we are going to discuss can begin to be used in toddlerhood and will continue to be useful up through age ten.

As we've said, discipline can be divided into two basic parts: learning good behavior and avoiding misbehavior. First you teach your child behavior that is good, whether it is hanging up his clothes or learning to be more self-assertive. It's behavior you approve of and want your child to learn.

P O S I T I V E   R E W A R D   S Y S T E M

The most important technique in teaching desirable behavior is the *positive reward system.*

You have probably seen trained animal acts such as dolphins, elephants, and bears at amusement parks like Sea World or Marineland and at circuses. But you may not be aware of how the animals are taught to do their tricks.

Let's say the trainer is going to teach a bear to play basketball. How does he do it? He doesn't use any of the typical methods that parents use with children. He doesn't yell at the bear. He doesn't scold. He doesn't lecture. He doesn't ground the bear. He doesn't spank the bear. He uses a positive reward system. And nothing else!

If the bear is in one corner of the court and the basketball is in the other, nothing happens until the bear heads toward the basketball. As soon as the bear heads in the slightest degree toward the basketball, the trainer rewards him with small pieces of meat, until by such successive steps he gets the bear to the basketball. Then, by the same method, he gets him to take the basketball over to the basket, raise it up in his paws, and shoot. The bear doesn't learn to do all of this in one lesson, of course. It takes a number of teaching periods before the bear has learned to do it without any hitches. When the trainer is teaching the bear to do the trick the first time, he has to reward him every step of the way. But when the bear has finally learned the trick completely, then the trainer only rewards him once, at the completion of the trick, when he shoots the basket.

Teaching an animal is based on a very simple psychological law: *Any action that is followed by a positive reward is strengthened and more likely to be repeated in the future.* This law has been found to work for just about every kind of animal you can think of, including human beings of all ages.

First you need to decide what types of desirable behavior you want to teach your toddler. Let me just mention a few you might choose: to keep his plate on his tray at mealtime, to keep away from the TV knobs, or to help you put away his toys.

For any child the most positive reward is your approval. For example, when you see him keeping his plate on his tray, smile at him and touch him lovingly—a little pat on the head, a squeeze, or a tickle behind the ear. You can also praise him by saying, "What a good job you are doing. You are keeping your plate on the tray." Do this at every meal and he'll be eager to conform.

The older toddler may have some extra incentive if he receives additional rewards. Make a chart and put it on the refrigerator door; whenever he finishes a meal without throwing his plate let him put a star, a sticker, or a happy face stamp on it. The family will notice and he'll be so proud.

At this age, your toddler will want the reward immediately. A delayed reward that is paid off at the end of the week, which works fine at a later age, will not work for a toddler. And don't be afraid that if you give your child rewards he will expect you to continue doing so forever. Eventually, his sense of accomplishment and the knowledge that you are pleased will be his payoffs.

The rewards we've talked about so far are useful for teaching the basic tasks that recur every day. Here is another one that you can use for special spontaneous situations. "Kim! Help Mommy gather up the clean laundry and put it in this big bag, and I'll do something special for you! I'll make a funny face (or dance a jig, or stand on my head)." She'll do the task, win your approval *and* get that extra treat you're promising. This may sound a little strange to you, but it works! As the saying goes: "If you haven't tried it, don't knock it!"

The positive reward system does something special for you as a parent, too. Instead of having one eye cocked for trouble, like so many parents, you have exactly the opposite viewpoint. You are constantly on the lookout for good behavior on the part of your child. And when you notice it and show your approval by your touch or smile, it will produce a happier and more positive relationship between the two of you. Remember that the teacher (parent) who praises and rewards will always produce better results than the teacher who criticizes and scolds.

So much for the ways in which you can get your toddler to engage in new and positive behavior. Now for the other side of the coin. What if she throws that plate off her tray anyway? How do you teach her to refrain from unacceptable behavior?

T I M E   O U T

The best technique for accomplishing this is called the *Time Out*—a time out from any positive reinforcement or reward. We discuss this method in detail in Chapter 20, "Discipline in First Adolescence," but feel that it can be introduced very effectively in toddlerhood.

Here is how it works. When your youngster is doing something that is unacceptable to you, ask her to stop at once. If that doesn't work, you give her a Time Out immediately. Or you can skip the warning and proceed immediately to the Time Out, if she already knows she's not supposed to do it. Say, "Cindy, you're throwing your plate and you need a Time Out . . ."

Say this matter-of-factly. Pick her up so that she is facing away from you (she won't mistake it for a hug) and put her in her playpen for one to two minutes (set a timer) or until she has stopped crying. If you don't have a playpen, her crib will do. Don't talk to her or pay any attention to her. Go on with your routine. When you take her out, don't talk about her misdeed, simply put her down and let her go on with her activities.

You haven't had to repeat your request ten to twelve times, becoming more and more frustrated and angry each time. And your toddler hasn't had the thrill of playing the "Toss the Plate" game with Mommy. She is learning that the undesirable behavior has no rewards—neither a negative nor a positive reaction. What a bore!

So, when used appropriately, the Time Out keeps a parent from becoming angry and doing or saying something both parent and child will regret. It also immediately provides the child with a chance to get some distance from the situation—a chance to start over without feeling too bad about herself. Use it consistently and you'll be amazed at how quickly she learns, especially if you've coupled it with the positive reward system.

R E V E R S E   T I M E   O U T

Now here's a method that you can use when your kids have been driving you up the wall and you see no relief in sight. It's called the *Reverse Time Out*, or Mother's Vacation in the Bathroom. It's not one you're going to use every day, only in extreme circumstances. You can use it with toddlers or the next stage up, first adolescence (the "terrible twos").

When you think you are going to go out of your gourd if your kids don't settle down, take a good book or magazine and slip quietly into the bathroom and lock the door. Sooner or later they will discover where you are and start pounding on the door and yelling for you. Merely let them know you are there, to reassure them. After that, do not respond. Continue reading. Wait until the pounding and the yelling stop and then step calmly out of the bathroom and say something like, "It certainly is nice to have it peaceful and quiet in the house." You are teaching them in a very powerful way that it is only peace and quiet that brings you out of the bathroom.

Note: If they have been pounding on the door for ten minutes and you are tempted to come out, DON'T! All you will be doing is rewarding them for pounding on the door for ten minutes.

SPANKING

Perhaps we had better say a few words about spanking. First let's define what we mean by spanking. We are against the idea of attacking a child physically in the guise of "spanking" her. We are against the use of a parental "weapon," such as a strap or a wooden rod. We are against hitting a child across the face. What we mean by spanking is a few whacks with the flat of the hand on the child's backside.

Some psychologists and psychiatrists believe it is a cardinal sin if you ever spank a child at all. A child-raising book on the other side of the fence advocates spanking as a way to establish parental authority. We think this is equally ridiculous. Spanking does establish a kind of authority of the parent over the child—Gestapo authority! But that kind of authority doesn't do much to promote a good parent-child relationship.

Every time you spank your child you are teaching her to fear and hate you and that physical force is a way to solve problems. It is a punishment that you will want to keep to a minimum.

Typically, a mother has had a bad day. She is seething inside at her child's behavior and she loses control over that "last straw." She gives the child a few whacks, gets the anger out of her system, and then she and the child can start over.

You may have heard the saying, "Never strike a child in anger." But we believe you should spank your child *only* when you are angry. Your child can understand it when you lose your temper and whack her. After all, she does that herself with her siblings and playmates!

If we were all 100 percent perfect parents we would never use spanking as a discipline technique. Over the long run it is very ineffective. It leaves us feeling guilty and also does not accomplish the positive goals that other techniques do. But none of us are perfect. So while we don't recommend spanking we do make allowance for it.

Many parents spank their children because they don't know any other technique for controlling behavior. But you are learning a number of techniques that will help you achieve your discipline goals without having to resort to spanking. The *Time Out* for your child and the *Reverse Time Out* for you are invaluable alternatives. If you do lose your temper, consider these immediate actions—count to ten, slowly; bang your head against the wall, gently; or clean a toilet, briskly. Try whatever works for you!

TYPICAL TODDLER BEHAVIOR

We would like to add one more thing about toddlers that may save you a certain amount of exasperation and desperation. Let's say that Mother comes upon her toddler pulling the pages out of one of her favorite books. She gets furious and whacks him because she believes he is defying her. Or, in another situation, a toddler is eating lunch in his high chair and drops his spoon on the floor. Mother picks it up. He promptly drops it again. Gritting her teeth, she picks it up again. Immediately he drops it once more. She is full of anger and yells at him, "Don't you dare do that again!" She thinks he is doing it to get her goat.

Both of these parents misunderstand the situation. The young toddler is not pulling the pages out of meanness. He is pulling out the pages as part of his exploration of the world—he wants to know what it feels like to pull pages out of a book. We are sure his mother does not like his research, but her child did not create the problem. She did, by leaving a book out where he can get at it.

The other toddler is not dropping his spoon on the floor to aggravate his mother, although it seems like that to her. He is doing a little experiment in physics to find out if the same thing will happen every time he drops a spoon on the floor.

Now if a two-and-a-half-year-old did either of these things the situation would be different. He probably *would* be defying Mother and trying to get her goat. But a toddler is not in a rebellious stage. He is a charming fellow who is not ordinarily given to defying his parents or trying to annoy them, so don't treat him as if he is. The toddler's whole life is focused mainly on one thing: exploring all of the universe that he can reach—pounding it, pulling on it, petting it, tearing it, knocking it over, tasting it, chewing it up, spitting it out, and sitting on it.

If you have your house and yard thoroughly childproofed, he can do this safely and delightedly. But if you make the mistake of putting something within range of his exploration that you don't want him to reach (a book, a vase, a glass knickknack), then you are responsible for the ensuing problem. Give him the right kind of environment and he will give you little trouble.

16

I N T E L L E C T U A L
S T I M U L A T I O N
I N T O D D L E R H O O D

When your child was in the stage of infancy, she was very curious about the world. She tried to discover all she could about it with her eyes, ears, mouth, hands, and body. But her discoveries were limited by her crawling range and limited, low-to-the-ground perspective.

In the stage of toddlerhood, all that is changed. Now she is upright and walking. And now her incredible curiosity knows no bounds.

Toddlerhood is the age of exploration. A scientist who has just discovered a new island filled with many new species of trees and plants and animals would not explore that island with any more zeal than your toddler explores her house or apartment and backyard—as long as you have childproofed it.

When you have childproofed your home, you need to fill it with interesting discoveries and playthings. You do not need to confine yourself to store-bought toys. Your child's playthings are her tools for finding out about the world, and there are all kinds of different materials that will help her in her research.

P L A Y T H I N G S   F O R   Y O U R   T O D D L E R

These can be scattered around the house or backyard. This may make your home resemble a junkyard, but if you can suspend your aesthetic sensibilities for just a year's time, you will be aiding your toddler enormously by providing these basic research materials for her.

''NATURAL''
MATERIALS

1. **WOOD SCRAPS** of different shapes and sizes.

> You can usually pick these up in the scrap pile where a building is being built, or in the scrap basket of a cabinet shop. Have the pieces cut up or cut them yourself in various interesting shapes and sizes. Be sure there are no splinters left. Also, put a few large plastic containers around, both indoors and outdoors, to hold the wood.

2. **ROCKS** from a river, lake, or ocean are particularly good because they have interesting shapes and handholds. They can be supplemented by some you buy at a landscape supply shop. As with the wood scraps, simply scatter them around the house and yard. Be sure none of

the rocks are small enough for your youngster to put in her mouth and choke on.

3. **TIN CANS AND PLASTIC CONTAINERS** of various sizes. These are particularly good for sand play in the outside sandbox, but they are handy inside as well. Be sure there are no sharp edges on the can.

4. **SAND.**
> *Sand is glorious magical stuff;*
> *I never can seem to get enough.*
> *I grab a fistful of nice warm sand,*
> *But somehow it slips right through my hand.*
> *I pack it with water in a cup*
> *And then I'm able to firm it up.*
> *Now I can press it tightly down*
> *And build myself a little town.*
> *A little town with houses and forts;*
> *To make it with water I have to use quarts!*

Sand is a special magic substance to a toddler. She loves to sift it and run her fingers through it. Sand is like no other substance she encounters in the world. If you build her an outside sandbox, make it as large as possible.

5. **WATER.** A small pool outside in good weather is great, but a bathtub has much fascination also. Your child discovers that some things float in water but others sink. You can help by providing food coloring or ice cubes so that she sees what these do to the water.

6. **MUD.**
> *Mother says*
> *That mud's a mess.*
> *But mud to me*
> *Is happiness.*

Many mothers are squeamish about allowing their toddler to play with mud; but if you can tolerate mud play, your youngster will find it a delightful substance. She can shape it and mold it, pound it and roll it, and squash it down flat.

Homemade play dough has much of the appeal of mud without the messiness. Here's the recipe: Mix two cups of flour with one cup of salt. Add just enough water to make it the consistency of bread dough. If it becomes too sticky, add more flour. By varying the recipe you can get dough of different textures. One or two drops of oil of cloves will help preserve it. It can then be stored in a plastic bag and will keep for approximately a month.

STORE-BOUGHT PLAYTHINGS (MOSTLY)

1. **WOODEN BLOCKS.** One of the most basic toys you can ever purchase for your child. Most parents get too few. Get at least seventy-five. Blocks lend themselves to all sorts of play.

2. **SMALL METAL CARS AND TRUCKS.** For use in the block cities your toddler constructs, either inside or in an outdoor sandbox.

3. A MINIATURE WORLD OF PEOPLE AND ANIMALS (FARM, WILD, DINOSAURS, ETC.). Get plastic, so the toys won't be damaged when they're left outside at night. Your toddler will choreograph the action of these people and animals for dramatic play. Since she is very conscious of her small size, she enjoys playing with people and animals much smaller than herself.

4. WATER TOYS TO FILL AND EMPTY. Bath toys for use in bath or pool. Pouring water from one size container to another will begin to give her a sense of proportions. Also, an old coffee percolator is for various reasons a never-ending source of fascination to a toddler. She uses it with sand; she uses it with water.

5. FITTING-TOGETHER TOYS. A box with different-shaped holes in its sides: square, rectangle, triangle, circle. It comes with objects that can be matched to the correct shapes and pushed inside the box.

6. STACKING TOYS. Circular toys which thread onto a long rod. Fisher-Price has some nice ones.

7. HOOK-TOGETHER TOYS. Trains and trucks with a hook on one end and a ring on the other.

8. DOLLS, SMALL TO LARGE. Childcraft, Galt Toys, and Fisher-Price have some excellent ones. Fisher-Price also has an interesting selection of small toy people in a variety of environments such as house, school, farm, and circus train.

The best dolls are those that do nothing and in which the play is in the child, not in the doll. Unfortunately, most dolls are the exact reverse of this. Avoid sexist stereotypes and make dolls available to boys as well as girls, but give either gender the freedom not to play with them. Not all children are interested in dolls.

9. DRESS-UP CLOTHES. Get clothes from Goodwill, the Salvation Army, garage sales, or wherever you can find them. Many times parents think that only girls want to dress up. This is not true. Your little boy enjoys dressing up and playing in Daddy-size clothes. Hats are important in the role playing, so try to find a wide selection.

10. HOUSEHOLD PLAY. Your child will follow you around as you do your housework, using her own small broom, dustpan, and dustcloth. She will also do these things by herself. Again, give both boys and girls a chance to do housework as play, but don't insist if they don't want to.

PHYSICAL PLAY

1. OUTDOOR CLIMBING EQUIPMENT. These include Cone Climber, Toddler's Gym, Commando Gym, and a scrambling net, as well as various other pieces of outdoor climbing equipment. Childcraft, Galt Toys, and Childlife Play Specialists have some excellent outdoor equipment.

    One fine piece of climbing equipment can be found in most houses. We call it stairs. Toddlers love to climb stairs. Many mothers fight this because they are afraid the toddler will fall. We suggest you let her climb under supervision at first, until she is sure enough of herself to climb safely.

2. SWINGING TOYS. An old car tire on a rope is one of the best outdoor toys yet invented.

3. THROWING AND CATCHING TOYS. Big, light, inflatable balls; balloons; and homemade bean bags filled with beans or lentils—each of these has distinctive play properties and your child enjoys all of them.

QUIET INTELLECTUAL PLAY

1. BOOKS. One of the finest things you can do for your child, as we have stressed repeatedly, is to read books to him. In toddlerhood most children are not ready for books with a continuous narrative or books that are too long. They love books that embody the "Label the Environment" game such as Richard Scarry's *Best Word Book Ever*. Beginning at about a year and a half, toddlers become even more enthusiastic about nursery rhymes. You can continue to use the Mother Goose rhymes, avoiding those whose concept or words are out of date or sexist. You can also continue reading Dr. Dodson's *I Wish I Had a Computer That Makes Waffles*. Or you can use the modern rhymes in "I Wish I Had a Computer That Makes Ice Cream Cones," which is a section of Dr. Dodson's book *Give Your Child a Head Start in Reading*.

2. MUSIC. Elsewhere we have suggested that you play recorded music of many different cultures to your baby. These same records can be played to your toddler. Now he can dance to them if he wishes. In addition, he can use percussion instruments, such as a xylophone or drums to play rhythms of his own.

3. DRAWING. If you feel comfortable with the idea, paint all four walls of your child's room with blackboard paint. He will then have a king-size blackboard on which to scribble endlessly and prepare himself for later learning to print or write. Give you child a chance to do finger painting too, if you can stand the mess.

With all of these, your toddler will have a wonderful group of toys to research and play with. Do him an additional favor. Rearrange his toys from time to time and they will seem like new to him. Weed out the broken ones and throw them away, unless they're something he is particularly attached to. Also, put a good-sized serendipity box in the family room, in which to keep all kinds of odds and ends—spools, wooden spoons, measuring cups, pan lids—these miscellaneous things add freshness to his playtime.

THE TODDLER AT PLAY

These are the materials your toddler needs in order to do a thorough job of exploring his world. He will look closely at them from every angle. He will feel them and rub them with his hands. He will put them in his mouth and gum them. He will examine them in every way he possibly can. For months he will play the role of explorer. You need only be an assistant. If he needs your help in some way, he will call on you, but you should not suggest to him what he should do. For example, here are a few things NOT to say to him. "Oh, look, Bryan, let's put these two blocks together and make a truck." Or, "These little houses will make a wonderful city, won't they?" Every time you do something like this, you are obstructing his natural instinct to explore.

Your toddler learns by sorting and classifying the objects in his world, like a botanist working on different kinds of plants, shrubs, and trees. He is mentally grouping the objects according to their similarities and differences, in the same way that a zoologist studies animals and a botanist studies plants. He may spend months in this kind of scientific exploration, and then his studies become more advanced. Whereas at first he merely examined keenly every object he could reach, now he tests out hypotheses using these objects to see what will happen.

For example, when he pushes a ball, it rolls, but when he pushes a wooden block, it does not roll. When he pushes a football, it rolls in a very strange fashion, different from the round ball.

In his scientific research, sooner or later he will try out Mother's Favorite Experiment—dropping food from his high chair. But as we said in the last chapter, he isn't being naughty. He is testing hypotheses. There are some things he needs help in doing, and he will usually call upon you. But as we mentioned before, he does not need an assistant who will take the lead away from him.

However, in your role as research assistant you will need to take the initiative in some ways. For example, your toddler's brother's room needs a lock to protect it from the diligent explorer. And as we said earlier, the bathroom also needs a lock unless you are willing to let part of his water play make use of the toilet bowl, and we doubt that you are.

THE OUTSIDE WORLD

In order for your child to expand his intellectual and creative horizons, you want to broaden his experience as much as possible. For example, try to view the shopping trip as a scientific expedition. By and large your child has seen few of these wonders before. It is fascinating for him to see the fresh fruits and vegetables, the cans, the frozen foods, etc. And a department store can seem like a fairyland palace. In fact, any shopping trip—to a lumber yard, to the Goodwill, to the drugstore—if you have the right focus, makes a fascinating scientific trip for him.

Take him on adventures. And use that word to describe them. Take him to places in his neighborhood such as the fire station, police station, a bakery, a welding shop. He will be fascinated by these new places and will probably enjoy coming back again because they offer him different things to look at. A very special adventure for him is the zoo, which probably has more interesting things than anywhere else. Here he can begin to learn the names of animals.

H   I   S   O   W   N   B   O   D   Y

In addition to all of the toys at your child's disposal, you want to teach him some things about himself, such as the parts of his body. You can touch the part of his body and say it out loud. At first he will merely absorb what you say, but later when you say, "What's this?" he will say, "nose," or "ear." Be sure to include the sexual organs, or your child will develop some unfortunate learning about the body parts you are *not* naming. By the time he's two, he should usually be able to locate and name his face, nose, ears, mouth, eyes, hair, chin, neck, tongue, teeth, shoulders, arms, hands, fingers, thumbs, elbows, chest, back, penis or vulva, anus, legs, knees, ankles, feet, and toes.

There are many things you can do to help him develop his language and learn to communicate. In many respects your toddler is like a new arrival in a foreign country who does not know how to speak the language but merely has a foreign phrase book. So when you talk with your child, you will want to use more than words. You and he will talk with gestures and body language as well. For example, if you say to him, "Matthew, now it's dinner time," point him in the direction of the table.

As he learns to talk, it's important not to correct his language. If you do that you will only make him self-conscious and hesitant about his speech. If he says "aminal" instead of "animal," which is a very common mistake of children, let it be. Sooner or later he will pronounce it right. If you correct him, that will discourage his language development, which begins with one-word sentences, then gradually advances to two-word sentences and continues from there.

Toddlerhood is probably the easiest stage of all in which to stimulate your child intellectually. He will do 90 percent of the work if you simply furnish him the material. It is such wonderful fun to watch this young being examining everything in his world and reacting with delight as he discovers what the world is like.

17

SPECIAL SITUATIONS IN TODDLERHOOD

In this chapter we will cover problems that often arise in toddlerhood and give you some suggestions for dealing with them. Some of these situations are similar to those we discussed in our chapters on infancy. In those cases, we will also refer you to the discussions in those chapters.

COMFORT HABITS

We talked about comfort habits in "Special Situations in Infancy," since this is usually when these habits first begin. However, their use peaks in toddlerhood and first adolescence.

Toddlers have a great deal of pent-up tension. They are at the peak of their anxiety over separating from Mother, and they are also in the midst of their struggle to master themselves and their environment. They will use their comfort habit (a blanket, a "lovey," a pacifier, thumb sucking, hair twirling) to help them relieve anxiety. The more motor-minded child often releases tension by rhythmic activities such as rocking, head banging, or head rolling.

These are all very normal activities. The need for them arises with fatigue, anxiety, sadness, frustration, or anger. As your child acquires better verbal skills and self-control, his need for comfort habits decreases. But don't be surprised to see them crop up again during times of stress.

If your child seems to be needing comfort so much that it keeps him from exploring his world or interacting socially, look for the cause of his anxiety. Try to change the stressful situation if you can. Give him extra love and support. If he continues to feel very anxious, you'll need to consult with your doctor for other possible solutions.

Overall, your child's use of comfort habits is a very resourceful way to deal with stress. Don't be concerned. And, above all, don't add to the stress by teasing or scolding him or trying to make him give them up.

ROCKING AND HEAD BANGING

There are two types of comfort habits that sometimes concern parents: rocking (on all fours or in a sitting position) and head banging. Because these are also self-stimulatory actions in children who have handicapping conditions such as mental retardation or autism, they have in some people's minds become associated with these conditions. But do not become alarmed. These habits are also very common in perfectly normal little boys and girls. The rockers and head bangers are often very intense, persistent, active children, who build up a great deal of tension and need more vigorous release. If your child seems perfectly normal in every way, if he relates to you and other people affectionately, is developing well, and behaves this way only when tired or frustrated rather than to entertain himself, the behavior will pass. However, rocking and head banging can be disruptive to the household, and there are measures you can take to keep things more peaceful.

If your child is a rocker, he can be pretty "earthshaking" at bedtime and in the middle of the night. The rockers often shake, rattle, and roll the crib right across the room and into the wall. Try some environmental control. For example, take the wheels off the crib. Set the crib on a rug or carpet. Pad the sides of the crib, for sound insulation and wall protection. Even better, put adhesive cork squares on the wall where the crib hits. Be sure all of the screws on the crib are especially tight and the metal parts are well oiled.

Some parents have found that rocking can be reduced by increasing the settling-down time with their child at bedtime. Try rocking together in a chair or gentle dancing together to soft music until the child is quite sleepy.

The head banger is the one who startles and concerns parents even more because the child can bang his head against the crib, wall, or floor hard enough to leave bumps. However, it is never hard enough to make the child cry; he's smarter than that. The head banger, as we said, is usually the more intense, persistent child and also may be particularly sensitive to music and have a good singing voice. He can sometimes be distracted from his head banging with music or by offering him a toy. Head banging usually occurs when the child is tired. At bedtime, hand banging may be decreased by the same tactics for rocking: soft music and gentle dancing or rocking with the child. This does not mean the head banging will totally disappear, since he may awake during the night and use it to settle himself back to sleep. Pad the crib so there will be less noise and let him bang. Most head bangers no longer need to do this by the time they are three years old and have developed good language skills.

T E M P E R   T A N T R U M S

Temper tantrums often begin to appear in toddlerhood, especially in the more intense, difficult-to-manage child. This child experiences an incredible amount of tension, and the tantrum is an explosion of the frustration and rage that have built up inside him. He doesn't have the communication skills to tell you how he feels or the self-control to channel the explosion into more acceptable outlets. He really has no control.

Screaming is a part of every tantrum, but some children will also run around the room wildly, accidentally knocking things over. Other children throw themselves on the floor, hitting, kicking, or even head banging.

Your child's tantrums can be so intense that they shake you right down to your toes. They usually fill you with anger and frustration at your inability to control him. If you are in a public place, you are also embarrassed by what you fear people are thinking of you and him. Remember that as hard as tantrums are for you, they are even harder for your toddler. At this age he is not having a tantrum to defy you. He has simply lost control, and this loss of control scares and overwhelms him.

PREVENTION

The best way to handle tantrums is to prevent them from happening. The typical time for a tantrum is when the child is tired, hungry, overstimulated, or, most of all, frustrated. You can avoid frustration build-up by steering him away from situations that exceed his capabilities, being as pleasant and tactful about it as possible; and by avoiding confrontations, though definitely setting limits.

Here is an example of frustration avoidance through environmental control. It is the end of the day and Mom is trying to fix dinner, answer the telephone, and keep an eye on twenty-month-old Timmy who is playing in the corner. He has a plastic milk bottle with a soggy raisin inside. He is tired and hungry. He has always been able to get raisins out of the bottle before, but this one won't come. He begins to whine, shaking the bottle violently, then banging the bottle on the floor as the whine becomes louder and louder. His mother can see the tension and frustration building. She excuses herself from the telephone and goes over to Timmy.

Mother: "Timmy is having a hard time." Timmy whines in a high-pitched voice.

Mother: "That old bottle is making you so mad, it won't let the raisin come out. Let's see. It looks like that old raisin is too sticky. Let's try another dry one that's not sticky. There it goes!" She slips a new raisin into the bottle, extracting the old one with the end of a spoon.

Mother: "I'll bet Timmy can do it now." Timmy grabs the bottle, turns it upside down in the way he's learned, and there it is. A big smile spreads over his face and relief is apparent. Disaster has been averted.

HOW TO HANDLE
A TANTRUM

What if this situation had occurred while you, his mom, were on the telephone with your back turned, tending a pot on the stove, not able to see Timmy's plight. His tension and frustration could escalate until finally he explodes in a rage, throwing himself on the floor, kicking and screaming and throwing the bottle across the room. Here it is, his first tantrum. What can you do? There are several lessons you can teach him, now that the tantrum has occurred. The first is that even though *he* is out of control, *you* are not. So you will not get angry and scold him, which only adds fuel to the fire and escalates his anger. You can teach him that his feelings are normal and acceptable. You can give him words to label his feelings, so that as he matures he can begin to use words rather than having to use kicking and screaming to let you know how he feels. You can help him gain control of himself.

Go over and sit on the floor beside him and gently pick him up, stroking and soothing him with the words, "Timmy, pull yourself together. I will help you."

He won't be able to settle down right away, but it helps to have you there beside him to hold and comfort him and to let him know that you accept him and understand his feelings. As he quiets down, you can give him the words he needs to learn to be able to handle these rages in a more acceptable fashion later. Say, "Poor Timmy has had a hard time. He wants that raisin, and that yucky old bottle won't give it to him. He feels so mad because he can't get it. That's frustrating!" And after he is calmer, if he indicates that he wants to persist in trying to succeed at the task, and it's possible, you can by all means help him. In this case, teach him some skills for getting the soggy raisin out of the bottle.

HOW NOT TO HANDLE A TANTRUM

There is one lesson you definitely do not want to teach him. You do not want to teach him that tantrums are worthwhile for controlling his parents. Let's say that the tantrum came about because you would not give Timmy a piece of candy that he badly wanted. Giving him the candy after the tantrum has subsided would teach him the wrong lesson.

Just as you do not want to reward a tantrum by giving your child something he has been denied, you should not punish it by denying him something which was originally intended, such as a walk or an outing in the park. It is better to go on about your business after a tantrum, making it as unimportant as possible.

Some children do not like to be held during a tantrum and become even more angry because their movement is being frustrated. This is often the child who tends to run around screaming and flailing his arms. In this case, try to protect him from harm. Also, remove breakables from the room so that he won't be ashamed later when he is back in control, because he has done damage. Stay calmly by and wait for him to subside. Then soothe him and use the same techniques for labeling his feelings. The lessons you can teach your toddler in these tense experiences are the first of many to help him develop self-control.

You may have heard that the best way to handle a temper tantrum is to ignore it, as you would with other bad behavior. This is appropriate for the older child who has tantrums but has some ability for self-control and communicating his feelings. However, with a younger child who is frightened by his lack of self-control, ignoring such behavior would seem almost heartless. Consider your own feelings if, for example, you have had a particularly frustrating day, you come home angry and frustrated, slamming the door and muttering to yourself, and your husband simply turns away and ignores you.

TANTRUMS OUTSIDE THE HOME

What do you do when your child has one of these temper outbursts while you are shopping? If you feel that everyone is staring at you and you are embarrassed, carry your toddler out to the car even if it means leaving a cartful of groceries sitting in the aisle. You can always come back to them. If the car is not readily available, go to the restroom where you can be more private until he is settled down. Then go on about your business, unless he is so tired and hungry that another outburst is likely to occur—in which case, give up on the shopping and go home. Do try to avoid taking him with you when he is about to be in such a state.

SLEEP PROBLEMS

We have said that sleep problems begin occurring in later infancy. These continue on into toddlerhood and are the result of the child's separation anxiety and the excessive stimulation he receives all day with his newfound independence. Additional sleep problems arise from the change in your toddler's need for daytime sleep; that is, the gradual moving from two naps a day to one nap a day. It's that in-between period, when he really needs one and a half naps, that can be the bear.

NAPS

The switch from two naps to one may require a great deal of patience and juggling on your part. You will really not be able to tell when and for how long your toddler will be sleeping during the day. Some toddlers stay awake after breakfast, only to go to sleep at 11:30 in the morning and sleep through lunch. Others go to sleep right after breakfast, wake up around 12:30 and eat lunch, but are no longer ready for an afternoon nap; then they run out of steam at 5:00. All of these require adjustments, either very early lunches or very early dinners.

Your youngster's one nap a day may be exceptionally long. You may need to wake him up in order to get your shopping done, pick up his older sibling, or do any of your other normal outside-the-house duties. If you do need to awaken your toddler, be sure to allow plenty of time before you expect him to do anything. He will be extremely grouchy and resistant. He won't want to eat, he won't want to get dressed, he won't want to move. He will need extra cuddling and soothing, probably for fifteen to thirty minutes before the show can get on the road. If you have not allowed for this time it can result in a confrontation which both of you would rather avoid.

BEDTIME RESISTANCE

Resistance to going to sleep at night often begins in late infancy, but if not then, it will begin in toddlerhood. The reason for this is that by nighttime your youngster is both overstimulated and overtired. Also, the whole family is home, and being with them is much more inviting than going to bed. The bedroom is dark, and somehow separation seems so final.

It is important not to change the bedtime ritual, which we discussed in "The Daily Care of Your Infant." Just realize that it may take longer now, with more rocking, singing, or soothing, especially if your child is the active type. It may take him thirty to forty-five minutes to unwind after his day. Some children handle the transition better by listening to tapes or records. If you can get the type of phonograph that plays the record over and over, you can prevent the trauma that occurs when the record ends. Your child will need a night light and some books or toys in the bed to entertain himself with. If he has had a nice long bath and a quiet story he will usually be relaxed enough to go off to sleep. Even if your child learned in infancy to settle down on his own at night, he will probably fuss now. But tuck him in, kiss him, and say good night.

If your youngster whimpers as you are leaving the room, don't turn back. Let him try to settle down on his own. Sometimes the crying becomes insistent enough that you know he is upset and scared. The bedtime lesson may have begun in infancy, but you need to continue to reinforce it now: You are available to him when he is scared, but he will not be allowed to leave his room. You expect him to be able to settle himself. Read our section on "Bedtime Blues" for more suggestions on how you can help.

Do not forget to praise him the next morning if he has settled down without crying. Reward him with something special: a sticker, a star, or a happy face on a chart. Continue rewarding and praising until he is consistent in settling down without fussing.

THE CRIB CLIMBER

This is the age of the crib climber. He is usually the difficult-to-manage child or the very motor-minded child. He makes bedtime even more miserable for you. If you have been able to keep him in the sleeping-bag nightwear in which there are no slots for feet, therefore decreasing his mobility, he is unlikely to climb out of the crib—he can't get his legs apart. If he refuses this kind of nightwear, then try lowering the mattress. If this fails, monitor him closely. Catch him in the act or catch him before he gets out of his room. Put him back into the bed matter-of-factly, without talking. Do this consistently, and he will learn that climbing out of the crib will get him nowhere. You may need to get yourself one of those portable intercoms so that you can hear the activity in his room and get in there before he gets out the door. Or try a gate at the door to keep him in until you can put him back to bed. Praise and reward him every time he stays in bed.

Sometimes, in spite of your consistently putting your child back to bed for a week or two, he persists in climbing out of his crib. Since this can result in falls and injuries, you had better put his mattress on the floor. Be extra sure his room has been childproofed, and keep him confined to his room with a gate. He will eventually fall asleep in spite of himself. You may find him sleeping on the floor and not his bed, but you can always move him. Again, don't forget to praise and reward him when he has shown appropriate behavior.

IF AT FIRST YOU DON'T SUCCEED...

When you first start using these techniques, expect your child to be fairly difficult for a few nights, especially if you have let him get up sometimes in the past. He is testing to see if you really mean it now. He will gradually learn that you do.

This learning may take several weeks. And bedtime problems may return after several months of calm if your youngster has had a particularly stressful time, such as the advent of a new baby, a move, an illness, or a new sitter. Simply repeat your routine until it takes hold again.

Sometimes a parent who has only one child, or whose schedule allows for extra time, will stay in her child's room until he is asleep. Or if the child is in a big bed, she will lie down with him and stroke or pat him until he is asleep. It is wonderfully comforting and reassuring for the child. In some cases this presents no problems, unless a new baby arrives on the scene, or the parent has to go out at night, or the parent is sick or unavailable. This usually results in some real problems in the child's getting to sleep, especially for the persistent child or the one who is slow to adapt. But if there are no such disturbing events, the child will gradually need to have the parent with him less and less as he approaches the end of his anxiety about separation, usually by the age of three. If this is something you want to do, by all means go ahead and do it. It does give you a nice cuddly time with your child. But be aware of the hazards!

If you start the routine of staying with your child and then find you've had enough before he is ready to give it up, tell him you can no longer do that and he is old enough now to go to sleep alone. Help him with the change by letting him know that after this story (or song or rocking) it will be sleep time and you will leave the room. Carry out the recommendations for bedtime resistance. It may take time, but if you stick to your guns he'll settle down. Use a positive reward system to help him learn more quickly.

STAYING WITH THE CHILD

It is perfectly normal to awaken briefly and fall right back to sleep several times at night. But your toddler may begin to have trouble falling back to sleep. The suggestions we've made in our "Infancy" section are still helpful now.

Another reason for a child's awakening at night at this age is nightmares, or night terrors. It is important if your child does wake up crying and frightened that you go to him as soon as you can in order to prevent the anxiety from escalating. Usually, just soothing and patting him is enough to get him back to sleep. Do not stimulate him further by taking him out of bed, feeding him, or talking to him excessively.

Night waking can also be caused by your toddler's teething, which can be quite uncomfortable. Use the suggestions offered in the teething section of "Special Situations in Infancy."

NIGHT WAKING

Here is a checklist to avoid other causes of night waking.

- Eliminate outside noises.
- Make sure that your child is not too cold or too warm.
- Make sure that he is not too wet (double diaper and use diaper liners).

HOW TO DEAL WITH NIGHT WAKING

• Make sure that his "lovey" or pacifier is where he can reach it.
• Make sure that he is well fed before bedtime.
• Put a cracker and water (in a bottle or a lidded cup) on a table or stool nearby, in case he is hungry in the night.

Some toddlers get up at night and wander around the house. This can be a dangerous situation. You can keep him in his room by using a gate at the door or a latch on the outside of his door. If you feel uncomfortable doing this, you can hang bells on his doorknob to awaken you. Put him back to bed matter-of-factly each time, advising him that wandering at night is not allowed.

The toddler often awakens early in the morning, much to a parent's chagrin. You can get a few more minutes of sleep if you have some toys on the table next to the bed, so he can entertain himself. Crackers and water by the bed will help tide him over until breakfast. However, an older sibling in the same room is infinitely more wonderful, since they will often play together for an hour or more. If you have an alarm clock that your toddler can hear, and if you go in to him as soon as it rings, he will soon learn that he can depend on that and not yell for you before the alarm goes off.

F E A R S   A N D   P H O B I A S

Because toddlerhood can be a time of anxiety, your toddler may begin expressing fears of things that he has previously never seemed concerned about. He may be frightened by loud noises such as sirens, the vacuum cleaner, or the lawn mower. Or he may become fearful of animals, especially dogs, snakes, or bugs. He may also be afraid of such things as the flushing of the toilet and the draining of the water in the bathtub, almost as though he's afraid he will go down along with the water. He is not putting you on: He is truly afraid of these things. They seem unreasonable to you, but they are very reasonable and real to him.

M A S T E R I N G   F E A R S

Your first step to help your youngster master these fears is to accept his feelings. You do *not* need to act afraid yourself, and if you happen to share his aversion to animals such as snakes, dogs, or insects, it would be best if you could mask it. But don't scoff at him, telling him not to be silly or not to be afraid. It won't work. Above all, don't force him into a situation he fears. However, you can reassure him. "Stevie, that dog scares you, doesn't he? He looks big and scary, but he won't hurt you. Come here. Mommy will hold you. You don't have to touch him, but Mommy can pet him." You have accepted his fear, reassured him, offered him comfort by holding him, but have also shown him that the object does not frighten you.

Sometimes if you know that your child has a fear of something it helps if you can prepare him for the situation before it occurs. For example, perhaps your toddler is afraid of thunder storms. So when you see that a storm is imminent, express your delight with nature's fireworks. You know your child is frightened during the storm, so make the situation as pleasant and comfortable for him as you can. Hold him snuggly in your arms with his favorite "lovey," rocking gently in a rocking chair, in a spot where you have a view of the sky. One word of caution: Do not sit directly in front of a window or in an open doorway, since that might actually expose you to lightning. As you hold and rock your child and you see lightning, anticipate the sound of the thunder, playing a game of making thunder noises and then laughing when it does occur. If he still seems frightened, acknowledge that thunder storms can be scary, but reassure him that he is safe. It may take more than one session, but you will gradually help him to overcome this fear.

Many children can overcome their fears by acting out the fearful situation or taking on the role of the feared object, such as playing that they are a dog, a snake, or a bug. *Remember that play is a child's way of working.* By playing out his fears he is *working* them out. When a child has been frightened by a large animal, such as a big dog that has leaped on him and knocked him down, he may also need gradual exposure to a smaller, quieter version of such an animal to overcome his fear.

PHOBIAS

Sometimes the child's fear can become so intense that rather than occurring only at the time the fearful situation is present, it is carried over into his imagination. If he is afraid of a dog, he may be afraid of toy dogs and pictures of dogs in books. He may even fear that there might be a dog on one of his outings, and refuse to take his usual walk. This fear is known as a phobia. This should be handled in the same way as other fears. Prepare your child for the possibility of the event, acting out what might happen and what he can do. Accept his fear, but at the same time reassure him that you will not allow him to be hurt. Play games in which he can become the feared object, and in that way feel he has some control over it. If possible, make the exposure to the feared object a very gradual one. Associate it with distracting and pleasant situations, such as cuddling and rocking during the thunderstorm. Or take him on a special outing to the mall and buy him an ice cream cone to lick on while looking in the windows of the pet shop with the puppies romping about.

If you use these techniques over a period of time, you will help your toddler overcome his phobia. If the phobia does persist in spite of these efforts and it becomes a deterrent to your social life, consult with your physician for a referral to a psychologist or a psychiatrist.

SIBLING RIVALRY

Toddlerhood is the first stage in which sibling rivalry raises its somewhat ugly head, since that is the earliest stage in which a younger sibling can arrive. Many people seem to be puzzled by rivalry among brothers and sisters. Some are convinced it does not exist. But I (FD) remember seeing a Punch and Judy show a number of years ago in which Punch asked the audience what he should do with a little baby. The three- and four-year-olds in the audience, many of whom were supposed by their mothers to be free of sibling rivalry would scream, "Flush him down the toilet!" "Kick him!" "Throw him over the fence!"

Sibling rivalry is something that all children have, and at times it consists of a fierce and deep jealousy and hatred of the other children in the family, particularly the younger ones. This jealousy and hatred may be covered over with a veneer of friendliness and goodwill, but it is there, just the same. This does not mean, however, that it is not also accompanied by a fierce and deep love, which will definitely show up should the sibling be threatened by an outsider.

Sibling rivalry is based on a simple psychological fact. When a child has enjoyed 100 percent of her parents' attention, she resents it deeply when some "intruder" comes into the family and takes away part of that attention.

HOW TO DEAL WITH SIBLING RIVALRY

Once you understand the reason for sibling rivalry, you can understand that it can be lessened but never eliminated. It is usually more intense in first children toward their younger siblings. One study found that every child in the family felt that the other children got a better deal than she did! A younger child especially does not understand how parents can have enough love to be divided up. And your toddler has no way of telling you she feels jealous. She will need your help. Remember too that the toddler is going through her own period of self-assertion and aggression, even with children who aren't related.

What can you do for the toddler who now has a young sibling on the scene? First you will have helped her a great deal if you have prepared her ahead of time for the baby's arrival. If she is still in a crib, don't displace her for the baby. Don't change her room around. Make the homecoming special by having the baby's father or baby-sitter take the baby as soon as you come home. Give your toddler your complete, undivided attention. Hold her, cuddle her, tell her how much you have missed her. Don't discuss the baby at all. Let your toddler decide when she wants to see or hold the baby. Her natural curiosity will take her there. Help her to feel like a big girl and let her do as much as possible in helping to care for the baby. Give her a doll baby to feed and care for while you care for the baby. But make sure that she has some special one-to-one time with you each day. In this way you are teaching her that there is enough of you to go around.

JEALOUSY

Nevertheless, there are going to be times when your toddler feels jealous but is not able to express it. You can help her to do this without bopping the baby on the head with a block or pulling his hair. You can lessen her jealousy by saying mildly nasty things to her about the baby. For example, "Babies can be pretty yucky sometimes. All they do is cry." This gives your toddler a chance to get out some of her hostile feelings toward the baby safely. If she handles her doll roughly or aggressively, give her some feedback. "Lucy doesn't like that baby. She's so mad that she feels like hurting him. Baby brothers make her mad too."

Be sure to avoid two mistakes that many parents make in handling sibling jealousy.

MISTAKES TO AVOID

1. They try to convince the older child that she is a big girl now and doesn't need to act that way. This is not usually very successful, because she figures that maybe if she acts like the baby she'll get as much attention.
2. When the older child expresses anger toward the baby, many parents try to shush her and tell her that it's her sweet little brother and she shouldn't talk that way. Well, she doesn't see the baby as her sweet little brother. She sees him as a crummy intruder who has taken away some of her mother's and father's affection.

So allow your toddler to vent any angry feelings that she has. And if she wants to regress back to being a baby and drinking out of a bottle, let her. It won't do her any harm, and she will soon grow out of it.

THE TODDLER AS YOUNGER SIBLING

On the other side of the coin, what if the toddler is the younger sibling? Imagine your preschooler's feelings when all of a sudden the immobile little baby sister he has just begun to really care about becomes a holy terror. She is constantly getting into his room and destroying his carefully built Lego-Land or block castles. Your toddler will also want to do many of the things her brother does. She furiously resents being shut out when her brother has a friend over.

Your toddler and preschooler may play together quite nicely for brief periods of time, but often you will need to divert the toddler's attention to her own activities in order to give the preschooler some privacy. Environmental control is definitely in order. This is an age when the older sibling may enjoy being in the playpen, in order to be protected from the toddler while he does some writing or drawing. If the children have separate bedrooms, put a lock on the preschooler's door—one that can be locked from the inside when he wants to have some quiet time to build or play on his own. The door should also be latchable from the outside to keep the toddler out of the room when her brother is away.

QUARRELING

Remember that all children quarrel. Brothers and sisters just have more opportunities to do it, and sibling rivalry adds the extra ingredient that makes the sparks fly. In most cases you should try to let the children settle their quarrels on their own, but this may be difficult as the toddler's reasoning abilities and empathy are not too well developed. If there is heavy squabbling and it seems that someone will be hurt, you will need to intervene. Try not to act as a referee and blame one or the other. Certainly if you have seen the whole altercation and know exactly what happened, there is no reason that you cannot make a judgment. But if you are not sure what happened, it is best to separate the children nonjudgmentally until the dust settles.

If it seems that your siblings are fighting more and more frequently, and that one seems to be starting it, that sibling may be feeling neglected. Sit down and help her to label her feelings. For instance, I (AA) noticed that Katie and Kimberly seemed to be at it more than usual. Katie did not miss a chance when she walked by Kimberly, who was twenty months old and often intent on her own pursuits, to shove her, pinch her, or give her other little "love pats." I realized that Kimberly had been ill with an ear infection, requiring extra rocking and soothing, at Katie's expense. One day Katie had been sent to her room for a Time Out after being particularly aggressive. I went to her at the end of the Time Out for a chat. It went something like this.

Mom: "Katie, you sure have been pretty mad at Kimberly lately. She is really bugging you."

Katie: "Yeah, I hate her. She is an old dummy girl. I wish she would get flushed down the toilet. She is an old poo-poo." [Katie was a four-year-old and really into bathroom language.]

Mom: "Yeah, I can understand that. Kimberly has been taking a lot of Mom's time since she has been sick. Doesn't seem like there is time for Katie anymore."

Katie: "Yeah, that's right. Nobody loves *me* anymore, just dummy old Kimmy."

Mom: "Since Kimmy has been sick I have missed having a special time with you too. Would you like to make a special date and go out to lunch with me to McDonald's?"

Katie: "I'd love it. Can Kimmy come too?"

Once the jealousy and anger were accepted, her deep-down love for her sister came through and she couldn't imagine going without her! This did not mean that they would now be friendly on a day-to-day basis, but there was hope for the future!

Remember that the only way you can get rid of sibling jealousy completely is to throw out one of the children. And surely you don't want to handle it that way! So simply resign yourself to the fact that as long as you have two or more children they are going to feel rivalry. Give them a chance to express the hostility they feel toward each other, but in words only, not in deed. And remember, despite their rivalry your children will have a loving and caring friend in each other if each feels appreciated and accepted for who she is.

B A B Y - S I T T E R S

We covered the topic of baby-sitters in our "Special Situations in Infancy," and we suggest that you read that section now if you have not already, since many of our suggestions apply to toddlerhood as well. At this stage there are also some additional concerns.

Remember that your toddler is an active child, into everything. You need a mature baby-sitter who can handle emergencies well. Leaving your toddler with a baby-sitter, even a familiar and loved one, often results in protests. Your child is at the peak of separation anxiety. She'll pull out all the stops to keep you home—crying, calling, clinging. It can break your heart and make you feel guilty. But it is good for you and your child to have some time away from each other, and good for you and your spouse to have time alone. It's also good for your child to learn to be with other caretakers and learn that when you leave, you will return.

It's not your child's protests at separating that you should be concerned about. It's her behavior during the separation. Does she settle down and play contentedly after a few minutes? Or is she sad and fussy the whole time? It's normal for a toddler to call your name and look for you at some time while you're away but for the most part she should be able to cope. If she isn't, you need to take a closer look at the situation. Is the sitter new? Have you recently moved? Has your child been separated from you for a long time recently because of hospitalization or your taking a trip without her? These can be very upsetting.

You may find it helpful to stay with your child and a new sitter for some trial visits until your youngster seems more comfortable with the situation. Then make your first outings very brief, an hour or so, to teach her that you will return. Be sure the sitter knows the routines and rituals and that she is engaged in a fun activity with your child when you leave. And continue to use the same leavetaking rituals developed during infancy, if they give her extra security.

What about long trips away from the children? You'll obviously need the most familiar and best-loved sitter you can get. Your prolonged absence is much harder for the toddler. If you can, avoid long trips during this period. But sometimes being away for more than a day or so is unavoidable. It helps if you leave your picture in your child's room. A tape of you reading one or two of her favorite bedtime stories as well as some words of encouragement and reassurance of your return also helps ease the sadness. Be sure to leave extra batteries for the tape recorder. Kimberly wore ours out listening to me (AA) on the tape while I was away. A phone call can cheer your child, but it isn't really quite as good as a tape, because with the tape, your toddler can hear your voice whenever she wants.

Be prepared for a rough time when you get home. I (AA) have had many a mother moan that the week away for a vacation almost wasn't worth what her toddler put her through on her return. Your toddler will feel angry with you for leaving and may ignore you at first. If she is an intense child, like our Katie, she may clobber you! Let her know you understand and accept her feelings. Be available for the extra holding and loving she'll need for the next few days. She'll get over her anger in a hurry and then will probably stick to you like glue.

ENVIRONMENTAL CHANGES

In "Special Situations in Infancy" we discussed environmental changes such as having company, traveling, visiting other people, and moving. We urge that you read this section, since our recommendations there hold true for the toddler. There are some special considerations in toddlerhood, however.

TRAVELING   One of these is traveling by car. Your toddler definitely does not like to sit still for long periods of time. And since she is also interested in being self-assertive and independent, she will balk at being in her car seat. You will need to be calm and matter-of-fact about it. Tell her that the car cannot go until she is buckled in her seat. Put her in it and buckle her in, despite the screams of protest. Try to distract her with toys, special books, and storybook tapes. If she yells, screams, and begs, ignore her even though it is a teeth-gritting experience. The minute she becomes quiet, pat her and praise her for being quiet. Try to get her involved in conversation and looking out her window. Do not let her out of her seat; you are only rewarding her and reinforcing the yelling and screaming. Smile at her and touch her often when she is sitting quietly in her seat.

Keep car trips short, with frequent breaks. Your toddler cannot stay cooped up in a car for more than two hours at a time. On long trips, plan to stop in places where she can run around—in a park, a zoo, or even a rest stop on the side of the road. Make your motel reservations in advance, and be sure a crib is readily available. Your toddler needs exercise, plenty of rest, and on-time meals to preserve your sanity and hers. Take her favorite comfort object along and have the spare available. Don't let her take her "lovey" out of the car at rest stops though, since it can inadvertently be left behind, creating a disaster. Have a grab bag full of favorite old toys and books and some new ones to help pass the time. Take easy snacks such as peanut butter crackers and juices that she can drink in her lidded cup, to tide her over until mealtime.

Some toddlers ride easily at night, sleeping comfortably in their car seat. If you have been blessed with such a child, you can make better time by driving at night. Remember, however, to put her into her pajamas so that she is in as familiar a situation as possible. Be realistic in your expectations, however. Travel with a toddler takes twice as long as it would otherwise.

For very long trips, traveling by air is the best alternative. Ask to bring your toddler's car seat on the plane in order to ensure her safety in the event of sudden bumps or jolts. Otherwise, belt her in or seat her securely on your lap during the trip. Be sure to have extra changes of clothing and extra supplies of food in case of delays.

MOVING   A major change like moving to a new home is particularly scary to the toddler. Use the same precautions as you would if she were an infant and be prepared for some regression and sleep problems with the change.

PETS

We discussed pets at length in "Special Situations in Infancy," and our recommendations for toddlerhood are the same but even more cautious. The toddler, in her exploring and aggressiveness, can get herself into some difficult situations with pets that bite. She also puts everything in her mouth, including dirt. If you already have a pet, keep it free of parasites and your toddler's play area free of pet feces to avoid infecting your child (see "Health Care").

ACCIDENT PREVENTION

The first thing you need to realize about accident prevention is that to compel your toddler to live in an exclusively adult house is highly dangerous for her. So the first thing you need to do with your house and backyard is to childproof it. This is so important that we stress it in two of our chapters on toddlerhood, and we go into even more detail about safety in our health care chapter. Please take the time to read it. You will be glad you did.

CHILDPROOF YOUR HOME

By childproofing your home, we mean to remove breakable or dangerous objects so that your youngster cannot get to them. She should be free to roam and explore the house, without danger to herself or your possessions.

Remember that your toddler's judgment and powers of observation are very limited. She cannot be taught yet to discriminate between what is safe and what is unsafe. And everything she discovers and researches goes into her mouth. The experts estimate that 60 to 90 percent of all accidents that seriously injure or kill very young children could have been prevented if the parents had taken proper precautions to childproof their house.

We are not going to provide you with an elaborate safety checklist, because you could check the items off the list and promptly forget about the day-to-day concerns for your child's safety. Instead, we want you to develop an awareness of the kinds of things that might be harmful to her. In a way, we want you to see your house the way your toddler sees it. You think of the aspirin in the medicine cabinet as the tablets you take one or two at a time for a headache. And you think of the vitamins in the kitchen cupboard as pills you take each day to keep you healthy. But your toddler will look at these bottles and see that they are full of a new and fascinating kind of candy, not knowing that eating a whole bottle of this candy can make her deathly sick. So make a systematic trip through your entire house, including the basement, backyard, and garage. Try your best to see it through the eyes of your toddler.

THE CAR

Your car can also be a source of great danger. It is amazing how quickly a toddler can release the emergency brake, lock herself inside, perhaps turn on the ignition, or fall out of a window. Never leave your toddler in the car while you run into a store on an errand. Always take her with you. Remember too that a car safety seat is a MUST, even though your toddler may object to its confinement. If you insist that she use it at all times, she will eventually adjust to it and automatically jump into it. You must be consistent, however.

PLAN AHEAD FOR EMERGENCIES   It is a wise idea to sit down with your spouse and think about emergencies ahead of time. Read our chapter on "The Well Child" to help prepare yourselves.

Remember too that any baby-sitter you hire should be as well informed as you are. This means also that the sitter should be mature enough to handle emergencies. A thirteen-year-old who has taken a baby-sitting course and is responsible and experienced with children would probably be the youngest sitter who could handle your toddler.

It may seem like a great deal of trouble to take all of these precautions. It is! But once you childproof your home and have prepared for emergencies, then feel free to let your toddler explore to her heart's content. You will have the security of knowing that your home is a safe environment for her. When you visit other people, keep your eyes open there too for potential hazards, and do as much childproofing as you possibly can. Don't expect to have long, lazy visits when you go with a toddler, however!

PART 4

F I R S T

A D O L E S C E N C E

18

OVERVIEW OF FIRST ADOLESCENCE

You often hear this stage called the "terrible twos." It is an accurate enough name, because kids are usually terrible at this age, between two and three (or even as early as eighteen months). But it is not a particularly helpful name, because it does not give parents any inkling as to *why* kids are so terrible at this age or how they can cope with them. We prefer the term *first adolescence*, because this stage is so similar to the *second* adolescence that occurs in the teenage years: a teenage child, in transition from childhood to adulthood, is rebellious and defiant, and his parents find him very unpredictable; he is very different from the child he was a few years earlier.

These things are also true of the first adolescent. He, too, is in transition—from babyhood to true childhood. He swings back and forth psychologically, moving up toward true childhood, and then regressing back to acting like a baby. He is feeling good enough about himself to make that final break with babyhood and will even try to achieve the maturity and independence of the next stage of development, the preschool stage. But it's not easy for him.

As a toddler, your child was not ordinarily rebellious and defiant. But as a first adolescent, he is. His favorite word seems to be "No!" Why is he so defiant? Because for the first time in his life he is attempting, through his behavior, his thoughts, and his feelings, to answer the question, Who am I?

Let's face it, first adolescence is not an easy or pleasant stage for your child or for you. But although your child's mood swings, rebelliousness, and negativism make life rough for you, don't forget that they are actually positive steps for him. And no matter how much it may sometimes seem that he is in a power struggle with you, he is not. His struggle is only with himself. And without this struggle he would remain stuck in babyhood. Try to look beneath the rebellious and stormy surface of his behavior and view it as a positive and dynamic thrust toward a strong and powerful self-identity.

A first adolescent reminds us of the exuberant words of Zorba the Greek: "Without a touch of madness a man will not have the courage to cut the rope and find out who he really is!"

EXPLOSIVE NATURE

The first adolescent's surging personality force can make him explosive at times. Not necessarily all the time. If that were so, probably none of us would survive to parent a second child. Some youngsters are mildly explosive. Some are horrendously explosive (you guessed it, usually the intense, persistent, difficult-to-manage child). But all are explosive to one degree or another. It can be quite shocking to your parental nervous system if this is your first child. You have been an adult for a number of years and have become used to dealing with adults. When you ask an adult a question, he answers you reasonably politely. He doesn't throw a building block at you. He doesn't burst into tears and start screaming. He doesn't yell, "I won't, I won't, and you can't make me."

But you can't change the explosive nature of your first adolescent, so you will simply have to get used to it. There are, however, some guidelines we can give to help you and your child during this time.

As we have said before, it's very important to distinguish between your child's actions and your child's feelings. Your child cannot control his feelings, but he can learn to control his actions. Your first adolescent needs to know what he is allowed to do and what he is not allowed to do. But he will need very firm guidance, given in the most diplomatic way possible, of course.

Does all this sound rather overwhelming? Don't be discouraged; nature is kind to us in many ways. She gives us some breaks in the struggle. The emotional battle begins slowly in most children, so that the just-two-year-old may even appear sedate, with a better emotional equilibrium than the toddler. The emotional struggle builds gradually in intensity, peaking usually at around two and a half years of age. This is when your child will probably go to extremes, from aggression to withdrawal, with the demanding, jealous, explosive behavior that gives the two-year-old his "bad" name. Then the intensity gradually decreases, so that by the time your child is three, he has become a happy, contented, friendly, settled little person with evidence of emotional and physical self-control. Just hang in there and wait out the storm.

We've said that the emotional turmoil of this period is related to your child's continuing psychological growth. Let's examine both the mental and physical maturing that is going on now.

PHYSICAL AND PSYCHOLOGICAL GROWTH

Your two-year-old looks like an advanced eighteen-month-old. She still has a tummy, short legs, and a head that seems large for her body. However, her posture and movement are much more refined. Her legs are not spread wide apart when she walks, and she does not need to lean forward as much to keep her balance when walking. In fact, she is learning to run. She will begin to slim down this year, and her growth continues at a slower rate. She will probably gain around three to five pounds and grow three to four inches.

Your first adolescent continues needing about thirteen hours of sleep a day but is well established now with one nap a day of one and a half to two hours. Some children require less sleep and begin dropping their naps during this year. However, they still need a quiet rest period to help them deal with the stress of growing up.

The two-year-old's skin is still immature, so still susceptible to infections, burns, and blisters. The child still loses more body fluids than the older child through her skin, and she remains at a higher risk for dry and chapped skin.

S K I N

The head size is about adult size by two years of age, and as her body grows through the year she begins to assume the proportions of an older child.

HEAD AND FACE

Although the two-year-old still bumps into things and needs a little bit of time to gauge the height of a table top or stairway, her depth perception is better than last year and continuously improves.

E Y E S

The first adolescent has the same problem with ear infections as the younger child, because the eustachian tube is still short and soft. When allergies or infections occur, it swells, causing a blockage and resulting in a buildup of fluid behind the eardrum, which may result in frequent ear infections or a hearing loss, which should be evaluated.

E A R S

By three years of age your child has approximately twenty baby teeth. She is a most adept little eater. And her tongue and lip control are so much improved that she can articulate quite intelligibly by the time she is three.

N O S E ,
M O U T H ,
A N D T E E T H

Your first adolescent can manufacture all the antibodies that adults can, but she has fewer than adults because she has not yet encountered all the infections we have. Antibody production is increasing, however, since she continues to have approximately six to nine infections a year. With the increasing development of antibody production, her lymphoid tissue (tonsils, adenoids, and the lymph nodes in the neck, armpits, and groin) continue to grow. This is not a cause for alarm, but merely indicates the body is doing its job.

I M M U N E
S Y S T E M

Your youngster's cardiovascular system is essentially mature, and her heart rate remains between 80 and 125 beats per minute, with an average of 105. Her blood pressure is usually 100/60.

CARDIOVASCULAR
S Y S T E M

Your first adolescent breathes at the rate of 22 to 34 breaths per minute, which is slightly slower than the toddler, indicating a greater capacity of the respiratory system. She still has a cartilaginous windpipe, which is soft and has a small diameter, continuing to make her more vulnerable to infections. A cold often results in infection of the lower respiratory tract as well (croup or bronchitis).

RESPIRATORY
S Y S T E M

GASTRO-INTESTINAL SYSTEM

The gastrointestinal system of the first adolescent is very much like that of the toddler. It is mature enough to handle a normal diet but still reacts to stress and is more vulnerable to infections. The stomach empties quickly, so she continues to need snacks during the day. The first adolescent is developing neuromuscular control and during this year will be showing regularity in the character and timing of her bowel movements. It is during this time that she shows the ability for voluntary control of her bowel movements and is ready to begin toilet teaching.

GENITOURINARY SYSTEM

The youngster's genitourinary system is essentially mature, and she is also showing signs of neuromuscular development in this area by being able to go for longer periods of time without urinating (two to three hours between wet diapers). Her wetting will gradually decrease from eight to ten times in twenty-four hours to three to seven times. She is ready to learn voluntary control of daytime wetting.

MUSCULOSKELE-TAL SYSTEM

The musculoskeletal system continues to be the one with the greatest growth, since the first adolescent is as active as the toddler. She continues to show steady improvement in the quality of her motor activity, becoming much less awkward and jerky.

NEUROLOGICAL SYSTEM

As we mentioned before, by the time your child is two years of age her brain size has reached 90 percent of adult size. There is still a great deal of neurological development going on, since the brain continues its maturation and refinement during the preschool years.

DEVELOPMENTAL MILESTONES

Let's talk about some of the developmental gains that you can expect during this year of transition. Remember, however, that developmental stages will be different for each individual child. So use them only as a guideline. Remember too that your child's temperament largely determines the way she interacts with her environment. Temperament is an important factor in individualizing development. We discuss this more fully in "The Daily Care of Your Infant"; you should read that section if you are unfamiliar with the concept.

The two-year-old is improving in all areas (motor, language, mental, and social) as she makes her transition from toddlerhood to childhood. Besides the emotional turmoil and struggle for independence going on in your child this year, her language development is also outstanding. It is the development of her ability to communicate verbally that assists your child the most in gaining self-control. She is learning to express her desires in a more grown-up way, and she definitely needs to have you listen and respond to her. She also needs a great deal of praise and reinforcement for the other skills that she is acquiring. Let's see what these are.

MOTOR DEVELOPMENT   The two-year-old is learning to run smoothly, and by the time she is two and a half she will be able to jump with both feet from the bottom stair, as well as being able to climb up and down stairs. Her balance is much better, but she is still unable to dart about rapidly or make quick turns. This is the year she can learn to ride a tricycle. She will love rough and tumble play, especially if she is an active, persistent child. An outdoor area in which she can run freely and safely is essential.

Your child now chews automatically and is quite adept with handling her tongue and lips to make new sounds. She will be found practicing these new sounds and words even without an audience. In the fine motor area she is much more refined. During this year she will go from being able to build a tower three to four cubes high to a six-cube tower. She is also learning to turn the pages of a book one page at a time, rather than in the hit-or-miss fashion of the toddler. At the beginning of the year she makes scribbling circular motions when she draws, but by the end of the year she can imitate lines and make circles. If given a pair of blunt-ended scissors, she can make snipping motions, but don't expect good coordination with the scissors yet.

LANGUAGE DEVELOPMENT   The jargon heard during toddlerhood is disappearing. The two-year-old is learning to speak in short sentences of three to four words. The rhythm and intonation are still not that of an older child and tend to be a little bit sing-song. This is the age in which your youngster particularly enjoys rhymes. In fact, her ability to use words is blossoming. During this year she may go from having a vocabulary of two to three hundred words up to a thousand words. Her articulation ability lags behind slightly, so she still speaks a lot of baby talk. This is adorable and cute, but it's very important that when you respond back to her you pronounce the words correctly, although *not* correcting her. There are just some sounds that she cannot say, and it only embarrasses and frustrates her if you try to get her to do it. If you use the correct pronunciation she will eventually be able to do it herself. The two-year-old is also becoming quite adept at using pronouns—particularly "I," "me," and "mine." Remember that this is the culmination of her drive for separateness and independence.

MENTAL DEVELOPMENT   The two-year-old shows an increasing attention span and an ability to sit for longer periods. She still likes to study and examine things, using her eyes and hands for learning. She is now showing increased ability to remember the past and to use it appropriately. She can use objects in such a way that they represent something they are not. For instance, you will see the two-year-old marching around with a pan on her head, being a firewoman. She has become imaginative and inventive, being able to play by herself for longer periods of time. Remember that with this play she is learning, and it is important work for her. She is also learning to manipulate blocks or cubes imaginatively, making a train by putting them in rows. By the time she is three years of age she will be able to add a block to the top of the train, to represent a chimney.

So you can see by her actions and in her play that she has developed a symbolic system. Her language and perceptions are far beyond that of a toddler. However, she still remains centered on herself. It is still difficult for her to distinguish her views from someone else's. For example, the two-year-old talking on the telephone will feel that it is quite appropriate to answer questions with a nod, firmly believing that the person on the other end can see her.

The first adolescent also gives inanimate objects her own human capabilities. For example our (AA) Katie, on being told that she was not permitted to eat a cookie that contained nuts, found it easier to accept when she assigned negative feelings to the cookie: "That cookie with nuts doesn't like me. He would make me sick." This is a perfectly normal perception and you shouldn't pooh-pooh it. You can also use it effectively to get over some rough spots as we will mention in the next section. By the time she is four years of age she will have outgrown that and will remind you, "Oh, Mom, my dolls don't have feelings! They are just toys."

SOCIAL DEVELOPMENT   Social development is taking place in several areas at this stage. Let's consider them.

FAMILY INTERACTION

The real landmark in your first adolescent's social development is her achieving independence and separateness. She has become extremely self-centered. Mom is still very important, but your child no longer sees you as an extension of herself. It is during this year that she gradually accepts separation from you. But it is not easy, and she continues showing the anxiety both in her sleep and in her everyday activities, as she did in toddlerhood. Handle her fears in the same way you did when she was a toddler.

THE DRIVE FOR INDEPENDENCE AND ITS HAZARDS

Temper tantrums and aggressive behavior peak during this period. Your first adolescent hates being thwarted and has a tremendous amount of tension because of her struggle for independence. This tension is released in explosions of rage and frustration: the temper tantrum and lashing out in physical aggression. Your youngster faces two *major* areas of social learning during this stage. These are learning self-control over her temper tantrums and aggression, and becoming independent in toileting. Because you can see her desire for autonomy, as well as her ability to achieve it, you will want to help her to learn these skills. We give you suggestions for teaching them in "Special Situations in First Adolescence."

Your first adolescent also has a strong need for constancy and structure in the outside world. It seems as though there is so much changing inside of her that she doesn't want change on the outside. She becomes more rigid and ritualistic. Everything and everybody needs to be the same. I (AA) can remember the wails that greeted me when I walked in on my two-year-olds with a new haircut! They *hated* any change.

PEER INTERACTION

Because of your child's separateness and independence, she is not always the most sociable of characters with her peers. "Sharing" is not in the two-year-old's vocabulary, and she probably should not be made to share. Let her friends bring their own toys when they come to visit, and let her take her own toys when she goes to a friend's house. Having two of everything when company comes is also fantastic, but it's not always possible.

By the time your youngster is two and a half years of age or closer to three, she becomes more interested in being social and learning the rules of the game. However, for the most part, she usually enjoys more solitary play. When with peers she probably plays alongside them, totally enjoying their company but not their interference.

She continues to show signs of developing empathy, however. She is genuinely concerned and upset by another's distress. But she won't be able to figure out what caused it or how to help fix it, although she may try. It is a good time to use feedback techniques to help her label the other person's feelings and give reasons why she might feel that way. This is the first step on the long road to becoming a sensitive, empathic adult.

LEARNING SELF-CARE   The two-year-old continues to develop self-help skills and wants to become more and more independent. Environmental control is essential, just as it was in toddlerhood. Think about your child's day and what obstacles she will encounter. Put yourself down on her level and look for the things that are most frustrating. Try to remove or alleviate those whenever possible. This helps her to be successful and certainly gives you fewer headaches.

Achieving independence in dressing and toileting are the more difficult skills to acquire. Your youngster can take almost anything off, but she continues needing help to dress. She doesn't know front from back or right from left. She can pull her pants up and down, however, which is essential for independence at the toilet. And she can help you with putting her shirt on. Socks can still be tough, and shoes often get put on the wrong feet.

You can help your child sort some of these things out with some teaching aids. Using nail polish, paint a happy face on the inside of her right shoe. Then paint a similar face on her right big toe to match. Teach her that clothes labels are in the back. If there are no labels, put marks on the backs of pants or shirts so that she can know the back from the front.

When teaching your first adolescent the "how" of putting something on, work backward in steps. We recommended this in "Overview of Toddlerhood," and it continues to be an excellent teaching aid. Children love instant success, and in this case, success is completing the task. For instance, when she is learning to put on a shirt, you get it on her up to the last sleeve, then let her finish the job. After she has mastered that, let her do that step and the step immediately before it (the first sleeve). Keep going backward until she can do the task right from the beginning.

Remember to praise and reinforce your child. This encourages her to be persistent. Don't push her, though. If you see she is having a hard time and becoming upset, distract her and help her get through it. You can effectively use her belief in animism for this. For example, "That old shirt is in a silly mood today! She wants to make it tough on you. Let me see if I can get her to behave." While you are making the necessary adjustments you can be talking to the wayward shirt: "Come on, silly shirt! Erin needs to wear you today." With this technique most children will forget their frustrations and be less likely to throw in the towel with howls of anger and tears.

Even though your child is gradually able to be more independent now, getting her to do these tasks when you need them done is another story. Again, the game playing that you had to use in toddlerhood is essential, but not always as successful. Dawdling has become an art. You can't rush the two-year-old. Sometimes it is because she really doesn't care about what she is doing. Other times it is because she has been stressed by too many demands or the task is too difficult. In a way, dawdling is a more passive and acceptable form of negativism than the temper tantrum. So when she does dawdle, take a look at what you are asking of her. Are you giving her enough time to complete the task? Are you interrupting her from something else especially nice? Are you asking her to do something that she is really not capable of doing? Try to correct any of these problems and your dawdler may become a more cooperative human being.

When your child's drive for independence, her love of imitation, her desire to have everything in its proper place, and her neuromuscular maturation are added together, it makes this the ideal time to begin toilet teaching. This can be an enjoyable experience or a total disaster, depending on how it is approached. We will give you some clues on how to approach it in our "Special Situations in First Adolescence" section.

Somehow, being completely independent in toileting marks the real culmination of this year. Being out of diapers seems to be the badge that marks the end of babyhood.

So what do we have here with this powerful, rambunctious, highly verbal little person in transition between babyhood and childhood? We have your first really big challenge as a parent. But let us give you a heartening word. Once you are past first adolescence, you won't come to any stage of childhood that is really difficult or tough for nine more years, until your child reaches the stage of pre-adolescence.

19

NUTRITION IN FIRST ADOLESCENCE

The first adolescent is in the throes of exerting his independence, and this applies to his eating habits as well. Because he continues to grow at the slower rate of the toddler, his appetite continues to be as sporadic as it was in toddlerhood. He may also dawdle and like fewer foods than before.

Children vary greatly in this stage. The easy-to-manage youngster, who can play quietly for fairly long periods of time, will obviously expend less energy than the more rambunctious two-and-a-half-year-old down the block, so there is a difference in what and how much each will eat. If you find yourself comparing your child's eating unfavorably with the eating of other first adolescents you know, stop and realize that your child is an individual. As long as he is healthy, growing, and happy, don't worry.

Your first adolescent is quite skilled at feeding himself with a spoon and drinking from a cup or glass. By two and a half he will be a very good chewer and can handle foods he couldn't when he was younger. Because he is more adept at feeding himself, his efforts take less concentration, which means that he can be more aware of what is going on around him. Sometimes he may be more interested in socializing than eating. He may talk excessively at his meals, spit food out to see how you will react, and occupy himself with feeding the dog. He may still not be aware enough of his surroundings to avoid knocking over his milk at almost every meal. These are accidents, however, and should be treated as such, without punishment. Your two-year-old is probably not ready to join the family for every meal and certainly is not ready to sit still for a whole meal.

During this year he will be ready to give up the high chair. A good sturdy booster chair (like those used in restaurants), the telephone book, or some pillows will raise him enough to sit at the big table with the family. Some children prefer kneeling in an adult chair.

You will miss the high chair, because at least you were able to belt him in. Once he has freedom, he may constantly try to get out of his seat and run around, darting back for mouthfuls of food. He is definitely not your most desired guest at a dinner function, and he is not ready for any concrete lessons in manners. But because he is becoming more aware, he certainly can begin to pick up some of the niceties of life from the role modeling of his siblings or other family members. You may begin to get some spontaneous "pleases" and "thank yous." Rejoice in them each time you do, because it will remind you of the light at the end of the tunnel this year, when he will turn three.

Mealtime is a good arena for environmental control. (See Chapter 15, "Discipline in Toddlerhood." Avoid having your first adolescent sit at the family table for long periods of time. Keep the dog out of the room during meals. Continue protecting the floor from spills as you have been doing. This is a good time to introduce a small table and chairs, which your two-year-old will revel in, especially at times when a little friend comes to share a meal with him. Little children really enjoy being able to eat with their feet on the ground.

Continue to use unbreakable utensils and dishes, keeping the fork and spoon small to fit your youngster's hands. He will still be most interested in using a spoon, but by the end of this year should be fairly adept at spearing food with a fork. He'll love using a straw, and this is a wonderful way to interest him in a new beverage he might otherwise refuse.

This remains an age during which he wants to touch and smell foods, particularly new ones. Finger feeding may still be his favorite method of eating, so remember that when you consider what to offer him.

W H A T

Your first adolescent can eat anything the family eats without having to have it pureed, mashed, or strained. You can give him his food in small, bite-size pieces or in strips that he can use as finger food. He can now digest broccoli, cauliflower, cabbage, and other foods that his system could not handle previously. He can chew well once he is two and a half, so small pieces of hard vegetables, fruit, gum, popcorn, or candy no longer need to be avoided. However, nuts are still on the "no-no" list until he is three or four.

Some family foods may need to be adapted, as they were with your toddler, in order to suit the child. If you are serving cooked vegetables with a very strong flavor, such as cabbage, you may want to cook his portion a little longer and rinse it more to weaken the flavor. If you are making a salad, serve the ingredients separately for him. It is difficult for him to handle vegetables in tossed salad form, but he can handle the raw vegetables as finger food and dip them into the salad dressing. In fact, he will probably still prefer raw vegetables to cooked, and may for several years. Since some nutrients are lost in cooking, he gets more from raw vegetables anyway. He probably still needs to drink his soups, with the solids sieved off and served separately in a bowl.

Your youngster probably still prefers the softer, moister foods; and chicken, hamburger, spaghetti with meat sauce, and hot dogs are favorites. Crackers, breads, and rolls are much loved also. It is important, however, that your child get a variety of textures, for a child who has been fed only soft foods may have a great deal of difficulty adjusting to crispier or chewier textures later.

If your child is healthy and has not learned to think of eating as a battleground, or food as something to be used as a weapon, he will eat what he needs if offered a variety of foods from the four basic groups (see Appendix F). They may be given in many different forms, in any order, and at any meal he wishes or that you are able to prepare. In Appendix F we have listed the dietary needs of the average hungry first adolescent and a sample of a daily menu. Remember that these are just examples, and you can fit your child's needs to your whole family. There is no need to make special meals for him as long as your family is offered a well-balanced meal that includes one food he likes.

If your first adolescent is not already familiar with sweets, he will begin to come in contact with them at friends' homes during this stage. This may worry some parents. If you have not read our section on sweets and junk food in Chapter 18, "Nutrition in Toddlerhood," it will be helpful to read it at this time.

Remember that any food can be a snack or can also be eaten at a meal. If he wants leftover pizza for breakfast, let him have it. He may then want oatmeal for lunch. This is not a time to be teaching him the "proper" order of meals. In another year he will be ready to listen to reason and conform to the group.

H   O   W

When offering food to your youngster, be sure he can handle it with a minimum of trouble. He can become easily frustrated and give up on eating if, for example, he has to chase the peas across the plate. You might try serving peas with mashed potatoes so that he can mix them. He may turn his nose up at a stew or casserole made by you, but his own creation may delight him. Similarly, he may not like scrambled or fried eggs, but be perfectly happy to have hard-boiled eggs in quarters so he can pick them up in his fingers. He may likewise enjoy his meat in strips, his potatoes as french fries, and his green beans as finger food. He may prefer his hot dogs in little chunks so that he can spear the pieces and dip them in the ketchup rather than having to struggle to keep a wiener in its roll.

Toothpicks are a great boon for introducing new foods. Your youngster will see toothpicks as a game and not realize that he has just speared and eaten a food that he has never had before. He may not like orange juice but may thrive on oranges which have been cut into wedges, or he may like the juice frozen in popsicle form. We have mentioned before that dips are very popular with young children and can be made from yogurt, cottage cheese, or sour cream, all of which help to meet his calcium needs. He may not be able to eat the lettuce in a salad, but she can handle chunks or strips of lettuce (and nearly all of the raw vegetables such as broccoli, cauliflower, mushrooms, cherry tomatoes, spinach, and carrots) quite well with her fingers. He wouldn't even consider trying some of these foods in cooked form.

As we mentioned previously, different textures make a meal more interesting for him. He enjoys the crisp crunch of a raw carrot with the soft moistness of mashed potatoes. Dry foods—such as a well-done roast, steak, or meat loaf—are hard to eat, and you may offer them with some moist food—such as vegetables in a cream sauce or mashed potatoes. Keeping in mind that children do prefer moist foods, meat that is medium to rare is more likely to be accepted at this age.

If your child prefers milder foods to tart ones, a combination of the two such as a tart orange and a milder banana mixture can be appealing. When mixing fruits use honey as a sweetener rather than sugar, since less is needed. Or add lemon juice, which brings out the natural sweetness of the fruit, thus requiring no extra sweeteners.

Snacks contribute significantly to your child's nutrition. Try using raw fruit or vegetables, chunks of cheese with bread or a cracker, or a hard-boiled egg given with a beverage (water, milk, juice). Other snack suggestions can be found in Appendix F. Time your youngster's snacks at least an hour or an hour and a half before meals, and keep fat and sugar content (hunger suppressants) low.

Your first adolescent is much more comfortable with familiar objects, including foods, just as your toddler was. Introduce new food with a favorite or familiar food and allow her time to get used to it. Many children won't even begin to try to eat a food until they have seen it about three times. When they do try it, they may in fact dislike it. Remember that you as an adult probably dislike certain foods, and respect your child's right to do likewise.

It is sometimes helpful to involve the first adolescent in shopping for new foods. Also, let her see how the new food is cooked and perhaps taste it during the cooking process. Likes and dislikes may change from day to day or week to week. And some children need more rituals in their food preparation than others. My (AA) Kimberly at two would not even consider a peanut butter sandwich unless it was cut into four small triangles. Some children want their food on their plates in exactly the same way at each meal. This will pass. She will be able to eat differently some day.

Toddlerhood and first adolescence are the times in which you are most likely to get into a vicious cycle over eating, but if you can get through this period without having mealtimes become emotionally laden, you will probably not have an eating problem with your child in the future. Keep the eating times pleasant, and pay attention to your child when she is eating and behaving well. Try to ignore undesirable behavior. If it becomes too extreme you can quietly and firmly remove her plate from the table, telling her that you see she seems to be finished. If she wants to continue, give her one more chance.

W H E R E

Although having your first adolescent at the family meals is not always desirable, you would certainly want to have her be a part of the family meal at least once a week and possibly every night. Gear the duration of her visit to her ability to sit still. You may wish to have her eat her main course earlier and let her join the family when it is time for salad or dessert.

One of your youngster's biggest and hardest tasks during this year is simply to learn to sit at the table until the meal is over. It often helps, when she is joining you at family dinner, to make it a special occasion and serve it in style with candles, pretty napkins, and nice china. Your two-year-old may feel it's a treat to be allowed to use the china and the glassware. In fact, doing this seems to bring out the best behavior of the whole family.

When you take your first adolescent out to eat, fast-food restaurants are still a good idea, to avoid waiting for a table. Or call ahead for your pizza.

H   O   W   M   U   C   H

There is one more thing to remember. Don't expect your youngster to clean her plate or even to taste everything on it. Studies show that the child who is forced to eat food she doesn't like will probably not learn to like it even in later life. Consider, too, that there are times when your child simply may not be very hungry. If she is given small portions she will stand a better chance of finishing her meal. She can ask for more if she is still hungry. If you give her small portions and she still does not eat them, respect her right to eat only when she is hungry.

If this not-eating-even-small-portions begins to be a routine thing, then you need to look more closely at what might be causing it. Perhaps her snack is too close to mealtime, or the snack is too high in hunger-suppressing fat or sugar. Perhaps it's a time of day when she is less hungry. Perhaps she has had some very inactive days and has not run off much steam, so she needs less food. This can happen, for example, when she can't go outside because of the weather.

On the other hand, she may have been excessively active and be overtired. Fatigue often curbs hunger. If you decide this is the case, you might want to have your active two-year-old come in and settle down in front of "Sesame Street" or "Mr. Rogers" before eating so that she can gradually unwind. Also look at the types of food she eats. If she likes fried foods, which have more fat than boiled foods, then she is getting many more calories and will not need as much quantity at her meals. Respect what her body is telling her about her energy needs. Loss of appetite can also be an early sign that your child is coming down with something, and many a mother has been able to anticipate the runny nose the next day simply by noticing her child's diminished appetite the night before.

20

DISCIPLINE IN FIRST ADOLESCENCE

Of the first five years of life, those of first adolescence are the most difficult for discipline. Sometimes it seems to parents as if the rebellious behavior of the first adolescent is deliberately programmed to do nothing but infuriate them. Even if you are lucky and have only a mildly obnoxious youngster to contend with, all first adolescents are difficult to handle. Here are some methods that may help.

You can try all of these techniques on your first adolescent and find that none of them work easily! What do you do then? Shoot yourself? No. You remind yourself that at three, things will be different and the discipline techniques will work well again. Don't give up on them just because you have run into the buzzsaw of first adolescence.

DISCIPLINE TECHNIQUES

Some of the discipline techniques for toddlerhood may continue to work with a first adolescent, so give them a try. *Environmental control* is still a key to avoiding conflicts or confrontations. If that cake isn't out there in plain view, he won't think of throwing a tantrum if he can't have it. *Distraction* is helpful, although the first adolescent may be a little more difficult to get off the track. *Game playing* makes an unpleasant chore more fun at any age. It's far easier to go down the hall to bed as an airplane than to have to be carried down kicking and screaming!

The *positive reward system* will be a mainstay for you during this stage. Catch him being good! Look for every chance to use it. Reward any behavior you like to see in him. He still wants your approval most and still warms to your touch. Give lots of pats, hugs, kisses, and squeezes every day. Stars, stickers, happy faces, and shiny new pennies may still work. But they may not. And you may need to substitute more concrete rewards: for example, five stars at the end of a week equals a trip to the park. There is one gimmick from toddlerhood that will usually continue to work in first adolescence. You can still offer your child the reward of seeing you make a funny face or dance a jig or stand on your head or do something else silly. The first adolescent will usually think that's as hilarious as the toddler did. Remember that the rewards should be given immediately after the desired behavior in order to reinforce it. You won't have to reward it forever. Once he has learned how to act and that it pleases you, he'll be glad to do it on his own. Praise for his good behavior will go a long way to making the desired behavior permanent. If he backslides a bit, just start again at the beginning.

Here is a new technique which usually works quite well at this age too. It's the method of giving your child *choices*, rather than giving her direct orders, for she loves to defy those. Say things to her like, "Jill, do you want corn or beans for lunch?" "Bill, do you want to stay inside and play on your indoor gym house or go in the backyard and play in your sandbox?"

But suppose this happens: You give your child a choice of corn or beans for lunch. She chooses corn. Then just as you start to get the corn out of the pantry she says, "No, beans!" You put the corn back and get out the beans. Immediately she shouts triumphantly, "No, corn!" What do you do? You arbitrarily pick one and say, "I know—you really want the corn." "How you know?" she says. "Because your voice sounded different when you chose the corn." Then you go ahead and fix the corn and ignore whatever outbursts or tantrums she throws.

Incidentally, teaching your child how to make choices—even if you have to help her along with them sometimes—will stand her in good stead later, because it gradually helps her to develop a sense of independence and responsibility.

HOW TO HANDLE UNDESIRABLE BEHAVIOR

Most parents handle misbehavior by punishment because nobody has taught them any better ways to handle it. The parent thinks that the punishment will stop the offending behavior and make the child behave differently in the future. Sometimes that's true. Unfortunately, most of the time it is not true.

As we mentioned in Chapter 19, punishment causes a child to fear and hate you—and the worse the punishment the more intense the fear and hate. I (FD) remember the four or five times when my father took me up to the attic and whipped me with his belt. He was even corny enough to say each time, "Son, this is going to hurt me more than it does you!" Believe me, there was no way I could figure out how he could have been more hurt than I was! After each whipping I was consumed with hatred for him, and fantasized all sorts of ways in which I would get back at him some day. It's been many years since those whippings, but I can still remember the depth of my angry feelings. It's very clear to me that none of those whippings made me want to behave better in the future.

So, even though parents have been punishing their children since the days of the cavemen, we don't want you to make their mistakes.

Another thing about punishment is that it violates the law of the soggy potato chip. Children will prefer a crisp potato chip to a soggy one any time. But if they have to choose between a soggy potato chip and no potato chip, they will usually choose the soggy one.

Children ordinarily prefer their parents' positive attention to negative attention. But if they have to choose between negative attention and no attention, they will usually choose the former. What does this mean when you spank your child? It means that the punishment, the negative attention, acts as a paradoxical reward, just like an ice cream cone or a quarter acts as a positive reward. We are not saying it works this way with all children. Some children are by nature so timid and shy they will be frightened enough of punishment to stop the misbehavior (or only do it when they are out of sight of their parents). But others seem to ask for a spanking. When? Usually when their mothers are very involved in a project that excludes them. Negative attention is better than none!

TIME OUT

If you don't use any form of punishment with your first adolescent, what can you do? The single best way of handling misbehavior will still be the *Time Out*. And since first adolescents are such a difficult age group to handle, you may find yourself giving lots and lots of Time Outs, until your child reaches the age of three and enters the more cooperative preschool stage.

The Time Out procedure, which will be used frequently during this stage, is essentially time out from any positive reinforcement. For the younger child this means being removed from his parent, to whom he is strongly attached. It can be in a chair facing a corner, a laundry room, a bathroom, a lighted walk-in closet, or his bedroom. Some children seem to enjoy their bedrooms enough so that a Time Out there does not seem to be a removal from positive reinforcement. But since many are devastated at being cut off socially, the bedroom can be used effectively. You'll have to see what seems to work best for you. The active child cannot sit still in a chair even for a few minutes so he'll definitely need another alternative. Whatever the location, it will need to be safe and contain nothing breakable.

Before using a Time Out for unacceptable behavior, examine the situation closely. Does the child understand why the behavior is not acceptable? If not, *teach him.* Keep the explanation short and simple. Offer an example of acceptable behavior, if appropriate. For example, when he's angry with his sister and wants to clobber her, have him pound some clay instead. Once you feel he understands, no future scolding or explanations are necessary. If he clobbers her, he receives one warning about Time Out. If he heeds it, give him an *immediate* positive reward. If he doesn't, give him an *immediate* Time Out.

When examining misbehavior consider too what seems to cause it. Look at the preceding events. Have you been too busy to pay attention to him when he *isn't* misbehaving? If so, the misbehavior may vanish when you take time to rectify that. A Time Out may not be necessary. You may simply be able to ignore him when he is misbehaving and move in quickly with attention when he isn't.

However, this can be difficult to do, especially if, by ignoring his misbehavior, bodily harm or destruction may befall a family member. So a Time Out will probably be necessary in many cases, usually in the case of aggression, tantrums, destructiveness, or disobedience.

Make sure your child is aware of the rules of Time Out. Be sure to tell him that you are doing this to teach him how to act and to avoid yelling, scolding, and spanking. He'll appreciate the latter reason. Especially if you *don't* yell, scold, or spank!

- After your warning has gone unheeded, *calmly* tell him that since he has hit his sister (or whatever the misdeed) he needs a Time Out.
- If he'll go on his own steam, great. Otherwise you'll have to use the minimum amount of assistance necessary. If it means picking him up and carrying him, do it with his back to you so that he doesn't think he's getting a hug!
- Set a kitchen timer (one minute per year of age—two minutes for a two-year-old, three minutes for a three-year-old) near by so he can hear it. This way he knows he can't be forgotten and you'll remember too. Keep the time short. It's been shown that the lesson is learned no more quickly with longer periods of isolation. And, he'll probably forget why he's there.
- You can expect some crying and angry talk. After all, he's not feeling happy about it. But if his actions are unacceptable (kicking the wall or throwing things, for example), tell him that the timer will not be set until they stop.
- If he tries to get out before the time is up, reset the timer. You may need to stand by the door and even hold it shut if resetting the timer doesn't deter him. If you are persistent, he will soon learn.
- Allow him one trip to the bathroom but advise him that the timer will be reset. At this age he'll need help in the bathroom so you'll have to go with him.
- The more-difficult-to-manage child will try everything to get your attention during Time Out. My Katie (AA) even vomited and soiled her pants! If he is required to help you clean up the mess before he can leave Time Out, he will quickly tire of it.
- Once Time Out is over do *not* speak about his misbehavior again. If he is angry with you, certainly acknowledge his feelings in an understanding way.
- Be on the lookout for good behavior during the few minutes after a Time Out so that he may receive a positive reward and feel good about himself again.
- Make sure that siblings respect the Time Out rules, too.

If parents can use Time Out and positive reward consistently, the child will gain a sense of security about what to expect. And it certainly cuts down on the time spent in negative interaction, such as scolding or spanking.

HANDLING REBELLION

The first adolescence stage is full of rebellion, defiance, and stubbornness; and *nothing* you can do is going to change that until your child outgrows it. Once you have decided you can't change her personality at this age, but can only contain it, half the battle is won. Spend as much time as you can together having fun rather than fights.

Unfortunately many parents are not this wise. They take personally the rebellion that is so characteristic of the first adolescent. We have heard many parents say, "I'm gonna show that kid once and for all who's boss in this family—and it ain't her!" Such an attitude can produce nothing but a vicious cycle. As the parent's actions force the child to become even more stubborn and obnoxious, the parent cracks down harder. And so it goes. Don't let yourself be trapped into such a futile battle with your youngster.

We don't want to give you the impression that there is no way to curb the "terrible twos." There is—but you will pay a heavy price for it later. We know a mother whose child never went through the typical rebellion of the terrible twos. She squashed any signs of rebellion immediately by laying an immense guilt trip on him. "You don't want to do things like that, do you? Your mother loves you so much and when you do something like that it makes her so unhappy she could cry. And you wouldn't want to make your mother cry, would you?" At this point, she would enfold him in her arms and snuffle quietly.

It worked. While the other kids in the neighborhood were normal rebellious first adolescents, hers was a sweet, almost demure child. But when the boy was old enough to go to kindergarten, the mother discovered what the price was. He had been in kindergarten for about a month when the teacher called her in and told her the boy had problems. She said, "He's painfully shy and isolates himself from the other children. And when they tease him he's almost totally unable to stand up for himself. I think it would be wise to take him to see a therapist." The mother was dumbfounded. She gradually came to realize that she had blotted out her child's ability to assert himself, not only with her, but with everyone.

If you want to discipline your child's behavior wisely, write down what you want to achieve. This will require making three different lists (and you will need to revise them each time your child reaches a new developmental stage). Be realistic. This isn't the stage for a lot of rules and regulations—just enough to keep him safe and others safe from him.

First, list the actions your child is doing that you approve of and want to see him continue doing. Since he is already doing these things, all you need to do is to reward him for continuing to do them.

Second, list the actions you wish your child were doing more of. You can set up a positive reward system to teach him to do these things. Be sure that they are actions he is capable of doing; and break learning tasks into small steps when possible.

Third, list the things you wish your child would do less of (or perhaps even stop). You can use the Time Out to handle these.

C O N T R O L L I N G   T H E   E X P R E S S I O N   O F   F E E L I N G S

So much for your child's actions. Now what about his feelings? Here the goals are different. We believe that the healthiest thing for a child is to express all of his feelings—both positive and negative—to his parents and his siblings. The ability to express both kinds of feelings is one of the foundations of good mental health. The inability to do so is one of the basic causes of many neurotic problems and psychosomatic diseases. The child who has learned not to express anger will be severely handicapped as an adult.

We are quite aware that there are places where children are not allowed to express anger, such as at school, church, scout meetings, etc. So you will probably need to tell your child, "Robert, you can get angry here in the family, but doing it at school may get you in trouble." (Some teachers, bless them, will allow children to express angry and unhappy feelings, but they are definitely in a minority.)

Some of you may be thinking, "But if I allow my child to get angry at me, what about respect?" By our definition, respect means that a child looks up to his parents and believes they know more than he does and can guide him. A little boy can certainly be angry with his father but still love and respect him, just as you can. It is much healthier to let a child get the unhappy feelings out in the open where they can be dealt with.

Even if you agree with this general philosophy, you may still find it difficult at first to permit your children to be open with their emotions. Very few adults were allowed to express themselves as children. I (FD) certainly was not. I had my mouth washed out with yellow soap several times for daring to express my negative feelings to my parents.

You may find it hard to give your children a freedom of expression that you never had. But let's assume that you decide to try. The way to do it is by using what we call the *feedback technique*. That is, you allow freedom for verbal expression and spoken feelings, but not negative actions in defiance of your rules.

Anger and balkiness are not the only emotions which can be handled by the feedback technique. Feedback is the best method of handling *any* feelings.

For example, if your first adolescent rushes in with a cut finger, crying that she must go to the hospital, you will only make her hysterical if you tell her to stop the nonsense, that all it needs is Bactine.

Using the feedback technique the scene might go something as follows:

Brenda: Mommy, I cut finger. I go hospital!
Mother: Let me see it. Goodness, that's awful. It's bleeding and you'll probably have to go to the hospital. That must hurt very much.
Brenda: It does!
Mother: Well, before you go to the hospital, the first thing to do is to put some Bactine on it and then put a Band-Aid on it. OK?
Brenda: OK.
(Mother disinfects and bandages the cut. Then she puts Brenda on her lap and gives her a big hug.)
Mother: How does it feel now?
Brenda: Better. Gonna get glass of cold milk before I go to hospital. (Nothing further is heard from Brenda about going to the hospital.)

Notice that the mother did not challenge Brenda's statement that she had to go to the hospital. She accepted it as Brenda's way of saying that she was very upset and her finger hurt a lot and she was scared. She did not attempt to make rational statements, as so many parents do. She simply responded by feeding back the feelings the child was sending. Since her mother did not challenge her emotional messages, Brenda had the opportunity to calm down and evaluate them herself and see that she did not really need to go to the hospital.

It is very hard for many parents to handle a child who is being irrational. Unfortunately, most try to counteract an irrational child with rational statements, which get them nowhere.

The irrational fears of children are no more susceptible to being dissolved by rational means than are the irrational fears of adults.

If at 3 A.M. your child enters your bedroom convinced that there is a lion in his room, it will do no good to try to talk him out of it. Instead, let him know that you understand his fears are real. Feed his fearful feelings back to him in your own words so he knows you understand. Then you might ask him what *he* thinks would be the best thing to do. If he suggests sleeping in your bed it may be a much simpler solution than to try to get him over his fear at 3 A.M. Just make it clear that this is a special thing you are doing for tonight only and that tomorrow night he will be back sleeping in his own room.

We've given you a number of discipline techniques in this chapter. If you have a very strong-willed child, none of them will be easy at this stage. But at least they will give you practice for the next stage—the preschool stage—when all of them will work well.

21

INTELLECTUAL STIMULATION IN FIRST ADOLESCENCE

In toddlerhood, it was easy to stimulate your child intellectually. But when your youngster enters first adolescence, everything is different. And because he is in transition from babyhood to childhood, you never know ahead of time what his unpredictable feelings are going to be. If his feelings tell him he wants to learn something, all systems are *go*. If his feelings tell him he doesn't want to learn something, all systems are *stop*.

If you want to teach your first adolescent something, the main thing you need to do is find out whether he is receptive. If he isn't, forget it. With that important limitation in mind, let's proceed with how you can offer intellectual stimulation to your youngster in this stage. He will still be interested in the materials and equipment suggested for toddlers, but he will also enjoy the extra activities we'll discuss now.

TELEVISION AND STORIES

Good movies or TV shows, such as "Sesame Street," are almost always helpful. I (FD) have a story about a little girl told to me by her grandmother. One morning when the girl was three, she brought the morning paper over to her grandmother and said, "Grandma, does that word say 'horse'?" The grandmother was dumbfounded because the word was "horse." She turned to another part of the paper and asked the girl, "What does that word say?" "Orange," said the girl without any hesitation. The grandmother was amazed and perplexed, until she realized that when her granddaughter was two years old, she had been allowed to watch "Sesame Street" every morning, mostly to keep her out of mischief for an hour. So please don't underestimate the potential value of good TV and good movies for your first adolescent.

But monitor what he sees on TV. Watch some TV with your child, then gradually begin to make comments about it, both positive and negative. When making negative comments, be sure you are not attacking one of your child's favorite programs. Feel your way gently, and don't overwhelm him with too many comments. Just do this occasionally.

Another tried and true method of intellectual stimulation is reading to your child. Again, you must respect his wishes if he pulls away and says, "Don't want a story tonight!" But the nights on which he does want a story, give it the full moxie. Put him on your lap and cuddle him as you read. Have him point out the parts of the illustrations. Ask him questions about the story. Remember, he is a year older than he was as a toddler, and a year more sophisticated. Just have respect for his negativism and don't push.

Your child will usually continue to be quite interested in nursery rhymes at this stage, so continue your reading of Mother Goose rhymes and *I Wish I Had a Computer That Makes Waffles*.

First adolescence may turn out to be a splendid time for you to tell stories as well as read them. For example, for several years I (FD) told my children stories from *The Adventures of Paul Bunyan*. I would read one of the stories to myself, get the main elements in my mind, and then retell it without the book to my kids.

One kind of story that will fascinate your child is a story you make up about yourself and your work. It need not be entirely factual. Feel free to have lots of exciting things happen to you in connection with your work, whether you are an accountant, a lawyer, a production line worker, a secretary, or a business person. Give your main character a different name; merely draw upon yourself and your knowledge of your occupation in building the story.

Stories about a child of your own child's sex and approximate age are also sure to be interesting. The stories do not have to be terribly dramatic—they can simply be about a little girl going to the playground with her father or mother, or about a boy building a high tower of blocks and going to the ice cream store for a special treat.

You can make use of comic strips to stimulate your child intellectually in a very interesting way. Children are usually fascinated by comics and love to have their parents read them to them. After you have read the comic and talked about it, cut the panels out with scissors and tape each of them to a separate piece of cardboard. Then put them before him in a mixed-up order. Ask him to put them together in the right order and then tell you the story.

You may think that such a thing will do little to further the intellectual growth of your child. Not so. This kind of game is used in the best adult intelligence test that exists, and in one of the two best intelligence tests for children. It reveals how intelligent the child is in his social perception of both children and adults, and psychologists who design the tests regard this perception as an important part of intelligence.

O U T I N G S

Continue taking your first adolescent to places he doesn't usually visit. Remember that his education can rise no higher than his experience. The broader his experience, the better his education. So take him to places such as your local fire station, police station, newspaper, welding shop, bakery, airport, and zoo. It's OK to revisit the ones he's seen earlier, for he will continue to find them fascinating and will also make new discoveries about them as his powers of observation increase. Remember the principle of positive reward and follow the visit with some kind of special treat. When you get home, you can make up a story or have him dictate a book to you about his visit. You can also use a tape recorder and interview him about the trip.

As you did when he was a toddler, expand his language and thinking by the piggyback method of adding words to what he says. For example, when he sees a model of a dinosaur at a museum and says, "That is a *big* animal," you can respond, "Yes, that is a very big animal. He's so big he's huge and enormous."

Wherever you and your child go in your ordinary use of the environment, try to make it an adventure instead of a dull trip, just as you did during his toddlerhood. Treat a trip to the supermarket as an opportunity for teaching him some new words, such as "in" or "out" or "walk in" or names found on cereal boxes. That way the trip can continue to be an exciting intellectual adventure for him. Incidentally, it will be a lot easier and more fun for you.

However, avoid overstructuring your child's life so that he doesn't have any free time. Your child needs time just to do nothing. A lot of children don't have that. They are always being bombarded by some kind of stimulation or learning chosen for them by adults.

ANSWERING QUESTIONS

Parents should also be careful not to stifle or ignore a first adolescent who asks a lot of questions. And first adolescents are very apt to do this. Next to "no," "why?" is usually their favorite word. Sometimes a child who asks a great many questions becomes a nuisance to the parent. Remember, though, that when your youngster is learning to ask questions, he is learning one of the most valuable ways in which he can develop his intelligence. This doesn't mean you have to qualify for sainthood when your child is in the question-asking stage. If his questions are beginning to get on your nerves, simply say, "No more questions today! Mother's had enough questions for now and she's all tired out. No more questions until tomorrow."

Try to avoid giving the impression that you think there is anything wrong with unusual questions, imaginary playmates, weird fantasies, or any out-of-the-ordinary mental processes you perceive in your first adolescent. These are merely part of his imagination. And if he has a more vivid and exotic imagination than the average child, maybe he will grow up to be an outstanding science fiction writer!

There's a world of difference between pushing your child and intellectually stimulating him. When you push him he will send you a message by body language. A bored, uninterested look on his face, a tapping of his foot, turning his body around in the opposite direction: All these things say clearly to you, "I don't want to hear any more of this; I want to do something else!"

CONCEPTS AND MUSIC

At this age, you can teach your child concepts such as colors, days of the week, and seasons of the year. Most of these can be taught by using nursery rhymes in *I Wish I Had a Computer That Makes Waffles.* Simply read him the rhyme that contains the colors or days of the week a number of times. When teaching different colors, you can mark white paper with different colored felt pens and ask the child what color you have used. If he shows marked resistance to any of these activities, drop it until a later age.

Since your first adolescent is not merely a cerebral child but is also in need of exercising his large and small muscles, you can dance and march with him to the music of different cultures that you played for him as a baby, as well as some new music you can buy for him, such as Sousa marches. You can take old tin cans, fill them with a number of rocks or large pebbles and seal up the top with masking tape. (You want to have the pebbles large enough so he can't choke on them.) Then you and he can use these primitive musical instruments as you dance or march to the music.

P E T S

You may want to introduce animals as pets to him at this stage. But remember that you are the one who will have to take care of the pet; do not expect him to do it. If you are willing to take on this responsibility, you may want to get him a dog, a bird, an aquarium with fish, a turtle, a rabbit, or a hamster.

In this chapter we have emphasized intellectual stimulation. But your child is still a child. He also needs to be hugged, to cuddle up on your lap from time to time, to run around the house and yell. He needs to do all the things that are important to the emotional life of a youngster of his age, so don't forget the emotional growth of your child while you are busy satisfying his intellectual needs.

22

SPECIAL SITUATIONS IN FIRST ADOLESCENCE

Many of the special situations occurring in first adolescence are similar to those in toddlerhood. So from time to time in this chapter we will refer you back to the toddlerhood section for further information.

COMFORT HABITS

The first adolescent continues to need the comfort object (blanket, toy, pacifier, thumb) or activity (hair twirling, rocking, head banging) that he did in late infancy and early toddlerhood to soothe him when he is distressed, tired, or frustrated. As he progresses toward the end of the year, he will probably need to resort to these habits less and less. However, when there is an environmental change or stress, you can be assured he will turn to them again. Please read the section on comfort habits in "Special Situations in Toddlerhood" for a more detailed discussion.

TEMPER TANTRUMS

Temper tantrums, which usually begin in toddlerhood, peak in first adolescence, and continue into the preschool years. Tantrums are seen more often in the intense, persistent child who is sensitive to all stimuli, and they are more likely to occur when he is overtired, overstimulated, or hungry. Preventing these situations can go a long way toward decreasing tantrums.

If you have not already read the section on temper tantrums in "Special Situations in Toddlerhood," we recommend that you read it now in order to understand the gradual change in the quality of tantrums as the child matures. It is the quality of the temper tantrum—the situation in which it occurs and the child's ability to handle that situation appropriately—that is the deciding factor in how you, the parent, should handle the tantrum. In the younger child, particularly the toddler, the frustration seems to be that of failure to accomplish what he wants. In the first adolescent, it seems to be more the result of being thwarted or denied. Often this tantrum takes on a defiant and rebellious tone.

Let's begin with some things you should *not* do in trying to cope with your child's tantrums.

If the tantrum is triggered by your refusal to let your child have his own way on some issue, do not now give in. A number of parents unfortunately do exactly that, not realizing that this rewards the child for having a tantrum. Remember: When a child is given a reward or payoff, the action will be strengthened and more likely to recur in the future.

Never try to reason with the child or even talk to him when he is having a tantrum. Above all, don't yell at him or attempt to get him over the tantrum by threatening to spank him or actually doing so. All of us have heard parents say to a child who is in the midst of a tantrum, "Stop that crying right now, or I'll really give you something to cry about!" This is like trying to put out a fire by pouring gasoline on it.

All right, what is the best thing to do when your child is having a tantrum? As we have said, your toddler did not have the verbal skills to communicate his angry feelings and was not yet able to exercise self-control. Therefore we suggested that you hold him gently during the tantrum, helping him get control of himself, if he would allow it. But once you feel that your child has the verbal skills to communicate his feelings and is showing the drive for independence and self-control, a different tactic is necessary. Youngsters who have the skills to control themselves need to learn that tantrums are not acceptable behavior. You can explain to your child that he is a big boy now. And it is time he learned to control himself when he is angry and frustrated.

While your child is still in the stage of learning control, keep your eye out to anticipate outbursts before they occur. When you see him working up to a tantrum, move in quickly. Help him put his feelings into words or more acceptable actions (pounding a pillow or jumping up and down, and saying "I'm so-o-o mad!"). When he does, reward him with praise and a hug. If necessary, use extra reinforcement—a star or sticker chart—for not losing control. Meanwhile, should a tantrum occur, ignore it. If you need to, walk out of the room until it is over. When it is over, do not mention it. Go on with what you were doing as matter-of-factly as possible. If you do this consistently, the tantrums should gradually fade out and disappear.

If your child throws a tantrum in the supermarket or department store or some other public place, try to handle the tantrum the same way as we suggested on page 218. Later that day, perhaps at night when he is getting ready for bed, you can talk about the day and about how angry and frustrated he felt. This will help him understand that you can accept his anger but not his actions. Help him look for some alternatives for his actions and let him know that you know he will be able to conquer this problem soon. Remember too that when he does behave well on an outing, positive reinforcement will go a long way in helping him learn his lesson.

F E A R S   A N D   P H O B I A S

The first adolescent continues to exhibit the fears and phobias that he did in toddlerhood, and they should be handled in the same way. As he approaches the preschool stage, his fears will change in quality, becoming more imaginary with fears of monsters, ghosts, and other scary creatures. Night lights and open bedroom doors are definitely in order. Sometimes he may even need a 40- or

60-watt bulb. Don't worry about this. It can be gradually decreased as your child lets you know he's ready. Needing a light is *not* a sign of weak character. How many adults have you known who need a crack of light at night in order to sleep more comfortably? If your child is afraid of specific shadows or sounds, lie down where he is and see if you can discover the source of the problem. Correct it, if possible. If not, show him what's causing it.

It is during first adolescence that the child is often exposed to water in the form of learning to swim. This can be a time of fear of the water, even though the year before he enjoyed it immensely. Accept his fear and respect it. Throwing the child into the water is definitely not recommended. Instead, give him gradual exposure to the water. Couple it with an entertaining and distracting activity such as playing with a toy, riding piggyback on Mom, or blowing bubbles like a motor boat. There's no rush. He has plenty of time to learn to swim.

SIBLING RIVALRY

Sibling rivalry can be particularly intense in this period because the first adolescent tends to be very jealous and demanding. For a discussion of sibling rivalry, please read that section in "Special Situations in Toddlerhood."

TOILET LEARNING

Toilet learning is a learning experience not only for children, but for the parents who are teaching them as well.

I (FD) like to keep up with what my colleagues in child raising are saying. So a few years ago I took incognito an evening course in parenting at UCLA, given by a local psychiatrist. From the types of questions and comments made by the audience, I guessed that about two thirds of them were college educated.

When we came to the section of the course dealing with toilet training, I was dumbfounded by the questions asked. One I remember particularly well. A well-dressed woman raised her hand and asked, "Is it all right to spank your child if he keeps having accidents when you're toilet training him?" Other women chimed in, "Yes, yes, is it all right to spank?" The psychiatrist assured the women that spanking was not necessary in toilet training a child.

I was shocked by these questions. Surely these mothers would not hire a piano teacher who spanked the child's hand with a ruler every time he made a mistake. And yet in all seriousness they wondered if it was all right to take a teaching process such as toilet learning and punish mistakes by spanking.

And yet as I thought about it more, it wasn't so surprising. The reason parents know so little about toilet training is the same reason they know so little about overhauling the transmission of their cars. Nobody has ever taught them how to do it. So here's a very comprehensive discussion on how to toilet train your child.

People have called this process *toilet training* for many years. But we prefer to call it *toilet teaching* on the part of the parents and *toilet learning* on the part of the children. By anchoring it to a teaching/learning process, we can make use of thousands of research studies on how to teach a child anything, from learning to read to learning to swim.

WAIT TILL HIS BODY IS READY

The first thing to remember when toilet teaching your child is that he cannot have a bowel movement (BM) unless his body is ready to. So it makes no sense at all to sit him on the potty when he's not ready and expect him to have a BM just because you've told him to. Even if you urge or scold him, he still can't.

And how do you think a little child feels when he is sitting on a cold potty and an adult has told him that it's time for him to have a BM, but he has no biological urge whatsoever to do so? Obviously, he feels he's expected to do something that he cannot do, and this tends to undermine his self-confidence about the messages he gets from his body. Since his parents are such powerful authority figures, he tends to feel the parent must be right and his body must be wrong. He now begins to feel, "Maybe I shouldn't trust my body anymore." This takes place on an unconscious level, because this little child can't yet consciously interpret all of his body's signals. But it affects him powerfully anyway.

The child may try hard to produce a BM to please his parents. But he is likely to take out his frustrations and upset feelings in other areas. Perhaps he develops new and irrational fears or has nightmares, whereas before he slept peacefully. Perhaps he develops eating problems or becomes generally balky about routines that previously went smoothly. He may work hard to conform to his parents' expectations in the bathroom, and succeed in learning. But while his parents boast to their friends how easily he was trained, they are completely unaware of the invisible connective thread between the toilet teaching and these new problems that have suddenly developed.

Perhaps your child is not such a docile person about toilet learning. Perhaps he's a rebel. When he learns (for you have taught him) that moving his bowels in certain ways and at a certain time and place seem terrifically important to you, and if he doesn't, he can make you angry, he knows that he can control and frustrate you by not moving his bowels the way you want him to. At this point the Battle of the Bowels has begun, and nothing good can come of it, for either parents or child.

So perhaps the most important message we want to give you about toilet teaching is never to put the child on the potty unless he indicates that he has had an unmistakable signal from his body that he has a biological need.

When we talk about toilet teaching your child we are talking about both bowel and bladder learning. There are differences in these physical and neural mechanisms. Bowel learning is usually easier than bladder learning, so it is wise to begin with that, although in extensive studies done by Dr. T. Berry Brazleton, about 80 percent of children learn both at the same time.

Before you begin to toilet teach your child, he needs to be sufficiently matured, physically and emotionally. For this reason it is wise to wait until he is two before you begin. As we have mentioned before, the child is usually not neuromuscularly able to control his sphincter muscles well until he is about this age.

Your child needs other skills to achieve independence in toileting also. He needs the mental skills of knowing that he has wet or soiled himself. Then he has to become aware when he is doing it and be able to tell others. Still later, he begins to anticipate when he is about to soil or wet. He needs the verbal skills to label his actions and communicate them to you. And he needs the motor skills of being able to walk, sit himself on the toilet, and pull his pants down. He acquires these skills during toddlerhood. In first adolescence he is ripe for learning to put it all together.

Just as you look for signs of your child's being physically and mentally ready, you must also look for his emotional readiness. It is important not to start teaching during a period when negativism is at its peak. Select a time when his general desire to please, his wish to imitate, and his wish to be independent seem particularly strong. Select a time when environmental stresses are at a minimum. Not only is it important for the child to be emotionally ready, but also for you to be emotionally ready. If you are in the midst of a great deal of stress, this is not the time to start.

KNOW WHEN HE'S EMOTIONALLY READY

Sometimes it is not so easy to determine whether your child is emotionally ready. For example, we (FD) attempted to toilet teach our older son, Randy, when he was about two years old. After a few weeks of trying, we came home one Saturday afternoon and heard a tale of woe from the baby-sitter. She said, "You'll never guess what Randy did. He had a big BM and he rubbed it all over his face and hands and then rubbed it all over Siggie [the dog] and then whatever was left he rubbed off on the fence." We decided that Randy was trying to send us a message. So we dropped the toilet teaching and started again at two and a half without any better success. We started it again at three years of age and he was toilet taught in several weeks. This certainly illustrates the fact that you can't teach a child until he is emotionally ready to learn.

On the other hand, some children will teach themselves in spite of the mother's desire not to tackle it at this time. Our (AA) Katie decided at twenty-four months of age that she would no longer wear diapers. She insisted on "big girl pants." I happened to be seven months pregnant with Kimberly, and I knew that Katie would regress to diapers as soon as the new baby was born. Also, I did not want to be bothered with bending over the toilet in my cumbersome state, cleaning out poo-poo pants, when disposable diapers were so convenient. I informed her that this was out of the question and that we would wait a while before she was ready for big girl pants. Katie is our intense, persistent child, remember? You guessed it! She did it herself. She was in training pants in a few days, having mastered the skills necessary for independence. Of course, it goes without saying that she also managed to fill her share of training pants with BM just to make sure that I got to do the washing!

USE A POTTY CHAIR AND TRAINING PANTS

In preparation for training, we suggest you buy a potty chair a few weeks before you plan to begin. We recommend a potty chair rather than a seat that fits over the toilet, since the height of the toilet is awkward for small children and some children become frightened by what to them is the scary roar and turbulence of a flushing toilet. It is easy for a child to get into a potty chair by himself, and the potty also lets him plant his feet firmly on the floor, a necessity for increasing his pushing force for having a BM.

Put the potty in the bathroom near the big toilet, so that he can sit on it while you are going to the bathroom. Remember that he learns a great deal by observing and talking with you about your toileting. First let him sit on the potty with his clothes on, so that he won't react to the cold surface. Then let him sit on it naked. He may love the potty seat so much he wants to carry it all around the house, using it to watch TV or color at a small table. Let him do it. He can even sit on it in the bathtub. (Of course, you'll have to be there to prevent falls.) And who knows? He may even urinate in it by accident—you know how baths are! He'll have his first success.

After he becomes used to this, buy or borrow training pants. You will need a good supply (two dozen if you can't wash every day). Make sure they are loose and big in order to be more easily pulled up and down. Have your child wear the training pants over his diapers and practice pulling them up and down, the way you do. This makes one less skill to learn when he is trying to concentrate on getting to the potty in time. Of course, if you are fortunate enough to live in a warm climate or to be teaching him during summer, you can avoid the problem of pulling pants up and down by putting the potty chair outside in the yard and allowing your child to run around naked or with just a shirt on. This simplifies matters immensely. Running around without pants also helps the child who hasn't quite connected it yet to actually *see* what is going on or coming out, so to speak. He can more fully understand the actions that go with the words.

When the time seems right, tell your child that when he needs to have a BM (or to pee) he can do it in his potty. Tell him he is old enough to be able to do this in the potty just like Mother and Daddy. Next, tell him he is a big boy now and that he can do it when and if he wants to. If you put training pants on him, make sure that there is a supply of clean pants in a lower drawer or on a shelf that he can reach easily, so that he can change his own pants.

REWARD HIM FOR SUCCESS

The psychological process of your teaching him and his learning is simplicity itself. You reward him for every time he successfully gets the BM in the potty chair. Your reward can be warm praise, hugs, kisses, clapping, and exultation; which are even more effective if accompanied by a treat. When he is unsuccessful, you simply say to him in a matter-of-fact voice, "Well, you missed out this time, but you will get it next time." It's only a question of time until your child learns to teach himself to use the toilet. To know that you will eventually be successful should make you feel much easier in your mind.

HANDLING PROBLEMS

On the other hand, you may find that after two or three weeks no progress is being made. Decide that he is not yet emotionally ready. Drop it for now, and resume it at a later time.

If you have been successful at teaching bowel control, but urinary control has not automatically followed, you can teach it separately. Bladder control has two aspects: waking control and sleeping control. For waking control, you will have to rely on the child's own biological signals that he needs to urinate. By talking to him about his body feelings after he has just urinated, he will learn what a full bladder feels like and use this as his signal to go to the potty. Again, please do not put your child on the potty at some chosen time of your own.

In order to have more frequent successes it often helps to increase the child's fluid intake during the training process. This gives him more chances for positive reinforcement and more rapid learning. As with bowel teaching, you reward all of his successes and ignore all of his failures.

If it is a boy you are teaching, do not use a deflector on the potty seat, since it can hurt him and diminish his desire to use the potty seat. Your little boy may want to urinate in the big toilet just like Daddy. If so, get a small step stool so that he can stand up facing the toilet. Don't be caught in the trap that says boys and girls are the same and must be taught sitting down. If your boy wants to urinate standing up, let him. If your little girl wants to try to urinate standing up, let her try until she discovers it doesn't work well for her.

Control of the bladder during sleep is dependent upon two achievements. First, the child must learn through daytime control to respond to tension in his bladder by tightening his sphincter muscles. Second, he must learn to keep his sphincter closed without waking up. Obviously, nighttime control is harder to establish than daytime control, so it takes longer.

Is there anything you can do to establish nighttime control? No, absolutely nothing. The natural maturing of the child's bladder will take care of the situation sooner or later. To make your life more bearable in the interim see the suggestions in "Home Treatment for Bedwetting."

This year your child will probably need help in wiping after BMs or urination. It is important to teach your little girl the proper wiping technique. Little girls who wipe from back to front are very susceptible to urinary tract infection because of the introduction of fecal material into the bladder. Teach your child to wipe from front to back and throw the tissue immediately into the toilet. This will have to be consistently reinforced and checked on throughout childhood.

It is important to vary the toilet conditions with your child, so that he does not require you to take his potty chair with him wherever you go. One family told me (FD) they were driving out in the country to go camping when their two-and-a-half-year-old suddenly announced that he had to go to the bathroom. Since there were no gas stations or other toilet facilities anywhere near, the father took the child into the woods by the road. "No, no," the little boy said, "this is not a bathroom!" It was all the father could do to talk him into doing the job there.

Still, on long trips where there may be no good stops, it is wise to take the potty along in case of emergencies.

Finally, we cannot stress too strongly the importance of not attempting to push or force the child to learn toileting. It will only harm the learning process.

LEARNING TO BE A SOCIAL BEING

First adolescence is the period just before preschool. And the preschooler is expected to be a social creature who gets along well with her peers and behaves appropriately. Don't think that this happens magically overnight on your child's third birthday! Becoming civilized is a long, slow process. It depends on what her learning situations have been in first adolescence. And those situations can affect her behavior in either a positive or negative way.

During first adolescence, when your child tends to be more defiant and rebellious, she can get herself into some pretty nasty situations with her peers and, sometimes, in public. If this negative behavior is inadvertently reinforced, it will appear more frequently. This is a vicious cycle. The child becomes more unpleasant to be around and spoils things for everyone else.

For example, let's consider the hungry two-year-old who is taken to a restaurant where there is a twenty-minute wait before the order arrives. She begins to fuss and cry for something to eat. Her parents try to distract her, talking and playing with her, but her fussing continues. It begins to increase in intensity, becoming wails, until finally her parents ask the waiter to bring them some crackers, which he does. The child stops fussing, and all goes well. However the next time the parents take her to a restaurant, even though she is not particularly tired or hungry, she begins fussing and crying immediately. Again she is rewarded or reinforced by the appearance of some crackers or cookies. This restaurant behavior continues to escalate until finally both parents agree that they should never take her to a restaurant, because she acts like such a brat.

What these parents are not aware of is that their child's first experience in the restaurant was a *learning* experience, and she learned all the wrong things. She learned that by fussing and crying she was able to get what she wanted. Had the parents been prepared for it as a learning experience, they could have been ready to reward the child for her behavior when it was appropriate. Anticipating that the child might grow restless and fussy, they could have taken crackers or fruit with them. As soon as they were seated in the restaurant, when she was quiet and looking around, they could have given her the food and remarked on how nicely she was behaving. If they did not have food with them, they could have gotten something for the child to eat on her first cry for food. Allowing the crying to escalate in intensity and duration only taught her that she must do this to get the attention she wants. The same holds true for behavior in any public place. Or at home too, for that matter.

However, this lesson is easier talked about than taught. When you go into a restaurant, department store, or grocery store, you have a task to accomplish, such as ordering the dinner, buying clothing, or getting the weekly groceries. You can't devote 100 percent of your attention to teaching your child.

PRACTICE OUTINGS

One solution to this is to take *practice outings* to various places solely for the purpose of teaching your child the appropriate behavior. It can be great fun for both of you. The trips not only teach your child appropriate behavior, but are also affectionate one-to-one interactions that are intellectually stimulating as well.

The key to these trips is to keep them short (no more than ten to fifteen minutes) and to use positive reinforcement. Explain to your child that the two of you are going on a special outing, to a store or a restaurant, and that it will be fun; but there are some rules she needs to know before you go. Be sure that when you talk to your child about the rules you are down at her eye level and have her full attention. State the rules simply and clearly. The most important rule is that she stay with you and not wander off. She needs to know that the purpose of the trip is not to buy anything. You will simply look around the store or restaurant and learn how big boys and girls act there. Tell her that she is not to pick up or touch anything without permission; these places are for looking, not for touching. Ask if she has any questions about it. Talk to her a little bit about what you are going to do there. She can get just as excited about going to this new place as she would to a zoo or a park. Pick a time when the establishment is not busy.

Upon arriving at your destination, get down to eye level with your child again, making sure you have her attention, and go over the ground rules again. When you go inside, involve your child in a pleasant conversation, talking about what you see and what she thinks about it. If she wants to look at a particular object, get down and look at it on her level. Try to see it through her eyes and teach her what you can about it.

You will need to praise your child very frequently, at least every two to three minutes. Be sure when you praise her that you state specifically the appropriate behavior she is exhibiting, such as not touching, or not begging for candy, or staying right next to Mommy. As you are giving verbal praise, make sure that you also give her physical reinforcement frequently, patting her on the head, squeezing her hand, rubbing her back.

When it is time to go, state matter-of-factly that you're sorry it is time to go because the trip was so much fun with her, and walk out to the car. If she walks out with you without fussing and begging to stay, be sure to praise her for that. After you are in the car you can talk to her about how pleased you were with how well she did and how it makes you feel like taking her with you on many more trips.

You may need many of these practice outings, and it may seem that it takes a lot of time, but it's worth every bit of it. It will save you time in the long run.

What should you do, however, if your child breaks one of the rules? If this is your first learning trip, remember that she is in fact still learning how to behave. You will need to stop, get down to her level, and remind her of the rules. Tell her this is a warning and that should she forget the rule again she will receive a Time Out. (Remember you are also teaching her that there are consequences when her behavior is inappropriate.) The Time Out should be for two minutes, be assigned matter-of-factly, and be in any space that you deem appropriate. To isolate her in a restaurant you might push her chair away from the table, or put her at an empty table. If she is quite loud and annoying, you could take her to the rest room and put her in a corner. In a grocery store you could place her in a corner or take her outside the store. The other alternative is always to return to the car. Time Outs should be matter-of-fact. If you have your timer with you, all the better. When the Time Out is over do not discuss the behavior. Simply go on with your visit, being sure to give her just as much praise and reinforcement for appropriate behavior as you did before she broke the rule.

Obviously you want to program your child for success on these trips. Be sure that she is healthy, well-fed, and well-rested beforehand. At home that night you and your child can talk about the trip with the rest of the family. Be quite liberal in your praise of her good behavior.

PEER INTERACTION

We have discussed peer interaction in our section on social development in "Overview of First Adolescence." We urge you to read that, in addition to this.

You can help your child develop social skills. First, you can help her feel good about herself, which you have been doing all along. Second, you can provide an environment for play with her peers that is fun and safe. The play group will need to have plenty to do, space to do it in, and freedom to move about without too much intervention (but with supervision). Usually if you keep the group small, this can be done. However, they definitely need to be supervised, since a group of two-year-olds can really get into some knockdown, drag-out fights. It is important to leave them alone most of the time, but also at times to give them plenty of positive adult attention. They will like this most if you actually get down and play with them at their level.

There are two types of behavior that concern parents when they see their child in action with other children: shyness and aggressiveness.

SHYNESS   Obviously, everyone is shy or anxious in a new situation with new people. The anxiety is gradually overcome as things become more familiar, and the person can enter in and have a good time. The child who is slower to warm up, which is a normal temperamental characteristic, may be inappropriately labeled shy. She just takes a little longer to get into things, but she is interested in watching. With a little gentle encouragement and time to adjust, she becomes very happy and involved, a part of the group. The shy child, on the other hand, remains afraid. This is an irrational fear and should be handled very much the same way as other fears that can occur during the first years of life. We have discussed some of these methods in "Special Situations in Toddlerhood." In summary, however, to help the shy child you will need to do the following:

- Accept the child's feelings; don't try to talk her out of them. They may seem unreasonable to you, but they are very real to her.
- When a social situation is forthcoming, whether at your house or at someone else's, you need to prepare the child in advance. This means telling her some things about the people who will be there and talking about some of the feelings that people have when they come into new situations. Explore some possible plans of action to help overcome these feelings.
- Help the child to conquer her fear by giving her exposure to smaller versions of the feared object. In other words, if she has difficulty with children her own age, let her play first with one younger child in your home, where she is safe and secure and can excel. Keep the social situations at this level until she seems happy and comfortable. When you think she is ready, go on to a group of four. Never have a group of three children. Three is a crowd at any age!
- When your child can happily handle this social situation, move on to teach-

ing her to play with children of her own age. You will need to find a play-mate who is not overly aggressive. After she is comfortable with one, she can be exposed to a group. Remember that after each of your child's play sessions, you need to praise and reinforce her for her successful interaction.

• Just as you would with other fears, it helps to have your child play-act situations in which *she* can be strong, brave, and a conqueror. This helps her to overcome her fear of the more dominant child by becoming one herself. She'll love this game!

It will take time to help your child overcome her shyness. She may always be a more cautious child who is quieter than others. The real key, however, is whether she is happy and has the ability to interact when she wishes to do so. If you can get her to this stage by the time she is ready to start preschool, you will have given her a good foundation upon which to develop good peer interaction during the important preschool years.

AGGRESSIVENESS The very aggressive child, on the other hand, can also be of great concern to her parents. Aggression is to be expected at this age, and peer groups of two-year-olds may have days of nothing but grabbing toys, hitting, and pushing, with screams of "Mine, mine!" When aggressiveness does occur it is important to acknowledge the child's feelings, but let her know that she cannot act on them in ways that hurt people.

As always, the best cure for aggression is that ounce of prevention—environmental control. Having playtime when the children are rested and well-fed avoids frayed nerves. Having their own toys and plenty of space to move about can also help to avoid conflicts. When conflicts do occur, and they will, remove your child from the situation by distraction, by giving her a Time Out, or by taking her home. Once you are home and the dust has settled, if she was an aggressor in the conflict you can talk to her about what happened and perhaps help her seek some alternative ways of getting what she wanted. Let her know again that physical force and hurting people are not acceptable. The next time she is about to be involved with a peer, go over some of these ground rules. Be specific about what she can and can't do. However, when she is playing and using appropriate behavior, be sure to praise and reinforce her immediately. All of us parents seem to feel that when children are playing together quietly, it's best to let sleeping dogs lie and not interfere. We breathe a sigh of relief for the moments of peace and quiet. However, remember that by doing so we are not strengthening this desired behavior. In fact, we may be weakening it, especially when we only react to the negative, inappropriate behavior. It's praise that strengthens and reinforces the desired behavior.

BABY-SITTERS

When you have a first adolescent, your needs in a baby-sitter are the same as for the toddler. We recommend that you read our earlier sections on baby-sitters if you have not already. However, in first adolescence, testing behavior can be a problem. It is important that your sitter know your house rules and be able to carry them out. Above all, she must have patience, coupled with the ability to enjoy the good qualities of the two-year-old.

E N V I R O N M E N T A L   C H A N G E S

Our recommendations concerning environmental changes now are basically the same as for toddlerhood. The two-year-old does not like change any better than the toddler. So you need to make extra provision for your child's adjustment to traveling, visiting, or moving. It is easier now, however, for her to deal with changes and for you to prepare her for them, since she is more adept in her communication skills. She is also more independent and more able to participate in a productive fashion. She can help pack her bag or look at brochures for sightseeing spots—pleasant distractions in case she is resistant to the change.

P E T S

We recommend that you read our section on pets in "Special Situations in Infancy," since our suggestions there hold true for the first adolescent as well. She is learning self-control, but it's not all there yet. A pet can be an endangered species in the hands of the first adolescent.

A C C I D E N T   P R E V E N T I O N

Again, we recommend that you read our section on accident prevention in "Special Situations in Toddlerhood" as well as in "The Well Child." The two-year-old is beginning to understand, but doesn't really yet know, what's dangerous. Coupled with her unpredictable behavior, this can be a problem.

Here are some special safety considerations for the first adolescent.
- Your child is now into more rough-and-tumble outdoor and indoor play. Safety glass and decals on glass doors are essential to protect her in her headlong play. She needs to be closely supervised on the playground. It is important to really check out playground equipment, both at home and at public playgrounds. Look out for projections, sharp edges, loose parts, spaces in which your child could entrap her head, and hard swings. Of course, always keep her out of the path of moving swings. A slide should not be higher than four feet from the ground. The surface underneath playground equipment should be soft, preferably sand or bark chips; *never pavement*. The play area should obviously be enclosed, in order to keep the child from darting out into the street.
- The two-year-old is still interested in exploring the universe, so you need to check for poisonous plants. She is too young to be educated about not eating unknown plants. She loves to be outside, and you must be aware of what is going on out there all the time. She should never be outside when a power mower is in use. Any object the lawn mower hits can become a high velocity missile. Children should not be anywhere in the area when a power mower is in use.
- The two-year-old is learning to ride a tricycle and loves riding other toys.

She will particularly want to get out into the driveway and the street, which you must not allow her to do. Because she is so much more independent and moves so much faster now, be particularly careful in shopping center parking lots. In spite of the fact that a mother needs eight hands, there are times when she has to face the fact that she has only two. When she is reaching into her purse to get her car keys, she has no hand available to hold on to her first adolescent. One of the tricks that I (AA) found helpful with my three girls was playing the game of "Don't Let the Car Get Away." The two-year-old loves to feel strong and powerful. I would tell them that the car might roll away from us, and could they please use all their strength and hold on to the car with both hands to keep it from getting away while I found the keys. They loved this game.

• You still need to continue supervising and childproofing your child's environment. Car seats, childproof caps, latches on cabinets and drawers, lowering the hot-water thermostat, and gates at stairways remain the order of the day. The two-year-old cannot be fully educated about avoiding danger yet. Your role is to protect her until she can be.

PART 5

PRESCHOOL

STAGE

23

OVERVIEW OF THE PRESCHOOL STAGE

All the stages we have covered so far have had a single developmental task. This stage is different. This one has nine different developmental tasks. And the years from three to six, the preschool stage, will have an enormous effect upon your child as he meets and attempts to master these nine tasks. They are:

- To fulfill his biological needs for both large and small muscle development.
- To separate himself from his mother.
- To learn the give and take of relationships with his peers.
- To develop a control system for his impulses.
- To learn to express or repress his feelings.
- To stabilize gender identity as a male or female.
- To work his way through the resolution of the "family romance."
- To develop his basic attitudes toward sexuality.
- To go through a period of development in which he is particularly responsive to intellectual stimulation.

Before we look closely at these tasks, let's see what children are like as they pass through the preschool stage.

THE THREE-YEAR-OLD

The three-year-old has passed through the psychological storm and stress of first adolescence and settled down into a period of equilibrium. Now that your child has made it successfully from babyhood into childhood, he no longer needs to be as domineering or dictatorial as he was in first adolescence. He is beginning to learn how to share, to take turns, and to be more patient with physical tasks such as stacking blocks.

The three-year-old is a delightful and wonderful person who is at peace with himself and his world. He loves his life, he loves his parents, and he feels positive about himself. However, in his passage to four he may hit a rough spot around three and a half years. He becomes more fearful, gets frustrated easily, begins whining, seems to need constant reassurance of his mother's love, and may even begin stuttering. This can come as a shock to mothers who may have felt that all the rough spots were over when they got out of the twos. What is happening is that the three-year-old is becoming more introverted, seeming to need to withdraw to gather strength for the expansiveness of the next stage—the four-year-old.

THE FOUR-YEAR-OLD

No mistake about it, four is an age of extremes! Dr. Arnold Gesell suggests that the key word to describe the four-year-old is "out-of-bounds." He is out-of-bounds in his motor behavior. He hits, he kicks, he sometimes throws fits of rage. He runs up and down stairs, careens madly through the house, and slams doors with a bang. He is out-of-bounds in personal relationships. He defies orders and requests. He chafes at all restrictions.

The four-year-old is out-of-bounds verbally also. His drive to talk is compulsive and powerful. He loves to sound off about anything and everything. He is fascinated by words and the sounds of words. He finds the use of bathroom words particularly funny. He will say to his mother, "Mommy, you know what I had for lunch today? I had a BM sandwich!" Following this four-year-old one-liner, he will dissolve in peals of laughter, knocked out by his own incredible wit. He especially likes exaggeration, nonsense rhymes, and humor. Play along with this streak in his nature. He will get much amusement when you ask him questions such as, "Do you have a horse in your pocket?"

Because of the personality characteristics we have just described, four-year-olds need firm parents. A weak or wishy-washy parent will be run into the ground by a four-year-old. And four thrives on variety. He needs a frequent change of pace. You need to sense when a situation is getting out of hand and have a new and interesting activity to present to your child.

THE FIVE-YEAR-OLD

Like three, five is an age of equilibrium. The difficult out-of-bounds behavior of the four-year-old has melted away. He is satisfied with himself, and others are pleased with him. He has returned to the spirit of cooperation and the desire for approval of others which he showed at three, only now he is at a higher level of sophistication.

Five loves his home and his mother and father, but he is also ready for enlarged community experiences. He enjoys playing with friends in the neighborhood. Kindergarten is ideal for him because he is capable of a great deal of intellectual work under the guidance of a skilled teacher. Physically, emotionally, and intellectually, he is a delight to have as part of the family. He functions so well it is only fitting that five should be the culmination of the preschool stage!

Now let's take a look at the physical and psychological growth taking place during these preschool years.

PHYSICAL AND PSYCHOLOGICAL GROWTH

During the preschool years your child is becoming refined emotionally, physically, and socially. This refinement is very apparent in his physical appearance. He is no longer the soft, rounded little youngster with the swayback and the large head. He is becoming slimmer and sleeker, with more adult proportions. It is during these preschool years that your child takes on the body build he is likely to have in adult life.

Physical growth during the preschool years continues its slowing-down period. Your child will probably gain three to five pounds and grow three to four inches between his third and fourth birthdays. Between his fourth and fifth birthdays he will gain another three to four pounds and grow two to three inches. And the following year, between five and six, he will grow at about this same rate.

SKIN AND HAIR

The preschooler's skin continues its slow maturation process, and now it is less susceptible to skin problems than before. However, it is not yet completely mature and is still somewhat susceptible to infection. Your child's hair is losing its baby fineness and also is beginning a darkening process.

HEAD AND FACE

Your youngster's face continues to grow proportionately longer, as it did during first adolescence. With this growth it totally loses its babyish appearance. The sinuses are developing rapidly, and it is during this period that sinusitis is more likely to appear as a consequence of an upper respiratory infection.

EYES

The preschooler continues to be somewhat farsighted but can easily accommodate for it. He has essentially normal vision. This is the time when vision screening should be done, because if an eye muscle defect (*strabismus*) is not picked up before the child is five, it is unlikely that a loss of vision resulting from it can be regained. Eye examinations are important and any sign of muscle imbalance should be checked. Usually by the end of preschool years, at age six, depth perception is mature.

EARS

Ear infections are still frequent in the preschool child, but they decrease as the child matures. The eustachian tube enlarges and assumes a more adult position. However the nasopharynx (the area behind the nose and the back of the throat) is still short and narrow. There is an increase in lymphoid tissue, such as tonsils and adenoids, which can cause a blockage of fluid that results in hearing loss or infection. If you have any suspicion that your child may have a hearing loss, have his hearing evaluated as soon as possible.

NOSE, MOUTH, AND TEETH

The child's nose grows forward, losing its pug appearance. Tonsils and adenoids increase in size, a response to body infections. The teeth remain essentially unchanged, although some of the baby teeth are lost at age five in some children.

IMMUNE SYSTEM

The immune system continues to develop, so infections in the preschooler are less severe than before. They tend to be more localized, with less chance of severe, total body infection, such as septicemia or sepsis.

CARDIOVASCULAR SYSTEM	Your child's heart continues to grow in size and efficiency. The pulse rate of the preschooler ranges from 75 to 120, with an average of around 80 beats per minute. His blood pressure is around 100/60.
RESPIRATORY SYSTEM	The growth rate of the preschooler's respiratory system continues slowly. The airways enlarge and the efficiency of the system improves. Because of the improvement in the immune system and the maturation of the respiratory system, respiratory infections tend to be localized in the upper respiratory tract and are less likely to move down into the lower respiratory tract.
GASTRO-INTESTINAL SYSTEM	The GI system still continues slow maturation, but digestion is essentially mature. Children may still react with GI symptoms when the body is stressed, however.
GENITOURINARY SYSTEM	During the preschool years the child is exhibiting more and more control over his urinary system. Sleeping and waking control becomes complete in most children by the age of five. However, nighttime control may not yet be achieved by approximately 10 to 15 percent of five-year-olds, particularly boys. A child usually voids three to seven times a day during the preschool years.
MUSCULOSKELE-TAL SYSTEM	The preschooler loses his tummy, because his abdominal muscles are stronger. He tends to have a mild swayback, but has a more upright posture. Flat feet usually become arched during this time. Toeing-in caused by foot abnormalities has corrected itself, but toeing-in caused by slight turning of the large bone (femur) in the upper legs may begin to appear during the preschool years. Knock-knees also are common in preschoolers. Both conditions usually disappear with growth, and without intervention. The bones still have a high cartilage content and are somewhat soft. This means they are less likely to break, and they heal easily when broken.
NEUROLOGICAL SYSTEM	The preschooler's nervous system continues to develop, but at a much slower rate. Sensory and motor functions are being refined, and this refinement is reflected in the developmental changes that occur throughout the preschool years.
DEVELOPMENTAL MILESTONES	MOTOR DEVELOPMENT The preschooler shows marked improvement in the quality of his fine and gross motor abilities. The three-year-old tends to be more reflective, quiet, and interested in fine motor activity and language skills. However, he likes gross motor activity, and during this year he learns to pedal a tricycle, begins to walk heel to toe, tries balancing on one foot, and learns to go upstairs by alternating his feet.

The four-year-old is exceptionally interested in motor activity; it goes with his exuberant, out-of-bounds behavior. He has much better control of his legs, and he loves athletic feats. He will probably want to ride a two-wheel bike with training wheels, and if he is exceptionally daring will want to take the training wheels off. They will probably have to be put back on, however. He enjoys a balance beam, and is skilled at heel-to-toe walking. He can come downstairs alternating feet, and he no longer needs to be watched as carefully on stairways.

The five-year-old comes across as a finished product. He is beautiful in his coordination and fluid movement. He hops, skips, jumps, and runs like the older child. He has a wonderful sense of balance, and is much less cautious in his gross motor activities. This is a wonderful age for gymnastic and dancing lessons. The five-year-old rides the two-wheel bike with training wheels. Some will learn to ride it successfully without the training wheels.

The preschooler's progress in fine motor skills is equally exciting. The three-year-old can draw a circle and gradually learns to make a cross, although he needs to have it demonstrated to him before he can do it. Four can draw a square, and five a triangle. He may be able to write some of the alphabet letters and numbers as well.

Preschoolers enjoy working with pencils and papers. The four-year-old can usually draw a primitive-type man with one to three parts. The five-year-old can draw a man with anywhere from three to six or more parts. Four is much more imaginative and abstract in his drawings, but five shows his literal and serious bent by trying to be quite realistic.

The preschooler's block building has improved, with towers of ten or more cubes. He makes bridges and buildings from cubes and can handle smaller and smaller building materials.

The three-year-old becomes adept at buttoning and soon handles buckles quite well. The four-year-old moves on to lacing, and the five-year-old may begin trying to tie his shoes. You will find that five is much less a dawdler when trying to do self-help activities that require fine motor abilities. He has become much more adept in this area and it is obviously less stressful for him.

LANGUAGE Just as fine and gross motor abilities improve in quality, language continues to blossom dramatically during the preschool years. It blossoms as your child's thinking and reasoning abilities expand, and it's exciting to observe. 90 percent of the preschooler's speech is intelligible. This is a welcome change from those early years when you had to try to get inside his head to figure out what he was trying to tell you!

Your three-year-old is still pretty self-centered, so about a quarter of the time his speech is a monologue, regardless of whether anyone else is in the room. Because he is moving from a stage of predominantly motor activity, he still uses a lot of motor movement in his expressive language. He has also not learned to modulate his voice and talks at a louder volume now than he will later in the preschool period.

Your three-year-old is extremely language oriented. He is less physically active and talks less than he did at two, preferring to listen more. He is learning through his language. He wants you to name everything. He is trying to get labels for his whole universe. Make sure that you give your child a name when he asks for it. But don't go into a long explanation about what it does. The three-year-old still enjoys chants and songs and tends to have a sing-song quality to his speech.

Stuttering begins to appear at around three and a half years in many children. This is normal during the preschool years, and it comes and goes, depending on the child and the situation. It usually occurs when the child's mind is working faster than his mouth can. Stuttering is often seen in a younger child with older siblings who hog the show, never letting him get a word in edgewise. If your child stutters, it is important not to react in an anxious manner. Give him time to talk. Make sure that older siblings respect that time and make sure he is not teased. The problem gradually disappears in the majority of cases by the time the child is five.

The four-year-old, as we have said before, loves to hear himself. This is the age of constant "why?" questions. Many times he wants to know the answer, but other times he just wants to get your attention or keep the conversation going. It can drive you daffy! If your child is doing this to you, let him know that you are happy to talk to him and answer his questions, but there are times when you can't handle it, and you would like for him to save them up for a better time. The four-year-old tends to be bossy, especially when talking to toys and animals, and he sounds very much like his parents. He is practicing his expressive language and social learning. It can be great fun to listen to, if you can laugh at how *you* sound to him!

The five-year-old, on the other hand, has fewer questions and is much more serious in his questioning. His speech is modulated and more adult in articulation, although not perfect. Children are not able to pronounce all of the sounds the adult can until they are about seven or eight. Five's language structure and rhythm are fairly adult, and you are unlikely to hear him use infantile speech.

THE MENTAL DEVELOPMENT of the preschooler is fascinating. He remains, in his separateness, an egocentric child. He is unable to perceive from another's perspective. Two preschoolers on opposite sides of a table will look at a picture of a boy standing with arms outstretched above his head (arms toward one child, feet toward the other) and argue about whether the boy is standing on his feet or his hands. Neither one will admit to the possibility of another perspective. And the five-year-old knows his own right and left but cannot project himself to distinguish it on another person.

The preschooler also shows a lack of logical reasoning, because he tends to center on only one part of an object or event. The most classic example of this is the inability of the preschooler to realize that an amount of water poured from a short, fat glass into a long, tall glass is still the same amount even though it appears higher in the skinnier glass. He can only think of tall and short, not width or diameter.

Another immaturity in the preschooler's thinking is responsible for some of his fears and worries. This is the age of magical thinking, when he has difficulty separating fantasy and reality. The preschooler thinks that for every thought he has, an action will occur. For example, the preschooler whose new baby sister suddenly becomes ill may seem to be taking it very hard. He may have wished that the younger sibling would disappear, and feel he is responsible for any harm befalling her. Or if the preschooler becomes sick after defying a parent, he may feel that his defiance has caused his illness. These are important aspects to consider when dealing with your preschooler's reactions to illness or injury.

There are gradual maturations in a youngster's mental abilities during these years. The three-year-old knows his first name, age, and sex. The four-year-old knows his first and last names and the name of the town he lives in. The five-year-old knows these as well as his telephone number and address. Three has an eye for form and shows a sense of order, while four tries to bring order to his thoughts. Three is ready to listen and learn, interested in labels. Four shows more ability to generalize and gives his own appropriate labels to words such as our (AA) Kimberly's announcing that a bunny rabbit was not a bunny rabbit but was a "bunnit." This showed a maturity in her ability; she was able to contract the words while knowing full well what the meaning was. Those are fun words to adopt, since they don't really represent baby talk and are clever and amusing creations.

The three-year-old who is able to discriminate colors becomes the four-year-old who can name colors and discriminate some letters and numbers. The five-year-old goes on to name letters and numbers and do simple arithmetic.

It is during the preschool years that one sees a development of the child's sense of time. This is probably one of the reasons it is easier for the preschooler to separate from his mother. He does understand that there is a "later" and what it means when his mother is coming back to pick him up. The three-year-old shows that he is beginning to understand the past and the future, but it is usually more immediate, such as "yesterday" or "tomorrow." The four-year-old, who has broadened his horizons, understands longer periods of time, such as "last winter" or "next summer." Four is also very aware of the daily sequence of events. A five-year-old is interested in the logistics of time. He will be able to tell time in a primitive way and be quite good at following the plot in a story. Along the same line, he will be able to pick up work that he left off the day before without having to start over again.

Handedness is developing during preschool years and is usually obvious by three. There is absolutely no need to change a "lefty" to a "righty." Allow him to develop his own way.

SOCIAL DEVELOPMENT is continuing at a rapid pace in many areas. Let's take a look at these.

FAMILY INTERACTION

It is during the preschool stage that most parents become aware of something studied extensively by Doctors Gesell, Ilg, and Ames: Children go through stages of equilibrium, in which they seem settled and organized, only to break apart and become unsettled in a period of disequilibrium or transition. (This is called having "up" phases and "down" phases.) The periods of disequilibrium seem like a time when the child needs to withdraw, maybe even taking a step backward and becoming more dependent. He seems to need to get as much energy as he can from the environment in order to gather his forces for the new development that is going on. When he is able to incorporate the new with the old, he then settles into a more calm and peaceful phase. These phases run their course, and each child has his own timetable. It is important that you as a parent know about these phases so that you can assist your child, particularly during some of the more difficult times.

Each up and down phase of the preschool years usually lasts six to twelve months. I (AA) always found it helpful to remind myself that the phase wasn't permanent, when one of my girls was in an ornery, difficult-to-get-along-with stage that was draining my energy. I also realized when one of my girls was going through a more settled phase that I would have about six months to collect myself and to regather my energies before the next challenging phase. So many moms who thought the preschool years would be all smooth sailing after first adolescence throw up their hands in dismay when their four-year-old acts "just like a two-year-old, only he can talk more and get into more!" They weren't prepared for that.

Let's take a look at general behavior patterns in the preschool years, recognizing that each child has an individual rate of development.

As we have said, the three-year-old is collected, happy, eager to learn, and friendly, very much like a one-year-old. However, in his passage to four he may hit some spots in which he resembles the fifteen-month-old in much of his behavior, whereas the four-year-old is very much like the eighteen-month-old. Four is full of himself, rough, impatient, quarrelsome, full of outward energy. At around four and a half he may show signs of turning inward, becoming less adventuresome and more serious. He seems very much as he did at twenty-one months, although more mature.

The five-year-old, as we've said, is settled, serious, poised. He has strong family feelings and is very cooperative, like the twenty-four-month-old. By five and a half to six, however, the unsettled period begins. The child begins to fall apart, becoming more quarrelsome, argumentative, and domineering, much like the two-and-a-half-year-old.

These behavior patterns in the preschool years are more obvious in some children than in others. The intense child, who does everything 200 percent, exhibits these changes in a way you can't miss. The more placid, adaptable child may be so easygoing that the phases are almost unnoticed. However, if your "good, sweet child" becomes an ornery little cuss, look at where he is in his development; perhaps he is getting into one of these unsettled phases. Understanding this should help you deal with him.

In understanding your child's behavior, also keep in mind his individual temperamental characteristics. This is just as important as understanding the behavior phases. Perhaps now is the time to reread the discussion of individual temperament in our chapter "The Daily Care of Your Infant."

The preschooler is going out into the world. The child who is slower to adapt to new situations will need considerate handling. Persistence in appropriate actions is becoming valued by others, and distractibility is less well tolerated. So the child with high distractibility and low persistence will need extra support and help, too.

Supporting and helping your preschooler through difficult times doesn't mean tolerating all his undesirable behavior. He needs to continue to learn the lessons about what is acceptable and what is unacceptable, at any stage. Discipline at this stage can be on a much more rational level. Your preschooler is ready to be reasoned with. He has a strong desire to please, and he loves to imitate his parents, siblings, and other significant adults. He sees you, his parent, as a separate human being, so you can begin to bargain with him. We discuss discipline more fully in our chapters "Discipline in Preschool" and "Special Situations of the Preschool Stage."

Your preschooler will respond to diplomatic demands that stress the positive, such as "We *do* need to brush our teeth before we go to bed," rather than "Don't go to bed without brushing your teeth." Your preschooler is also ready to take the consequences of some of his actions. For example, if it is cold outside and he doesn't wish to wear a coat, let him go outside and find out for himself how cold it is. Let him make the decision that he needs a coat, rather than having it become a battle of wills. (Just make sure that he will not be putting himself in danger.) Your preschooler will sense that you are treating him with respect and will in turn act in ways that will earn your respect. A child who is trusted to act appropriately will, for the most part, live up to that trust.

Obviously your preschooler is still very much a child and will still have accidents, resulting in breakage, spilling, or other similar minor disasters. Your preschooler has a developing conscience. If he accidently breaks something, he will be sorry and needs no further discipline. Help him learn to be responsible for himself by either cleaning the mess up or using some of his own money to replace the broken object. However, keep this type of payment very light. Your goal is not to have your preschooler feel guilty, only responsible. Let him know that you, too, feel bad when things are broken, but that accidents happen and even to adults.

Preschoolers by nature tend to be louder and more boisterous than other children. This can cause many a headache for parents, particularly by the end of the day. What actually happens is that as the preschooler becomes louder and louder (since he has difficulty controlling the volume of his speech), his parents, peers, or siblings become louder and louder in response. But remember that the preschooler loves to imitate. If the adult is able to notice what is happening and begins to talk in a soft, quiet voice, sometimes even exaggerating it into a whisper, the preschooler will soon follow. Use this trick to give yourself some peace and quiet on rough days.

PEER INTERACTION AND PLAY

The preschooler is much more interactive with his peers than ever before. However, during the early preschool years he is still not civilized and needs to be supervised in groups, since physical aggression can get out of hand—or foot or mouth, for that matter!

Your three-year-old is learning to take turns, but it is not easy. When there is only one swing and three preschoolers, getting a swinger to give it up is tough. One way to help ease the pain is to tell everyone that you will all count to ten, or any other number that seems appropriate, and when you reach the end, the swingers will change. Another way is to set the kitchen timer for a period of one to two minutes. When the timer rings, the next child gets a turn. Somehow this seems more objective and fair to preschoolers than having an adult seemingly arbitrarily say that their turn is over. They can learn how to set the timer themselves and to count themselves, and no longer need adult intervention.

The three-year-old is able to share much better than the two-year-old, but still may have some tough moments. If your three-year-old has a particularly precious toy or possession that he does not relish sharing, then put it up out of reach before his friends come over to play. When sharing does become a problem, a technique of substitution can be very helpful. For example, if Janet has the only toy coffeepot and Susie wants it, you can tell Susie that Janet needs the coffeepot right now and that perhaps Susie could set the table for a tea party. Also, using such terminology as "needs" or "has to have" seems to work infinitely better than saying "wants" or "insists," just as it does with adults. Remember, too, that even though your three-year-old enjoys playing in groups, he still enjoys being alone. So don't force him into interactive play with his peers. Allow him to play alongside his peers in parallel play as much as he wants.

The four-year-old seems to have an insatiable drive to play with other children. He may want to be at a friend's house or have a friend over all the time. He is quite good at taking turns and at group play; however, his out-of-bounds behavior is very evident in his interaction. He is very verbally assertive, often fooling peers and adults into thinking that he is more mature than he is. In his play with peers he often engages in tall tales and boasting, such as "My daddy is smarter than your daddy!" This horrifies parents who put adult values on what the children are saying. However, it is merely a game, an exercise in verbal skills for a four-year-old. This is the age of extremes, remember.

The four-year-old has an active imagination, and this is the age when the imaginary companion may show up. The imaginary companion may be a human or an animal. If it is an animal, the child may even take on some of the qualities of the imaginary companion. It is as if he were trying on a new identity. An imaginary companion can serve primarily as a good friend, but can also serve as a conscience or a scapegoat for the child. Children who have imaginary companions are often more imaginative and social children. They are not necessarily lonely, something parents worry about. Children who have imaginary companions are often working on their self-control and developing their conscience. It seems to be much easier for them to like themselves if they can put their bad feelings onto imaginary companions, their scapegoats.

You can go along with your youngster's imaginary companion in a play or pretend fashion, and it can be a lot of fun. However, it is important to let your child know that *you* know this is a pretend being. You will go along with it only in a make-believe fashion and not at the expense of others. For instance, I (AA) remember growing up with my brother Rick, who had an imaginary friend, Harvey. The family enjoyed knowing Harvey through Rick, but drew a line when Harvey took one of the chairs at the dinner table. We were a large family, with six children, and there were no extra chairs around! My mother asked Rick to please tell Harvey that he would be fed later because all the seats were taken. He did it very ceremoniously, while the family giggled with him. An imaginary companion may continue with the child on into the early elementary school years, but the five-year-old is probably the most adept at this type of play, carrying it out to perfection.

The five-year-old really needs other children too, and he plays well in much larger groups. He can now play organized group games well and can play by the rules *fairly* well. There isn't a five-year-old in the world, however, who loves losing. They *all* hate it! It is still important at birthday parties and in situations where prizes are awarded that each child receive a little something.

The five-year-old understands sharing and taking turns and is much more able to organize his play in a more adult fashion. His conversations with his friends are more serious and literal. Preschool play can involve some cruelty both verbally and physically, since the preschooler is still not good at respecting other people's feelings. "Three's a crowd" is still a problem.

You can, however, develop empathy in your preschooler by pointing out how another person might feel in various situations. It can also be done through play, by playing games in which he takes on the role of another person and pretends to be him. This is called *role taking* or *role playing*. You can also assume his role. Let him see how it makes him feel. It is in this way that he learns that other people have perceptions and feelings that are different from his.

This social understanding is usually mastered by the time the child is seven years of age, but the preschool years are a crucial time to begin the lesson. It has been shown in studies that preschoolers who are taught role taking are much more helpful toward others, making them more successful in society.

The preschooler uses play to try on adult roles, embodying every facet of living. Preschoolers will have make-believe weddings, babies, fights, and all the other excitement of the adult world.

Your preschooler also uses play to release tensions, by reenacting events that have caused him fear or anxiety. It's also helpful for you if you can listen to him while he is playing, since he may not be able to let you know how he feels in words.

It is important to listen to your child's play but not to interfere or try to direct him. But you may make a few comments using the feedback technique if you think it will be helpful. For instance, the preschooler who has been particularly sweet and nice to his brand new baby brother might be playing house with his dollhouse. In his play, the baby leaves with the grandparent while the older child stays home with the parent. You could make a comment such as "It looks like the baby needs to get out of the house. Now the big boy gets his mommy and daddy all to himself." You might then ask him how that big boy feels about the baby, allowing him to discuss negative feelings about his sibling in the third person. He can thus get the feelings out, get your reactions to them, and find out whether you'll accept them *and* him.

Many parents are distressed at the amount of violence that preschoolers exhibit in their play. It is important to remember that the violence shown in preschool play is not truly adult-type violence; it is often just a game. Remember, when they say "I'm gonna kill you," they have no idea of the permanence of death. Aggression and experimenting with ways to deal with it are part of their learning. If you remove toy guns from them, they will use a broom handle, a stick, or their fingers to "shoot" you. Some children could care less about these kinds of games; others are really into them (usually boys or active and aggressive girls).

It would be appropriate to sit down and talk to your child about how you feel about guns, and killing and violence particularly, if it seems the play is getting out of hand or your child is playing these games excessively. When violent events are seen on TV or talked about at home, take the opportunity to talk about it with your child. Discuss the rights and wrongs of this type of behavior. Just as your youngster learns to work out his aggressive feelings in his play, he also learns through you what is appropriate and right. There is much controversy over the effects of TV and movie violence on children. If you feel that your child is using excessive amounts of violence and aggression in his play, and he is watching a lot of violence on the screen, it would be appropriate to curtail the TV or movie violence in order to decrease his exposure.

LEARNING SELF-CARE   The preschooler is making rapid progress toward complete independence in self-care. You need to make the environment as supportive as possible for this independence, but recognize that he still needs some assistance. In order for him to be independent in grooming, you need to look at his environment through his eyes. Remove obstacles, if you can. If you want him to dress and undress himself, make sure that the clothes are easy to get. Are they hanging on a low rod? Are they in a drawer that is easy to open and close or, possibly even better, on an open shelf? Are hooks low enough for him to hang his clothes on? Are his clothes easy to manage and do they allow him freedom of movement?

To avoid hassles in your youngster's fight for independence, get shoes that slip on or buckle. He is not ready to tie shoelaces. Can he reach his toothbrush and the sink? Brushing teeth can be made fun if you use those disclosing agents that color the "dirt" pink, making a visible target for his brushing.

Bath time for the preschooler is still a lot of fun. He can pretty much handle it by himself, including trying to wash his hair. It's much more exciting for him if there is a mirror in the bathtub in which he can see himself and experiment with many different hair styles when his hair is soapy. You will need a creme rinse to keep the knots out of the hair, and use a wide-toothed comb to make combing out less painful, so that hair washing is not dreaded. Most preschoolers still need help with hair combing—they forget they have a back to their head!

Just as you are making the environment one in which your child can become more independent, you also need to be giving your child a greater sense of independence by allowing him to make choices. This can be done easily in the area of self-care. It is important to remember, however, to be careful about how you present these choices. If there is something that he has to do and there is really no yes or no choice, present it in such a way. For example, if he has to brush his teeth, then give him the choice of "Do you want to brush your teeth before your bedtime story or after your bedtime story?" Ask him, "Do you want to wear this outfit or that outfit to nursery school tomorrow?" rather than giving him a whole closet full of clothes to choose from.

However, a word of warning: As he matures, the preschooler will quit falling for that gambit and will want to choose from the whole closet. I (AA) have found this to be one of the more frustrating and traumatic issues of the preschool years. It seemed inevitable that Kelly, Katie, and Kimberly during these years would come out on the hottest day of summer dressed in their heaviest woolen outfits, and vice versa. I knew that I should let them suffer the consequences of their choice, but I couldn't see them doing it for the whole day. I finally learned that cleaning out the closets and leaving only the seasonal clothes in was the environmental control that I needed to keep my sanity.

The three-year-old continues to need some assistance with dressing, still having problems with back, front, right, and left. He handles buttons and zippers fairly easily. The four-year-old dresses himself without much assistance, although he is certainly not into color coordination. Right or left foot and shoe may still give the five-year-old problems, but he is usually quite independent otherwise. Tooth-brushing and hair combing still require adult intervention, at least for checking on some of the hard-to-reach spots.

The preschooler can take a bath independently as long as an adult is nearby. Many preschoolers want privacy and resent adult intervention. It is important to teach your child which is the hot tap and which is the cold tap so he will not turn on the hot and burn himself.

In the toileting area, by three years of age most children have control. But daytime accidents are certainly not unusual, since the three-year-old tends to hold off going to the bathroom too long and often doesn't quite make it. If this is a recurrent problem, it may help to have some type of positive reinforcement to encourage him to pay attention to his body signals. Give him a happy face, a star, or some other appropriate token when he does make it to the bathroom on time.

Your three-year-old is able to care for himself in the bathroom but is not a terrific wiper, so he may need to be checked on. The four-year-old, on the other hand, insists on privacy and usually resents being wiped. The four-year-old is really "into bathrooms." He is very much interested in bodily functions and curious about all bathroom activities. The five-year-old is totally independent and also more self-conscious about his bathroom activities.

MEALTIME   Civilized behavior at mealtime is not to be expected in the young preschooler. In fact, the three-year-old may need to eat alone or only with siblings for the majority of his meals. It is best not to put him into a situation in which he is not going to do well, and the dinner table is one of those situations. The young four-year-old may also be in the same predicament. He is usually not able to control his talking and wriggling very well. He is much more easily distracted at four than he is at four and a half or five.

By four and a half or five, the child is more able to control himself and to sit at the table without constantly jumping up. He can finally manage talking and eating at the same time. Have clear-cut guidelines as to what is appropriate behavior at the table. Remember, the most effective teachers are the adult role models he lives with. Use positive reinforcement when you catch him being good and positive instructions such as, "We sit in our chairs at mealtime. We talk when our mouth is not full. We like to let other people finish what they are saying before we talk." These are much more effective than the "don'ts."

Use a Time Out when your youngster has broken one of the rules, but use it only twice. The third time, remove his plate without comment and don't feed him until the next meal. Remind him of the rules before the next meal, and praise him frequently whenever he practices good behavior.

SLEEP   In the area of sleep, the preschooler is making some changes. He is beginning to drop his nap, although he may still need a rest period. Make it a game such as a "play nap" or a "play rest" and allow him to fix his pillows and blankets on the floor in the shape of a house, a bus, an airplane, or a train. He may snuggle in and inadvertently fall asleep.

The three-to-four-year-old begins having nightmares or night terrors (very intense nightmares from which the child does not wake and which the child does not recall). Putting the preschooler to bed takes more time than it did earlier, and the bedtime routine is often around thirty minutes long. In a study on preschool sleep done at Cornell, it was found that almost a third of the three-year-olds needed a night light, with this need increasing at age four and decreasing by age five. Almost half of the children at age three and four took toys or blankets to bed. This need decreased by age five. Three-quarters of the preschoolers regularly called out at least once after being put to bed, and it took them at least thirty minutes to fall asleep. Waking at night was not at all an unusual occurrence and was likely to occur one or more times a week during the preschool years. This was often associated with nightmares or night terrors.

The occurrence of bad dreams is believed to be due to the fact that the preschooler has a lot of imagination and is more likely to worry. Using the nighttime ritual that was established in the earlier years is important, making allowances for the additional needs of the preschooler. For example, the preschooler who is able to awaken in the night to go to the bathroom may be afraid to go, even though he has a light on. He could be helped by having a potty by his bed and some environmental comforts: Let him have a light on as long as he wants it; let him have a radio, record player, or tape recorder, or books and toys beside his bed. He will listen to his radio or play with his toys and gradually settle himself down.

When your child has nightmares and wakes up crying, get to him as quickly as possible so that he will not get himself worked up and can go back to sleep with a little soothing or patting. When he has a night terror he will seem very "out of it," not really knowing what is going on or appreciating the fact that you are there. He may be staring into space and screaming in absolute terror. Try to soothe him and not waken him. It is important not to panic. Some children with night terrors begin running around and don't know where they are. It is important to hold that child and even rock him. It may be necessary to awaken him by dabbing cool water on his face in order to get him under control. If he wakes up, soothe him and then matter-of-factly put him back to bed.

Night terrors are more likely to occur when the child has been sick or is overtired. It is important if you have a baby-sitter to let her know how to handle these situations, since they can be very frightening. Also, should they become very frequent, discuss them with your physician. In rare instances they may be a result of a seizure disorder.

The preschooler is much more likely to come into his parents' bed in the night because of nightmares or other fears. Whether or not he should be allowed to sleep in his parents' bed is a controversial subject. It should be an individual decision, based on your needs and your child's needs. Some professionals advise against allowing the child to sleep in the parent's bed. They feel that this encourages the child's dependency on his parents or is too stimulating for the child, who is in the middle of the "family romance" during the preschool years. Another concern is that the child's coming into the parents' bed may interfere with their sex lives or privacy. Should the child be distressed, the parent is advised to go to the child in his own room, leaving once he has been comforted.

On the other hand, other professionals feel there is no reason not to do what seems to come naturally: allowing the child to get into bed with his parents when he is troubled. It often seems the most comforting thing for him. Once he has settled down he can be moved back to his own bed or remain with you, if it does not disturb you. This usually does not become a persistent need. It disappears on its own as the child matures. Having the child in bed can also be a warm and snuggly feeling for parents as well. But it can get crowded, especially if you have more than one preschooler! If it seems that your child is beginning to want to get into your bed too much, or if it is interfering with your needs, use your own judgment about stopping it. Tell him that it is interfering with your ability to sleep and that it tends to make you grouchy the next day. When he comes in, take him back to his own bed. If necessary, wait until he falls asleep. Then return to your bed. He will gradually stop if you do this consistently.

INDEPENDENCE OUTDOORS Your child is also learning to be independent in the neighborhood during the preschool years. The three-year-old can play in a fenced-in yard without having his parents there supervising him at all times. The four-year-old is able to go to a neighbor's house, if it doesn't involve crossing the street. The five-year-old can learn to cross the street, if it is not a busy one, and go over to a friend's house unaccompanied. But he is still not ready to handle a bicycle or tricycle in the street. However, you will need to make many "learning trips" with him, practicing crossing the street, to be sure he can handle himself and knows your safety rules, before he can be given his wings.

D E V E L O P M E N T A L   T A S K S

Let's take a look now at how you can help your preschooler master the nine developmental tasks of this stage, which we listed at the beginning of this chapter.

Your preschool child is an energy factory. She takes in raw materials in the form of food; out of these she manufactures huge supplies of energy. Then she needs to release this energy. She needs to walk, run, jump, wriggle, climb, and be on the go.

So provide your preschooler with plenty of play space and play equipment, both indoors and outdoors, to allow her to expand her boundless energy and

FULFILLING BIOLOGICAL NEEDS

develop her physical skills. The equipment recommended for toddlers is still appropriate. If a child is compelled to be unnaturally quiet and "good" during her preschool years, she will be at a disadvantage with her grade-school classmates later. She will lack the basic muscular coordination which is necessary for developing skill in the games and sports of school. So when you're giving your child's mind a chance to grow and expand during the preschool years, be sure you give her body an equal chance. Give her lots of opportunities to climb, to become physically dexterous, to walk, to run, and to yell.

SEPARATION FROM MOTHER

During the stage of first adolescence your child is not yet ready to separate from her mother. For this reason it is generally not a good idea to send your two-year-old off to nursery school. But when your child becomes three or thereabouts (some are ready at two and a half and others not until three and a half or four), things are different. She now wants to become more independent. An easy way to help her do this is to send her to a good nursery school. A skilled teacher can help even a shy child to separate from her mother. If for any reason your child cannot attend nursery school, then you can help her accomplish this developmental task by encouraging her to venture out and play with neighborhood children. It is a BIG STEP for your child to become independent of you. It is a step that is accompanied by considerable trepidation on the part of the child. For a while she feels very ambivalent about it. Part of her wants to launch out into her newfound independence, but part of her wants to stay back and cling to the security of her mother. She will need help in making this big step.

PEER RELATIONSHIPS

When you analyze the reasons that people are fired from jobs, you will find that in most cases it is not for the lack of technical competence, but for inability to get along with their colleagues. Certain things they do rub other people the wrong way. And these difficulties in interpersonal relations can be traced back to the preschool years, when many children have difficulty in adjusting to the new world of their peers.

As we have said, during the preschool stage an important part of your child's social development is learning the give and take of relationships with other children. She finds that the world of peer relationships is dramatically different from the world of her family. She may be accustomed to conning her mother and manipulating her, but she may find that such tactics do not work with her peer group.

Peer relationships have a new set of rules and demands. The child may find that she is not always accepted by her peers, as she is in the bosom of her family. Sometimes peers accept her and other times they do not. So she needs a whole new set of relationship skills. She needs to learn to put her feelings into words, to stand up for her rights, to share, to take her turn, and to assert herself without resorting to pushing or hitting.

No child is born with these social and emotional skills. They must be learned and they must be mastered in early childhood in order for them to be effective in adult life. We have mentioned in our section on social development what you might expect in your child's peer interaction at different age levels in the preschool years. The most important ingredient for success is exposure to peers. Having play groups at your home and at friends' homes is an excellent way to begin, and nursery school is an ideal place for refining socializing skills.

The suggestions given in "Special Situations in First Adolescence," about how to help your child over rough times in peer interaction, still hold true for the preschooler. The shy preschooler and the aggressive preschooler require the same sort of intervention. The young preschooler who has a lot of difficulty sharing can learn to do this more smoothly by playing with an older child (five or six years of age), who is less likely to feel threatened by the preschooler's seeming selfishness.

We will discuss more fully the pros and cons of nursery school in "Special Situations of the Preschool Child."

AN IMPULSE CONTROL SYSTEM

During her preschool years your child also needs to learn to develop an impulse control system. A very young child is a primitive creature with no control at all over her impulses; if another child wrestles a toy from her, she may hit the other child with a toy to get it back. But as your child reaches her third birthday, she is actively working on controlling herself. Remember, that was one of the tasks of first adolescence. If she was successful at this, she will be showing some signs of emotional and physical self-control by three years of age. But it takes time to develop control, usually about three more years.

There are two major mistakes parents make in teaching impulse control to their preschool child. First, some parents make no demands at all for control. If their child hits another child, they say nothing. The result is that when the child is six, she still has pretty much the same impulse control she had at age two. Most parents, however, tend to err in the opposite direction; they pressure the child to learn to control her impulses too fast. Three is a good time to work on learning more control (but don't expect the lesson to be completed), since it is an age of equilibrium.

EXPRESSING FEELINGS

The years between two and six are the years in which your child learns either to express her feelings or to keep them stuffed inside. In Chapter 20, "Discipline in First Adolescence," we first suggested that you allow your child to learn to express both her positive and negative feelings. What we said in that chapter continues to be very important during the preschool stage.

It's not until about age seven that your child can fully understand that other people have feelings also and that she should respect those feelings. And from the age of six on, during middle childhood, she will begin to understand better that there are times and places to express feelings and times and places to keep them to herself. But in the preschool years, your main concern is to help your child learn to express her feelings. You can continue using the feedback system to make the process easier for both you and her. You can also continue developing her empathy, so that she can become more aware of the feelings of others and of her effect on them.

GENDER IDENTITY   In our overview of the stage of toddlerhood (Chapter 13), we talked about what we call *positive gender raising*. If you have not recently read that chapter, do so now; for everything it discusses applies to your family throughout each stage of your child's emotional and intellectual growth. Positive gender raising is an important part of your child's healthy gender identity. Valuing and respecting both sexes will help her to feel solid and comfortable as a member of her own sex.

THE FAMILY ROMANCE   During the years from three to six, both boys and girls go through a normal stage of development which we call "the family romance." Whereas a little boy's previous relationship to his mother has been solely a babyish and dependent one, around the age of three his feelings about her begin to change. At this time he develops new romantic feelings about her. If he is open about this, he will say things such as "Mommy, when I grow up I'm going to marry you, and Daddy can go away somewhere." These romantic feelings are nature's way of getting the boy ready for his eventual role as a husband to some future wife.

Unfortunately, there's a catch to this. The family romance is also a family triangle. He comes to realize that his father has a relationship to his mother that he doesn't have, and he feels jealous. If a father is unaware of his child's psychological task, he may take it all personally, not realizing that this is a stage that every young boy goes through. In a normal family situation, the little boy gradually realizes that his fantasies of being a replacement for Father are not going to come true. So he finally begins to adopt the attitude, if you can't lick 'em, join 'em. He decides that since he can't be Father, now he will settle for *being like* Father.

By the time most little boys are six they have resolved the family romance and passed successfully through this very important phase of development. Deep within the boy are now unconscious images of the type of woman he will later want to marry as well as the type of husband he will be to such a woman.

The little girl goes through the process of the family romance in the same way, only the characters are reversed. She wants to marry Daddy, and Mother is the rival. Finally she resolves this by realizing that she cannot have Daddy, and she begins to imitate and emulate Mother.

EARLY SEXUALITY   For over twenty years I (FD) have been treating people of all ages and backgrounds suffering from different types of psychological difficulties: marriage problems, depression, anxiety reaction, phobias, and so on. For each of these people, I have taken a personal life history. One of the standard questions I ask is, "What kind of sex education did you get at home?" The answer is always the same: "I didn't get any sex education at home." Yet it is in the first six years of life that our basic attitudes toward sex are formed.

Sexual attitudes and problems are often the result of our inability as parents to talk in a relaxed way about sexual information with our children.

Even a parent who believes that masturbation is perfectly normal may find difficulty in handling the situation when he finds his young child playing with his sexual organs. Your three-year-old boy is taking a bath and you discover that he is fondling his penis. In earlier times people believed that nothing like this occurred until teenage days. But now we know that pleasure in playing with sex organs is a part of the normal development in the preschool stage. It doesn't mean he's oversexed! What's the best way to handle this situation? Ideally, leave your child alone. Later he can be taught not to practice this behavior in public. If it still bothers you, we suggest you talk with your doctor or any professional who has experience in dealing with children.

Sex play is a common and natural occurrence during the later preschool years. It is not "sexual" in the adult way. It usually involves playing "doctor," and is children's way of learning *all* about each other.

Some parents become alarmed and even feel disgusted at what seems to them "dirty play." They may punish or scold the children, stopping them immediately. Others feel less alarmed and can deal with it matter-of-factly. They can acknowledge the children's interest in knowing the differences between the sexes and initiate a conversation about it, getting some health-related books with pictures for illustration. The children are in this way encouraged to talk freely and ask questions, a good beginning for their future sex education. The children can be encouraged to come back again to ask questions anytime. This decreases the need for sex play. If you can handle it in this way, sex play will gradually decrease as your child matures. It will no longer be necessary.

Another aspect of the sex education of young children concerns nudity in the home. We feel that for a youngster up to the age of four to five, an open policy toward nudity is fine if the parents are comfortable with it. It may make for a more healthy attitude toward sex if children and parents are free to be nude, or partially nude, around the home while the children are preschoolers. Later on, things change. The child may begin to be stimulated by the sight of her nude parent. The parent usually senses this, feels uncomfortable, and becomes more modest. The child should never be chastised for her feelings. Simply avoid being undressed in her presence. If she walks in on you, matter-of-factly express the need for privacy. As children mature, usually between the ages of four and seven, they themselves develop modesty. At this time, for example, your child may want the bathroom door closed when she is taking a shower. You should respect her right to privacy, too.

The issue of sex education for our young people is a very important one, and in our chapter "Discipline in Preschool," we have some additional suggestions on the subject.

SENSITIVITY TO INTELLECTUAL STIMULATION

The preschool stage is a particularly important one for your child's intellectual growth. The kind of stimulation she receives during this period determines the basic skills and attitudes toward learning that she will carry with her the rest of her life. You can define your child's intelligence very simply as "her storehouse of basic learning skills." Each time you increase her basic learning skills, you increase her intelligence.

What's the best way of making sure that your child receives an optimal amount of intellectual and emotional stimulation during the preschool stage? One of the best ways is to enroll her in a good nursery school when she is three years old and able to be away from mother. Of course, if you can't afford nursery school or if there isn't a good one near you, you will need to make other arrangements, which we will discuss in our chapter on preschool stimulation where we describe in detail how you can set up the equivalent of a good nursery school in your own home.

During the years from three to six an enormous amount of development is taking place in your child. She has worked through and mastered nine developmental tasks. And very crucial developmental tasks they are. Many of the attitudes and much of the learning she acquires during these three years will remain with her the rest of her life.

24

It is during the preschool years that your child finally begins to like a wide variety of food, cuts down his dawdling, and begins to move toward better table manners. Unfortunately for nutrition, however, this is also the age when a lot of yummy, chocolaty, rich foods get extra value in your child's eyes because of TV blitzkrieg commercials. Peer pressure becomes a factor, too. You will hear, "But Mom, Artie gets sugar-coated cereal, so why can't I?" With this increased exposure to sugar, however, also comes the increased ability of your preschooler to be reasoned with. He will listen to your explanation about tooth decay and may even become a little fanatic about avoiding it. But your task is not always that easy. Chances are you will need to remember to be the "gatekeeper," and control the food that comes into your home.

Your youngster is now ready to sit at the table during family meals. Although he is working on learning manners, that should not be the overwhelming topic at the dinner table, for it can become an area of conflict that interferes with pleasant food consumption. Earlier we suggested some methods of teaching your child manners. He will also absorb some from being with the rest of the family at mealtime. If you, his role models, are accustomed to saying "please" and "thank you" at the table, your preschooler will probably also say "please" and "thank you." But at times he will need a gentle reminder.

Your youngster can now learn to serve himself at the table and pour his own drinks, and he is very adept at handling a fork and a spoon. He is probably not ready to use a knife for cutting, but he certainly will want to try using a knife for spreading. You may have to grit your teeth while he makes giant holes in the bread when he spreads butter. You can make his job easier by using soft margarine or by softening the butter before putting it on the table.

Your youngster now like to fetch his own snacks at home, so keep them available in the refrigerator or in a cupboard or drawer where he can help himself. Some preschoolers gradually drop their need for snacks, and others continue the need. All nursery schools and day-care centers have snack times. Your child can handle delays in meals more easily now, because he has a greater capacity to control his behavior. Although he still needs regular mealtimes, that structure can now be loosened up.

Your child can do quite well when eating out in restaurants as long as the service is fast and the meal does not exceed a half hour to forty-five minutes. It is still wise to order ahead for a pizza, because that twenty-minute wait can be intolerable even for a preschooler. Fast-food restaurants will probably still provide the easiest experience in eating out.

W H A T

Your preschooler can now eat all the foods that the rest of the family eats, including nuts. There is no reason to avoid any kind of food with your youngster unless he is allergic to certain foods. However, he still prefers simple foods and may have a limited list of likes for a while longer. His favorites are likely to be hamburgers, hot dogs, spaghetti, pizza, and peanut butter.

In Appendix F we have suggested a diet for a healthy preschooler. We remind you that this is simply a suggestion of the types of foods he should be offered. What he eats may vary from day to day. If he still likes a snack, as most preschoolers do, remember to incorporate it as part of his overall nutrition plan. If he does come into contact with more sweets than you feel are good for him, simply find out what he has eaten and discreetly remove the food that has the highest sugar content from the following meal or meals. Things will balance out in the long run.

Encourage your child to eat the foods that are high in sugar content at his meals rather than as snacks. Other foods help wash the teeth, and fat consumed with the meal coats the teeth and protects them further, thus enhancing the odds against tooth decay. Get him into the habit of drinking water or rinsing his mouth after a sweet, particularly a chewy and sticky one. At home, you can brush his teeth after sweets or have him brush them. Sweets and junk food are defined in Chapter 14, "Nutrition in Toddlerhood."

Now that your child sometimes eats at friends' houses, you may be in for a surprise. He will eat some things there that he will not eat at home, perhaps preferring the way they are prepared or presented, or eating them simply because his friend does. Let him tell you what he likes about the food—and you may learn something new.

In preschool your youngster will probably be learning facts about nutrition, which can back up your ideas at home. He can learn what foods have value for protein, carbohydrate, fat, and certain vitamins and minerals, and what foods have high sugar content. He can become a partner in planning the meals, if he knows that there have to be foods from each group. Teaching by involving him in the planning is more likely to interest him in eating intelligently.

H O W

Your child is learning to appreciate foods for their different appearances, flavors, and textures, and can verbalize his feelings about it. Colorful food (especially orange, yellow, red, and green) is particularly enjoyable and he appreciates the decorative touch of a sprig of parsley. He also enjoys sandwiches cut into different shapes and likes cutting them himself.

At the family dinner table your child is learning as much about people and relationships as he is about eating, so try to make mealtimes as friendly and congenial an experience as possible. This isn't always easy when your youngster sometimes gets tired of trying to manage his utensils properly, becomes restless when sitting, and wants to revert to more primitive ways of behaving.

Having special family dress-up meals will continue to excite your preschooler and entice him into showing his best behavior. One way I (AA) have found to make learning manners more fun has been to declare that one meal a month, usually a dinner, will be considered the "pig meal"—the one at which the children can practice their *worst* table manners with gusto. It creates a lot of giggles and groans, and gives them an appreciation of why we try to use good table manners.

Your youngster appreciates any imaginative, creative approaches to the preparation and presentation of food and enjoys helping with the preparation. As recommended earlier, *Feed Me I'm Yours* by Vicki Lansky can help you prepare foods your child will enjoy, and contains recipes that he himself can do. He is excited about learning and doing adult tasks. In cooking, he will want to try new recipes and become your partner in providing good nutrition for himself and your family.

25

D I S C I P L I N E I N P R E S C H O O L

In the chapters dealing with discipline in earlier stages of development, we confined ourselves to methods of promoting "good" behavior and discouraging "bad" behavior. In this preschool stage we extend our teaching goals far beyond simple day-to-day behavior. The things you are going to teach your child now will affect his entire future life. Happily, these years from three to six are golden years for your child's learning.

Please get a pencil and paper and take a few minutes out of your busy life. Imagine that your child is now twenty-seven. What kind of person do you want him to be at that age? Don't read any further in the book. Just write down the different aspects of character and personality you would like him to have when he is twenty-seven.

We hope you played fair and wrote down your list before coming back to the book.

Although each child and parent is unique, here is our stab at a list that you might have made. (These qualities are not in order of importance.)

When he's twenty-seven I want my child to be:

1. Courteous
2. Ethical, with a good value system.
3. Able to communicate well with other people.
4. Able to give and receive physical affection.
5. A good reader who really likes reading.
6. Able to write simply and clearly.
7. Able to handle math well.
8. Able to speak up and assert himself.
9. A good sex partner.
10. Curious about many things.

1. You want to teach your child to be courteous. Anyone who has had much contact with kids between seventeen and twenty-two would probably agree that in many respects we have raised a generation of discourteous louts.

If you want your child to be courteous and well-mannered, you will need to teach him. And you will need to start early. Age three is an ideal time. Here's how to do it.

Sit down with your three-year-old when you have some quiet time and say something like this: "Peter, today I'm going to teach you a very important thing. I'm going to teach you about courtesy and manners." Talk about why we need to practice courtesy. If you've been helping him develop his empathy as we suggested in our "Overview of the Preschool Stage" chapter he will understand how much better a courteous person can make him feel.

"Let's start by learning how to say 'please.' The rule is: When you're asking for something, you need to say 'please.' If I want you to do something, I say, 'Peter, will you come to lunch now, please?' You can practice saying it to me. You can say, 'Mommy, may I play outside, please?'"

Then you and Peter can practice role-playing different situations where you say "please" to each other. This leads naturally to "thank you." Every time you ask him "please" do something and he does, say "thank you" afterward. At your second teaching session, you can call his attention to "thank you." You can then role-play situations where he says "thank you" when somebody—his teacher, a friend, a friend's parent—gives him something or does something nice for him.

At a later session you can explain to your child that there is another way to say "thank you," which is to write somebody a little note when she has done something nice for him. You can ask him, "Do you want to thank somebody who has done something especially nice for you?" Perhaps his grandfather and grand-mother who live in another state have given him some dandy birthday presents.

"OK, now here's how to write a thank-you note. Since you haven't learned to print yet, you can dictate it to me and I'll print it." This is the final result:

> Dear Grampy and Grammy: Thank you for the nice
> presents you sent for my birthday. I especially liked
> the Lego set.   Love, Peter.

You should conclude each of your teaching sessions with a positive reward. Give him a hug, read a story, ride bikes, or play a game. Or take him to the play-ground or the library.

At the next lesson, teach Peter to say simply, "You're welcome" when someone says "thank you" to him. Use role playing for this, as you did for practicing "please" and "thank you."

At your next session you can teach him to compliment other people. Begin by explaining what a compliment is—something nice you say about somebody, that makes them feel good—like telling his friend George at nursery school that he is a good trike rider, or telling his Grandma he likes the cookies she bakes.

Role-play some of these compliments. Then make this suggestion to him: "I want to see if you can think of some more things next week to compliment some-body on. When you think of something you like about somebody, tell me and I'll write it down in this notebook. And at the end of the week I'll have a special surprise for you for thinking of nice things to tell people."

Close this lesson by telling your child that he's very good at thinking of com-pliments, and reward him.

As you are writing down your child's compliments from day to day, compli-ment him for thinking of them. At the end of the week, praise him and reward him with something like a trip to the toy store for something special. (Unless he didn't think of any compliments at all, which would be very unusual. In that case you say, "I'm sorry you didn't think of any compliments at all. Maybe we'll try it another time." Then drop it, because he's telling you the idea doesn't appeal to him for some reason.)

You can also use role playing and positive rewards to teach your youngster to say "excuse me" if he accidentally bumps into somebody, or if he wants to pass somebody in an aisle, or if he makes a mistake that inconveniences someone.

In teaching your child any kind of behavior or value system, remember that he will learn best from what he sees you do, rather than what you tell him to do. So be sure you role-model what you want him to learn. At first it's a good idea to point out to him when you are being courteous to someone. If you say to a friend, "Marie, your home-baked bread tastes wonderful," you can say to your child, "I'm giving Marie a compliment." When you thank the checkout clerk at the market when she hands you your change, you can let your child practice saying "thank you" too. And treat your child with courtesy, saying "please," "thank you," "you're welcome," and "excuse me," which, incidentally, is very good for his sense of self-esteem.

When using the positive reward system in teaching, remember that by the time your child is about five, he will respond to gold stars or happy faces on a chart, adding up to a tangible reward after a certain total. Children under that age will need a more immediate treat.

Teaching your child courtesy now will give him a valuable head start for getting along with people socially, at school, and on the job.

2. *You want to teach your child to be ethical, with a good value system.* Age five is a good time to begin.

Here's how *not* to teach your child these things. Do not simply try to impose an absolute system of right and wrong on him and force him to swallow it. Even if he does accept it now, sooner or later (probably in adolescence) he will rebel and throw it over, because it is not genuinely his.

Instead we suggest you teach your child to *think* about ethics, something very few parents do. For example, a boy is in a grocery store and sees some candy he wants. Nobody is looking so he stuffs it in his pocket and takes it out of the store. Although he may be worried that someone will catch him, he doesn't think about how he would feel if he were the owner of a store and someone stole something from him. That's the kind of ethical thinking you need to teach your youngsters.

Put it to him in the form of a game. "Ben, here's a new game we can play. It's called 'What Would You Do?' Here's one for you. You are in a grocery store. You buy some groceries for two dollars. You give the grocer five dollars, and he gives you back four dollars by mistake—that's one dollar too much. What would you do?" Let him tell you what he would do and why. Do not be judgmental. Let him give his honest opinion.

Suppose Ben says, "I wouldn't do anything, because he made the mistake and gave me a dollar too much." Then you can say, "Well, I would have done something different." Tell him what you would have done, without saying that his solution is wrong or bad, and why. You don't teach your child to be ethical by making him feel guilty.

Newspapers and magazines are excellent sources of ethical examples. Just read a story—for example, one about widespread cheating on college campuses to-day—and ask your child what he would do in that situation.

You can use newspapers and magazines in this way from the time your child is five until he is almost eleven. At eleven, children typically become too rebellious for this technique to be effective.

Unfortunately, there are not many children's books on ethics and morality. There is one good series, though—*Value Tales,* by Spencer and Ann Johnson, published by Oak Tree Publications of San Diego, California—consisting of more than twenty titles. See Appendix B for some of them. You can start reading these books to your child at age three or four, using each as a springboard for discussion of that particular value.

If you follow all the suggestions that we have given you, beginning in the preschool stage, your child should have a good background in ethics and morality, and a good value system.

3. You want your child to grow up to be able to communicate well with other people.

This is one of the important factors for success in marriage and in work. If you asked most parents whether they want their children to grow up to be successful communicators, they would say, "Well, certainly." But you will find that these same parents give their children very little opportunity to express their own thoughts and feelings. Their view of an ideal parent-child relationship is one where the parents do most of the talking. They expect their children to be passive, quiet, submissive creatures until the age of twenty-one, at which time they will magically blossom forth as fluent communicators.

So the first way to teach your child to be a good communicator is to allow her the freedom to express her thoughts and feelings. The second way is to use the feedback technique to let your child know that you are really listening and really care about what she thinks and feels.

Next, teach her how to draw other people out and get them to talk. Use the interview technique. You can begin this when she is five and continue to nearly eleven. Tell her how TV and newspaper reporters interview people; use role playing to illustrate how they ask questions and discuss, using the feedback technique, the answers they get. Then role-play a situation in which you interview your child; use a tape recorder, and play it back to her so she can hear how the interview sounds.

When you are sure she understands the technique, have her do a few interviews at school (without telling the people what she is doing). She can tell you what she's learned about them when she comes home. Tell her that after three interviews she will get a prize or a treat.

If your child has had practice from age five to eleven interviewing people, this should prove of great benefit to her as a teenager, when awkwardness with the opposite sex often sets in. Tell her that people always like to talk about themselves, and they will like her if she gives them a chance to do it.

4. You need to teach your child to be able to give and receive physical affection.

The habit of physical affection begins in infancy when you caress your baby. Continue to use lots of body contact as she grows older. Put your affection and love into words, too. Say things like, "I'd sure like to give you a hug!" And be sure to get her in the habit not only of being hugged but of hugging back.

5, 6, and 7. You need to teach your child the skills of 1) reading and loving books; 2) being able to write simple, clear English sentences; and 3) being competent in mathematical computations.

Whereas we have been talking about social skills up to now, reading, writing, and 'rithmetic are academic and work skills. Although these particular skills are discussed in the chapters on intellectual stimulation in toddlerhood and preschool, they are mentioned briefly here because they are part of your ultimate goals for your child. We suggest that you pay careful attention in those chapters to the step-by-step directions for teaching these intellectual skills to your child.

8. You need to train your child to be self-assertive. Millions of adults in the United States today are paying good money for courses in self-assertiveness because their parents raised them to be unassertive.

The real problem is that most parents want their kids to be quiet and passive and not make waves—or, as some of us were told when we were young, "Children should be seen and not heard." That kind of upbringing causes many children to become acquiescent.

If you want to raise your child to become a confident, assertive adult, you must do three basic things:

First, refrain from squashing your child's thoughts, feelings, and actions.

Second, encourage her to make choices. Ask your child what she would like to have for dinner or what movie she would like to watch. Most parents simply tell the child what she's going to eat, what movie she's going to see, and where they're going out to dinner. And be sure that you do let your child have her choice fairly often, even if sometimes it's not exactly what you would have preferred.

Third, applaud your child when she is being an individual—that is, holding to her opinion or asserting herself against someone who is trying to put her down: her peers, outside people in authority, even you! Very few parents view a child saying "No, I don't want to!" as a valuable instance of self-assertion. But a child who always obeys her parents without a murmur will not grow up to be an assertive adult.

When we say that you should praise your child for the assertive things she does, obviously we are not talking about antisocial acts. We are obviously talking about assertiveness that is within the bounds of legal and ethical restraints.

We know how hard it may be for you not only to allow your child to be assertive, but also to give her approval for it. But if you can manage to sit on some of your natural inclinations and do it, you will end up with a child you can be proud of when she becomes an adult.

9. You can teach your child to be a good sex partner when she grows up.
Now hold on! Don't have a stroke. We are not suggesting you teach her to be

a junior sex fiend at age five. No, we are talking about teaching her the attitudes and feelings she needs in order to grow up to be an adult without sexual hangups.

The people who have studied the sexual attitudes and behavior of our adults find that they leave a lot to be desired. For example, sex researchers Masters and Johnson estimate that severe sex problems affect approximately 50 percent of American marriages. From our clinical experience we would agree with that estimate.

One of the troubles is that our society is so ambivalent about sex education. Some school systems have sex-education courses in junior high and high school. But the classes are taught at a very superficial level, and concentrate more on what we call "sexual plumbing" than anything else. If an instructor has the guts to delve into the sexual areas the kids really want to know about, he is usually fired.

This type of ambivalent attitude of, "Yes, we do want to teach our kids about sex, but no, we really don't want them to learn anything," is summed beautifully in a cartoon that shows a young boy hanging his head, shamefaced, and his father standing over him tapping his report card on the table. The father says in a stern voice, "Now what's this I hear about you getting an A in sex education?"

We ask you to examine your own learning of sexual facts and attitudes. If you are like many other people in the United States, your parents told you absolutely nothing about it; at school you learned nothing. You learned a few things from your peer group, which is much like the blind leading the blind. Finally, when you actually began to engage in sexual behavior your learning was strictly trial and error. And in sex, trial and error can be damaging to relationships as well as costly in terms of unwanted pregnancies or venereal disease.

You may think that nothing to do with sex goes on with a child until puberty, at about thirteen. Wrong. The most important years for learning sexual attitudes and feelings are the first five years of life. The things we're going to tell you about helping your child to have a healthy, happy, and hangup-free life as an adult begin long before the preschool stage. For the teaching of healthy sex attitudes begins when your child is born.

When your baby is feeding, cuddled within her mother's arms, she is acquiring her first and most basic feelings about bodies and skin contact. When her father hugs her or cuddles her or pats her, she is acquiring warm positive feelings about the first man in her life. Once these feelings are built up, positive or negative, they are hard to change.

Sooner or later, you will start teaching your youngster the parts of her body, as we discussed in an earlier chapter ("Intellectual Stimulation in Toddlerhood"). We're sure you have all seen mothers doing this. But have you ever heard a mother, as she goes through the parts of the body, say "Put your finger on your vulva," or "Put your finger on your penis."?

What is the inner emotional experience of a little child when her mother teaches her, carefully and painstakingly, the names of all her body parts except one? Probably that "This part of me down here must be bad, because my mother never taught me its name."

It's important that your child learn the names of all the parts of her body, including her sex organs. And as she grows older, it's important that you talk about sex as simply and openly as you do any other subject.

The next important phase of sexual development concerns questions. Children vary enormously in how they ask questions about sex. Some children have already picked up fears of the subject and will shy away from asking any. Other children will ask a lot.

You should try to answer your child's questions about sex simply, clearly, and matter-of-factly. So if she asks you, "Where do babies come from?" your answer should be given in the same straightforward way that you would respond to, "What makes the grass grow?" or "Why are rocks heavier than flowers?" Give simple, short answers. If she wants more detail, she will ask you. For example, if she asks, "Where do babies come from?" you can answer, "They grow inside the mother, in a special place called the uterus." Don't go into things like the husband having intercourse with the wife and the baby being born of the union of the sperm and the egg. You will want your child to know all of these facts sooner or later, but that's not the question she is asking you at age three. So answer only her question and nothing more.

One question a child usually has trouble with is how the baby gets out of the mother. If your child asks you this question, ask her to guess before you tell her the correct answer, so that you can find out her misconceptions and clear them up. She may guess that the baby comes out of the "BM hole" or the belly button. Then you can tell her, "No, it doesn't come out of the BM hole. We call that the rectum. And it doesn't come out the belly button. The mother has a special baby hole like a tunnel. This baby hole is very stretchy. When it's time for the baby to come out, it can stretch big enough for the baby to come through the tunnel. After the baby is born, then it can unstretch and go back to the way it was."

Even if your child asks a lot of questions, her knowledge of sex will be only piecemeal if it is derived solely from your answers. We suggest you read her a good book on the subject, which will give her a clear overview of sexuality, the individual, and the family. There are various good books, but the one we like best is *The Wonderful Story of How You Were Born,* by Sidonie Gruenberg. You can read it to your child once when she's three, once at four, and once at five, or any other times she might ask for it. In order to counteract the guilt and misinformation that circulate in our society, it is usually necessary to give sex-related information to a child more than once.

When your child turns five you can start another type of sexual education, which very few families in America use. Most families talk together at the dinner table about such things as the news of the day or their plans and activities. But subjects relating to sex are never mentioned. Once again, the implication is that sex must be nasty, since the family never talks about it.

Your family can be different. When you take your child to farms and zoos he'll have the opportunity to observe the animal kingdom's sexual activities. Let him discuss them with the family at the dinner table. Handle his questions and concerns openly.

We believe firmly that the more openly and honestly you can discuss sex with your children, the healthier an attitude they will have and the happier they will be as sexual adults.

10. Teach your child to be curious about many things.

In one sense, curiosity is not something you need to teach your baby. She already has it.

But from the age of two to the age of five you will need to play a more determined role in helping your child develop an active and powerful curiosity. Keep up the visits to places she would not ordinarily see without you. All these things enlarge her understanding of the world.

The public library is one of your greatest allies in developing your child's curiosity. Concentrate particularly on nonfiction books that tell about things that are new to her: animals that she doesn't already know about; anthropology for very young readers, such as stories about ancient Mexico or ancient Egypt; books like *What's Inside of Me?;* or a book that traces the plumbing of the house from the bathroom and kitchen down to the sewer. Try to expand the reading of the book into a discussion.

You can use your daily newspaper or magazines such as *Time* and *Newsweek* to expand your child's horizons. Find a story that you think would interest her—not one about the president and Congress or about a shift in foreign policy, but one about a bear that escaped from a zoo, or a volcano that just started erupting, or a gun chase between cops and robbers. You can read the story at family dinner and perhaps start a discussion on it.

Later on when your child learns to read, you can have her find stories she likes, then tell about them at dinner. She could be given some appropriate reward each time she does this.

If you do these things in the first five years, you will help your child develop a strong and active curiosity, the main driving force that will enable her to become a well-educated and successful person.

Now that we have discussed these ten subject areas, which many parents would be surprised to see included under the heading of discipline, we want to conclude by describing two orthodox approaches to discipline which can be used during the preschool years. One concerns teaching a child desirable behavior, the other, avoiding misbehavior.

T E A C H I N G   D E S I R A B L E   B E H A V I O R

First is the method of contracting. This is really an extension of the positive reward system which we described in our chapter on "Discipline in Toddlerhood." The positive reward system is still a powerful way of teaching desirable behavior. It not only applies to your preschool child but also will continue to be a valuable tool in your child's teen years. Naturally, the rewards change as your child matures. He'll let you know what he likes. But the positive reward system is unilateral, because the parents decide the behavior that they want to teach and the rewards that they will use to motivate their child.

Contracting is bilateral rather than unilateral. The contract is an agreement between parents and child. The child agrees to behave in a certain way, and the parents agree to do something for him in return. But precisely what the child will do and what the parents will do is a matter for negotiation.

Here is how it works. Let's say you want to teach your four-year-old son to say thank you. You know that the circus is coming to town in two weeks, and he will want to go. So you and he negotiate the following contract: "Darryl agrees to learn to say thank you. Mommy and Daddy agree to take him to the circus with a friend when it comes to town in two weeks." Signed by Darryl, Mommy, and Daddy.

The contract must be written down, and both parties must sign it. (You can help your preschooler make an X or a happy-face drawing or a capital letter that stands for his name.) Make an original and a carbon. The main reason for writing it down is so that any misunderstandings can be cleared up simply by looking up the contract and seeing what it says. Also, a written document is psychologically more impressive to a young child.

The big advantage of the contract is that the child is usually highly motivated to carry it out, because he participated in negotiating it. When you have agreed to the final terms of the contract you can say, "OK, it's a deal!" Your child will like that. Pretty soon you will hear him saying to you, "Mom, I've got a deal for you!" meaning he has worked out in his own mind a contract he would like to see accepted. This is a good sign, for it means he has accepted the basic idea of contracting.

There are other advantages to contracting. Starting at the five-year-old level enables the child to get accustomed to it, so that it will be easier for you to use in the teenage years. This in turn helps prepare your child for the real world of business negotiating in adult life. His knowledge of contracting and the art of give-and-take negotiating will also stand him in good stead later in his personal relationships.

A V O I D I N G   M I S B E H A V I O R

The next method, the mutual problem-solving technique, teaches your child to avoid undesirable behavior. Like contracting, it involves negotiating an agreement with the full cooperation of the child, although the negotiations are more complex. It too ends with a signed contract.

The mutual problem-solving technique can be used from about age five through adolescence. It is particularly helpful in resolving situations where there is a conflict between parent and child. Here's a typical problem with a five-year-old. Let's see how parents would handle it with old-fashioned methods. The family is eating dinner.

FATHER: "Tony, it's Friday and time for you to take the trash out. You were supposed to do it this morning but you didn't, so I'm reminding you now."

TONY: "Aw, gee, Dad, I gotta take care of my turtle tonight."

FATHER: "Turtle? Ha! Since when did your turtle ever keep you from doing something you really want to do? C'mon now, go on and do it, right now!"

Tony shuffles reluctantly out the back door.

FATHER: "See, Peggy, what did I tell you? You've just got to be firm with children and then you don't have any trouble with them."

Ten minutes later Mother speaks: "John, I surely don't think it can be taking Tony all this time to take out the trash. I wonder what's happened to him?"

FATHER: "I'll go see." (He goes out the back door and sees that the trash is still there. He hears some hammering in the garage and goes to investigate.)

FATHER: "Tony, what are you doing out here in the garage? You're supposed to be taking out the trash!"

TONY: "Gee, Dad, I started building this cage for my guinea pig and I must have forgotten all about the trash!"

FATHER: "Well, isn't that convenient! I'm sick and tired of you paying no attention to what I say." (Grabs him by the scruff of the neck and pulls him along to the back porch.) "Now grab that trash can and take it out to the alley right now or you're going to get a good spanking!"

(Tony, crying and sniffling and darting looks of hate at his father, does as he's told.)

FATHER: "There! Now wouldn't it have been been a lot simpler for all of us if you had done the job right at the beginning?"

Tony says nothing, but his face speaks volumes.

Let's analyze this little parent-child scenario. It is a classic example of parent winning and child losing. And what has been accomplished? Well, technically, the trash has been taken out. But at what price? Tony is furious with his father. It will not be too surprising if he does something sneaky to get back at him. He will not be highly motivated to take out the trash in the future. And the experience has been unpleasant for Father as well.

Now let's look at this scenario again, with a different ending.

FATHER: "Tony, it's Friday and time for you to take the trash out. You didn't do it this morning so I'm reminding you now."

TONY: (Starting to cry) "You're always picking on me!"

MOTHER: "Yes, you didn't need to say it in that tone."

FATHER: "What do you mean, *that tone?* I simply reminded him to take the trash out. Is that a crime?"

TONY: "You just hate me! I'm going to my room!" (Runs upstairs to his room.)

MOTHER: "Now see what you've done! You could have some consideration for his feelings, you know."

FATHER: "I'm going to get him." (Father goes upstairs and takes a weeping Tony by the arm and deposits him back in his seat.)

FATHER: "Now there! Nobody hates you. I simply reminded you to take the trash out."

TONY: "You do too hate me!" (Tony crawls underneath the table.)

FATHER: "Look, I don't have to take this. I work pretty darn hard all day and I just don't have to take this kind of stuff when I get home. I'm going to solve this whole lousy problem very simply. *I'm* going to take the trash out myself from now on. And Tony can stuff crayons up his nose or do anything else he wants, but he won't have to burden himself with such a tough, hard job as taking out the trash!"

(Tony starts crying more loudly under the table.)

In this scene the child wins and the parents lose. Tony has done a terrific job of manipulating. When his parents give in to Tony, they are doing a good job of teaching him that if he persists in whining, crying, complaining, and wheedling, he will sooner or later get his way.

Children raised in homes where child power wins and parent power loses are usually selfish and demanding. Their power ploys may be successful with their parents, but they find their peer group resents them.

Now let's see how the whole thing could be handled by the mutual problem-solving technique.

FATHER: "Tony, I'd like to talk something over with you. I think we've got kind of a problem here. You know it's your job to take the trash out every Friday. But a lot of the time you don't do it. And when Mother or I remind you, you say you will, but many times it still doesn't get done. Isn't that what happens?"

TONY: "Yeah, I guess so."

FATHER: "Well, I'm going to tell you about a way we can solve this problem. Here's how we do it. First we state exactly what the problem is. The problem is that Tony has the job of taking out the trash but often it doesn't get done. Is that a correct way of stating the problem, Tony?"

TONY: "Yeah, I guess so."

FATHER: "OK. Now, all three of us, you and Mother and me, try to think up ideas that will solve the problem. And the rule is that nobody is allowed to criticize or find fault with anybody else's idea. We'll try to think of as many ideas as we can. Even ideas that are kind of crazy or wild are OK. Mother will write each idea down and number it. This way of thinking up ideas is called *brainstorming* in business. So let's do some brainstorming. Who has some ideas of how we can solve this problem?"

TONY: "Let somebody else take out the stupid trash!"

MOTHER (Writing down the ideas): "We can just let the trash pile up and nobody take it out."

FATHER: "We can pay somebody else to take it out."

MOTHER: "We could advertise in the paper, 'Garage sale of trash this week'!"

FATHER: "We could give a present of a big can full of trash each week to Tony, in addition to his allowance!"

TONY: "You could pay me each week for taking out the trash."

FATHER: "OK, I think we've got enough ideas. Now we need to go over the ideas and see if there is one, or more than one, that we can all agree on. If even one person doesn't agree, it knocks that idea out. We have to have 100 percent agreement, or otherwise we won't all be behind the idea and work to make it succeed.

"One. Let somebody else take out the trash."

(Tony votes yes, Mother and Father vote no.)

"Two. Let the trash pile up and nobody take it out."

All three vote no on that one.

One by one each idea is taken up and voted down, until they come to the idea of paying Tony to take out the trash. Tony votes for this one and Mother and Father say they might vote for it, depending on how much Tony would be paid.

TONY: "How about a dollar each time?"

MOTHER: "Way too much! How about a dime?"

TONY: "But, Mom, what can I buy for a dime?"

MOTHER: "I guess you really can't buy much for a dime these days. You've got a point there, Tony."

FATHER: "OK, Tony, suppose we make it a quarter. If we do that, I'll vote for it."

MOTHER: "So will I."

TONY: "OK, let's make it a quarter."

This contract can be written very simply: "Tony agrees to take the trash out every Friday after dinner, and Dad agrees to pay him a quarter afterward." Signed by Tony and Dad and Mother.

The advantages of having used mutual problem solving are quite clear. First of all, nobody loses, neither Tony nor his parents. Since punishment is not used, there are no bad feelings. Because the negotiation process is used, all three have good feelings about working together to solve the problem. Tony is being given a valuable lesson in how to solve problems with other people. And, as in regular contracting, he will be much more highly motivated to take out the trash now, since he participated in the negotiation process.

Some of you may feel, "Why should I have to pay my child to do something that he ought to do without pay?" Well, since adults don't work for free, is it really such a surprising idea to pay our children for work they do? And it gets children into the habit of working to earn money, which is what they will be doing as adults.

It's a good idea to start using mutual problem solving early with a child, so that he's pretty familiar with it by adolescence, when it is *the* method of choice for resolving conflicts between parents and teenagers.

Incidentally, this is also a good technique for solving problems where no conflicts exist. It might be that the family has a problem scheduling time for something special they all want to do. Or a problem about how one of the children can earn money for an expensive pair of track shoes that his parents can't afford to buy him. In situations like this, family brainstorming sometimes comes up with some very creative solutions. A contract is often not necessary or even appropriate.

We want to close this chapter by stressing again that the three years of the preschool period are probably the most ideal time to teach your child *anything*, particularly the skills and attitudes that will influence the rest of his life. In the years before three his intellectual grasp of many things is still hazy. And in the years from six on he is more resistant to teaching. But in the years from three to six his mind is more open to being taught *anything* than it will be for the rest of his life. Take advantage of that open and teachable mind!

26

INTELLECTUAL STIMULATION IN PRESCHOOL

For many years, professionals working with children have known that the first five years are the most important for the emotional development of the child. But it is only recently that research has shown that the first five years are also the most important for intellectual development.

We can experiment with lower animals to a degree which, of course, is impossible with human beings, and much of what we now know about children was first revealed in studies of such diverse animals as dogs, cats, rats, monkeys, ducks, and birds. Many animal experiments have demonstrated that when animals are given stimulation in infancy, they develop mentally at a more rapid rate and become more intelligent than other animals that have not been stimulated.

For example, research at the University of California at Berkeley shows conclusively that an enriched early environment in white rats produces superior problem-solving adult animals. Tests of the rats in later life reveal that those that received early stimulation are more intelligent and can solve problems better than their nonstimulated litter mates.

Now, research at the human level confirms what we have found with the lower animals. Stimulation or lack of stimulation in the early years of childhood has an important effect on their adult behavior and intelligence. One major researcher specializing in the preschool years is Dr. Benjamin Bloom, of the University of Chicago. In his book *All Our Children Learning* (New York: McGraw-Hill, 1981), Dr. Bloom summarizes a massive body of research which shows that children develop 50 percent of their intelligence by the age of four.

This means that the more intellectual stimulation you can give your child in the first five years of life *without pushing or pressuring him,* the brighter and more intelligent he will become. He will have a higher IQ as an adult.

Way back in Chapter 3, "Good News for Parents," we talked about the research of Dr. Dolores Durkin, who found that children who entered school knowing how to read had one thing in common. They all had at least one parent—usually the mother—who had provided an intellectually stimulating home environment for them.

Let's look again at some of the things these mothers did for their young children.

- They read a great deal to them.
- They had materials around the house that stimulated their children's interest in reading and writing: pencils, felt pens, white paper, colored paper.
- They had books, both bought and from the library.

- They had a blackboard in the home.
- They stimulated their children's curiosity about words by pointing out labels and signs and then explaining what the words meant.
- They helped their children learn to print.

In short, Dr. Durkin found that early readers are not a special kind of child. In personality, intelligence, and everything else you cannot tell early readers from nonearly readers. Rather, early readers have a special kind of parent.

You too can be a special kind of parent, for it is easy and fun to do. If you have been following the suggestions of this book throughout your child's earlier developmental stages, you already are that kind of parent. And the probability is that your child already has a head start, not only in school but in life.

In analyzing the learning that goes on in the preschool period, Dr. Bloom explains that the child's environment has its greatest effect on him during his period of most rapid change, which is in his preschool years. And there are three areas of intelligence in which your child can make great gains during his preschool years: language, thinking, and mathematics.

LANGUAGE

Your child's language development can be divided into two aspects: oral language and written language. You have been stimulating and enriching her oral language all along by talking with her and listening to her. A very important thing you can do as well to stimulate your child's language development is something we have been stressing throughout the book. Continue reading to her. Take library trips on a regular basis—she'll love it.

The second thing you can do to stimulate your child's language development is to help her learn how to print. When she shows an interest, usually around three and a half, get an alphabet book that has the letters in both capitals and lowercase, and a fat felt-tip pen, which is easier to use than a pencil, pen, or crayon. Start with the capital letters, since they are easier to print. You don't have to start at A and go all the way to Z. Begin with the letters that are easiest to make, and then go on to the harder ones. Here's one possible order you might want to use to teach her the capital letters: I, L, X, T, H, F, E, A, M, V, N, P, U, C, W, O, Q, D, Y, Z, B, K, J, R, S, G.

Children often want to learn how to print their own name. If this interests her, teach her those letters. Give your child lots of time to learn the capital letters. It will probably take many months. But there is no rush. You're not on a schedule.

The lowercase letters are, with a few exceptions, quite a bit harder to learn. Don't try to teach them until your youngster has learned all the uppercase letters. Begin by showing your child that she already knows nine lowercase letters, for these are exactly the same as the capitals only smaller: c, i, o, s, u, v, w, x, z (except that i has a dot over it).

She may spend hours working on her writing and not be at all interested in the letter sounds. Most children need to master writing before they can go on into reading. But if you can label objects around the house with printed words, write little notes in her lunch box, or help her write greeting cards she'll easily make the transition into reading. And it will make sense to her.

You can go one step further and have her dictate her thoughts or a little story to you. You should write it clearly and correctly. When possible, put it into booklet form and leave room for her own illustration. Then read it back to her. By watching you write she is learning many skills—how to write letters correctly, how to read and write from left to right, and finally to recognize letters and words. It also teaches her that words have meaning and are not mysterious.

The third thing you can do to stimulate your child's language development is to teach her to make her own books.

The fourth thing you can do to stimulate your child's language development is to arouse her curiosity about words. You can, on trips to the market, point out words on cereal packages, frozen pizza, and cracker boxes. When you see a direction sign, you can call her attention to the words on the sign. NO LEFT TURN, EXIT, STOP, FOR SALE, TOY STORE. When you are watching TV together, call her attention to words on the screen. If you direct her attention to words naturally and matter-of-factly as you come across them, it will not be long before she will start asking what a word says. This curiosity is an important element in learning to read.

Probably the most basic learning skill we can teach a child is how to think. And what is thinking? Thinking is simply using your mind—to reason, reflect, problem-solve, imagine, anticipate, remember, and other activities of that nature. There are two important kinds of thinking. Thinking of the left hemisphere of the brain and thinking of the right hemisphere. Left-hemisphere thinking is logical and analytical. It proceeds step by step through a conscious process. Right-hemisphere thinking is not logical or analytical, but unconscious and intuitive.

How can you teach your child left-hemisphere, logical thinking? First, you need to provide raw materials for her to use. The most basic kind of raw materials are sensory experiences, and you are already providing some of this if you have been following our suggestions all along. For example, encourage your child to feel and become aware of different textures. Help her to learn to listen to all of the varied sounds of her environment, both natural and man-created. Help her to see beauty in commonplace things—the configuration of water as you hose down a car, the peeling paint on a garage wall. An awareness of the sensory world is your child's most basic foundation for thinking.

In addition to giving your child a wide range of sensory experience, you also need to provide her with a variety of materials as stimuli for her thinking. Make available to her lots of paper, crayons, felt pens, coloring books, scissors with blunt ends, stacks of old magazines, a scrap box for collage materials, Lego or similar construction toys, play dough and clay, books, a blackboard. Let her use the materials and experiment with them herself. Don't feel you have to sit down and teach her. Just be available for help if she wants it. It's also important for her early intellectual development to be exposed to a wide range of firsthand experience, for a child's thinking can extend no further than her experience.

A good way to broaden your preschooler's experience is to continue to take her on adventure trips with you into the community. Even places you have taken her when she was younger will continue to have meaning for her. As she grows, she will understand more and more about what she sees. So take her again to the bakery, the zoo, the fire station, the newspaper, the shoe repair shop, the dressmaker, the police station, the airport.

Now we turn to the thinking of the right hemisphere. Here we are trying to help your child develop the intuitive, imaginative, and unconscious part of her mind. When your child creates something, it means that out of unstructured materials she is forming a structure that originates within her mind. This is why it is so important for your child to have access to unstructured materials. These can be crayons, paint, clay, play dough, paper, collage, blocks, Legos, pans, dirt, and the like. You will notice that most of these are the same tools that your child needs for learning logical thinking as well. The difference is in how the materials are used. In developing logical thinking, crayons, for example, might be used for working in coloring books or for printing. But in developing your child's creative thinking, your child provides the structure out of her own mind. She creates a picture with crayons on a blank piece of paper. Or makes delicious-looking mud cakes out of dirt and water. In this kind of play, the structure is in the child, not in the materials.

Remember that you are not trying to teach your child to be an artist by using these unstructured materials. You are letting her develop the creative part of her mind. You are helping to build her self-confidence by letting her learn that she can create order and structure from unstructured materials. You are increasing her sensitivity, her awareness, her originality, and her powers of flexibility.

The freedom of your child's feelings plays a large role in the development of her intellect. Teach your child that there is no such thing as right or wrong, good or bad, when it comes to her feelings or thoughts. Good and bad are confined to actions, to outward behavior, not to inner thoughts and feelings. When you encourage the expression of your child's feelings, you help her develop access to her unconscious mind. And from the unconscious come the creative hunches and ideas of right-hemisphere thinking.

Feed your child's imaginative life. Besides nonfiction books, read her such wonderful fiction as *Winnie the Pooh, The Twenty-One Balloons,* or *Charlie and the Chocolate Factory.* (There is a list of recommended books of fantasy for preschoolers in Appendix B.) You can feed your child's imagination not only through books on fantasy but through nonverbal activity such as music, dance, and art. These creative activities give her a chance to express feelings and develop her imagination and fantasy life.

M A T H E M A T I C S

Mathematics is a vital area in which to stimulate your child during her preschool years. Unfortunately, when we hit the topic of mathematics we run head-on into a lot of parental anxieties. The parent is afraid she will not be able to do a good job of teaching her child because her own adult math skills are on such a shaky foundation. You can relax. We're going to suggest you teach math to your preschooler in a way that assumes you know nothing at all about the subject. You can use the special Cuisenaire Rods Parents Kit, which is designed for that purpose. It can be obtained from one of the stores that sell by mail.

The wooden rods are different colors and lengths, and you use them in playing a series of games with your child. You will find this a fascinating and delightful toy, and you will probably wish you had had the advantage of learning arithmetic with it when you were a child.

Remember too that your child is experiencing number concepts every day. She'll be counting to make sure she got as many jelly beans as her brother and while she may not get the numbers right she'll learn the concept of "same," "more," or "less" if you can line them up for her. If she's allowed to help you with measuring out quantities while you cook together she'll even be learning fractions!

So there you have it: oral and written language, thinking, and mathematics. These are the three most important areas of learning for school and later life. And you can give your child a head start in all of these by intellectually stimulating her in the preschool years.

And it can be fun, too, if you are not too serious about it. Let your child proceed at her own rate. She is in a stage when the thrill of learning is what motivates her. Too much pressure can rob her of that. Provide the materials and the experiences and watch her go!

27

SPECIAL SITUATIONS OF THE PRESCHOOL STAGE

In this chapter we will be discussing special situations that you may encounter during your child's preschool stage, both those that are carry-overs from first adolescence and toddlerhood and some that are new.

COMFORT HABITS

The comfort habits adopted by the younger child, whether it be the need to hold a special object, such as a blanket, toy, or pacifier, or to engage in a particular activity, such as thumb sucking, rocking, hair twirling, or head banging, will continue to be apparent during the preschool years. As before, your preschooler uses these habits when she is distressed, tired, or frustrated. The need for them decreases during these years but may be particularly apparent when she is faced with a new situation, such as starting preschool.

There is no reason that your child should not take her comfort object to preschool, or engage in her comfort activity during stressful times. Trying to get her to give this up only increases her stress. You can be of most help to your child when you accept her comfort object in a loving way. A more detailed discussion of comfort habits can be found in "Special Situations in Toddlerhood."

TEMPER TANTRUMS

Temper tantrums first begin to appear in toddlerhood, peak in first adolescence, and often continue in the preschool years. They are most apparent during unsettled times, as we mention in our overview of this stage. Tantrums now should be handled in the same way you handled them during first adolescence.

FEARS AND PHOBIAS

The preschooler has an active imagination and can come up with new fears and worries that the first adolescent couldn't conceive of. This accounts for some of the preschooler's nighttime fears and problems with sleeping (which we discuss in "Overview of the Preschool Stage." Youngsters in this stage can also become very concerned about death, either the death of their parent or themselves. They also worry about keeping themselves whole and uninjured.

It is during the older preschool stage that children begin to be concerned about why one sex has a penis and the other doesn't, often worrying that perhaps it has been cut off or removed in some harmful way. Because of their concern about their bodies, preschoolers are particularly difficult to handle when getting shots, having splinters removed, or any other procedure that they perceive as invasive to their bodies. These concerns coupled with their magical thinking also makes them worry when they see someone who is crippled or blind, or in some other way perceived as injured. They fear that if they are around that person or touch him they might "catch it."

When you are aware of how your preschooler thinks, you can do much to alleviate his fears. Using play is one of the most effective tools for this. In our chapters "The Well Child" and "Health Problems in Early Childhood" we talk about how to deal with your child's concerns about a doctor visit or medical procedure.

Along the same lines, if your child is going to be exposed to someone who has had something drastic happen to his body, talk to her ahead of time and prepare her for it. Explain that it is not "catching" and that it will not happen to her. The child who is particularly fearful may need to be exposed to the feared object or person in small doses, as we mention in "Special Situations of Toddlerhood."

A concern that commonly crops up in the preschooler is the fear of fire in her own home. This fear often arises after firemen have visited the nursery school to show films about fires and how to handle them. These are very important in educating the child, but they can also create much anxiety. When this program is going on at your child's school, you can help her by letting her talk about her fears. Playing "fire" is a very helpful mechanism for conquering your child's fear and relieving her tension. Help her act out what to do in the case of fire, by using a dollhouse. Our (AA) Katie needed to play "fire" in her dollhouse for weeks to get over her fear.

Accept your child's fear, recognize that it is not unreasonable in her mind, and help her to conquer it. These are your goals in this stage.

S I B L I N G   R I V A L R Y

Sibling rivalry obviously exists during the preschool years, and we discuss this fully in "Special Situations in Toddlerhood." It is important to note here, however, that you should consider the issue of sibling rivalry before sending your preschooler off to nursery school or day care when a new sibling arrives. A young preschooler could perceive that her being out of the home after a new baby arrives only confirms her worry that you no longer care about her. Your preschooler likes babies and can be an excellent help in taking care of the new baby. She may feel quite grown-up about it if she isn't overburdened. Don't be surprised, however, if your child who has seemed so mature regresses and becomes more dependent with the arrival of a new sibling.

Preschoolers make wonderful friends for their siblings. They are particularly good too at helping a younger one make the transition into a new situation just by being present.

A D O P T I O N

Because of the preschooler's interest in babies and where babies come from, this is a good stage to make your adopted preschooler aware of her origin. The most important factor is your own feelings about it and how you convey them.

Your preschooler will ask if she grew in your tummy. Treat the adoption as a natural process by explaining that she grew inside another mother's tummy—in a special place called the uterus. Explain, if it is so, that you were unable to grow a baby and very much wanted one. Another mother who could grow a baby wasn't able to take care of her, but you could and you wanted very much to do it. So you adopted her. She may not ask any more questions about it for a while, and there is no need to overemphasize it.

Pitfalls can occur when parents stress that the adopted child was "specially chosen." She may feel that if she should change in any way she may no longer be chosen. The worry about being given up can occur in any child who is adopted. She needs to know that you are her mother and that you will always take care of her and love her.

There are books that are very helpful to parents in dealing with the issue of adoption. We list several of these in our Appendix D. Also, assistance can often be obtained from the local adoption agency or family service agency should you need it.

L E A R N I N G   T O   B E   A   S O C I A L   B E I N G

In our chapter "Special Situations in First Adolescence," we discuss teaching your child how to behave in public places by taking practice outings with her. If your preschooler is having difficulty with appropriate behavior in public places, we suggest you read this information for some ideas on how to help her. Even though your child seems to have learned how to behave during first adolescence, the lesson may be forgotten. She will need gentle reminders prior to each outing as to what you expect of her.

Reminders are in order also for any social functions she attends. Talk to her about good behavior before she goes. Be specific. If necessary, role play so that she can see more clearly just what you are talking about. Also, go over with her any problem behavior that may have occurred in the past, in order to avoid it this time. For example, acknowledge that it is difficult to go home when you are having a good time, and work out with her a system for letting her prepare herself for it. This may mean telling her five minutes in advance, and then helping her put playthings away before leaving.

When your child behaves appropriately or is in the process of behaving appropriately on these social outings, be sure to praise and reinforce her immediately. It is much more effective for her to receive encouragement while behaving well. Should she forget some of the social graces, you can give her some tactful cues by doing them yourself. For example, when leaving, say "Thank you. Kristy had a nice time." Kristy may pick up the hint for her own "thank you." But if she doesn't, forget it. Don't make an issue of it at the time, but discreetly discuss it with her afterward. You are setting a courteous example yourself, and that is very important.

DEALING WITH STRANGERS

The preschooler is much more outgoing with other adults than she was at a younger age. And since she is more likely to be on her own in the outside world, she needs some safety rules for dealing with strangers. Your goal is to educate her but not make her fearful.

Tell her what a stranger is. Assure her that it is perfectly acceptable to chat with strangers when she is beside you. But when she is alone or with other children, she should not talk with strangers even though they seem nice. Tell her to return home or to come right to you should she be approached. Assure her that most people truly care for children and would not hurt them, but some people have a problem and might do so. Since no one can be sure who is who, she should avoid talking with someone she doesn't know.

ANNOYING BEHAVIOR

It is during the preschool years that we adults begin to expect our children to become more responsible and grown-up. Behavior that doesn't fit these expectations can become very annoying. We shall discuss this here, with some suggestions on how to deal with it.

WHINING

We have mentioned before that whining begins to appear at around three and a half years of age, a time when the child is particularly unsettled and more easily upset. The whining habit sometimes begins without your realizing it. Perhaps the child's request made in a normal voice is not met right away. She repeats it in a whiny voice. The parent complies, not realizing or appreciating the change in voice tone. Naturally, this reinforces the whining.

Whining is much more likely to occur at a time when a parent is especially busy, tired, or impatient herself. It is an annoying noise, and stopping it right away may seem imperative. So parents give in. One day they take stock and realize that in fact their child is a persistent whiner, and it's driving them crazy.

It is time then to have a heart-to-heart talk with your child. Tell her that whining is unpleasant and makes you feel angry and upset with her. Let her know that when she uses that whiny tone, you will not listen. This means that you as a parent need to train yourself to pay attention to your child when she is talking in an appropriate tone of voice. And you must make up your mind not to give in to a whining voice.

Practice some role playing so that your child gets the hang of it. Reinforce her appropriate voice by responding to it (which of course does not mean giving her everything she wants whether it's appropriate or not). If your child persists in whining in spite of this, you may need to set up a Time Out system so that each time she whines she is placed in Time Out. Remember to do this matter-of-factly and *not* as a punishment. ("Oh, I hear that whiny voice again. I guess Sharon needs a Time Out for a few minutes.") And couple your efforts with a positive reward system for not whining, in order to make them more effective.

LYING

Lying is not uncommon in the preschool years. We have already mentioned the four-year-old, who is full of tall tales and boasting. She may be teasing, exaggerating, or simply enjoying her imagination. These are what we call "fish-tales." Don't worry about them. Go along with them good-naturedly, but let the child know that you recognize it as exaggeration and tall tales.

During preschool years a child may also lie in order to get what she wants or to avoid the consequences of a misdeed. If you know that your child has done something wrong, do not ask her to tell you "yes" or "no." This may only foster a lie. Instead, discuss it with her in such a way that she knows you know the truth. For example, when you come home to find lipstick all over your bathroom walls, don't ask, "Erica, did you do that to my bathroom walls?" This is almost sure to get you a "no" response. Simply say, "Erica, I see that you have made a mistake and written all over the walls. I am mad about that."

If there is a situation in which you are not sure about the truth, and your child is truthful, praise her for being so. She will still need to be responsible for her actions, but perhaps the consequences could be lighter because she did tell the truth. You are in this way reinforcing her good actions.

STEALING

The preschooler may begin to take things that don't belong to her. To an adult this is stealing. To her it is merely acting on a wish that she have something. It is important not to overreact to these situations but to begin a lesson about respecting other people's property. Go with her to return the item, and on the first transgression you can apologize for her. If her actions continue, however, she will need to do the apologizing. This usually causes her embarrassment enough not to do it again.

If your child has been in the habit of "borrowing" toys and other delights from her friend's house, watch her while she is there. When you see her begin to take something, talk to her about how you understand her feelings about wanting it, but taking it is not appropriate behavior. Reinforce her for showing control when she does.

The older preschooler, around five, is ready to learn a little about ethics. We discuss this in our "Discipline in Preschool" chapter.

DAWDLING

Dawdling becomes most aggravating during the preschool years (though diminishing by around five years), especially when you are trying to get your child ready for school in the mornings. It occurs most often with dressing and at meals.

Here are some suggestions to help your child with this problem.

1. Dressing

Make sure your child can do what you ask her to do. If she can, then give her a reasonable amount of time to do it in. Establish a routine; things are easier for her with structure. For example, in the morning it might be:

a. Get up
b. Go to the bathroom
c. Get dressed (set timer for fifteen to twenty minutes—the child who is a slow mover will need longer)
d. Eat breakfast

Be sure to praise her while she is dressing. Do not nag or mention her not dressing.

At first, reward her with a happy face, a star, or a story when she has dressed before the timer rings. This helps her to establish a routine. Later, simply getting dressed and eating breakfast will be reward enough for her.

Some children are easily distracted, so remove as many distractions as possible from the environment, like TV or other siblings.

Should your child be unable to complete her dressing in time, and if you are in a situation in which you can keep her at home, do not allow her to go to school. Again, do this matter-of-factly, and not as a punishment. If your preschooler enjoys school (and she would not be going if she doesn't), it will take only one day out.

However, if you have to be elsewhere and your preschooler must go to school, go ahead and dress her. Don't discuss it. Give her breakfast. Should she not have time to finish it, she will have to go without it. She won't starve to death! Do not make an issue of it then. That evening, go over with her what is appropriate dressing behavior and work on a positive reward system to encourage it.

2. Mealtime

Dawdling at mealtime can occur in several circumstances. You may be expecting her to eat more than she can handle. She may be nagged to hurry to keep up with her older siblings. She may have learned to get attention at mealtime by dawdling. Or she may simply be a slow mover, by temperament, and she needs longer to eat. Explore the possibilities and define just exactly what is causing the slow eating behavior. If dawdling seems to be her way of getting attention, then consider doing the following:

- Praise her when she is eating; ignore her when she is not.
- Set a reasonable time limit for the meal. Use the portable kitchen timer and inform your child that when the timer rings, the meal is over and her plate will be cleared without further comment. If she is accustomed to getting a snack between meals, give her the usual one, no more.
- Reward her with stars or happy faces when she does finish on time. She'll soon develop the habit of doing so and you can gradually stop the tangible rewards. She'll be reinforced by her feelings of accomplishment.

P E E R   I N T E R A C T I O N

We discuss peer relationships in "Overview of the Preschool Stage," and we suggest you read that section now if you haven't already. Also, if your preschooler is either excessively shy or overaggressive, read "Special Situations in First Adolescence" for some suggestions on how to help her overcome it. Remember that during the preschool stage one of your child's developmental tasks is to learn the give-and-take of peer relationships. Your job is to make her environment one in which she can learn it most positively and effectively.

NURSERY SCHOOL (PRESCHOOL)

As we have said before, nursery school is an ideal place for refining social skills. This is essential for an only child or for a child who lives where there are no playmates her age. For children living where there is limited play space both inside and outside, nursery school would offer more expansive horizons for playing.

At around three years of age a child is usually ready to become independent, if only for a part of each day. And most mothers could use a break from their preschoolers, no matter how much they enjoy them. Nursery school provides a break that can be most beneficial to you and your child, especially to your child's intellectual and social growth.

SCHOOL READINESS

Some children start nursery school between two and a half and three years of age. But one of the keys to having a good nursery school experience for you and your child is knowing whether she is ready to handle it. Is she able to talk to familiar adults? Can she separate from you in familiar surroundings? Does she want to play with other children? Is she toilet taught? Most schools require that children be out of diapers or close to it. Some schools will accept children in diapers and offer assistance in toilet teaching, but you need to make sure that their methods are the same methods you intend to use. Remember, the school will have her for only a few hours a week; you will have her the rest of the time.

If you can answer "yes" to those questions, your child is probably ready. If not, it would be better to wait awhile and give her more experiences at home.

SELECTING A NURSERY SCHOOL

In selecting a nursery school that will be enriching and satisfying for your child, there is no one who can do it better than you. You know your own child's individuality—his temperamental characteristics, what he likes, how he faces new situations, and his strengths and weaknesses. In choosing a nursery school, all of these must be considered. You also have to meet your own needs. You must take into account the cost, the school's schedule, the distance to and from school, the availability of other mothers in your neighborhood to form a car pool, and if you are working, facilities for after-school care. In the next section we will discuss different types of preschools that may be available. Obviously, if you live in an area that has only one or two preschools, your choices will be limited. But at least your decision making will be easier.

In deciding whether a particular preschool is right for your child, do not just interview the director and go by what she says. You might get a clear, well-thought-out description of the philosophy of the curriculum of the nursery school. But on the other hand you might get a snow job. Remember that the director is telling you what the teachers and children are *supposed* to be doing. It is much better for you to see what the teachers and children are *actually* doing.

We feel the only really good way to choose a good nursery school is to narrow the list down to three or four (if there are that many available), and then take off three or four half days and observe each class in action. What vibes do you pick up from the teacher and the children? Is she an effective teacher? An effective teacher often gets down eye-to-eye with the child. She senses when the children are not with her and can switch activities. She knows and respects each child's individuality. (For example, the child who needs structure and firm discipline will be treated differently from the child who is slower to adapt to new situations.) A good teacher listens, understands the child's feelings, and helps him express them. She also expresses her own feelings and knows how to make effective use of her voice. She talks quietly to keep the children quiet, but if necessary, she raises her voice to get their attention. She sounds very talented, doesn't she?

Remember, however, that teachers are human. They have bad days just as you do. If you have felt that a teacher was lacking in some skills you might talk to her afterward. Ask her how her day was. She may in fact tell you that she has had a really rough day and invite you to come back another time.

Take a look at the activities in the classroom. Are they meaningful, or are they merely busy work? Look at the teaching materials. Are they varied? Do they help children learn gross motor skills, fine motor skills, language, music, drama, socialization, science, art, and preacademic skills?

What is the atmosphere in the classroom? Are the children happy? Are they involved? But don't look for the children to be doing something together all the time. Remember that they are still learning to deal with group situations. Some may be doing things by themselves, or with a small group. And in a normal group, you will see aggression as well.

Look at the amount of structure in the school. Too much structure would stifle a shy child, while too little would be chaotic and frightening for him. A very active, aggressive child needs a school with structure, but one that also allows a great deal of time for gross motor activities in wide open spaces. He needs to work out some of his energies in order to be ready for the quiet times. Most young preschoolers cannot decide for themselves when they need to rest or to play outdoors, and a good school will have a schedule that alternates physically active times with quiet times.

Find out how the school disciplines. Observe to see if what they say they do is in fact what they do. Do the children understand the rules? What happens if they break them? Ask the children. If they don't know, then it's probably not clear. If they do know, they will enjoy telling you, and with gusto.

Ask about the school's first-day policy. Are parents encouraged to stay with their child? If the child is having a problem with separation, are they permitted to stay on subsequent days? If you have a child who is cautious or slow to warm up, this is particularly important. It can be very frightening for him if the school requires that you just drop him into this new situation.

There are other concerns that you might need to look into before choosing a nursery school. If your child has to be withdrawn from the school, what is their refund policy? What is their policy on illness? If they allow children to come to school when they have colds, it means that if your child has only a slight cold he need not stay home. On the other hand, he will be more exposed to other children's illnesses. Are the snacks nutritionally sound?

You may think that four half days spent sitting in different nursery schools is an awfully lot of time to spend. But we don't know of any other way to do it. This goes for picking out a day-care center as well as a nursery school.

These same principles should also be followed if you are shopping for a good private kindergarten instead of a public kindergarten. Incidentally, most private kindergartens fill up rapidly, so don't wait until April and expect to get your child in in the following September. Check with the schools in your area to find out their deadlines.

Most preschools operate a half day, usually in the mornings. The children come two to five days a week, with younger chlidren usually coming less frequently. A day-care center is tailored to working parents. They can drop the child off at 6:30 or 7 A.M. and pick him up again at 5:30 or 6 P.M., at the end of the working day. In a day-care situation, the child is of course fed and is required to take a nap. Because the child spends so much of his day there, it is especially important to choose his day-care situation carefully. We discuss this more completely in our chapter "The Mother Working Outside the Home."

TYPES OF NURSERY SCHOOLS

There are many types of nursery schools, particularly in larger communities. We will list some of these here so that you can know a little more about them.

- A *church-affiliated nursery school* will usually have a good teacher-to-pupil ratio and be less expensive than some of the private schools. The atmosphere is usually warm and caring. The disadvantages are that the teachers may not have degrees, and religion may be taught that does not coincide with your beliefs.

- A *cooperative play school* is one in which parents help with the teaching, allowing them to meet other parents and to see their own child in the perspective of a group. It also lets them remain in contact with their child, which is an obvious advantage for the child who has difficulty separating. And it allows the father to get involved, since weekend work is often required. The disadvantages are that the parents must participate, which may interfere with their own schedules. There may be less structure, and conflicts can occur when parents use disciplinary techniques with your child that you do not agree with. Also, at first some children may be self-conscious about having their parents present.

- A *private nursery school* that is not church related may be medium-priced to very expensive. It may have a very impressive physical plant with good equipment but have less outdoor play space, since its taxes are higher than for a church group. Some of these schools are very academically oriented and overemphasize testing and evaluation prior to bringing the child in, which is an unnecessary trauma for parent and child at this young age. There also may not be much socioeconomic mix.

- *Montessori schools* are usually more expensive. The teachers are usually college prepared and Montessori trained. If you are not familiar with Montessori's philosophy, we suggest you read Maria Montessori's excellent book, *The Secret of Childhood*. The advantage of a Montessori approach is its emphasis on the learning process, which is done in such a way that it is helpful for all children, including slow learners. Children are helped to become independent, and the atmosphere is one of quiet and order, which may carry over into the home. Some of the disadvantages are that socialization and imagination are not as encouraged as at other kinds of schools. The school takes children as young as two and a half or three and requires that they come five half days a week, which can be too many hours or days for some children.

PREPARING YOUR CHILD FOR SCHOOL

Next to choosing your child's school, preparing him for it is most important. It is usually possible for you and your child to visit the classroom during the school year prior to his enrollment so that he can see the physical plant, meet the teacher, and understand more fully what you have been telling him about it. If this isn't possible, then perhaps you could at least arrange for your child to meet the teacher. This is particularly important if your child is slow at adapting to new situations.

Tell your child in advance about the basic rules and routines of the school. Role play with him what will be happening. He should know, for example, that if you will be staying on the first day, you will not be there to play with him; you are going to sit on the sidelines while he begins to become comfortable with the group. Talk to him about how proud you are that he is growing up and ready to go to school. Tell him about the part of the school day that he will like best. Leave out the part that he might not like, such as taking a rest. He may not like to do that at home, but it may be novel for him in a group, so you don't really know how he is going to feel about it.

If a child has a little friend to go to school with him, he can feel much more comfortable. If you don't know anyone attending the school, ask for the names of a few children in your area that you might get in contact with during the summer so that your child can get to know someone.

Buy something special for your child to take to school. If your child feels that you have a positive feeling about the school, he will go in with a positive feeling. But don't make any rash promises such as that he'll just love it or have fun or make a lot of new friends, since he may not, in the beginning.

Let your child know that even though you may stay with him the first day, you will gradually stay less and less because he is growing up and won't need you as much in the subsequent days. Be sure that you do in fact carry out what you have told him. Stay with him on the first day of school if he needs it. Make yourself as invisible as possible and encourage him to become involved with the teacher rather than cling to you. However, remember that the slow-to-warm-up child may stay on the sidelines for some time, just taking in the action. Don't do what you may feel inclined to do, which is to push or coax him to get into the group. Remember, it may take him a little longer, but he will do it eventually. The effective teacher will not try to coax or pull your child into the group but rather will respect his need to "case" it.

When you see that your child is getting involved in an activity and enjoying himself, let him know that you will be leaving and that you will come back. If he is a child who cries at home when you leave but is happy while you are gone, you may expect the same thing at nursery school. Sometimes the leave-taking ritual you use at home helps your nursery school child to handle your leaving. Use it if you possibly can.

Taking a comfort object to school is helpful, too. And some children are helped by having their mother leave a belonging of hers at the school with them so that they know she will come back.

You *know* your own child and what he needs. If you find yourself feeling inadequate in the presence of school personnel, remember: you are the person who is most knowledgeable about your child's needs. Try to be assertive, and stick to your guns in a very polite fashion. It will be good for you and your child.

It is important to maintain communication with your child's teacher, so that she can know what has been going on at home and you can know what has been happening at school. The teacher who knows that there has been stress for a time at home because of illness, death, or marital problems can be a very effective ally. She can be attuned to your child's special needs at that time, avoiding potential problems.

Pick up your child early rather than late if he is having difficulty lasting out the school day. In fact, you might want to shorten the day in the beginning. When your child begins to resent your coming early, you'll know that he has settled in. Remember too that if your child becomes ill and has to stay home, he may have the same problem separating again, even though it has not happened for a while before the illness.

Obviously, if your child has never been separated from you before it would be wise to begin doing this during the summer before school, in small play groups in the neighborhood or at church with a mother's day-out program.

SCHOOL DIFFICULTIES

Sometimes, no matter how much you have done to prevent it, the school isn't right for your child or your child isn't ready for school. You will be able to sense when this is so. Your youngster will come home unhappy and he won't want to go to school in the morning. If your child begins behaving like this, talk to him about his school and let him tell you what is happening. Again, dramatic play may be the way to find out, if your child has difficulty expressing his feelings to you. (See "Overview of the Preschool Stage.") Or simply sit in the classroom and observe; this will give you a sense of what is going on. Talk with his teacher. It may be something as simple as your child's feeling that he needs a snack. Most teachers will work with you and help you to come up with a solution when there is a problem.

If your child's difficulties continue, take him out of school and wait awhile. Enroll him in a different school after a month or so. You will probably find that his extra maturity and your new knowledge of what appeals to him have helped you to select the perfect place for him. There is no reason for a child to be unhappy in school just to prove he can sit something out. This is not the time for character building; it's the time for enrichment and joy.

P E T S

The preschooler is ready for pets. He can learn to be responsible, *but not totally*, for a pet. Obviously, in choosing your pet, consider your own preschooler: what he likes, what he is capable of, and whether he has a history of allergies. Talk to a veterinarian about the different types of pets that might be appropriate. Find out what their care entails. Remember that even though your child will assume some responsibility, you will be the major caretaker. Is it something you are ready to tackle right now? Every puppy grows into a dog, and every kitten becomes a cat. In our health-care section we discuss animal-borne infections. Discuss this with the veterinarian, too.

B A B Y - S I T T E R S

The preschooler is an easier charge for the baby-sitter. Accident prevention and safety are still important, but since the preschooler is more easily reasoned with and more in control of himself, he takes less constant watching. It is important that your sitter be a fairly mature person (thirteen years or older is usually appropriate) who enjoys kids, who will play with them and read to them and be able to follow your house rules for discipline. Be sure that she has all the emergency numbers and knows how to reach you. She needs food, drink, and also a blanket if you are staying out late. Be sure to show her where all the vital things in the house are, such as the thermostat, the fuse box, and a working flashlight in case the power goes off.

We also urge you to read our baby-sitter section in "Special Situations in First Adolescence."

E N V I R O N M E N T A L   C H A N G E S

The preschooler is learning to be a social being and is ready for company and outings, as we have already discussed. If he is still having some difficulty we suggest you read the section in "Special Situations in Toddlerhood" about practice outings.

Moving and vacations can still be upsetting to a preschooler, particularly one who is slow to adapt. Preparing him for these events is essential. Talk to him about the trip. Plan it out with him. If you are moving, show him or tell him about his new school. Show him his new house or a picture of it. Let him help you with the packing and unpacking. These things are as essential now as they were in the stage of his first adolescence.

A C C I D E N T   P R E V E N T I O N

It is important that you read our section on accident prevention in our chapter "The Well Child."

The preschooler is now ready to be reasoned with and can be educated about danger. However, he has *not* completed his lessons yet, and you still need to protect him. You still need safety latches and safety caps. You still need to lower the hot-water thermostat and check out playground equipment. These all continue to be keys to your child's safety. And your preschooler still enjoys running around the house as much as he did in first adolescence, so decals on the glass doors and safety glass continue to be essential.

Your youngster is now learning to become more independent in the neighborhood. Teach him about safety rules. And have safety learning trips around the neighborhood. As you walk together, let your child tell you what he needs to be watching out for, such as cars, bikes, or sharp objects in the street.

Your preschooler is probably more comfortable around water now but he is still at an age where he needs to be watched. And here is one other word of caution, in this day of hot tubs and spas. Parents often feel that since their child is a preschooler and as big as he is, he can be left unattended in a hot tub or spa. However, in many of these tubs there is a suction outlet on the bottom that has been known to trap young children by sucking their hair and holding them under, resulting in injury or drowning. If your child is around a hot tub or spa, do not allow him to go in alone. Cover the suction outlet with an elevated grate so that the child cannot become entrapped.

Playing with matches is something that a preschooler is more able to handle and is interested in. So teaching fire safety is essential. Bicycle safety is equally essential. Many children have been injured on a bicycle because of shoelaces or long garments getting caught in the spokes. Checking your preschooler's toys for safety hazards and keeping him from playing with toys such as darts or bows and arrows is also important.

The car safety rules that we have discussed previously continue to be important: Use seat belts, lock the car when your child is riding in it, never leave the keys in the car, and never leave your child in the car unattended. These precautions will go a long way toward keeping your preschooler safe.

PART 6

SPECIAL
PARENTING
SITUATIONS

28

THE MOTHER WORKING OUTSIDE THE HOME

Mothers who are employed outside the home are often referred to as "working mothers" or "part-time mothers," in contrast to "full-time mothers" whose work is at home. But rest assured, the mother who stays at home works, and in a job that is often more taxing and frustrating than outside employment. At the same time, the outside-working mother also has responsibility and concern for her child on a full-time basis. So let's forget the terms "working mothers," "full-time mothers," and "part-time mothers." *All* mothers are working mothers. And *all* mothers are full-time mothers.

This question of terminology helps underline the fact that the issue of the outside-working mother vs. the full-time homemaker is a controversial one. And for mothers, it can create guilt on both sides of the fence. It's kind of a "darned if you do and darned if you don't" situation. And it seems that everybody else wants to get in the act too and tell the mother what to do. Traditionalists push the mother to stay home. On the other hand, some feminists imply that a woman who does not go to work outside is letting her sisterhood down.

We say, make your own decision. You are the one who is concerned, and your decision should be made by weighing needs: your child's needs, your needs, your spouse's needs, and the needs of the family as a whole. In any case it is not an irrevocable decision. It can certainly change as circumstances dictate.

Almost half of all American mothers with children under the age of six are now employed outside the home. Most of these mothers work because of financial need. Others work to continue in their careers. Some realize that they would not be content staying at home full time. They find that outside interests make them happier and better-adjusted people (and better mothers). All of these reasons for working are certainly valid.

As we've said, many people, including outside-working mothers, believe that the mother who works outside the home is harming her child. This criticism overlooks the fact that many a stay-at-home mother may be so busy running a volunteer organization, organizing bake sales and book sales, or performing civic duties that she has little time for her child.

It is ridiculous to believe that a mother who works outside the home automatically is doing a bad job of child raising. She may, it is true, spend less time with her children than an at-home mother. But it's the quality of time, not the quantity of time, that is crucial. If a stay-at-home mother yells and scolds her children a lot, that is not particularly helpful. If a woman spends her time at home overprotecting her children, that doesn't make her a good mother either. It is really *how* a mother spends her time with her children that counts. So should you decide to be employed outside the home, you will need to give special attention to how you are spending the time that you do have with your child.

Your attitude about your outside employment is another important factor in ensuring your child's well-being. Studies have shown that if the mother working outside the home is happy with her job, accepting it as a natural thing to be done, the mother-child interaction will be no different from the interaction should she not be working. A child gets her cues from her parents, above all. If you accept something as a matter of course, your child will too.

Before we talk about the various caretaking options and the choice of a caregiver, let's discuss the timing of your decision to work at an outside job.

WHEN TO RETURN TO WORK

Some mothers have to go to work soon after their child is born. However, it is preferable to wait until you and your baby have had at least three months together. If you have a choice about when to go back to work, there are several aspects to consider. First of all, as we have said, the infant of around eight months of age is beginning a phase of separation anxiety which is fairly intense until eighteen months of age. It continues, although in a lessening degree, until age three. Obviously, this period, especially until eighteen months of age, is a more difficult time for her to have you gone. Once she is three she is more independent and is able to separate from you more easily, for short periods anyway. However, a child can adjust to her mother's working at any age, if she has good substitute care.

Your child's temperament and her special needs would also play a role in your decision. Adjusting takes more time for a child who is slower to adapt, and a more gradual change may be better for her. If you have a child who has a chronic illness or special problems requiring frequent visits to doctors or therapists, this also makes it more difficult for you to begin work. And beginning work at a time of family stress increases the stress for your child. So in times of a marital crisis, a death, a new baby, a move, or any other environmental change, postpone going back to work if at all possible.

GOOD SUBSTITUTE CARE

Once you have made the decision about when to return to work, you need to give thought to the ingredients necessary for good substitute care for your child, which is an important element in helping you to feel happy about your employment, and is essential for the child's well-being. Lack of it causes guilt.

Regardless of where your child is cared for there are certain necessary qualities to look for in the caregiver herself. The caregiver should be a warm, friendly person who likes children and can be affectionate with them. She should be interested in you, your child, and your ideas about parenting. You should not feel inadequate about your role as a mother after talking with her. And you certainly shouldn't feel that you need to abdicate your responsibility as a mother to her.

The ideal caregiver should have these qualities plus some knowledge about child development. This is often hard to find. But you can share your knowledge with her. Or ask her to read our chapters pertaining to your child's stage so she will have some information on child development. You can tell her how it applies to your child. She too can share her experiences with other children with you. There should be good communication between you and the caregiver. By treating each other with respect you can build a solid relationship. This goes a long way to meeting one of the crucial needs of a younger child: the permanence of a caregiver. Young children need stability and time to become attached and feel secure.

There are various kinds of care available. Studies show that 60 percent of children under six are cared for by a relative in the home of the child or the home of the relative. 30 percent receive care in a home with a small group of other children (which is called family day care) or in a neighbor's home. Only 10 percent are cared for in large group centers. Now let's take a look at these different types of substitute care and their advantages and disadvantages.

• *A relative.*

A relative is more likely to think as you do, and you will know ahead of time how the relative reacts and interacts with children. Your child will probably already have a good relationship with her and the relationship is certainly a permanent one. Naturally you would want the same qualities in a relative that you would in any other caregiver. The relative may keep your baby in her home or come to your home. In her home, you would need to look for the same things you would want in a family day-care center.

At a relative's home, your child can be cared for when she is sick, and there is less chance of her being exposed to infection from other children—unless your relative has a large family herself.

There is often more flexibility in the hours with a relative. And she may be more available to chauffeur your child to different functions when the youngster is old enough for them. This arrangement is usually less expensive, too.

A disadvantage is that relatives feel freer to give unwanted advice and it can be difficult when you disagree with them about child-rearing methods.

• *A baby-sitter/nanny in your home.*

This is obviously a more expensive arrangement than most. However, it provides consistency for your child and less chance of infection. In some cases, it may provide you with some help with the housework so that you can spend more time with your child after work.

To go about finding such a caregiver, ask other people—other parents, your minister, your doctor, or the school principal. You can also advertise in your local paper. Interview several caretakers before deciding on one. Ask her for at least two references, and contact them. You will learn a great deal from talking with other parents she has worked for. You'll want to know the ages of the children she cared for and how the children liked her. How long was she there? Why did she leave? Is she dependable and honest? Does she smoke or drink? Would the reference feel comfortable hiring her in your situation?

If possible, have this caregiver come and spend some time with you and your child over several weeks, so you can see how she acts with the child and how the child responds to her. Also, you can show her how you want your child to be treated. Does she seem to take over and make you feel left out? If so, perhaps she is not a good candidate.

This arrangement gives the same flexibility as a caregiving relative.

• *Family day care, or small group day care.*

Your child is cared for by a woman in her private home who is also caring for other children, usually two to eight, in a small-group setting. Qualifications for this type of person are the same as those we have already mentioned. It is important before you decide on a particular person that you get to know her. Observe at least half a day in her day-care center.

Recognize that the caregiver is not going to be just like you, but she should be someone whom you can relate to and communicate with.

Observe the children in the setting. Are they happy? Or are they crying a lot? How does the caregiver handle them when they are upset? Does she recognize that they have individual differences and acknowledge these?

How does the caregiver structure the day? Are there periods of quiet interspersed with physical activity? Does she have a good play area outside? Does she have enriching toys and books around within the children's reach?

Is the environment safe? How does she handle emergency situations? Does she take medical information on your child? What would she do if your child were sick? Does she have insurance to cover the children? Is her place clean but not so immaculate that children don't fit in there?

Talk to other parents whose kids attend that center so that you can find out how satisfied they are.

One benefit of the family day-care situation is that it is by nature as similar to a home away from home as you can get. Another benefit is that it may be near your home or work (and you might be able to continue breast feeding your baby should you be doing so).

Usually older children (toddlers, first adolescents, and preschoolers) enjoy being with other children, which is an added benefit. Being in contact with more children does increase the number of infections in children under twenty-four months of age. However, most of these caregivers will take your child even if she has a cold or minor infection whereas a large-group day-care center may not.

Family day-care situations are often more flexible in their hours, giving you some leeway should you have to work late. These settings can be in the home of a friend, a neighbor, or someone you have heard about from others. In some states these settings are licensed; in other states, not. If yours are, check with the authorities to see if there have been any reports against them.

• *Large-group day care.*

There are several types of large-group day care:

Custodial care: This kind of day-care center is nothing more than a baby-sitting service offering no educational or developmental experiences. It is extremely cheap but definitely a poor environment for your child.

Comprehensive child development center: This setting is usually federally subsidized; if not, it is extremely expensive. It offers a comprehensive package—educational care, health care, and nutritional care. Family counseling and education are often offered, which you may not need. However, should you have a child with a developmental disability or a handicapping condition requiring special care, this type of center would be advisable.

Developmental day-care center: This type of center offers a stimulating environment with a wide variety of materials. It is manned by trained personnel and may even offer medical care by having a nurse available. The center is often coupled with a preschool or at least provides transportation to and from a preschool so that your child may have preschool experience as well as after-school care.

When deciding on a day-care center you will need to visit each for a half day and observe. Are the children happy or is there a background of fussing and feuding? How do the caretakers interact with the children? Do they recognize individual needs? Are they interested in the children as individuals? How do they discipline? And how do they show their affection? Is there a rocking chair in the day-care center? Remember at this age many children still need rocking when they are distressed.

What is a typical day like? Do they alternate periods of activity with periods of quiet? Are there creative outlets or do they have to perform everything in a regimented way? Is their artwork displayed on the wall? Is it a bright, cheerful environment, with enriching toys, books, and puzzles that the children can reach? Is there plenty of play space, both inside and out?

Is the center safe? How do they handle medical situations? What do they do if your child is sick? Is the facility clean? How do they practice hygiene? How do they handle nasopharyngeal secretions and fecal wastes? Remember that infections are increased two to three times in a large-group day-care setting. But the spread of infection and diarrhea can be reduced by proper handling of waste and hand-washing techniques.

Your child will need to have snacks and lunch there. What kind of meals do they offer? Are they nutritious?

Talk to other parents and see how they like the day-care center. How do their children like it?

Talk to the director. How much training has she had and how much training has her staff had? What is the ratio of children to staff? The ratio for a child under two should be no more than 1 : 4 and for the three- to five-year-old, no more than 1 : 7. How permanent are they? Remember that, especially if your child is an infant or a young toddler, she will really need *one* consistent caregiver. In fact, consistent caregivers are an important need for any child under the age of five.

Does the center allow time for the parents and the caregiver to communicate news at the changing of the guard in the early morning and late afternoon? It is important that you have time to tell your child's caregiver what has been going on at home and for her to tell you what has been going on in the center.

Obviously, finding the right substitute care situation for your child entails a lot of work and a lot of looking around.

In addition to the considerations we have already raised, the type of care that is right for your child often depends upon the age of the child.

An infant needs physical love with a lot of cuddling, holding, and stroking. He needs someone who is responsive and consistent, who will provide stimulation and certainly not use physical punishment. The caregiver must be responsible and able to handle emergencies. Obviously, an ideal situation for an infant would be to be cared for at home by his mother and father, who could arrange their work schedule so that one or the other is always available. This is certainly less expensive, but often allows little time for them as a couple. Other suitable situations would be to be cared for by a relative or a baby-sitter in the home. Family day care is also a possibility if the caregiver has enough time to meet the infant's needs well. Some large-group day-care centers will take infants. However, this is less desirable than the other possibilities.

The toddler (one to two years old) or *first adolescent* (two to three years old) needs a caregiver who will provide a lot of love and individual attention. She must have enough energy to keep up with this little guy, because he needs consistent discipline and loving attention. He obviously would do well in his own home with one of his parents, a relative, or a baby-sitter. Family day-care centers are also a possibility, since this age enjoys being with other children—if there are not too many others and the ages are compatible. Large-group day-care centers are also a possibility, *if* they are good ones.

The preschooler, aged three to five, can handle large-group settings. He will also enjoy either a family day-care center or his own special caregiver in her home or at his home. This child can also have his day care provided by a preschool, if his mother is working part time (for information on preschools or nursery schools, see "Special Situations of the Preschool Stage."

If you are planning to work part time rather than full time, this should make your day-care situation much easier. However, sometimes mothers with part-time work fall into the trap of depending on many different and temporary baby-sitting situations. The child still needs permanence in his caregivers. He can certainly become attached to several caregivers at a time, but each one must be a stable part of his environment. Having many new sitters will unsettle him. So if you are going to have part-time work, try to make sure that your child's substitute caregivers are people he can count on knowing and caring for for a long time (at least a year).

There is no evidence of any differences in emotional development between children whose mothers work part time or full time or at home when substitute care has been good.

P R E P A R A T I O N

Once you have decided to go back to work and have chosen your substitute care there is much you can do to smooth the way, lessen the load, and prevent pandemonium. Prepare your child in advance and ease his transition. Streamline your household. Work on the trouble spots—getting everyone up and out in the morning and getting everyone back and in for the evening. In giving you some suggestions here I (AA) have drawn on my experiences as an outside-working mother and the experiences of the many mothers I have encountered over the years.

It is important to prepare your child for the change, assuming he is old enough for explanations. Tell him that Mommy, like Daddy, is going to be going to work. You will be going out in the morning and coming home at night just like Daddy. This is a concrete fact your child has been experiencing since he was a baby, and he can understand.

Assure him that you love him, that you will miss him, and that you will be thinking of him while you are at work. If you can, promise to call him on the phone during the day. Tell him that you will miss him at lunchtime, and you will send him little love notes in his lunch box that his caregiver can read to him. Tell your child what you will be doing at your work. If possible, take him to your work place and let him see what it is like. If appropriate, have pictures that he's drawn or pictures of him in your work place so that he can see that he is very much a part of it.

When you talk to your child about starting work, remember that your attitude is more important than words. If you are matter-of-fact, confident, and cheerful, he will accept it. However, recognize that the preschooler, who is more able to express himself, may let you know his feelings of anger, rejection, or frustration at the change. Accept his feelings. Try using his play to act out your going to work so that he can work out his feelings. Let him play with the dollhouse, showing the mommy and daddy going to work and the child going to the appropriate caregiver. Play this with him as much as he wants. He may then begin to play it by himself. He may be very anxious at first and require a lot of reassurance. But once everything is settled and you are at work, he will accept the change and carry on with his normal activity. You can use play later too if your child seems unhappy and you wonder if it's because of his substitute care. Let him play baby-sitter or school. Suggest that he be the sitter or teacher. Then listen.

MAINTAINING THE PARENT-CHILD BOND

Many mothers worry that they will lose their child when they go to work—that the caregiver will take her place in his heart. Rest assured this will not happen. Studies have shown that the mother-child bond remains as strong as ever in spite of the child's being cared for by another person. A child can be attached to many caregivers without decreasing his primary attachment to his mother. He will always seek his mother when he needs help.

Sometimes the child who is angry with his mother for leaving him (especially during his stage of separation anxiety) will punish his mother when she comes to pick him up by clinging to the caregiver and seeming to not want to go to his mother. Remember that this is perfectly normal and that he still loves you first and foremost.

You can encourage a feeling of closeness between you and your child even while you are away at work. You can call him on the phone from the office, and you can leave tapes of yourself reading or talking to him so that he can listen to you while you are away. Meet him for lunch some days if you possibly can. But *most of all,* when you are with him at home be available to him. Let him know how glad you are to see him and how you miss him.

COPING WITH HOME CHORES

Obviously, certain problems arise when you have a job outside the home. Compromises have to be made, because you cannot devote as much time to your home and family as you could before you worked, and you cannot devote as much time to your job as you could when you did not have a husband and children.

It's time for weeding out the unnecessary. Flexibility is the name of the game, and it's not easy. The mother who works outside the home has taken on *another* job, not just *a* job. Studies show that most husbands assume very little responsibility for household chores even when the wife is working outside the home. However, this is changing, and that's a benefit for both the child and his father. Men are becoming more willing to compromise their work situation for family needs. More divorced fathers are being awarded custody or joint custody of their children, having to care for them while working too. Maintaining a household and nurturing children is becoming less of a female role. But the change is a slow one. Women still assume the large part of this responsibility, whether working outside the home or not. So if you have a husband who does pitch in and help, *cherish him.* If you don't have such a jewel, you may have to make changes in a gradual way. Obviously, if your husband is against your working, this is going to be an added obstacle.

If you can afford it, get the household chores such as laundry, cleaning, and meals done by an outside source. If you can't, then streamline your work at home. Buy only permanent-press clothes. Use comforters instead of bedspreads. Have hooks all over the house to make it easy for your child to hang up his clothes, toys, and various other items.

Your preschooler can assume some responsibilities for certain chores. Use the positive reward system to encourage him. He can certainly help with taking out the garbage, pulling the comforter up on his bed, putting his dirty clothes in the clothes basket, and clearing the table. It's important, however, when he is learning a responsibility that you be extremely clear as to what he is to do. Reread our suggestions on learning self care. Then supervise him until he can do it well. Remember to use the positive reward system (praise, stars, happy faces) along the way and even once he has got it. Above all, *don't* do it over after he has done it. This would only serve to discourage him and make him less likely to want to tackle anything new.

Shelves are the key to survival with a preschooler, since they very seldom want to put things into drawers. Color-code his shelves and teach him which things go with which colors.

Getting up and out in the morning is often one of the most irritating times of the day. I (AA) will give you some suggestions here that have helped other mothers. The suggestions are somewhat tongue-in-cheek, however, since I haven't always been able to carry them out myself. I simply cannot stand getting up early in the morning, even if it means allowing myself more peace and quiet before the chaos begins. However, if you can, it will simplify the morning.

- Be up and dressed yourself before the kids get up. Many young children wake up on their own in the morning. If yours doesn't, buy him an alarm clock.
- If you have established a morning routine as we suggested in "Special Situations of the Preschool Stage," your child will get dressed before breakfast. If you haven't a routine, try to establish one. This may take some special work on your part for a while, but it does pay off if you can stick with it.
- Pack lunches and set the breakfast table the night before.
- Make breakfast simple.
- Have your child choose his clothes and lay them out the night before so that when he is a grouchy little bear in the morning he won't have to decide what to put on.
- Make sure that anything anyone needs to take with him is set out and ready to go, to avoid that last-minute looking. This includes you!

Even with all these suggestions you can expect a little chaos in the morning, because there is always some little hitch that is unexpected. Just grin and bear it. We said that flexibility is the name of the game, but you can't survive without a sense of humor, too.

TRANSITIONS

Another trouble time is the transition from work to home. How I (AA) envied my husband when he would come home from his work at the hospital, flop into a chair, and turn on the TV. I had rushed home from work, been set upon by children all talking and asking for something different, tried to talk to my baby-sitter about what had transpired during the day, and begun dinner all at the same time. By the time dinner was over I was a basket case. The quality of my parenting wasn't what I wanted it to be, so I decided to do some sorting out and make my work-to-home transition time easier on us all.

I (AA) have now found that it helps if the children have a snack such as cheese and crackers or fruit or frozen yogurt before I come home, so that the need to prepare dinner is not so urgent. Another nice idea is to share the snack with my children after I come home. This gives us time to sit down and talk while we nibble.

At times when I (AA) have had a particularly trying day, I find it helpful to unwind by sitting in the car for a few minutes before I go in, if only to read something I particularly want to read or collect my thoughts. Other mothers have found that changing into more comfortable clothes as soon as they get home helps them begin to relax. I also find that lying down in a reclining chair with a couple of children on my lap while we watch "Sesame Street" or "Mr. Rogers" is a good transition. Some mothers relax by bathing or showering when they get home, with or without children. Bicycling, walking, or any other activity that can be done with children can also be helpful. What you are trying to do is shake the worries and the responsibilities of the work world and be able to focus your attention on your children. Dinner can wait until later.

QUALITY PARENTING

We close with some thoughts about quality parenting versus quantity parenting. This is an important concept for all parents, but is especially important for the mother (or father) working outside the home. It's really quite simple: *Enjoy your child when you are with him.* Don't let parenting become just hard work (there's plenty of that anyway).

Does this mean you have to set aside long periods of one-to-one fun time? No, it can be done along with the day-to-day tasks of managing a household. While you are working at home, include your child in your activities. Listen to him while you're folding clothes. Share your thoughts with him while sweeping the floor. Stop and help him when he needs a hand. These are fun moments that parents can experience all the time. But this certainly doesn't mean you would never set aside some special private time like a quiet talk at bedtime or an outing for just the two of you.

So if you are a mother who is away from home all day at an outside job, don't feel guilty about the quantity of time you have with your child. Enjoy him every chance you can.

29

THE SINGLE PARENT

We have said that being a parent involves mastering a number of complex skills. With single parenting, still more skills are involved. A single parent is (usually) a woman who is under great economic pressure and must perform heroic feats to keep her family above water financially. She is operating under enormous time pressure as well. She is juggling her work, her children, and her own social life.

Therefore, in this chapter we will talk about single parenting in terms of the mother with custody, the father without custody, and the widowed single parent. And since the overwhelming number of single parents are divorced mothers with custody, let's begin there.

THE MOTHER WITH CUSTODY

Every single divorced mother contends at first with a tremendous sense of loss. The University of Washington has created a rating scale, from greatest-difficulty to least-difficulty, of life events that people encounter. The most powerful stress that can hit a person, according to this scale, is the loss of a spouse, through death or divorce. The divorced mother is in fact dealing with the death of a marriage, and she will do some grieving. Even if both parties wanted the divorce—even if it was she who wanted out of the marriage—she still has to contend with this sense of loss.

A divorce is a severe blow to both partners' self-image, no matter whose idea it was. Both husband and wife end up feeling rejected. It is important for a divorced mother to establish new relationships with people who value her and find her worthwhile.

One of the most terrible and gut-wrenching things a divorced mother must contend with is loneliness. She can't rely on her old married friends, because she finds that they drop away quickly. She must look for new friends among the ranks of other single mothers and single fathers.

And for the woman who does not already have a well-paying job or career, the financial squeeze after a divorce is usually the toughest stress of all.

When you put all these stresses together, it is no wonder that if you are a single mother, you may be experiencing a deep feeling of copelessness. You simply feel unable to cope with your finances, your time, your job, and your children. And you are particularly worried about the effect the divorce will have upon your children.

We can clear away one of your sources of stress right now by telling you to forget the ridiculous bogeyman myth that divorced homes produce psychologically maladjusted children. Many people seem to believe this in spite of the fact that there is no scientific evidence to support it. As a matter of fact, some studies have shown a higher percentage of maladjusted children in intact homes than in single-parent homes.

Of course, single-parent homes can't all be lumped into the same category any more than intact homes can. The stresses in single-parent homes differ in degree from one situation to the next. But regardless of the specific situation, all divorced single parents face many problems in common.

Let's talk about the relationship of you as a single mother with your ex-husband. Let's assume the best possible situation. Your ex-husband does not hassle you at all. He sends his child-support payments regularly and visits the children regularly. So, since he is not giving you a hard time, let's talk about your economic problems.

If you are just barely scraping by financially, and deeply worried about it, this is obviously going to interfere with your ability to do a good job of parenting. You will undoubtedly need to find work, and this is good for your psyche as well as your economic situation. However, even with a job, the more things you know how to do for yourself around the house or with your automobile, the better off you will be financially. Check out nearby colleges and adult-education programs to see if they offer courses on taking care of your car and making simple household repairs.

One way in which you can save money is to try out the barter system. Make a list of every skill you have to trade and then see if you can find someone who will exchange that skill for something you need done. If you're a good cook, you can exchange a fine meal for having part of your car fixed. Or exchange meals in return for lessons in car maintenance. You could trade typing term papers for the college student down the street who could mow your lawn or clean windows in exchange.

It may also be important for you to start looking at your children in a new way. With all your problems, much of the time you may see your children as an overwhelming burden. And it's very understandable that you would feel this way. But imagine what life would be like if you had no children. Your children offer you love and the warmth of human contact. Children also give structure to your life. And you need that structure. Especially when the terrible first feelings of the divorce overwhelm you. Immersed in the lives of your children, you get your mind off yourself and your own feelings of desolation.

Next, you need to find groups in which you can be with people who are friendly, compatible, and emotionally supportive. For instance, if you like the outdoors and hiking and camping, the Sierra Club has several Sierra singles' sections. Parents Without Partners is a national organization formed entirely of single parents. Here as well you can find some new companions.

We have mentioned these two organizations because they have branches in many states. But you will also find local singles clubs. In addition to these groups and clubs, don't overlook evening classes in an activity that particularly interests you and where you are likely to meet other people who share your interests. And remember that you need to make friends with women as well as men.

Now that you have the full responsibility for the children, you may feel particularly unsure of the way you are handling them. Basic information about child raising, such as you will find in this book, will help you battle this insecurity.

Or perhaps you are feeling that the whole divorce was a dreadful mistake. "We should have stayed together and stuck it out." Predivorce counseling can help prevent these particular feelings, but if you haven't had such help before the divorce, get it afterward. Either individual or group counseling can help you work through difficult feelings as well as give you confidence about handling the children alone. You need it for both your sake and the children's.

You not only need to learn to handle your own feelings; you need to learn how to handle your children's feelings about the divorce. Many times children seem at ease and relatively happy following a divorce. This is usually a facade. Underneath their quiet exteriors, your children are feeling hurt, abandoned, lonely, and angry. They too need to mourn a loss—the ending of their family as they knew it. This is true even if there was not a great deal of warmth in the family to begin with and the children did not get much affection from their father.

Two main factors determine how well your children will get through the divorce process psychologically. The first is the children's own ability to handle stress. The second is the amount of parental psychological warfare that they are subjected to during and after the divorce.

The ability of a child to handle stress is determined largely by his own self-esteem and self-confidence. A child who lacks these inner resources will be overwhelmed by hostility between his mother and father and by the divorce itself. On the other hand, a child with strong self-esteem is much less dependent on his parents for his internal well-being. He will be extremely unhappy at their stress and at the divorce; but since he has plenty of psychological strength within himself, he can ride out his parents' troubles.

Another crucial ingredient in the child's handling of stress is his ability to express his own angry feelings. The child who buries these feelings will be more severely affected by the divorce. The child who is able to expose his angry feelings will gradually get them out of his system.

The second factor, and probably the most important one, that determines how a child will survive the divorce process is the way in which his parents relate to each other during this painful time. Some parents are able to confine their hostility to each other. They do not let it spill over onto their child. The child knows that his parents are very angry at each other, but they are not angry at him. It is unfortunate when parents are not sufficiently mature to be able to keep their children separate from the wrath they feel toward each other.

Some parents do not take their problems out on their child but they do each try to get the child on their side. The child then becomes a pawn in the game of divorce chess. This is a truly horrible situation, because the child ordinarily loves both parents and the last thing he wants is to be forced to take sides.

There are many permutations and combinations of parents and children in divorce chess. But they are all bad. And the children are the chief losers.

Although all divorces are different and all children of divorce react individually there is one sense in which most of the children are alike. Studies have shown that no matter how good or how bad the marriage, the children would nearly always like to see the marriage put back together. No matter what their age, they have very little comprehension of the psychological strain on each parent which led them to separate. And it is amazing how long the children of divorced parents can cling to the fantasy notion that their parents will get back together again and the family will be as it was. Even after one or both of the parents remarries, and the new families are psychologically healthy, the children will still yearn for the return of the old family, no matter how many tensions it contained.

How can you best handle your child so that he can make his way through the unhappy divorce process and emerge in good shape on the other side? First, remember that it's only an old wives' tale that children of divorce are psychologically scarred. This is true for some children, but it is by no means true for all children. And if you handle your child well, it need not be true for him.

If you have a child who does not yet have a lot of psychological resources such as self-esteem and self-confidence, he will need a great deal of special reassurance, preferably from both of his parents, that he is a loved and valuable person. Give your child a chance to vent his unhappy feelings of suffering and anger. Say to him things like, "I know it makes you feel just terrible that Daddy and I are going to get a divorce and not live together anymore. But Daddy will come to see you a lot and he will still love you as he does now. Daddy and I are getting a divorce from each other, but we are not getting a divorce from you, and we never will." Then encourage him to tell you his unhappy feelings.

Above all, resist the temptation to bad-mouth your spouse. It will only put your child on the spot. He does not want to have to choose between the two of you and, in effect, that's what you force him to do if you engage in mud slinging.

Your child will need a long time to ventilate his anguished feelings about the divorce, perhaps six months or a year. So give him time to do this. If he still seems overwhelmed and cannot bring his grief to a conclusion, we suggest you take him to a professional for help: a psychologist, psychiatrist, or other counselor.

If you do the kinds of things we have suggested here, there is no reason why your child cannot finally emerge from the divorce process as psychologically healthy as he was before the divorce began.

Sooner or later you will probably find a man with whom you develop a deep relationship that leads toward marriage. And you will discover that your children probably have mixed feelings toward your husband-to-be. On the one hand, your children want a new father surrogate in their lives if they have been several years without a father. On the other hand, they have had you all to themselves for a while and they will not like the idea of giving you up.

When the going gets rough, try to remember that you have a great deal going for you as a single parent. Children of divorce are still children. They have the same stages of development and respond to the same discipline strategies as other children. If you have learned these stages and strategies, you are going to be far ahead in guiding and handling your children, whether in an intact family or a single-parent family.

T H E   F A T H E R   W I T H O U T   C U S T O D Y

Men are awarded custody of their children in an infinitesimally small percentage of cases—as low as two or three percent in some states. So we will discuss the without-custody parent in terms of the father.

How does the father's post-divorce shock differ from the mother's, when she has the children? The custodial parent loses only the role of spouse. But the parent without custody loses two roles—spouse and full-time parent. Of course, if the father without custody is not particularly interested in the children anyway, the loss of the parental role is no big thing. But if the children mean a great deal to him, the loss of his parenthood comes as a shattering blow. He too needs to grieve and to rebuild his life with a new emotional support system.

I (FD) know a divorced father who, in order to compensate for the loss of his children, asked some married friends with children if he could eat dinner with them one night a week. They agreed. Every so often he took the whole family out to dinner to pay them back. He really looked forward to that one dinner a week. It gave him the feeling of belonging to a family again, for a short while.

In this situation we want to stress one very positive point: You may end up having a better and deeper relationship with your children now than you did in your previous, intact family. When you are with your children now, you are free of the emotional war with your wife that may have been going on when you were married. You may also put more time and effort into your relationship with your children as a divorced father than you did as a married father. Many fathers have said that they first really began to know their kids after the divorce.

We want to warn you about a psychological land mine that many fathers encounter in relation to visitation ground rules. Many judges tell the father they are granting him "reasonable visitation." But what this means is, if your ex-wife is reasonable, you will have reasonable visitation. If not, you will quickly discover that it means whatever visitation she wants to dole out to you. Do not accept "reasonable visitation." Get your rights pinned down specifically. Only then will you know where you stand. A definite visitation schedule gives structure and order to your relationship with the children; they know when they can count on seeing you. This gives them something predictable to look forward to.

We suggest you arrange a home-away-from-home for your children when they come to visit—a space that is theirs alone. If you live in a house, set aside a special room for them. If you live in an apartment, perhaps you can afford to rent one with an extra bedroom. If this is too much for your financial resources, then fix up a special corner of your apartment for them, where you can decorate the wall with their drawings and keep their playthings stored.

Do some planning for the time you spend with your children. Some fathers pick their children up and take them to a movie or an arcade and then think, "Holy Smoke, what am I going to do with them next?" Many fathers who have spent very little time with their children when they were in an intact family find that interacting with the kids alone for long periods makes them feel inadequate. At first, plan activities that will not require you to talk a great deal with each other. You may be better off taking them to sports events or movies, where you can enjoy being together but not have to converse for great stretches of time. If you find at first that you're not too comfortable being alone with your children, let each of them bring a friend along on outings or even on long trips together. This eases the atmosphere and takes much of the heat off you.

Remember that it's very important for you to understand your children and their stages of development. Read up on the psychology of children. Learn the discipline techniques.

So far we have been assuming that your ex-wife is not hassling you. But the sad fact is that if you are a father who loves his children, and your ex-wife is bitter and vindictive, she can cause trouble for you in any number of ways.

Here are a few tips for difficult times with your ex-wife. If she lies in court about things you have said or not said, then communicate with her only by telegram or nightletter, with a confirmatory copy to yourself. Take a friend with you when you go to pick up the children. If they're not available to you, you have a witness to confirm the fact. If your wife is badmouthing you to the children, just trust that the truth will emerge in the future.

Do not retaliate by maligning her to them. This is bound to boomerang, and as we said earlier in this chapter, is very bad for your children. Simply let the children have a firsthand perception of you as a loving, understanding, and fun person. And as they grow older, their mother's tactics may backfire. A young child may be afraid to talk back to his mother, but as an adolescent he may begin to stand up to her and tell her what he feels you are like, as opposed to what she has said about you.

T H E   W I D O W E D   S I N G L E   P A R E N T

Our society shuns the reality of death. Therefore, you will have to have the courage of breaking with this cultural taboo and talking openly with your children about death. If you are a mother whose husband is undergoing a long terminal illness, you need to be open in telling the children that he is dying. Many hospitals have hospice professionals who can help families deal with the imminent death of a member, and we would advise you to seek out such help if it is available. But suppose your husband dies unexpectedly—of a heart attack or in an accident. Then you must help the children face the abruptness of this reality.

Whether your husband's death was expected or unexpected, your most important job is to help your children grieve. We suggest that you read our section on children and death for more information on how to do this.

The other most important thing for you to do is to create or retain order and structure in your life. If you already have a job, continue working. If you don't have a job, get one. The fact that you have to get up in the morning and meet certain expectations in connection with your job is psychologically good for you. Even if, financially, you don't need to work, we still suggest that you get at least a part-time job. This will force you to involve yourself in the world of adults, which keeps you from hiding away in the tight little circle of your family.

Some newly widowed mothers think of their children as a burden to carry on top of all their feelings of loss. In one sense the children are undeniably a burden. But their love for you is an abundant psychological reservoir to draw from. And the responsibility of the children, like the demands of a job, will force you to keep going. Coping with your children and their problems will take your mind off your own. You must also, however, find a way to take regular time away from your children. If you aren't ready to start dating again, then this free time might be spent with women friends.

When you are ready to begin dating again, you will need to face a new problem—guilt. No matter how logically you know that it's time for you to have men in your life again, you may still feel that dating means neglecting your children or betraying your dead husband. It may take time to get these feelings out of your mind, but it is important for you to do so and to resume your full life again.

There is another problem you will have in raising your children at this point in your life. Both a boy and a girl need a father surrogate. Your boy needs a man to identify with and model himself after. And your girl needs a father surrogate to serve as a model for the man she will ultimately marry. Perhaps you can find a relative or in-law who can play an active male role with your children. A man you are dating cannot play this role unless you and he have settled down to a steady relationship. And we recommend that you not bring the men you are dating into your children's lives very much until you are ready to settle into a steady relationship with one of them.

Now suppose you have been seeing a man for some time and you have decided to get married. Your children may even have asked you, "Why don't you get married so we can have a daddy like other children do?" But on the other hand, they have had you all to themselves for several years and they probably don't want to give you up. Much of the negative side of their feelings may suddenly burst out after you are married. Help your fiancé to understand that your children may have confused and irrational feelings, so he will be able to deal with their hostility later and will not take it personally. If possible, invest in a few sessions with a professional counselor for you, your fiancé, and your children.

So that's the good and the bad of the situation, single parent, whether you are widowed or divorced, with or without custody. It is hard to be an effective single parent, harder than being an effective parent in an intact family. But in spite of the problems, you can still lead a rich and happy life with your children.

30

S T E P P A R E N T S

If you are a stepparent, you are one of twenty-five million in America. And you may be raising not only your spouse's children but your own as well. That can be quite a task.

In many respects, stepparents and biological parents are the same. They are both parents. They both need a lot of knowledge about the physical and psychological development of children in order to care for and guide them well. But the psychological world of the stepparent can be quite different from the psychological world of the natural parent.

THE STEPPARENT WITH NO PREVIOUS CHILDREN

Let's begin by considering the stepparent who has no biological children of her own. Let's say she is about thirty-one, and she marries a forty-two-year-old man with two boys, age two and five. Whereas her husband has had plenty of opportunity to grow up easily and naturally with his children, she has had none. And she is expected to put on the mantle of instant parenthood without any trouble. Well, obviously, it doesn't usually work that way. The husband has feelings and ways of handling the children that are "built into his bones" by this time, and he has an ongoing relationship with them. The wife has none of these, and no training in parenting. And when you are suddenly a parent, without parenting skills, the adjustment can be a jolting one. To help with this adjustment, we suggest that in addition to reading this chapter you read our discussion of children of divorce.

EMOTIONAL ADJUSTMENTS

In the first few years a blended family is an incredibly complex set of emotional relationships. A child feels one way toward his biological father and another way toward his stepfather. And the same thing for his natural mother and stepmother. The father feels one way about his natural son and another way about his stepson. The same with the mother. A woman simply can't feel the same about someone else's child as she does about her own, at least not right away. As somebody once said, there are too many people in a stepfamily!

There certainly is jealousy in a blended family, especially if the family contains both the mother's and father's children from their previous marriages. (In a biological family, the jealousies are much more simple and straightforward.) In the blended family there are not only jealous feelings, but ambivalent feelings also. And it's hard to adjust yourself to a family in which nearly everybody has very mixed feelings about everybody else.

Of course, we are not saying that these whirlpools of jealous and ambivalent feelings cannot be overcome. They can. And quite happily too. But in order to overcome them you have to realize that they are there and know what to do about them. Stepparents typically do not anticipate all of these problems. Before the wedding they tend to overlook the existence of the stepchildren. Oh, they know they are there, of course. But they do not know they are *really* there because they haven't yet experienced all of the emotional wrenchings and jostlings that take place when the family actually moves in together.

Another problem is that the stepfamily is haunted by ghosts from the biological family. For example, no matter how difficult and conflict-ridden a marriage may have been, almost all children of divorce wish they could have the old family back again, and this irrational ghost hovers over many blended families.

Another type of ghost inherited by the stepparent family is the ragbag of problems created by the earlier biological family. There he is, seven-year-old Gregory, and the stepfather thinks to himself, "I'm not responsible for what he's like. His father and mother are. But I'm the one who's got to get him over these mistakes and these disastrous ways of meeting people." It is this stepparent's job to learn to discipline and love this child whose problems he had no hand in shaping.

T H E   R O L E   O F   T H E   S T E P P A R E N T

Too often the role of the stepparent is fuzzy and ambiguous. The stepmother can never take the place of the child's real mother, living or dead. On the other hand, the stepmother is more than just a friend who happens to live in the same house and occupy the same space as the child. So what is she exactly? It is not easy to carve her own role.

If you are thinking about a marriage that will make you a stepparent, there are some things you should consider in advance. Did your prospective spouse's marriage end by death or divorce? A dead parent is even more likely to be idealized than one who is still alive. However, more marriages end by divorce than by death, particularly marriages where the children are still young. And fortunately for you as a prospective stepparent, younger children appear to have an easier time adjusting to new situations. Also, divorced parents usually remarry in a shorter period of time than widowed parents. So the child of divorce has had less time to adjust to life with a single parent, and is not as likely to feel that the stepparent is an intruder.

If the child's parents are divorced, this usually means she has an alternate place to visit or live if things get rough for her in her new home. A child whose other parent is dead has no such safety valve. The other side of this coin is that an older child can sometimes manipulate her new family by threatening to go back to the other parent.

Another consideration is whether or not you are already a parent. If you are a parent, then you have had a certain amount of "seasoning," and you know what children are like at different ages. But if you haven't had children and suddenly you become a stepparent, you will probably feel like you've been hit in the face with a cold mackerel. It's like the story of the soldier who was in combat for the first time and shouted out to his buddies, "Hey, they're really firing at us!" That's what it feels like to have your first confrontation with your new stepchild, even one who lives with you only on weekends and vacations.

Having a stepchild often brings you yet another personality to deal with—your spouse's ex. Some of those confrontations can boggle the mind. You may even think to yourself, "I didn't count on this when I married Eddie. It was just going to be him and me and a lovely marriage." But of course there's no way to predict these things ahead of time. You may find your stepchild's other parent very easy to get along with. Or she may be just the opposite. And you'll never know until you have your first encounter with her.

The age and sex of the children play a great part in how well you and they are going to relate to one another. Young children can relate well. But what if you inherit a thirteen-year-old along with the five-year-old? Remember that even if the teenager were still in her biological family she would be in a state of rebellion as a typical part of her adolescent development. Apart from being a stepchild, she may well be uncooperative, belligerent, and defiant. So if you marry a parent with a teenage child, you will probably have to deal with her feelings of jealousy and hostility. The feedback technique should prove very helpful in dealing with her feelings. Naturally, you do this on a much more sophisticated level with a thirteen-year-old than with a five-year-old.

The sex of the child is important too, since a child between the ages of three and six is going through the stage of the "family romance." For example, a four-year-old girl is likely to be jealous of her new stepmother's relationship with Daddy, and a little boy of his stepfather's relationship with Mommy.

No matter what the age or sex of the child, you as a stepparent should expect a certain amount of hostility and standoffishness. It's a good idea for you to get to know the child during the courtship. Knowing her bad points probably won't keep you from wanting to get married, but it will prepare you somewhat for the problems. Knowing her good points will aid you in developing loving feelings sooner. And letting her get to know you may soften her feelings toward you somewhat. Don't count on it, because it can go either way. But at least you can get the relationship started, so you both know what to expect. The worst possible thing you could do would be to concentrate entirely on the person you are going to marry, and just assume that the children will tag along lovingly and obediently after the wedding.

Some prospective stepparents make the mistake of trying to rush into a relationship with the child. We guarantee that coming on too strong will make the child back off. Your approach should be low-key and casual. Don't bring a gift the first time you meet the child. She will tend to be suspicious of this. When you do begin to give her gifts, don't make the first gift too expensive. At first you can find out from your spouse-to-be the things that the child likes. In the appendices of this book you will find suggestions for toys, books, and records appropriate for each age group.

I F   I T ' S   N O T   L O V E   A T   F I R S T   S I G H T

But suppose the worst happens. You have tried very hard to get your prospective stepchild to like you. But obviously she doesn't. And suppose you don't really care much for her yet either. What should you do? We think it helps to remember this: Almost every stepchild will see you as upsetting her status quo, even if she is quite young, and the feelings are not fully conscious. You may be trying very hard to win over your prospective stepchild and establish a relationship, but perhaps all she can see is that you are going to change things. Keep this in mind, and use the feedback technique as a way of solving it, if she is at an age where you can use it—first adolescence or older. If she's too young for the feedback technique, then you will just have to offer her affection, and let her feelings gradually come around.

To use the feedback technique, when the child withdraws or sulks or gives you a bad time, you might say something like, "Linda, I guess it's very hard for you to think of me marrying your daddy and becoming a part of the family." If she doesn't respond, don't press it. Try again another time.

It would be a wise investment for you and your prospective spouse to have a few sessions with a professional counselor. A psychologist, psychiatrist, or social worker will be able more easily than you to bring to the surface the problems that your blended family needs to face. We recommend this to everyone who is planning a marriage that will make him or her a stepparent.

T H E   L A R G E R   S T E P F A M I L Y

So far we have just been talking of a very simple case of a new stepparent and a new stepchild. But what if there are going to be two, three, or even four new stepchildren? Or what if two sets of stepchildren are going to live in the same family?

Questions descend on this prospective stepfamily like a cloud of mosquitoes. What are the new kids like? Will they like me? Will I like them? Will I get to keep my own room? Will Mom like any of them better than me? These are very real questions and are not to be taken lightly. In an intact family, children compete for parental attention. The rivalry of stepsiblings is much more exacerbated. These problems are in urgent need of the feedback technique. And in need of the family council as well, which is something you might start doing together as a family as soon as it becomes certain that the marriage will take place.

The family council is a very helpful technique for enabling family members to get over their grouches and learn to be closer. It meets once a week and includes all children aged three or older. Parents and children take turns being the president of the council. Even a child of five can take her turn in leading the council. She can ask everyone to air their gripes, but she may need help from others on how to solve the problems.

The family council is especially helpful for a stepfamily. Both parents and children ventilate their angry and jealous feelings and get them out of their system, so that positive and loving feelings can take their place. The family council establishes a regular forum for settling disputes and conflicts that arise within the family. It also serves as an orderly talkabout within which the two original families can learn to blend into a new family with its own unique life-style. Do not vote in the family council. Voting means someone wins and someone else loses. And that interferes with the harmony of the family. All decisions made in the family council should be unanimous. If you can't get a unanimous decision at one family meeting, then hold that issue over until the next meeting.

S O M E   C O M M O N   Q U E S T I O N S

There are so many issues in stepparenting that we cannot possibly cover them all. Let's take the rest of the chapter to cover a range of questions you may have as a prospective stepparent. For example, should you invite the young children to the wedding? If the children are over three, we believe you should definitely include them in the wedding. If you don't invite them, they will probably feel hurt and left out. But, of course, don't force them to come.

If possible, find a new place for the family to live—a house or apartment where neither family has lived before. Parent and children who have lived in a home have a certain feeling of territoriality. They tend to regard it as *"my* house." The stepchildren and even the other parent may feel like outsiders. When a stepfamily starts out fresh in a different home, then neither family has prior claim on it. You may think that this is a minor matter. We assure you it is not.

What should a child call her new stepparent? Don't ask a stepchild to call you Mother or Daddy. She already has a mother or father and will resent your asking. Probably the best thing is to ask her to call you by your first name. Sometimes a child will begin by calling you by your first name and then later, entirely on her own initiative, change to Mom or Dad. And that's great.

Often the subject comes up as to whether or not to legally adopt the stepchild. We would usually advise you not to. Don't even consider it unless the other parent shows absolutely no interest in the child. If that parent is still living, you cannot adopt the child without his or her legal consent anyway. If the other parent is making regular contact with the child, it would be a mistake even to bring up the subject. If the child is old enough to understand what is going on (five years of age or older), she may not want to be adopted. Deep down she may have a sense of identity with her original name. With a very young child, assuming you have the natural parent's consent, there is probably no reason not to adopt. With an older child, each situation must be judged separately. Certainly there is something to be said for giving the child the same last name as her parents. Even though there is probably no longer any stigma attached to her having a different name, having the same name may make her feel more a part of the family.

What about stepparents and discipline? Naturally, discipline for the stepchild should follow the same basic rules as discipline in an intact family. But often a parent feels more hesitant about disciplining her stepchild. Don't fall into that trap. Be firm, steadfast, and equal in your dealings with all your children. Remember that discipline is teaching. It is also a sign of your love for your children.

What about the effect on a blended family if husband and wife have a new child of their own? First of all, we think your decision about whether or not to have a child should certainly not be determined by what you imagine the effect will be on any other children in your family, stepchildren or not. If having a child is important to you and your new spouse, then have it. If not, don't. But keep in mind that your stepchild may fear that you and your spouse may love the new baby more. This is true of natural siblings, of course, but even more true of a stepchild. You may need to take extra care to let her know that the baby will not replace her in your affections. By all means, read our section on sibling rivalry.

We have been talking mostly about the live-in stepchild. But there is another kind, and we should not forget her: the stepchild who comes only for a day, a weekend, or for vacation. We suggest you set up a regular schedule of visits for her and stick to it whenever possible. This creates a sense of stability for the child as she swings back and forth between households. You and your spouse also need to agree on ground rules that will apply to all of the children when the stepchildren are visiting. Be sure all the children understand what they are.

Try to provide a space for your visiting stepchild to call her own, and have it ready for her when she arrives. This space is her territory. She can keep some special toys and playthings there. Also, it's very important to understand the feelings of a visiting stepchild for the parent she lives with. You may not get along with her mother, but the child loves her. The woman is, after all, her mother. So resist the temptation to say anything negative about the other parent in the family. It will only backfire.

We have tried to give you an overall view of stepparenting. In so doing we have pointed out that it is harder to be a successful stepparent than it is to be a successful intact parent. We think we would be doing you a disservice if we implied otherwise. We have also tried to point out the psychological land mines scattered throughout stepparent territory, so you will know where they are and be able to avoid them. But don't worry too much about the negative factors. If you know the psychology and physiology of the stages of development, and if you know the psychology of guiding children through positive discipline, then you can end up doing a better job as a parent than many parents with intact homes are doing.

PART 7

TEN COMMANDMENTS FOR PARENTS

31

T E N
C O M M A N D M E N T S
F O R   P A R E N T S

We have covered an enormous variety of topics in this book. We have tried to include everything you might ever need to know in order to raise your child successfully and happily in the first six years of life (and keep your sanity!).

But we don't want you to be so overwhelmed by the details of parenting that you miss some of the main points. This final chapter is a summary of the main ideas of this book—what we think are the most important things to remember about child raising.

Here are our Ten Commandments for parents.

1. *Children are people.*

They have arms and legs and bodies and heads and bones and muscles and nerves and blood vessels, just like other people.

But children are *little* people. They view the world through the eyes of little persons—their parents and other adults are giants. And children's perception of time is vastly different from the time perceptions of big people. Children know only one kind of time—the here and now. The future does not exist for them. Children have their own kind of logic, quite different from adult logic.

Since the world of children is very different from the world of adults, it is important not to assume that simply because you understand the world of adults you also understand the world of children.

One of your most important jobs as a parent is to study your children and learn about them. Understand what makes them happy, afraid, or angry; understand what makes it fun for them to learn and grow.

Imagine that your children are like a charming little race of primitive people who have come to live with you temporarily and you are studying them earnestly and carefully, the way an anthropologist would study a new and strange race of natives. You will really have to do this if you are going to learn about your children and understand them. And if you do not understand them, how can you teach and guide them through the years until they become adults?

2. *Your child is unique.*

One of the troubles with books like this one is that they deal with children in general. When we speak of the typical behavior of a four-year-old we are speaking of four-year-olds in general. But, of course, there is no such thing.

Remember that there is not a single other child in the world who is like your child. Therefore, a description of a typical four-year-old may describe only part of your child's behavior.

Why is your child unique? For two reasons, one biological and one psychological. Biologically your child is an absolutely unique combination of genes. Psychologically your child occupies a unique position in the family. Even though you deal fairly with all of your children and love each of them, the first child's psychological life space is different from the second child's and so on. Starting from the very beginning, the people and events in each child's life continue to shape him uniquely, just as he has an effect on his environment and on other people.

This one-of-a-kind combination of genes plus psychological environment means that each of your children is as unique as his fingerprints.

So respect your child's uniqueness. Don't try to fit him into a preconceived mold of what kind of kid you think he ought to be, or what some child-raising book says he ought to be.

3. *Parenting is a learning process.*

When you are learning to parent, which is a new and complex skill for you, it's no different from learning to play golf or bridge, or to operate on the innards of a car. Truthfully, we think parenting is a more complex skill than learning to be a lawyer or a doctor. In fact, it is so complex that we believe parents haven't really learned much about child raising until they have raised their first child through adolescence.

Obviously, when people are learning to play golf or bridge, or to be a competent auto mechanic or lawyer or doctor, they make many mistakes, probably thousands. It's impossible to learn a complex skill any other way.

The weird thing is that so many parents expect the impossible of themselves— to learn to be parents without making mistakes! And they are dreadfully upset when they find they have done something "wrong." Do yourself a favor and expect to err as you learn to parent. We can assure you that the authors of every book in existence on child raising (including this one) have blundered from time to time in raising their children.

Be kind to yourself. If you slip up, forgive yourself. Teachers, ministers, judges, businessmen, authors, congressmen, presidents—they all make mistakes. Don't you, a poor miserable parent, have the same right?

4. *Don't get tied down to a set of rules.*

That also includes those set forth in this book. After all, raising a child is a human relationship, and human relationships can't be reduced to a set of rules. We have said that your child is unique, but so are you, his parent! Your relationship with him is different from that of any other two people; don't make the mistake of trying to fit it into a rigid mold. Think of the rules we have given you only as guidelines.

5. *The years before six are the most important years of your child's life.*

During this period, attitudes and habit patterns are established which will last through life. This is when your child's basic personality structure and his ability to relate to other people are molded. This is when his gender identity is formed, as well as his ability to relate to the opposite sex. An enormous number of very basic aspects of your child's personality are shaped during this early time.

Not only is personality shaped in early childhood, but the intelligence is formed also. Dr. Benjamin Bloom has amassed research evidence to show that approximately 50 percent of a child's intelligence is developed by the age of four. The oral and written language your child develops by six will probably influence his language development throughout his life. His general role model for problem solving and his intellectual approach to understanding the world are also developed in his first six years.

6. *Learn to distinguish between feelings and behavior.*

When you are setting limits to guide your child's behavior, it is very important that you understand the distinction between her inward feelings and her outward actions. By inward feelings we mean such things as love, fear, anger, joy, loneliness, and excitement. By outward actions we mean anything the child does that can be observed by another person, such as walking, talking, hitting, hugging, singing, and sleeping.

We separate feelings from actions because it is reasonable to expect a child to control her actions, according to her age and stage of development. It is not reasonable to expect her to control her feelings, for thoughts and feelings come into her mind unbidden and she has no control over them.

With regard to your child's actions, it's important for you to decide on reasonable rules and limits. Your child should know what she is allowed to do and what she is not allowed to do.

No one magic set of rules is *the* correct set. Parents differ widely. Some are more easygoing; some are more strict. It is important that you feel comfortable with your own rules and can explain the reasons for them to your child if she asks.

7. *Give your child the right to express feelings.*

The freedom to express all her feelings is one of the greatest gifts you can give your youngster. It enables her to get negative feelings out of her system and replace them with positive feelings, helps her to build positive self-esteem, and acts as a safety valve when hostile feelings build up.

Some parents generally approve of expressing feelings, but are uncomfortable with the idea of allowing their child to express negative or hostile feelings, especially toward them. Giving your child the right to express her feelings, including negative ones, will in no way lessen her respect for you. On the contrary, it will increase it, for she will see that you feel secure enough as a parent to allow her the democratic right to express her feelings as a junior member of the family. These are the same kind of democratic rights that you as an adult have as a free citizen of your country.

8. *Draw a sharp distinction between punishment and discipline.*

Although many parents use punishment, it is actually a very ineffective method for curbing undesirable behavior. Discipline, on the other hand, is teaching. When you discipline your child you teach her to employ desirable behavior and to avoid undesirable behavior. There are various effective methods of teaching desirable behavior, such as the positive reward system, contracting, and environmental control. The positive reward system is the most effective. There are also different methods for teaching a child to avoid undesirable behavior, such as the Time Out, the feedback technique, and the mutual problem-solving technique. The Time Out method is probably the most effective of these.

In guiding your child toward the ultimate goal of self-regulation, reinforce her positive moves. Behavior that is reinforced is strengthened and tends to be repeated. So reward your child when she acts independent, self-assertive, creative, and loving. Do not reinforce her when she acts timid, whining, uncooperative, violent, or destructive.

9. *You are your child's most important teacher.*

In order for your child to develop her maximum intellectual potential, she needs intellectual stimulation from you at home, particularly in the crucial first six years of life. This is of enormous importance for the optimum development of her intelligence. Stimulating her language development, exciting her interest in words and language and books, teaching her to print, playing games with her that teach her to think logically and grow in her understanding of mathematics— all these are part of the rich intellectual basis you can give your child by the time she is six years old.

The curriculum at home during your child's first six years is far more important than the curriculum in the schools she attends after her sixth birthday. You need to offer her a wise choice of toys, books, and records.

10. *Parents have rights too!*

In the process of raising your child, don't forget this important fact. Raising a child is no easy task, but it mustn't become so heavy an obligation that you forget about your own needs.

Parents have the right to put their marriage ahead of their child raising sometimes. When parents put all of their energies into parenting and neglect the marriage relationship, the twenty-year divorce is often the result; The children leave the nest, and the parents discover that the marital relationship is not strong enough to endure.

We would grow stale at our regular jobs without vacations. Although people do not realize it, the same is true for parenthood. Once in a while Mother and Father should leave the children with a grandparent or baby-sitter and take off for a night, weekend, or even longer.

Above all, you have the right to be human—to have bad days; to be cross, illogical, biased, and opinionated; to be furious with your children on occasion; and to feel like flushing them down the drain sometimes.

The authors of this book have certainly had all these feelings, and have given themselves the right to have them, without feeling guilty. We urge you to give yourself that right too!

NOTE: We have covered an enormous amount of ground in this book, and we hope we have answered all the questions that a parent might ask. However, if you do have questions about raising your child which we have not covered in this book, you can write to us in care of our publishers, Simon and Schuster, 1230 Avenue of the Americas, New York, New York 10020. We cannot promise to answer each letter individually, but we can promise to answer in future books.

PART 8

HEALTH CARE

32

T H E W E L L C H I L D :
R O U T I N E H E A L T H C A R E
F R O M B I R T H T O A G E 6

One of the most important things you can do to keep your child healthy and well is to assure good health care. This requires a partnership between you and the professional with whom you have chosen to work. You will feel better if you have selected your doctor before your baby is born, and know that you have confidence in her. You may or may not have a choice between a pediatrician or a family practitioner. If you do, make sure you know the difference between the two.

A family practitioner is a physician who has completed medical school and served an internship and possibly two additional years of residency in family practice. The advantages of this experience are that the family practitioner is trained to treat both adults and children and can work with the family unit as a whole. *A pediatrician* is a physician who has had a year of internship and two years or more of residency in pediatrics. A pediatrician has more expertise than a family practitioner in the area of children's medicine. A pediatrician has extra training in the developmental needs of the child. You can use the AMA Directory at the library to find out if they have passed their specialty boards.

Prior to your baby's birth you might want to interview several physicians and discuss such matters as the type of delivery method you have chosen and your choice of breast or bottle feeding. Also, make sure to ask if she minds how many questions you ask as a patient and how much teaching of the parents is done in her practice. You will want to know how available she is and what kind of coverage by another doctor is provided if she has to be away for any reason. Does she have a time during the day when you might telephone with some question that is not an emergency?

It is important to find out the fees, the office hours, whether there is an area for well babies which is physically separate from the area for sick children, the name of the hospital that she is affiliated with, how many patients she might see in an hour, and if she offers any parenting classes. When you come away from the interview you should ask yourself how well you related to her. What kind of "vibes" did you get from your interview? Good? Poor? Lukewarm? Remember that this is a person you will be working with for a long period of time. You will be dealing with a topic of great emotional importance to you: your child. You need to feel that you can easily discuss your concerns and be heard.

You and your doctor give your child two types of care in order to keep him well: *well-child care* and *ill- or injured-child care.*

Well-child care, discussed in this chapter, is a form of preventive medicine in which the physician observes, immunizes, and screens the child while teaching the parents about accident prevention, exercise, nutrition, and normal growth and development. *Ill- or injured-child care* is defined and covered in depth in our chapter, "Health Problems in Early Childhood." Finally, our first-aid section tells you how to handle an injury or serious illness requiring immediate action.

Much of the following information, particularly in the physical examination section, applies to your child in the first two or three years. That's when medical supervision for wellness is carried out with the most frequency. As your child grows into his fourth and fifth years, he will probably be having routine check-ups less often. However, all of the information in this chapter is important for you to know, even if your child is already in the late preschool years. And some of it—for example, playground safety, accident prevention, and preparing for emergencies—definitely applies to him.

Sometimes mothers complain to me (AA) about the frustrations of taking their baby to the doctor for their routine checkups. It can be harrowing.

For example: Your toddler Joey's appointment is scheduled just after his nap-time, which he has refused to take today. So he is behaving like "the bear of the year." When you finally manage to get to the doctor's office, the waiting room is full of runny-nosed kids. Of course Joey heads straight for them, and you envision sleepless nights ahead when he, too, will come down with whatever they have. Once inside the sterility of the doctor's examining room, Joey refuses to take off his clothes or let you do it. He refuses to get on the scales and throws himself on the floor in a rip-roaring tantrum.

You are sure that the nurse thinks you are the worst mother possible, because you seem to have no control over your child. The doctor, whom Joey has seemed to enjoy on previous visits, has no success in getting the toddler to settle down for the physical examination, which is carried out nonetheless.

You had wanted to discuss your concerns about Joey's lack of appetite, his screams of woe when his familiar baby-sitter arrives, and his negative behavior. But, unfortunately, Joey is weeping and wailing and your mind is only on how you are going to handle the DPT shot he is about to receive. Joey gets the shot, screams bloody murder, clings to you, and promptly falls asleep.

By the time you get home an hour and a half later, you are a basket case. I can sympathize with this experience, because I have been there one or two times myself. But there are ways to make the well-child visit more pleasant for everyone.

THE PHYSICAL EXAMINATION

First, it helps if you understand the components of well-child care and know what to expect inside the examining room.

Your doctor follows your child's growth, development, and physical well-being through the routine physical examination. This includes periodic measurements of height, weight, and head circumference. The height and weight are plotted on growth charts to make sure that your child is growing normally and that no un-usual trends are developing. We recommend that you ask for one and keep it at home so that you can follow your child's progress yourself. If you don't under-stand how to plot it, simply ask the nurse or doctor on your first visit to assist you with reading the chart. The trends that your doctor looks for are very excessive weight gain or weight loss, or unusual changes in height.

The head circumference is particularly important in the first two years of life because it is a clue to brain growth, which is very rapid during this time. Very rarely, some of the bones in the head will fuse too early, not allowing the head to grow properly. The term for this is *craniosynostosis*. This can be corrected surgically, which is often necessary in order for the child's brain to grow. At the other extreme, sometimes the system producing fluid to bathe the brain and the spinal cord becomes obstructed. A backup of fluid occurs. This is called *hydrocephalus* and results in a very large head with excessive pressure on the brain tissue. Again, this can be corrected surgically and must be done early in order to prevent brain damage.

As part of the physical exam the doctor checks your child's head to observe any abnormalities in the fontanelle, or soft spot, another clue as to what is happening in the brain. He checks your child's ears, eyes, nose, and throat for signs of infection or loss of ability in hearing or vision. It is sometimes hard to notice vision and hearing problems at home, and your child can lose a lot of ground if they are not picked up early enough.

The doctor listens to your child's heart and chest to check for heart or lung problems. Congenital heart disease may first be diagnosed on the basis of the abnormal sound of blood flow through the heart. This sound is called a murmur. Your doctor may mention that he hears a murmur, but that there is nothing to worry about; he will probably call it "functional," "benign," or "innocent." The child has a thin chest wall, so it is much easier to hear the blood as it flows through the heart. When the heart rate is increased with fever, excitement, or exercise the flow of blood through the heart is much more rapid. The sound then is louder, producing a murmur. *This type of murmur does not signify heart disease.* So this is what your physician is usually talking about when he mentions a functional murmur. The word itself tends to scare mothers half to death. If your doctor says something about a murmur and you feel frightened, be sure to discuss it with him until you feel comfortable. Remember, no question is a stupid question when it involves your child's care.

Your youngster's abdomen is checked to make sure that the liver and spleen are normal and that there are no other unusual masses. Your baby's genitalia are checked for possible hernias, undescended testes, or low-grade infections that could result in adhesions of the foreskin or labia minora.

The child's hips are checked carefully, particularly in the first year of life, to rule out any possibility of dislocation of the hips. This problem can be handled fairly easily if detected early but will result in damage to the hip joint and cause walking problems if not. If there is a dislocation, the mother usually notices that it is difficult to diaper the baby because she has problems getting his legs apart. Your doctor also checks for any abnormalities of the legs or feet such as excessive toeing-in or bowlegs. Most babies do not have perfectly straight feet and legs, since their bones are soft and pliable and they have been molded in the uterus. They will straighten out during the first year, in most cases.

Your doctor also observes your child's ability to move about, use language, interact socially, and learn, which are all important aspects of development.

YOUR OBSERVATIONS AND CONCERNS

Your observations and concerns are a very important part of well-baby care, since you know your child better than anyone else could. When you share this information with your physician, you help him to know your child better. Sometimes your mind goes blank when you see the doctor. Write down your questions and concerns before the visit and bring the list with you. Your doctor can help you with management problems that occur as your child grows, and he can also help to guide you as to what to expect in the months ahead.

IMMUNIZATIONS

Immunizations have made one of the most significant contributions to the control of disease in childhood. The infections they prevent have been the leading causes of illness and death in children in years past. Because immunizations have done such a good job of prevention, we tend to become complacent, and begin to wonder if it is really necessary to take our child in for such treatment. However, you will not question the need for immunizations if you fully understand them, what the diseases are that they combat, and what the specific side effects and risks of the immunizations are.

The body fights invading germs by producing antibodies. Immunizations give the child germs in a weak, modified form that do not make the child ill. However, the body produces antibodies just as it would if the child had been infected with the normal germs. These antibodies then protect the child if he comes into contact with the real germs. He will either not get the disease or will get it in a very mild form.

When the whole population is immunized, the incidence of infection is very rare. This does not mean, however, that the germs no longer exist. They are still there, just waiting for a susceptible victim. By immunizing your child you do your bit to keep the occurrence of these diseases rare. However, no immunization is 100 percent effective in preventing the disease or 100 percent without side effects.

The diseases that your child will be immunized against are diphtheria, pertussis (whooping cough), tetanus (lockjaw), polio, measles (rubeola), German measles (rubella), and mumps. Let's take a look at each of these diseases, the immunization, and the possible side effects or risks of the immunization.

DPT

The DPT shot is a three-in-one shot that gives immunity against diphtheria, pertussis, and tetanus.

DIPHTHERIA is an infection that affects the throat, nose, and skin and is quite contagious. The complications of this infection include heart damage and paralysis. It can be treated with antibiotics, but approximately 10 percent of the patients who acquire diphtheria will die. Reactions to the diphtheria immunization are extremely uncommon and are usually limited to a slight swelling at the injection site.

PERTUSSIS (WHOOPING COUGH) has a very high mortality rate among infants (see pp. 400–1). Antibiotics have been used with some success, but immunization has been the important measure for controlling it. Side effects of the pertussis vaccine include redness and swelling at the injection site, fever, and malaise for twenty-four to forty-eight hours. These can be treated with Tylenol and cold compresses. Convulsions or shock have been reported at a rate of 6 per 10,000 immunizations. When these occur, the pertussis vaccine should absolutely not be included in any subsequent immunizations. Also, babies who experience high temperatures (greater than 105° F), extreme sleepiness, or excessive crying (crying or screaming for three or more hours) probably should not receive any subsequent pertussis vaccine either.

The risk of the disease still far outweighs the risks of the vaccine. But if you are concerned, discuss the situation with your physician.

TETANUS (LOCKJAW) is a very dangerous illness. Tetanus vaccine is one of the most effective of all the immunizations. Serious side effects are extremely rare. Usually there is no more than local swelling with heat. Your child may lose appetite or be slightly fussy and irritable for several hours after the injection. But Tylenol and local cold compresses help alleviate this.

POLIO VACCINES

POLIO is a viral infection which can result in paralysis and sometimes death. Because it is a virus, antibiotics are not effective in treatment. The only weapon against polio is immunization. At the present time there are two types of vaccine: oral vaccine (Sabin), which has a live polio virus, and a vaccine which is given by shot (Salk) and contains an inactive or dead virus. The oral vaccine is currently used routinely in the United States. It should not, however, be administered to anyone with an immune problem or anyone who lives in a family with other members who have an immune problem. After the oral vaccine is administered the child sheds the polio virus in the stool, and susceptible contacts could get an infection this way. Very rarely (1 in 8 million cases) a person may develop paralysis due to the polio vaccine. This is usually due to their having a rare disease which predisposes them to developing infection.

The injected polio vaccine is an alternative to the oral vaccine in households with susceptible individuals. This is a choice that you should discuss with your physician. Again, the risks of side effects are minimal compared with the risks of contracting the disease.

MEASLES, MUMPS, RUBELLA

Another three-in-one shot that your child will be receiving at fifteen months of age is the combination measles, mumps, and rubella vaccine.

MEASLES is a virus disease in which the mucous membranes of the eyes, nose, and throat become inflamed, followed in a few days by high fever and rash. With this immunization there is no danger of spreading the vaccine virus to susceptible individuals. Side effects of the vaccine occur in about 5 to 15 percent of those receiving it. About the sixth day they may develop a fever of around 103° or higher and this may last as long as five days. Sometimes a transient rash and mild joint pain will be noticed. Encephalitis has been noted in 1 in 1 million recipients of the vaccine. However, children acquiring natural measles run the risks of encephalitis at a much higher rate—1 per 1,000. The illness that this vaccine prevents can have serious results. The vaccine should not be given to anyone who has immune problems.

Before the measles vaccination there were 400 to 500 deaths a year due to measles, and far more often there were horrible complications such as encephalitis, pneumonia, convulsions, and blindness. The disease is most devastating in the first year of life.

RUBELLA is a mild illness with a fever and rash which does not affect the developed child or adult but has a devastating effect on the fetus in early pregnancy. The deformities include heart defects, blindness, deafness, and retardation. The immunization program is intended to protect those children yet to be born, hence recommended for unimmunized women at least two months prior to conceiving. A small percentage of children may react to the vaccine with transient rash, fever, swollen glands or, rarely, joint pain.

MUMPS infects and causes swelling of the salivary gland, the testes in males, and the ovaries in females. It can also cause encephalitis, but far less frequently than with measles. Mumps have been known to cause abortions in early stages of pregnancy as well.

Reactions from the MMR vaccine are extremely rare; self-limiting ones such as fever, rash, or itching may occur.

There are other vaccines available for diseases encountered abroad or periodically, in epidemics. These are special situations that you will need to discuss with your physician at the appropriate time. If you have any concerns about a particular immunization, your physician or your health department should be able to explain in detail the risks, benefits, and current recommendations.

SCREENING

Routine eye and hearing tests are done to screen for difficulties. At twelve months of age your child also receives a tuberculin skin test, since tuberculosis is still common in some parts of the country. Routine tuberculosis screening will probably be done every one to two years after that. If your child is having problems with eating, possibly resulting in low iron intake, a blood test for anemia (low blood) will be done. Your doctor will check your child's urine and blood if other findings indicate the need to do so.

ENCOURAGING EXERCISE AND GOOD NUTRITION

Our society, unfortunately, is increasingly inactive. Many people believe that the preschool years are the time to teach a healthy attitude toward exercise.

Make every attempt to see that your child exercises every day, especially if he tends to be a "sitter." Preschoolers love music and marching. Walking or biking with your child on a daily basis is another excellent way to promote exercise.

There are some necessary precautions to keep in mind when your child is exercising or playing hard in hot or humid weather. Children do not adapt to temperature extremes as effectively as adults. For example, your child is not able to sweat as well. He burns up more energy and loses more heat from his body. It is important that he drink fluids (three ounces of cold tap water for every thirty minutes of exercise) and that he wear lightweight clothes in the heat, changing sweat-saturated ones frequently. The child who is obese, has gastrointestinal infection, diabetes, congestive heart failure, cystic fibrosis, or malnutrition is at much greater risk for heat exhaustion.

As for promoting good nutrition, just follow our suggestions in the nutrition chapters in this book. Remember not to force food on your child; let his hunger set the pace. And remember to keep mealtimes as pleasant as possible and to set an example of good nutritional eating yourself.

ACCIDENT PREVENTION

Because accidents are the leading cause of injury and death in the young child, we have addressed it throughout the book. We summarize it again here since it is an important part of well-child care. Education for safety training is an ongoing process and the young child needs protection until he has mastered the ability to recognize danger. The hazards change according to the child's development. They also change according to the family situation. Accidents are more likely to occur when mothers are tired or sick and unable to keep as watchful an eye as usual. Any change in family routine such as moves, vacations, parental stress, company, or baby-sitters can also increase the likelihood of accidents. Obviously, if you have taken precautions to accident-proof your home you will have a lower incidence of disaster even when the family routine is disturbed.

Go through your home room by room, looking for and removing any poisonous substances and objects that could result in suffocation, choking, falls, burns, or electric shocks. Here are some safety suggestions for each room.

Kitchen. Make sure that all cords and appliances are out of reach, most particularly the coffee pot. Turn pot handles toward the back of the stove. Simmer on the front burners and do your high-heat cooking on the back burners. Watch for children when you are drinking or eating something hot. Hot coffee spills are leading causes of burns. Make sure knives and other sharp utensils are out of reach. Make sure all household cleaners, bleaches, and chemicals are locked up and out of reach. Be careful when using them; a child can move quickly and drink from an open bottle in no time. Never leave a child alone in the kitchen in a high chair or on a table or counter in an infant seat.

Living room. Make sure all plants are nonpoisonous. Appendix F provides a list of poisonous plants. Ashtrays should be cleaned out and alcoholic beverages cleaned up after parties. Breakable objects and things with small removable parts should be out of reach. Sharp corners on tables, especially glass tables, should be padded (foam tape or rubber corners can be obtained from the hardware store).

Child's room. Make sure that all equipment bought for the child meets safety standards. Never use plastic bags for toys or to waterproof mattresses. Do not leave a very young baby in a crib with a pillow or any loose blankets. Place the crib away from windows where window shades, curtains, or cords could result in choking or suffocation. Make sure also that the crib is not near any heating device that could result in burns. Keep away from the crib all boxes or furniture which your baby could climb on to in order to get in or out of the crib. All toys should be checked to make sure that there are no small removable parts that can be swallowed or aspirated.

Bathroom. Never leave a young child in the tub unattended. Keep all cleaning agents, cosmetics, and medications out of reach, preferably in locked cabinets. Turn the hot-water heater below 130° F to avoid burns. Cover the hot-water tap with a rag to prevent contact burns against the hot metal during baths. Make sure there are skidproof rugs on the floor so that your wet child climbing out of the tub does not slip and fall. Use rubber bath mats or abrasive treads inside the shower or tub to prevent slipping. Never leave a tub of water just sitting; a younger child might wander in. Make sure razors and electrical appliances are out of reach.

Laundry room, garage, utility room, workshop, basement. Keep all chemicals out of reach and under lock if possible. Use original containers, never soft drink or milk bottles. Dangerous tools should be kept out of reach and disconnected. Do not allow your child to play in the dryer or around old refrigerators or freezers. Take doors off of such appliances if they are not in use. Don't allow children to play games of running under the garage door when it is closing.

All rooms. Protect your child and yourself from falls by keeping floors clear of toys and other objects. If possible, avoid scatter rugs. Do not keep floors too highly waxed, and clean up spills immediately. Stairways should have gates at the top and bottom and be in good repair. Make sure that balconies and bannisters are in good condition and that windows are fitted with childproof latches. Beds and furniture should not be used for bouncing on.

Cover unused electrical outlets with special plugs or heavy electrical tape. Make sure that frayed cords and broken or loose plugs are fixed. When disconnecting an extension cord from an appliance, don't leave the cord plugged in to the wall. Make sure all electrical appliances are kept away from water. Lock up firearms of any kind. Never keep them loaded.

Your child's clothing can also be hazardous, particularly long skirts, scarves, or untied shoelaces. Buy flame-retardant nightwear.

Be sure your home has a safe heating system and reliable smoke detectors. Have home fire extinguishers, if possible, and be prepared with a plan for escape should fire occur.

Playground. Playground equipment should be checked and rechecked on a regular basis for sharp objects, splinters, or rough corners. Slides should not be higher than four feet, and ideally playground equipment should be in areas with soft surfaces such as sand, pine chips, or grass. Playground safety rules should be taught and reinforced frequently. Cover the sandbox when not in use (to prevent its being used as a litter box). Check the play area for poisonous plants and sharp objects. Keep the child inside when mowing the grass since hard objects hit by a mower become high-velocity missiles!

Street. Young children should be taught the hazards of the street, and riding toys in the street should not be allowed.

Car. Using federally tested restraints and/or seat belts is a must. Keep car doors locked, whether the car is in motion or parked. Children should not be allowed to play with the controls in the car at any time, since they will begin to consider it a toy.

Children should not be left alone in a car, especially with the windows rolled up—in hot weather the car becomes an oven in a matter of minutes. Never leave the keys in the ignition while you hop out for "just a minute." Electric windows can be hazardous; mechanical windows are ideal. Car doors "eat fingers."

Water. The incidence of drowning is high with small children. Make sure that all pools, including wading pools, are protected from the crawling infant and the young child either by an unclimbable fence or a cover or emptying. (And an empty pool certainly must be surrounded by a locked, unclimbable fence.) *Vigilance* is the key with the nonswimmer. If you own a pool, consider buying an alarm system that sounds when anything heavier than five pounds falls into the pool. If you live in an area where you can swim all year round or where your child is around water frequently, consider swimming lessons. But an infant or very young child *can never be considered a good swimmer*. So do not get a false sense of security. Even those who have had lessons require vigilance.

Filled scrub buckets, vaporizers, and diaper pails can be dangerous for the crawler or the toddler. She may not have the strength to pull herself out, should her curiosity pull her in.

It sounds so scary when you put all the hazards together, but don't go to the extreme of overprotecting your child and never allowing her to experience the world. Simply accident-proof the environment and keep alert. Accident prevention should become a habit, not a fear.

DENTAL CARE

Your physician can tell you about the amount of fluoride already in your drinking water and whether your baby will need a fluoride supplement. Usually babies who are breast-fed will be given a fluoride supplement unless they are drinking fluoridated water in between feedings. As we suggested in our chapter "The Daily Care of Your Infant," begin cleaning your child's teeth and gums as soon as his first tooth appears. Wipe them with a wet washcloth or gauze pad. Or use a toothbrush with soft bristles. If your child is taking a fluoride supplement, don't dilute it with juices or milk. Give it to him when his teeth are clean for maximum effectiveness.

You will want to choose a dentist for your child. There are dentists who specialize in working with children—pedodontists—and their offices are usually equipped to handle children very effectively. However, a general dentist who has a great deal of patience and caring can also work with young children.

You should plan on taking your child to the dentist sometime between the ages of two and three years, unless she has problems before then. At this time the dentist can assess the general condition of the teeth and whether they are coming in right. He will probably begin topical fluoride on the outer enamel, a procedure which is usually repeated once a year. Your dentist will look for signs of early crowding of the teeth, malocclusion, cavities, or congenital problems involving the teeth. Usually the first visit is one in which the dentist is presented as a friend and the teeth are looked at and perhaps brushed. For the first couple of visits you should go into the treatment room with your child to provide security and comfort. After the visit to the dentist, take your youngster for a special treat. Remember the positive reward system! Obviously, good preventive care is important even at the earliest age. Keeping the teeth and gums clean and decreasing the amount of sugary foods in contact with the teeth are essential for good dental health.

KEEPING A HEALTH RECORD

We strongly advise you to keep a health record for each of your children, to help you keep track of how they have been doing. The American Academy of Pediatrics has the *Child Health Record,* which covers medical records, dental records, and immunization schedules, and also has height and weight charts from infancy to adulthood. We recommend that you ask your physician about the possibility of obtaining the publication. It comes in small booklet form and has a pocket for additional papers. If your doctor does not have one, write the American Academy of Pediatrics, 1801 Hinman Avenue, Evanston, Illinois 60204, and request one. Obviously, other child-health record books would also suffice.

HANDLING THE DOCTOR VISIT

As we have said, a trip to the doctor or dentist with your young child can be fraught with hazards. There definitely is no way to guarantee that every trip will be smooth sailing. But here are some tips that will help.

When taking your child to the physician, dress her in clothes that are easy to take off and put back on. Be prepared in the event of a wait. This means bringing food, drink, toys, her "lovey" and books. Also, we recommend asking for the first afternoon appointment, since the wait is likely to be shorter then. And there are likely to be fewer sick children waiting, which means less exposure for your child.

Once your baby has begun her immunizations, particularly after twelve months of age, she may become fearful and anxious when going for a checkup. Remember too that from six months to about twenty-four months your child is going through stranger and separation anxiety. Unless your child has had to make frequent visits because of illness the doctor usually falls into the "stranger" category. If your child is anxious, your physician will probably conduct much of the physical examination with her seated on your lap and will certainly allow you to stand at the examining table and comfort her through any exams or procedures.

Make it a policy never to lie to your child about whether or not a procedure will hurt. Do not elaborate about the hurt. We have found that saying that a shot will make an "ouch" for just a second and then get better seems to help. It is also helpful to buy a toy doctor kit for your child and play doctor with her at home, performing the examination that the doctor gives, with dolls, stuffed animals, or your child as the patient. When your child becomes quite good at the game you will probably get a few free examinations yourself.

If your child is very fearful of injections, then get a syringe (ask your doctor for one) and play giving injections to each other, including wiping the skin with alcohol (sometimes it is that cold alcohol feeling that scares them more than the shot) and applying an adhesive strip bandage and saying "ouch" when necessary. When you have a preschooler who has had to have many shots, playing this game usually won't satisfy her unless in fact there is a needle on the end of the syringe! Obviously, the child must be supervised during this game, and a soft doll or stuffed animal can be the subject.

This same procedure holds true for dental visits. When you play "the dentist game," your child will love tapping around in your mouth!

There are also books that help to prepare the child. Two books by Jane Watson are geared to the child ages two to five. These are *My Friend the Dentist* and *My Friend the Doctor*. Billy Pope has written *Let's Go to the Doctor's Office*, and Harlow Rockwell's *My Dentist* may also be helpful. "Mr. Rogers" has wonderful TV shows on going to the dentist and going to the doctor, which we highly recommend. The American Society of Dentistry for Children offers free pamphlets on dental care and preparing for a trip to the dentist. You can write for these to the American Dental Association, 211 East Chicago Avenue, Chicago, Illinois 60611.

If you need to talk with your doctor about some concerns that require one-to-one attention and no interruptions, you'll need to arrange to be childfree. This means either bringing a baby-sitter to keep your youngster in the waiting room, or scheduling a separate appointment for the talk. Your doctor will be amenable to this, and we urge you to try it. It's *so* hard to listen through the wails of a child.

BEING PREPARED FOR ILLNESS OR INJURY

Another important consideration in the health care of your well child is that of being prepared should illness or injury occur. It's tough to look up phone numbers, search for supplies, and soothe a screaming child all at the same time. We encourage you to take the time now to read the following section. Discuss it with your doctor to see if he has any changes or additions he'd like you to make.

We recommend that you post your first-aid recommendations and emergency numbers on the refrigerator door, by the telephone, or in some other central spot so that they become a familiar sight. You might even read them on a regular basis as you are putting away groceries or waiting on the phone. Posting the information also makes it more available for visitors or baby-sitters, should you not be there. We are putting the first-aid measures in a separate chapter later in this book. You can tear out the pages, punch a hole in the corner, put a ring or string through them, and hang them up next to your other emergency information. Or you can photocopy the pages and use that set for hanging up.

If you have not yet taken the CPR (cardiopulmonary resuscitation) course offered by the Red Cross, we strongly urge you to do so. You cannot learn it from books.

In the same vein, learning to take a temperature and read a thermometer before your child is burning up with fever helps to relieve some of the stress and anxiety when you are first confronted with that situation. And discuss emergency measures with your doctor—does he want you to call him or the rescue squad first? Which rescue squad does he recommend, if you have a choice?

EMERGENCY NUMBERS

Emergency numbers are those which you would need in the event of illness, injury, fire, choking, drowning, or poisoning. Post the numbers near the telephone, apparent to everyone in the family and any baby-sitter. The numbers that you should have on this list include the poison control office, the office and home of your doctor and dentist, the rescue squad (it would be helpful to add the time it takes to reach your home), fire department, police department, pharmacy (the nearest and/or the all-night pharmacy, preferably one that delivers and allows charges), your nearest neighbors, and the hospital emergency room (distance from the house to the emergency room).

FIRST-AID SUPPLIES

Your first-aid supplies should be kept together, in a portable box such as a tackle box, which can be locked or kept out of the reach of children. It should be restocked as necessary, and everyone in charge should know where it is.

Stock the first-aid box with the following:

Adhesive strip bandages (assorted sizes)
Butterfly bandages
Nonadhesive sterile dressings or "film"-type dressings (Telfapad)
Adhesive tape (1″–1½″ wide)
Sterile gauze pads (2″ × 4″)
Tourniquet supplies (a short sturdy stick and an old, but clean, necktie)
Aspirin and/or Tylenol
Hydrogen peroxide
Rubbing alcohol

Ammonia
Calamine lotion
Rectal thermometer
Sharp needle
Sharp scissors
Tweezers
Tongue depressors
Syrup of ipecac
Ice bag
Meat tenderizer
Anaphylactic kit if known allergies
Antibacterial ointment (Betadine, Bacitracin, Neosporin)

Knowing how to take your child's temperature is a necessity. The three ways to take a temperature are: orally (by mouth), rectally (by rectum), or by underarm (axillary). (There are devices on the market which measure temperature by placing a strip on the child's forehead. At the present, they have not been found to be as reliable as these we discuss.)

TAKING A TEMPERATURE

Most children under five years of age have difficulty keeping an oral thermometer (long, narrow bulb) in their mouths. But it is worth trying to teach your child after she is three years old. When taking the temperature orally, place the bulb of the thermometer under the side of the child's tongue and have her close her mouth. The thermometer should remain under the tongue for four to five minutes.

The rectal temperature is the most accurate, but it is also the most traumatic. Toddlers, particularly, do not relish this. A rectal thermometer has a short, round bulb. Lubricate the bulb heavily with petroleum jelly. Place the child on her tummy over your lap or on a changing table or bed. With one hand hold the child at the base of her spine and with the other *gently* slip the thermometer into the rectum. Never force it; the rectal wall can perforate. It should be inserted into the rectum until the bulb is fully covered. Leave the thermometer in place for three minutes. Never leave the child alone with the rectal thermometer inserted. There is a natural tendency for the child to expel the thermometer.

The third method, under the arm, is the least traumatic for the child, and we recommend it for most cases. You can use either an oral or a rectal thermometer. The bulb should be placed under the arm well up into the armpit and held in place against the body by the arm. You may have to hold your child's arm down if she is uncooperative. The thermometer must stay in place for ten minutes. You can hold your child on your lap and rock or read to her while you wait.

The average normal temperature by mouth is 98.6° F (37.0° C), by rectum 99.6° F (37.6° C), by the axillary method 97.6° F (36.4° C). Body temperatures fluctuate during the day—it is usually lower in the morning and peaks in the late afternoon or evening. There are individual variations, and variations according to your child's age. Don't be concerned if your child's temperature is one degree above or below average.

Be sure the thermometer is shaken below the 95° mark before you use it. After using, wash the thermometer with soap in tepid water and rinse with alcohol before storing. The amount of mercury in the thermometer is not dangerous, so don't worry if it breaks. Your child will enjoy chasing the mercury balls around.

Post your emergency information and become familiar with it. Stock and lock your first-aid box. Read our "First Aid" section. Talk to your doctor. Take a CPR course. Learn how to take your child's temperature. Then you will be well prepared to deal with emergency situations.

33

H E A L T H   P R O B L E M S   I N   E A R L Y   C H I L D H O O D

In this chapter we will first address general information that might be needed to care for a sick child—what to do when he becomes ill, how to handle a hospitalization, and what to do if your child has a chronic illness or impairment. We will follow these sections with information on specific health concerns which may occur in early childhood.

W H A T   T O   D O   W H E N   Y O U R   C H I L D   B E C O M E S   I L L

No matter how well and carefully you take care of your child, he is bound to come down with some of the childhood aches and pains and contagious illnesses. There's just no getting around it. And when he does, you'll need to know:

- the signs and symptoms of illness
- how to work with his doctor
- how to care for your sick child

SIGNS AND SYMPTOMS OF ILLNESS

When you are a new parent it may be difficult to tell at first when your child is really ill. After you have been through a couple of illnesses, however, you will probably be an expert and be able to tell long before the doctor when your child is coming down with something.

The following signs and symptoms are often seen with illness:

- HEAD: Appearance of the soft spot—sunken or bulging.
- EYES: The eyes look "sick"—glassy, sunken, dark circles.
- EARS: A discharge or swelling is seen or the child is pulling on his ears.
- BEHAVIOR: The child becomes lethargic, sleepy, and uninterested in things around him. Or he may be sleeping poorly, be irritable, and not respond as usual to soothing.
- CRY: The cry changes—becomes high-pitched, hoarse, or excessive.
- SKIN: The skin appears flushed, bluish, gray, pale, or sweaty, or has unusual rashes or seems extremely dry.
- BODY MOVEMENTS: The child develops chills, trembling, stiffness, or convulsions.
- VOMITING OR DIARRHEA.

- URINE: There may be blood in the urine or it may have a peculiar odor. The child may have pain on urination or have decreased urine output.
- APPETITE: The child may have a change in appetite, usually a decrease.
- TEMPERATURE: The body temperature can go up with exercise, excitement, or heat exposure, but an elevated temperature is also a sign of illness. In young infants, the body temperature may drop instead of rise with illness.
- HEART RATE: If the heart rate is greater than 130 or less than 60, this is abnormal.
- RESPIRATORY RATE: The respiratory rate increases with activity and decreases with sleep. A normal respiratory rate for the newborn and infant is 50 to 60 breaths per minute. This may be irregular in the first few months of life. At a year of age the respiratory rate is 25 to 35 breaths per minute, and at five years of age it has decreased to 30 or fewer breaths per minute. If the child has any difficulty with breathing, such as having to work harder to get air in or out, noisy breath, or hard coughing, there is a problem.

WORKING WITH THE DOCTOR

It is important that you sit down and discuss with your physician under what circumstances she would like you to call. It is obviously important, especially with a young infant, to err on the side of calling too much rather than too little. When you call, it also helps to be prepared with the information that the doctor is going to need. Jot down pertinent information as follows:

- The child's *name, age,* and the *ongoing condition.*
- Your child's *temperature,* how long it has been that way, and what treatment you have used.
- Any *signs and symptoms* noted from the list given above.
- Any *medication* or *treatment* that you have already given.
- The name and number of your *pharmacy.*

If your doctor gives you advice over the phone, write it down on the same paper you have jotted your other notes on. Be sure to repeat it back to the doctor so that she is sure and you are sure that you are on the same wavelength. Follow your doctor's suggestions, and if you find they are not effective, or if you need more explanation, call her back. Remember that this is a partnership, and your doctor should not be a "silent partner."

CARING FOR THE SICK CHILD

Caring for a sick child is one of the most trying times of parenthood. All your routines are ruined, your child feels miserable, and you feel concerned. Eventually you may become so fatigued that you feel angry and resentful toward your child for putting you through this. It's not an easy time for either of you. But fortunately, children usually bounce back quickly and within a few days are back to their usual selves. Let's consider some of the things that can be done to give you smoother sailing.

MEDICATIONS   One of the first things you must know is how to give medications. If you have ever gone through the frustrations of trying to get your screaming child to swallow that "good, delicious medicine" only to have him spit or vomit it all over you, you know what we mean. Here are some guidelines according to the child's age:

NEWBORN TO THREE MONTHS: The ideal way to administer medication is through a nipple. Position the baby on your lap so that his head is supported and both of your hands are free. (This is the en face position; see illustration.) Using an infant seat is another possibility. Draw the medicine up in a syringe or a dropper. Place a nipple in the baby's mouth and then drip the medicine into the nipple while the baby is sucking. Follow it with some water to make sure that all of the medication is out of the nipple. If the baby is unable to suck, then the medication can be given directly with a syringe or a dropper. Be sure the medicine is deposited in the center back portion of the mouth. You may place it along the gums, toward the back of the mouth. The medication is more easily given in small amounts, when the infant is hungry.

THREE TO TWELVE MONTHS: Children this age usually prefer taking the medication directly from the nipple or syringe. The syringe is particularly helpful with the teething child, who will probably enjoy chewing on it while the medicine is being slowly pushed in. Have the child sit on your lap in a physically comforting way, which helps him to relax. Chilling the medication in the refrigerator prior to giving it makes it more pleasurable.

ONE TO THREE YEARS: Giving the medication through a nipple may not be effective now, although your child may still accept the syringe. This is an age when the child is becoming increasingly independent and does not want to be forced. Try giving the medication in a very small shot glass or medication cup, and follow it with something he particularly enjoys drinking or eating. Let him assert himself by choosing what it is he wants to take to wash down the medicine. Praise him when he has done well. Remember that resistive behavior is at a peak and you will need to be firm and consistent. Give choices when possible, such as, "Do you want to sit in the chair or on my lap to take your medicine?" If the child cannot tolerate the bad-tasting liquid, then mix the crushed tablets or the capsule contents with a favorite food (such as ice cream or applesauce) to disguise the taste. Unfortunately this is not a foolproof method. But more and more better-tasting chewable tablets are being produced and will ease the situation. Simple, honest explanations of why the medication is being given and what it will do are also in order.

THREE TO SIX YEARS: It is more difficult to disguise the taste of medicine in food in this age range, but now your child can be making the transition to pill taking. Using a favorite soft candy can be helpful in this. For example, cut a jelly bean in half and play a swallowing game in which the child swallows the jelly bean without chewing it. You should also be explaining the relationship between the cause of the illness and the treatment. Reward the child when he has done what he has been told.

When medication is prescribed for your child, it is important to discuss with the doctor or the pharmacist any precautions or suggestions about when to give the medication and whether certain foods should be avoided at that time. Be sure you understand what the medication is for. Check the label to be sure it is the strength your doctor recommended. If the label says "Shake Well," shake it well. Sometimes the medication settles to the bottom, leaving only the watery solution on the top. Measure the medicine precisely. The pharmacist can give you devices for doing so, such as a syringe or a calibrated test-tube-like device with a lip on it for drinking. Last, but not least, if you think your child may be allergic to the medication, let your doctor know.

FEEDING YOUR CHILD   Most children do not want to eat when they are sick. Feeding time can be a chore if you worry excessively about your child's decreased appetite. He will probably prefer to drink fluids that he particularly enjoys, however. Consider your child's symptoms and then think about how you would feel if you were in his shoes and what you would particularly enjoy. Fix that and offer it to him. Don't nag. Be patient; he will eat again. Children with fevers, sore mouths or throats, or general malaise usually love ice cream, pudding pops, popsicles, and cold drinks. Children with stopped-up noses and bad colds usually like something warm like hot tea, hot soup, or hot cocoa.

HIS NEEDS, YOUR NEEDS, FAMILY NEEDS   Getting your child to rest and stay in bed is not a problem when he feels miserable. Let him decide how much moving around he can do. He should be able to pace himself, unless he is nagged constantly about taking it easy. Then, even if he is tired he may continue going just to prove his independence. Children, if left alone, will rest and sleep as much as they need.

One of the biggest problems is keeping the child happy when he doesn't feel like moving around and playing. TV, books, quiet games, play dough, crayons, and paints are the old standbys. Have them available and offer them to him, but don't force him to play. He may start something and not finish it. Be understanding but not overly solicitous. Let him know that you understand how miserable he feels, but do not allow him to express his misery in unacceptable behavior such as throwing things, hitting, or biting. He needs to know that the same rules for behavior apply whether he is sick or not. Do expect some regression, however. He will want to be rocked, held, kissed, and sung to more than usual. Surely you can remember feeling that way yourself when you have been sick, even as an adult. Hasn't the thought ever run through your mind when you felt totally wiped out, unable to move: "I want my mother."

Mother is the person the child wants nearby if Mother is the primary caretaker. It is important to let your child know that you are available and that you will change your plans in order to give him more time and care. It won't be for long. One of the problems, however, is that Mother has only a certain amount of energy. Conserve that energy as much as possible. When your child sleeps, you sleep if you can. If your child is so ill that he is waking up during the night, we would advise you to sleep in the room with him. That way you won't have to keep getting up and coming into his room. It also keeps you from disturbing your husband's sleep. This is especially good, since he can perhaps be of assistance in assuming some of the other household duties that you are neglecting. Don't worry about getting your child into the habit of having you sleep in his room. Once he is better, you will both know it, and you can matter-of-factly state that it is time for you to go back to your own bed. If you are convinced and firm about it, there should be no problem.

If there are other siblings in the house, they will be experiencing feelings of jealousy over all of this increased attention for their brother. Recognize this and help them to express it. Reassure them that if they were sick too you would do exactly the same thing for them. Also, help them to see some of the negative aspects of being sick. There is a charming little book called *I Wish I Was Sick, Too* by Fritz Brandenburg. It certainly helped smooth the ruffled feathers in my family when one of ours was sick.

Last, but not least, don't forget yourself. You need a break if your child has been sick for a while. Get out of the house when you can, if only for a walk!

HOSPITALIZATION

Hospitalization is a traumatic event for a young child. It is an extreme break from his normal routine; and he is separated from home, family, and friends, in a totally strange and scary environment. Your child's hospitalization is very difficult for you as well. You are anxious and concerned for his welfare, and your own normal routine is a shambles.

If it is at all possible, avoid a hospitalization for your young child. Of course, sometimes it is essential. And, obviously, nothing can take away the stress completely. But there are ways to make things easier for you and your child. It requires understanding how hospitalization affects a child, and then doing what you can as a parent to decrease the psychological trauma for him.

The child of five or under is the most traumatized by hospitalization. Afterward, he will exhibit undesirable behavior changes for weeks, sometimes months. This is the age of greatest dependency on his parents, and he is immature in his ability to understand what is going on. However, there are differences in reactions in children, depending on their ages. Let's look at these:

NEWBORN TO FOUR TO SIX MONTHS. Even if a young infant is separated from his mother, he will handle a hospitalization fairly well if he receives good nurturing and stimulation while there. It's you, his mother, who suffers from the separation. Whenever possible, you should stay with your baby and assume as much of his care as you can. This helps to relieve your anxiety and keep up your confidence in your ability to care for him.

FOUR TO SIX MONTHS TO THREE YEARS. Around four to six months your infant is capable of discriminating strangers. He becomes anxious in their presence. This blossoms into an anxiety about separating from you, an anxiety that lasts until around three years of age. Separation from Mother is really stressful for this child! Nothing in the hospital care can make up for your absence. You need to be with him and care for him as much as possible. Other things to consider in this age child are his extreme motor drive, as well as his fight for independence from eighteen months to three years.

FOUR YEARS TO SIX YEARS. The child from four to six years can handle temporary separation a little better, but still needs his parents very much. During these years he has the added misery of his fantasies and fears, which really work overtime during a hospitalization. He is not only upset by the separation, but scared to death about what is happening to him. Let's explore his fears:

a. He is in the age of magical thinking, so he may feel responsible for his own illness. He remembers that Mom said he'd get sick if he ate all that candy. Lo and behold, he is! He may view the hospitalization as punishment for his misdeeds.

b. He may be afraid that his parents have abandoned or rejected him. After all, how could his powerful parents allow this horrible thing to happen to him if they cared about him?

c. He is at an age when his body is very important to him, and he may be afraid he will be mutilated or lose a part of himself. When blood is drawn he may feel they're taking away an integral part of him. He may put up more of a fight than he did at age two. Shots are an invasion of his body and confirm his fears.

d. The self-control he worked so hard to get in his first few years seems lost when he is experiencing vomiting, diarrhea, or incontinence with his illness. He may be placed in a bed with side rails or in a crib, and restrained from free movement as well. Remember that motor activity is very important to the preschooler, too.

Put all of this together and add to it the general scariness that even grownups can feel in a hospital, not to mention some physical discomfort and pain connected with the illness. No wonder your child needs a parent with him! Not only does he need your presence, he needs your empathy to help him deal with his fears.

Now that you understand what is traumatic about hospitalization for your child, you will understand the essential ingredients for helping him cope and thus speed his recovery. If you can decrease his fears and anxieties during hospitalization, he will be less affected by it and will behave better in the weeks afterward. These essential ingredients are his preparation for the experience, your presence while he is there, your calm reactions, and his expression of his feelings.

Obviously, much of what we recommend below does not apply to the infant. Use your own judgment as to what your child needs.

1. Preparation.
   - Prepare your child for hospitalization two or three days before he's to be admitted. This gives him time to ask questions and express fears, but not too much time to worry about it. Obviously, if it is an emergency admission you can't explain much in advance. Ask the hospital staff for any teaching materials they might have, to help you tell your child what to expect. You can say to him that the doctor feels he needs to go into the hospital to make his problem better. Assure him that you'll be with him, if you will. Tell him you love him and that in no way is he responsible for his illness.
   - Explain what happens in the hospital. Gear the explanation to your child's level of comprehension. The younger the child, the less he can take in.

But even the one-year-old will benefit by looking at pictures or playing doctor and hospital with you. His favorite Teddy could get sick, go to the hospital, and come home again. It helps to use story books as a beginning. Your doctor or the library may have some. Here are some suggestions: *Curious George Goes to the Hospital* (three to eight years) by H. A. and Margaret Rey; *The Hospital Story* (three to ten years) by Sarah Bonnett Stein; and a coloring book called *The Hospital Book* (four to ten years) by Barbara Haas.

- Go through a hospital day, what his bed will be like, meals on trays, urinals and bedpans if he'll need them, IVs and shots if he'll get them. Don't lie if he asks about pain. Tell him if it'll hurt, but assure him that it's for just a little while. Tell him he can certainly cry if he wants to and you'll be there to help him. Tell him about the more enjoyable parts of the hospital—TV, toys, books, and other kids to play with. Don't overdo it, though. It's not going to be a picnic.

- Many hospitals have teaching programs to help explain hospitalizations to children. Ask about these. This is especially important for surgical procedures. Having anesthesia is one of the scariest things to children, and the more they understand, the better. If there is no program, find out what will be done and rehearse or role-play it with your child at home.

- Use play materials to help prepare him. Doctor kits and dolls or puppets that can be doctors, nurses, families, patients, and even animals who get sick will all help. At first, get down with him and show him what will happen by acting it out. He may ask you to do it over and over again and then begin playing it by himself. Be sure to take the play materials to the hospital, since more explanations may be in order later.

- When he is to have a procedure, explain it to him just ahead of time. Tell him what it has to do with his problem. Don't lie about how it will feel or how he'll feel afterward. Tell him the truth, and assure him you'll be there.

- Let him help pack his bag so he can add favorite toys, comfort objects, and family pictures. Be sure to let him choose the clothes he wants to wear home, an assurance that his stay is temporary.

- Last but not least, do all you can to build up his self-esteem before hospitalization. He'll need a good reserve to cope. To help boost your child's self-esteem, take every opportunity to let him make decisions. Praise him frequently. Let him go into that hospital feeling like he's terrific!

2. Your presence.
- All children five and under need a parent with them in the hospital, most ideally to stay night and day. If there are young children at home too, it is better to make arrangements for someone to care for them in a familiar environment than to leave your sick child alone in the hospital. Most hospitals now have facilities for parents to spend the night in the room, often providing cots or chair beds for parents to sleep on. If these are not available, you will need to insist that you are staying. Sleep on an air mattress, such as that used on camping trips, if necessary. Be firm in your knowl-

edge that your presence is the very best thing that can happen for your child while he is in the hospital. Obviously, if your child is in an intensive care unit it is not appropriate for you to spend the night there. There should be facilities for you to sleep near the unit, however, so you can be available to your child when he is awake and wants you.

• If you or some member of your family cannot arrange to spend the night with your child, the next best step is to have unlimited visitation. Visit as frequently as possible. Bring his siblings if you can. It is extremely important that your child have tape recordings of you reading stories to him and letters and phone calls from you, as much as possible. Be sure to tell the staff all of his quirks and idiosyncrasies, his likes and dislikes. Do this preferably in the presence of the child, so that he sees you as working with the staff and "passing the baton."

3. Your calm reactions.
  • Try to appear calm. Children get their cues from their parents. If you are anxious, your child becomes anxious. Obviously you will be feeling upset and concerned, but you can relieve much of your anxiety by becoming as informed as possible. Find out everything you can about what will be happening. Write down your concerns and fears, and ask the doctor or nurse for a private conversation to discuss them. There is no sense in worrying needlessly.
  • Do as much of your child's care yourself as you can. This helps to relieve your anxiety and makes the situation more natural for him. If you're not sure how to handle something, ask the nurse. She appreciates your help, too.
  • Allay your child's fears, especially if he feels his illness is his fault. Act as confident and as cheerful as you can, even if he should be upset with you for a while. Children feel very angry with their parents if they have been left alone in the hospital or if they have had to undergo a painful procedure or operation. They will react by rejecting them or by being very nasty to them for a few days afterward. This can make parents feel very guilty and upset, afraid that their child will never love them again. Don't worry, he'll be all over you in a few days. Stay calm and reassure him that you love him. Acknowledge that he is angry with you and that you understand.
  • Recognize that he will regress and return to more infantile behavior during his hospital stay. These are not negative behaviors, just his way of coping with his increased feelings of dependency. Baby talk, thumb sucking, a return to the bottle or pacifier, a need for holding and rocking, may all be expected. Accept these and don't nag or tease him.
  • Foster his sense of self-esteem and self-control by letting him help in his own care. Let him make any decisions he can. Let him answer the staff's questions when he can. If he has to be disrobed for something, let him keep his socks on if he wants to. It helps to make him feel more intact.
  • Help to make his hospital environment as much like home as possible. Bring his pillow and pillowcase. Let him wear his own clothes. Ask that

any procedures be done in a treatment room, rather than his bed. That way he can feel that his bed is safe, his own protected space.

- Be present for any procedures you can. If he is having surgery, ask if you can accompany him until he's asleep and be there when he awakens.
- Work with the staff in a friendly and trusting way. Be confident in *your* knowledge about what your child needs. If there is a problem, share it with the staff. They may be very busy and overlook something, but they are interested in your child's welfare too. You need to work as a team. Sometimes the hospital staff can forget how important the parents are: gently remind them.
- Tell your child if you have to leave for a while. Never slip away to avoid hearing him cry. He'll really feel abandoned then. Of course, he'll cling and cry when you leave. He may also cry when you come back. But that doesn't mean he doesn't need you. He's only sharing his feelings with you and needs your understanding.
- Don't overindulge your child. He needs to have the same limits on his negative behavior that he had at home. He needs to like himself and have others like him too.

4. Expression of his feelings.
   - Understand how your child might be feeling. Remember he might feel angry with you, guilty, sad, afraid, rejected, and frustrated. Encourage him to express these feelings. If he can express them verbally, wonderful! If not, you can respond to the emotions you see in his face. Accept his feelings and don't belittle them or tell him he shouldn't feel that way. Let him know you understand.
   - Most young children cannot verbally express their feelings. Use the type of play we mentioned earlier to help him communicate. The key to a child's emotions is through his play and, when he can draw, his artwork. Self-expression through play serves many purposes. It provides a release of hostile and guilty feelings; it's a means of desensitizing him to the trauma he has experienced; and it's a way of putting him in control of the situation, if only in play. Many hospitals have personnel trained to help children use play effectively—nurses, recreation therapists, child life workers. Ask them to help you. If they're not available, supply the medium for his play with the toys he has taken with him to the hospital. Give him the toys and let him play the way he wants. It's natural for him, and he needs no instruction. He may or may not want you to interact. Self-expression through play will be important in the hospital and once your child goes home. No matter how much has been done to alleviate the trauma of hospitalization, he will still have fears and feelings about it for weeks and perhaps months, even after his convalescence.

CONVALESCENCE

The convalescent period is one in which your child exhibits behavior that is not pleasant for anyone. If you were able to prepare him for the hospitalization, were with him during it, and helped him express his feelings while keeping your own under control, he will have fewer problems. However, he may continue the regressive behavior from his hospitalization—feeding and sleep disturbances, urine and bowel incontinence, or the need for a bottle or pacifier. He may seem excessively aggressive, dependent, demanding, and fearful. Nightmares or night terrors may become more frequent. Of course, much of this depends on what has happened to him in the hospital, how long he spent there, and what his personality was like going in. Some children can sail through with very few of these problems, and others seem to have a harder time of it.

When your child comes home from the hospital you can expect a difficult period because he has been gone for a while. He may be very angry and clingy at the same time. That's perfectly normal. It will get better. Settle him back into his old routine as quickly as possible. Set limits and give him structure.

As far as possible, let your child convalesce somewhere where the action is, so that he doesn't feel isolated. Get him toys and games in which he can use motor abilities as much as possible. Continue to give him the opportunity for expressing his feelings: modeling clay, dolls, animals. Even have a group of children over to play hospital. He can teach them all about it. And keep in mind that most children bounce back much more quickly than adults. Soon the pain and stress of hospitalization will be but a distant memory for both of you.

WHEN YOUR CHILD HAS A CHRONIC ILLNESS OR IMPAIRMENT

Sometimes the parents of a young child are faced with the shocking news that their child has a chronic illness, such as diabetes mellitus, cystic fibrosis, leukemia, or some other type of physical illness that cannot be completely cured and requires a lifetime of treatment and intervention. Or the news may be that their child has a developmental disability, such as mental retardation, cerebral palsy, autism, hearing loss, vision loss, epilepsy, or some other impairment that interferes with his developing in the normal fashion. Again there is no cure, and the child and the family need to learn to cope with the child's problems and his special needs.

In this situation, it is not only the child who has special needs. The family does too. And in fact, to help the child, the whole family must be considered.

The family's goal is to remember that the child is *first* a child. He needs to accomplish the developmental tasks of all children, though he has additional needs as well. He needs to be treated as normally as possible. That's easy to say, but often difficult to carry out. The road is a bumpy one.

The more a child understands about his problem, the easier it is for him to do what is expected of him and to gradually become independent himself. Accentuate the positive, however. He is a normal child, with just an ill or impaired part. Emphasize what he *can* do. If he feels particularly low about himself, help him notice that other people have differences too. Point out that other people wear glasses, have braces, and have other types of physical differences.

If your child is experiencing frequent illnesses and may require several hospitalizations, read our sections on caring for your sick child and hospitalization. The information there is intended to avoid some of the pitfalls that may result in your child's developing undesirable behavior, further complicating his chronic problem.

Many parents wonder what to tell siblings about their child's problem. Don't try to disguise your feelings, since the children can detect that there is something going on. However, it is important not to frighten them, which can happen if your grief is so intense and uncontrollable that you are unable to talk about it calmly. Sometimes it helps to tell them about the problem while you are going about some other activity, which can serve as an external control. Obviously what you tell them and their reaction depend upon their level of verbal development. Keep it simple, in language they can understand. Encourage them to talk about the problem and listen to them. Listen when they talk to others about it.

Remember that although the siblings will feel sad and will grieve for their brother or sister, it may not be in a way that you might expect. Children who are tense and upset often act out by being silly or fooling around. They act like they don't care. If you notice a change in the siblings' behavior, consider that this might be their way of dealing with their sadness.

An additional problem for preschool-age siblings may be the discomfort or embarrassment of their peers around a child who looks or acts different. In this situation, many parents have found that an open approach is most helpful. Talk to your children's friends or classmates about the problem. Let them ask questions. The child who is different should be presented as a person with the likes and dislikes of other children. If a child has need of adaptive devices, such as leg braces, splints, or a wheelchair, allow the other preschoolers to touch the appliances.

Do not deny the child's problem but stress his assets. Just as your own children's attitudes are shaped by your attitudes, your children's friends will respond to your positive feelings about your child. Remember too, normal preschool children may feel fear when they are exposed to "different" children. Sarah B. Stein has written an excellent book, *About Handicaps*, which can help deal with that issue.

Let's not overlook the grandparents. You may be looking to them for support and they may not be able to provide it. They may deny the problem or, not being able to understand it, they may feel in need of comfort themselves.

And, last but not least, we must consider the needs of the mother and father. You will go through many emotional stages while learning to cope with your child's problem—shock and disbelief; grief and sadness; anger, guilt, or blame; apprehension and anxiety. Both of you may not experience the same emotions at the same time. Individuals handle crises differently: Women usually verbalize feelings more easily. Men tend to avoid their feelings, and, in doing so, many men avoid the home front, leaving the mothers to carry most of the load. All of this stress can strain a marriage. It is important to recognize this and seek outside help.

Parent support groups play an important role in helping parents deal with these feelings and anxieties. The other parents in the group have usually all experienced the same feelings or are presently experiencing them. It helps to be together, to share each other's feelings. It is safe to ventilate there. And other parents can often help the new members to be more realistic in their expectations of themselves and of their child. If these groups do not meet your needs, consider seeking the help of a professional counselor as well.

One caution: As the parent of a chronically ill or disabled child, you will get much advice from many different sources. In fact, you can be inundated with advice, often conflicting and confusing. It is important to have one primary adviser for you and your child, someone you respect and trust to help you sort things out. Use all the *support* systems you can get, however. This is what you need to get you over the rough spots. Acceptance of your child's problem and learning to cope effectively with it will come; maybe in bits and pieces, but it will come.

Much has been written about this subject, and we urge you to read the literature recommended to you by the special-interest groups that apply to your particular situation. We also recommend an excellent book by Audrey T. McCollom, *Coping with Prolonged Health Impairment in Your Child.* Ms. McCollom has done a beautiful job of looking at how families cope with the bad news of their child's problem. She gives suggestions for meeting the child's particular needs in each developmental stage. We encourage you to read it for in-depth discussion and suggestions.

HEALTH CONCERNS

Now we will cover some of the health concerns that may crop up in early childhood. We have grouped these concerns according to the body system that is affected: *general*, covering concerns that may apply to more than one area or system of the body; *head, neck, and chest; gastrointestinal; genitourinary; skin;* and *musculoskeletal.* We will give brief descriptions of the problems and, when appropriate, home treatment. Both this and the following chapters are basically for reference, if and when needed. Emergency situations are covered in our section on first aid.

Obviously we cannot cover everything that could occur in your child's first years. We encourage you to pursue further with your doctor anything you want to know more about: any sign, symptom, or problem that your child has. Your understanding and knowledge of what is going on and what to expect is crucial in maintaining your child's health.

GENERAL

ALLERGIES For our own protection, our bodies are geared to respond when harmful foreign substances are contacted. This response is in the form of antibodies, which our bodies produce to fight infection. (See our discussion of immunizations.) This is obviously beneficial. But the allergic individual has not only this response, but a second one, which is not so beneficial. This is a hypersensitive, or allergic, response, which may occur when he is in contact with either harmless or harmful substances. He produces antibodies to both.

The substance causing an allergic reaction is called an *allergen.* When this allergen comes into contact with the body's antibodies, a substance called histamine is released from the cells. It causes small blood vessels to enlarge and to leak fluid into surrounding tissue, which swells. There may be muscle spasm in a limited area. Mucus is usually produced. The symptoms depend on where the allergen meets the antibody. If it is in the nose, the child will have *allergic rhinitis*. If it's on the skin, he may have *hives* or *eczema*. If it's in the lungs, he will have *asthma*. If it's in the blood, caused by an insect bite or medication, he will have skin reactions, lung reactions, nasal reactions, and possibly *anaphylactic shock* with swelling of the airways and cardiovascular collapse. The allergic individual may also have tissues which are hypersensitive even without an allergen-antibody reaction. For example, his lungs may have an asthmatic response to cold air or exercise. And his skin may develop a reaction by simply being stroked.

Allergies tend to run in families, although they may vary from individual to individual. For example, the father may have hay fever while the child has eczema or asthma. If there is a strong family history of allergy on either side of the family, you should observe certain precautions to lessen your child's chances of developing allergies.

PREVENTIVE MEASURES FOR ALLERGIES:

- Breast-feed your child, and avoid eating allergenic foods such as cow's milk, soy products, egg whites, and seafood while you are nursing. Milk substitutes such as Nutramigen or goat's milk may be advisable (consult your doctor about this). If you use goat's milk, be aware that the powdered form may be deficient in some essential vitamins—thiamine or folic acid—and a supplement will be needed.

- Do not start your child on solid foods until after six months of age, avoiding allergenic ones when you do. These would be cow's milk, wheat, egg whites, citrus fruits, chocolate and seafood. They can be added after one year of age.

- Do not acquire pets. If you already have pets, keep them out of your child's room.

- Dust and vacuum your child's room regularly. See the hay fever section for further details on avoiding mold, mildew, and house dust exposure.

- Avoid woolens, feather pillows, and chenille bedspreads.

- Every child needs stuffed animals, but buy the ones that are washable and are not stuffed with animal hair. Wash them once a week and dry them thoroughly.

Let's consider some of the forms in which allergies are manifest.

ASTHMA

Asthma is characterized by wheezing, which is due to spasm of the muscles in the small air passages in the lungs (bronchospasm). This spasm makes it difficult for the child to get the air out of his lungs once he has taken it in. The lungs become overinflated and the chest expands, sounding like a drum when you tap it. The wheezing is the sound you hear when the air is being pushed out. The bronchospasm may be brought on by exposure to allergens, by infections, exercise, or inhalation of cold air.

Asthma can range from mild to severe. The child with asthma should be under the care of a physician, who will probably prescribe medication to dilate the airways. The medication is usually Theophylline, which is taken orally. There are also hand-held inhalers, which must be used carefully. They have not been recommended for children under six years of age, but it has been our experience that a child of three or older can be taught to use the inhaler properly. They are especially good when the bronchospasm comes on suddenly, such as during sleep or exercise.

Home treatment consists of preventive measures and treatment of an attack.

PREVENTIVE MEASURES FOR ASTHMA:

- Avoid pollen, if it's the culprit, and air condition your child's room (use an electrostatic precipitator only if necessary). If possible, keep your child indoors when the pollen count is high or when it is windy. But don't let this keep him from being with the other kids. Do not cut the grass when your child is around during pollen season. Shampoo and shower your child every night during the pollen season. If you have an outside pet, pollen will be on its hair too.

- Be aware of other things that might trigger an attack—dust from turning on the furnace, paints, perfumes, smoke from a log fire, aerosol sprays, fertilizers, tobacco smoke, animal danders, feather pillows, flowers, or Christmas trees.

- Following the suggestions given in the section on hay fever for decreasing exposure to mold, mildew, and house dust.

- Give your child his medication on a regular basis and keep appointments for checkups even though he is not having problems. The level of medication in the blood makes a difference in preventing attacks. So as your child grows he may need to increase his medication in order to maintain the proper level.

- Teach your child relaxation methods and breathing exercises that can be used when bronchospasm begins. They may circumvent or shorten an attack. Ask your doctor about these.

- Encourage exercise even if it means that your child must use an inhaler or take medication beforehand. Exercise is good for asthmatics, including exercise that requires sustained activity, such as swimming or long-distance running. This type of exercise won't hurt him and may be helpful. You may have to make some special adaptations. Our (AA) Katie has asthma and loves sports. We recently went snow skiing for the first time and she had a great deal of difficulty in the cold, dry air of the mountains. The inhaler and her medication were helpful, but not enough. We found a foam-rubber face mask which kept the air she was breathing warm and moist. She looked like Darth Vader, but was off on the slopes with no more wheezing!

- Remember that your main goal is to promote a sense of wellness in your child. Do not let the asthma become an invaliding condition. If your child is wheezing but still feels like playing, allow him to do so after giving him the necessary medications. Read our sections on hospitalization and chronic illness for more suggestions on helping your child cope with his illness. Also, for more information, contact the American Lung Association, 1740 Broadway, New York, New York 10019.

HOME TREATMENT FOR ASTHMA ATTACK:

- *Stay calm.* Being short of breath can make the child anxious, and if you appear anxious too this only amplifies it.
- Follow the steps recommended by your physician. If these do not work, *call your physician* for further instructions.
- Increased fluid intake is recommended to keep the normal lung mucus from becoming sticky. Have the child drink half a glass of clear fluids every hour he is awake, if he can.

ECZEMA

Eczema, or atopic dermatitis as it is often called, is characterized by red, dry, itching skin. When scratched, the skin begins to weep, then characteristically crusts over. It may become infected. This condition usually begins in infancy and becomes less severe by age five. It may recur at puberty. When the condition persists, the new skin comes in thick and rough. It is usually found on the back of the knees and in the front of the elbows, behind the ears, and on the face and neck. It can be aggravated by infection, food allergy, exposure to other allergens, sweating, emotional stress, or excessive contact with water. Most children with eczema are allergic individuals, but some are not. Those who are allergic may develop asthma or hay fever later in life.

HOME TREATMENT FOR ECZEMA:

Home treatment is based on maintaining good skin care and avoiding allergens.

- Keep your child's fingernails clipped short and keep his hands clean to avoid infection. He may need to keep mittens or gloves on, especially when sleeping.
- Dress your child coolly to avoid sweat retention, and use cottons. Wool tends to aggravate itching.
- Do not bathe your child longer than ten to fifteen minutes. Do not use soap on any areas of rash. Young children basically do not need soap, but if your child is very dirty, use a mild soap such as Neutrogena. Avoid shampoos. Use the same soap for hairwashing.
- After the bath while he is still damp, lubricate his skin with a cream such as Keri, Nivea, Lubriderm, or Eucerin (this should be stored in a warm place in order to make it more spreadable). Do not use oils such as Vaseline, Crisco, or Wesson Oil since they can make the rash worse. Swimming in chlorinated pools may aggravate it. Lake and ocean swimming are fine, if the cream is applied afterward.
- Avoid excessive heat and cold, as in hot showers or below-freezing temperatures, which can trigger eczema. Dry air is also an irritant, so a humidifier is helpful.
- Carpets, especially those containing wool, can be very irritating and the young child should not play on them.
- Steroid creams are the treatment of choice. Use as directed by your physician.

- The itching is usually worst at bedtime. Aspirins or antihistamines can be helpful.
- Food allergies can also cause eczema. An elimination diet may be necessary.
- Follow the precautions given in the section on hay fever in order to decrease exposure to environmental allergens.
- Hyposensitization injections are not beneficial for eczema.

HAY FEVER (ALLERGIC RHINITIS)

Allergic rhinitis, or hay fever, is the most common allergic problem. The symptoms are watery, itchy eyes; stuffy, runny nose; sneezing; and headache. The allergens may be pollens, foods, house dusts, molds, house mites (frequently found in mattresses and impossible to eradicate), and animal danders. Allergic rhinitis can be distinguished from a head cold by noting the nasal discharge. In rhinitis, the nose is swollen internally and the discharge is watery and clear. It is also accompanied by itching. In a head cold, the nose is usually obstructed by a thick, mucousy discharge. Allergic rhinitis is also accompanied by frequent short sneezes, while the head cold usually is associated with one or two large sneezes.

HOME TREATMENT FOR ALLERGIC RHINITIS:

- If the child is allergic to pollen, avoid the pollen: Air-condition the house, shampoo and shower the child every night before bedtime during pollen season, and avoid handling pets that have been outside in pollen season.
- Make sure that as many allergens as possible are removed from the house, particularly from your child's bedroom. Mites are tiny organisms that feed on human skin particles and are found in abundance in carpets and mattresses as well as in house dust. They are highly allergenic. Damp-mop the floors and vacuum the carpets several times a week. There is a product on the market called Dust Seal, which can be put on fabrics and carpeting to decrease dust buildup. Keep the bedroom and closets free of dust collectors by putting those items away in drawers. Keep only clothing in the closet. Wash curtains and stuffed animals frequently (once a week). Cover pillows and mattresses with zippered plastic covers. This does nothing to eliminate the mites that are found in mattresses but it decreases the chance of their causing problems. A hyposensitization vaccine for the house mite is being developed; hopefully this will provide relief in the near future.
- If your child has to use the humidifier or vaporizer because of a head cold, make sure that the vaporizer has been cleaned recently, since it is an excellent growing place for molds.
- Make sure that the filters on air conditioners and heaters are changed frequently. You may even need to seal off the duct in your child's room. Use an electric baseboard heater if necessary.
- If your child has antihistamine medication, give it to him at the first sign of sneezing or sniffing, since it is most effective if started early. If you know that your child is going to be exposed to pollen, give him the medication before he is exposed. One of the side effects of antihistamine is drowsiness. This will decrease after one or two weeks. Do not discontinue the drug if your

child seems drowsy; decrease the dosage temporarily. Discuss the appropriate antihistamine with your physician. Some can be obtained over the counter; others need a prescription. Nasal sprays or nose drops do not help hay fever, since they are washed out of the nose by all the secretions that are being produced. However, new nasal-spray products have been developed, which, if given on a regular basis, can prevent allergic rhinitis. Consult your doctor.

- Hyposensitization (allergy shots or desensitization) has been found to be very effective in some cases. Unless the allergic problem is quite severe, hyposensitization would probably not be started until after the child is around four years of age because the frequent injections required can be traumatic.

- If your child's eyes are itchy and watery, some additional treatment may provide relief. Irrigate the eyes for several minutes with cool water and apply two drops of a vasoconstrictor eye drop such as Visine, Clear Eyes, or Murine Plus. Another effective home remedy is cold compresses applied over the nose and the eyes until the itching subsides. To calm your child, use a reassuring voice and manner. Itching can make him frantic and rubbing his eyes and nose sometimes makes it worse, particularly if the allergen is on your child's hands. Wash his hands well with soap and water as a precaution.

HIVES (URTICARIA)

Hives are discussed in chapter 33.

ANEMIA   Anemia is caused by an insufficiency of hemoglobin, which is an essential protein in the blood and is responsible for carrying oxygen to the cells in the body. The insufficiency is basically due to a decreased production or increased loss of red blood cells, which contain hemoglobin. During the newborn period the baby may have anemia because of bleeding at birth or a blood incompatibility, resulting in the destruction of red blood cells. But after this period, and particularly after six months of age, the most common cause of anemia is iron deficiency. Children who are anemic because of iron deficiency are frequently children who are consuming large quantities of milk and getting no solid food.

The symptoms of anemia are pallor, fatigue, increased incidence of infections, and, in severe cases, heart enlargement and heart failure. Physicians screen for anemia by doing blood tests known as hematocrit or hemoglobin tests. Iron deficiency anemia is treated by iron supplements, either by injections or orally. This type of anemia can be prevented by adequate iron in the diet.

Other rare causes of anemia are those due to an abnormal hemoglobin protein, resulting in red blood cells that are easily destroyed. An example of this is sickle cell anemia, more commonly seen in the black race. This is not due to iron deficiency but is an inherited abnormality. Early symptoms of this are anemia accompanied by fever and swelling of hands, feet, or joints. Early screening is important. This type of anemia is a chronic problem since there is no cure. For help in coping with a chronic illness, read our section on it. Frequent hospitalizations are often necessary, and we suggest you also read our "Hospitalization" section. For more information contact:

CENTER FOR SICKLE CELL ANEMIA
COLLEGE OF MEDICINE, HOWARD UNIVERSITY
520 W STREET, N.W.
WASHINGTON, D.C. 20001

ANIMAL DISEASES TRANSMITTED TO HUMANS   There are a number of diseases that can be transmitted to children by infected household pets or rodents. It is important to be aware of these should your child become ill after exposure to such an animal.

Dogs and cats can have *hookworm* and *roundworm* infections, which can be transmitted to humans by way of their feces. These can cause skin eruptions (cutaneous larva migrans) or an internal infection (visceral larva migrans) producing malaise, fever, anemia, cough, and liver and lung problems. Children acquire these by contact with soil contaminated by the feces of an infected animal. Another parasitic infection acquired from cats is that of *toxoplasmosis*. It is usually asymptomatic but may produce symptoms resembling mononucleosis. It is acquired by contact with cat feces or the consumption of poorly cooked meat from an infected animal. Cats and, less frequently, dogs with *ringworm* or *mange* may infect humans, resulting in skin eruptions. A dog or cat can also harbor the *Streptococcus* germ, which is responsible for strep throat.

Rabies is acquired by the bite of a diseased animal, usually a dog, skunk, or raccoon. *Rat bite fever* can result from the bites of diseased rats or mice (including guinea pigs, hamsters, or gerbils) and, occasionally, cats or squirrels. This illness is characterized by fever, rash, and swollen glands one to three weeks after a bite.

Animals such as turtles, chicks, and ducklings may be infected by the *Salmonella* germ, which is responsible for gastroenteritis, typhoid fever, or localized infections in the brain (meningitis), bones (osteomyelitis), or skin (abscesses) in humans. Children get the infection by not washing their hands after handling these animals or their feces. Pet birds may also harbor a germ which can result in a lung infection (ornithosis), causing high fever, cough, and muscular pain (myalgias).

Obviously this does not mean you should never have pets. But make sure that your pets are acquired from a reputable dealer. Give them good veterinary care and keep them free of infection, parasites, or worms. Teach your children to practice good hand washing after handling animals. Keep their play area free of feces and the litter box off limits.

If your child becomes ill with the signs and symptoms mentioned, be sure to advise your physician of any possible contact with animals.

ANTIBIOTICS   Antibiotics are medications that are useful in combating bacterial infections. They play no role in the treatment of viruses. Antibiotics are prescribed for specific illnesses and should not be used except under a physician's recommendation. Some antibiotics, such as penicillin and Keflex, are absorbed better in the fasting stage. Others, such as erythromycin, should be given with food to maximize absorption. With some, such as ampicillin, it makes no difference. Ask your doctor or pharmacist about timing.

It is important to give antibiotics exactly as instructed. One common mistake parents make is to stop the antibiotics as soon as the child seems to feel better, usually after three to four days. This often results in the infection's recurring. The antibiotics *must* be given on schedule, until the bottle is empty. Make a chart for days and times the medication is to be given, and hang it on the refrigerator door to remind you. I (AA) know only too well the need for doing this, as I am as forgetful as the next person!

APPETITE LOSS Most children lose their appetite with most minor illnesses. This is not harmful. If your child has lost his appetite because of illness, let him select what he wants and let him decide how much he can eat.

BREATH HOLDING A breath-holding spell can be very frightening to parents and to anyone else observing it. Breath holding occurs in about 5 percent of children and usually starts between six months and two years of age, disappearing by age four or five. The spells are brought on by crying because of pain, fear, frustration, and other stresses. You'll notice that this happens during the age range when children are likely to have temper tantrums and have difficulty controlling themselves, resulting in frequent crying.

Many children hold their breath when crying, sometimes becoming blue around the lips. However, a true breath-holding spell goes one step further to include passing out for a few seconds. Only a small percentage of children do this. An even smaller percentage may have a few muscle jerks while they are unconscious. The scariest thing that comes to the parent's mind is often, "My child has epilepsy!" But breath-holding spells have absolutely nothing to do with epilepsy. The attacks are harmless and will stop by themselves. However, if your child is breath holding and he is less than six months old, if it lasts longer than one minute, or if he has rhythmic muscle jerks, *consult your doctor*. This is not a typical breath-holding spell.

HOME TREATMENT FOR BREATH HOLDING:

- Apply a cold, wet washcloth to your child's forehead until he starts breathing again. There is no need for resuscitation. Time the length of the attack with the second hand on your watch to be sure it is less than one minute. When your child wakes up, it's imperative that you show a relaxed attitude. Do not appear frightened, even if you are. If a temper tantrum precipitated the attack, do *not* give in to what he wanted, since you are only reinforcing his breath holding. You can give him a hug and a kiss, however, and let him know that you care about him.
- As a preventive measure you could use environmental control to avoid situations in which your child will be likely to lose his temper or his ability to control himself. Examples of these are fatigue, hunger, boredom, and overstimulation.

CANCER Cancer can occur in many areas of the body. It is caused by an excessive growth of certain abnormal body cells, which overcome the normally growing cells. In a young child the more frequent types of cancer are those of the nervous system in the abdomen (neuroblastoma), of the blood cells (leukemia), and of the cells in the eye (retinoblastoma).

There have been many advances in the treatment of cancers, using surgery, radiation, and/or chemotherapy. This has resulted in an increase in remission rates and some long-term cures. The child often has frequent hospitalizations, and we recommend that you read our section on this in order to decrease that trauma for your child. There are often family support groups available that are of great assistance. Ask your doctor about such groups. They will not only help you to deal with the fear, but will also give you ways to make your child's life as normal as possible. For further suggestions, read our section on chronic illness.

CHILD ABUSE AND NEGLECT   Hundreds of thousands of children are abused or neglected each year. The most likely individuals to be the abusers/neglectors, in decreasing order of frequency, are parents, extended family, friends, acquaintances, and strangers. Abuse may be physical, sexual, or emotional. Neglect may be physical or emotional. A child may suffer one type or some combination thereof. Often only one child in the family is the scapegoat.

Any of us, given the right circumstances, could become a child abuser when social isolation, financial difficulties, or frequent emotional stressors are coupled with a child whose needs place extreme demands on our patience and tolerance. But usually it is a parent who was raised by abusive or neglectful parents, never having received the nurturing essential to the growing and developing child. So the majority of abusing and neglectful parents are not insane, psychopathic, or seriously mentally ill. Rather, they are people who are very needy themselves. They need someone to love and nurture them, to make them feel worthwhile and bolster their image of themselves. Unfortunately, they too often turn to children to provide this. The tables are turned, and the children must become the nurturers. So, many abused children often have a pseudomaturity and are very protective of their parents. However, when their own developmental needs get in the way of meeting the parents' need, abuse or neglect is likely to occur.

Certain characteristics seem to place a child at higher risk for abuse. He may have special needs, such as those accompanying a chronic illness or handicap. Or the child may have a temperament that is difficult to manage. Or he may simply have a temperament that does not mesh with his parents' temperaments. The child may have been unwanted, illegitimate, or adopted. He may even look very much like a relative who is much disliked.

Dr. Barton Schmitt, an expert on child abuse, has pointed out that children are at higher risk during those developmental periods in which a child's behavior is likely to frustrate and stress even the most empathetic parent:

- The period of colic in the first few months.
- Persistent night waking in the first years of life. The child who is very sensitive to external stimuli is more likely to do this.
- The period of intense separation anxiety (six to eighteen months) in a child who is more cautious, slower to adapt, and clingy.
- The crawling and toddling exploration period, especially for the curious child with a short attention span.

- The period of first adolescence, with its negativism.
- The period of decreased hunger (eighteen months to three years), with the child's refusal to eat. Parents don't understand it and try to force feed.
- Toilet teaching, especially if the child is not ready.

Almost all parents have feelings of anger or even rage at some time when dealing with their children. When they are angry they are more likely to spank, particularly if they themselves have been spanked as children. But when the parent goes out of control, physical punishment can result in injury or death.

The question is often asked, "What is the distinction between spanking and physical abuse?" There is no exact answer. We feel that a spanking is something done only with the hand, never with an object. The child is slapped on his hand or his buttocks and never more than one or two "pops." These are given without force enough to leave bruises or welts. In our society, spanking is most often used as an emphasis for "no," particularly in matters of safety.

What if a parent does get out of control and uses more physical force on her child than she ever intended? She usually feels very guilty and terrible about having done so. Sometimes such a parent is resourceful enough to seek help in order to be able to avoid similar situations in the future. She talks about the situation with family and friends, she calls someone in to baby-sit or help out when she is under stress. In some cases, she seeks professional help. She could also contact a local protective service or social services department for information, or contact a parent group such as Parents Anonymous for help and support. She could check into the availability of a crisis nursery to which she could take her child when she feels she can't stand it anymore. Obviously, it takes a great deal of courage to be able to take the first step.

It should go without saying that although we have been using the pronoun "she" for the parent, we could as easily have said "he." Fathers are equally likely to be the abusing parent, for all of the reasons we have described.

When parents continue to abuse or neglect their child, it is usually because a support group is not available and they do not have the resourcefulness to correct the problem on their own. To safeguard the children, authorities have established a hot line for reporting suspected abuse and neglect. The caller can be anonymous, so that if she is a part of a support system for that family she can report the problem without jeopardizing her position. It is sometimes the only way to help parents and child. The aim of treatment is not to dissolve the family, but to mend it.

ABUSE OR NEGLECT BY SUBSTITUTE CAREGIVERS

Today many more mothers are working outside the home, leaving their children in the care of others. They are concerned about how their children are cared for in their absence. While very rare, abuse and neglect have occurred in these settings. How can a parent avoid this or know if this is happening? Reread our sections on selecting a substitute caregiver and selecting a preschool. Check the situation out thoroughly before putting your child in their care. Once he is there, watch carefully for any signs or symptoms that something is amiss.

After the initial period of adjustment, if your child is being well cared for, he should be happy to go to the substitute caregiver. Is he becoming *more* anxious and clinging instead of *less*? Does he seem more upset at home, requiring more comforting, and is he possibly regressing in his behavior? Is he having more frequent nightmares? Does he have more temper outbursts than usual? Take the time to observe him in the day-care setting. Talk to other parents who have children there to see how their children are feeling. Use the child's play, as we have mentioned previously in our "First Adolescence" and "Preschool" chapters to help him express some of his fears and concerns.

Talk to your child's doctor about your concerns. He may give your child a complete physical examination to look for signs of physical or sexual abuse.

If there are no signs of physical or sexual abuse, your child may be reacting to emotional abuse or neglect, something more difficult to assess. Or it may simply be that your child's caregiver is not the type of person your child can relate to. In any event, if your child remains unhappy, remove him from the setting.

COMMON CONTAGIOUS DISEASES OF CHILDHOOD There are eight infectious diseases that are more common to children than to adults. These are mumps, measles, German measles, chicken pox, fifth disease, roseola, strep throat/scarlet fever, and whooping cough. Several of these have been nearly eradicated with the use of immunizations, but all are still around and children may still be exposed to them.

MUMPS

Mumps is a viral infection of the salivary glands (parotid glands), which are located directly below and in front of the ear. The swelling may occur on one or both sides of the jaw, preceded by a mild headache and fever for several days. To distinguish mumps from a swollen lymph gland, feel for the edge of your child's jaw beneath the ear. In mumps, you will not be able to feel it. Also, chewing and swallowing may produce pain, and spicy or sour foods may make the pain worse. There are rare complications, which include encephalitis, pancreatitis, kidney disease, deafness, and involvement of the testicles or ovaries. However, these complications are far more frequent in adults than in children. Infection with mumps results in a lifetime immunity. No medicine will directly kill the mumps virus. But the mumps vaccine has made a dent in the incidence of the disease. The vaccine is not 100 percent effective, however, and so even if your child has been vaccinated she still runs a slight risk of getting the mumps.

INCUBATION: 12–24 days.   DURATION: 6–10 days.
COMMUNICABILITY: 5–7 days before to 9 days after swelling begins.

HOME TREATMENT FOR MUMPS:

- Give your child aspirin or Tylenol for her discomfort, and put cool compresses on her cheeks.
- Avoid feeding her sour or spicy foods.
- Your child may be very sensitive about her appearance. Don't laugh; she doesn't find it funny.

MEASLES (RUBEOLA, OR RED MEASLES)

Measles, also called rubeola or red measles, is a viral illness that begins with a fever; itchy, red eyes that are sensitive to the light; hacking, irritative cough; and malaise. A skin rash appears three to five days later around the hairline, face, and neck, and behind the ears. The rash is pink, blotchy, and flat. It gradually moves downward to the chest and abdomen and finally to the arms and legs. There is mild itching. Complications of measles are common: Ear infections and pneumonias require antibiotic treatment because they are due to bacteria. The pneumonias can be very serious, as can encephalitis, which can leave permanent damage. Rarely there may be a problem with blood clotting so that bleeding occurs, which is apparent as dark purple splotches in the skin.

INCUBATION: 10–24 days.   DURATION: 7–10 days.
COMMUNICABILITY: 4 days before the rash to 4 days after the appearance of the rash. (Please read "Exposure to Infectious Diseases.")

HOME TREATMENT FOR MEASLES:

- Aspirin or Tylenol can be used to relieve fever or pain.
- A cough suppressant is also helpful; ask your doctor about which one.
- Dim lighting in the room makes the eyes more comfortable, but bright light will not blind the child as has been commonly believed. Soaking the eyes with a warm saline solution may also ease the discomfort.
- Your child should be isolated until the end of the contagious period. Any unimmunized child who has been in contact with the measles should be brought in to the doctor immediately for immunization or gamma globulin. This is particularly true for young infants.

COMPLICATIONS WITH MEASLES:

If complications arise with measles you should *call your doctor immediately*. Symptoms of encephalitis are headache, vomiting, convulsions, and/or lethargy. Pneumonia may cause a breathing problem and a high respiratory rate. The blood-clotting problem may show up as nosebleeds, bleeding from the mouth or rectum, or bleeding into the skin. An earache or sore throat should also be treated by the physician.

Measles, like mumps, has been almost eradicated with immunizations.

GERMAN MEASLES (RUBELLA, OR THREE-DAY MEASLES)

German measles, also known as rubella and three-day measles, is a viral illness that is relatively mild. It begins with two to three days of malaise, with enlarged lymph nodes at the back of the neck. A rash then appears on the face, consisting of flat or slightly raised pink to red spots. It next spreads to the trunk, then to the arms and legs, where it becomes larger and patchier. The fever is very mild and joint pains sometimes occur.

INCUBATION: 14–21 days.   DURATION: 3–6 days.
COMMUNICABILITY: 5–7 days before symptoms appear, to 5 days after.
CAUTION: Pregnant women should avoid any contact with a rubella patient if

she is not sure she has immunity, either from a vaccine or a previous infection. A woman can find out if she is adequately protected from the disease by having blood tests to check for antibodies to rubella.

HOME TREATMENT FOR GERMAN MEASLES:

- Give your child aspirin or Tylenol for her fever or malaise.
- Keep her isolated from pregnant women.

CHICKEN POX (VARICELLA)

Chicken pox is still very much with us, and many of us mothers wish they would develop a vaccine for it. It spreads very easily between brothers and sisters who are in close proximity; over 90 percent catch it. Chicken pox is spread by droplets from the mouth or throat or by direct contact with contaminated articles of clothing. It is not spread by dry scabs. Unlike measles, the child will probably have no symptoms before the rash appears, though occasionally there is some fever for about twenty-four hours. The rash appears in stages. Flat, red splotches, which quickly become raised and look like pimples, are seen first. These develop into small blisters, called vesicles. They look like tear drops on a red base and are easily scratched off. When they break, a yellow crust or scab is formed. It takes only a few hours for this to happen, but the crust lasts approximately nine to thirteen days. It is itchiest at the beginning of the crusting period. The vesicles appear in "crops," usually two to four crops within three to six days. They usually appear on the head and are more extensive over the trunk, but they can be found in any orifice—ears, mouth, eyes, or genitals! There may be just a few, or there may be scores of them. Complications are rare, but encephalitis, with symptoms of convulsions, headache, lethargy, or stiff neck, can occur. Secondary infection of the lesions by bacteria also occasionally occurs. Chicken pox rarely recurs, but the virus causing chicken pox persists and may flare up to cause *shingles* (herpes zoster) later in life. A child may contract chicken pox from a person with shingles.

INCUBATION: 10–20 days.   DURATION: 7–10 days.
COMMUNICABILITY: One day before spots appear to about 6 days after. Once the final crop of vesicles is all crusted and scabbed, your child is no longer contagious.

HOME TREATMENT FOR CHICKEN POX:

- The illness must run its course, but you can treat the itching and fever. Do not use aspirin for fever—there is now a possible link to Reye's Syndrome. Please read our section on "Home Treatment for Itching" for some suggestions.
- It is important to cut your child's fingernails or put gloves or mittens on her hands to prevent scarring from scratching. And keep her hands and skin as clean as possible (use antibacterial soaps such as Dial or Safeguard).
- Lesions in the mouth feel better when the child gargles with salt water (¼ teaspoonful of salt to 1 cup warm water).

Chicken pox is generally a mild disease, but it can be devastating to anyone with any abnormality of the immune system, or to someone undergoing chemotherapy for diseases such as cancer. For these children, avoid exposure at all costs. If exposure occurs *contact your doctor.*

FIFTH DISEASE (ERYTHEMA INFECTIOSUM)

Fifth disease is included in the common childhood illnesses because it has a rash that is sometimes confused with the other childhood illnesses causing rashes. It gets its name, *fifth,* because it is fifth after the four most common childhood illnesses—measles, German measles, mumps, and chicken pox. Fifth disease is extremely mild and the rash is its only symptom. At first it appears that the child has slapped cheeks. After four or five days, a lacelike rash spreads to the backs of the arms and legs and may tend to come and go for days or even weeks, most particularly after a warm bath or shower. There is no fever, but the child may have mild joint pain. Fifth disease is thought to be caused by a virus and is very contagious.

INCUBATION: 6–14 days.
DURATION: 4–7 days plus possible recurrences noted.
COMMUNICABILITY: Not known, but it is quite contagious.

HOME TREATMENT FOR FIFTH DISEASE:

- None is needed. If your child develops a rash similar to this with no fever there is no need to make a trip to the doctor's office. Because of the mild nature of the illness, isolation is not needed.

ROSEOLA

Roseola is a contagious viral illness commonly seen in children under three, but it can occur at any age. It is characterized by several days of sustained high fever, which sometimes triggers a convulsion. The convulsion is due to the fever and does not indicate epilepsy. As the fever is disappearing or has disappeared, a rash appears, which is pink and flat or slightly raised. It is seen on the chest, stomach, or back first and then spreads to the arms and neck; but it is rarely seen on the face or legs. The rash lasts about a day. Roseola is basically a mild disease, but encephalitis can be a very rare complication. Symptoms of encephalitis are convulsions, headache, or severe lethargy. Obviously, *your physician should be contacted.*

INCUBATION: 10–14 days.   DURATION: 5–6 days.
COMMUNICABILITY: Variable.

HOME TREATMENT FOR ROSEOLA:

- Treatment of the fever is the main thrust since apart from that, the child feels well. The high fever should not last more than four or five days.
- *Contact your doctor* if fever is associated with any of the conditions given on page 405 in our section on fever.

STREP THROAT AND SCARLET FEVER

Strep throat is a sore throat caused by a bacterium called *Streptococcus*. The sore throat can also be accompanied by a rash, and when this occurs the illness becomes scarlet fever. In addition to the sore throat, scarlet fever usually begins with fever, weakness, headache, and stomachache. There can also be nausea and vomiting. Within one to three days a red rash appears on the neck, in the armpits, and on the groin, then spreads over the face, trunk, and arms within twenty-four hours. It is a very fine rash, with the feeling of fine sandpaper. The area around the mouth is pale, and the skin creases in the elbow and armpit are quite red. The throat is red, the tongue becomes swollen and red, and there may be swollen glands in the neck. The rash persists for five to six days and results in peeling, especially of the palms of the hands, which may last for a month.

INCUBATION: 1–5 days.   DURATION: 6–8 days.
COMMUNICABILITY: 1 day before symptoms appear to 6 days after. After 24 hours on antibiotics (such as penicillin), the child is no longer contagious.

TREATMENT FOR STREP THROAT:

- Your child needs to be seen by the doctor so that antibiotic treatment can begin.
- The infection is quite contagious, and the other children in the home will need to be observed or even have a throat culture to rule out infection.
- Treat the fever as suggested on page 406 and the sore throat as suggested on page 426.
- Offer fluids frequently.
- The disease will get better without antibiotics, but the antibiotics are given to prevent a serious complication:
  a. *Rheumatic fever*. Rheumatic fever used to be one of the leading causes of heart disease in adults who had had a strep infection in childhood. It is due to an immune reaction to the strep germ in the throat. But since the advent of penicillin and good treatment for streptococcal infections, rheumatic fever and consequent heart disease is rarely seen.
  b. *Glomerulonephritis*. This is a term used to describe a kidney disease resulting from an immune reaction to the strep germ, whether it is in the throat (strep throat) or on the skin (impetigo). The symptoms vary in severity, but include high blood pressure; fluid retention causing puffy eyes, hands, and feet (edema), and dark bloody urine. The long-term prognosis for recovery is excellent. Penicillin has been helpful in preventing this disease, but not as effective as it has been in preventing rheumatic fever.
- Recurrent strep throat is sometimes found in families with pets (such as a dog, cat, or bird) who harbor the strep germ. Pets respond well to penicillin treatment just as people do, so pets should receive it if they are infected.

WHOOPING COUGH (PERTUSSIS)

Because of the immunization program against it, the incidence and severity of whooping cough has greatly decreased. However, it is still of some concern because immunization provides neither permanent nor absolute protection. Whooping cough can still occur, although in a milder form, in some previously immunized people.

Whooping cough is a bacterial illness with three stages. The first is the catarrhal stage, lasting one to two weeks. In this stage it is like a cold, with clear mucus discharge from the nose and a mild, dry cough. The second stage is the paroxysmal stage, lasting two to four, or more, weeks. During this stage the child has the characteristic paroxysms of coughing—five to ten *hard* coughs without a breath in between. The coughing is so hard that the child usually gags and vomits afterwards. It is the paroxysmal coughing plus vomiting that arouses the suspicion of whooping cough. In most cases, but not all, after the series of coughs the child makes a crowing or whooping noise as she tries to catch her breath. The cough usually occurs at night, but may be brought on by exertion, sneezing, eating, or drinking. In between coughing spells the child may seem quite well. The third stage is the convalescent stage, lasting one to two weeks. During this stage the symptoms gradually subside although the paroxysmal-type coughing may recur with any respiratory infection for many months.

Whooping cough can be very serious in young children (under seven years of age) and especially in infants. It can be complicated by pneumonia, otitis media, and, sometimes, brain involvement. So it is especially important to *contact your doctor* if your child develops paroxysmal coughing or has been exposed to someone with whooping cough, even if he has already been immunized.

The doctor can use several laboratory tests to confirm the diagnosis. He will then begin antibiotic treatment. The antibiotic will lessen the severity of the disease if given during the catarrhal stage, but will only decrease communicability if given as late as the paroxysmal stage. If a young child or infant has been exposed to whooping cough he will need a booster shot (if he hasn't had one in six months) and prophylactic antibiotics to prevent or decrease the severity of the illness.

INCUBATION: 6–20 days.   DURATION: 6–8 weeks.
COMMUNICABILITY: Onset of catarrhal stage to 4 weeks after its onset. Very contagious. Isolation for 7 days after antibiotic therapy or, if on no therapy, for 3 weeks after paroxysms begin. (Please read "Exposure to Infectious Diseases.")

HOME TREATMENT FOR WHOOPING COUGH:

- Problems occur during the paroxysmal stage because of exhaustion from coughing and poor nutrition from vomiting. Avoid situations which seem to induce coughing if possible. Children seem to do better in cool moist air so use of the cold-air vaporizer is recommended. Cough medicines are usually not helpful.
- Feed the child frequent small meals and offer them after a vomiting episode.
- Offer fluids frequently.
- *Contact your doctor* immediately if symptoms of pneumonia, otitis media, dehydration, convulsions, lethargy, or coma occur.

CYSTIC FIBROSIS Cystic fibrosis is a hereditary disease, but at the present time there is no way to detect it prenatally. Should someone in the family have it, genetic counseling is very much in order.

Cystic fibrosis results in a production of abnormally thick secretions in the gastrointestinal and respiratory tracts. There is also excessive sodium (salt) loss in the sweat. Cystic fibrosis usually becomes apparent in infancy in the form of GI problems or chronic respiratory infections. In some cases it may not be picked up until later.

Treatment requires a group of professionals with a team approach. Many advances have been made, and now children with cystic fibrosis can expect to live into adulthood in many cases.

Frequent hospitalizations are often required, however. We urge you to read our hospitalization section in order to decrease this trauma for your child. Family and peer support groups are also very helpful. Ask your physician about them. We also suggest you read our chronic illness section for help in dealing with a chronic illness. The more you learn the easier it will be to help your child. For more information contact:

NATIONAL CYSTIC FIBROSIS FOUNDATION
3379 PEACHTREE ROAD, N.E.
ATLANTA, GEORGIA 30326

DIABETES MELLITUS Diabetes mellitus, known more often simply as diabetes, is a chronic disorder that is a result of insufficient production of insulin by the body. Sugars are essential for body energy, and insulin is a hormone essential for metabolizing these sugars. When there is insufficient insulin, sugars cannot be used for energy and they build up in the blood stream, resulting in a condition known as hyperglycemia, or high blood sugar. The sugars are eventually excreted in the urine, rather than being burned for energy. This condition is diabetes mellitus. (It is unrelated to *diabetes insipidus*, which is a rare disorder caused by an insufficiency of a hormone supplied by the brain).

There seems to be a predisposition for diabetes mellitus in some families. We do not know what the predisposing factor is, but it seems to be triggered by stress or viral infection, resulting in the disorder. Diabetes can occur at any age. However, new cases occur more frequently in children between the ages of five and six years, and between the ages of eleven and thirteen years. These are both times of stress: One is the age of entering school, the other the age of early puberty.

The signs and symptoms of diabetes are frequent urination, renewed bedwetting, excessive thirst, weight loss in spite of a good appetite, and/or fatigue.

There is no cure for diabetes. The treatment goals are to try to maintain the blood sugar in a normal range in order to avoid secondary damage to blood vessels. This potential damage is atherosclerosis (hardening of the arteries), which can result in vision loss, kidney malfunction, hypertension, cardiac problems, and other circulatory disorders. The objectives of treatment are also to keep the child in good physical condition, with plenty of exercise and maintenance of a normal weight.

The child with diabetes requires daily shots of insulin and a good structured diet plan. The parents and the patient need ongoing education in order for them to continue maintaining the optimum treatment. The child with diabetes needs to learn to manage his own treatment as much as possible. While he can never lead a totally "normal" life, he is certainly able to be as active and fit as any other child if the treatment programs are successful.

There are parent organizations and associations for helping families learn about and deal with diabetes. Ask your physician or nurse for information about these organizations. Also read our sections on hospitalization and chronic illness. The more you learn the easier it will be to help your child. You should definitely contact this organization:

AMERICAN DIABETES ASSOCIATION
2 PARK AVENUE
NEW YORK, NEW YORK 10016

EXPOSURE TO INFECTIOUS DISEASES With some infectious diseases it is particularly important to take action as soon as you suspect your child has been exposed. Exposure to meningitis and encephalitis is addressed in chapter 33. In this section we will discuss tetanus, tuberculosis, measles (rubeola), whooping cough, and hepatitis.

TETANUS

The question of tetanus arises most frequently. The bacteria are present in dust, soil, and waste matter. They grow only in the absence of air, so puncture wounds are the injury with the greatest likelihood of causing tetanus. The symptoms of the disease are severe muscle spasm especially of the head and neck (thus, lockjaw), and the mortality is as high as 40 percent even when treated with antibiotics and tetanus immune globulin. In our first-aid supplement we note which injuries might require a tetanus booster. The decision to give it depends on the child's immunization status and the type of wound. Whenever in doubt it is important to *call your doctor* to discuss it.

TUBERCULOSIS

Tuberculosis is a disease that is more common than often believed. It is seen most frequently in urban areas with crowded living conditions. If your child has been exposed to someone with tuberculosis, *contact your doctor*. He will probably want to do a tuberculosis skin test on your child first. If the skin test is positive he will probably follow it with a chest X-ray. It is important to have your child go through these screening methods, to be sure she has not become infected.

MEASLES (RUBEOLA)

If your child has not been immunized and is exposed to measles, *contact your physician*. Because of the risks in measles infection, exposed children should receive measles immunoglobulin. It is effective if given within six days of exposure. Measles is contagious for about four days before the rash appears and for four days after the rash appears. Your physician may also feel that a measles vaccine would be appropriate, although these have not been felt to be effective if given later than two days after exposure. However, if your child was exposed to casual acquaintances rather than to siblings or close friends, the vaccine may be effective. If your child is over fifteen months of age and is given the immunoglobulin, she should return to the doctor two to three months later for the complete immunization. (Please read our discussion of measles in the "Childhood Diseases" section.)

WHOOPING COUGH (PERTUSSIS)

If your child has been exposed to someone with whooping cough, *contact your doctor* even if she has been immunized. The immunization does not give complete protection. Since it can be a serious disease in young children, your doctor will begin treatment. (Please read our discussion of whooping cough in the "Childhood Diseases" section.)

HEPATITIS

If your child has been exposed to someone with hepatitis, *call your physician.* It is contagious until two weeks after the jaundice (yellow skin) clears. Sharing a car pool, attending a nursery school or day-care center, or living in the same house with someone who has hepatitis is considered close contact. Your physician will probably want to give your child a gamma globulin shot and will advise you to keep your child away from the infected person, being sure to keep eating and drinking utensils separate. If you are caring for a child with hepatitis in your home and have another child, be sure always to wash your hands after handling the sick child.

FEVER   Fever is an elevated temperature. It is not always a sign of illness, however. Normal body temperatures vary from person to person; also, your child's temperature might vary as much as 1.5° F (.75° C) from its usual level without being significant. Temperatures vary during the day, being lowest in the morning. Excess clothing, exercise, anxiety, excitement, and, in the case of oral temperatures, warm foods can raise the body temperature to abnormal ranges.

Some children respond to illness quickly and develop very high temperatures, and others develop only a low-grade fever, if any. The amount of fever is not a reliable indicator of the severity of the underlying infection. Although fever is often a signal of illness, it is also a good sign; it indicates that the body is responding to the infection. In fact, fever seems to be associated with the mobilizing of the body's forces to fight the infection. It is now felt that trying to lower the temperature when it is 102° F or less may actually prolong the illness.

Fever is an oral temperature of over 100° F (37.8° C), a rectal temperature of over 101° F (38.4° C), or an axillary (underarm) temperature of over 99° F (37.2° C). (For ease of reference, body temperatures discussed in this section are rectal.) If your child's temperature is hovering around 102° F or less, check it again in about half an hour. The correction of temperature-raising situations such as overheating, exercise, anxiety, or eating warm foods will allow the body temperature to return to normal in about that time. Remember too that your child may develop a fever for one to two days after DPT immunization and about a week to ten days after the measles immunization.

There are certain conditions associated with fever that require *calling your doctor as soon as they occur*. They are the following:

- Young infant (less than four months)
- Temperature higher than 104° F
- Stiff neck, severe headache, or seizure (convulsion)
- Purple rash or spots on the skin
- Difficulty with breathing
- Difficulty awakening the child, or the child seems confused
- Urinary problems or swelling of eyes, hands, or feet
- Redness of the skin around the eyes or in the sinus area

There are other situations that are not quite so urgent, but which your doctor would probably want you to *contact him* about:

- Fever lasting three or more days
- Fever recurring after temperature being normal for one day
- Fever with an earache or discharge from the ear
- Fever with a greenish-yellow discharge from the nose
- Fever with a sore throat and swollen glands

Obviously, if your child doesn't have these symptoms but has fever and looks sick to you, by all means *call your doctor*.

Fever in itself is not harmful; the complications are what we are trying to avoid. One of these complications is the *febrile fit* (also *febrile convulsion* or *fever fit*). The febrile fit is a convulsion associated with a rapid elevation in body temperature, usually to a high fever (104° F or higher). It has been seen, however, in children with a temperature lower than 104° F, but in whom the temperature has changed very rapidly. About 3 to 5 percent of all children experience a febrile convulsion between the ages of six months and six years. We are not certain why some children have this problem, but the seizure is thought to be due to overheating of the brain, causing some short circuits of the electrical impulses.

The signs of a febrile fit may be stiffening of the body, eyes rolling back, rhythmic jerking of one or several extremities, jerking of the head, and loss of control of urine and bowels. It usually lasts one to five minutes, and your child may be sleepy afterward. The fit is not a serious problem and does not result in brain damage. If your child has a fit, follow the first-aid instructions for convulsions, being sure to take measures to reduce the fever. *Call your physician*, since he will probably want to make sure nothing else is going on to cause the convulsion. He may need to do a spinal tap to rule out an infection of the nervous system such as meningitis or encephalitis. Fewer than 50 percent of children who have one febrile convulsion have a second, and fewer than 25 percent have more than that.

Another complication of high fever can occur with temperatures higher than 105° F, which can result in severe overheating of the brain and subsequent brain damage. In children, the problem arises if the temperature stays around 107° F for several hours. These temperatures are usually seen in patients with severe heat stroke, and are uncommon when fever is due to infection.

HOME TREATMENT FOR FEVER:

The objectives of treatment are to make your child more comfortable, to control her fever while she is asleep, and to keep the temperature down to around 102° F. There are several ways to accomplish this.

- Take your child's temperature by one of the methods described in "The Well Child." Remember to tell your doctor which method you used—oral, rectal, or axillary.
- Medications used to lower temperature are aspirin, which comes in chewable and tablet form; and acetaminophen (Tylenol or Liquiprin), which comes in liquid, chewable, and tablet form. The liquid form of acetaminophen comes in drops and syrup. The drops are much more concentrated than the syrup, so it is important to differentiate the two when you are treating your child. Both aspirin and acetaminophen are poisonous when taken in too high doses. They should be kept out of the reach of children and be used only as advised. They are usually given every four hours. For bedtime, when your child will be sleeping for a longer period of time and you don't wish to wake her up, or in a child who has a history of febrile convulsions, your doctor may advise you to give both aspirin and acetaminophen together every six hours. This has been shown to give a longer-lasting effect—about four hours of fever control. If your child is vomiting or unable to take anything by mouth, then aspirin suppositories, in two- and ten-grain sizes, and acetaminophen suppositories, in two- and ten-grain sizes, are also available. They can be cut to the appropriate dose for your child. The following is a dosage table, using the common brand names for fever medications:

    These are the dosages based on an average-size child. If your child is smaller or larger than average, or if she has lost a lot of fluids by vomiting or diarrhea, you will need to *check the dosage with your physician.*
- Sponging is a very useful and effective way of bringing down a fever. It must be used with fever medicines, however, as it is only temporary; it need not be done unless the temperature remains higher than 104° F one hour *after* fever medicine has been given. There are several ways that a child can be sponged. But *never* use alcohol, just lukewarm water.

    a. *A bath.* If your child is not sleepy and is feeling up to a bath, the simplest way to bring down her fever is to put her in a tub of lukewarm to tepid water. You may want to start with a little warmer water and gradually cool it, so that the water will not feel too cold to her when you first put her in. Shivering raises the temperature. Putting some of her toys in the tub will help her to have a good time. Keep her in the tub for twenty to thirty minutes. Squeeze water with a washcloth or sponge over her back and chest, especially in the armpits and around the neck. Putting a cool, wet washcloth on top of her head will also help. Recheck her temperature about one hour after she is out.

    b. *Sponge bath.* You can give a sponge bath to a sleepy child or to one

	Tempra/Tylenol (acetaminophen)	Liquiprin (acetaminophen)	Tempra/Tylenol (acetaminophen)	Tylenol (acetaminophen)	Baby Aspirin (aspirin)
	Drops— 1 gr/0.6 ml	Drops 1 gr/1–2 ml	Elixir— 2 gr/1 tsp (5 ml)	Chewable— 1¼ gr	Chewable— 1¼ gr
less than 6 months	C O N S U L T		Y O U R	P H Y S I	C I A N
6 months	0.3 ML	0.6 ML	¼ TSP (1.25 ML)		
1 year	0.6 ML	1.2 ML	½ TSP (2.5 ML)	1 TABLET	1 TABLET
2 years	0.9 ML	1.8 ML	¾ TSP (3.75 ML)	1½ TABLETS	1½ TABLETS
3 years	1.2 ML	2.4 ML	1 TSP (5 ML)	2 TABLETS	2 TABLETS
4 years	1.5 ML	3.0 ML	1¼ TSP (6.25 ML)	2½ TABLETS	2½ TABLETS
5 years	1.8 ML	3.6 ML	1½ TSP (7.5 ML)	3 TABLETS	3 TABLETS

who is too sick to be put into the tub. Cover the bed with a plastic or waterproof sheet and then cover that with a large towel or flannel blanket. Undress the child completely and cover her with another towel or lightweight blanket. Put an ice bag or a cool washcloth on her forehead. (*Do not* put an ice bag on a baby's soft spot since it can cool the brain excessively.) Change the washcloth as it warms up. Immerse five or six bathtowels in lukewarm water in a large basin or sink and wring them out. Wrap each body part in a towel—arms, legs, neck, and torso (be sure the armpits and groin are covered). Change the towels as soon as they become warm from the heat of the child's body. Do this for twenty to thirty minutes. Recheck your child's temperature in about thirty minutes.

- Dress your child in lightweight clothing such as pajamas or a T-shirt. When she is sleeping, cover her with a sheet or lightweight blanket. Too much covering on the skin prevents heat from escaping through the pores.
- High body temperatures result in fluid loss, so it is important that your child be offered fluids frequently. Most children prefer cold drinks, cracked ice, sherbet, or cold popsicles at this time. Milk should be avoided since it can cause a stomach upset. Keep track of your child's urine, as to how much and how often she urinates. Normal urination output is an indication that she is getting adequate liquids.

FREQUENT ILLNESSES   The average child has six to nine viral illnesses a year. This is not true in the first year of life, because infants are not exposed to a great number of people from whom they might contract a virus. However, once the exposure increases, and particularly after your child begins day care or pre-school, it may seem that she has one long infection after another, especially in the fall and winter months. Think about it—if each infection lasts about a week and most of them fall during the school year (nine months), your child will have a viral illness about one week per month! Often the infection is so mild that she would really not be considered ill. At other times the infection seems prolonged, because secondary bacterial complications such as ear infection or sinusitis may occur. There are many different viruses, and having an infection with one does not protect you from an infection with another. Viral illnesses may occur back to back, giving you a child who is sick for four to five weeks, but probably with four different viruses—a mother's nightmare. I (AA) can sympathize with this, as our Katie gets an infection every three weeks from September to June, without fail.

One of the concerns that parents have when their child has repeated infections is that perhaps the body's immune defense mechanisms are not functioning. In very rare cases this is true, but those children usually have severe infections of the lungs or skin, and poor growth. Of course, if, in your family history, a child died at a young age from a severe infection, your physician would probably want to check your child carefully.

PROBLEMS OF GROWTH AND DEVELOPMENT   In this section we will discuss the more common issues and problems that can arise in early childhood in the areas of physical, mental, emotional, and social growth.

BEHAVIORAL CONCERNS

Most parents worry when their youngster starts exhibiting behavior they feel is undesirable. But we suggest you read again the "Overview" and "Special Situations" chapters appropriate to your child's age. Be sure that the behavior that bothers you is not in fact a very normal one, such as separation anxiety, fear of strangers, inability to go to sleep, or refusal to eat. You also need to consider your child's individual temperament and notice how she reacts to her environment in her own special way.

If you are still concerned about your child's behavior after rereading these chapters, then you need to talk to your doctor and seek some assistance. Identified early—the earlier the better—behavior problems can be managed quite well. Let's discuss some of the major ones.

HELPING THE CHILD COPE WITH DEATH   Dealing with death of a loved one is difficult at any age, and it is especially hard for the child under five, who is confused about what death is. Because of TV, most young children have had some exposure to the words "die," "dead," and "kill." They have heard about it in books or have discussed it in relation to animals. However, most children under three, though they may use the words in their play, have no concept of what they are saying. Children between three and five still have a difficult time in understanding death as a final, permanent process. They think it is temporary and that the dead person or pet will be coming back.

Children can be very frightened by their misperceptions of death. For example, if a child has experienced the death of someone close to her and has been told that death is like going to sleep, sleep can become something dreadful to her. If a child is ill and cannot move very well, she may be afraid that this is a precursor to death. With her magical thinking, the preschooler may feel that her angry or bad feelings are causing her own impending death or that she is being punished for something she has done. A young child's greatest worry about death is that she will be separated from her mother and father and never see them again. It's the separation that frightens her, not the death itself.

Preschoolers are extremely curious and they ask a lot of questions about death that are difficult to answer. They wonder where the dead person goes, what happens to him, is he coming back, and why can't the parents fix him like a toy can be fixed. It is important that their questions be answered as literally as possible. It helps to explain that death is like having a broken toy that can't be fixed, that the person or pet is very old, very weak, or very sick, and no matter how much people try he couldn't get better. If religion and the discussion of heaven are a natural thing for you and your family, this is certainly very helpful for children. However, if the child is told that she will go to heaven if she is good, you may see some bad behavior begin to occur. She may fear that if she is good she will automatically have to leave you and go to heaven *right now!* Many times it helps to illustrate death by using the plant world as an example. Show a young bud being formed, growing into a flower, and eventually dying. It is important to point out that another flower will not grow back in exactly the same place, for no one or nothing can be replaced exactly.

When a young child experiences the death of someone close, the grief reaction will differ from child to child. A child may seem not to grieve at all, accepting it matter-of-factly and readily. She may seem to be very self-centered. This can make the adults feel angry. They need to recognize that the child is not able to understand the true meaning of death, and at this age she really is concerned about being taken care of. She may go on about her day-to-day life at first in what seems to be a normal fashion. But after a few weeks to a few months, she may begin to show some changes in her behavior as the permanency of the loss becomes more apparent. Then the grieving will begin to look more like an adult's—depression, clinging, possibly withdrawal. Some children become overly aggressive, fearful, and anxious. They become very anxious about the possibility of their own death or the death of a parent as well. Some children are very upset from the beginning. Children also feel angry with their parents in the event of the loss of someone close, because they wonder why the parent can't fix it or make it better, since they regard their parents as omnipotent.

As we have mentioned before, the preschooler needs to be assured that in no way could she have been responsible for the death. And she needs to be reassured that she is loved and will be cared for as always. The preschooler needs to be encouraged to express her feelings, and as always, play is one of the best tools for this if she is not particularly verbal. Provide her with the toys or dolls necessary to reenact the events, and let her play out the scenes with them. She will eventually get into it if she needs an outlet for her feelings. It is also helpful for a child to see the grief of those close to her, if it is not too intense or out of control. That can be frightening.

Parents often wonder about allowing their child to attend a funeral. There is no pat answer; but usually, funerals are too confusing and frightening for infants, toddlers, or first adolescents. The preschooler may attend a funeral if it is important to the parent for her to do so. She will need to be prepared for the funeral ahead of time with an explanation of what to expect. And as with other situations, the attitude of the parents will have a greater impact on the child than will the events of the funeral itself. The child needs to know that if she becomes uncomfortable she will be able to leave. It is important at the time of the funeral, when the family is very disorganized, that someone not so affected by the loss help to care for the child so that she is not forgotten in the shuffle.

After the death and the funeral, the child should be allowed to cherish her memories. It is important not to take away all the reminders of the loved one nor avoid talking about the loved one. It is through the memories that the child can see that although the loved one cannot be replaced, he can still be remembered. It is wise also if the child loses a pet that she be allowed to grieve for that pet and not have an immediate replacement. It is through the loss of the pet that the child begins to learn about the concept of death, and also learns that nothing can ever be exactly replaced. With the death of a pet, it might be helpful to have a brief funeral for the animal, so that a farewell may be said by the child or the family. This does not have to be a burial service, but a memorial service in which a few words of praise and farewell are said about the beloved pet.

Here are some excellent books for children that deal with the subject of death. They can be read to your child during the preschool years when she is wondering about death, or in the event of a loss.

THE DEAD BIRD, by Margaret Wise
ABOUT DYING, by Sarah B. Stein
THE TENTH GOOD THING ABOUT BARNEY, by Judith Viorst
CHARLOTTE'S WEB, by E. B. White
TALKING ABOUT DEATH: A DIALOGUE BETWEEN PARENT AND
CHILD, by Earl Grollman.

HYPERACTIVITY   Please read our section on Attention Deficit Disorders for a discussion of hyperactivity.

POOR PERSONAL-SOCIAL INTERACTION   There is much personal-social behavior that requires further evaluation. Obviously, the child who is harmful to himself or who exhibits bizarre behavior will come to the physician's attention quickly. A less obvious situation that requires evaluation is when the child seems to have the inability to interact with others, including his parents, often avoiding eye contact and not seeming to need physical affection. The exceedingly shy child who has severe terror on separating from a parent even in a familiar setting should also be evaluated further, as should the exceedingly aggressive child with poor peer and family interaction.

BOWEL OR BLADDER INCONTINENCE   Loss of bowel and bladder control after being totally trained for several months can occur in the young child in stressful stiuations, such as the addition of a new sibling or the loss of a loved one. If stresses are not obvious and the child is having bowel or bladder incontinence, it would be a good idea to discuss the situation with your physician. Together you might look for other causes of these changes. Physical causes need to be ruled out first. If none are found, your physician may treat it or a referral to a psychologist or psychiatrist may be necessary.

SELF-STIMULATION BEHAVIOR   Many parents are concerned about their children's self-stimulatory behavior, such as constant rocking or head banging. Remember that your child begins to use such self-stimulatory behavior as comforting maneuvers in the period from seven to twelve months of age. The behavior is usually seen when the child is tired or frustrated. It is not a cause for concern, and it decreases and disappears by three to five years of age. However, if rocking or head banging becomes persistent even when the child is not tired or frustrated, and if this seems to replace any other activities, you obviously need to discuss this with your physician and look for possible causes.

Thumb sucking in the first five years of life is of no concern, since it is a perfectly normal comforting device, as is hair twisting or stroking a blanket or toy. Hair plucking, however, usually occurs when the child is angry or frustrated. When it persists, look for causes of excessive stress, and try to find more appropriate ways for him to learn to deal with anger or frustration.

DEVELOPMENTAL CONCERNS

Most of the disorders discussed in this section are rather marked. But often parents have concerns about unusual or trying behavior in the areas of sleeping, eating, toileting, aggression, peer interaction, compliance, or independence. To relieve your worries, we recommend that you read the earlier chapters which describe normal behavior and various methods of discipline appropriate to the age of your child. But if you are still concerned talk to your doctor. She can assess your child to be sure everything is progressing normally. If it appears that your child is not doing well in some area, get another opinion from a specialist. There are speech pathologists, who evaluate language and speech. Audiologists evaluate hearing. Both physical therapists and occupational therapists evaluate motor function. The physical therapist also works extensively with assessing strength, balance, posture, and body movement. The occupational therapist is very skilled in assessing perceptual motor abilities as well as feeding problems or other problems in activities of daily living. And psychologists are trained in the area of cognitive, or intellectual, abilities as well as emotional development. Ask your doctor for a referral to someone with whom she has worked or who has a good reputation for working with kids.

If you are concerned about your child, it is important to have an evaluation done. Early identification and intervention can be very helpful in many developmental problems. It gives the child every chance for remediation, especially in the area of hearing and vision. And it helps avoid secondary problems that can arise as a result of a developmental lag.

DEVELOPMENTAL DISABILITIES

A developmental disability is a disorder that results from impairment to a child's nervous system at some time during maturation in the uterus, during the birth process, or during the child's developmental course to adulthood. A developmental disability may be very mild to very severe. There are many types of disabilities, but the most common are attention deficit disorder (minimal brain dysfunction), autism, cerebral palsy, epilepsy, hearing impairment, mental retardation, spina bifida, and visual impairment. We will discuss each of these.

Raising and caring for a child with a developmental disability is often difficult and anxiety producing. It is a chronic situation, and it requires ongoing care and concern. Remember that any child with a disability is a *child* first. He needs every opportunity to experience a normal childhood, in any way he can. Let him experience everything he can, even if it isn't exactly the way other kids do it. A blind child can creep around and explore, but he will experience more bruises. A deaf child can "listen" to a book as you read it to him, but he will do this by watching your face, looking at the book's pictures, or seeing the story acted out. The child with cerebral palsy can learn to feed himself, but he may be a little messy. The parents' attitude is crucial for the child's development. Have a "can do" approach and your child will try whatever he can. Overprotect him and he'll be afraid to try.

There are national organizations for each of the different developmental disabilities. These special-interest groups usually involve parents, professionals, and other concerned citizens. They can provide invaluable information, educational materials, and sometimes referrals to parent groups. We include the appropriate organization in each section that follows. We also list literature that we have found to be helpful for parents. The more you know and understand about your child's disability, the easier it is to cope with. Parent support groups also provide an invaluable service—not only for moral support and knowing you're not alone, but also for practical tips on day-to-day management. We encourage you to join a group. And if there isn't one in your locality, consider forming one.

To find services for evaluation and treatment, contact your physician, your state or local health department, your state developmental disabilities council, or even your local schools. Your motto may need to be "Persistence is a virtue." *You* are your child's best advocate.

The following are national organizations that are interested in helping anyone with a developmental disability.

COUNCIL ON EXCEPTIONAL CHILDREN
1920 ASSOCIATION DRIVE
RESTON, VIRGINIA 22091

MARCH OF DIMES BIRTH DEFECTS FOUNDATION
1275 MAMARONECK AVENUE
WHITE PLAINS, NEW YORK 10605

A helpful publication that includes most developmental disabilities is:

THE EXCEPTIONAL PARENT
296 BOYLSTON STREET
BOSTON, MASSACHUSETTS 02116

ATTENTION DEFICIT DISORDER (Minimal Brain Dysfunction, Learning Disability, Hyperactivity) The most common behavior problem that comes to the doctor's attention in these first few years is hyperactivity. There is obviously a wide individual range in normal activity, from the very quiet, placid child to the very physically active child. When a child is in fact abnormally active, or hyperactive, this is usually only part of a group of symptoms. When decreased attention span and impulsive behavior are grouped together with physical hyperactivity, the problem is known as *attention deficit disorder,* or ADD. There is no single cause for ADD, but it is thought to involve some areas of brain function and so it has also been called *minimal brain dysfunction* (MBD). Hyperactivity is also seen in children with mental retardation, brain damage, emotional problems, or hearing loss. These diagnoses need to be ruled out.

The child who is hyperactive moves all the time, not just in playing or school but while sleeping, watching TV, or reading. He may have a history of moving all around the bed as an infant, learning to climb out at an early age. The quality of his activity is not productive when compared with the normally very active child, who can, in fact, accomplish a great many tasks. He is very easily distracted, unable to concentrate on one thing for very long. He may be impulsive, have trouble waiting his turn, and need a great deal of supervision.

ADD is seen four to six times more often in boys than in girls, and it occurs in about one in fifteen to twenty children. It can persist into adulthood and can result in additional emotional problems if not dealt with early. The child often has some learning disability because of the poor attention span coupled with problems processing either visual or auditory information. Not all children with ADD are learning disabled however. Nor do all children with a learning disability experience hyperactivity, short attention span, or poor impulse control.

This condition is very frustrating for the child and his parents alike. The sooner treatment can begin, the greater the relief for everyone. ADD *can be helped.* Environmental changes need to be made to provide the child with clear structure and limits. Behavior management, using the positive reward system and Time Out recommended throughout our book, has proved quite effective.

The Feingold diet is a diet developed for the treatment of hyperactivity. Dr. Feingold found that because of sensitivity to certain dyes and additives many children who were hyperactive responded to a special diet in which these food dyes and additives were removed. The Feingold diet is not effective for most causes of hyperactivity, but it is not harmful and is worth a trial. However, it is very difficult to maintain. Allergy to common foods may also be a culprit to consider.

Medications such as Ritalin, Cylert, and Dexedrine are also helpful for ADD. But they should not be given to a young child unless he has had a complete evaluation by professionals specializing in the area of child development, who follow the child consistently, both on and off the medication, to decide whether it is truly needed. If you suspect your child has ADD, a comprehensive evaluation involving several professionals (psychologist, developmental pediatrician or neurologist, speech pathologist, occupational or physical therapist) is very important. It is sometimes difficult to diagnose and once diagnosed needs consistent treatment and follow-up.

Families with this problem need ongoing support and parent groups have been organized for this purpose. Ask the professionals about any groups available. Contact the national organization (see below) for further information, too.

Organization: ASSOCIATION FOR CHILDREN WITH LEARNING DISABILITIES
4156 LIBRARY ROAD
PITTSBURGH, PENNSYLVANIA 15234

Literature: *THE HYPERACTIVE CHILD AND THE FAMILY,* BY JOHN F. TAYLOR. A GUIDE TO DAY-TO-DAY LIVING. (AN EVEREST HOUSE BOOK) DODD, 1983.

LIVING WITH CHILDREN OR *FAMILIES,* BOTH BY GERALD PATTERSON. EXCELLENT PROGRAMMED TEXTS FOR TEACHING PARENTS THE INS AND OUTS OF BEHAVIOR MODIFICATION. THEY DEAL IN DEPTH WITH THE POSITIVE REINFORCEMENT SYSTEM. A HELPFUL GUIDE FOR THE PARENT OF A CHILD WITH ADD SINCE BEHAVIOR MANAGEMENT CAN BE VERY DIFFICULT. RESEARCH PRESS, 1976.

AUTISM   Autism is a disorder that becomes apparent in infancy or early childhood. The parent may notice that her infant resists cuddling, avoids her gaze, and is irritable. As he matures he may continue to avoid eye contact and seem to avoid close relationships with people. He may spend considerable time manipulating objects in a repetitive fashion, such as twirling a top or spinning a wheel. His social unresponsiveness is a very distressing situation for his parents. As the child develops, his language also may be impaired, so while he seems to understand some things, he does not understand everything and his spoken language is not entirely normal. The child with autism seems to be unable to perceive or interpret facial cues or speech tones. The autistic child often exhibits *echolalia,* or parroting. For example, when a mother asks her child, "Do you want a cookie?" The child repeats, "Do you want a cookie?" It is difficult to measure the intellectual potential of a child with autism, but his native ability may range from retarded to very bright.

The exact cause of autism is unknown. It is thought to be the result of an impaired function of the brain due to a trauma (or *insult*) to the brain in utero, infancy, or very early childhood (before three years). It is definitely *not* caused by poor parenting, as used to be believed.

The diagnosis of autism is not always easily made. Parents often suffer much heartache, going from one doctor to another for an answer. A child with suspected autism usually needs to be referred to a developmental center, where a group of knowledgeable professionals can assess him and help the parents find the best treatment program possible. As in all developmental disabilities, there is no cure. But much progress has been made in helping autistic children learn to interact in appropriate ways and develop more effective language. Autistic children usually need specialized treatment programs, and the sooner the program is begun, the better the chance for improvement.

Organization: INFORMATION AND REFERRAL SERVICE FOR AUTISTIC
AND AUTISTIC-LIKE PERSONS
306 31st STREET
HUNTINGTON, WEST VIRGINIA 25702

Literature: *AUTISTIC CHILDREN: A GUIDE FOR PARENTS*, BY LORNA
WING. AN EXCELLENT RESOURCE. CITADEL PRESS, 1974

CEREBRAL PALSY   In plain English, cerebral palsy means loss of muscle function (palsy) due to a brain (cerebral) disorder. The damage in the brain may arise from infection, injury, decreased oxygen supply, toxic agents, or bleeding.

The effects of this brain damage vary from individual to individual. There may be extensive involvement, with little ability to move the body, or involvement of only one small area of the body, such as one limb. The loss of muscle function may be mild to severe. Because brain damage is not always limited to the area of the brain controlling muscle movement, other areas of the brain may be affected as well. So a child with cerebral palsy has a higher risk of having a seizure disorder, mental retardation, a hearing impairment, a visual impairment, or a learning disability.

Cerebral palsy is not a progressive problem, such as the muscle problems seen in muscular dystrophy ("Jerry Lewis" kids). While there is no cure for cerebral palsy, the child and his family can receive excellent help from the many professionals who are knowledgeable and committed to working with them—neurologists, pediatricians, orthopedists, physical therapists, occupational therapists, speech pathologists, educators, nurses, social workers, and nutritionists. In some cases, all may need to have some input. In other cases, only a few would need to be involved. Because of the number of professionals required, the evaluations and services are more efficiently handled with an interdisciplinary approach.

The aim of the professionals is to work with the family and the child in order to maximize the child's potential for as normal a life as possible. There are many activities of daily living, such as feeding, toileting, and self-care, that are hampered by poor muscle control. The child is more dependent on his parents than are other children, and this can hurt his development of a good self-concept. Professionals do everything they can to help the parents care for him and, when he is ready, to help him become more independent. Their goal also is to make sure that this child has every chance to get up on his feet and walk, should that be a problem. Walking may need to be assisted by supportive devices (orthoses) or even a surgical procedure.

Sometimes children with cerebral palsy have difficulty with the muscles needed to talk. In this case the goal is not only to improve the child's muscle control through therapy, but also to develop communication devices that will help him communicate his needs and thoughts.

Organizations: UNITED CEREBRAL PALSY ASSOCIATION
66 E. 34th STREET
NEW YORK, NEW YORK 10016

NATIONAL EASTER SEAL SOCIETY
2033 W. OGDEN AVENUE
CHICAGO, ILLINOIS 60612

Literature: *HANDLING THE YOUNG CEREBRAL PALSY CHILD AT HOME*,
BY NANCY FINNIE. AN EXCELLENT RESOURCE. THE AUTHOR

ADDRESSES MANY DIFFERENT LEVELS OF SEVERITY, SO DISCUSS WITH YOUR THERAPIST WHICH SECTIONS OF THE BOOK WOULD BE APPROPRIATE FOR YOUR CHILD. A. WHITMAN, 1975.

HOWIE HELPS HIMSELF, BY JOAN FOSSLER. A BOOK ABOUT A CHILD'S DRIVE FOR INDEPENDENCE. GOOD FOR READING TO A CEREBRAL PALSIED CHILD AND HIS SIBLINGS. DUTTON, 1975.

EPILEPSY (SEIZURE DISORDER) Seizures, or convulsions, are the result of a temporary electrical short circuit in the brain. They may occur in a child who has a high fever resulting in febrile convulsions or febrile fits. In this case, the child does not have a specific area of the brain that is a problem, and the EEG (electroencephalogram) is totally normal. It is believed that these seizures are due to immaturity in the child's nervous system, which she outgrows. This is *not* epilepsy.

Epilepsy exists when an area of the brain contains abnormal nerve cells that tend to be "trigger happy." When they begin discharging their electrical activity inappropriately, the electrical impulses spread like a brush fire, and soon a whole area of the brain is doing the same. This discharge results in a seizure, which can lead to unconsciousness, unusual sensory experiences, or involuntary movements as the muscles clench or contract. These abnormal areas of the brain usually cause abnormal brain wave patterns on the EEG, and there will be repeated seizures. Most children with epilepsy have normal intelligence and their seizures can be controlled quite effectively with medication. The seizures often disappear completely after several years, requiring no more medication. A small percentage of children, however, have epilepsy as a part of a general brain problem, including cerebral palsy and/or mental retardation. Their seizures are more difficult to control. The treatment for seizures is covered in the "First Aid" section.

It is important to remember that the child with epilepsy is a child first. She needs to be treated as normally as possible. She should be encouraged to participate in childhood activities, with safety precautions. For example, if she has frequent seizures that cause her to fall and hit her head, a special helmet may be needed for protection. She may swim, but she will need close supervision. When she has a seizure, maintain an air of calmness and behave matter-of-factly. Be sure you know what to do when a seizure occurs. Take a CPR course and be prepared for any emergency. Because she may have a seizure resulting in incontinence, always have a change of clothing handy. Change her, give her a hug, and let her proceed with her activities.

Try to become as knowledgeable as you can about your child's medications and their side effects. For instance, dental care is very important with some seizure medications, especially Dilantin, which causes swelling of the gums. Seizure medications may also affect Vitamin D and folic acid metabolism, resulting in rickets and anemia. Consult your doctor about the need for a supplement.

Above all, try to educate those who will be around your child. Their attitudes and interaction with her can be positive, if they are free of superstitions and fears. Your child's feelings of self-worth and self-esteem depend upon her interaction with others as well as with you, her family.

For further discussion on coping with a chronic problem, read our section on chronic illness. Talk to your doctor or nurse concerning local resources, especially support groups.

Organization: EPILEPSY FOUNDATION OF AMERICA
                4351 GARDEN CITY DRIVE
                LANDOVER, MARYLAND 20785

HEARING IMPAIRMENT   A hearing impairment can be mild to severe. As we have stressed before, it is very important to identify a hearing impairment early and begin treatment right away. During the first three years of life particularly, a hearing impairment can interfere with the development of language.

If your child has been found to have a hearing impairment, the teamwork of a speech pathologist; an audiologist; possibly an ear, nose, and throat specialist; and your pediatrician is needed to work out the very best treatment plan. He may or may not require a hearing aid, but he will certainly require intensive language stimulation and stimulation of his other senses, especially touch and sight, in order to learn more fully.

Sometimes on learning that their child can't hear, parents stop talking to him. They forget that talking involves not only sound, but also facial expression and gestures. These are very important for him in learning to communicate with you. He can learn to imitate your facial expressions, and he can feel sounds by touching your throat and your mouth while you talk. If he is making sounds, imitate those too; let him feel them. His senses of vision and touch are a great help to him in learning to communicate. So be sure to talk extensively to your child, even more than you ordinarily would. A good speech pathologist is essential in helping you do as much as you can for your child.

Again, parent groups for support and for tips on day-to-day living are also extremely important for the family with a child with a hearing impairment.

Organization: INTERNATIONAL ASSOCIATION OF PARENTS OF THE DEAF
                814 BAYER AVENUE
                SILVER SPRINGS, MARYLAND 20910

Literature: *DEAF LIKE ME,* BY THOMAS AND JAMES SPRADLEY. A
                MOVING STORY OF A YOUNG CHILD WITH A HEARING LOSS,
                AND HER FAMILY. RANDOM HOUSE, 1978.

MENTAL RETARDATION   Mental retardation is a term used for a condition in which there is an impaired ability to reason and learn. It ranges in severity from profound retardation, in which the individual remains at the level of an infant, to retardation just below normal, with the ability to complete almost all subjects in school except the most academic.

Mental retardation can result from a genetic or chromosomal defect such as Down Syndrome; an infectious process in utero or later, such as rubella or meningitis; toxic agents; injury to the brain; a metabolic disorder; or decreased oxygen supply. In many cases, the cause is unknown.

Down Syndrome (DS) is one of the more commonly found causes of mental retardation. It is the result of extra chromosome material on chromosome 21. It is not known what causes this in most cases, but in a small percentage the syndrome is inherited. The overall incidence of DS in the population is about 1 in 600. However, it has been noted that the incidence increases with parental age (over thirty-five years for the mother and over fifty-five years for the father). If a family has a child with Down Syndrome, genetic counseling is essential in order to find out whether it is, in fact, the type that can be inherited. Amniocentesis can be done in early pregnancy to detect the presence of a fetus with DS.

The child with DS is characterized by a particular facial appearance—a slight slant to the eyes and a rather flat face. He may have a large tongue and is typically small for his age. Most children with DS have some degree of mental retardation. It may range from borderline to severe but is usually in the moderate-to-mild range. A few individuals with DS have been found to be in the normal range intellectually.

Much work has been done on early stimulation and educational intervention with children with Down Syndrome and other forms of mental retardation. The results are very encouraging. We urge you to contact the national organizations in order to find out as much as possible about the resources and parent groups available to you.

Organizations: ASSOCIATION FOR CHILDREN WITH DOWN SYNDROME
589 PATTERSON STREET
EAST MEADOW, NEW YORK 11554

NATIONAL ASSOCIATION FOR DOWN SYNDROME
BOX 63
OAK PARK, ILLINOIS 60303

Literature: *HE'S MY BROTHER,* BY JOE LASKER. A SIBLING'S STORY OF HIS RETARDED BROTHER. A. WHITMAN, 1974.

LIKE ME, BY A. J. BRIGHTMAN. THIS IS A TEXT WITH PICTURES ILLUSTRATING THE FEELINGS OF A RETARDED CHILD. LITTLE BROWN, 1976.

SPINA BIFIDA   Spina bifida (*neural tube defect, myelomeningocele*) is a disorder caused by a defect in the development of the spinal column in utero. It varies in severity. The extent of the defect may be so mild that it is only apparent in X-ray; or it may range to very severe, with a large sac of spinal fluid, spinal cord, and nerves exposed on the child's back. In the most severe cases the child will have severe nerve damage with loss of control below the level of the defect. This results in bladder and bowel incontinence and paralysis of the lower extremities. Sometimes spina bifida is associated with hydrocephalus ("water on the brain"). Some children with spina bifida have some degree of mental retardation, but the majority of children are not retarded.

The exact cause of spina bifida is not known, but it is evident that there are combined genetic and environmental factors. Once spina bifida has occurred in a family there is an increased risk of its happening again, so genetic counseling is very much in order. Studies can be done in the first stages of pregnancy in order to detect spina bifida in the fetus.

Many professionals need to be involved with the evaluation and treatment of a child with spina bifida. This is best done with an interdisciplinary approach at one center, in order to avoid fragmentation and provide optimal care. The disciplines that might need to be involved would be neurosurgery, neurology, pediatrics, urology, orthopedics, physical therapy, education, psychology, nursing, and social work. While there is no cure for spina bifida, there is much that can be done to help these children lead as normal a life as possible. They can be taught to care for themselves in all respects and helped to lead fulfilling lives.

Organization: SPINA BIFIDA ASSOCIATION OF AMERICA
343 SOUTH DEARBORN, SUITE 319
CHICAGO, ILLINOIS 60604

Literature: *A GUIDE FOR HELPING THE CHILD WITH SPINA BIFIDA,* BY E. J. MYERS. VERY HELPFUL FOR FAMILIES. C. C. THOMAS, 1981.

VISION IMPAIRMENT Vision impairment ranges in severity from very mild to total loss. There are many causes of vision impairment, some occurring in utero and others occurring during the child's development. As with any developmental disability, early identification and intervention is essential. When a child is visually impaired, he needs to use his other senses to their fullest.

Children who are visually impaired develop differently from those who are not. This is illustrated beautifully in a study done by Selma Fraiberg, which she has described in her book *Insights from the Blind.* The child who is blind and without other handicaps goes through the same developmental stages as the sighted child, but with much different timing and sequencing.

The needs of the child with visual impairment are the same as those of any other child. In the first two years of life, one of his needs is to become emotionally attached to his parents. This can be difficult if the child does not use his eyes to contact his parents. Therefore, extra time should be spent with holding, carrying, and talking to the baby. Because eye contact is such a positive reinforcer for a parent, parents with visually handicapped children often need extra emotional and social support from other parents and professionals.

The child with a visual impairment needs to actively explore his environment in order to improve his sense of touch and hearing. He should be encouraged to be independent—to learn to feed himself, even if it is terribly messy, or to look for his toys himself by using his hands. He also must tolerate more bumps and bruises than the child with good vision. And because he is unable to get the visual cues, the child with visual impairment needs a great deal of language stimulation.

In the preschool stage, peer interaction for this child is essential. Also, to develop independence, he needs to learn to help himself in toileting, dressing, and bathing. The blind child has difficulty with orienting himself and needs extra work in learning the concepts of up, down, and under. He may also, if he is quite impaired, need to learn techniques for being safely mobile in his world.

These are just a few of the needs of the blind child. Many more suggestions and aids are available from special-interest groups.

Organizations: NATIONAL FEDERATION OF THE BLIND
1800 JOHNSON STREET
BALTIMORE, MARYLAND 21230

AMERICAN FOUNDATION FOR THE BLIND
15 W. 16th STREET
NEW YORK, NEW YORK 10011

Literature: *ELIZABETH,* BY SHARON ULRICH. THE STORY OF A BLIND CHILD'S ADAPTATIONS TO A PRESCHOOL LEARNING PROGRAM, WRITTEN BY THE MOTHER. UNIVERSITY OF MICHIGAN PRESS, 1972.

GET A WIGGLE ON; MOVE IT!!!, BY RICHARD DROUILLARD AND SHERRY RAYNOR. AAHPERD, 1978.

RAISING THE YOUNG BLIND CHILD, BY S. KASTEIN, J. SPAULDING, AND B. SCHARF. A BEAUTIFULLY DONE GUIDE TO DAY-TO-DAY LIVING AND LEARNING WITH A BLIND CHILD. HUMAN SCIENCE PRESS, 1980.

WEIGHT PROBLEMS

UNDERWEIGHT If your child is lean, that is no cause for concern unless he has a sudden weight loss or is gradually falling below the normal range. If he is, your physician should be contacted so that an evaluation can be made. Weight loss can result from reduced food intake, reduced calorie intake, or poor absorption of food. These conditions may be caused by excessive vomiting or diarrhea; excessive dilution of the formula; easy tiring during sucking and eating because of illness; or poor suck because of abnormal muscle control in the mouth area, as is seen in cerebral palsy. Weight loss can also be caused by infections with persistent fevers, or the extra muscle movement in neuromuscular disorders such as athetoid cerebral palsy.

Some children have weight loss because of behavior problems that result in a refusal to eat. Refusal to eat can occur when a child is depressed or sad, but it can also occur when the family is uptight about food intake and coaxes or nags excessively. This problem is most likely to arise in a period when the child in fact decreases his food intake normally (because of illness or a slower period of growth). If this happens with your child, your physician can help you plan a course to avoid further problems.

OVERWEIGHT The question of the overweight child has received a great deal of study in recent years. If your child is overweight, you can usually see rolls of fat around the tummy, thighs, and upper arms. Remember that the infant is supposed to have rolls of fat; but he should begin to thin out once he is walking. The most scientific way of assessing a child's possible obesity is by measuring the skin folds in the upper arms or over the shoulder blades.

You can use your growth chart to see whether your child's weight is in the right proportion to his height. However, a very muscular child can be mistaken for an obese child if only the growth chart is used. Muscle is quite heavy, but it is lean weight, which is not at all the same as obesity, or excess fat. A sudden weight gain or a gradually increasing proportion of gain is cause for examination by the doctor and possible treatment.

In studying children who are overweight, researchers have found that often these children do not consume as many calories as the normal or underweight child. The difference is exercise. The overweight child moves much less than the other. It would seem then that if your child has a tendency to be overweight, increasing his exercise would be advisable. Obviously, you could modify his diet by decreasing sweets and fats. But remember that a baby less than one year of age should continue to receive his regular formula. No skim milk or low-fat milk should be used.

REYE'S SYNDROME   Reye's syndrome is a serious illness, the cause of which is unknown. It seems to be associated with a preceding illness of chicken pox, influenza, or an upper respiratory infection. There is *some* evidence, although it is not conclusive, that links the use of aspirin during these illnesses to a higher incidence of Reye's. The illness begins with persistent vomiting three to seven days after the preceding illness and may be accompanied by lethargy, sleepiness, or confusion. The child becomes ill quite rapidly and *needs to be hospitalized* as quickly as possible. There is extensive involvement of the liver and marked swelling of the brain. This used to be nearly always fatal, but newer techniques and treatment have lowered the mortality rate greatly. The incidence of permanent brain damage after Reye's syndrome is extremely small, so when a child recovers she is not likely to have any further problems.

SUDDEN INFANT DEATH SYNDROME (CRIB DEATH)   Sudden infant death syndrome (SIDS), also known as crib death, is still one of the main unsolved problems of early infancy. SIDS is the sudden and quiet death of an infant who has been essentially well. The death is unexplained even after an adequate autopsy. There appears to be no one single cause for these deaths. In some cases it may be due to an abnormality in the nervous system, which causes the baby's respiratory system to stop or the cardiac system to malfunction. In other cases it may be due to seizures, abnormalities of the immune system, or abnormalities of the respiratory system.

There does seem to be a higher incidence of SIDS in low-birth-weight babies, male children, and children from lower socioeconomic levels. However, it can be found in all walks of life.

Most of the babies die at home while they are asleep. They do not cry, and there is no evidence of a struggle. Most have been totally well when they were put to bed. Others might have had only a mild upper respiratory infection.

SIDS is a *rare* occurrence, but a devastating one. The parents often find it very difficult to avoid feeling guilty, even though they in no way could have done anything to prevent the death. Physicians are rallying more quickly now, and giving the parents the autopsy results as soon as possible. They try to maintain contact with the parents for continued counseling and support and give repeated reassurance that the parents are not responsible in any way for their child's death.

Organizations have been developed to help parents of SIDS victims. The National Foundation for SIDS, Inc., is at 310 South Michigan Avenue, Chicago, Illinois 60604. If you or anyone close to you has lost a child from SIDS, it is important to contact a local organization. At a time like this, it helps to know you are not alone.

TRAVEL SICKNESS (MOTION SICKNESS) Travel sickness is due to a familial sensitivity of the balance center in the inner ear. It is not related to emotional problems and is a fairly common condition in young children. The child complains of nausea and not feeling well while riding in a car, plane, train, or boat, or even on amusement park rides.

PREVENTIVE MEASURES FOR TRAVEL SICKNESS:

- Bonine tablets in a chewable form can be bought at the drug store. They are 25 mg tablets, and a child aged three to six years can take a half tablet. Give it one hour before traveling or going to the amusement park. It will last eight hours.
- When riding in a car, have your child sit in the front seat and at window level. On a plane, select a seat near the wings or the center of the plane.
- Rather than feeding your child large meals while traveling, let her snack frequently during the day.
- Spinning-type rides at the amusement park should be avoided.

WORMS *Pinworms* are the most common type of worm infestation. Pinworm infections are found worldwide and are commonly seen in whole families. About 10 to 15 percent of the world's population is probably infected, although it is difficult to tell. The infection is very common in preschoolers and young children, who are more likely to put their hands in their mouths after playing with their bottoms.

Pinworms live in the rectum. At night the female worms come out, lay their eggs around the anal region, and sometimes migrate to the vagina. This results in intense itching in the anal and vaginal region, causing restless sleep. The children scratch in their sleep, get eggs under their fingernails, and can infect other close family members and friends in this way.

The worms are very small (¼–½ inches; 6–12 mm) and a greyish white in color. They may occasionally be seen in the genital and anal region at night if the parent goes in and inspects while the child is itching. The worms may look like lint or normal secretions, but can be differentiated by the fact that they move. Most often a diagnosis will have to be made by a physician. If you suspect that your child has pinworms, apply a piece of transparent tape to the skin around his anus, then peel the tape off and save it for the doctor. Do this first thing in the morning, before washing your child. The tape picks up the eggs and the doctor can identify them with a microscope.

A pinworm infection can be eradicated with medication, and steps must be taken to reduce the chance of reinfection. For three days the child should wear pants under his pajamas, and every morning you should put him in the bathtub, then remove his pants and rinse his bottom off carefully. Make sure he scrubs his hands and fingernails before he eats and after he goes to the bathroom. (Machine-washing sheets, bed linens, clothing, and towels will kill any eggs on them.) The pinworm eggs can be found on the bedroom floor, so vacuum or wet-mop the floor during this time. If a family member should be infected by the child it will take a month for symptoms to appear.

We have mentioned previously that children can be infected by worms carried by infected dogs and cats. There are other worms—*roundworms* and *hookworms*— that are specific to humans. Both can be acquired by contact with soil that is contaminated with infected human feces. This is obviously not a risk in areas with good sanitation. Should a person be infected with hookworms or roundworms, he himself is not contagious and there is no reason to isolate him.

Let's look first at the respiratory tract, since this is the most common site for illness in the first few years of your child's life. We will describe the common respiratory symptoms, the infections that cause them, and home treatment where applicable.

HEAD, NECK, AND CHEST

RESPIRATORY TRACT

SYMPTOMS

These are some of the symptoms you may notice when your child is having respiratory problems.

CHANGES IN BREATHING
- Your child may be breathing faster than usual.
- The child may have to work harder to get air in and out. This usually shows up as nostrils flaring and skin being sucked in at the area between the collar bones and between the ribs.
- The child's breathing may be noisy—wheezing, grunting, or crowing.

These symptoms can indicate a variety of problems. If the child makes snoring, gurgling sounds when breathing in but is not in distress or working hard, then the congestion is probably in her upper airway (the nose, or perhaps the tonsillar area with swollen tonsils or adenoids). This may cause the younger baby more difficulty, since she is primarily a nose breather and may have trouble switching to mouth breathing. The younger baby also breathes through her nose while she feeds, so nose or tonsil congestion will cause difficulties when she is sucking on the bottle.

If the problem is farther down the airway, either in the area of the voice box (larynx) or the upper windpipe (trachea), you might hear a raspy sound when she breathes in, perhaps like a foghorn. This is known as a "croupy" sound.

The child may be working hard to get air in but have no other symptoms. This can mean she has aspirated, or inhaled, a small object into her windpipe, and it is blocking the airway. When the child is working hard to get air in but also has a fever and a rapid rate of breathing, and she has recently had a cold, pneumonia is a possibility. *In both of these situations, call your doctor immediately.*

When the child is having trouble breathing out, especially if she is making a wheezing sound, she is likely to have asthma or bronchitis. *Contact your doctor.*

Call your physician immediately if your child is experiencing any change in breathing accompanied by shortness of breath, anxiety, fever, or color change (turning pale, bluish, or dusky).

HOARSENESS   The hoarse child has a raspy voice and often cannot speak above a whisper. The following are possible causes for hoarseness:

- Aspiration or inhalation of something into the windpipe. *The doctor should be contacted as soon as possible.*
- In an infant who has *not* recently had a cold, hoarseness may indicate some type of congenital abnormality or possibly hypothyroidism. *Your doctor should be contacted for an evaluation.*
- In an older child who has not recently had a cold, hoarseness may be the result of a benign nodule on the voice box due to voice strain. This is usually seen in the "yellers and screamers." If it persists, *your physician should be contacted.*
- Inflammation of the trachea or larynx (called tracheitis or laryngitis) accompanying a cold may cause hoarseness. This is usually nothing to be concerned about. However, should it continue longer than two weeks, contact your doctor.

COUGH   There are two basic types of coughs. The first is dry, hacking, or tight, in which no mucus is produced. The second is wet, or productive, in which mucous material is produced.

- The cough of an upper respiratory infection (the common cold, also called a URI) begins as a dry, irritative cough. This is usually the result of an irritation in the back of the throat (the pharynx). The cough may be worse at night when the child is lying down and excessive mucus from the nose drains down the throat and windpipe (trachea).
- A wet, productive, cough is usually seen in lower respiratory problems, such as pneumonia or bronchitis.
- The child with asthma usually has a dry, tight cough which requires a great deal of effort.
- If the child has not had a cold and suddenly develops a dry, irritative cough, the possibility that she has inhaled something into her windpipe needs to be considered. Obviously, *your physician should be contacted as soon as possible.*

SORE THROAT   A sore throat almost always accompanies an upper respiratory infection, or cold. There are different types:

- The sore throat of a URI or laryngitis is usually raspy and burning.
- If your child has a very severe sore throat with difficulty in swallowing, especially if the glands in the neck are swollen, you should *contact your physician.* These are the symptoms of strep throat, although these symptoms may also indicate a viral infection.
- The child who complains of a sore throat, particularly on awakening in the morning with clearing during the day, is probably experiencing drainage from the nose at night.
- The child with a sore throat and any type of rash *should be checked by the physician* to rule out strep throat or scarlet fever.

See "Home Treatment for Colds" for home treatment suggestions.

RUNNY OR STUFFY NOSE   The nasal mucosa (mucous membranes) may become swollen and produce excessive secretions (rhinitis) under many circumstances:

- In an infection, such as a URI.
- As a allergic response—hay fever or allergic rhinitis.
- As a chemical rhinitis caused by irritants such as smoke or toxic gases, by swimming in a chlorinated pool, or excessive use of nosedrops or sprays.
- As a vasomotor rhinitis because of temperature change, fatigue, or tension causing a change in blood vessel tone which results in swelling.

INFECTIONS   Now let's take a look at some of the respiratory infections that cause these symptoms.

UPPER RESPIRATORY INFECTION (URI, OR COLD)   As we have said, most children from one through five have six to nine colds per year, as they come in contact with the many viruses responsible for URIs. Each cold your child gets is caused by a different virus, and there are over a hundred strains. Unfortunately, antibiotics do *not* kill these viruses.

The peak seasons for cold viruses seem to be autumn, winter, and spring. And the child who is poorly nourished, fatigued, or under a great deal of stress has a greater chance of catching cold when exposed to a virus. A virus is spread from person to person, usually from hand to mouth. Therefore, if you have a cold or someone else in the family has a cold, hand washing after contact would help cut down the exposure.

Once your child is exposed to the cold virus, the incubation period is one to four days, which is a very rapid onset. Before she even develops symptoms she will be contagious for one to two days. This is the reason a cold spreads so effectively. Some children can feel miserable with a cold and develop a fever; others seem to sail through the infection. The symptoms usually last five to seven days. And then your child is ready to catch the next cold!

A cold causes swelling of the respiratory tract. Because children have short, narrow eustachian and airway tubes and an ineffective cough, they are more likely to develop complications. These complications are most commonly ear infections (otitis media), bronchitis, croup, pneumonia, or sinusitis.

HOME TREATMENT FOR COLDS:

- If your child has a fever and is not eating well, it is important to offer her cold fluids, ice cream, or popsicles as frequently as she can take them. Tylenol can be given if her fever exceeds 102° F or if she is feeling bad.

- You can treat the nasal stuffiness with decongestants, either topical (such as .025% Afrin or ⅛% Neo-Synephrine) or systemic (such as Sudafed or Naldecon). This helps decrease nose blowing and irritation of the skin under the nose. It also improves feeding in the young infant, who depends on her nose for breathing while sucking. And it helps make the child more comfortable in general. Apply petroleum jelly or skin cream around the nose to decrease the chance of irritation.

- A decongestant also helps relieve the nighttime cough if it is due to drainage from the nose. The cough can also be relieved by increasing the humidity in the air. Use a vaporizer (cold air) at bedtime. Because the younger child cannot cough well and tends to keep mucus in her lungs, your doctor would probably not prescribe a cough suppressant. (Occasionally, a suppressant will be prescribed for a persistent, dry, hacking cough if it interferes with sleep.) An expectorant is really of little help.

- As we have said, your child will probably have a sore throat with her cold. Sucking on hard candy (such as a lollipop) or popsicles and gargling with warm salt water (¾ teaspoon salt to 1 cup warm water) can also be of some comfort. Local anesthetic sprays are sometimes prescribed, but some children are allergic to the anesthetic (such as benzocaine) so we do not recommend it.

- Milk has been found to thicken the secretions in some children. With a child over six months of age, give clear liquids. Consult your doctor with a younger child.

- There is no need to limit your child or make him stay in bed (an almost impossible task with a young child). Allow him to limit himself; he'll settle down and rest if he needs it. Keep him home from school until he has no fever. He may play outdoors at anytime in nice weather.

- If hoarseness develops, increase the humidity with a vaporizer or a steamy bathroom, try to get your child to rest her voice, and let her suck on hard candy or a popsicle.

- If your child is having a cold for the first time, *call your physician for suggestions* for over-the-counter medications. These will probably include a nasal decongestant. Decongestant nose drops are effective, without any side effects, but *only* for three to four days. Then instead of shrinking, the tissues begin to swell. Some of the systemic or oral-type decongestants can have side effects, making your child either very drowsy or more irritable.

- *Your doctor should be contacted* if your child has a fever and is an infant under four months of age; if she is older than four months and has a fever for more than three days; if she has an extremely sore throat or an earache; if she develops a thick, greenish-yellow discharge from her nose lasting more than a day; if she develops a thick or wheezy cough; is lethargic; is eating very poorly; has difficulty breathing; or seems quite ill. She may have developed a secondary bacterial infection and require antibiotic treatment.

BRONCHITIS Bronchitis is an infection of the lower respiratory tree, involving the bronchi (the smaller tubes coming off the windpipe); it usually involves the windpipe as well. Bronchitis sometimes accompanies an upper respiratory infection, and also may be seen with influenza, measles, scarlet fever, and whooping cough. Bronchitis infections are usually caused by a virus, but in some cases bacteria are the culprit. The symptoms are frequent, dry, hacking coughing two to three days after a cold. The child may complain of her chest hurting or burning. She may have paroxysms of coughing, which cause her to gag and vomit. In a few days the cough becomes quite wet and productive, and the mucus becomes yellow or green. Breathing develops whistling or wheezing sounds, usually on breathing out. The illness lasts for approximately five to ten days and the cough gradually disappears. If your child develops these symptoms, *you should contact your physician.*

HOME TREATMENT FOR BRONCHITIS:
- Home treatment for bronchitis is the same as that for a cold.
- If her chest seems very full, contact your doctor. He may suggest using postural drainage, a technique for loosening secretions. His nurse may demonstrate it.

PNEUMONIA Pneumonia is an infection of the lower respiratory tree, involving the alveoli (the small air sacs). It may be caused by a virus or by bacteria.

Pneumonia is usually preceded by a mild cold for a few days. The child then becomes sicker, with higher temperatures, possible chills, breathing problems, loss of appetite, and lethargy. Some children complain of abdominal pain, and their tummies may be bloated. This can be from swallowing air, or it can be due to decreased function of the intestines because of the lung infection.

Your child will need to *see the doctor.* Blood tests and X-rays may be necessary to establish the diagnosis and the cause of the infection—virus or bacteria. If a bacterial infection is present, antibiotics will be prescribed.

HOME TREATMENT FOR PNEUMONIA:
- Most children do not require hospitalization, and home treatment is the same as for a cold or bronchitis.

CROUP Croup is a term referring to a group of infections that affect the windpipe, voice box, and surrounding areas. It causes hoarseness, a brassy cough, and a crowing (or foghorn) sound when breathing in. In children under three years of age, croup is usually a viral infection. In older children, it is most commonly a bacterial infection and requires antibiotic treatment. It usually follows a few days of a mild cold but may also occur rather suddenly. A mild case of croup would have only a barking or brassy cough and some hoarseness. It can usually be treated at home. *Call your doctor* to check.

HOME TREATMENT FOR CROUP:
- The child needs humidity twenty-four hours a day. If a humidifier is not available, put pans of water in the room or hang wet towels in the room.

Make sure that she drinks plenty of fluids (offer half a glass per hour). The fluid should be clear. Some bottle-fed children have problems sucking when they have croup, and may have less difficulty on a cup.

• Cough medicines are not very effective for this type of cough. Sucking on a lollipop or taking a drink of lemon juice with a little sugar water (concentrated lemonade) does as well.

• If your child has a fever higher than 102° F, Tylenol or aspirin could be given.

PROBLEMS WITH CROUP   If the croup progresses, which means increased swelling of the airway, *immediate* treatment by your doctor may be needed. The symptoms are an increased crowing noise, drooling because of problems in swallowing, and evidence of respiratory distress (hard breathing, or change of color). *Call your doctor right away.*

It is important that you or another adult sleep in the same room with your child when she has this cough, in order to tend to her as quickly as possible. When children develop breathing problems, they quickly panic. Panic and crying increases the obstruction. If you are there and can act in a calm, reassuring manner, you can alleviate the panic and improve the problem. Should your child develop the crowing noise, it is important that she be placed in a room with warm mist. The best place is the bathroom, with a hot shower running to steam it up. Take a rocking chair into the bathroom and rock and sing to her while she steams. Your husband can be calling the doctor in the meantime. Often the child will settle down and fall asleep in twenty or thirty minutes in the steam room, and then sleep through the night. You obviously should have the humidifier going in her room, as close as possible to where she is sleeping.

There is a form of croup involving the epiglottis (a flap of tissue at the base of the tongue that prevents food from getting into the windpipe during swallowing). The epiglottis can cause an acute obstruction, which often requires immediate hospitalization. A child with this problem will not improve as markedly in the steam room.

In the event your doctor decides that the child does need to come into the hospital for observation and treatment, you will need to stay with her for the entire time. You may need to get into the mist or oxygen tent with her should she need one. Those things are very scary to young children, and panic only serves to make the problem worse. You may get some flack from hospital personnel, but stand firm. This is your child. Fortunately, most cases of croup do not require hospitalization, and the child will recover very nicely after three to five days. She may experience several more attacks of the crowing noise, but she will rapidly improve when you take her into the steam room.

Some children seem to have a tendency to get croup and may get it with every cold. It also tends to occur in families.

INFLUENZA   Influenza is an infection very much like the common cold, only the viruses (influenza A and influenza B) are much more powerful and usually cause more muscle ache and fever. Vaccines have been produced for these specific viruses. But immunization lasts only one to two years, and the vaccines themselves can cause a brief period of mild illness. Influenza vaccination is not necessary for healthy children; however, it is indicated for children with certain chronic illnesses because they are at greater risk. These chronic illnesses are heart disease, lung disease (cystic fibrosis, tuberculosis, asthma), neuromuscular disease (involving weakness of the respiratory muscles, such as muscular dystrophy or cerebral palsy), kidney disease (nephrosis, glomerulonephritis), and metabolic problems (diabetes). There is a medication on the market (amantadine hydrochloride) which has been shown to be helpful in fighting influenza A, if given prior to exposure or early in the course of the illness.

Call your doctor as you would for a cold.

HOME TREATMENT FOR INFLUENZA:
- Home treatment for influenza is essentially the same as for a cold: humidity, increased fluids, and fever reduction. (Since the use of aspirin with influenza has been associated with an increased incidence of Reye's syndrome, it is recommended that Tylenol be used instead.)
- Influenza can result in serious lung problems, so it is very important that your child be kept as quiet as possible during the illness and convalescence. Because she will feel so much more miserable than she does with a regular cold, this probably won't be so difficult.

SINUSITIS   The sinus chambers, which open into the nose, serve to warm and humidify the air as it passes through the nose. Not all of the sinus cavities are developed in early childhood, but the ones on either side of the nose in the cheek area and in the eye area are developed. With any cold these can become blocked and congested, as they do in adults. This causes a chronic runny nose, occasionally pain, and mouth breathing. Sinusitis is also commonly seen in children with hay fever.

HOME TREATMENT FOR SINUSITIS:
- Sinusitis symptoms can be relieved by having your child inhale warm mist, in a bathtub or shower; by placing warm, wet washcloths over her nose; and by putting hot water in a humidifier and letting her breathe the mist as it comes out. This may be enough to open up the blockage with no further problems.
- If problems do continue, nose drops are helpful (such as .025% Afrin or ⅛% Neo-Synephrine). When you administer nose drops, the child should be lying down with her head in your lap and turned to the side. Put the nose drops in the lower nostril so that they may go into the sinus opening. Repeat on the other side with her head turned the other way. Wait a minute before she gets up. These nose drops taste bad when they go back down the throat, so having a nice drink afterwards often helps.
- If you are planning an airplane trip, be sure to give your child a dose of nose drops half an hour to an hour before takeoff. If the flight is longer than about three and a half hours, give your child another dose half an hour to an hour before landing (if the drug is to be used every three to four hours). The decongestant prevents sinus pressure discomfort from changes in altitude.

- If your child complains of pain with the sinusitis, which is unusual in younger children, give her aspirin or Tylenol. Some children respond to warm, wet cloths over the sinus area; others may respond to ice bags. Oral medications are usually not necessary for sinusitis, but if your child is allergic, taking her regular allergy medicine may be helpful.

PROBLEMS WITH SINUSITIS:
- Sometimes sinus congestion can become complicated by a secondary bacterial infection, resulting in a yellow-green, purulent discharge from the nose; fever; and redness or swelling of the skin overlying the sinus. In infants it typically causes redness and swelling around the eyes. *Contact your physician immediately,* as antibiotics will be necessary. Occasionally the symptoms of bacterial infection are not quite so obvious, and your child will feel quite well but have chronic bad breath and yellow-green nasal discharge. Your physician should be contacted.

PHARYNGITIS (SORE THROAT)   Pharyngitis, or sore throat, is one of the most common symptoms in early childhood. It is usually experienced with any respiratory infection, and it varies from a mild burning or raspy feeling to marked pain, especially on swallowing. If your child has swollen glands in the neck area and pus on the tonsils, *contact your physician* to check for the possibility of a strep infection, which requires antibiotic treatment. If persistent fever accompanies the sore throat and your child feels poorly for longer than two to three days, you should again contact your physician to rule out a strep infection.

Occasionally the sore throat involves areas around the tonsils, resulting in an abscess, which needs *immediate treatment.* The signs of this are excessive drooling and difficulty swallowing.

The tonsils grow markedly larger during early childhood, because this is when they are needed most to fight infections. Enlarged tonsils alone are nothing to be concerned about; they are simply doing their job.

HOME TREATMENT FOR PHARYNGITIS:
- Treatment for a sore throat is mainly supportive. This means giving your child aspirin or Tylenol to reduce pain, letting her drink cold liquids and eat cold foods such as popsicles or ice cream, and letting her suck on hard candy.
- Avoid using anesthetic sprays, because your child can develop an allergy to them.

TONSILLECTOMY AND ADENOIDECTOMY   Remember that the tonsils and adenoids are very important in early childhood—they are responsible for mobilizing forces to fight infections. However, there are occasions when these tissues can present problems. Occasionally, tonsils or adenoids can be so large that they obstruct the airway, especially when the child is very relaxed, as in sleep. Symptoms you might notice are restless sleeping, with snoring. When this condition goes unnoticed for a long time, the child may develop chronic pulmonary problems and possibly even enlargement of the right side of the heart, which pumps blood to the lungs. In such a situation, the need to remove the tonsils or adenoids is obvious.

When your child has chronic or recurrent infections of the tonsils, particularly strep, or when there are chronic peritonsillar abscesses (abscesses of the tonsils, spreading to the surrounding throat tissues), then tonsillectomy is again necessary.

There are some instances, however, when taking out the tonsils or adenoids is a controversial issue. (And tonsils and adenoids do not necessarily need removal together, in any case.) Your pediatrician and your ear, nose, and throat doctor may not agree; and you may need to get several other opinions. Such a controversial instance might be when your child has recurrent chronic ear infections that are unresponsive to medical therapy, and her hearing is affected. Other such cases are those in which the adenoids are causing chronic obstruction of the nasal passageways or there are chronic recurrent swollen glands in the neck. More and more careful study is being given to these medical situations, so that the preferred choice can be more easily determined.

OTHER HEAD, NECK, AND CHEST PROBLEMS

HEAD

ALOPECIA (HAIR LOSS) Alopecia, or hair loss, can be total or partial. It can be caused by many things, some of which we don't understand. One type of alopecia, seen more commonly in infants, is that caused by the child's always lying in one position in bed and rubbing the hair, causing breakage. Another type of alopecia occurs when the child uses hair twirling or hair pulling as a comfort method, gradually picking herself bald. Little girls may suffer hair loss from excessively tight ponytails or braids that create excessive traction on the hair near the forehead. Extremely high fever or severe emotional stress may result in a diffuse hair thinning or hair loss, as does chemotherapy. Occasionally, fungal infections of the scalp as well as seborrheic dermatitis also result in patchy hair loss. Very rarely, hair loss is the result of a congenital defect.

In the case of congenital alopecia, the hair will not grow back. But in most other cases, the hair will return when the cause of loss is removed.

HEADACHE Headaches are extremely unusual in the young child. If your child complains of a headache, or if your very young child holds her head and cries with pain, it is important to *call your physician* for an evaluation. Obviously a headache may occur with a febrile (feverish) illness, which involves many aches and pains—head and muscles included—but most young children do not complain of their head hurting at these times.

INJURIES Injuries to the head are discussed in "First Aid."

MENINGITIS AND ENCEPHALITIS The central nervous system consists of the brain, spinal cord, and its surrounding membranes (meninges). Inflammation of the central nervous system may result from many causes—toxins, infections, tumors. Inflammation involving the brain is called *encephalitis;* if it involves the membranes, or meninges, it is called *meningitis;* and *meningo-encephalitis* refers to a combination of the two.

Encephalitis is characterized by headache, fever, and drowsiness. Nausea, vomiting, seizures, coma, and paralysis may also be present. *Meningo-encephalitis* is essentially encephalitis with the added involvement of the meninges, resulting in a stiff neck as well as the other symptoms of encephalitis. Encephalitis is not contagious. In children it is usually the result of a viral infection or ingestion of a toxin, probably lead. *Call your doctor* for immediate evaluation if symptoms occur. Treatment varies with the cause of the inflammation. The illness may range from mild, with only a headache and fever, to severe, resulting in permanent brain damage or death.

Meningitis is seen more frequently in children than in adults. It is usually the result of infection by bacteria and, occasionally, viruses. The symptoms in an infant include irritability, a high-pitched cry, no appetite, vomiting, drowsiness, and/or a bulging soft spot (fontanelle). A stiff neck is often not present. In the young child the symptoms may be a stiff neck, headache, nausea, vomiting, fever, drowsiness, photophobia (avoidance of light), seizures, and/or evidence of neurological impairment such as blurred vision, tremor, or loss of function. *This disease is a medical emergency.*

In infants and young children the infection often follows several days of a URI or GI upset. After seeming to get better, the child may become sicker, developing some of the above symptoms. In other cases there may be no preceding infection.

The child must be admitted to the hospital for immediate antibiotic treatment. With appropriate treatment most cases will do fine. When effective treatment has been delayed, however, permanent neurologic damage may occur in some of the cases, especially in the younger patient.

Some types of bacterial meningitis are contagious, and protective medication (antibiotics or vaccines) may be necessary for all household and day-care nursery contacts. *Ask your doctor* about this.

EYES

BLOCKED TEAR DUCT   A blocked tear duct is extremely common in young infants. The symptoms are a continually watery, tearing eye with some mucus collecting in the corner, which may cause the eyes to be stuck together after sleep. This is usually not noticed until the child is one to two months of age, since babies do not produce tears until that age. When there is a blockage, it is in the duct that leads from the tear sac into the nose and is usually caused by a plug of cells and mucus. Ninety percent of these will open by six months of age without any intervention by an ophthalmologist (probing of the duct).

If your child has a blocked tear duct, it is important to *consult your physician*. He will probably suggest that you massage the duct frequently in order to clear out the blockage. Before doing massage, be sure to wash your hands so that you don't introduce any bacteria into the eye. Massage by pressing gently downward in the inner lower corner of the eye. Any mucus that collects in the eye can be wiped out with a clean washcloth or cotton ball. If the eye begins to become puffy or red, your physician should be contacted and the massage stopped.

CONJUNCTIVITIS (PINKEYE)   Conjunctivitis, also called pinkeye, is an inflammation of the conjunctiva, which is the membrane lining the inner surface of the eyelids and the eye. The symptoms that can occur include burning, itching, redness (bloodshot eyes), tearing, and pus that causes the lids to stick together. There are many causes of conjunctivitis—eye irritants, such as chlorine in water, smog, or smoke, which can irritate the conjunctiva and result in burning and redness; allergies, which cause redness, itching, and tearing; a foreign body in the eye. Viral and bacterial infections are also common causes of conjunctivitis.

HOME TREATMENT FOR CONJUNCTIVITIS:

- Conjunctivitis caused by chemical irritation is best treated by eliminating the irritant, then washing the eyes out in the same way as you would for a foreign body. Relief can also be obtained by using a long-acting vasoconstrictor in the form of eye drops, such as Visine, Clear Eyes, 20/20, and Murine Plus.
- With viral or bacterial infections, the eye will be bloodshot and have purulent material (pus) that may cause the lids to stick together in the morning. This can be very frightening for a young child and it is important that you maintain a calm and reassuring manner. Unstick the lids by soaking a cotton ball in warm water and wiping the eyes with it gently, using a different cotton ball for each eye. Try to prevent your child from rubbing her eyes if possible.
- These infections are very contagious and can be spread from one eye to the other and to other members of the family. It is important that the child with conjunctivitis have her own towel and washcloth and that her bed linens be washed frequently.
- If eye medications have been prescribed by your doctor, we suggest these methods for giving them. When applying ointments or eye drops, be sure eyes are clear of liquid or dried pus. Use cotton balls and warm water. To apply the medication, hold the child's lower lid down and ask her to look up to the ceiling. Put a line of ointment or set two drops in the lower lid. Have the child close her eyes for two minutes and have a tissue or cotton ball handy for overflow. For a young child who has never had this treatment before, it can be frightening, and you might want to demonstrate it on your own eye first. A method that may work for the infant and toddler is to put the drops in the inner corner of the eye when her eyes are closed and while she is lying flat on her back. When she opens her eyes, the drops will run in. If it doesn't work, you'll need someone to hold her eyes open while you put the drops in. Be prepared for some yelling!

Viral conjunctivitis. The viral infections causing colds or the measles usually result in an accompanying conjunctivitis, a viral conjunctivitis that affects both eyes. They do not require antibiotics and usually clear within two or three days. There is a virus, herpes simplex, similar to that causing a cold sore, which can cause a serious infection in the eye. The eye becomes very red and the child complains of pain and discomfort with the eye. The problem is usually in one eye alone. It may cause decreased vision. When pain and decreased vision are present, *the child should be taken to the doctor immediately.*

Bacterial conjunctivitis. Bacterial eye infections have very much the same symptoms as viral infections, but often occur in only one eye. They require antibiotic treatment in order to clear them up. When your child has conjunctivitis without any signs of a cold, or without signs of clearing after several days, *contact your doctor.* He may prescribe eye drops that need to be given every two hours, or an ointment that lasts longer but interferes with vision. (See the preceding page for suggestions on giving medication.)

INJURIES   Injuries to the eye are discussed in "First Aid."

STYE   A stye is an infection of an eyelash follicle, very much like a pimple in any other part of the body. It begins as a sore, swollen, red area on the eyelid and comes to a head with a pimple in two to three days. It is usually caused by bacteria, commonly staphylococcus (staph).

HOME TREATMENT FOR STYE:

- A stye can be very uncomfortable for a young child, and the discomfort can be alleviated by Tylenol or aspirin and warm compresses to the eye, for five minutes, four times a day.
- It is important that the child be kept from rubbing her eyes as much as possible, as rubbing will spread the bacteria and other styes may arise. It is equally important if you, the parent, have the stye that you wash your hands carefully before handling your infant or young child, as you too can spread the bacteria. There is an over-the-counter medication called Stye, which may help prevent the spread. It will not cure the stye, however.
- If your child has frequently recurring styes, it is important to *discuss this with your physician* for possible underlying causes.

SWOLLEN EYES   Swollen eyes can be the result of allergies, insect bites around the eyes, infections in the sinuses around the eyes, or excess fluids in the body caused by kidney or heart problems. If your child has swollen eyes, it's important to *consult your physician* to establish a cause unless you know for sure it is an insect bite or a known allergy.

VISION PROBLEMS   When a child has a vision problem there are several different signs and symptoms you might notice. One common problem is crossed eyes, although this is difficult to determine with a young infant, because many infants appear cross-eyed at times. However, a child who has permanent turning in (cross-eyed) or turning out (walleyed) of one or both eyes should be evaluated by the doctor. This is called *strabismus,* or *squint,* and usually indicates a problem in the eye muscles. If one eye is "lazy" and does not focus, the child will begin to use the good eye solely, and the lazy eye may lose its vision because of disuse. This is called *amblyopia.* It is a preventable form of blindness, and for this reason *your child should be seen as early as possible by your doctor.*

Fortunately, it takes time for amblyopia to develop. If the problem is picked up by five years of age, the visual defect can usually be corrected. The treatment is patching of the good eye in order to make the child use the weak eye, glasses, or, occasionally, corrective surgery.

Other abnormal movements of the eyes warrant an *examination by the doctor.* If the movements are very jerky or if by two months of age the child is unable to look at any object nine to twelve inches away and follow it for a brief period of time, contact your doctor. In an older child, symptoms of this same visual problem might be a cocking of the head to look at objects, or an inability to manipulate small objects.

If you notice that the pupil of the eye appears cloudy or grayish white, *your doctor should also be contacted.* This is usually the symptom of a cataract. Cataract is extremely rare in young children, but if it is present, it definitely impairs vision.

Sitting too close to the TV or reading a book in poor light will not injure your child's eyes. However, if your child constantly has to hold the book close to her face to read, she may be nearsighted. *Consult your doctor.*

EARS

EARACHE   An earache can result from several conditions. Earaches are most commonly caused by buildup of fluid in the child's middle ear. The middle ear is drained by the eustachian tube, which carries fluid into the nose and throat. In young children this tube is soft, short, and narrow, and easily obstructed by any inflammation or irritation. In infants who are given bottles in bed, milk may back up into the tubes because the child is lying down, and may cause irritation and inflammation.

An inflammation of the tube can also be the result of allergies and colds. The eustachian tube can also become obstructed because of collapse, which can occur when there is excessive negative pressure, such as when flying in airplanes.

When the tube becomes obstructed by inflammation or collapse, fluid tends to build up in the child's middle ear. The buildup of this fluid is called *serous otitis media.* The child may complain of an earache, crackling or popping noises in the ear, or feeling stuffy-headed. You may notice that she does not seem to hear as well, often turning the TV up louder or talking loudly herself.

If your child complains of these symptoms, *she should be evaluated by your physician.* He may prescribe decongestants or, if your child is allergic, antihistamines. Occasional serous otitis media is to be expected during early childhood, and it is nothing to be overly concerned about.

Chronic serous otitis media, on the other hand, is one of the leading causes of hearing loss in young children. It may require prescribed decongestants, insertion of a small plastic tube in the eardrum to allow drainage or, in severe cases, removal of the adenoids if they are blocking the tubes.

Acute otitis media is another cause of earache. A child with serous otitis media is a candidate for an infection, because bacteria or viruses can grow rapidly in the fluid that collects in the middle ear. This results in acute otitis media, which is a painful, purulent or pus-secreting infection behind the eardrum. The majority of these infections are bacterial. This is potentially alarming, since if the infection is untreated, it can progress to involve the mastoid area (behind the ear) and even the brain.

These bacterial infections cannot be seen, but they are usually accompanied by some symptoms. The child may complain and cry, holding on to her ears. She may pull or tug on her ears, be more irritable, or have a fever. If the eardrum ruptures, a purulent discharge from the ear may be noted. When a young infant or baby has had a cold and several days later begins to be increasingly irritable, pulling on her ear, *your physician should be consulted as soon as possible* in order to begin antibiotic treatment if it is needed. It is imperative to treat these infections without delay.

Another cause of earache is an infection of the ear canal, *external otitis,* often called *swimmer's ear.* This is a bacterial infection of an already irritated canal. The canal may have been irritated by an accumulation of water, soap, and shampoos, or from an object's having been poked into the canal, breaking the skin. It often occurs after swimming in pools. This is not because the chlorine is insufficient, but because the chlorine is so strong that it not only kills the bacteria in the water but also kills the normal bacteria in the ear canal, allowing abnormal, infection-causing bacteria to take over.

The symptoms of swimmer's ear are itching of the ear canal and pain when the ear is rubbed or manipulated. (Serous otitis media and acute otitis media, on the other hand, do not cause pain with movement.) The ear can become red, and the canal swells shut. Lymph nodes enlarge behind the ear, and there may be a foul-smelling white discharge.

HOME TREATMENT FOR SWIMMER'S EAR:

- Most of the time, swimmer's ear can be dealt with quite effectively at home if white vinegar is used at the first sign of a problem. Vinegar is very acidic and creates an environment in which bacteria cannot thrive. Using a medicine dropper, fill your child's ear canal with vinegar. Keep her on her side for five minutes to allow the vinegar to remain in close contact with the canal. Then repeat with the other ear. Do this twice a day.
- If possible, have your child avoid swimming until all the symptoms are gone.
- If she must swim, use a white-vinegar rinse in the ear canal after each session.
- If the ear does not respond to the vinegar treatment within two to three days, or if it becomes more painful or red or has a purulent discharge, *contact your physician.* He will probably need to prescribe an antibiotic and steroid combination of ear drops, and in some cases your child will need an oral antibiotic.
- The child who gets recurrent swimmer's ear should take prophylactic ear drops every time she finishes swimming. A one-to-one mixture of white vinegar and 70 percent ethyl alcohol, or 3 percent boric acid and 70 percent ethyl alcohol can be used instead. Alcohol should never be used with an acute (painful) swimmer's ear, since it can worsen the pain.
- Drying the ears carefully after swimming is also helpful. A hair dryer set at a low speed and warm temperature can be helpful in accomplishing this.

The collapse of the eustachian tube from excessive negative pressure (such as on an airplane) can usually be prevented by having your child swallow frequently while you gently pinch her nose closed. With a young baby, give her a bottle to suck on while you gently close her nose for brief periods. The child who has a cold is more likely to have problems with flying and should be given decongestants prior to going on the airplane.

Similarly, a temporary earache can occur from playing outside in cold weather.

On coming inside, the cold air inside the middle ear warms up and expands, causing pain. It helps to chew gum or a cookie or suck on a pacifier. The pain should subside in one to two hours.

HOME TREATMENT FOR MIDDLE OF THE NIGHT EARACHE   Sometimes an earache occurs at night and your child may need help for her discomfort, but not be sick enough to call the doctor until morning. The earache is probably due to swimmer's ear or acute otitis media since serous otitis media doesn't cause severe pain.

- Give your child Tylenol.
- Do not use eardrops.
- Apply heat to the ear with a heating pad, hot-water bottle, or warm, wet washcloth.
- Wipe up any discharge from the ear with a clean wet cotton ball or washcloth. Do *not* attempt to clean the ear canal.
- Call the doctor in the morning.

EAR DISCHARGES   Several kinds of discharges may be noted in a child's ear:

- The most common discharge noted in the young child is that of earwax. Everyone has earwax. It is essential for keeping the ears healthy since it keeps dirt, dust, and insects off the eardrum. It also protects the lining of the ear canal and has been found to have some immunological properties in it that help to kill germs. There is absolutely no need to clean earwax out with anything, even a cotton swab. The wax is constantly being made and gradually works its way out to the opening of the ear canal. Simply wipe your child's ear with a warm, wet washcloth. Putting anything into her ear only serves to make the wax go farther into the canal and sometimes impacts it against the drum, resulting in a hearing loss.

  Young children are often the culprits in impacting earwax, since they love to put fingers and other objects into their ears. If your child seems to have a hearing loss, and you see a large quantity of earwax when you look inside the canal, there are ways to get it out. If the wax is hard, soften it by using baby oil or mineral oil (three drops twice a day for two or three days). There are also over-the-counter wax-softening agents, which are more expensive but not necessarily more effective. One of these is called Cerumenex, which sometimes, if left in for a long period of time, causes a skin reaction. If you use Cerumenex be sure to rinse it out of the ear after twenty minutes.

  Another trick is to apply a warm (not hot) heating pad to the earlobe for twenty minutes to soften and melt the wax. Once the wax is soft it can be irrigated out *gently* with a rubber ear syringe or in a shower, using water that is close to body temperature. If there is a possibility that the eardrum has been perforated (has a hole in it), *do not* irrigate the ear with water. If the earwax does not come out or the child still has difficulty hearing, *contact your physician.*
- A bloody discharge from the ear would indicate that the canal has been cut by a sharp object, or the eardrum has been perforated by a blow to the ear or by a sharp object.
- A child with an ear infection (acute otitis media) and a drum perforation

will have a purulent yellow or white discharge. The discharge will be a dry crust on the earlobe or pillowcase in the morning.
• Swimmer's ear also results in a discharge that is commonly white and foul smelling.

If your child should have any of these discharges from the ear (except earwax), *contact your physician.*

HEARING LOSS   There are two types of hearing loss. One is that caused by *nerve damage,* in which the sound waves reaching the nerve are not carried to the brain to be interpreted. The young child with this type of damage is usually born with it, or she may have acquired it suddenly because of infection of the brain, a high fever, or after taking an antibiotic that causes damage to the auditory nerve.

The second type of loss is a *conductive* hearing loss. This means that there is a blockage somewhere in the ear that interferes with the sound waves' reaching the auditory nerve. The blockage may be something in the ear canal, such as wax, a foreign object, or an infection causing swelling. The problem may also be in the middle ear, where a buildup of fluid is interfering with the sound-wave transmission.

These hearing losses can be either sudden or gradual in their appearance. The early detection of a hearing loss is crucial to the child. Many hearing experts believe that, particularly during the first three years of life, normal hearing is essential to the normal acquisition of language, which is essential to learning. They feel that even a mild hearing loss during these years may be responsible for some of the learning disabilities that show up later in the school years.

Detecting a hearing loss in a young infant can be done now with the use of special tests. However, you as a parent are the best screener for a hearing loss. For example, with an infant under three months of age, observe your child's response to noises such as a handclap, a telephone, or a whistle. The child with normal hearing might blink, open her eyes wide, start sucking, or move about.

The infant who has even a severe hearing loss may coo and gurgle and even develop babbling by around six months of age. However, she will not proceed to the next step, and the babbling will stop shortly after six months.

In an older child, possible signs of a hearing loss are slow speech development, paying little attention to conversations or to someone calling her, turning the TV up very loudly, or talking loudly herself. In the child with a conductive hearing loss, in which fluid builds up in the ear and then recedes, the hearing loss may fluctuate and the symptoms come and go. If you have any suspicion at all that your child is experiencing a hearing loss, *contact your physician right away.* The earlier you can do something about it, the better for your child. An audiologist can test the hearing of very young children, even a newborn, so don't "wait until he is older."

INJURIES   Injuries to the ear are discussed in "First Aid."

NOSE

CONGESTION   If your child's nose is stuffy with no discharge, it is probably blocked by dried mucus and some swelling. Warm tap water or salt water (⅛ tsp. salt per 3 oz. water) nose drops are helpful in getting the mucus out. Administer the nose drops as discussed before. The mucus can be removed by using gentle nasal suction with a suction bulb that you buy in a drugstore. Or if your child is old enough, have her blow her nose by compressing one nostril gently, alternating nostrils with each blow.

If the water nose drops are not effective you may use over-the-counter commercial decongestant nose drops. See "Home Treatment for Colds."

If your child's nose is runny with a clear discharge, she has either a cold or an allergy. If she has a cold, the runny nose may be accompanied by fever, sore throat, or general malaise. If she is allergic, she will probably not have a fever but may have itching and excessive sneezing. The natural remedy for a runny nose is sniffing and swallowing. However, if you or your child cannot tolerate this, then the child can be taught to blow gently as described above. With the young child, you can use a suction bulb. We recommend the use of decongestant nose drops, particularly at bedtime, so that the discharge does not run down into the pharynx and cause an irritative cough. The decongestants are more effective for colds than for allergy, however. The allergic child responds better to antihistamines. *Discuss this with your doctor* and see which antihistamine he would recommend. Some of them may be bought over the counter.

If your child has a runny nose with a purulent (yellow-green pus or mucus) discharge, you will need to *call your physician*. This can indicate a secondary bacterial infection of the sinuses that may require antibiotic treatment. If your child has a chronic purulent discharge, a foreign body may have become lodged in the nose and caused irritation. Discuss this with your physician.

INJURIES   Injuries to the nose are discussed in "First Aid."

MOUTH

BAD BREATH   Good dental hygiene and toothbrushing can eliminate bad breath in almost all cases. However, there are situations that can produce bad breath regardless of toothbrushing. These are infections of the sinuses, mouth, and throat. Bad breath can also be caused by a foreign body lodged in the nose or by tooth decay, and when accompanied by a chronic cough may indicate a chronic lung infection.

CLEFT PALATE AND CLEFT LIP   This is a common congenital malformation caused by the incomplete development of the roof of the mouth (palate). It may also involve the upper lip and extend up into the nose. While usually apparent at birth, small defects may not be detected until later. Its exact cause is unknown, but it is thought to be due to environmental factors combined with a familial predisposition. Genetic counseling is recommended.

Feeding is a problem in infancy and special intervention techniques may be needed before corrective plastic surgery can be done. Treatment requires many professionals—speech therapist, ear, nose, and throat specialist; plastic surgeon; audiologist; nurse. These needs are best met by an interdisciplinary team working together. They will assist the family with feeding techniques and ensure optimal speech and language development.

INJURIES   Injuries to the mouth are discussed in "First Aid."

SORES (LESIONS)   Mouth sores can be caused by bacteria or by a virus or fungus. The fungus that causes mouth lesions is *candida,* or *monilia.* It also causes thrush, which we have discussed previously. The most common viral infection causing sores in the mouth is herpes simplex. The first infection of herpes simplex is usually quite severe and involves the lining of the mouth, the gums, the tongue, and the lips. The sores start as small blisters, which become very red and develop a white ulcerated center. These are extremely painful and the child develops swollen glands in the neck and a high fever. The herpes virus lies dormant in the skin and will recur with fever, illness, stress, or sunburn, but without the severity of the first infection. The subsequent sores are commonly on the lips only and are called cold sores or fever blisters.

A bacterial infection causing sores in the mouth is called trench mouth, but this is extremely uncommon in young children.

The most common sores in the mouth are canker sores. The cause of canker sores is unknown. It is thought that in some people, outbreaks may be due to sensitivity to certain foods; in others, they may be due to trauma, such as biting of the cheek. Canker sores are usually separate, single sores. They can be quite painful and appear as small red ulcers on the lining of the mouth. There is no fever, and the glands do not get swollen as they do with herpes.

HOME TREATMENT FOR MOUTH SORES:
- The treatment for sores in the mouth is basically supportive. The child is uncomfortable. It is difficult for her to eat solid foods and particularly spicy foods. Because she refuses food, she tends to become dehydrated, so it is important to offer her cold fluids frequently as well as cold, bland foods such as ice cream, pudding, and popsicles. You can also give her aspirin or Tylenol for the discomfort.
- If your child continues to have a great deal of pain, and her food and fluid intake is very poor, *your physician should be contacted.* He may prescribe some topical anesthetics that can be used until your child is feeling better— for example, Orobase with a steroid in it or viscous xylocaine. Sometimes a child can tell when she is getting a recurrent herpes, or fever blister. Applying ice to it in the early stages for ten minutes at a time, three times a day, has been found by many to promote faster healing. Others find that applying alcohol with a cotton swab four times a day also speeds healing. However, the child may object strenuously, since it does sting. The sores will crust over but remain visible for approximately one to two weeks.

Fever blisters (cold sores) are brought on by fever, sunshine, or stress. You can eliminate one source by putting a sunscreen on your child when she is at the beach or outside for a long time.

TOOTHACHE Toothaches are preventable if dental hygiene is practiced and regular dental care is begun after two or three years of age. A toothache is caused by a cavity that has progressed far enough to involve the nerves of the teeth or involve an infection or abscess.

HOME TREATMENT FOR TOOTHACHES If your child has a severe toothache accompanied by a fever or swelling of the face, *contact your dentist immediately.* He may need to prescribe antibiotics as well as eliminate the source of the problem. The pain can be relieved by aspirin or Tylenol and hot compresses or a heating pad over the area.

NECK

SWELLING The most common cause of swelling in the neck is swollen glands. These glands are lymph nodes, which are extremely important in producing defenses against infection. The lymph nodes grow quite rapidly during the first few years of life, and when the child has an infection they may double or triple in size. After the infection is over, it may take a month for the lymph glands to return to normal. All children have a few pea-size lymph nodes in their neck or in the backs of their necks throughout childhood. Sometimes the nodes become quite large and tender, usually from a bacterial infection. *Contact your doctor.*

Another source of swelling in the neck is the thyroid gland, although this is unusual in young children. The swelling can consist of a small nodule or cyst; or the whole gland can swell, such as with a goiter. *Contact your doctor* about any inexplicable swelling in your child's neck.

HEART DISEASE Infants and small children do not have heart attacks as adults do. However, babies are sometimes born with heart defects that are the result of problems in the development of the heart in utero. This condition is called *congenital heart disease,* and there are many different types. Some defects are detected at birth, others later in childhood.

There are other heart defects acquired later in life. These are the result of damage to the heart as a result of *rheumatic fever,* a complication of an untreated strep infection. Fortunately, with the use of antibiotics this type of defect is less and less frequent.

There have been major advances in correcting heart defects. And once a defect has been corrected, most children go on to lead active lives. If your child has a heart defect, *consult your physician* about the necessity for antibiotic treatment during dental work or infections.

Because children with heart problems often need to be hospitalized in the early years, we suggest that you read our section on hospitalization in order to minimize the trauma for your child. If your child's heart problem results in a chronic impairment of normal function we suggest reading our section on chronic illness for suggestions on helping him deal with this.

ABDOMINAL PAIN The causes for abdominal pain change with the age of a child. In "Special Situations in Infancy," we discuss colic, probably the most common cause of abdominal pain in infants. Both infants and older children can have abdominal pain with vomiting and diarrhea, as in gastroenteritis with the stomach flu. But it is more common in the infant.

GASTRO-INTESTINAL SYSTEM

Other infections can also produce abdominal pain, even though the abdomen itself is not infected. These are infections such as sore throat, ear infection, pneumonia, and excessive coughing. A child with hepatitis (inflammation of the liver) may also have abdominal pain, usually in the right upper corner of the belly, often accompanied by nausea and vomiting, and sometimes yellow jaundice. Abdominal pain can also be a result of obstruction in the intestine, which will produce colicky pain and vomiting without diarrhea. Appendicitis can also cause abdominal pain, although appendicitis is not too common in children. A child with appendicitis will usually complain about pain around her belly button and characteristically will not want to move. She is likely to have decreased appetite and may have nausea, vomiting, and fever. The abdominal pain of appendicitis usually prevents sleep, whereas abdominal pain from other causes will not.

Ulcers can occur in young children, although uncommonly. The main symptom is usually pain in the upper abdomen, which continues for many days. There may be vomiting of dark material or blood. Abdominal pain can also result from the swallowing of an object which has become lodged in the esophagus, the stomach, or the intestines. Ingestion of poison or drugs can also result in abdominal pain, and should be considered if your child has unexplained symptoms.

Take your child to your physician immediately if she has any of the following: abdominal pain with black or bloody stools or vomitus; a history of having swallowed an object in the last few days; a recent abdominal injury; a possible poisoning.

You would also want to *call your doctor* if your child is experiencing abdominal pain which has lasted for four to six hours, or is accompanied by vomiting and no bowel movements, or is accompanied by yellow jaundice; call too if she has pain in one special part of the tummy, or the pain is accompanied by a bad cough, a sore throat and swollen glands, or a rash.

HOME TREATMENT FOR ABDOMINAL PAIN:
- If the abdominal pain is accompanied by diarrhea and is not severe, you could first treat her for the diarrhea and wait and see. If your child has nausea, vomiting, and diarrhea, treat her for those as well. These symptoms more than likely indicate gastroenteritis and do not require immediate medical attention.

CONSTIPATION   Constipation in infants is discussed in our chapter "Special Situations in Infancy." In a young child, constipation can result in various symptoms. One or several of these may be present: The child has to strain very hard and is unsuccessful in passing a stool. The child has pain with the passage of stools. The stools when passed are usually hard and quite large.

Large, hard stools may tear the anal opening, causing an anal fissure that can be quite painful. This may cause your child to withhold stools to avoid pain. The anal fissure may also result in bright red blood showing up on the toilet paper or the outside of the stool. A severe diaper rash, or an illness involving lesions on the anus such as chicken pox, may also cause pain. Stools can also become quite firm and hard if the child is experiencing dehydration because of decreased fluid intake with an illness, or sweating a lot during high activity in the heat of summer. In the process of being toilet trained, the child may hold back her stools in a power play or out of fear. Some medications can also result in constipation, antihistamines being one of the culprits.

There are some children who seem to have a physiologic tendency toward constipation, and have chronic problems.

If constipation is untreated it can progress, with the accumulation of larger and larger quantities of stool in the bowel. This causes the bowel to stretch like a balloon and lose its elasticity, making it even more difficult to expel the feces. The child may then develop a fecal impaction. When this occurs the child may seem to be having diarrhea, as liquid stool can escape around the impaction and soil the child's pants. The child is not aware of passing any stool until her pants are dirty. When this occurs it is called "soiling." *Prompt medical attention is necessary.* Your physician will look for any possible causes of poor bowel control, and a long-term treatment program will be instituted to retrain the bowels and correct the problem. The medical term for this condition is *encopresis.*

HOME TREATMENT FOR CONSTIPATION:

- If your child is experiencing constipation, it would be helpful to explore all the possible causes before beginning any treatment. Removing problem medications, offering her increased fluids, or waiting for her to feel well enough to take increased fluids may cure the problem.
- Home treatment for simple constipation is primarily dietary change. Although it is important to increase your child's fluids, avoid giving her milk. Milk can be quite constipating, as can other dairy products, such as cheese and ice cream.
- Fruits and vegetables are very effective laxatives, especially if eaten raw, and preferably with their peels. Be sure your child gets fruits and vegetables three to four times a day. However, in some children, apples and bananas can be constipating. This will require some experimenting. Some good fruits and vegetables are prunes, figs, raisins, peaches, pears, apricots, cabbage, celery, and lettuce. The juices from these fruits and vegetables are also good. They can be mixed with water or with sodas such as 7-Up or Sprite to make them tastier. Increasing the bran content of the diet with bran cereals, muffins, graham crackers, whole wheat bread, or oatmeal is also helpful. Try the dietary changes for three days.
- Do not use laxatives, suppositories, or enemas without consulting your physician, as they can irritate the gut and become habit-forming. If your child's elimination has not responded to the dietary changes by the end of the third day, or if she is having a lot of abdominal pain and cramping, *call your physician.*

If your child has an anal fissure, applying an ointment such as zinc oxide or Preparation H to the anus prior to a bowel movement can help alleviate some of the pain. Obviously you also want to keep the stools as soft as possible, using the dietary recommendations above. Healing of the anus can be promoted by having your child sit in a warm bath for fifteen minutes, three times a day.

If your child has a diaper rash, you need to treat that as well as the constipation it may be causing. See our section on diaper rash in "Special Situations in Infancy."

If your child seems to be having extra difficulty passing stools, let her have a firm surface for her feet, to give her increased leverage: Either put her potty chair on the floor or, if she is using the large potty, give her something upon which to rest her feet.

DIARRHEA   Diarrhea is a common symptom in young children. The definition of diarrhea is the sudden onset of runny stools. For diarrhea in infants, see page 000. In the older child with diarrhea, the stools may vary from soft to runny. They are often green in color and have a foul smell.

Diarrhea in children is usually caused by a viral infection of the gastrointestinal system—*gastroenteritis*. It is usually accompanied by a fever, fatigue, irritability, and sometimes vomiting. The lining of the gut, or intestines, which controls absorption of lactose (the sugar found in milk), is injured by the virus. Milk cannot be digested and moves rapidly through the gut, resulting in diarrhea. Fatty foods suffer the same fate. Gastroenteritis usually lasts for three to five days and requires no special medication.

The intestines also react with diarrhea in the presence of infection elsewhere, especially in the very young child, who has an immature gut. Certain foods if taken in excess—vegetables, raw fruit, fruit or vegetable juices, bran, or bran products—can also result in more liquid stools. Decreasing the intake of those foods will correct the problem. Antibiotics, especially ampicillin, are also known to produce diarrhea because they kill the normal gut bacteria. Acidophillus milk or yogurt replace these bacteria. Give these to your child if loose stools develop with antibiotics.

The child should be seen by a doctor immediately if she has any of these symptoms: severe diarrhea (the stools occurring one an hour or more frequently); blood, mucus, or pus in the stools; persistent abdominal pain occurring other than at the time the stool is being passed; dehydration, with decreased urine output, dry skin, dry eyes, sunken eyes, and dry mouth; rapid breathing. *Call your doctor* if she has diarrhea and fever for longer than two days; or diarrhea persisting for more than four to five days; or if she has become incontinent when no longer in diapers.

HOME TREATMENT FOR DIARRHEA:
- Home treatment for diarrhea consists of dietary changes. In the young infant who requires milk, especially the child under six months of age, the dietary changes are suggested in our chapter "Special Situations in Infancy."
- For the older infant and young child, the following dietary changes are recommended: Discontinue your child's milk for one week. Offer her liquids frequently, in the form of Gatorade, Pedialyte, half-strength fruit drinks, half-strength sodas, gelatin water (mix in one quart of water), and popsicles. A bland diet consisting of saltines, dry toast with jelly, bland soups, eggs, noodles, cottage cheese, yogurt, cheese, or cooked fruits should be instituted for at least four to five days or until there is no diarrhea for a day.
- Do not add milk or ice cream until a week has passed. Avoid fatty or greasy foods.
- To avoid irritation around the anus, wash carefully after each diaper change and protect the area with zinc oxide or petroleum jelly. Sitting in a tub of warm water is also soothing.
- Diarrhea can be contagious when caused by a virus or bacteria. It is important that you practice good hygiene, washing your hands after every diaper change.

DISCOLORATION OF THE STOOL There are many circumstances that can cause discoloration of the stool. The most common cause is the ingesting of substances that turn brown feces black. Such substances are iron, Pepto-Bismol, licorice, charcoal, and black-colored dirt. These would usually be no cause for concern. However, black stools can also result from bleeding in the intestines. These black stools are of a different quality—tarry and sticky. If your child begins to pass black stools, it would be advisable to *call your physician*. Save a stool for him to examine, if possible.

Stools can be red after beet ingestion, and undigested vegetable particles can sometimes be seen in the stools. Neither of these are cause for alarm.

NAUSEA AND VOMITING Nausea and vomiting are not uncommon in young children. They usually accompany any gastrointestinal infection, often in conjunction with diarrhea. Vomiting is of special concern in the young infant, who may become dehydrated quickly. The signs of dehydration are dry and sunken eyes, dry skin, dry mouth, and production of very little urine, which is darker in color. *Your doctor should be contacted immediately* if dehydration occurs.

If vomiting occurs with blood in it, or if the vomitus looks like it has coffee grounds in it (actually, old blood) and is accompanied by pain or fever, this may be the sign of an intestinal blockage. Obviously, this too requires *immediate medical attention*.

Persistent vomiting, usually *not* associated with pain or fever, may be the first sign of Reye's syndrome. It is of particular concern if the child has had a URI, influenza, or chicken pox in the past three to seven days. *Call your doctor right away*.

The young child who is very excited, upset, or under stress may also vomit. Sometimes medications that your child is taking cause nausea and vomiting. If your child vomits while on a new medication, *check with your doctor*.

Vomiting may also be a symptom of other problems, such as poisoning, urinary tract infections, meningitis, or head injuries. As discussed elsewhere, all of these require *immediate medical attention*.

HOME TREATMENT FOR VOMITING:

- If your child is vomiting, she should not have solid foods. Offer her clear liquids in small doses, frequently. It is important to keep your child's fluid intake as high as possible, as she is losing fluid with the vomiting. However, do not offer more than one to two tablespoons at a time, as it may just come back up. Popsicles are good in this situation, as are ice chips. When your child begins to feel like eating again, increase the amount of clear liquids and then begin adding gelatin desserts, applesauce, and bland foods until she is feeling better.

URINARY TRACT PROBLEMS This section deals with the five most common urinary tract problems: pain and frequency, retention, wetting, problems with the urine stream, and changes in urine color or odor.

GENITOURINARY SYSTEM

PAIN AND FREQUENCY

These are the most common urinary symptoms in young children. In a child of two and a half to five years, abnormal frequency is urination eight or more times a day.

One cause is a bladder or *urinary tract infection* (*cystitis*). If she wipes from back to front, a young girl can contaminate the urethra (the tube through which urine passes from the bladder to the outside) with the bacteria from the stools. This often results in a bladder infection. In boys, a bladder infection is more often due to an internal problem in the urinary tract, causing blockage and excessive pooling of urine. In both girls and boys, internal structural problems need to be looked for and treated. *Call your doctor.*

A bladder infection can also result from urethral irritation often caused by too much soaping of the area during bathing, and by bubble baths. This can be avoided if your child is encouraged to urinate after her bath, if bubble baths are avoided, and if your child spends less of her bathtime in soapy water. Shampoo and soap her just before she gets out of the tub. These suggestions apply to both boys and girls. No soap should be applied to the genitals at all. The urethral opening can also be irritated by too much heat and humidity, and if your child has this problem it could be alleviated by keeping her in white cotton underpants so that there can be more air circulation. Also, let her sleep without underpants at night.

Urethral irritation can also result from excessive itching from pinworms, which causes your child to rub and traumatize the area. You can relieve her discomfort by having her soak for fifteen to twenty minutes at a time in waist-high warm water to which ½ cup of white vinegar has been added.

Bladder infections are likely to recur in about 80 percent of young girls, requiring close follow-up and treatment. However, most children go on to grow up without any serious complications, so it is not a cause for undue concern. Occasionally, bladder infections can also involve the rest of the urinary tract up into the kidneys (*pyelonephritis*). This is obviously more serious, and the child will have the symptoms of a bladder infection but appear much sicker, with nausea, vomiting, fever, and abdominal or back pain. In some cases this infection can become chronic, resulting in permanent kidney damage and chronic illness with frequent hospitalizations. We suggest reading our sections on chronic illness and hospitalizations if this applies to your child.

Stress and worry can also result in urinary symptoms—usually frequency, with a need to go to the bathroom every fifteen to thirty minutes. There is no cause for alarm. The problem will get better when your child's anxiety decreases.

PROBLEMS WITH THE URINARY STREAM

It is important to watch your child urinate if possible. If the urine comes out in dribbles or there is a very weak stream with frequent stopping and starting, then the possibility of a congenital stricture needs to be checked. The stricture can result from the foreskin being too tight or a narrowing in the urethra or in the valves of the bladder. *Contact your doctor.*

RETENTION

The child of two and a half to five years urinates three to seven times daily. Retention, or lack of urination, can occur because of pain caused by urethral irritation or a bladder infection. Try putting the child in a tub of warm water for about fifteen to twenty minutes. As the water dilutes the urine as it comes out, the pain may be alleviated. If retention persists, *contact your doctor*. Lack of urination can also be a result of dehydration, which we have discussed previously. Or it can be due to a kidney disease known as glomerulonephritis.

URINE COLOR AND ODOR CHANGE

When the urine is bright red or cola colored it must be checked for the presence of blood. This can occur with infections, kidney stones, or trauma to the kidneys or bladder. Urine can also turn pink or red after the ingestion of beets or some medications, such as Pyridium, cascara, and senna. The urine can also turn a brownish color from dehydration or from ingestion of rhubarb, cascara, or senna. A dark yellow color can be the result of jaundice, dehydration, or ingestion of aspirin, sulfa drugs, excessive carrots, or squash. A green urine may be seen after ingestion of a yeast concentrate or vitamin B-complex pills. *Call your doctor* and discuss it with him on the phone to be sure. When there is a urinary tract infection, mothers often suspect it first on smelling their young child's urine. It is a foul smell, unlike the ammonia smell of soppy diapers.

WETTING (ENURESIS)

Obviously, the most common type of wetting in the first five years of life is bed-wetting. At five years of age approximately 15 percent of children still have some bed-wetting; at six years of age 10 percent still have some. In a child who is fairly well trained, you will probably find that nighttime wetting occurs most often when she is overly tired, coming down with an illness, or already ill, or has become cold in the night (cold temperatures result in increased urine production and hence more wetting).

If your child is still wetting the bed at five years of age (and your boy is much more likely to have this problem than your girl), this is really no cause for alarm. However, if either your boy or girl has remained dry for months and suddenly begins wetting the bed again, you should *contact your physician for an examination* for a urinary tract infection. Occasionally, with the introduction of a new sibling into the household or some unusual stress, bed-wetting will recur, then clear up once the stressful situation has improved.

Having accidents and wetting her pants is a common occurrence in the young child under five. This usually happens when she is playing outside and can't make it inside in time. Again, there is no cause for concern and no reason to scold or reprimand your child. However, if your child has been dry in the daytime and suddenly begins wetting or dribbling in her pants on a rather regular basis, it may well be the symptom of a urinary tract infection. She will need an exmination.

HOME TREATMENT FOR BED-WETTING:

- There is no need to buy any of the devices advertised in magazines. They put too much emphasis on the problem and make the child feel less than adequate. The best treatment is "tincture of time."
- The following suggestion may be helpful: Buy a large, rubber-backed flannel pad in a baby department or fabric store. Let your child sleep on top of the pad, with the sheet underneath. Then if your child does wet at night, remove the wet pad, and a dry sheet is available underneath without your having to change the bed.
- Decrease your child's fluid intake after supper, especially avoiding caffeine drinks (remember how coffee acts as a diuretic on you?), such as cola, Mountain Dew, tea, or chocolate. Be sure your child goes to the bathroom at bedtime, and see if you can arouse her enough to go to the bathroom again when you go to bed.
- If your child does wet the bed, make light of it. There is no need for scolding or reprimand. She feels worse about it than you do, as it is quite uncomfortable.

SWELLING AND TENDERNESS   Swelling or tenderness of the external genitalia is usually caused by trauma, or injury. This is discussed in "First Aid." Swelling in the groin or scrotum may also be the result of a hernia and *requires a medical examination*. Sometimes the testicles can get turned on themselves (testicular torsion), causing severe pain and requiring immediate medical attention. A common cause of swelling in the scrotum in infant boys is a *hydrocele*. This is a collection of clear fluid above the testicle, usually due to pressure during delivery. It clears on its own in six to twelve months and requires no surgical intervention.

PENIS   The most common problems with the penis in the young infant are due to circumcision. This is discussed in "The Daily Care of Your Infant." The uncircumcised child can have difficulties with the foreskin. Sometimes if the foreskin has been pulled back, it remains stuck. This can cause a constriction and subsequent swelling and pain. This requires *contacting the physician immediately*. If the foreskin is swollen and red, it is usually due to irritation caused by bathing with soap. Washing with water alone will usually clear this up.

There is usually no need for retracting the foreskin when bathing your child, as he usually urinates in the bathtub and has an erection prior to urination. With an erection the foreskin retracts normally. Remember, however, that the foreskin is not able to be completely retracted until the child is several years old. It is a gradual process. Don't force it. If any discharge, pus, rash, or pustule is seen on the penis, *your physician should be contacted* for possible antibiotic treatment.

VAGINA   Vaginal bleeding is usually due to lacerations from an injury or a foreign body. Treatment for this is discussed in "First Aid." Newborn vaginal bleeding is usually due to the mother's estrogens, which simulate a slight menstrual period in the baby. A vaginal discharge in a young child is usually a reaction to the retention of a foreign body in the vagina. This is usually quite foul smelling and the vagina is often inflamed. The foreign body can often be seen with a flashlight if your child is placed in a knee-chest position on the bed so that her buttocks are in the air. Wait a minute or two and the vagina will relax and fall open, allowing fairly good visibility. If there is a foreign body, your *physician should be contacted.* You should not try to remove it yourself.

Discharge can also occur with inflammation of the vagina caused by retention of sand or dirt, pinworm infestation, or bubble bath irritation. Infection by a fungus (monilia) will also result in inflammation and a cheesy-white discharge. This requires antibiotic treatment.

HOME TREATMENT FOR VAGINAL INFLAMMATION   Most inflammations of the vagina can be relieved by vinegar soaks (½ cup vinegar to a tubful of waist-high warm water) for fifteen to twenty minutes, several times a day.

BLISTERS   Friction blisters usually occur on the child's foot, especially since he cannot tell you realistically whether new shoes fit. If he really likes the shoes, he will suffer agony in order to get them.

S   K   I   N

PREVENTION AND TREATMENT OF BLISTERS:
- When your child is breaking in a pair of new shoes, have him wear heavy socks and cover rubbing areas with adhesive strip bandages to prevent blisters. You can also put a piece of moleskin tape onto the tight places in the shoe itself, to cushion those areas.
- If a blister does occur, do not open it. It will dry out and peel in one to two weeks. Put a strip bandage over the blister until it is healed.

BURNS   Heat and chemical burns are discussed in "First Aid."

SUNBURN

Sunburn is a result of prolonged exposure to the sun, and the best treatment is prevention. Children should always wear a sunscreen and not be exposed to the bright sun for a long period of time. If sunburn is severe the child will blister (second degree burn) and may have fever, dizziness, and visual problems (can't keep the eyes open or look at the light). You will need to *call your physician,* as these can be serious complications.

Prevention of sunburn also has the added benefit of preventing skin cancer in adult life, so the use of sunscreens on a regular basis gives your child that added protection. Ask your pharmacist about the different types of sunscreens. If your child is fair, such as a blond or redhead, he will need much more protection than the brunette child, whose skin is darker.

HOME TREATMENT FOR SUNBURN:
- Treatment for serious sunburn is discussed in "First Aid."
- Home treatment for minor sunburn consists of treating the pain, which usually begins six hours after exposure and lasts for forty-eight hours. Cool baths with Aveeno or other colloidal oatmeal (1 cup per tub), or baking soda (½

cup per tub) are often helpful. Careful, the colloidal oatmeal can make the tub slippery.

- No ointments or creams should be applied the first day, because they cause retention of heat and a worse burn. They are very helpful, however, when peeling begins, as they are quite soothing. Avoid ointments containing topical anesthestics (the -caines—such as Solarcaine, Lanacane, and Americane), as they may irritate the skin and also sensitize it.
- Aspirin is helpful for relieving the pain.

INFECTIONS

BOILS

The boil is an infection of a skin pore or hair root caused by the *Staphylococcus* germ. It starts as a tender red lump, which gradually comes to a head after five to six days. It can be quite painful until it drains.

Boils can usually be handled at home, but you would need to *call your doctor* for any of the following: the boil is accompanied by fever or has red streaks spreading out from it; the child is an infant (with a higher possibility of a blood infection, or sepsis); there are several boils (more than two); the boil is on the face (a higher risk of severe complications, with spread of infection to the brain); the boils are recurrent; or the boil has come to a head and has not started draining (and needs lancing).

HOME TREATMENT FOR BOILS:

- Home treatment for boils is warm compresses for fifteen minutes, three times a day, to relieve the discomfort. Aspirin or Tylenol is also helpful.
- Wash the area with antibacterial soap (such as Dial or Safeguard) and shampoo with an antibacterial shampoo (such as Dial shampoo). This is especially important if your child has recurrent boils.
- A boil will usually drain itself, but if it does not, it may need to be lanced. *Your physician should be contacted* about this.
- When the boil is draining it is quite contagious and is spreading staph germs. At this time you should cover the boil with a sterile 4″ × 4″ gauze pad and change it three to four times a day, washing with antibacterial soap and cleaning the surrounding skin with 70 percent alcohol each time.
- Keep your child's linens separate and wash them with Lysol or with chlorinated bleach (if they are colorfast).

FUNGAL INFECTION

The most common fungal infection of the skin in childhood is ringworm. Ringworm is not caused by any type of worm, but is simply a fungus that seems to like some skins and not others. It is not a sign of poor hygiene and you do not need to be embarrassed if your child has ringworm. It starts as a small, red, circular spot that gradually enlarges and develops a raised border, with scaling and lighter color in the center. It may often be confused with eczema or other skin problems. If you are not sure what it is, you should *contact your physician* to confirm your suspicions. You also need to contact your physician if the ringworm is on the scalp, as it is very difficult to treat there.

HOME TREATMENT FOR RINGWORM:
- In order to treat ringworm at home you need Tinactin cream, which can be bought over the counter. Apply the cream two times a day for several weeks, until the ringworm has disappeared. You should expect some healing within a week, but it may take many weeks before it totally disappears.
- If the spot is not healing by the end of the week, *call your physician*, as it may not be ringworm.
- It is important for your child not to scratch ringworm, as it can cause a bacterial infection, such as impetigo. Keep her nails short and wash her hands as frequently as possible with antibacterial soap.
- Ringworm is not as contagious as impetigo. There is no reason your child cannot go to play group, nursery school, or the day-care center.

IMPETIGO

Impetigo is a superficial skin infection usually caused by the *Streptococcus* germ but occasionally by the *Staphylococcus* germ. It appears as a small red sore with a golden colored crust. It spreads easily but can be quickly treated. It won't permanently scar, but the child may have a blemish on the skin for six to twelve months. Impetigo is a very common occurrence, especially in the summer months when the skin is less protected by clothing. Insect bites are common, and the skin can be broken by cuts or scratches. A frequent site for impetigo is under the nostrils when the skin is irritated by frequent nose blowing during a URI.

HOME TREATMENT FOR IMPETIGO:
- One of the best treatments is prevention. Bathe your child with an antibacterial soap, such as Dial or Safeguard, every day in the summer to help keep down the bacteria. If your child has insect bites or any cuts on the skin, it is important to wash carefully around those areas.
- If your child gets impetigo in spite of this, you will need an antibacterial ointment such as Betadine or Bacitracin, which can be bought without a prescription. Before using the ointment, however, it is important to get the crust off of the sore, as the germs are collected underneath. To do this, soak the child in a warm bathtub for twenty minutes and gently wash in the area with antibacterial soap. This should remove the crust. Don't scrub, as this hurts and may in fact spread the infection by rubbing the germs in further. Don't worry if there is some bleeding when the crust comes off. If you start working on the crust as soon as it begins to appear, you will have less trouble than if it has grown and become harder.
- After the crust has been removed, put the antibacterial ointment on four times a day, being sure to wash the sore with antibacterial soap before the ointment is applied.
- Keep your child's fingernails short and wash her hands frequently with antibacterial soap. Remind her not to pick at the sore, as this causes further spreading. Exposure to air promotes healing, but if your child is a picker, cover the sore with an adhesive bandage.

- Because of the contagiousness, keep your child's linens and towels separated from the rest of the family's. They should be washed with Lysol or a chlorinated bleach to kill the germs.
- Keep your child out of large groups of children, such as the day-care center, play group, or nursery school, until the sores have been treated with antibiotic ointment or oral antibiotics for twenty-four hours.
- It should improve within forty-eight hours and be well in a week.

PROBLEMS WITH IMPETIGO:

- You will need to *call your physician* about the impetigo in the following circumstances: If the child is an infant; if the impetigo is severe (four or more sores); if the child has any signs of blood in the urine or kidney probblems; if the impetigo has spread to the family; or if the impetigo is the kind that begins as blisters (this is usually due to *Staphylococcus* and will not respond to home treatment). You'll need to call too if it gets worse on home treatment or isn't completely well after one week of treatment. Your doctor will often prescribe oral antibiotics in these cases.

WOUND   If your child has had a cut or a wound you can expect an area of pinkness or redness around the edge approximately ⅛ inch, or .3 cm, across. The pain and swelling peaks on the second day and can be helped with warm saltwater compresses (½ teaspoonful salt per pint of water). Dry well with a hair dryer set on the warm setting.

If a wound has been contaminated there is a greater chance of infection, and this will usually occur within twenty-four to seventy-two hours. If the wound is infected, the area of redness will be wider and increasing in size with time. It will be quite tender, and there may be fever or may be red streaks coming out of the wound area. If this occurs, *contact your physician as soon as possible.*

INSECT BITES

CHIGGERS

The chigger is a very small mite, which is also known as a red bug. (The red bug itself can often be seen in the center of the sore.) It prefers areas bound by clothing, such as the waist. The bites result in severe itching.

HOME TREATMENT FOR CHIGGER BITES:

- The best treatment is prevention, by using insect repellants or by bathing immediately after being outside.
- A-200 and Cuprex will kill the larvae but will not relieve the itching.
- The itching regimen should be used to give relief.

LICE

Lice are not prejudiced; they can be found in every social class. They are very much a fact of life. The louse is a very small (1/16 inch) bug. It is gray to black in color, and it scurries around rapidly. If your child has lice you are more likely to notice head scratching and see only white spots on the hair shaft, rather than seeing the bugs. These spots are called nits, and they are clusters of louse eggs. They resemble dandruff, but they are sticky and difficult to remove from the hair shaft, unlike dandruff which can be shaken off. They prefer the warmest areas of the scalp, usually behind the ears and on the back of the neck.

HOME TREATMENT FOR LICE:
- Over-the-counter remedies for lice can be effective. These are A-200, Rid, Cuprex, and Triple X. Follow the instructions carefully. Repeat in one week since they may not be 100 percent effective in killing the eggs.
- At the time of treatment be sure to wash the child's linen, clothing, brushes, and combs in hot water with Lysol or chlorinated bleach (if it's colorfast). Vacuum or wet-mop your child's room at the same time to get any nits off the floor. Items that can't be washed can be set aside for two weeks. Lice can't live for over three days off the human body. Nits hatch in about one week.
- Nits can be removed from the hair by loosening them with a one-to-one vinegar and rubbing alcohol solution and combing with a fine-tooth comb. Unfortunately, some maintain their stickiness and need to be picked off—a tedious job. Follow this with a shampoo. If the nits are not removed, they will open in one to two weeks and result in a reinfection.
- Eyelashes often contain the nits, and obviously they cannot be treated. Putting petroleum jelly on the eyelashes every night at bedtime for two weeks will prevent the louse larvae from growing once the nits hatch, in one to two weeks.
- Check other members of the family. If there are any scalp sores, rashes, or excessive itching, they should also be treated. The whole family may *feel* itchy once lice are found in a child, even if they don't have lice. This is a normal psychological reaction to the idea of bugs in your hair!
- If your child does not respond to over-the-counter medications, you may need something stronger and should *consult your physician*, who will probably prescribe Kwell, a more potent type of medication.

SCABIES

Scabies is a skin irritation caused by a very small mite similar to the red bug, or chigger. It too knows no social boundaries. It is spread by person to person or from cloth items to persons. The mite burrows under the skin, causing a raised, red tunnel which may blister. The mite lays its eggs in the tunnel, especially in warm spots such as between fingers, in elbow and knee creases, in groin creases, and in armpits. The burrow is very itchy and will have many scratch marks over it because of the vigorous scratching that results.

HOME TREATMENT FOR SCABIES:
- The itching can be treated with the itching regimen, but your child will probably also need a prescription medication, such as Kwell.
- Scabies is quite contagious, but the incubation period is one month. So when it occurs in a family, or with close contacts, everyone should be treated at

the same time as the patient. Your child can return to his large-group activities such as play group, day care, or preschool after one treatment with Kwell.

• After the treatment, be sure to wash all linens and clothing in hot water, which will kill the mites. Any items that are not washable should be put away for at least five days, as mites cannot live off of the body that long.

RASHES, ITCHING, AND SWELLING   Because itching is a common symptom with many skin disorders, and the treatment for the itching is the same for each disorder, we will discuss this treatment now in order not to have to repeat it each time.

HOME TREATMENT FOR ITCHING:
• Itching is thought to be caused by the release of a chemical called histamine in the skin cells. If the child has a disorder that results in itching, it may be relieved for long periods of time by taking a hot bath. The heat from the bath causes the cells to release their histamine, depleting the histamine for six to eight hours, during which there is no itching.
• There is intense itching during the hot bath; the child should remain in the bath until the itching has subsided. The problem can be helped by adding Aveeno, or any other colloidal oatmeal (1 cup per tub), to the bathwater. The colloidal oatmeal can be slippery. Baking soda (½ cup per tub) or cornstarch (1 cup per 4 cups cool water added to the bathwater) are other alternatives.
• Itching is also relieved by taking aspirin or antihistamines (an over-the-counter product such as Chlor-Trimeton does nicely).
• Apply cold compresses or an ice bag, or rub the itching area with an ice cube, for fifteen minutes for immediate but short-lived relief.
• Calamine lotion also is a tried-and-true remedy. Lotions containing calamine plus another substance such as antihistamine are not any more helpful and can result in sensitizing the child to the antihistamine. Topical anesthetics containing benzocaine (such as Dermoplast, Lanacane, Americaine, and other -caine type of names) are not recommended, for the same reasons.
• Remember to keep your child's nails short. Keep hands and skin clean using an antibacterial soap such as Lifebuoy, Dial, or Safeguard.

CHILDHOOD ILLNESSES RESULTING IN RASHES

Illnesses causing rashes are discussed on pages 397–400.

DIAPER RASH

Diaper rashes are discussed in "Special Situations in Infancy."

ECZEMA

Eczema is discussed on page 389.

HIVES

Hives look like mosquito bites. They are pinkish to white spots with raised borders and flat centers, which are intensely itchy. Hives are a result of an allergic reaction to almost anything, even to heat, cold, or stress. If the hives are accompanied by systemic reactions, such as shortness of breath, wheezing, or dizziness, *your physician should be called immediately*, as this is an emergency.

Sometimes hives can be a result of drug reactions. If your child is taking a medication and begins to have hives accompanied by joint pains or swelling, stop the medication and *call your physician*. One medication that is commonly used with children is ampicillin. This causes a fine, red rash on the trunk and occasionally the face in about 10 percent of children taking it. This is not an allergy to ampicillin or penicillin, but a reaction to the toxins causing the infection. It usually occurs three to six days after ampicillin has begun. If your child does develop a rash on ampicillin it is important to *contact your physician* to discuss it. If it is the rash we mention, he will probably tell you to continue using the medication.

If hives are accompanied by fever or any joint swelling or pain, *your physician should be contacted*. This may be the result of an infectious process going on in the body. Otherwise, if your child has hives you can begin some detective work at home. See what precedes the presence of the hives. Avoid the substances if you do find the culprit. When your child has hives, relieve the itching by using the regimen we have recommended.

NEWBORN RASHES

Newborn rashes are discussed in "Your Newborn Baby."

POISON IVY AND POISON OAK

Poison ivy is a skin reaction to the oil of the plant. This is called a *contact dermatitis*. The reaction can be expected twelve to forty-eight hours after the contact. The skin will get itchy and red and may develop blisters or some oozing. Typically it appears on exposed skin following a period of being outdoors in a field or forest.

HOME TREATMENT FOR POISON IVY AND POISON OAK:

- The best treatment is prevention. Teach your child to recognize the plants and make sure any property where your child might be unattended is free of poison ivy or poison oak. Remember that even in the winter when the leaves are off, the plant can cause a reaction.
- If your child has been outside in a field or forest, give her a good shower, or wash exposed areas at least three times with soap. If bathing facilities aren't available, use an alcohol-based cleaning tissue (such as Alcowipe) for washing. Your child's clothing and your dog's fur can also contain the plant oil, so these also need to be washed.
- If your child does get poison ivy, the itching regimen is in order. *Call your physician* if the poison ivy is severe, if your child can't sleep, or if she has a previous history of a severe infection. In these cases your doctor may prescribe steroids.
- Sometimes poison ivy can become infected with bacteria and turn into impetigo because of scratching. Washing your child with antibacterial soap and

keeping her nails short and clean would help to prevent this. But should it occur, *your physician should be contacted.*

PRICKLY HEAT

Prickly heat is discussed in "Special Situations in Infancy."

MUSCULOSKELETAL SYSTEM (BONES, JOINTS, AND MUSCLES)

BOWLEGS AND KNOCK-KNEES   Children's legs normally progress from being bowlegged when they first walk to becoming knock-kneed by around three to five years of age. This is no cause for concern. Your doctor will check for these things on the routine visits. The only concern would be if this development does not follow the normal age sequence, if the problem is severe, if it occurs only on one side, or if there is a family history of short stature and bowlegs or knock-knees. (This is usually due to rickets, or insufficient vitamin D, resulting in soft bones and poor growth.)

FLAT FEET   Flat feet are normal in infancy and early childhood. With walking, the arch muscles strengthen and the arch continues to form but is not totally developed until adulthood. Arch height varies from individual to individual. One in seven children never develop an arch. Loose-jointed and heavier children often appear somewhat flat-footed. However, many children who appear flat-footed can be seen to have an arch when their feet are hanging free while sitting or while they are standing on their toes.

The only cause for concern and treatment for flat feet is if they are very painful or stiff, or so severe that the foot turns over on itself.

HIP DYSPLASIA   *Congenital dysplasia of the hip* means abnormal development of the hip joint. This may be a complete dislocation or may be a situation in which the head of the femur (the long bone in the upper leg) is partially displaced (subluxed) from its position in the joint. The cause is unknown, and it is more common in girls than boys. It is also associated more frequently with breech presentation, suggesting that uterine position can be a possible contributing factor.

Your doctor will check your child for hip dysplasia during the first year of life, since it is during this time that it can be found and treated most easily. If it is found, the child will be referred to an orthopedic surgeon, who will recommend devices that keep the hips in a position in which the joint can develop more normally. This usually takes only six weeks if the child is young. However, if the child is older before the hip problem is picked up, the treatment takes longer to correct.

INGROWN TOENAIL   Ingrown toenail is a result of tight shoes or of failing to cut a toenail straight across. Both of these can result in pressure to the underlying skin, with redness and pain at the nail edge.

HOME TREATMENT FOR INGROWN TOENAIL:
- Pain from an ingrown toenail can be relieved by soaking in warm salt water (1½ tablespoons of salt per quart of water) for fifteen to twenty minutes, three times a day, which shrinks tissues and may prevent infection.

- While soaking, massage the skin away from the nail to relieve the swelling.
- If the skin is infected, use an antibacterial soap, such as Dial or Safeguard.
- If the corner of the nail is irritating the skin, cut the nail back.
- After soaking, lift the nail up with dental floss and wedge a small amount of cotton between the corners of the nail and the underlying skin. This allows the nail to grow over the skin rather than into it.
- For comfort, let your child wear sandals or go barefoot. If shoes must be worn, protect the area by taping cotton to the toe to prevent rubbing.

LIMP   A limp in young children is usually due to ill-fitting shoes; a sliver, a cut, or bruise on the bottom of the foot; or an intramuscular injection in the thigh or buttocks. If your child's limp is not due to one of these causes, and especially if it is accompanied with fever, swelling, or decreased range of motion in the joint at the hip, knee, or ankle, you should *call your physician* for an evaluation.

PAIN AND SWELLING   The most common cause of pain in muscles is from strenuous exercise or a viral illness. This is known as *myalgia*. The most common cause of pain in joints, or *arthralgia*, is the result of an injury or a viral illness. In children, the *"nursemaid elbow injury"* is not uncommon. This is a result of a sharp pull or yank to the child's arm, usually to keep him from falling or stepping out in front of a car. The elbow snaps, and a small arm bone becomes dislocated at the elbow joint. This can be quite painful. The child refuses to use the arm and keeps the elbow bent. There is no visible sign of injury, but the child will refuse to reach up for anything, even a lollipop. You will need to *take your child to the physician* in order to have the bone put back in place, which is a simple maneuver. The physician can teach you this maneuver so that if it happens again, and it well might, you can treat your child at home.

Joint pain accompanied by swelling, heat, and redness is *arthritis* and usually is a result of an infection or an immune disorder. *Your physician should be called as soon as possible.*

HOME TREATMENT FOR MUSCLE AND JOINT SORENESS:
- Home treatment for soreness in muscles and joints is hot baths and Tylenol.
- Aspirin should be avoided, as it may relieve underlying arthritis and delay diagnosis.

PIGEON-TOES (INTOEING)   Intoeing, or pigeon-toes, are common in childhood. If your child is pigeon-toed, you should take him to the physician for an examination so that you can understand the reasons for it. There are three possible reasons for pigeon-toeing: *Metatarsus adductus* (hooked foot), *tibial torsion*, and *femoral torsion*.

Pigeon-toeing in infancy is usually due to the metatarsus adductus, or hooked foot, as we mentioned in our chapter on the newborn. This is due to positioning in utero, and it will get better on its own. In rare cases it might need casting.

Tibial torsion becomes apparent during the first year of life and is a result of a bone (the tibia) in the lower leg failing to rotate from an inward position to an outward position during the first year. This causes the foot to turn inward. It can be seen when the child is sitting and the leg is dangling. The outer ankle bone will be in front of the inner ankle bone. This usually gets better on its own, but your doctor may prescribe some methods to keep the feet turned out while the child is asleep, such as tying the pajama sleeper heels together or tying shoe heels together so that the feet turn outward. In rare cases, a special splinting device may be necessary.

Femoral torsion occurs when the large bone (the femur) in the upper leg twists inward at the hip, again resulting in the lower leg turning in and pigeon-toeing. This is commonly seen at around five to six years of age and is usually outgrown, requiring no treatment.

SHOE PROBLEMS   Shoe problems are a very common concern with the young child who is just beginning to walk.

PREVENTION OF SHOE PROBLEMS:

- *Barefoot* is the best situation for any foot, especially a young child's. However, he also needs protection from sharp objects and the cold, so a shoe is often necessary. Buy shoes that are as close to being barefoot as possible. They need to be flexible, for freedom of movement, and soft. Buy them large enough to be loose around the toes. The soles should be flat and rubber in order to prevent slipping and skidding. High-top shoes are unnecessary.
- If your child needs special party shoes (and how we mothers love to get our little girls dressed up in patent leather shoes), they will have slick soles, which often slip. This can be remedied by putting adhesive tape on the soles, the toes, and the heels. This is necessary only until friction itself has rubbed the soles rough. Or you can very lightly sandpaper the soles, toes, and heels.

34

F I R S T A I D

EMERGENCY TREATMENT FOR THE ILL OR INJURED CHILD

C O N T E N T S

INITIAL ASSESSMENT	**461**
INJURY OR ILLNESS	**461**
ABDOMINAL INJURY	461
Blow to the Abdomen	461
Open Wound	461
Swallowed Foreign Body	461
*AMPUTATION	461
BITES AND STINGS	462
Animal or Human	462
Bee, Wasp, Hornet, or Yellow Jacket	462
Black Widow Spider, Brown Recluse Spider, Scorpion	462
Marine Animals	462
Biting Fish	462
Stings	462
Tick	462
*Snake	462
Nonpoisonous	462
Poisonous	462
*BLEEDING, SEVERE	463
Arterial	463
Venous	463
BONES: FRACTURES/DISLOCATIONS	463
*BURNS	464
Thermal	464
Chemical	464
Sunburn	464
CHEST INJURY	464
Open Wound	464
Rib Injury	464
*CHOKING	464
COLD EXPOSURE	465
Frostbite	465
Hypothermia	465
*COMA	465
*CONVULSIONS (SEIZURES, FITS)	465

* Major Emergencies

*DROWNING   465
EAR   465
    Foreign Body   465
    Injury   465
*ELECTRIC SHOCK OR LIGHTNING   465
EYE INJURY   466
    Chemical   466
    Foreign Body   466
    Trauma   466
EXTREMITIES (ARMS, LEGS, HANDS, FEET)   466
    Bruised or Jammed Finger or Toe   466
    Finger Caught in a Ring or Small Object   466
    Smashed Finger or Toe   466
    Sprain   467
    Strain   467
    Torn Nail   467
FAINTING   467
GENITALS   467
    Foreign Body   467
    Injury   467
*HEAD INJURY   467
    Laceration   467
    Severe Injury   467
    Mild Injury   468
*HEAT REACTIONS   468
    Heat Exhaustion   468
    Heatstroke (Sunstroke)   468
MOUTH INJURIES   468
NOSE   468
    Nosebleed   468
    Foreign Body   468
    Injury   468
*POISONING   468
    Ingested   468
    Inhaled   469
*SHOCK   469
SKIN INJURY   469
    Bites and Stings   469
    Bruises   469
    Burns   469
    Cut or Scratch   469
    Foreign Body   469
        Fishhook   469
        Sliver   469
    Puncture Wound   469
    Scrape or Abrasion   469
TEETH   470

INITIAL ASSESSMENT

If your child should be injured or become suddenly ill, do not lose control yourself. Stay calm, even if you are not. You may feel lightheaded, because when you are afraid your body reacts by rushing blood away from the brain and into the muscles to prepare for action. Don't scream. Speak in a calm, reassuring voice, and you will find that this helps you as well as your child.

In many of these situations, you will need to use the techniques of *mouth-to-mouth resuscitation* and *external cardiac massage*. If you do not know these techniques now, we *urge* you to TAKE A CPR CLASS, where you will be able to learn and practice them.

Take time to assess the situation. If the injury seems serious, do the following:

1 Check the child's BREATHING. If he is having problems use mouth-to-mouth resuscitation.

2 Check his PULSE (for a baby, below the left nipple; for an older child, at the large artery on the side of the neck). If no pulse can be felt, use external cardiac massage.

3 Consider the possibility of a BACK or NECK INJURY, and do not move the child in that event. If injury is suspected, see "Fractures/Dislocations."

4 Check for BLEEDING. Serious bleeding should be controlled by using methods on page 463.

5 Check for signs of POISONING—chemicals lying around, or burns or stains on the child's mouth. If present, see "Poisoning."

6 Consider the possibility of SHOCK if the child has been seriously injured. See "Shock."

INJURY OR ILLNESS
ABDOMINAL INJURY

BLOW TO THE ABDOMEN

• If the child has had a severe blow to the abdomen, he may have injured his internal organs. Internal bleeding may result, requiring immediate intervention.

• These are symptoms of serious injuries: thirst, shock, listlessness, bruising of the abdomen or flank, bluish discoloration of the navel or flank, abdominal pain and swelling, urinating or vomiting blood. Call your physician or the rescue squad.

OPEN WOUND

• Control bleeding by applying direct pressure on the wound with gauze or a clean cloth. *Call the rescue squad.*

• If a knife or other weapon protrudes from the wound, *do not* remove it; it may bleed uncontrollably.

• If organs or intestines protrude, *do not* replace them. Cover with a moist pad or cloth.

• *Do not* give the child anything to drink. Treat for shock.

SWALLOWED FOREIGN BODY

• Most swallowed foreign bodies make it to the stomach and are passed in normal bowel movements in 3–4 days. If possible, check all bowel movements for the object until it is passed (not as easy as it sounds). *Do not* give the child laxatives.

• Call your physician if your child has swallowed any of the following: a metal object the size of a nickel or larger, a sharp object, or a battery (because of toxic chemicals inside).

• Call your physician if your child has the following symptoms: difficulty with swallowing, increased salivation, gagging, discomfort in the throat or chest, excessive coughing, choking or difficulty with breathing, abdominal pains, or vomiting.

• If the foreign body hasn't passed as far as you know in 7 days, don't worry; you probably just missed it. However, if any symptoms such as vomiting or abdominal pain develop, call your physician.

AMPUTATION

• If a limb or extremity is amputated, control the bleeding as directed in "Bleeding" section.

• Call your physician immediately, and (following his instructions) carefully rush the child to the hospital.

• Also, immediately wrap the amputated part in a wet clean cloth or a sponge. Place it in a plastic bag or plastic wrap; pack this in ice and take it to the hospital with you. It is sometimes possible for amputated parts to be reattached.

• Call ahead so they are prepared to act as soon as you arrive.

BITES AND STINGS

Animal or Human

• Wash the wound with clean water and soap for 5 minutes. Do not use antiseptics or ointments.

• If the skin has been cut or penetrated, particularly if there is a deep puncture wound, contact your physician. A tetanus shot or antibiotics may be necessary, particularly for human bites.

• If possible, in the case of animal bites, catch the animal (carefully) and keep it alive for observation for rabies.

Bee, Wasp, Hornet, or Yellow Jacket

• If the child is bitten by a bee, hornet, wasp, or yellow jacket, there is a possibility of an anaphylactic reaction (an allergic reaction causing shock). Check for difficulty with breathing, wheezing, tightness of the chest or throat, hives, swelling, or itching elsewhere. This is especially important if the child has a history of allergies. If a symptom is present, proceed as follows:

• If the bite is on the arm or leg, put a constricting band between it and the heart, tight enough to make the veins stand out but loose enough to allow a pulse.

• If the stinger is still present, remove it by scraping it off with a fingernail. Apply an ice cube to the site.

• If an anaphylactic kit is available, give the child subcutaneous (under the skin) epinephrine. If not, give a dose of any medication containing antihistamine (Dimetapp, Benadryl, Chlortrimeton, Coricidin, Actifed). Get the child to an emergency room immediately.

• If there is no anaphylactic reaction and the bite is painful, scrape the stinger off with a fingernail. Use tweezers or a sterile needle if necessary. Rub the area with a cotton ball soaked in a meat tenderizer solution, if possible. Otherwise, an ice cube is helpful.

Black Widow Spider, Brown Recluse Spider, Scorpion

• Apply a venous tourniquet between the bite and the heart, tight enough to make veins stand out but loose enough to allow a pulse. Apply an ice pack to the bite. *Call your physician.*

• Catch the spider or scorpion if possible and bring it to your physician.

• Do not let the child walk or exercise. Use mouth-to-mouth resuscitation if necessary.

Marine Animals

BITING FISH • Wash the bite with soap and water for 10 minutes. Contact your physician, if there is a laceration or puncture wound, for consideration of a tetanus shot.

STINGS Whether or not your child has a systemic reaction to the sting, do the following:

• Apply a venous tourniquet between the bite and the heart, tight enough to make the veins stand out, but still loose enough to allow a pulse.

• Remove any stingers present by wiping them off with a towel or cloth. Neutralize the toxin reaction by applying a strong solution of meat tenderizer or ammonia to the area. For a stingray wound, soaking in very hot water helps to destroy the heat-sensitive toxin. Remove any spines or barbs as you would a sliver.

• Remove the tourniquet after applying the neutralizing chemical and removing the barbs. This means after 15–20 minutes, or after an hour if you are using hot water. Keep the tourniquet on if generalized symptoms develop, and *call your physician.*

• After removing the tourniquet, wash the area with soap and water for 10 minutes. Call your physician if the laceration requires sutures.

Tick

• If imbedded, soak and cover it for 30 minutes with nail polish, petroleum jelly, or margarine, and the tick may loosen its grip and back out. If not, try holding a cotton ball soaked with gasoline or alcohol on the area for 3–5 minutes. Or, carefully touch a lighted cigarette to the tick's back. (Don't do this before washing off the oil or gasoline you've already tried!) If this isn't successful, grasp the tick's body with tweezers and roll it forward until it loosens its grip. If the head is left in the skin, remove it as you would a sliver. Wash the site with soap and water afterward.

• Observe the child for fever or rash in the following week. Call your physician immediately if either occurs (rarely, ticks transmit Rocky Mountain Spotted Fever).

Snake

NONPOISONOUS • Treat it as a puncture wound, and contact your physician concerning the need for a tetanus shot.

POISONOUS • Work quickly. Apply a constricting band above the bite (not too tight). If the veins do not stand out, the tourniquet is too loose. If the hand or foot turns white or blue or the pulse disappears, the tourniquet is too tight.

• Get to an emergency room or to a doctor as soon as possible. Keep the child quiet. Do not let him walk or thrash about (which increases blood flow). During transportation keep the bite lower than the rest of the body, if possible.

• If you are more than 30 minutes from a hospital or physician and you are sure the snake was poisonous (fang marks present), and there is swelling in the area or the child's tongue is quivering, some venom must be removed. Apply a tourniquet, as noted above. Keep the patient quiet. Clean the wound with alcohol. Sterilize a knife or razor blade over an open flame. Make a shallow vertical incision ½″ long over each fang mark (do not cut deeply or crisscross).

• Try to squeeze out the venom for 1–2 minutes. Using a suction cup or your mouth (if it is free of open sores), draw the venom from the wound. *Do not* swallow the venom. Do this for at least 5 minutes and preferably 20–30 minutes. Rinse the skin with water after each suction.

• Wash the wound thoroughly with soap and water. Apply cold compresses or ice wrapped in a cloth. *Do not* pack the wound in ice.

BLEEDING, SEVERE

ARTERIAL

Act quickly. If blood is spurting or pumping from the wound, it is arterial.

1 Lay the child down with feet elevated (10″–12″).

2 If you know arterial pressure points, apply strong direct pressure to the artery between the wound and the heart. Otherwise, apply sterile gauze or a clean cloth (a towel or handkerchief) over the wound and apply direct pressure, with the palm of the hand if necessary.

3 If the bleeding cannot be controlled by direct pressure, as with an amputated or mangled extremity, then saving the life is the primary consideration. Apply a tourniquet as follows:

a. Use a ½″–2″-wide piece of cloth (a necktie will do), and place around the limb slightly above the wound. If a joint is nearby, position the cloth above the joint.

b. Wrap the cloth tightly around the limb and tie a half knot.

c. Place a 4″–5″ piece of sturdy wood or small knife on the knot and complete the knot on top of it.

d. Twist the stick or utensil in a circle until the bleeding stops.

e. Tie the stick in place so it won't unwind before you reach the hospital. *Do not loosen* the tourniquet until medical care is available.

VENOUS

If the blood is not spurting with the heartbeat, it is venous.

1 Have the child lie down with his feet elevated 10″–12″.

2 Apply direct pressure to the wound for 10 minutes, using the palm of the hand and sterile gauze or a clean cloth.

3 While doing this, elevate the injured part higher than the heart unless there is evidence of fracture.

4 After the bleeding is controlled, bandage the dressings tightly in place. Do not remove the bandage until the child is under medical care.

BONES: FRACTURES/DISLOCATIONS

Any deformity of an injured part usually means a fracture or a dislocation. Do not move the part without splinting it.

• If the bone is showing through the skin, cover the wound with a sterile dressing or a clean cloth.

• *Shoulder or arm:* Make a sling of triangular cloth.

• *Leg:* Use pillows, boards, or magazines for rigidity; pad with cloth. Do not tie the splint too tightly. Immobilize the injury in the position found.

• *Neck Injury:* Do not move the child until the rescue squad arrives with the appropriate brace or board. Put sand bags, bricks, or books on each side of the head so it cannot be turned. If the child is in danger and must be moved, support the neck and keep the head and back straight.

• *Back:* Don't move the child until the rescue squad arrives. If the child must be moved, move as in the neck injury with head, neck, and back kept straight.

BURNS

THERMAL

1 If the child's clothes are on fire, throw him to the ground with flames uppermost and cover him immediately with a blanket, rug, or coat. If these are not readily available, throw yourself over the child quickly. The flames will die without burning you.

2 Immediately put the burned part in cold tap water (*not ice water*) or pour cold tap water over it for 30 minutes. This will relieve the pain. *Do not* break any blisters. If the limbs are burned, raise them higher than the child's heart. Cover the burn with a non-adhesive dressing such as a Telfapad or plastic wrap. *Do not* use ointments, greases, or powders. (The juice of the aloe vera plant is not harmful and may be soothing for minor burns.)

3 If the burns are extensive, get the patient to the hospital or to the doctor at once. If the burns are limited, call your doctor.

4 Treat for shock, if it is present.

CHEMICAL

• Immediately remove the contaminated clothing and rinse the exposed part of the body with clear water for 20 minutes, using the shower or tub. *Do not* rub the skin.

• Cover the burns with a clean nonadhering dressing or cloth such as a Telfapad or plastic wrap. Call your doctor.

SUNBURN

• *Do not* put ointments or creams on for the first 24 hours since it increases heat retention.

• Call your physician if sunburn is severe (blisters, fever, dizziness).

• Give cool baths with Aveeno oatmeal (1 cup/tub) or baking soda (½ cup/tub) to relieve pain. Aspirin or Tylenol may be given, also. Avoid topical anesthetics since they may be sensitizing.

CHEST INJURY

OPEN WOUND

• If a knife or other weapon protrudes from the wound, don't remove it before reaching the hospital. It could bleed uncontrollably.

• If the wound is open, seal the opening as soon as possible using plastic wrap or aluminum foil (non-porous). Make it airtight with adhesive tape or plastic wrap. *Call the rescue squad.*

• If part of the chest bulges out when the child breathes out and the chest wall collapses on breathing in, there are several broken ribs. Hold a pillow or towel over the chest to keep it from bulging, and lay the child down on that side.

• Treat for shock.

RIB INJURY

• If the child has pain when he breathes or when the rib area is touched, take him to the hospital.

• To relieve some of the pain, splint the chest by bringing his arm on the injured side against his chest, with the fingers touching the opposite collarbone. Hold it there.

CHOKING

If the child can breathe, speak, or cough, *do nothing*. Encourage him to cough and reassure him.

If the child can't breathe or cough, or if he passes out:

• Open his mouth and see if there is an object in the back of the throat that can be removed with fingers or tweezers (this is rare). Do not put your finger deep into the mouth, because it can force the object to go down further. *Call the rescue squad immediately.*

• For an infant, place him face down over your arm, with his chest on your palm and his head lower than his trunk. Rest your arm on your thigh to brace it. Give four rapid, firm blows with the heel of the hand between the shoulder blades. If this is not successful, roll the child over and, keeping his head down, give four chest compressions as in CPR.

• Treat a larger child in the same way, except that you will have to kneel on the floor and drape him across your thighs to give back blows. If these are unsuccessful, proceed to the Heimlich Maneuver.

HEIMLICH MANEUVER

1 Stand behind the child. Place your arms around him, just below the rib cage. Make a fist and put it thumb-side-in against the bottom of the breastbone. Cover your fist with your other hand.

2 Give a bear hug with a sudden upward jerk at a 45° angle, to squeeze the air out of the chest

and blow the lodged object out. Give four quick thrusts.

If this maneuver is unsuccessful after three tries, begin mouth-to-mouth resuscitation.

COLD EXPOSURE

FROSTBITE

• Frostbitten skin is cold and white, and feels numb or tingly.
• Warm the frozen part against the body until you get the child indoors. Then immerse the frozen part in warm water or cover it with warm compresses. When it becomes flushed, discontinue warming.
• Move the affected part to stimulate circulation. Keep frostbitten toes or fingers separated with a clean cloth or dry gauze. Call your physician.
• Have the child drink a warm drink, such as soup, tea, or cocoa.

HYPOTHERMIA (BODY TEMPERATURE LESS THAN 95° F)

• Symptoms of hypothermia are persistent or violent shivering; slow, slurred speech; drowsiness; trembling hands.
• Get the child to a warm place; remove her clothes and put her in a sleeping bag or bed. Warm her body through skin-to-skin contact with you, and if possible add another person.
• Give the child warm sweet drinks or soup. Call your physician.

COMA

• If the child is unconscious or difficult to arouse, consider a possible head injury or neck injury. *Call the rescue squad.*
• Check for possible poisoning. Bring the bottle to the doctor if there is one.
• If breathing is slow and weak or if the skin is bluish, begin mouth-to-mouth resuscitation.

CONVULSIONS (SEIZURES, FITS)

• Lay the child on his side on a soft surface, with his head lower than his hips (put a pillow under his torso). Remove any objects from his mouth. Do not force anything into his mouth.
• Breathing stops momentarily and a bluish color is commonly seen during seizures. Resuscitation is usually not necessary. The seizures should stop after 5 minutes. Report it to your physician.
• If the seizures persist longer than 5 minutes and the child is blue, *call the rescue squad.*

DROWNING

• *Call the rescue squad.*
• Give mouth-to-mouth resuscitation as soon as possible. Continue it until the child is brought to a medical facility. Children have survived long immersions, especially in cold water.
• Vomiting is common. If it occurs, immediately turn the child on his side or face-down to keep liquid from entering a lung.

EAR

FOREIGN BODY

• If a live insect is in the ear canal, kill it by pouring in alcohol. Remove it by irrigating the ear canal with water (a shower or the kitchen tap will do nicely).
• For any other object, turn the child's head so that the ear canal is pointed toward the floor, and then shake the head (*gently*). The object may fall out. If this does not work, call a physician.
• Do not put any device into the ear canal, including the child's finger.

INJURY

• Call your physician about any injury to the ear, especially if any of the following occur: swollen earlobe, decreased hearing on the affected side, bleeding from the ear canal, earache, or if a pointed object has been inserted into the ear canal.

ELECTRIC SHOCK OR LIGHTNING

• *Break contact.* Turn off the power if possible; or separate the child and the current using a dry, nonmetallic object such as a broom, a chair, or a cushion. *Call the rescue squad.*

• Begin mouth-to-mouth resuscitation and cardiac massage if breathing or heart has stopped.

EYE INJURY

CHEMICAL

• For a chemical splash in the eye, immediately wash out the eye with plain water (in the bathtub or shower, with an eye cup, or by putting the side of the child's face in a pie pan), and continue for 15 minutes. Do not use drops or ointment.

• Bandage the eye shut with a gauze pad to relieve pain.

• *Call your physician.*

FOREIGN BODY

• A particle in the corner of the eye can be removed gently with a moistened cotton swab or cotton ball.

• For a particle under the lower lid, pull the lower lid out and touch it with a moistened cotton swab or cotton ball. If that doesn't work, pour water on it.

• For a particle under the upper lid, have the child open and close her eyes with her face submerged in water (use a bathtub, sink, cake pan, or pie pan).

• For a young child, hold her over the sink and pour water in her eye with her eyelids opened. *You may need help to hold her!*

• Call your physician if the child's vision has not returned to normal after resting for an hour, if tearing and blinking persist for more than 2 hours, or if pain or the sensation of grittiness persists. A serious infection can occur if a foreign body remains embedded.

• Bandage the eye shut with a gauze pad to relieve pain.

TRAUMA

• Call your physician if the eye has been injured and there is a cut on the eyelid or eyeball, persistent pain, blurred vision in either eye, double vision, or constant tearing, or if the object that hit the eye was a high-speed object (such as a rock from a lawn mower ricochet, or a baseball).

• If the eyeball has been cut, *do not* wash out the eye. If it is bleeding, apply a pressure dressing. If not, bandage the eye shut with a gauze pad. Keep the child's hands away from his eye.

• If the child has an object penetrating his eye, *do not* try to remove it. Call your physician or the rescue squad. Hold a paper cup or glass over the eye to keep the child's hands away from it.

• If there is only bruising and minor swelling, apply an ice bag or cold compresses for 20–30 minutes. If the child develops small hemorrhages in the white of the eye or a black eye, she will need to be examined.

EXTREMITIES (ARMS, LEGS, HANDS, FEET)

BRUISED OR JAMMED FINGER OR TOE

• Soak the bruised hand or foot in ice water for 1 hour, removing it every 15 minutes to prevent frostbite.

• Check the range of motion at the joint. If decreased, call your physician.

• You may splint the injury by taping the finger or toe to the next digit for immobilization. Do not tape them too tightly, or they may swell.

FINGERS CAUGHT IN A RING OR SMALL OBJECT

• If the object is sharp, do not try to remove it by pulling on it. Try to cut the object in two with wire cutters.

• Remember that the finger will swell between the enclosing object and the fingertip. Try removing it by lubricating the finger with soap, jelly, or grease. If this is not successful, soak the finger in cold water for 5 minutes. Then hold the finger in the air for 5 minutes and massage downward toward the ring. Repeat this three times and then try grease again.

• If none of these are successful, call your physician.

SMASHED FINGER OR TOE

• A smashed finger or toe, with a blood clot under the nail, is extremely painful. Soak the hand or foot in ice water for 1 hour, removing it every 15 minutes to prevent frostbite (putting a toy or marbles in the water helps pass the time).

• Give the child aspirin or Tylenol. If blood is oozing from under the nail, encourage it by squeezing it or milking the finger. This will ease the pressure buildup under the nail and decrease the pain.

• After soaking, keep the hand or foot elevated to decrease swelling. If the clot is extensive and the pain is severe, a hole may need to be put in the nail to release the blood. This is usually done with a red-hot paper clip or wire. Call your physician for advice and instructions.

SPRAIN (BRUISING, PAIN, AND SWELLING OF TISSUES AROUND A JOINT)

• Immobilize the area with a blanket, a splint, a pillow, or an elastic bandage. Do not bandage too tightly, since sprains swell.

• Elevate the injured part and apply cold compresses or an ice bag covered with a towel to decrease swelling.

• Keep the child off the injured part.

• If there is marked pain or swelling, call your physician.

• Give Tylenol for pain.

STRAIN (PAIN FROM PULLED MUSCLE)

• Have the child rest. Apply warm, wet compresses.

• Give Tylenol for pain.

TORN NAIL

• A torn fingernail or toenail is very painful. Hold the child on your lap and comfort her while holding the affected finger or toe firmly with cloth or gauze.

• After the child has calmed down, take a look. If there is a small tear, just leave it alone and tape it with an adhesive strip bandage. If it is torn almost through, cut along the line of the tear with nail scissors or clippers. If the whole nail is hanging, remove it; it is a site for infection if taped on.

• Soak the finger for 20 minutes in cold water. Apply an antibiotic ointment such as Bacitracin or Neosporin and cover it with a nonstick dressing such as a Telfapad for 3 days.

• Soak the finger once a day in warm salt water (½ tsp. to 1 pint) for about 15 minutes. Rebandage with a new pad and antibiotic ointment. On the 4th day, a new bandage, without antibiotic ointment, is all that is needed.

• Within a week the soaking and bandaging can be stopped. It will take 1–2 months for a nail to grow back.

FAINTING

• Keep the child flat, and turn his head to one side.

• Loosen the clothing around his neck and remove any objects from his mouth.

• Call your physician.

GENITALS

FOREIGN BODY

• If the child has a foreign body lodged in the vagina, it may cause bleeding or a foul-smelling discharge. Call your physician if you suspect one.

INJURY

• Control bleeding by direct pressure with gauze or a clean cloth.

• Call your physician if there is bleeding for longer than 10 minutes after direct pressure, if there is difficulty with urinating, if there is vaginal bleeding, or if there is a possibility that an object has penetrated the vagina.

• Otherwise, wash the area by placing the child in a tub of warm, slightly soapy water for a few minutes then apply an ice bag or cold compresses for 30 minutes. Treat cuts or abrasions as listed under injuries to the skin.

• If there is pain with urination because of the injury, put the child in a tub of warm water to dilute the urine as it is passed.

HEAD INJURY

LACERATION

• Scalp wounds bleed excessively, even though the injury may be slight. Apply gentle, direct pressure with gauze or clean cloth to control bleeding.

• Prop the child on a pillow to keep his head and shoulders higher than his heart to help stop blood flow. *Do not* bend his neck. If there is *any* suspicion of a neck injury, keep him flat.

• When blood flow is stopped, bandage with gauze in place.

• Call your physician.

SEVERE INJURY

These are symptoms of *severe* head injuries: unconsciousness, vomiting, convulsions, paralysis of a limb, oozing of bloody or watery fluid from the ears or nose, unequal pupils, skull deformity, persistent headache. *Call your physician and the rescue squad immediately.*

• Keep the child lying down with his head turned to one side so that fluid may drain out in case he vomits.

• If an object has pierced his skull, *do not* remove it. *Call the rescue squad.*
• Watch for signs of shock and treat it.

MILD INJURY

• Reassure the child and keep her quiet.
• Call your physician for instructions. Follow them carefully since the seriousness of a head injury cannot always be determined immediately.
• Use an ice bag to reduce swelling.

HEAT REACTIONS

HEAT EXHAUSTION

• The symptoms of heat exhaustion are moist skin, muscle cramps in the limbs and abdomen, normal or subnormal temperature, dizziness, fainting, weakness.
• Cool the child with fans or a moist cloth in a cool room. Give her sips of salt water (1 tsp. salt per glass) or Gatorade every few minutes for 1 hour.
• Follow this treatment with a sweetened beverage.

HEATSTROKE (SUNBURN)

• Heatstroke is caused by overexposure to the sun or by excessive heat exposure even without the sun. It is a *very serious* condition and can be life threatening. The skin is hot, flushed, and dry, and the body temperature is extremely high—105° F or more. There may be fainting, delirium, or unconsciousness.
• Cool the child as rapidly as possible, in a cool place. Put her in a tub of cool water or wrap her in wet, cool towels or sheets. Use a fan if possible.
• If the child is conscious, give her cold water with 1 teaspoon of salt to a glass, or give her Gatorade.
• *Call your physician or the rescue squad.*

MOUTH INJURIES

The mouth heals beautifully in 3–4 days, with rare exceptions.
• Apply ice to the wound, or have the child eat a popsicle or drink ice water. Give aspirin or Tylenol if pain persists. Avoid spicy foods. Rinse the mouth well after eating.
• Call your physician if any of these conditions exist:

1 The wound continues to bleed longer than 10 minutes.

2 The child has fallen on a sharp object such as a pencil, stick, or spoon.

3 There is an injury to the back of the throat, or the soft palate.

4 There is a cut that is split open and deep.

• Pressure can be applied to wounds of the tongue or cheek by pinching both sides of the tongue or cheek together with a gauze pad.

NOSE

NOSEBLEED

• Have the child sit down and lean forward, so the blood won't go down her throat and so she can spit it out of her mouth.
• Gently pinch the lower part of the bleeding nostril (or nostrils) closed for 10 minutes, and apply cold (ice water) compresses to the nose. If the bleeding persists, pack the nostril with cotton and pinch for 10 more minutes.
• If the bleeding still persists, call your physician.
• If the nose appears broken, follow the above instructions. Once the bleeding has stopped, continue applying cold compresses to minimize swelling and call your physician.

FOREIGN BODY

• Have the child blow her nose vigorously while pinching the unblocked nostril. Call your physician if this is unsuccessful.

INJURY

• Call your physician if these symptoms occur after a nose injury: the skin is split open, clear fluid continuously drains from the nose, breathing is blocked on one side, the central dividing wall inside the nose is crooked, the nose looks broken or crooked, or a nosebleed does not stop after 20 minutes of direct pressure.
• Otherwise, apply an ice bag or cold compresses to the nose for an hour. Give aspirin or Tylenol as necessary for pain.

POISONING

INGESTED

• Find out what has been ingested and *call the poison control center, physician, hospital, or rescue squad promptly.*

• If so instructed, drive the child to a medical facility. Bring the package or container with intact label, and a pan to collect vomitus to show to the doctor.

INHALED

• Get the child into fresh air. If he is not breathing, begin mouth-to-mouth resuscitation. *Call the rescue squad.*

SHOCK

• Serious injuries produce shock and the child with such an injury should be observed for the symptoms: nausea, dizziness, cold, clammy skin, listlessness, breathing change (weak, irregular).
• *Call your physician or rescue squad.*
• Lay the child down on a blanket and cover him with a blanket.
• If there is *no* neck or back injury, elevate his legs about 12″ unless it is painful.
• *Do not* let him eat or drink.

SKIN INJURY

BITES AND STINGS

• See "Bites and Stings" section.

BRUISES

• Apply cold compresses for 20–30 minutes for a severe bruise. *Do not* put ice on the skin.
• If the bruise is from a wringer-type injury or from catching a limb in the spokes of a wheel, *call your physician immediately.*

BURNS

• For skin burns, including sunburn, see "Burns" section.

CUT OR SCRATCH

• If the wound is superficial, wash it thoroughly with soap and water for 5 minutes. Rinse it well, and expose it to the air if possible.
• If the wound is in an area that will get dirty, cover it with an adhesive strip bandage or gauze for 12 hours.
• If the wound is deep, apply direct pressure to the cut to stop the bleeding. If the bleeding does not stop after 10 minutes of direct pressure, or if the deep cut is on the face or hand, call your physician for possible suturing.
• If the part is amputated, see "Amputation" section.

FOREIGN BODY

FISHHOOK • Do not attempt to remove a fishhook from a child's face. Call your child's doctor immediately. If a fishhook is imbedded elsewhere, do the following:

1 Push the shank through the skin until the point appears, then cut off the barbed end with clippers or pliers in order to remove the shank from the wound.

2 Wash the wound with soap and water for 10 minutes and bandage. Call your physician for a possible tetanus shot.

SLIVER • Slivers can be removed with a needle and tweezers that have been sterilized with alcohol or a flame. Wash or soak the skin with soap and water before and after removing the sliver.
• If the sliver is deeply imbedded, or is difficult to see and to remove (such as glass), it would be considered a puncture wound and your physician should be called, to consider a tetanus shot.
• If the child is very sensitive and the sliver is very painful, numb the area with an ice cube before removal.
• If a sliver can't be removed, soak the extremity in warm soapy water for 15 minutes, 3–4 times a day. It will often work its way out. If it doesn't, and becomes infected, consult your physician.

PUNCTURE WOUND

• Call your physician to consider a tetanus shot. Soak the wound in hot water and soap for 15 minutes.

SCRAPE OR ABRASION

• Wash the abrasion with soap and water for 5 minutes (soak in the tub if he won't let you touch it). Swab it several times with wet gauze to remove all the dirt. Some particles may need to be removed with tweezers. Tar can be removed by rubbing with petroleum jelly. Pieces of loose skin should be cut off with clean scissors. Then rinse the wound well.
• If the wound is small, expose it to the air. If it is large, cover it with a nonsticking dressing. If the

wound was dirty, call your physician to consider a tetanus shot.

• Change the dressing after 12 hours. After 24 hours, leave the wound open for faster healing.

• No antiseptic ointments or sprays are needed. Tylenol or aspirin can be given for the pain.

TEETH

• If a tooth has been knocked out and it is a permanent tooth, put it in cold milk (any kind will do) or a specimen of the child's saliva to take to the dentist. It can be put back in.

• Call your dentist if the teeth are chipped, if there is a fracture line, if the tooth is displaced, or if the tooth becomes sensitive to hot or cold fluids over the next few days.

• If the tooth is jarred and the gum is bruised, treat the injury locally with ice or a popsicle. If any of the teeth are slightly loose, feed the child a soft diet for 3 days.

• Aspirin or Tylenol can be used for pain.

APPENDICES

A Parent's Guide to Children's Toys

It is unfortunate that the quality of toys in America seems to be going down rather than up. For instance, good wooden toys are hard to find. King Plastic rules the toy industry. One wonders whether some day in the future it will be impossible to find children's wooden blocks anymore because they've all been replaced by plastic imitations that are cheaper to manufacture!

Worst of all, fewer and fewer toys are designed to stretch a child's imagination and creativity. More and more they violate the dictum that the play should be in the child and not in the toy. Battery-powered atrocities continue to flood the toy stores.

So if many of today's toys are shoddy and uncreative, what can you do? Answer: Make your own toys for your children! We urge you to look carefully at Appendix E, "A Parent's Toy Factory." The simple but creative handmade toys described there will be better for your youngster than many of those you can buy in a store, and have an important added feature: You made them yourself and that is a very special bonus for your child!

The development of electronic and computerized toys is one bright hope for the future of the toy industry. Already on the market are thinking and spelling games for young children and electronic baseball, football, and basketball games for older children. We foresee the day when we will have a myriad of delightfully creative thinking games for preschoolers; when we will teach science, history, logic, and almost anything else by computerized games. Watch for these wonderful kinds of toys and games. They have much to offer our children.

There is one aspect of toy buying on which we want to urge you parents to stand firm. Every year, from Thanksgiving to Christmas, your children will be deluged by the annual TV blitz of toy ads. And you will be besieged by tearful little faces, saying, "Oh, Mommy, you've got to get me Dr. Dreadful's Mink-Lined Torture Chamber for Christmas!" Nine out of ten of the toys advertised on TV are the worst sort of junk. Don't be pressured into buying your child something you think is uncreative and junky, and probably expensive to boot.

Pick out the toys you want your child to have; don't let the TV commercials do it for you. Choose toys you think are creative and durable, with a long play value. And if your child at Christmas complains bitterly that he didn't get Dr. Dreadful's Torture Chamber, use the feedback technique. Tell him you have chosen the toys you think he will have the most fun with for a long time, and let it go at that.

However, the toy scene today is not completely bleak. There are a few companies still producing well-designed and durable toys with lots of play value. While we might fault one or two of their toys, in general we can recommend their whole line.

These are the companies we recommend:

Fisher-Price specializes in toys for babies and for children under the age of six. The whole Fisher-Price line is well designed and durable; the toys all have excellent play value.

Tonka Toys specializes in cars, trucks, and earth-moving equipment. These are well designed and will withstand very hard usage by a preschooler.

Childcraft, which in our opinion is one

of the top toy companies in the United States, is available in retail stores, but sells mostly by mail order.

Other toy companies that sell through retail outlets make individual good toys; we will mention some on the following pages.

Interestingly, some of the best toy companies in America sell only by mail order. Those of you who live in rural areas or in small towns, where the selection of toys in accessible stores is limited, should welcome the opportunity to buy good toys by mail order. But even those of you who live in big cities can in this way obtain toys that you might not be able to find in local stores.

All the following companies are excellent. Their catalogs are usually free, and we suggest you send for a catalog from each. Many of them have a toll-free number.

CHILDCRAFT, 20 Kilmer Road, Edison, New Jersey 08817. Phone: (800) 631-5652. Childcraft has a good Dome Climber and the Toddler's Gym.

CHILD LIFE PLAY SPECIALTIES, 55 Whitney Street, Holliston, Massachusetts 01746. Phone: (617) 429-4639. This top-notch company specializes mainly in outdoor play equipment: tree houses, jungle gyms, firemen's gyms, and a ladder jungle. You can also get the play equipment in the form of a kit, put it together yourself, and save 20 percent.

THE CHILDREN'S DESIGN CENTER, Geyser Road, Saratoga Springs, New York 12866. Phone: (800) 833-4755. Superb design characterizes all Children's Design Center toys.

COMMUNITY PLAYTHINGS, Rifton, New York 12471. Phone: (914) 658-3142. Community Playthings are used a great deal by nursery schools, which says a lot for the sturdiness of their construction!

CONSTRUCTIVE PLAYTHINGS, 1040 East 85th Street, Kansas City, Missouri 64131. Phone: (816) 444-4711. The firm stocks a wide variety of good toys, including the dome climber and indoor gym house.

DEBO TOYS, 24401 Redwood Highway, Cloverdale, California 95425. Phone: (707) 857-3693. This company makes a set of handcrafted natural wood animals for ages three to six.

DIFFERENT DRUMMER WORKSHOP, Solon, Maine 04979. Phone: (207) 643-2572. Different Drummer's brochure states: "We take pride in the quality of our work and will gladly repair or replace any toy which breaks in the course of normal play." Good wooden toys are hard to find, so this company is a particularly valuable source.

EDUCATIONAL TEACHING AIDS, 3905 Bohannon Drive, Menlo Park, California 94025. Phone: (415) 322-9934. Lock 'N' Stack Blocks, Superblocs, Educubes, Snap Wall, dollhouse and dollhouse furniture, puppets and Versa-tiles (educational games in reading readiness, language arts, and math) are all of top-notch quality for preschool children.

GALT TOYS. This company is one of the best in England, and they now have a branch in the United States at 63 Whitfield Street, Guilford, Connecticut 06437. Phone: (203) 453-3366.

JONTI-CRAFT EDUCATIONAL PLAY EQUIPMENT, 416 Summit Avenue South, Sauk Rapids, Minnesota 56379. Phone: (612) 251-7503. This company specializes in wood toys.

LEARNING GAMES, INC., Box 820-C, North White Plains, New York 10603. Phone: (914) 428-7336. This company puts out the extraordinary Cuisenaire Home Mathematics Kits, as well as Quick Master Chess, an excellent way to teach a child as young as five how to play chess.

MILO PRODUCTS CORPORATION, Grantham, Pennsylvania 17027. Phone: (717) 766-6451. This company manufactures Dado, the modular space block. These precisely cut, oil-finished, birch plywood blocks allow children to build almost anything their imaginations can conceive of.

NOVO TOYS, 11 Park Place, New York, New York 10007. Phone: (212) 255-

1061. Novo's catalog is an encyclopedia of fun toys that are also educational.

PLAYPER CORPORATION, Box 312, Teaneck, New Jersey 07666. Phone: (201) 836-7300. This company manufactures only one piece of play equipment: Fun Covers. Start out with empty half-gallon milk cartons, tape Fun Covers around them, and you will wind up with a miniature city that preschool children will love. A most ingenious idea, with enormous creativity and play value for your child.

THE TOY WORKS, Middle Falls, New York 12848. Phone: (518) 692-9666. This firm specializes in antique-style dolls with features hand-printed on natural fabrics. You can purchase them ready-made, or more inexpensively in sew-it-yourself kit form.

WOODEN TOYS BY R. VOAKE, Toymaker. Thetford Center, Vermont 05075. Phone: (802) 785-2837. Another craftsman of quality wooden toys. These toys are built for rugged play, and are usually big enough for a young child to ride on.

Now let's proceed to an analysis of what toys are appropriate and helpful for your child at each age and general stage of development. Remember, of course, that each child is different and you must allow for individual variations and taste. We also will not repeat toys that have already been named in our previous chapters.

INFANCY (FROM BIRTH UNTIL THE CHILD LEARNS TO WALK, USUALLY AROUND THE END OF THE FIRST YEAR)

Here are some good toys that can aid babies greatly in their sensory exploration of their environment:

BABY TRAINER (Childcraft)

BUSY BOX or ACTIVITY CENTER WITH A NUMBER OF THINGS TO DO (Fisher-Price; Gabriel). For roughly ages three to eighteen months. One of the best and most practical toys ever designed for the baby and toddler. You will find this toy especially helpful if you're taking your baby on a long trip.

CRADLE GYM (Fisher-Price; Children's Design Center)

CRIB MOBILES, bought or homemade (Fisher-Price has some excellent ones)

MODULAR CRIB ROD (Childcraft)

MUSICAL CAROUSEL OR MUSICAL MOBILE (Fisher-Price)

MUSICAL PULL TOYS THAT HANG FROM THE CRIB (Fisher-Price)

RATTLES (Fisher-Price; Children's Design Center)

RUBBER SQUEEZE TOYS (Fisher-Price; Children's Design Center)

SMALL, SOFT TEXTURE BALL (Calico Clutch Ball, Children's Design Center; Childcraft's Clutch Ball)

SOFT, CUDDLY TOY ANIMALS OR DOLLS (Fisher-Price; Childcraft)

SPONGES FOR BATH PLAY

TEETHING TOYS (Child Guidance; Fisher-Price)

TUB AND POOL TOYS (Fisher-Price)

TODDLERHOOD (FROM THE TIME THE CHILD LEARNS TO WALK TILL APPROXIMATELY THE SECOND BIRTHDAY)
OUTDOOR PLAY EQUIPMENT

(Obviously, some of the toys we list below can be used both outdoors and indoors. These two categories are only approximate.)

CARDBOARD BOXES big enough for toddlers to get inside

CLIMBING HOUSE and CLIMBING FRAME (Galt Toys)

DOME (or CONE) CLIMBER (Childcraft; Constructive Playthings) is the best single item of outdoor play equipment you can buy for a toddler. Based on Buckminster Fuller's geodesic dome concept, it can safely support the weight of as many children as can climb on it. It is terrific for a toddler's large-muscle development. Put a piece of cloth or canvas over it and it can serve as a playhouse, tent, tepee, or anything else your child's imagination can dream up. It will last for years.

HOLLOW WOODEN BLOCKS

LARGE WOODEN or METAL CARS, TRUCKS, and EARTH-MOVERS (Different Drummer Workshop; Wooden Toys by R. Voake; Tonka Toys)

AN OLD COFFEE PERCOLATOR (especially delightful for toddlers!)

PLASTIC TOY PEOPLE AND ANIMALS for sand and water play

PLAYHOUSE, bought or homemade

SANDBOX AND SAND TOYS: cups, spoons, pie pans, sifters, etc.

SLIDE

SMALL BUT STURDY BOARDS, sanded down

SMALL BUT STURDY SHOVEL for digging and sand play

TYKE BIKE (Playskool)

WATER TOYS: plastic boats, dishes, scoops, measuring cups, etc.

INDOOR PLAY EQUIPMENT

CARDBOARD BOXES of various sizes (from your friendly neighborhood market)

DRESS-UP CLOTHES (Goodwill, Salvation Army, or your own closet!) Both girls

and boys like to dress up and play out adult roles.

HAMMERING AND POUNDING TOYS (Playskool; Childcraft)

HOLLOW CARDBOARD or PLASTIC BLOCKS for building (Galt Toys; Constructive Playthings, Fun Covers bricks by Playper)

INDOOR GYM HOUSE (Childcraft "Toddler's Gym"; Constructive Playthings; Novo Toys). We consider this the single best piece of indoor play equipment for a toddler. It has a ladder, a slide, a tunnel for crawling through, and a "house" inside. It's great for large-muscle development.

LARGE BEADS to string

MUSIC BOXES (Fisher-Price)

PULL TOYS of various sorts. Toddlers love these, and Fisher-Price excels at making them.

SOAP FLAKES or LIQUID DETERGENT for water play, plus water play toys listed in "Outdoor Play Equipment" above

SOFT, CUDDLY TOY ANIMALS AND DOLLS. Many commercially produced dolls are terrible. The play is not in the child, but in the doll, which cries, wets, or dances the rhumba. But Childcraft has three nice ones: Terry Teddy, Terry Baby, and Bunny Ball, a toy rabbit. Other good dolls can be obtained from Galt Toys, Fisher-Price, and the Children's Design Center.

STACKING AND NESTING BLOCKS (Playskool; Fisher-Price)

TOY CARS and TRUCKS that come with toy people (Fisher-Price)

TOY XYLOPHONE (Fisher-Price)

VERY SIMPLE PUZZLES (Fisher-Price; Childcraft)

FIRST ADOLESCENCE (FROM APPROXIMATELY THE SECOND TO THE THIRD BIRTHDAY)
OUTDOOR PLAY EQUIPMENT (SEE TODDLERHOOD TOO)

Again, some of these toys can be used indoors if you have the room.

DART-ABOUT RACER (Constructive Playthings)

EASEL for painting and drawing outside. Make an easel that will go on a fence in your yard; see suggestions below about paper and paint.

FIRST WAGON (Childcraft)

FOURWAY TRANSPORT (Community Playthings) is one sturdy wooden truck kids can ride on in four different ways.

A LARGE RUBBER BALL for outdoor play

NOTCHED PLAY PLANTS (Childcraft) fit together without posts, bolts, or pegs. They can be used to build various types of playhouses, taken apart, and used again.

PLAY-ALL (Childcraft). A remarkably versatile toy. These curved sections of unbreakable polyethylene can combine in different ways to form a sit-astride seesaw, a rolling circle, an individual rocker, or a reclining seat.

RIDE 'EM CAR (Childcraft) is very durable, sturdily built of one-inch heavy-gauge tubing.

SNAP WALL (Childcraft). Big, colorful panels for building play structures with swinging doors and crawl-through hatches.

WORKHORSE TRICYCLE (Community Playthings) is called a "workhorse" because it is built to last for a long, long time.

INDOOR PLAY EQUIPMENT (SEE TODDLERHOOD TOO)

BLOCKBUSTERS BLOCKS (Childcraft; Educational Teaching Aids). Large, light-weight blocks made from corrugated cardboard. These blocks are sturdy enough to stand on, yet easy for a young child to manipulate.

BRISTLE BLOCKS (Playskool). Colorful plastic shapes with flexible interlocking bristles that can be pressed together to form all sorts of constructions.

CLAY, bought or homemade

CRAYONS and CHALK

FINGER PAINTS. Watercolor felt-tip pens (fat ones); water-soluble paint and large, sturdy paintbrushes; and an easel.

PAPER. At this age your child will be perfectly happy to paint right over the printing on ordinary newspaper.

PLASTICINE

TOYS DEALING WITH SOUNDS AND MUSIC
Rhythm instruments: cigar boxes and pans to beat; tin cans with pebbles or dry beans in them to shake; drums, cymbals, triangles, bought or homemade
Toy xylophone or accordion
Inexpensive record player or tape recorder. Fisher-Price has nice ones.
Inexpensive records the child can play by herself.
(You can play good children's records for your youngster on your own record player.)

OTHER EQUIPMENT YOU MAY WISH TO GET

BULLETIN BOARD for your children's paintings and drawings

CHILD-SIZE TABLE OR DESK on which to paint and draw

STURDY CHILD-SIZE CHAIRS. We recommend Efebino children's chairs, sold by the Children's Design Center. They are well designed and constructed of molded plastic reinforced with fiberglass, come in attractive colors, stack easily, and are very durable.

THE PRESCHOOL STAGE (FROM APPROXIMATELY THE THIRD TO THE SIXTH BIRTHDAY)
OUTDOOR PLAY EQUIPMENT
(SEE FIRST ADOLESCENCE TOO)

IRISH MAIL (Childcraft; Constructive Playthings)

ROPE LADDERS or CARGO NETTING

TREE HOUSE, built near the ground, with ladder and slide

TUNNEL OF FUN (Childcraft; Constructive Playthings) is constructed of durable, nonflammable fabric on a spring steel frame. Children can crawl through it, hide in it, or use it as a tent.

WAGONS (Childcraft; Community Playthings)

CONSTRUCTION TOYS

METAL and PLASTIC CARS, TRUCKS, and EARTH-MOVERS for block play or sand play (Fisher-Price; Tonka)

MINIATURE INTERLOCKING WOODEN RAILWAY with MINIATURE CARS (Galt Toys; Educational Teaching Aids; Constructive Playthings) This toy is durable and kids really go for it.

PLAYTOWN (Galt Toys). This is a heavy vinyl base on which children can arrange and rearrange the buildings of their play cities.

PUT-TOGETHER CONSTRUCTION TOYS
   Lego
   Giant Tinkertoy (Gabriel). Kids love Tinkertoy, but they love Giant Tinkertoy even more!
   Swedish Variplay Set (Community Playthings). Unstructured building pieces will stimulate a child's imagination.
   Tinkertoy (Gabriel)
   Young Erector Set (Gabriel). Be sure not to get the regular Erector Set, which is for children six and older.
   NOTE: There are three excellent construction toys for preschoolers made in Europe: Brio, Bilofix, and Baufix. But there are very few toy stores in the United States where you can find them.

TOOLS: hammer, saw, etc., plus nails and screws. Don't get toy tools. Get real ones that a child can use under supervision.

VERY SMALL METAL CARS AND TRUCKS (Tootsietoy; Corgi; Matchbox)

WOODEN CARS and TRUCKS for use in the block cities your child will create (Different Drummer; R. Voake, Toymaker; Childcraft; Community Playthings; Constructive Playthings)

TOYS FOR ROLE-PLAYING AND CREATIVE FANTASY DEVELOPMENT

ADVENTURE PEOPLE by Fisher-Price. Similar to the Play Families line.

DOCTOR KIT, HOSPITAL KIT

DRESS-UP CLOTHES (Salvation Army; Goodwill)

FISHER-PRICE PLAY FAMILIES. Your child can engage in constructive role play through the use of these little toy people in a variety of environments. They are very helpful on trips.

FLANNEL CUTOUTS and FLANNEL BOARD (educational supply store)

FLEXIBLE FAMILY FIGURES for dollhouse or block city play (Childcraft)

HAND PUPPETS (Childcraft; Educational Teaching Aids)

PLAY STORE (Childcraft). Expensive to buy, but you can try your hand at making a simple one yourself.

PUPPET STAGE (Childcraft; Galt)

TOYS FOR A HOMEMAKING CORNER AND FOR DOLL PLAY

CHILD-SIZE PLAY STOVE, SINK, and REFRIGERATOR, bought (Jonti-Craft) or homemade

CHILD-SIZE POTS AND PANS, SILVERWARE (Childcraft)

DOLLHOUSE, DOLLS, and FURNITURE. Childcraft has an excellent open-top modern dollhouse and equipment. Even a very young child can manipulate the furniture and dolls easily.

OTHER DOLLS

Childcraft has anatomically accurate little brother and little sister dolls, and a number of other very fine dolls.

The Children's Design Center has an anatomically correct boy doll that can aid a parent in toilet training. After the doll drinks from his bottle, you push a button on his back and he's ready for the potty.

Playskool's Dapper Dan and Dressy Bessy are excellent dolls. Dressing and undressing these dolls gives preschoolers valuable practice in working snaps, zippers, buttons, and ties.

ARTS AND CRAFTS EQUIPMENT (SEE FIRST ADOLESCENCE TOO)

CLAY, bought or homemade

COLORED TISSUE PAPER and SCRAP MATERIALS for making collages.

ETCH-A-SKETCH (Ohio Art Company). A "classic" creativity toy for children. Very useful to take on trips.

GLUE and PASTE

GUMMED PAPER STICKERS and SEALS

LIGHT-COLORED PAPER to paint and draw on; bright-colored construction paper

VARIOUS MATERIALS FOR BLOCK PRINTING: oranges, lemons, carved potato, wire, key, leaf, etc.

TOYS AND EQUIPMENT FOR INTELLECTUAL ENRICHMENT

READING and LANGUAGE DEVELOPMENT
Cardboard signs with familiar words printed on them: door, chair, table, TV, etc.

Games to aid in reading readiness and language development (Childcraft has a number of excellent ones). Magnetic letters and numerals (Fisher-Price; Child Guidance; Childcraft). Use these on the door of your refrigerator.

Matching games that teach the child shapes, colors, and relationships (Childcraft has many of these).

MATTEL TLC (Teach and Learn Computer) for ages three to six. This computerized educational toy, in our opinion, is the best single cognitive stimulation toy presently available for preschoolers. It is built upon the positive reward system described earlier in this book. Even when a child gets the wrong answer, the computer's human voice encourages him by saying "That was a tough one! Now listen and try it again."

Plastic letters and numerals (Mattel).

Put-together, take-apart clock (Child Guidance) to aid your child in learning to tell time.

Puzzles of all sorts (Fisher-Price; Childcraft).

Rubber stamps of letters and numerals, plus stamp pad and paper.

Sandpaper letters and numerals. Cut your own out of cardboard or wood and glue the sandpaper on them.

MATHEMATICS and NUMBERS
Math readiness games (Childcraft). The Childcraft catalog has nine solid pages of math games for young children.

The Cuisenaire Home Mathematics Kit (Learning Games, Inc.). A great educational toy to introduce your preschool child to math in a fascinating way. A step-by-step instruction book for parents is part of the kit. Address: Box 820-C, North White Plains, New York 10603. Phone: (914) 428–7336.

SCIENCE
Science materials from Childcraft and Constructive Playthings. Both companies' catalogs contain several pages of excellent science materials for young children.

Magnets

MUSIC and DANCE TOYS

Childcraft has a fine selection of rhythm and musical instruments for young children: maracas, rhythm sticks, finger cymbals, sand blocks, tambourines, triangles, cymbals, an African koko drum, tomtoms, wood xylophones, steel drums, and bongo drums.

B

A PARENT'S GUIDE TO CHILDREN'S BOOKS

One of the finest gifts you can give your child is the love of books and reading. The purpose of this appendix is to help you do just that. It is a bibliography, classified by ages and stages, for selecting books from the library or the bookstore; it is a guide to both fiction and nonfiction for children from infancy to age six.

There are many more books on this list than you could possibly read to your child in the first five years of her life. Please don't feel overwhelmed by the number of books recommended. We have included so many titles because we want to offer something for every taste.

Only a very large library would have all these books. But your library, whatever its size, is bound to have some. And they can get you any book on this list even if it is not in their collection; just ask to have it ordered for you on interlibrary loan.

In addition to using this bibliography as a guide, it's a good idea to get to know the children's librarian. If you need a good book on the zoo for your three-year-old, or a funny children's novel for a five-year-old, she can suggest titles. If your library doesn't have a children's librarian, then the main librarian can be very helpful.

We suggest you take your youngster on weekly visits to the public library, beginning at age two or three. Since preschool books are short, you will probably read a whole book to your child each night at bedtime, and you will need to go to the library about once a week to get new books. When you and your child go regularly together, you are enrolling her in the most wonderful and inexpensive university she will ever attend: the Lifetime University of Public Libraries.

Some parents are penny-wise and pound-foolish when it comes to children's books. They take their children to the free library, but never *buy* them books of their own. This is a mistake. You buy toys for your child—if you don't buy books as well, she will naturally come to the conclusion that toys are much more important than books.

You may not live near a convenient bookstore that has an ample selection of children's books, but you can buy them by mail. One of the excellent sources in the United States is the Children's Book and Music Center, 2500 Santa Monica Boulevard, Santa Monica, California 90404. Phone: (213) 829–0215. They have a very comprehensive selection of children's books—over 15,000, in fact. All are available by mail. Send for their free catalog of books and records. The salespeople are quite knowledgeable, and if you have any special needs in books or records for your child, they will be glad to talk with you by telephone. We cannot recommend the services of this store too highly; it is an oasis of old-fashioned personalized service.

Another resource with an excellent selection of children's paperback books is Scholastic Book Service, 904 Sylvan Avenue, Englewood Cliffs, New Jersey 07632; or 5675 Sunol Boulevard, Pleasanton, California, 94566. Their free catalog lists more than 500 good paperbacks.

Here is the bibliography. Use it, but don't be limited by it.

INFANCY AND TODDLERHOOD (FROM THE TIME YOUR BABY BEGINS TO STAY AWAKE FOR LARGER PERIODS TILL THE SECOND BIRTHDAY)
BOOKS FOR LABELING THE ENVIRONMENT

The Cat in the Hat Beginner Book Dictionary, Dr. Seuss (Random House, Inc.). A first-rate picture dictionary for playing Label the Environment. The meaning of a thousand words is illustrated by Dr. Seuss in his unique style.

Richard Scarry's Best Word Book Ever (Western Publishing). Richard Scarry is in a class by himself when it comes to books for young children and this is one of his best. By the use of this book your child will acquire a vocabulary of 1400 words. Also consider Scarry's *Early Words* and *Little Word Book* (Random House, Inc.)

Sears or Montgomery Ward catalog, toy catalog, or *trading stamp catalog.* Many people would not think of these as books, but your toddler will! And he will delight in using them to play Label the Environment.

NURSERY RHYMES

Brian Wildsmith's Mother Goose, Brian Wildsmith: Franklin Watts Inc.; also paperback. Traditional Mother Goose rhymes delightfully illustrated by the well-known British artist.

Hi Diddle Diddle: Scholastic paperback. Mother Goose rhymes.

I Wish I Had a Computer That Makes Waffles, Fitzhugh Dodson: Oak Tree Publications Inc. Contains modern educational nursery rhymes which teach counting, zero, addition, subtraction, days of the week, family relationships, colors, nonsexist attitudes, as well as other important concepts. Special section for parents tells how to teach your child to write her own do-it-yourself nursery rhymes

and free verse poems. With stunning illustrations by Al Lowenheim. For ages one and a half to six.

MISCELLANEOUS

Anybody at Home?, H. A. Rey: Houghton Mifflin Co.; also paperback

Baby's First Golden Books: Western Publishing Co., Inc.

Baby's Lap Book, Kay Chorao: E. P. Dutton Inc.

Baby's Toys and Games, illustrated by N. Jo Smith: Platt & Munk

Farm Animals Board Book: Grosset & Dunlap

Find Out by Touching, Paul Showers: Crowell

The Giant Nursery Book of Things That Go, George Zaffo: Doubleday & Co., Inc.

The Touch Me Book, Pat and Eve Witte: Western Publishing Co., Inc.

Who Lives Here?, Pat and Eve Witte: Western Publishing Co., Inc.

BEDTIME BOOKS

Bedtime, Beni Montresor: Harper & Row, Publishers, Inc.

Bedtime for Frances, Russell Hoban: Harper & Row Publishers, Inc.; also paperback

A Child's Goodnight Book, Margaret Wise Brown: A & W Publishers, Inc.

Dr. Seuss's Sleep Book, Dr. Seuss: Random House, Inc.

Goodnight Andrew, Goodnight Craig, Marjorie Weinman Sharmat: Harper & Row Publishers, Inc.

Goodnight Moon, Margaret Wise Brown: Harper & Row Publishers, Inc.; also paperback

FIRST ADOLESCENCE (FROM APPROXIMATELY THE SECOND TO THE THIRD BIRTHDAY)

At this age some children have progressed into the preschool stage in their reading preferences; others still prefer toddler books. So use the list flexibly, and let your youngster be your guide.

It is important for you to make your reading to your first adolescent a cooperative affair. Your child does not take a passive approach to a book—he likes to look at it and touch it, and enjoys having you point things out in the illustrations.

A first adolescent usually has a few favorite books which he wants you to read to him over and over again. Sometimes it is difficult to get him to let you read a new book. And you may be in big trouble if you change a phrase or leave out a sentence.

ABC AND COUNTING BOOKS

ABC of Buses, Dorothy Shuttlesworth: Doubleday & Co., Inc.

ABC of Cars and Trucks, Anne Alexander: Doubleday & Co., Inc.

Anno's Alphabet, Mitsumasa Anno: Crowell

Brian Wildsmith's ABC, Brian Wildsmith: Franklin Watts Inc.

Brian Wildsmith's 1, 2, 3's, Brian Wildsmith: Franklin Watts Inc.

Brown Cow Farm, Dahlov Ipcar: Doubleday & Co., Inc.

Bruno Munari's ABC, Bruno Munari: Collins & World

Count and See, Tana Hoban: Macmillan Publishing Co., Inc.

Counting Carnival, Feenie Ziner and Paul Caldone: Coward-McCann

Curious George Learns the Alphabet, H. A. Rey: Houghton Mifflin Co.; also paperback

Dr. Seuss's ABC, Dr. Seuss: Beginner Books; a division of Random House

The Nutshell Library, Maurice Sendak: Harper & Row Publishers, Inc.

Richard Scarry's Find Your ABC's, Richard Scarry's Best Counting Book Ever, and *Richard Scarry's ABC Word Book,* Richard Scarry: Random House, Inc.

What Do You Think I Saw? A Nonsense Number Book, Nina Sazer: Pantheon Books, Inc.

BOOKS ABOUT SOUNDS

Bow Wow! Meow! A First Book of Sounds, Melanie Bellah: Western Publishing Co., Inc.

I Hear: Sounds in a Child's World, Lucille Ogle and Tina Thoburn: American Heritage Publishing Co., Inc.

It Does Not Say Meow, Beatrice DeRegniers: The Seabury Press, Inc.

Look Around and Listen, Jay Friedman: Grosset & Dunlap, paperback

The Noisy Book, Margaret Wise Brown: Harper & Row Publishers, Inc. (if your child likes this one, try the author's other "Noisy" titles, such as *The City Noisy Book, The Quiet Noisy Book, The Winter Noisy Book,* etc.)

What Does the Rooster Say, Yoshio?, Edith Battles: Albert Whitman & Co.

What I Hear, June Behrens: A & W Publishers, Inc.

NURSERY TALES

Catch Me and Kiss Me and Say It Again, Clyde Watson: Collins & World

It's Raining, Said John Twaining, N. M. Bodecker: Atheneum Publishers; also paperback

Tall Book of Nursery Tales, illustrated by Feodor Rojankovsky: Harper & Row, Publishers, Inc.

ANIMAL STORIES

Animal, Animal, Where Do You Live?, Jane Moncure: Child's World

Animals and Their Babies, David Roberts: Grosset & Dunlap

A Birthday for Frances, and the "Frances" series, Russell Hoban: Harper & Row, Publishers, Inc.; also paperback

Brian Wildsmith's books: Franklin Watts

Bruno Munari's Zoo: Collins & World

The Cat in the Hat series by Dr. Seuss: Beginner Books, a division of Random House

Harry the Dirty Dog, Gene Zion: Harper & Row, Publishers, Inc.; also paperback

Little Bear, Else Minarik: Harper & Row, Publishers, Inc.; also paperback

No Ducks in Our Bathtub, Martha Alexander: The Dial Press, Books for Young Readers; also paperback

Puppies Are Like That, and others by Jan Pfloog: Western Publishing Co., Inc.

The Runaway Bunny, Margaret Wise Brown: Harper & Row, Publishers, Inc.; also paperback

The Story About Ping, Marjorie Flack: The Viking Press; also Penguin paperback

Swimmy, Leo Lionni: Pantheon Books, Inc.; also paperback

The Tale of Peter Rabbit, Beatrix Potter: Frederick Warne & Co., Inc.

BOOKS ABOUT THE CHILD AND THE EVERYDAY WORLD

Big Red Bus, Ethel Kessler: Doubleday & Co., Inc.

The Carrot Seed, Ruth Kraus: Harper & Row, Publishers, Inc.; Scholastic paperback

Daddy Book, R. Stewart and D. Madden: McGraw-Hill, Inc.

The Day Daddy Stayed Home, Ethel and Leonard Kessler: Doubleday & Co., Inc.; also paperback

Days with Daddy, Pauline Watson: Prentice-Hall, Inc.

A Friend Is Someone Who Likes You, Joan Walsh Anglund: Harcourt Brace Jovanovich, Inc.

Friends, Satomi Ichikawa: Parents Magazine Press

Grover and the Everything in the Whole, Wide World Museum, Norman Stiles and Daniel Wilcox: Random House, Inc., paperback

Have You Seen My Mother?, Anne Maley: Carolrhoda Books, Inc.

Just Me, and others by Marie Ets: The Viking Press; also Penguin paperback

Summer Night, Charlotte Zolotow: Harper & Row, Publishers, Inc.

Umbrella, Taro Yashima: The Viking Press; also Penguin paperback

We're Going to Have a Baby, Doris and John Helmering: Abingdon Press

MISCELLANEOUS

Don't Forget to Come Back, Robie H. Harris: Alfred A. Knopf, Inc.

I Am Adopted, Susan Lapsley: Bradbury Press, Inc.

The Temper Tantrum Book, Edna Preston and Rainey Bennett: The Viking Press

The Very Hungry Caterpillar, Eric Carle: Collins & World

THE PRESCHOOL STAGE (FROM APPROXIMATELY THE THIRD TO THE SIXTH BIRTHDAY)

These are golden years for reading to a child. Your youngster will respond eagerly to his chance to have his mother or father read to him.

Be sure you strike a balance between

fiction and nonfiction. Don't let your youngster get fixated on one type of book; nonfiction gives him valuable information about his real world and fiction stretches his imagination and his creative thinking.

BEFORE AND AFTER BOOKS.
YOU CAN READ THESE TO YOUR CHILD *BEFORE* HE LEARNS TO READ; *HE* CAN READ THEM AFTER HE LEARNS TO READ.

Several publishers have published series of these books, and all of them are good. Look for the imprints.

BEGINNER BOOKS, published by Random House. Authors include P. D. Eastman, Dr. Seuss, Al Perkins, Stanley and Janice Berenstain, Helen Palmer, Bennett Cerf, and others.

LET'S READ AND FIND OUT SCIENCE BOOKS, published by Crowell. This series is excellent; the scientific information is accurate and up-to-date and the illustrations are eye-catching. Authors include Paul Showers, Roma Gans, and Franklyn Branley.

I CAN READ BOOKS, published by Harper & Row. Authors include Syd Hoff, Edith Hurd, Carla Greene, Nathaniel Benchley, Russell Hoban, and Lillian Hoban. In addition to general titles, they also publish I Can Read sports books, Early I Can Read books, I Can Read science books and I Can Read mystery books.

SCIENCE BOOKS, published by McGraw-Hill. These include a number of titles by Tillie Pine and Joseph Levine, and others by Herman and Nina Schneider, Jeanne Bendick, Norman Anderson, and J. Schwartz.

BEGINNING TO READ SERIES, published by Follett. This series includes many titles by Margaret Hillert. Most of the books in the series are available in paperback as well as hardcover.

BEGINNING SCIENCE SERIES, published by Follett. Most of the books in this series

deal with earth science and astronomy. Several titles are authored by Isaac Asimov.

THE LET'S FIND OUT BOOKS, published by Franklin Watts. Authors in this series include Valerie Pitt, Martha and Charles Shapp, and David Knight.

STEPPING INTO SCIENCE SERIES and THE TRUE BOOK SERIES, published by Children's Press.

SEE AND READ BIOGRAPHY SERIES, published by G. P. Putnam's Sons. Primarily famous figures in American history—presidents, black leaders, inventors, explorers, etc.

SCIENCE IS WHAT AND WHY SERIES, published by Coward-McCann. Books by Sally Cartwright, Melvin Berger, and others, about such things as sunlight, sand, sound, and stars.

WONDER BOOKS EASY READERS SERIES
1 *Adventures of Silly Billy*, Tamara Kitt
2 *The Birthday Party*, P. Newman
3 *The Boy, the Cat, and the Magic Fiddle*, Tamara Kitt
4 *Jokes and Riddles*
5 *Let Papa Sleep*, Crosby Bonsall and E. Reed
6 *The Monkey in the Rocket*, Jean Bethell
7 *Question and Answer Book*
8 *A Surprise in the Tree*
9 *When I Grow Up*, Jean Bethell
10 *Will You Come to My Party?*, Sara Asheron

BOOKS DEALING WITH INTELLECTUAL OR EMOTIONAL DEVELOPMENT

In addition to fostering your child's language development, these books will stimulate her general intellectual development. They are arranged according to the particular aspect of development they deal with; because some books cannot be categorized precisely, you may find a particular book listed in more than one place.

TEACHING VALUES AND
ETHICS TO CHILDREN

BOOKS ABOUT GRANDPARENTS

Grandfather's Story, Mervin Marquadt: Concordia Publishing House

Grandfathers Are to Love and *Grandmothers Are to Love,* Lois Wyse: Parents' Magazine Press, boxed set

Grandma Is Somebody Special, Susan Goldman: Albert Whitman & Co.

Grandma's Beach Surprise, Ilka List: G. P. Putnam's Sons

Grandmother Orphan, Phyllis Green: Thomas Nelson, Inc.

Grandmother Told Me, Jan Wahl: Little, Brown & Co.

Grandmothers, Glenway Wescott: Atheneum Publishers

Grandpa, Barbara Borack: Harper & Row, Publishers, Inc.

Grandpa and Me, Patricia L. Gauch: Coward-McCann

Grandpa, Me and Our House in the Tree, Barbara Kirk: Macmillan Publishing Co., Inc.

Grandpa and My Sister Bea, Joan Tate: A & W Publishers, Inc.

Grandpa's Farm, James Flora: Harcourt Brace Jovanovich, Inc.

Grandpa's Ghost Stories, James Flora: Atheneum Publishers

Grandpa's Indian Summer, Jan Wahl and Jeanne Scribner: Prentice-Hall, Inc.

Grandpa's Maria, Hans-Eric Hellberg: William Morrow

Granny and the Baby and the Big Gray Thing, Peggy Parrish: Macmillan Publishing Co., Inc.

Granny and the Indians, and *Granny and the Desperadoes,* Peggy Parrish: Macmillan Publishing Co., Inc.; also paperback

I Have Four Names for My Grandfather, Kathryn Lasky: Prentice-Hall, Inc.

I Love My Grandma, Steven Palay: Raintree Publishers, Inc.

Mary Jo's Grandmother, Janice Udry: Albert Whitman & Co.

My Grandfather and I and *My Grandmother and I,* Helen Buckley: Lothrop, Lee & Shepard Books

My Grandpa Died Today, Joan Gassler: Human Sciences Press Inc.

Nana Upstairs, Nana Downstairs, Tomie DePaola: G. P. Putnam's Sons; also Penguin paperback

Simon's Extra Gran, Pamela Oldfield: A & W Publishers, Inc.

Watch Out for Chicken Feet in Your Soup, Tomie DePaola: Prentice-Hall, Inc.

Why Are There More Questions Than Answers, Grandad?, Kenneth Mahood: Bradbury Press, Inc.

William's Doll, and *My Grandson Lew,* Charlotte Zolotow: Harper & Row, Publishers, Inc.

THE ALPHABET AND LEARNING
TO READ

ABC of Monsters, Deborah Niland: McGraw-Hill, Inc.

All About Arthur: An Absolutely Absurd Ape, Eric Carle: Franklin Watts

Alligators All Around, Maurice Sendak: Harper & Row, Publishers, Inc.

Alphabrutes, Dennis Nolan: Prentice-Hall, Inc.

Follett's Picture Dictionary, Alta McIntire: Follett Publishing Co.

The Headstart Book of Knowing and Naming, Shari Lewis and Jacqueline Reinach: McGraw-Hill, Inc.

I'll Teach My Dog 100 Words, Dick Gackenbach: Harper & Row, Publishers, Inc.

Jane Moncure's Series of Five: Child's World. A series involving play with alphabet letters.

Jane Moncure's Series of Ten: Child's World. This is a series about the sounds of alphabet letters.

Loud-Noisy, Dirty-Grimy, Bad and Naughty Twins: A Book of Synonyms, Sylvia Tester: Child's World

The Magic World of Words: Macmillan Publishing Co., Inc.

Never Monkey with a Monkey, Sylvia Tester: Child's World

Pooh's Alphabet Book, A. A. Milne: E. P. Dutton Inc.; also Dell paperback

Silent E Man: Sesame Street Book of Letters: Random House, Inc.

What Did You Say?, Sylvia Tester: Child's World

Zag: A Search Through the Alphabet, Robert Tallon: Holt, Rinehart & Winston

SENSORY AWARENESS AND PERCEPTUAL ACUITY

Do You Move As I Do? and *Do You See What I See?,* Helen Borten: Abelard-Schuman

The Headstart Book of Looking and Listening, Shari Lewis and Jacqueline Reinach: McGraw-Hill, Inc.

The Listening Walk and *Follow Your Nose,* Paul Showers: Crowell

My Five Senses, Aliki: Crowell; also paperback

Things We Hear, Anthony Thomas: Franklin Watts

CONCEPT FORMATION: SEASONS OF THE YEAR

The Jane Moncure series: Child's World

The Bears' Almanac, Stanley and Janice Berenstain: Random House, Inc.

Let's Find Out About Fall, Let's Find Out About Spring, and *Let's Find Out About Winter,* Martha and Charles Shapp: Franklin Watts

Summer Is, Charlotte Zolotow: Abelard-Schuman

Sunshine Makes the Seasons, Franklyn Branley: Crowell

Winter Bear, Ruth Craft: Atheneum Publishers

Wintertime for Animals, Margaret Cosgrove: Dodd, Mead & Co.

A Year Is Round, Joan Walsh Anglund: Harcourt Brace Jovanovich, Inc.

CONCEPT FORMATION: COMPARISONS

Fast Is Not a Ladybug and *Heavy Is a Hippopotamus,* Miriam Schlein: A & W Publishers, Inc.

High Sounds, Low Sounds, Franklyn Branley: Crowell; also paperback

Over, Under and All Around, Sylvia Tester: Child's World

Playing with Opposites, Iris Grender: Pantheon Books, Inc., paperback

Push, Pull, Empty, Full: A Book of Opposites, Tana Hoban: Macmillan Publishing Co., Inc.; also paperback

So Big, Eloise Wilkin: Western Publishing Co., Inc.

Up Above and Down Below, Irma Webber: A & W Publishers, Inc.

The Very Little Boy and *The Very Little Girl,* Phyllis Krasilovsky: Doubleday & Co., Inc., paperback

CONCEPT FORMATION: CLASSIFICATION BY SHAPE

Hello, This Is a Shape Book, John Trotta: Random House, Inc.

A Kiss Is Round, Blossom Budney: Lothrop, Lee & Shepard Books

On My Beach There Are Many Pebbles, Leo Lionni: Astor-Honor

The Shape of Me and Other Stuff, Dr. Seuss: Random House, Inc.

Shapes and Things and *Circles, Triangles and Squares,* Tana Hoban: Macmillan Publishing Co., Inc.

Square Is a Shape: A Book About Shapes, Sharon Lerner: Lerner Publications Co.

The Wing on a Flea, Ed Emberley: Little, Brown & Co.

CONCEPT FORMATION: CLASSIFICATION BY COLOR

Ant and Bee and the Rainbow, Angela Banner: Franklin Watts

The Color Factory, John Denton: Penguin, paperback

The Color Kittens, Margaret Wise Brown: Western Publishing Co., Inc.

The Great Blueness and Other Predicaments, Arnold Lobel: Harper & Row, Publishers, Inc.

Green Says Go, Ed Emberley: Little, Brown & Co.

Is It Red? Is It Yellow? Is It Blue?, Tana Hoban: Greenwillow Books

Little Blue and Little Yellow, Leo Lionni: Astor-Honor

Orange Is a Color, Sharon Lerner: Lerner Publications Co.

Richard Scarry's Color Book, Richard Scarry: Random House, Inc.

See What I Am, Roger Duvoisin: Lothrop, Lee & Shepard Books

CONCEPT FORMATION: NUMBERS AND COUNTING

Anno's Counting Book, Mitsumasa Anno: Crowell

Ants Go Marching, Berniece Freschet: Scribner's

Berenstain Bears' Counting Book, Stanley and Janice Berenstain: Random House, Inc.

I Can Count and *I Can Count More*, Dick Bruna: Methuen, Inc.

Moja Means One: The Swahili Counting Book, Muriel Feelings: The Dial Press, paperback

One Is No Fun, But Twenty Is Plenty!, Ilse-Margaret Vogel: Atheneum Publishers, paperback

One Is One, Tasha Tudor: Rand McNally & Co.

One, Two, Three: An Animal Counting Book, Margaret Wise Brown: The Atlantic Monthly Press

One, Two, Three with Ant and Bee, Angela Banner: Franklin Watts

Ten Little Elephants: A First Counting Book, Robert Leydenfrost: Doubleday & Co., Inc.

CONCEPT FORMATION: TIME

Do You Know What Time It Is?, Roz Abisch: Prentice-Hall, Inc., paperback

Just a Minute: A Book About Time, Leonore Klein: Harvey House, Publishers

Time, Harlan Wade: Raintree Publishers, Inc.

Time: A Book to Begin On, Leslie Waller: Holt, Rinehart & Winston

Time and Clocks, Herta Breiter: Raintree Publishers, Inc.

Time and Mr. Bass, Eleanor Cameron: Little, Brown & Co.

What Time Is It?, John Peter: Grosset & Dunlap

CONCEPT FORMATION: BASIC SCIENCE CONCEPTS THAT TIE A LARGE NUMBER OF EVENTS TOGETHER IN ONE CONCEPT

Atoms, Melvin Berger: Coward-McCann

The Fresh Look Series, J. Curtis: British Book Centre. Includes titles on the solar system, gravity, evolution, atoms and molecules, and water

Friction and *Electricity*, Edward Victor Follett

Gravity Is a Mystery, Franklyn Branley: Crowell

Heat and *Friction*, Howard Liss: Coward-McCann

Heat All Around, Energy All Around, Gravity All Around, Friction All Around, Tillie Pine and Joseph Levine: McGraw-Hill, Inc.

Levers, Heat, Sound, and *Electricity*, Harlan Wade: Raintree Publishers, Inc.

Motion, Seymour Simon: Coward-McCann

OTHER GENERAL BOOKS ON SCIENCE

Animal Habits, George Mason: William Morrow

Dr. Beaumont and the Man with the Hole in His Stomach, Beryl and Samuel Epstein: Coward-McCann

Earthquakes, Charles Cazeau: Follett Publishing Co.

In the Days of the Dinosaurs, Roy Chapman Andrews: Random House, Inc.

Insects Do the Strangest Things, Leonora and Arthur Hornblow: Random House, Inc.

First Fact books, Lerner Publications Co. Subjects in the series include Animal Attackers, Monkeys and Apes, Spaceship Earth, Volcanoes, the Sea, and Rockets and Astronauts.

Let's Look at Insects, Harriet Huntington: Doubleday & Co., Inc.

Let's Look at Reptiles, Harriet Huntington: Doubleday & Co., Inc.

Nature at Its Strangest, James Cornell, Jr.: Sterling Publishing Co., Inc.

Nature's Squirt Guns, Bubble Pipes, and Fireworks: Geysers, Hot Springs, and Volcanoes, Alice Gilbreath: David McKay Co., Inc.

Sounds All About, Illa Podendorf: A & W Publishers, Inc.

Where Are You Going with That Energy?, Roy Doty: Doubleday & Co., Inc.

THE MAGIC OF WORDS AND
THE MAGIC OF BOOKS

Beginning Search-a-Word Shapes, Dawn Gerger: Grosset & Dunlap

Books Are Fun, Geri Shubert: Western Publishing Co., Inc.

CDB!, William Steig: Simon & Schuster; also Dutton paperback

Fun with Words, Richard Scarry: Golden Books, a division of Western Publishing Co., Inc.

I Like the Library, Anne Rockwell: E. P. Dutton, Inc.

The Magic Word Book: Random House, Inc., an Electric Company book

The Magic World of Words!: Macmillan

Nailheads and Potato Eyes, Cynthia Basil: William Morrow

Play on Words, Alice and Martin Provenson: Random House, Inc.

Rabbit and Pork: Rhyming Talk, John Laurence: Crowell

Watchamacallit Book, Bernice Hunt: G. P. Putnam's Sons

What a Funny Thing to Say, Bernice Kohn: The Dial Press

NONSENSE POEMS

Reading nonsense poems aloud to a child is a splendid way to get him interested in words and language at an early age. You can begin reading these books to your youngster when he is about three or four years old.

Alligator Pie, Dennis Lee: Houghton Mifflin Co.

At the Top of My Voice, Felice Holman: Scribner's

The Book of Nonsense, Edward Lear: Garland Publishing, Inc.

Cats and Bats and Things Like That, Gill Beers: Moody Press

Cats and Bats and Things with Wings, Conrad Aiken: Atheneum Publishers

Dinosaur Do's and Don'ts, Jean Polhamus: Prentice-Hall, Inc.

Laughable Limericks, edited by Sara and John Brewton: Crowell

Nuts to You and Nuts to Me! An Alphabet of Poems, Mary Hoberman: Alfred A. Knopf, Inc.

The Owl and the Pussycat, Edward Lear: Atheneum Publishers; also paperback

The Pobble Who Has No Toes and Other Nonsense, Edward Lear: The Viking Press

Poetry for Chuckles and Grins, edited by Leland B. Jacobs: Garrard Publishing Co.

The Scroobious Pip, Edward Lear, completed by Ogden Nash: Harper & Row, Publishers, Inc.

Problem-Solving

Help!, Susan Riley: Child's World

Mom's New Job, Paul Sawyer: Raintree Publishers, Inc.

Sometimes I Worry, Alan Gross: A & W Publishers, Inc.

Up Day, Down Day, Jacquie Hann: Four Winds Press

What Can You Do with a Shoe?, Beatrice DeRegniers: Harper & Row, Publishers, Inc.

What If I Couldn't: A Book About Special Needs, Janet Kamien: Scribner's

What Makes a Shadow?, Clyde Bulla: Crowell

What Would You Do?, Leland Jacobs: Garrard Publishing Co.

Why: A Book of Reasons, Irving and Ruth Adler: John Day

Why Can't I?, Jeanne Bendick: McGraw-Hill, Inc.

Why Didn't I Think of That?, Web Garrison: Prentice-Hall, Inc.

Why and How: A Second Book of Reasons, Irving and Ruth Adler: John Day

Children's Emotions or Special Problems

Angry, Susan Riley: A & W Publishers, Inc.

Big Sister and Little Sister, Charlotte Zolotow: Harper & Row, Publishers, Inc.

The Boy With a Problem, The Man of the House, Don't Worry, Dear, All Alone with Daddy, and *My Grandpa Died Today*, Joan Fassler: Human Sciences Press, Inc.

The Dead Bird, Margaret Wise Brown: A & W Publishers, Inc.

Dentist and Me, Joy Schaleben-Lewis: Raintree Publishers, Inc.

Emily and the Klunky Baby and the Next Door Dog, Joan Lexau: The Dial Press

Feelings Between Kids and Parents and *Feelings Between Kids and Grown-ups*, Marcia Conta and Maureen Reardon: Raintree Publishers, Inc.

I Don't Care, Marjorie Sharmatt: Macmillan Publishing Co., Inc.

I Hate It, Miriam Schlein: Albert Whitman & Co.

I Have Feelings, Terry Berger: Human Sciences Press, Inc.

I Feel, George Ancona: E. P. Dutton, Inc.

I Won't Be Afraid, Joan Hanson: Carolrhoda Books, Inc.

I'm Running Away, and *Lie*, Ann Helena: Raintree Publishers, Inc.

Love Is a Special Way of Feeling, Joan Walsh Anglund: Harcourt Brace Jovanovich, Inc.

Me Day, Joan Lexau: The Dial Press

Mom's New Job, Paul Sawyer: Raintree Publishers, Inc.

Mommy and Daddy Are Divorced, Patricia Perry: The Dial Press

My Mama Says There Aren't Any Zombies, Ghosts, Vampires, Creatures, Demons, Monsters, Fiends, Goblins, or Things, and *The Tenth Good Thing About Barney*, Judith Viorst: Atheneum Publishers, paperback

The Quarreling Book and *The Hating Book*, Charlotte Zolotow: Harper & Row, Publishers, Inc.

Sometimes I Get Angry, Sometimes I'm Jealous, and *Sometimes I'm Afraid*, Jane W. Watson: Western Publishing Co., Inc.; also paperback

Sometimes I Like to Cry, Elizabeth and Henry Stanton: Albert Whitman & Co.

That Makes Me Mad!, Steven Kroll: Pantheon Books, Inc.

This Room Is Mine, Betty Wright: Western Publishing Co., Inc.

Timid Timothy, Gweneira Williams: A & W Publishers, Inc.

Where Is Daddy? A Story of a Divorce, Beth Goff: Beacon Press

Will I Ever Be Good Enough?, *I'll Get Even*, *I Dare You!*, *Sometimes It Scares Me*, and *Was My Face Red*, Judith Conaway: Raintree Publishers, Inc.

Will I Have a Friend?, Miriam Cohen: Macmillan Publishing Co., Inc.; also paperback

MATHEMATICS

About the Metric System, Alma Filleo: Child's World

The Greatest Guessing Game: A Book About Dividing, Robert Froman: Crowell

How Did Numbers Begin?, Mindel and Harry Sitomer: Crowell

How Little and How Much? A Book About Scales, Franklyn Branley: Crowell

Humphrey, the Number Horse, Rodney Peppe: The Viking Press

Mathematics series by Vincent O'Connor: Children's Books, a division of Raintree Publishers, Inc.

Measure with Metric, Franklyn Branley: Crowell; also paperback

Numbers, Signs and Pictures: A First Number Book, Shari Robinson: Platt & Munk

Solomon Grundy, Born on One Day: A Finite Arithmetic Book, Malcolm Weiss: Crowell

Zero Is Not Nothing, Harry and Mindel Sitomer: Crowell

SCIENTIFIC METHODS
FOR PRESCHOOLERS

ABC Science Experiments, Harry Milgrom: Macmillan Publishing Co., Inc., paperback

Adventures with a Cardboard Tube, Harry Milgrom: E. P. Dutton, Inc.

Berenstain Bears' Science Fair, Stanley and Janice Berenstain: Random House, Inc.

Finding Out with Your Senses, Seymour Simon: McGraw-Hill, Inc.

Got a Minute? Quick Science Experiments You Can Do, Nina Schneider: Scholastic, paperback

Greg's Microscope and *Benny's Animals and How He Put Them in Order*, Millicent Selsam: Harper & Row, Publishers, Inc.

The Headstart Book of Thinking and Imagining, Shari Lewis and Jacqueline Reinach: McGraw-Hill, Inc.

How Can I Find Out?, Mary Bongiorno and Mable Gee: Children's Press

Look! How Your Eyes See, Marcel Sislowitz: Coward-McCann

Magnify and Find Out Why, J. Schwartz: McGraw-Hill, Inc.

Prove It!, Rose Wyler and Gerald Ames: Harper & Row, Publishers, Inc.

Simple Science Fun: Experiments with Light, Sound, Air and Water, Bob Ridiman: Parents Magazine Press

BOOKS ABOUT RELIGION

Unfortunately, good books about religion for preschoolers are very scarce. Here are a few; there should be more.

A Book About God, Florence Fitch: Lothrop, Lee & Shepard Books

Children's Prayers for Today, Audrey McKim and Dorothy Logan: Association Press

Mitzvah Is Something Special, Phyllis Eisenberg: Harper & Row, Publishers, Inc.

Religion for children by Mary Alice Jones. An excellent, highly recommended series: Rand McNally & Co., paperback

Know Your Bible
Tell Me About God
Tell Me About Jesus

Told Under the Christmas Tree, Association for Childhood Education International: Macmillan Publishing Co., Inc.

Wineglass: A Passover Story, Norman Rosten: Walker & Co.

The Self-Concept

All by Myself and *About Me*, Jane Moncure: Child's World

Any Me I Want to Be, Karla Kaskin: Harper & Row, Publishers, Inc.

The Boy with the Special Face, Barbara Girion: Abingdon Press

But Names Will Never Hurt Me, Bernard Waber: Houghton Mifflin Co.

Hooray for Me!, Remy Charlip and Lillian Moore: Parents Magazine Press

How I Feel, June Behrens, A & W Publishers, Inc.

Katie's Magic Glasses, Jane Goodsell: Houghton Mifflin Co.

Look at Me Now, Jane Watson: Western Publishing Co., Inc.

My Five Senses and *My Hands*, Aliki: Crowell

To Be Me, Barbara Hazen: Child's World

Relationships within the Family and with Peers

Alexander and the Terrible, Horrible No-Good, Very Bad Day, Judith Viorst: Atheneum Publishers

But What About Me?, Sandra Love: Harcourt Brace Jovanovich, Inc.

Confessions of an Only Child, Norma Klein: Pantheon Books, Inc.; also paperback

Couldn't We Have a Turtle Instead?, Judith Vigna: Albert Whitman & Co.

Daddy, Jeanette Caines: Lothrop, Lee & Shepard Books

Feelings Between Kids and Parents, Feelings Between Brothers and Sisters, and *Feelings Between Friends*, Marcia Conta and Maureen Reardon: Raintree Publishers, Inc.

Friday Night Is Papa Night, Ruth A. Sonneborn: The Viking Press

Gorilla Wants to Be the Baby and *Why Couldn't I Be an Only Kid Like You, Wigger?*, Barbara Hazen: Atheneum Publishers

How Your Mother and Father Met and What Happened After, Tobi Tobias: McGraw-Hill, Inc.

I Love My Mother, Paul Zindel: Harper & Row, Publishers, Inc.

I Want Mama, Marjorie Sharmatt: Harper & Row, Publishers, Inc.

If It Weren't for You, When I Have a Little Girl and *When I Have a Son*, Charlotte Zolotow: Harper & Row, Publishers, Inc.

I'm Going to Run Away, Joan Hansen: Platt & Munk

It's Mine: A Greedy Book, Crosby Bonsall: Harper & Row, Publishers, Inc.

It's Not Fair, Robyn Supraner: Frederick Warne & Co., Inc.

It's Okay If You Don't Love Me, Norma Klein: The Dial Press

Mommies and *Daddies*, L. C. Carton: Random House, Inc.

Mommies Are for Loving, Ruth Penn: G. P. Putnam's Sons

My Daddy Is a Cool Dude, Karama and Mahiri Fukama: The Dial Press

My Sister, Karen Hirsh: Carolrhoda Books, Inc.

She Come Bringing Me That Little Baby Girl, Eloise Greenfield: J. B. Lippincott Co.

Somebody Else's Child, Roberta Silman: Frederick Warne & Co., Inc.

The Terrible Thing That Happened at Our House, Marge Blaine: Parents Magazine Press

The Way Mothers Are, Miriam Schlein: Albert Whitman & Co.

We're Very Good Friends, My Brother and I, P. K. Hallinan: A & W Publishers, Inc.

The Community and Community Helpers

Ask Me What My Mother Does, Katherine Leiner: Franklin Watts, Inc.

Busy Town, Busy People and *Richard Scarry's Busiest People Ever*, Richard Scarry: Random House, Inc.

Clean Streets, Clean Water, Clean Air, Cynthia Chapin: Albert Whitman & Co.

I Know an Airline Pilot, Muriel Stanek: G. P. Putnam's Sons

I Know a Bus Driver, Genevieve Gray: G. P. Putnam's Sons

I Know a Dentist, Naomi Barnett: G. P. Putnam's Sons

I Know a Librarian, Virginia Voight: G. P. Putnam's Sons

I Know a Nurse, Marilyn Schima and Polly Bolian: G. P. Putnam's Sons

I Know a Plumber, Polly Curren: G. P. Putnam's Sons

I Know a Zoo Keeper and *I Know a Grocer*, Lorraine Henriod: G. P. Putnam's Sons

Jobs People Do, and *People Who Help People*, Jane Moncure: Child's World

Nothing Ever Happens on My Block, Ellen Raskin: Atheneum Publishers

Policemen and Firemen: What They Do, Carla Greene: Harper & Row, Publishers, Inc.

Truck Drivers: What They Do, Carla Greene: Harper & Row, Publishers, Inc.

Who Are the People in Your Neighborhood?: Random House, Inc., a Sesame Street book

THE LARGER COMMUNITY: THE WORLD

A Book of Planet Earth for You, A Book of Astronauts for You, and *A Book of Outer Space for You*, Franklyn Branley: Crowell

Children Everywhere, David Harrison: Rand McNally & Co.

Space: A Fact and Riddle Book, Jane Sharnoff and Reginold Ruffanis: Scribner's

Where in the World Do You Live?, Al Hine and John Alcorn: Harcourt Brace Jovanovich, Inc.

The World Is Round, Anthony Ravielli: The Viking Press

The World We Live In, Arkady Leokum: Grosset & Dunlap

You Will Go to the Moon, Mae and Ira Freeman: Random House, Inc.

RICHARD SCARRY

Richard Scarry deserves his own special category. His charming and wonderful books teach children about the world and the people who live in it. Your child will get terrific intellectual stimulation from them. We have listed many already. Ask your librarian about others.

All Day Long: Western Publishing Co., Inc.

At Work: Western Publishing Co., Inc.

Busy, Busy World: Western Publishing Co., Inc.

Hop Aboard, Here We Go!: Western Publishing Co., Inc.

Nicky Goes to the Doctor: Western Publishing Co., Inc.

On the Farm: Western Publishing Co., Inc.

On Vacation: Western Publishing Co., Inc.

Rabbit and His Friends: Western Publishing Co., Inc.

Richard Scarry's Cars and Trucks and Things That Go: Western Publishing Co., Inc.

Richard Scarry's Favorite Mother Goose Rhymes: Western Publishing Co., Inc.

Richard Scarry's Great Big Mystery Book: Random House, Inc.

Richard Scarry's Great Big Schoolhouse: Random House, Inc.

FICTION AND FANTASY

We list a few here but there are many excellent books available. Each year a book is given a special award (the Caldicott award) for illustrations. A similar award (the Newberry award) is given for story content. Ask your librarian about these.

And to Think That I Saw It on Mulberry Street, Dr. Seuss: Vanguard Press, Inc.

Anno's Journey, Mitsumasa Anno: Collins & World

The Biggest House in the World, Leo Lionni: Pantheon Books, Inc.; also paperback

Blueberries for Sal, One Morning in Maine, Make Way for Ducklings, Burt Dow, Deep Water Man, and *Lentil*, Robert McCloskey: The Viking Press

Corduroy and *A Rainbow of My Own*, Don Freeman: The Viking Press; also paperback

The 500 Hats of Bartholomew Cubbins, Dr. Seuss: Vanguard Press, Inc.

Frederick, Leo Lionni: Pantheon Books, Inc.; also paperback

Horton Hatches the Egg, Dr. Seuss: Random House, Inc.

The House on East 88th Street, Bernard Waber: Houghton Mifflin Co.; also paperback

Inch by Inch, Leo Lionni: Astor-Honor

The Little House and *Mike Mulligan and His Steam Shovel*, Virginia Burton: Houghton Mifflin Co., paperback

Little Toot, Hardie Gramatky: G. P. Putnam's Sons; also paperback

Madeline, Ludwig Bemelmans: The Viking Press; also Penguin paperback

The Snowy Day, Ezra Jack Keats: The Viking Press; also paperback

The Story of Babar; Babar and His Children; Babar the King; and other Babar books, by Jean de Brunhoff: Random House, Inc.

The Summer Night, Charlotte Zolotow: Harper & Row Publishers, Inc.

Where Have You Been?, Margaret Wise Brown: Hastings House, Publishers, Inc.

Where the Wild Things Are, Maurice Sendak: Harper and Row, Publishers, Inc.

COLLECTIONS OF STORIES, TALES, OR FOLKTALES

The Book of Greek Myths, Edgar and Ingri D'Aulaire: Doubleday & Co., Inc.

Castles and Dragons: Read-to-Yourself Fairy Tales for Boys and Girls, compiled by the Child Study Association of America: Crowell

I Can Choose My Bedtime Story, edited by Mary Parsley: Grosset & Dunlap

Joan Walsh Anglund Storybook, Joan Walsh Anglund: Random House, Inc.

Kate Greenaway Treasury, Kate Greenaway: Collins & World

Night Noises and Other Mole and Troll Stories, Tony Johnson: G. P. Putnam's Sons

Told Under the City Umbrella, Told Under the Magic Umbrella, and *Told Under the Green Umbrella*, Association for Childhood Education International: Macmillan Publishing Co., Inc.

POETRY FOR PRESCHOOLERS

A Child's Garden of Verses, Robert Louis Stevenson: Franklin Watts, Inc.

Cricket in a Thicket, Aileen Fisher: Scribner's; also paperback

Hailstones and Halibut Bones, Mary O'Neill: Doubleday & Co., Inc.; also paperback

I Can't, Said the Ant, Polly Cameron: Coward-McCann

I Met a Man, John Ciardi: Houghton Mifflin Co.; also paperback

Listen, Children, Listen: An Anthology of Poems for the Very Young, edited by Myra Cohn Livingston: Harcourt Brace Jovanovich, Inc.

Nibble, Nibble, Margaret Wise Brown: A & W Publishers, Inc.

Something Special, Beatrice Schenk De-Regniers and Irene Haas: Harcourt Brace Jovanovich, Inc.

When We Were Very Young and *Now We Are Six*, A. A. Milne: E. P. Dutton, Inc.; also Dell paperback

Where the Sidewalk Ends: Poems and Drawings, Shel Silverstein: Harper & Row, Publishers, Inc.

You Read to Me, I'll Read to You, John Ciardi: J. B. Lippincott Co.

NONSEXIST PICTURE BOOKS

It's important to help our children grow up thinking of themselves and others in free, nonsexist ways. One way to do this is to read nonsexist books to them.

Some people think you should read only completely nonsexist books to your children. We disagree. Many good children's books are sexist. If a book is good, we feel you should go ahead and read it to your child. If the book also happens to be sexist, point out and discuss the sexist stereotypes with him. For example, discuss why it is wrong to imply that it is a weakness for boys to cry and that girls should be taught to be submissive and quiet.

Around and Around Love, Betty Miles: Alfred A. Knopf, Inc.; also paperback

A Bedtime Story, Joan Goldman Levine: E. P. Dutton, Inc.

Betsy and the Chicken Pox, Gunilla Wolde: Random House, Inc.

Bodies, Barbara Brenner: E. P. Dutton, Inc.

Grownups Cry, Too, Nancy Hazen: Lollipop Power Press

I Am a Giant, Ivan Sherman: Harcourt Brace Jovanovich, Inc.

Louie, Ezra Jack Keats: Greenwillow Books

Lucky Wilma, Wendy Kindred: The Dial Press

Mary Alice, Operator Number Nine, Jeffrey Allen: Little, Brown & Co.; also Penguin paperback

Max, Rachael Isadora: Macmillan Publishing Co., Inc.

My Mother the Mail-Carrier, Inez Maury: The Feminist Press; also paperback

The Steamroller, Margaret Wise Brown: Walker & Co.

Swinging and Swinging, Fran Manushkin: Harper & Row, Publishers, Inc.

The Wizard's Tears, Anne Sexton and Maxine Kremin: McGraw-Hill, Inc.

NONSEXIST EASY READERS

All Kinds of Families, Norman Simon: Albert Whitman & Co.

And I Mean It, Stanley, Crosby Bonsall: Harper & Row, Publishers, Inc.

Animal Fathers, Russell Freedman: Holiday House

Delilah, Carole Hart: Harper & Row, Publishers, Inc.

Did the Sun Shine Before You Were Born?, Sol Gordon and Judith Cohen: Okpaku Productions

Eliza's Daddy, Ianthe Thomas: Harcourt Brace Jovanovich, Inc.; also paperback

Fiona's Bee, Beverly Keller: Coward-McCann; also Dell paperback

He Bear, She Bear, Stanley and Janice Berenstain: Random House, Inc.

I'd Rather Stay Home, Carol Barkin and Elizabeth James: Raintree Publishers, Inc.

Is This Your Sister? A True Story About Adoption, Catherine and Sherry Bunin: Pantheon Books, Inc.

The Missing Piece, Shel Silverstein: Harper & Row, Publishers, Inc.

The Most Delicious Camping Trip Ever, Alice Bach: Harper & Row Publishers, Inc.; also paperback

New Life: New Room, June Jordan: Crowell

GAME BOOKS

Preschool children love games. These books offer a delightful array you can play with them, many when you travel.

Finger Plays for Nursery and Kindergarten, Emilie Poulssen: Dover Publications, paperback

A Hole, a Box and a Stick, Gladys Y. Cretan: Lothrop, Lee & Shepard Books

Jack Kent's Hop, Skip and Jump Book, Jack Kent: Random House, Inc.; also paperback

Little Boy Blue: Finger Plays Old and New, Daphne Hogstrom: Golden Books, a division of Western Publishing Co., Inc.

Two Hundred Two Things to Do, Margaret Sedlied: Regal Press; also paperback

MISCELLANEOUS

COOKING FOR YOUNG CHILDREN

Cool Cooking, Esther Hautzig: Lothrop, Lee & Shepard Books

I Am a Cookbook, Em Riggs and Barbara Darpinion: J. P. Tarcher, Inc.

Kids Cooking: A First Cookbook for Children, Aileen Paul and Arthur Hawkins: Archway, paperback

Kids Cooking Without a Stove: A Cookbook for Young Children, Aileen Paul: Doubleday & Co., Inc.

Teddybears' Cookbook, Susanna Greta: Doubleday & Co., Inc.

WALKER AND CO. "OPEN BOOKS" FOR ADULTS AND CHILDREN

Each of these books by Sara Stein contains a story that can be read aloud to a child. In addition, running beside the story is a text for the parents that makes clear the childhood fears being dealt with and explains how an adult can further explore the story with the child through questions and discussion.

A Hospital Story
About Dying
Making Babies
That New Baby
Who'll Take Care of Me?

WESTERN PUBLISHING READ-TOGETHER PAPERBACK BOOKS

This is another series of books specially designed for parents to read aloud to their preschoolers. The authors are Jane Werner Watson, Dr. R. E. Switzer, and Dr. J. C. Hirschberg. (Western Publishing)

My Friend, the Babysitter
My Body—How It Works
Sometimes I'm Afraid
Sometimes I Get Angry
Sometimes I'm Jealous

MAGAZINES FOR CHILDREN

We do not want to close this appendix without mentioning some good magazines for children. Since children get little mail, it is always exciting when a magazine arrives. They will be delighted when you read these magazines to them in the preschool years. And they will particularly enjoy doing the cutouts, puzzles, and other activities featured in the magazines.

Highlights for Children. 2300 West Fifth Avenue, Columbus, Ohio 43216. Ages two to twelve.

Humpty Dumpty's Magazine. Parents Magazine Enterprises, 52 Vanderbilt Avenue, New York, New York 10017. Ages three to seven.

Jack and Jill. 1100 Waterway Boulevard, Box 567B, Indianapolis, Indiana 46206. Ages five to twelve.

Sesame Street Magazine. Children's Television Workshop, 1 Lincoln Plaza, New York, New York 10023. Text in English and Spanish. Ages three to five.

C

A PARENT'S GUIDE TO
CHILDREN'S RECORDS

Many wonderful children's records will promote your youngster's emotional and intellectual development in a variety of ways—records like Sam Hinton's *Whoever Shall Have Some Good Peanuts,* Pete Seeger's *Abiyoyo,* Ann Barlin's *Dance-a-Story,* or many of the other great records you will find listed in this appendix.

There is one unfortunate catch to this list, however. Approximately 999 out of 1,000 of the parents reading this will not be able to find *any* of these records in local record stores or in department stores. Wherever you look, you will find a very small section labeled "Children's Records." And in that section you will find a group of children's records that are banal, trite, cutesy, and bad, bad, bad.

We do not have space to go into detail as to why it is so difficult to find good children's records when so many are produced. Let's just accept it as an unfortunate fact of life and see what we can do about it.

The Children's Book and Music Center, the store recommended in Appendix B for buying children's books by mail, has literally thousands of excellent children's records and cassettes to choose from. Simply write and ask them to send you their free catalog, which lists not only the records and cassettes in this appendix, but many more that space prevents us from including. If you need help in finding a particular kind of record for a child, you can phone them and describe your needs and they will suggest something appropriate. Their phone number is (213) 829-0215.

Parents are much less familiar with children's records than they are with toys or books, and you may not be aware that a good record or cassette can be used for developing many oral language skills: vocabulary building, logical thinking, memory training, and developing listening skills.

Here are the records and cassettes that can mean so much for your child's development in his first six years of life.

INFANCY AND TODDLERHOOD (FROM BIRTH TO APPROXIMATELY THE SECOND BIRTHDAY)
A CHILD'S FIRST RECORDS

These direct, rhythmic, and uncluttered recordings cover sensory, vocal, physical, and emotional responses. They are excellent for the earliest years.

A Child's First Record, Frank Luther: Vocalion

Activity Songs, Marcia Berman: Tom Thumb

Best of The Baby Sitters, The Baby Sitters: Vanguard

Children's Creative Playsongs, Vol. I, Teddy Bears: Stepping Tones

I'm Not Small, Marcia Berman and Patty Zeitlin: Educational Activities

Little Favorites, male and female voices: Bowmar

Loving and Learning from Birth to Three, Diane Hartman Smith: Joy

Lullabies and Other Children's Songs, Nancy Raven: Pacific Cascade

Music for One's and Two's, Tom Glazer: CMS

Nursery and Mother Goose Songs, male and female voices: Bowmar

Seagulls: Music for Rest and Relaxation, Hap Palmer: Educational Activities

Songs and Play Time with Pete Seeger, Pete Seeger: Folkways

Songs to Grow On for Mother and Child, Woody Guthrie: Folkways

You'll Sing a Song and I'll Sing a Song, Ella Jenkins: Folkways

MUSIC OF MANY CULTURES FOR INFANTS

Only recently have we learned from research studies how sensitive babies are to their environment, and how discriminating their hearing is. For this reason we believe parents are wise to play music of other cultures to their young children. Although your baby may not show any outward response to the music, you may be sure that the music he hears is being filed away in his tiny computer brain and he will remember it later.

African Drum, Chant and Instrumental Music: Nonesuch

Bailes Folkloricos de Mexico: Peerless

Fiesta Mexicana, Javier de Leon: Monitor

Flower Dance (Japan; includes koto, shamisen, drums): Nonesuch

Flower Drum and Other Chinese Folk Songs: Monitor

Hora—Songs and Dances of Israel, Guela Gill: Elektra

International Folk Dance Mixer (includes music from Africa, Denmark, Israel, Italy, Russia, Scotland): Gateway

Jazayer (Egypt): Jazayer Co.

Lilacs Out of the Dead Land (Greece), Manos Hadjidakis: Philips

Musical Instruments of Africa, Vol. I: Strings: Kaleidophone

Russian Folk Dances of the Moiseyev Dance Company: Monitor

Songs and Dances of Vietnam: Monitor

The Sound of the Sun (Trinidad), The Westland Steel Band: Nonesuch

FIRST ADOLESCENCE AND THE PRESCHOOL STAGE (APPROXIMATELY THE SECOND TO THE SIXTH BIRTHDAY)
ACTIVITY RECORDS

These recordings help the child to loosen up and develop more freedom of body movement through rhythmic activities. They may be used by children alone or with adults. The music is vigorous and lively and encourages young children to respond to it by activity and movement.

Action Songs for Indoor Days, David White and Terry Gris: Tom Thumb

Activity and Game Songs for Children, Vols. I and II, Tom Glazer: CMS

Castle in My City, Patty Zeitlin: Educational Activities

Dance-a-Story records, Ann Barlin: RCA. A series of eight storybook and record combinations. One side of each record consists of narrative and suggests different movements to go with the melody. The reverse side has only music; here the children are free to interpret the music as they feel it. The total package includes storytelling, dramatization, pantomime, and rhythmic play. Some of the titles are *At the Beach, Balloons,* and *Flappy and Floppy.*

Getting Bigger Every Day, Soundpiper Music: Soundpiper Records

I Like Sunny Days, Soundpiper Music: Soundpiper Records

Machines and Things That Go, Jon Frommer: Pacific Cascade

Many excellent recordings by Ella Jenkins: Folkways

Many excellent recordings by Hap Palmer: Educational Activities

Moving Makes Me Magic, Yvonne Johnson and Betty Mosley: Folkways

Rainy Day Dances, Rainy Day Songs,

Marcia Berman, Patty Zeitlin, and Ann Barlin: Educational Activities

Say Hi, Soundpiper Music: Soundpiper Records

The Small Dancer: Bowmar

We All Live Together, Vols. I and II, Youngheart Music Education Group: Youngheart Records

FOLK SONGS

Abiyoyo and Other Story Songs for Children, Pete Seeger: Folkways

Children's Greatest Hits, Vols. I and II, Tom Glazer: CMS

Little White Duck, Burl Ives: Columbia

Many other excellent recordings by Pete Seeger: Folkways

Peter, Paul, and Mommy, Peter, Paul and Mary: Warner Bros.

Really Rosie, Carole King: Ode

Songs to Grow On, Woody Guthrie: Folkways

Through Children's Eyes, The Lime-lighters: RCA

Whoever Shall Have Some Good Peanuts, Sam Hinton: Scholastic. This is our favorite record for preschoolers, sung in Sam Hinton's unique style.

FOREIGN LANGUAGES

These records help a child learn a foreign language through music.

Building Spanish Vocabulary Through Music, Vols. I and II, Eddie Cano: CP Records

Folksongs for Children of All Ages (Spanish-American children's songs), Jenny Vincent: Cantemos

Lo Mejor de Cri-Cri (Spanish): Arcano

Songs in French for Children, Lucienne Vernay: Columbia

INTELLECTUAL STIMULATION

Acting Out the ABC's: A Child's Primer of Alphabet, Counting and Acting Out Songs: Disneyland

All About Numbers and Counting, Ray Heatherton: Miller-Brody

Alphabet in Action (consonants and vowels taught through songs and motor activities), Michael Gallina: Kimbo

Ballads for the Age of Science: Motivation. An excellent series that introduces children to science concepts in a fascinating way. Titles include *Energy and Motion Songs, Space Songs,* and *Weather and Climate*

Children's Basic Concepts Through Music, Bob Kay: Stallman

Counting Games and Rhythms for Little Ones, Ella Jenkins: Folkways

Dance, Sing and Listen with Miss Nelson and Bruce: Dimension 5

14 Numbers, Letters and Animal Songs, Alan Mills: Folkways

Learning Basic Skills Through Music, Vols. I, II, and III, Hap Palmer: Educational Activities

Math Readiness: Addition and Subtraction, and *Math Readiness, Vocabulary and Concepts*, Hap Palmer: Educational Activities

Musical Math: Beginning Concepts, Ruth White and David White: Rhythm Productions

Musical math records: Tom Thumb

Addition/Subtraction
Multiplication

Noisy and Quiet, Big and Little, Tom Glazer: RCA

Sing a Song of Sounds (developing auditory perception through songs and motor activities), Michael Gallina: Kimbo

Singing Sounds, Vols. I and II (simplified phonics set to music): Bowmar

Songs of Safety/Manners Can Be Fun, Frank Luther: Vocalion

MUSIC APPRECIATION

A Child's Introduction to the Orchestra: Golden

The Small Listener: Bowmar

Sparky's Music Mix-up: Capitol

Tubby the Tuba, Danny Kaye: MCA

NONSEXIST RECORDS

These records help children build new concepts and self images free from sexist stereotypes.

Action Songs for Indoor Days, David White and Terry Gris: Tom Thumb

Free to Be You and Me, Marlo Thomas and Friends: Arista

Hurray for Captain Jane (stories), Tammy Grimes: Caedmon

Mommy Is a Doctor, Patty Zeitlin: Educational Activities

When I Grow Up I Want to Be, Bob Kay: Stallman

RECORDINGS BY TV PERSONALITIES

Mister Rogers: Pickwick—an excellent series. Children enjoy listening to these during a quiet time.

Sesame Street: CTW (Children's Theater Workshop)—many excellent recordings.

RECORDS TO PROMOTE POSITIVE SELF-CONCEPTS

These records help build positive self-esteem and enable children to grow both emotionally and socially.

Candy Band Sings "Play Me a Song," Candy Band: Folkways

Everybody Cries Sometimes and *Won't You Be My Friend?,* Marcia Berman and Patty Zeitlin: Educational Activities

I Have a Friend in You and *Who Am I?:* Wise Owl

It's a Happy Feeling and *I've Got a Reason to Sing,* Ruth and David White: Tom Thumb

Mommy . . . Gimme a Drinka Water, Danny Kaye: Capitol

Songs Between Friends, Wanda May and Tom Guy: T.G.I.D. Publications

STORY RECORDS

The stories on these records will hold even the youngest listener's attention. You can find books in your library or bookstore to accompany the records. Children usually enjoy seeing pictures in the book as they are listening to the story on the record.

Babar the King/Babar and Zephyr, Louis Jourdan: Caedmon

"Caps for Sale" on *Listening to Picture Books:* Classroom Materials

Catch a Little Rhyme, Eve Merriam: Caedmon

Curious George stories, Julie Harris: Caedmon

Dr. Seuss stories, Marvin Miller: Pickwick

Frances Stories, Glynis Johns: Caedmon

Frederick (plus several other stories), Carol Channing: Caedmon

Grimm's Fairy Tales, Joseph Schildkraut: Caedmon

Happy Stories for Gloomy Days, Frank Luther: Vocalion

Higglety Pigglety Pop, Tammy Grimes: Caedmon

Just So Stories, Boris Karloff: Caedmon

The Little Engine That Could (also *Winnie-the-Pooh*), Paul Wing: RCA Educational

Little Toot Stories, Hans Conreid: Caedmon

Lyle, Lyle, Crocodile, Gwen Verdon: Caedmon

Madeline stories, Carol Channing: Caedmon

Peter Rabbit, Goldilocks, and Other Great Tales for Growing Boys and Girls, Paul Wing: RCA Educational

Stories for Rainy Days, Frank Luther: Vocalion

Story of Ferdinand, Gwen Verdon: Caedmon

The Three Little Pigs and Other Fairy Tales, Boris Karloff: Caedmon

Winnie-the-Pooh, Carol Channing: Caedmon

Winnie-the-Pooh and Christopher Robin, Frank Luther: MCA

Where the Wild Things Are, Tammy Grimes: Caedmon

Why Mosquitos Buzz in People's Ears and Other Tales, Ruby Dee and Ossie Davis: Caedmon

The following records come packaged with books:

The Bears' Picnic, the Berenstains: Caedmon

Scholastic record and book sets. These include many classics such as *Hansel and Gretel* and *The Emperor's Clothes*, as well as some original stories by contemporary children's authors.

Storyteller Company series of cassette and book packages. These include many of the Grimm fairy tales.

D

A PARENT'S GUIDE TO BOOKS ON PARENTING

It would be foolish to think that you could pack into this or any other book everything that parents of preschool children need to know about parenting. If anyone tried to do that the book would probably run to five thousand pages, and would look so forbidding no parent would want to read it.

But obviously there are many things you might want to know that we have not had space to delve into or have only touched on lightly. For example, suppose you are the parents of twins. Or suppose you are planning to adopt a child. The purpose of this annotated list of books on parenting is to help you find just about any kind of information you might need in raising your youngster.

We recommend every book listed here. This doesn't mean we agree 100 percent with everything in them. But on the whole we believe each book is a competent and sound discussion of some aspect of child raising. We have also tried to select for this bibliography only those books we think are interesting and readable.

BOOKS ON CHILD PSYCHOLOGY

These books cover the stages of psychological development in the first five years.

The First Three Years of Life, Burton White: Avon, paperback. An impressive book based mainly upon the results of the Harvard Preschool Project, of which Dr. White was the director. He speaks candidly on such topics as methods of handling children, good toys for children, and so forth.

How to Father, Fitzhugh Dodson: New American Library, paperback. Many mothers have profited greatly from this book which was originally written for fathers.

How to Parent, Fitzhugh Dodson: New American Library, paperback. Dr. Dodson believes this is the most comprehensive guide to both the intellectual and emotional development of the child in the all-important first five years of life. But he could be biased.

Infant and Child in the Culture of Today, Arnold Gesell, Frances Ilg, Louise Bates Ames: Harper & Row, Publishers, Inc. A revised version of one of the most influential books on child psychology in the United States. Typical traits of each age, up to five, are summarized in the form of both a behavior profile and a "behavior day."

Infants and Mothers and *Toddlers and Parents,* T. Berry Brazelton: Dell Publishing Co. These two books give valuable insights into the development of infants and toddlers, respectively. Dr. Brazelton examines problems that can occur during these stages, as well as the wide range of normal behavior.

The Magic Years, Selma Fraiberg: Scribner's, paperback. This excellent book is written from the psychoanalytic point of view. Within that frame of reference it does a fine job in describing the psychological development of a child in the first five years of life.

Your Baby and Child from Birth to Age 5, Penelope Leach: Alfred A. Knopf. A comprehensive book, with beautiful illustrations, describing the development and needs of the child up to age five. Dr.

Leach writes clearly, forcefully, and with humor. Her basic point of view on bringing up children is to avoid "going by the book" and learn to "go by the baby."

Your Two Year Old, Your Three Year Old, Your Four Year Old, and *Your Five Year Old,* Louise Ames and Frances Ilg: Delacorte Press. These four books are updated versions of the well-known Gesell studies.

BOOKS ON DISCIPLINE

Changing Children's Behavior, John D. Krumboltz and Helen B. Krumboltz: Prentice-Hall, Inc. Shows how to strengthen existing good behavior as well as how to develop and maintain new behavior. Challenges both the permissive and authoritarian approaches. The book shares with us the viewpoint that any behavior, whether good or bad, is learned and therefore can be changed.

How to Discipline with Love, Fitzhugh Dodson: New American Library, paperback. Describes a number of different discipline techniques, and contains examples of how to apply these techniques to everyday situations. Discusses many subjects not usually covered in other books on discipline: how to desensitize yourself to a child's annoying behavior through the use of "negative thinking," how to teach ethics and morality, and the rights of parents. The book also covers the special discipline situations of single parents, working parents, and stepparents.

Living With Children: New Methods for Parents and Teachers, Gerald Patterson and Elizabeth Gullian: Research Press. Based on the same principles of positive reinforcement discussed in our book, this unique programmed book is like a teaching machine in book form; because of this it is particularly easy to read.

Parent Effectiveness Training, Thomas Gordon: New American Library, Plume paperback. Dr. Gordon's "active listening" technique and his "no-lose" method of solving problems between parents and children. We think this is a book every parent should read.

Positive Parenthood, Paul S. Graubard: The Bobbs-Merrill Co., Inc. Tells you how to change undesirable behavior such as tantrums, bad habits, the inability to get along with others, and irresponsibility.

BOOKS TO HELP YOU UNDERSTAND HOW TO STIMULATE CHILDREN INTELLECTUALLY

Give Your Child a Head Start in Reading, Fitzhugh Dodson: Simon & Schuster. After a brief explanation of why so many American children read badly, this book gives specific step-by-step instruction to parents in the simple and pleasurable ways that they can teach twenty-two different prereading skills to their children.

Give Your Child a Superior Mind, Siegfried Engelmann and Therese Engelmann: Simon & Schuster. The Engelmanns give easily understood advice on teaching a child science, arithmetic, and math concepts, and how to print and read. In our opinion, this is the best book to help parents of preschoolers maximize the intellectual development of their child.

How to Raise a Brighter Child, Joan Beck: Pocket Books, paperback. This clear and interesting book tells you step by step how a parent can provide intellectual stimulation for a child up to the age of six.

I Wish I Had a Computer That Makes Waffles, Fitzhugh Dodson: Oak Tree Publications. A book for parents and preschool children to use together, beginning at a year and a half and continuing until six. It is a guide for parents in how to develop their child's oral language skills. It also contains forty-eight brand new modern and nonsexist nursery rhymes written by Dr. Dodson—the first to be written since Mother Goose in 1765.

A Parent's Guide to Children's Reading, Nancy Larrick: Pocket Books, paperback. This book contains an excellent bibliography for children up to the age of twelve.

Thinking Is Child's Play, Evelyn Sharp: Avon, paperback. The first half of this book describes how young children learn to think. The second half contains forty games with which parents can teach logical thinking to young children.

BOOKS TO GUIDE YOU IN PLAYING WITH CHILDREN

The Complete Book of Children's Play, Ruth Hartley and Robert Goldenson: Crowell, paperback. It's a shame that few parents know of the existence of this classic. Not a single important aspect of children's play is neglected.

Housebuilding for Children, Les Walker: The Overlook Press. Shows children how to build six different houses all by themselves, with instructions and drawings that are clear and easy to follow.

The Rainy Day Book, Alvin Schwartz: Simon & Schuster, paperback. This is really two books in one. On the one hand it is a comprehensive guide to rainy-day activities for children, on the other a how-to-survive handbook for their harassed parents.

Your Child's Play, Arnold Arnold: Simon & Schuster, an Essandess paperback. This unique book will give you a better understanding of your child's play and enable you to better participate in it.

DIVORCE, BLENDED FAMILIES, AND CHILDREN

Not so long ago there were practically no books written to help parents understand the effect of divorce on children or how they could do a good job as single parents. It is heartening to see the number of books now available which deal with the subject of divorce from the perspective of both parents and children.

The Boys and Girls Book About Divorce, Richard Gardner: Bantam. This excellent book is written for children themselves to read. But parents can also read it and gain insight into how their children feel about divorce.

Daddy Doesn't Live Here Anymore, Rita Turow: Doubleday & Co., Inc. This is a sensitive book covering all phases of the divorce process. It also includes an invaluable list of helpful agencies for divorced parents and their children.

The Divorce Experience, Morton Hunt and Bernice Hunt: McGraw-Hill, Inc. Based on a nationwide survey and an extensive series of in-depth interviews, this is without doubt the most up-to-date discussion of divorce today.

Going It Alone, Robert S. Weiss: Basic Books. This book, based on reports from single parents—divorced, widowed, and those who have had children out of wedlock—provides great insight into the family life and social situation of the single parent. How to organize the single parent household, the problems of raising children, and the problems of establishing a life within the community are discussed.

Living in Step, Ruth Roosevelt and Jeanette Lofas: Stein & Day Publishers. This splendid book explores all the subterranean psychological currents that beset the stepfamily, and offers suggestions for achieving a truly blended family.

Mom's House, Dad's House: Making Shared Custody Work, Isolina Ricci: Macmillan Publishing Co., Inc. This valuable book deals with a plan which only mature divorced parents will be able to handle successfully—that of making shared custody succeed.

The Parents Book About Divorce, Richard A. Gardner, M.D.: Doubleday & Co., Inc. Written by a psychiatrist with long experience in treating the children of divorce, this book approaches divorce mainly from the standpoint of protecting the children's psychological welfare. It offers realistic guidance on how and when the children should be told, how to deal with feelings of guilt and shame on both the part of the parents and the children, and how to settle custody and visitation problems.

Single Father's Handbook, Richard H. Galey, Ph.D. and David Koulack, Ph.D.: Anchor Press/Doubleday. Both authors are psychologists and separated fathers who have experienced the guilt, anger, and despair that other separated or divorced fathers experience. They offer some practical solutions to problems that separated fathers often face.

Stepparenting, Jean and Veryl Rosenbaum: Chandler & Sharp Publishers, Inc. Equally as good as *Living in Step,* this book, by a psychiatrist husband and his psychoanalyst wife, is an excellent and sophisticated explanation of all the emotional mine fields to be found in stepparenting. It is full of sound and practical advice.

WORKING MOTHERS AND DAY CARE

The Day Care Book, Grace Mitchell, Ph.D.: Stein & Day Publishers. Here is a book that will help you prepare your children for the day-care experience, as well as help you find and evaluate the best possible care for your children. The placing of children in a day-care situation often leaves parents feeling guilty and neglectful. This book shows you how to cope with these feelings.

The Working Mother's Complete Handbook, Gloria Norris and Joann Miller: E. P. Dutton, Inc. A complete guide for mothers who work either by choice or necessity. It will help you learn to balance your life between working and mothering. It offers solutions to the many problems that a working mother faces.

FOR PARENTS OF TWINS

Having Twins, Elizabeth Noble: Houghton Mifflin Co. This is a complete guide for couples who learn in pregnancy that they are to be parents of twins, triplets, or other multiple births. It includes everything parents need to know about prenatal nutritional requirements, the latest medical research in the area of multiple births, how to meet the double duties involved in clothing, bathing, and feeding twins, and a listing of twin organizations and research centers as well as much other valuable information.

BOOKS ON RAISING BLACK CHILDREN

For many years child-raising books were written as if all American children were lily white and being raised in a lily-white environment. Finally, books on parenting have begun to catch up with the fact that black children are also being raised in the United States. Here are two fine books for black parents to use in raising their children.

The Black Child: A Parent's Guide, Phyllis Harrison-Ross and Barbara Wyden: David McKay Co., Inc. This book is written for both black and white parents. It covers the special problems of the black child. It also offers guidelines to white parents to help them raise children who can accept both racial differences and racial similarities. A very fine book.

Black Child Care, James Comer and Alvin Poussaint: Pocket Books, paperback. An excellent book, which covers the development of a hypothetical black child from birth through adolescence.

FOR PARENTS PLANNING TO ADOPT A CHILD

The Adopted Family, Florence Rondell and Ruth Michaels: Crown, revised edition. Contains two books. Book I, *You and Your Child: A Guide for Adoptive Parents,* gives excellent and down-to-earth advice on all phases of adoption. Book II, *The Family That Grew,* is a picture book and story to read to the adopted child and to use in explaining the situation to him. Highly recommended for all adoptive parents.

Adoption and After, Louise Raymond: Harper & Row, Publishers, Inc. Covers all phases of adoption including specific procedures for telling the child he is adopted. An excellent book.

Successful Adoption, Jacqueline Plumez: Crown. In our opinion this is the best single guide to adoption. After taking the reader on a careful step-by-step journey through the adoption process, Dr. Plumez concludes the book with a complete list of state and regional adoption agencies, resources for foreign adoptions, and state-by-state rundowns on average waiting time, availability of records, etc. If you're thinking of adopting, this is a must book for you.

THE MENTALLY RETARDED CHILD

Play Activities for the Retarded Child, Bernice Carlson and David Ginglend: Abingdon Press. Discusses how to help a mentally retarded child grow and learn through games, music, arts and crafts, and other play activities.

SEX EDUCATION IN THE HOME

Sex Education for Today's Child, Arlene S. Uslander, Caroline Weiss, and Judith Telman: Association Press. Here is a book that will be invaluable in your efforts to help your growing children achieve a sensitive, informed, and livable attitude toward sexuality. It will help you deal with such problems as the discussion of the new atmosphere of sexual freedom, using the correct words comfortably, and helping children to ask the right questions.

The following are books for parents to read to preschool children or for the grade-school children to read themselves. All of them are excellent.

A Baby Is Born, Milton Levine and Jean Seligman: Golden Books, a division of Western Publishing Co., Inc.

Before You Were a Baby, Paul Showers and Kay Showers: Crowell.

Growing Up, Karl de Schweinitz: Macmillan Publishing Co., Inc.

GENERAL BOOKS ON PARENTHOOD

Child Safety Is No Accident, Jay M. Arena, M.D., and Miriam Bachar: Haw-

thorn Books. Here is an easy-to-use, up-to-date, informative book about why children have accidents, how to prevent these accidents, and how to handle a crisis should one arise.

Daughters, From Infancy to Independence, Stella Chess, M.D., and Jane Whitbread: New American Library. A comprehensive guide to successfully raising a daughter to be an independent, responsible, and loving woman.

He Hit Me First, Louise Bates Ames and Carol Chase Haber: Dembner Books.

This book, co-authored by a splendid team of mother-granddaughter psychologists, offers many helpful suggestions for coping with this problem.

How to Fight Fair With Your Kids . . . And Win!, Luree Nicholson and Laura Torbet: Harcourt Brace Jovanovich, Inc. This fine book deals with a problem every family faces—anger and hostility within the family—and presents a number of methods by which hostility can be overcome and constructive relationships established.

How to Grandparent, Fitzhugh Dodson: Harper & Row, Publishers, Inc. The first book for grandparents that transcends the sentimental and tells grandparents things they really need to know about the care and management of today's children. A valuable five-part appendix gives grandparents assistance in wisely choosing toys, books, and records for grandchildren.

The Parents Book of Toilet Teaching, Joanna Cole: Parents Magazine Press. We believe every parent who has yet to toilet teach her child or is in the middle of toilet teaching should own a copy of this comprehensive book. It covers everything a parent needs to know about the subject, describing simply and clearly a step-by-step method for toilet teaching a child, and conveys a relaxed feeling of reassurance.

Parents' Yellow Pages, A Directory by the Princeton Center for Infancy: Anchor Press/Doubleday. A priceless collection of information on the whole range of problems that face parents during their children's first eight years of life.

E

A PARENT'S TOY FACTORY

You parents can do something about the deplorable state of toy designing and manufacturing in the United States. You can start your own Parent's Toy Factory! This appendix is your guide to making a number of inexpensive toys for your children.

ROCK ANIMALS AND ROCK PEOPLE

Nothing is easier than finding rocks. You can find them anywhere—in your own backyard, along a river, or near a lake. They don't have to be smooth or symmetrical, although that usually helps. They can range in size from a large pebble to one the size of your fist.

You can use just one rock for the face and body of your animal or person, or you can add legs and a head by gluing other rocks to the first one. Use sturdy nontoxic glue.

For coloring the faces or bodies on the rocks, acrylic paints have several advantages. First, they are water soluble and much easier to use than oil paints. They take approximately twenty minutes to dry, which gives you plenty of time to correct mistakes. Once dry, they are exceedingly durable. You can buy acrylic paints in any art store.

Make your decoration of the rocks simple and childlike. No artistic ability is required. Here are some of the things you can do:

You can paint only the features on the rock and leave the rest the natural color. Or you can paint the whole rock a solid color. Once you have painted the features, you may want to cover the entire rock with acrylic clear gloss to give it a nice shiny look.

Not only will your children delight in having you manufacture rock toys for them, but they will love to make them themselves, with your help.

STUFFED DOLLS AND STUFFED TOY ANIMALS

With a good doll or stuffed animal the child can use his imagination and creativity to the fullest because the toy has no built-in gimmicks to distract him from his own imaginative use of it. But there are very few such dolls on the market; most come equipped with cutesy little gimmicks that dictate the way in which the child must play.

So if ever there was a toy that needs to be produced by the Parent's Toy Factory, it's a good doll or stuffed animal. And you needn't be an expert seamstress, either—your child isn't going to care if a seam is crooked. You can use any kind of sturdy cloth for the outside of the doll, such as lightweight corduroy, heavy cotton, lightweight denim, terry cloth, gingham, plush, fleece, velveteen, or synthetic suede or leather.

Start collecting remnants of colorful materials to use for making the body of your toy. Simply cut the cloth to get the basic shape you want. You need enough material to make two sides of the animal, though the colors don't necessarily have to match. Cut the two sides exactly the same shape but a little larger than you want the finished toy to be.

A fish is one of the easiest shapes to begin with. Get some children's coloring books that have big pictures of animals to guide you. But don't get hung up on the idea that you have to get a shape just right. A young child won't care.

While you're at it, why not try making fanciful animals with weird shapes? You can call them "friendly monsters." Often the child will love these more than realistic animals such as a fish or an elephant.

The best stuffing for your doll is polyester fiber, which you can get at a fabric store or the yardage department of a department store. Sometimes you can purchase a big bag of it very cheaply. Polyester fiber has definite advantages over foam rubber in stuffing a toy animal. It is nonallergenic and easy to wash.

Sew up most of your doll or animal; stuff in your polyester fiber filling; then sew the rest of it up.

When putting in the details of the face (eyes, nose, mouth), you have a choice between using embroidery before you stuff the toy or using an indelible marker afterwards. If you wish to go to the trouble of embroidering, fine. But it is certainly much easier and faster to use an indelible marker after the toy is completely stuffed. You can buy all colors of markers at a stationery store; most supermarkets and large drug stores also have a good selection.

Do not sew on buttons for eyes, for a young child may work these loose, put them in his mouth, and choke on them.

Above all, remember that your doll or stuffed animal does not have to be beautiful. It will be beautiful to your child because you made the toy just for her. You can tell her there isn't a single other doll in the world like it.

Here are some very simple designs you can use:

The hands can be made with the fingers open or with only a thumb and a round glove effect for the fingers.

Here are some fanciful animal shapes you can make:

So far, we have talked only about stuffed toys *you* can make. But you and your youngster *together* can make some delightful dolls and animals.

Take a sturdy box and put all sorts of scraps in it: odd pieces of wood, cloth, spools, plastic bottles, cardboard boxes, and so forth. Also have on hand wax crayons, acrylic paints, and glue. Then see what fanciful creatures your child and you can dream up by gluing together some of these things and decorating them with crayons and acrylic paints. These toys will be much more thrilling to your child than store-bought creations, because she has made them herself. And they will do much more to develop her creativity and imagination than anything you could get in a store.

LARGE HOLLOW WOODEN BLOCKS

Every good nursery school or kindergarten has a set of large hollow wooden blocks, and children love to play with them. But, sad to say, very few homes where there are preschool children have such blocks for either indoor or outdoor play.

They are really very easy to make. You need only nail six boards together (half-inch plywood is probably best) in different sizes, such as 1' × 2' or 1' × 3'. Leave an open space between two boards on one side of the block so your child can grip the block more easily.

When you have finished nailing the block together, sand it down to remove any splintery surfaces. You can varnish or shellac it if you wish, but it's not absolutely necessary.

You will be amazed to see how much play value your preschooler gets out of this simple set of blocks.

WOODEN-HEAD PUPPETS

No elaborate skills in woodworking are necessary to create these unique puppets. Make them out of pine, the softest and easiest wood to work with. You can make them as large as a foot square, or much smaller. But the basic shape is the same: a wooden face topping a thin strip that the child can grasp.

The procedure is simple. Cut the pine board to shape and then sand it thoroughly. You can put in the facial features with wax crayons or acrylic paints. If you choose the latter, get a thin nylon paintbrush and cut the bristles very short; this will make it easier to paint lines on the wood. You can leave the rest of the wood unpainted, or you may want to cover the whole thing with clear acrylic gloss. Experiment by drawing on the appropriate size paper until you have figured out a whole cast of puppets that can be used by your child to act out a story. You and he can plan the characters together. Here are some suggestions:

Before you actually cut your wood, make some experimental hand puppets out of cardboard in different sizes. By doing this, you can find out which size your child likes best; some children prefer smaller ones, some larger ones.

If you want, you can build a simple stage for puppet plays. The stage is basically a piece of fence with a large hole cut into it, like this:

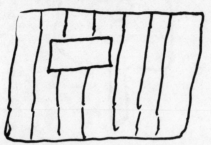

PLAY PEOPLE

This is another easy-to-make toy, using part of a pine plank as a base. Find reasonably large pictures of people in magazines and glue them to pieces of pine wood. Then cut out around each person with a scroll saw or an electric jigsaw if you have one. Paint over the whole figure with clear acrylic gloss as a protective coat for the picture. The gloss acts as both a glue and a clear paint.

When you have done this, you need only one thing more, something to make the figure stand up. Cut two rectangular pieces of pine large enough to form a base for a figure. Nail them to the front and back of the figure, as pictured below.

WOODEN SIGNS

These are not, strictly speaking, toys, but they are something your youngster will love. Start with an old familiar pine wood plank, one foot wide, and cut it down to the size you want. You will need a woodburning tool, which can be purchased in any hardware or toy or hobby store. Decide what you want the sign to say and then burn it into the wood. Here are some examples:

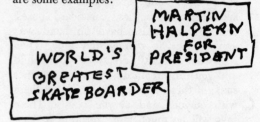

For an added touch, glue a picture of your child on the sign. Then paint the whole thing with acrylic colors and finish it with clear acrylic gloss.

CHILDREN'S BOOKS

There are two kinds of homemade children's books your child will enjoy, the kind you make for her, and the kind you help her make for herself. Let's start with the kind you make.

First, get a liberal supply of 8″ × 10″ paper—white or colored, depending on your preference. Then get a batch of old magazines with a lot of pictures in them. You might as well start saving old magazines now and asking other people to save theirs for you. Once you start making books for your child, you'll probably become addicted.

Equip yourself with a pair of scissors, a jar of glue, a small tin can, and an inexpensive paintbrush. Cut out any pictures you think are interesting and any words or phrases you think you might use in the book. Your book can be about anything—dogs or horses, cats or dinosaurs, animals of the forest, airplanes, flying saucers, little boys and girls, firemen or policemen—anything you think your child will be interested in. The age and sophistication of the child will determine to a great extent not only what subjects you choose, but also your selection of cutouts for the content of the book.

Once you have cut out enough pictures and words, begin assembling them on the pages of your book. You will not usually be able to complete what you want to say merely through the cutouts. You will probably need to use extra words, which you can put in with a black felt marker pen. The final result could look something like this:

The easy way to glue the pictures on is to pour some glue into a small can and apply with the brush. When all the pictures and words have been glued to the sheets of paper and the extra words have been printed in with the black felt marker pen, your child's book is ready for binding.

Either buy a binder in a stationery store, or, if you want something more elaborate, punch two holes in the pages at the appropriate places, and then saw two quarter-inch plywood boards for the cover. Drill holes in the boards at the right places and, using a stout string or twine, tie the pages of the book to the board covers. Then you can paint or stain the cover.

Now for the type of book your child writes with your help. Explain that she can make a book out of the pictures and words you both cut out of old magazines.

When you have amassed a fair-sized collection, spread them out on the floor and help your child decide what subject she wants the book to cover and what pictures and words and phrases she wants to use in her story. Whenever words are needed in the story that are not cut out of the magazines they can be printed in by your youngster. If she is too young to print well, she can dictate to you and you can print for her with the large black felt marker pen.

It is important to let her say what she wants, in her own way. Do not criticize her efforts, or you will discourage her from attempting further books. Don't worry; if she continues to write books with you, her ability to express herself clearly will improve. So just let her write down what she wants to say, regardless of mistakes.

When she has finished the book, make copies of the pages before you put them in a binder. You can send these copies to her grandparents or other relatives. You can even ask the people to whom you are sending the book to call or write or send her a dollar. This use of the positive reward system should strengthen her desire to do more books in the future.

You can do another kind of book with your child to promote his use of written language—one that comes entirely out of his own ideas. This type of book is best for ages three through five or six. Tell him you are going to help him write a book about himself. On an 8″ × 10″ piece of paper, print the first sentence: "This book is about Gordon." Then ask, "Now what else do you want to say about Gordon?"

"I like ice cream," your child says. You print that as the second sentence.

"What do you want to say in our next sentence?"

"Gordon likes to go fishing." And you print this sentence.

If he seems stumped at this point, you can easily stimulate more responses by asking such questions as, "What does Gordon hate? What movies does he like? What TV shows does he like? What kinds of secret wishes does he have? If he could do anything he wanted for one whole day, what would he do?" And so on.

It is Gordon's book, not yours. So don't try to improve it. Just print it as he tells it to you.

When you have finished, you can give it a title: The Story of Gordon, or The Book About Gordon.

The writing of these books can help a great deal in motivating a child to write, and in building self-confidence in his ability. Be sure to keep a copy of every book or letter he writes. You will be surprised, when he is twenty-five, how both of you will look back with delight on the books and letters you helped him write when he was three or five!

"BIG BOX"

This is the simplest and yet one of the most creative toys ever dreamed up for a child. Remember our principle that if 90 percent of the play is in the child and 10 percent in the toy, it is a good toy. Here is one toy in which that principle is certainly true. It is simply as huge a box as you can find (the kind a refrigerator or washing machine comes in, for example.) You can use it in two basic ways. First, you can merely give it to your child in its raw shape and let him figure out all the things he wants to do with it. (He will usually astound you with the number of novel uses he finds for the Big Box!)

Second, you can present Big Box to him and tell him that you will help him make whatever he wants out of it. Be prepared with a sharp cutting knife, a box of wax crayons (the thick kind), and a black felt marker. He will tell you what doors and windows he wants to cut out of it, etc. Try to let him do as much of the coloring and marking as possible. Your job is only to assist him with what he has difficulty with.

CARDBOARD DOLLS AND PLAY FIGURES

We've talked about making stuffed cloth dolls and animals. You can also make dolls and play figures out of cardboard.

Cardboard boxes can be found in nearly any market. All you need in addition to the box is a liberal supply of old magazines with pictures, some scissors, a sharp knife such as an X-acto knife, glue, an inexpensive applicator brush, and felt markers in several different colors.

Browse through the magazines and cut out figures or partial figures of people: grownups, teenagers, babies, athletes, fire fighters, police officers, or astronauts, as well as any kind of animal. You don't have to have a complete figure, because you can fill in what is missing with the felt marker.

Glue the cut-out figure to the cardboard, and when the glue has dried, cut it out carefully with the X-acto knife.

If you want your dolls or animals more sturdy, make a base for them out of wood. Simply cut a notch across the block of wood so that the cardboard doll or animal will fit in the notch. If you have a sophisticated workshop, you can use your electric saw to make what is known as a "dado" cut in the wooden block. But you can do the same thing with an ordinary hand saw.

In addition to dolls or animals made from magazine pictures, you can create your own animals by drawing them on the cardboard. If you can't draw a dog that looks like a dog you can draw fantasy animals, such as a mumpus, a gleech, or a swoon. Since nobody knows exactly what a mumpus, a gleech, or a swoon looks like, whatever you draw will be just fine.

You can draw hundreds of animals and make up your own names for them, and your preschool child will just love them. In fact, he can join in making up names for the imaginary animals. Be sure to draw an eye on each fantasy animal. The eye makes the animal look more alive.

Here are some examples of the shapes your animals might take:

Once you have drawn your fantasy animals on the cardboard, cut them out with the X-acto knife. A good way to finish them is to cover them with a sheer acrylic gloss, which gives them a protective coat and brings out the brilliance of whatever colors you have used.

I think you will discover that cardboard is a good medium to use, because it's so easy to cut. It is also light. This makes it easy to transport a box of cardboard figures from one house to another, or to take them on a trip.

You can use your cardboard fantasy animals either as they are or with the wood block base described above.

CARDBOARD CITIES AND WOOD CITIES

You can make buildings out of any size cardboard boxes; you will find different kinds in drugstores, shoe stores, supermarkets, hardware stores, and so forth. You can paint the windows and doors on the box or cut them out with an X-acto knife. You can also make movable doors or windows by cutting only three instead of four sides of the opening.

You can decorate the houses by using a colored felt marker, wax crayons, or acrylic paint.

When you finish, you will have a group of buildings of different shapes and sizes, such as these:

Obviously, you can make the same kind of buildings and cities with larger cardboard boxes as you can with smaller ones. But it's probably easier to start with the smaller ones to get the feel of it.

You can also try your hand at making a wooden city. The ideal place to acquire wood scraps for buildings is a cabinet maker's shop, or perhaps the scrap box of a lumber yard. Construction sites are also often a gold mine for wood scraps. What you are looking for are scraps approximately 1″ × 2″ to 2″ × 3″, or larger pieces that can be cut into those lengths.

If you can't find free scraps, you can have a lumber yard cut some for you. You can also get them to cut dowels of three-quarters to one inch thickness into short lengths of two or three inches, or you can do the same yourself with an old broomstick.

Each wood scrap can be a single building, or you can glue two or more sides together to make a larger building. As with previous projects, you can color or paint doors and windows and decorations on your wooden buildings.

Here's how some of your buildings will look:

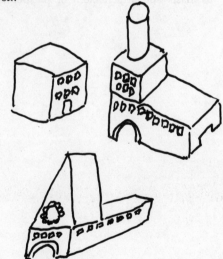

Let your child play on the floor with the buildings of her tiny town, or you can make a plywood base for her. Its size depends on how large you made the buildings. Perhaps three feet square would be good; half-inch-thick plywood is sturdy enough. Mark out streets on it, which you can color green. It will also enhance your toy city if you buy some small cars and trucks and other vehicles, such as Tootsietoy or Matchbox cars and trucks.

WOODEN BOATS AND CARS

Wooden boats and cars are very simple to make and will afford your child many hours of play value. Let's start with boats.

The basic structure is simplicity itself. You cut out two "boat shaped" pieces of wood, one larger than the other, and glue or nail them together; then you glue a piece of broomstick or doweling on top. Here's what it looks like:

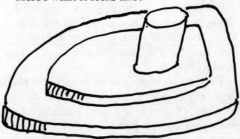

The boats can be as elaborate as you wish. You can glue on very thin dowels as masts and attach cloth or plastic sails in vivid colors. You can increase the size of the cabins and paint doors and windows on them.

Cars and trucks are also easy to make out of wood. For the body, use a chunky piece of wood of whatever size you want. The wheels can be made by cutting a large dowel into thin pieces.

Join the wheels to one another by thin dowels underneath the car. Attach the dowels to the underside of the car by steel brads that are big enough to let the dowels turn freely.

No matter how elaborate your cars and trucks are, they will all be variations of the same basic idea: a single piece of chunky wood with four round wheels attached under the vehicle, like this:

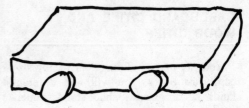

FOOD SOURCES OF VITAMINS
VITAMIN A

Milk (cow and human)
Cheddar cheese
Liver (beef or chicken)
Liverwurst
Butter, margarine
Apricot
Orange
Egg
Peach
Watermelon
Carrot
Squash
Sweet potato
Green pea
Spinach
Tomato

VITAMIN C

Milk (cow and human)
Broccoli
Brussels sprouts
Cabbage
Cantaloupe
Citrus fruits
Potato
Tomato
Strawberry

VITAMIN D

Most vitamin-fortified foods (milk, evaporated and homogenized; infant formula; margarine; cereals)

VITAMIN E

Milk (cow and human)
Egg
Ground beef
Liver
Chicken breast
Potato
Whole wheat bread
Margarine, butter
Strawberry
Orange
Green bean

VITAMIN K

Green leafy vegetables
Meats
Dairy products

THIAMINE
(VITAMIN B₁)

Milk (cow and human)
Infant cereals, high protein or rice
Oatmeal
Rice, enriched
Bread, whole wheat or enriched white
Macaroni, enriched
Pork
Hamburger
Liver (beef or chicken)
Green pea
Great northern bean

RIBOFLAVIN
(VITAMIN B₂)

Milk (cow and human)
Infant formula

Cheddar cheese
Infant cereals, high protein or rice
Oatmeal
Macaroni, enriched
Liver
Beef or chicken
Broccoli
Green pea
Spinach

PYRIDOXINE
(VITAMIN B₆)

Milk (cow and human)
Infant cereals, high protein or rice
Liver (beef or chicken)
Beef
Chicken
Peanut butter
Egg
Bread, whole wheat or enriched white
Green pea
Tomato
Squash
Banana
Orange
Strawberry

FOLATE OR FOLACIN

Milk (cow and human)
Yogurt
Eggs
Liver (beef, lamb, or pork)
Kidney (beef)
Tuna fish
Ground beef
Spinach
Broccoli
Beet
Romaine lettuce
Brewer's yeast
Bread, whole wheat or enriched white
Orange or orange juice
Banana
Apple

COBALAMIN
(VITAMIN B₁₂)

Lean meat
Liver

Eggs
Fish
Milk (cow and human)

PANTOTHENIC ACID

Meat
Eggs
Cereals
Fresh vegetables
Milk (cow and human)

BIOTIN

Organ meats
Dairy products
Eggs
Cereal grains
Milk (cow and human)
Legumes

FOOD SOURCES OF IRON AND CALCIUM
IRON*

Iron-fortified infant formula
Infant cereals, high protein or rice
Beef
Chicken
Liver (beef or chicken)
Liverwurst
Frankfurter
Egg
Pork and beans
Peanut butter
Bread, enriched white
Macaroni, enriched
Carrot
Orange
Canned pears

*It has been found that iron-containing foods are better absorbed when taken in conjunction with a food product containing Vitamin C, such as orange juice, tomato juice, or a potato. It is not absorbed as well when taken with caffeine-containing products—cola drinks, tea, or chocolate.

CALCIUM

The young child needs one to one and a half cups of milk per day in order to supply adequate calcium for growth. If the child does not like milk there are other sources of calcium. We list these here:

½ cup of milk = 1″ cube of cheddar cheese
½ cup of milk = ½ cup yogurt
½ cup of milk = ½ cup cottage cheese
½ cup of milk = 2 Tbsp. cream cheese
½ cup of milk = ½ cup ice cream
½ cup of milk = ½ tsp. calcium substitute

SUGGESTED DIETARY NEEDS OF THE CHILD FROM 1 TO 5 YEARS OF AGE
(From Basic Food Groups)
PROTEIN FOODS

3 servings per day consisting of:

1 egg or
1–2 oz. poultry or fish or
¾ to 1 oz. of cheese or
1–2 Tbsp. peanut butter or
1 frankfurter with roll or
½ cup baked beans or
1 cup dry cereal with 4–6 oz. milk or
½ cup cooked cereal or
1 cup yogurt, made from whole milk

VEGETABLES AND FRUITS

Fruit: 1 citrus fruit or other vegetable or fruit rich in Vitamin C. This can be served from a can (4–8 Tbsp.), raw (½–1 small), or as juice (3–4 oz.).

* Vegetable: 4–5 servings, including one green leafy or yellow. This can be given cooked (1–4 Tbsp.) or raw (1–2 pieces).

* Fruit and vegetable servings may be substituted for each other if the child refuses to eat one or the other.

DAIRY PRODUCTS

Milk or milk equivalent, 1–1½ cups per day. (Powdered skim milk (2 Tbsp. = 4 oz.) may be incorporated into other foods to supply the needs.)

BREAD AND CEREALS

3 servings per day consisting of:

½–1 slice of whole grain bread or
½–1 cup dry cereal or
¼–½ cup of spaghetti, macaroni, noodles, or rice or
2–3 crackers or ¼–½ cup cooked cereal at each serving

SAMPLE MENU FOR A YOUNG CHILD
BREAKFAST

1 high-protein food
1 fruit, preferably citrus (4 oz. orange juice, 1 orange, or ½ grapefruit)
Milk, 6–8 oz. (may be given with cereal)
Bread with butter or margarine

LUNCH

1 serving of protein food
Vegetables, 2 servings (1 raw and 1 cooked or 2 of either)
Bread, 1 slice with 1 tsp. butter
Milk, 6–8 oz.
Dessert—serving of fruit or a pudding containing milk, eggs, or fruit

DINNER

1 serving of protein food
Vegetables, 1 or 2 cooked or 1 raw
Bread and butter, 1 slice with 1 tsp. butter
Milk, 6–8 oz.
Dessert

SNACK SUGGESTIONS

Dry cereal out of a box or with milk
Raw vegetables or vegetable juice
Fresh fruit or fruit juice
Crackers or bread with cheese
Graham cracker with peanut butter or
    cream cheese

Cream cheese or cheddar cheese chunks
Nuts (if your child is 4 years or older)
Ice cream, frozen yogurt, or sherbet
Yogurt
Milk
Pudding
Hard-boiled egg

APPROXIMATE REFINED CARBOHYDRATE CONTENT OF POPULAR SWEET FOODS EXPRESSED IN AMOUNTS EQUIVALENT TO TEASPOONFULS OF SUGAR (AS COMPILED BY THE AMERICAN DENTAL ASSOCIATION)

Food	Serving	Sugar Equivalent
* Hershey Bar	small size	7 tsp.
Chocolate fudge	1½ in. square	4 tsp.
Chocolate mints	1 medium	3 tsp.
Chewing gum	1 stick	½ tsp.
Lifesaver	1	⅓ tsp.
Chocolate cake	1 slice of 2-layer, with icing	15 tsp.
Angelfood cake	1 slice	6 tsp.
Doughnut, plain	3 in. diameter	8 tsp.
Cream puff with icing	1 avg. custard filled	5 tsp.
Crackers	1 cracker	½ tsp.
Macaroons	1 large	3 tsp.
Brownies	2″ × 2″ × ¾″	3 tsp.
Gelatin	½ cup	4 tsp.
Baked custard	½ cup	4 tsp.
Ice cream	⅛ quart	5–6 tsp.
Sherbet	⅛ quart	6–8 tsp.
Apple pie	medium slice	12 tsp.
Cherry pie	medium slice	14 tsp.
Pumpkin pie	medium slice	10 tsp.
Chocolate sauce	1 Tbsp.	4½ tsp.
Jam	1 Tbsp. level	3 tsp.
Jelly	1 Tbsp. level	2½ tsp.
Syrup, maple	1 Tbsp. level	2½ tsp.
Pancake	1 average	3½ tsp.
Honey	1 Tbsp. level	3 tsp.
Chocolate milk	1 cup, 5 oz.	6 tsp.
Cocoa	1 cup	4 tsp.
Coca-Cola	1 bottle, 6 oz.	3⅓ tsp.
Ginger ale	6 oz.	4⅓ tsp.

Peaches, canned	2 halves in juice	3½ tsp.
Apricots, dried	4–6 halves	4 tsp.
Dates, dried	3–4 stoned	4½ tsp.
Raisins	¼ cup	4 tsp.
Orange juice	1 cup	2 tsp.
Fruit cocktail	½ cup	5 tsp.
Grape juice, sweetened	½ cup	3⅔ tsp.

* Candy runs from 75 to 85 percent sugar. Popular candy bars are likely to weigh from 1 to 5 ounces and may contain 5 to 20 teaspoonfuls of sugar.

MORE COMMON POISONOUS PLANTS*

Bird-of-paradise flower—seeds, pods
Bleeding-heart—foliage, roots
Burning bush, wahoo—fruit leaves
Calla lily, dumb cane, elephant's ear— all parts
Chinaberry—bark leaves, seeds
Christmas rose—all parts
Chrysanthemum—all parts
Croton—seed
Daffodil, jonquil, narcissus—bulb
Daphne—all parts
Elderberry—leaves, roots, bark
Foxglove—leaves
Holly, black alder—berries
Hyacinth—bulb
Jack-in-the-pulpit—all parts
Jerusalem cherry—fruit
Jessamine—all parts
Jimsonweed—all parts

Laburnum, golden chain—leaves, seeds
Lady's-slipper—hairs of stems and leaves
Lantana—all parts
Laurel—all parts
Lily of the valley—leaves, flowers
Mistletoe—all parts, especially berries
Morning-glory—seeds
Mulberry, red—green berries and sap
Nightshade—berries, leaves, and roots
Oleander—leaves, peas
Poinsettia—leaves, stem
Pokeweed, pokeberry—all parts
Potato—green tubers, new sprouts
Privet—berries and leaves
Rhododendron—all parts
Rhubarb—leaves
Spanish broom, Scotch broom—seeds or leaves
Star anise, Japanese—all parts
Star-of-Bethlehem—all parts
Sweet pea—all parts, seeds
Wisteria—pods
Yew—all parts

* Consult your Poison Control office or your pediatrician for a list of other plants which may be indigenous to your area.

I N D E X

Abandonment fears, at four years to six years, 380
Abdomen, of newborn, 39
Abdominal injury, first aid for, 461
Abdominal pain, 441–42
Abilities, of newborn, 42
Abnormal movements, of eyes, 434–435
About Dying (Stein), 410
About Handicaps (Stein), 385
Abrasion, *see* Scrape or abrasion
Abscess, breast, 80
Academic skills, and preschooler, 300
Accident prevention
    from birth to six years, 367–69
    in first adolescence, 268–69
    in infancy, 173–75
    and preschooler, 325
    in toddlerhood, 229–30
Acne, 36
Active child, with baby-sitters, 226–227
Active sleep, 55, 126–27, 130
    see also REM sleep
Activity level, 104
Acute otitis media, 435
Adaptability, 104
ADD (attention deficit disorder), 412–14
Adenoidectomy, 430–31
Adoption
    and preschooler, 315
    and stepchildren, 350
Adulthood goals, and preschooler, 296–303
    arithmetic, 300
    communication, 299
    courtesy, 296–98
    curiosity, 303
    ethics, 298–99
    physical affection, 299–300
    reading, 300
    self-assertion, 300
    sex education, 300–302
    writing, 300
Adult intelligence, 28

Adventures of Paul Bunyan, The, 254
Affection, *see* Physical affection
Aggressiveness, 267
Ainsworth, Dr. Mary, 112
Air conditioners, and allergic rhinitis, 390
Airplane trips
    and ear problems, 436
    and sinusitis, 429
    see also Long trips
Alcohol, 71, 74
Allan, John A. B., 115
Allergens, and eczema, 389–90
Allergic rhinitis (hay fever), 387, 390–91, 425
Allergies, 92, 138, 140, 386–87
    and breast feeding, 76
All Our Children Learning (Bloom), 308
Alopecia (hair loss), 431
AMA Directory, 361
Ambivalence, in blended family, 347
Amblyopia, 434
American Academy of Pediatrics, 370
American Dental Association, 371
American Diabetes Association, 403
American Foundation for the Blind, 420
American Lung Association, 388
American Society of Dentistry for Children, 371
Ames, Dr., 279
Ampicillin, 455
Amputation, first aid for, 461
Anal fissure, 443
Analgesics, 75
Anal stenosis, 167
Anaphylactic shock, 387
Anemia, 366, 391–92
Anesthesia, 381
Anesthetic sprays, 430
Anger
    of children after divorce, 341
    of parent, 27–28
Animal diseases, transmitted to humans, 392

Annoying behavior, and preschooler, 316
Antibiotics, 74–75, 80, 166, 365, 392–393
    for diarrhea, 444
    for meningitis, 432
    for pneumonia, 427
    for sinusitis, 430
    for strep throat, 400
    for URI, 426
    for whooping cough, 401
Anticonvulsants, 75
Antihistamines, 75, 439, 454, 462
    and allergic rhinitis, 390–91
Anxiety, in toddlerhood, 190–91
Apgar score, 43
Appendicitis, 442
Appetite
    vs. hunger, 132
    loss of, 393
    of sick child, 376
Areolar engorgement, 79
Arithmetic, and preschooler, 300
Arm fracture/dislocation, first aid for, 463
    see also Extremities
Arterial bleeding (severe), first aid for, 463
Arthralgia, 457
Arthritis, 457
Aseptic method, for bottle feeding, 94, 95
Aspirin, 75
Association for Children with Down Syndrome, 418
Association for Children with Learning Disabilities, 414
Asthma, 75, 387–89, 424
Atherosclerosis, 402
Atopic dermatitis, *see* Eczema
Attention deficit disorder, *see* ADD
Attention span, 104
Autism, 414–15
Autistic Children: A Guide for Parents (Wing), 415
Axillary temperature, 373

Babbling, of babies, 28–29
Babies
    babbling of, 28–29
    bath for, 125–26
    breast-fed vs. bottle-fed, 76, 78
    classifying by behavioral style, 25
    and language, 29
    nursing styles of, 70
    sleep of, 126–31
    thin vs. fat, 133
    see also Newborn
Baby
    in first few weeks, 103–4
    fussy, 83
    handling, 110–17
    handling when crying, 112–14
    holding, 110–11, 116
    holding bottle, 98
    imitating, 150
    interaction with, 116–17
    as personality, 104–5
    picking up, 110–11
    physical play with, 117
    soothing, 117
    talking to, 149–50
    types of, 115–16
    wrapping, 111–12
    see also Daily care; Delayed baby;
        Diapering; Infancy; Playing
        "baby"; Premature baby; Re-
        tarded baby; Sick baby
Baby cereal, 138
Baby Exercise Book, The (Levy), 151
Baby Learning Through Baby Play
    (Gordon), 151
Baby-sitters, 331–32, 334
    in first adolescence, 267
    and preschooler, 324
    and separation anxiety, 169, 170–
        171
    and toddlerhood, 226–27
"Baby" teeth, 38
Baby walkers, 110
Back fracture/dislocation, first aid
    for, 463
Back injury, first aid for, 461
Bacterial conjunctivitis, 434
Bad breath, 439
Baked goods, 197
Barefoot, 458
Barnes, Dr. George, 69–70
"Barracudas," 70
Barter system, for mother with cus-
    tody, 340
Basement, and accident prevention,
    368
Bassinet, 106, 127
Bath, 72, 154
    for babies, 125–26
    for fever, 406

and itching, 454
Bathroom, accident prevention in,
    368
Bathtime problems, in infancy, 168
Bath toys, 211
Bathtub, 107
Bed, of baby, 127
Bedtime blues, for babies, 130–31
Bedtime resistance, in toddlerhood,
    219–20
Bed-wetting (enuresis), 447–48
Bee sting, first aid for, 462
Behavior
    of abused child, 394–95
    vs. feelings, 357
    in infancy, 55, 104–5
    and nutrition, 141
    reinforcement of, 358
    self-stimulation, 411
    during separation for baby-sitters,
        227
    of sick child, 375
    see also Annoying behavior; Unde-
        sirable behavior
Behavioral concerns, 408–11
    bowel or bladder incontinence,
        410–11
    coping with death, 408–10
    personal-social interaction, poor,
        410
    self-stimulation behavior, 411
Behavioral style, classifying babies
    by, 25
Best Word Book Ever (Scarry), 212
Bibs, 137
Bicycle safety, 325
Biological family, vs. blended family,
    347
Biological needs, and preschooler,
    287–88
Biological temperament, 26, 31
Birch, Dr. Herbert, 25, 104, 105
Birds (pet), 392
Birth to six years, see Routine health
    care
Birth to three months, 58–59
    daily care for, 110–16
    intellectual development at, 58–59,
        147–51
    language development at, 58
    motor development at, 58
    social development at, 59
Bites and stings, first aid for, 462–63
    animal or human, 462
    bee, wasp, hornet, yellow jacket,
        462
    black widow spider, brown recluse
        spider, scorpion, 462
    marine animals, 462
    snake, nonpoisonous, 462

snake, poisonous, 462–63
    tick, 173, 462
Black race, 391
Black-widow spider, 462
Bladder control, 262–63
Bladder incontinence, 410–11
Bladder infections, 446
Bleeding, 461
Bleeding (severe), arterial and ve-
    nous, first aid for, 463
Blemishes, 36
Blended family
    vs. biological family, 347
    jealousy and ambivalence in, 346–
        347
    new child in, 350–51
Blindness, 44, 412
    see also Vision impairment; Vision
        problems
Blink reflex, 58
Blisters, 449, 452
Blocked tear duct, 432
Blocks, wooden, 210
Blood clotting, 44
Blood sugar, and diabetes mellitus,
    402
Blood tests, for newborn, 45
Bloom, Dr. Benjamin, 28, 308, 309,
    357
Blotches, 35, 36
BM, see Bowel movements
Body
    and intellectual stimulation in in-
        fancy, 150–51
    at three to six months, 152–53
    in toddlerhood, 214
Body movements, of sick child, 375
Body temperature, 373
    and fever, 404, 405–6
    of sick child, 376
    see also Temperature
Boils, 450
Bonded maid service, 47
Bonding, 43, 47, 52–53, 103
Bones: Fractures/dislocations, first
    aid for, 463
    see also Musculoskeletal system
Books
    for pretoddler, 156–57
    in toddlerhood, 212
    see also Reading
Bookshelves, 175
Bottle-in-bed habit, 98–99
Bottle feeding, 45, 91–101
    aseptic method for, 94, 95
    and baby holding bottle, 98
    and bottle-in-bed habit, 98–99
    vs. breast feeding, 76, 78
    choosing bottles, 91
    to cup drinking, 99–100

formula for, 91–93
giving, 95–96
and nipples, 97
and playing "baby," 101
propping bottles, 97–98
and refrigeration, 97
schedule for, 96
single-bottle method for, 94–95
terminal heating method for, 93
weaning from, 99, 100–101
Bottles
  baby holding, 98
  choosing, 91
  propping, 97–98
  out of refrigerator, 97
Botulism, 139
Bowel incontinence, 410–11
Bowel movements (BM), 158–59,
    185, 260
  and breast feeding, 83
  and swallowed foreign body, 461
  see also Toilet learning; Toilet
    teaching
Bowlegs, 456
Brain damage
  in cerebral palsy, 415
  after Reye's syndrome, 421
Bran, 443
Brandenburg, Fritz, 379
Brazelton, Dr. T. Berry, 105, 140,
    260
Breast
  of newborn, 38
  preparing, for breast feeding, 66–
    67
Breast abscess, 80
Breast feeding, 42, 43, 45, 64–90
  advantages of, 64
  and allergies, 387
  attitude toward, 64–65
  avoiding during, 74
  both breasts for, 69
  vs. bottle feeding, 76, 78
  and breast-fed baby, 78
  and breast problems, 78–82
  and burping, 122
  and clothing, 73
  colostrum, 70
  components of milk in, 75–76
  and drug intake, 74–75
  facts vs. myths, 65–66
  and father, 65
  foods during, 74
  and fussy baby, 83
  getting started, 67
  and home front, 72
  and infant problems, 82–83
  let-down reflex, 70–71
  and liquids, 73, 74
  and manual (hand) expression, 72

nursing patterns for, 69–70
nursing positions for, 67–68
and nursing support groups, 89–90
and nutrition, 73
other mothers and, 66
and physical abnormalities, 82
preparing breast for, 66–67
rewards of, 77–78
schedule for, 76–77
and special situations, 83–89
and poor sucking, 82
support for, 66
time for, 68–69
and vitamin supplements, 74
  see also Nursing; Weaning
Breast infection, 80
Breast problems, and breast feeding,
    78–82
Breast pump, 79
Breast rejection, 88
Breasts
  both, for breast feeding, 69
  flabby, 82
Breath, bad, 439
Breath holding, 393
Breathing, 461
  and breast feeding, 68
  of newborn, 38, 40–41
  see also Respiratory tract symptoms
Breathing exercises, 388
Breech delivery, 36
Brightman, A. J., 418
Bronchitis, 424, 427
Brown recluse spider, 462
Bruises, 469
Bubble baths, 446
Bureau drawers, 174
Burns, 175, 368, 449–50
  first aid for, 464
Burping, 122–23
  and bottle feeding, 95–96
  and breast feeding, 122
B vitamins, 196
  see also Vitamin B_{12}

Caffeine, 74
Calamine lotion, 454
Calcium, 65, 73, 139
  in toddlerhood, 197
Calm reactions, to hospitalization,
    382–83
Calories, and sweets, 197
Cancer, 393–94
Candy, see Hard candy
Canker sores, 440
Canned fruits, 197
Caplan, Frank, 63
Car, accident prevention in, 174, 229,
    269, 325, 369
  see also Driving car

Carbohydrates, 132, 133
Cardiac massage, external, 461
Cardiopulmonary resuscitation, see
    CPR
Cardiovascular system
  in first adolescence, 235
  in infancy, 57
  and preschooler, 276
  in toddlerhood, 185
Caregiver, 22, 330–34
  family day care, 332, 334
  large-group day care, 332–33, 334
  parents as, 102–3
  relatives, 331, 334
  see also Baby-sitters; Child abuse
    and neglect
Carey, Dr. William, 131
Carpets, and eczema, 389
  see also Rugs
Carriers, infant, 108, 149
Car seat, 50, 107
Cataract, 435
Cats, 172–73, 423
  diseases of, 392
Center for Sickle Cell Anemia, 392
Central nervous system immaturity,
    in infancy, 166
Central (straight ahead) vision, 55
Cephalohematoma, 37
Cereal, 138
Cerebral palsy, 412, 415–16, 420
Cesarean section, 36
  and breast feeding, 83
Changing table, 106
Charlie and the Chocolate Factory,
    311
Charlotte's Web (White), 410
Chemical burns, first aid for, 464
Chemical rhinitis, 425
Chess, Dr. Stella, 25, 104, 105
Chest
  first aid for, 464
  of newborn, 38
  see also Head, neck, and chest
    problems
Chicken pox (varicella), 398–99
Chiggers, 452
Child abuse and neglect, 394–96
  by caregiver, 395–96
Child Health Record, 370
Childproofing, 229, 269
Child raising, nonsexist, 180–81
Children
  biological temperament of, 26, 31
  characteristics of, 104–5
  and death, 344, 408–10
  after divorce, 339–42
  first six years of, 356–57, 358
  intelligence of, 28–30
  most important teacher of, 358

Children (*cont.*)
  as people, 355
  personality of, 31, 356–57
  reading skills of, 29–30
  rights of, 357
  temperament of, 104–5
  traumatizing, 25
  types of, 83, 85, 105, 113, 116–17,
    249, 385, 394, 412
  uniqueness of, 355–56
  see also Chronic illness or impair-
    ment; Health problems; Sick
    child; Stepchildren; Well-child
    care
Child's room, accident prevention in,
  368
Choice of foods, in toddlerhood, 200
Choices, in first adolescence, 247
Choking
  and breast feeding, 82
  first aid for, 464–65
Chores, *see* Home chores
Christmas tree, 175
Chronic illness or impairment, 384–
  386
Chronic serous otitis media, 435
Church-affiliated nursery school, 321
Churchill, Winston, 48
Circumcision, 39, 44–45, 121, 448
Cleaning hands and face, 125
Cleft lip, 439
Cleft palate, 439
Clip-on baby chair, 136
Cloth diapers, laundering, 119–20
Clothing, 368
  and breast feeding, 73
  for fever, 407
  see also Dress-up clothes
Clotting, blood, 44
Cold, *see* URI
Cold sores, 440
Cold weather
  and earache, 436–37
  first aid for, 465
Colic, 83, 167–68, 394, 441
Collapsible stroller, 109
Colostrum, 66, 70
Coma, 465
Comfi Baby Products, 108
Comfort habits
  in first adolescence, 257
  of preschooler, 313
  and separation anxiety, 170
  in toddlerhood, 215
Comic strips, 254
Commercially prepared baby foods,
  138–39
Commercially prepared formulas, 92
Common cold, *see* URI
Communication, and preschooler, 299

Compliments, and preschooler, 297
Comprehensive child development
  center, 333
Computer, 29
Concepts, in first adolescence, 255–
  256
Conductive hearing loss, 438
Congenital abnormality, 424
Congenital dysplasia, of hip, 456
Congenital heart disease, 363, 441
Congestion, of nose, 438–39
Conjunctivitis (pinkeye), 432–34
  bacterial, 434
  viral, 433
Constipation, 159–60, 442–43
Contact, with newborn, 43, 52
Contact dermatitis, 455
Contagious diseases, 396–401
  chicken pox, 398–99
  fifth disease, 399
  measles, 85, 365–66, 397, 403–4,
    405
  mumps, 85, 366, 396
  roseola, 399
  rubella (Geman measles), 85, 366,
    397–98
  scarlet fever, 400, 425
  strep throat, 400, 425
  whooping cough (pertussis), 365,
    400–401, 404
  see also Infectious diseases
Contraceptives, oral, 75
Contracting, and preschooler, 303–4
Convalescence, after hospitalization,
  383–84
Convulsions (seizures, fits), 465
Cooperative play school, 321
*Coping with Prolonged Health Im-
  pairment in Your Child* (Mc-
  Collom), 386
Cords, and baby, 174
Cornell, study on preschool sleep at,
  286
Coughing, 424
  and whooping cough, 401
Cough medicines, 75
Cough suppressant, 426
Council on Exceptional Children, 412
Counseling, 345, 386
  for child after divorce, 342
  for mother with custody, 341
  for stepparents, 349
Courtesy, and preschooler, 296–98
Coveralls, 137
Cow's milk, 76, 92
  see also Milk
CPR (cardiopulmonary resuscita-
  tion), 372, 461
Cracked nipples, 81
Cradle cap, 56–57, 165–66

Cradle gym, 152
Craniosynostosis, 363
Crawling, 154–55, 394
Creams, and eczema, 389
Creativity, *see* Right-hemisphere
  thinking
Crib, 106, 117, 127, 368
Crib climber, 220
Crib death, *see* SIDS
Crib gym, *see* Cradle gym
Crossed eyes, 37, 434
Croup, 427–28
Crying, 41, 112–14
  and breath holding, 393
  of sick child, 375
Cuddling, in infancy, 52
Cuisenaire Rods Parents, 312
Cup, 136
  from bottle feeding, 99–100
  and nutrition, 143
Curiosity, and preschooler, 303
Curious George Goes to the Hospital
  (Rey/Rey), 381
Custodial care, 332
Cut, first aid for, 469
Cyanosis, 44
Cystic fibrosis, 402
Cystitis, *see* Urinary tract infection

Daily care (infant), 102–31
  basic equipment for, 105–10
  bathing, 125–26
  bathing and cleaning, 125–26
  at birth to three months, 110–16
  burping, 122–23
  circumcision care, 121
  cleaning hands and face, 125
  dental hygiene, 124
  diapering, 118–20
  dressing and undressing, 121–22
  feeding, 122
  in first few weeks, 103–4
  handling baby, 110–17
  hiccups, 123
  hygiene, general, 124–25
  navel care, 120–21
  outdoors, 123–24
  at six to twelve months, 117
  sleep, 126–31
  at three to six months, 116–17
  see also Routine health care
Dairy products, 443
Danger, *see* Accident prevention
Dating, and widowed single parent,
  345
Darwin, Charles, 48
Dawdling, of preschooler, 317–18
Day-care center, 321
  see also Family day care; Large-
    group day care

Dead Bird, The (Wise), 410
Deaf child, 412
Deaf Like Me (Spradley/Spradley), 417
Death, 344, 408–10
  vs. divorce, 347
Decongestants, 426, 439
Deep sleep, 55
Dehydration, 445, 447
Delayed baby, and breast feeding, 85
Democratic rights, 357
Dennis, Dr. Wayne, 53
Dental care, 124, 369–70
Dental health, and breast feeding vs. bottle feeding, 76
Dentist game, 371
Depression, postpartum, 50
Depth perception, 55
Dermatitis, atopic, *see* Eczema
Dermatitis, contact, 455
Desirable behavior, and preschooler, 303–4
Developmental concerns, 411
Developmental day-care center, 333
Developmental disabilities, 411–21
  ADD (attention deficit disorder), 412–14
  autism, 414–15
  cerebral palsy, 412, 415–16, 420
  Down Syndrome, 85, 417–18
  epilepsy, 393, 416–17
  hearing impairment, 417, 438
  mental retardation, 417–18
  spina bifida, 418–19
  vision impairment, 419–20, 434–35
  weight problems, 420–21
  see also Behavioral concerns
Developmental tasks, and preschooler, 287–92
Diabetes insipidus, 402
Diabetes mellitus, 402
Diapering, 39, 118–20
  changing, 118–19
  cleaning while, 119
  equipment for, 118
  and plastic pants, 119
Diaper rash, 119–20, 164–65, 443, 454
Diarrhea, 56, 74, 85, 133, 160–61, 442, 444
  of sick child, 375
Dietary change
  and constipation, 443
  and diarrhea, 444
Different child, 385
"Difficult to manage child," 105, 113, 116–17, 249
Diphtheria immunization, 364
Discipline
  vs. punishment, 357

and stepchildren, 350
Discipline, in first adolescence, 246–252
  controlling expression of feelings, 250–52
  rebellion, 249–50
  techniques, 246–47
  time out, 248–49
  undesirable behavior, 247–48
Discipline, in infancy, 144–46
  and intellectual stimulation, 146
  and rapport, 144–45
  and spanking, 145–46
Discipline, and preschooler, 296–307
  adulthood goals, 296–303
  desirable behavior, teaching, 303–304
  misbehavior, avoiding, 304–7
Discipline, in toddlerhood, 202–8
  distraction, 204
  environmental control, 203
  positive reward system, 204–6
  reverse time out, 206–7
  spanking, 207
  time out, 206, 207
  and typical toddler behavior, 208
Discoloration, of stool, 445
Dishwasher compound, 175
Dislocations, first aid for, 463
Disposable bottles, 97
Disposable diapers, 119
Distractibility, 104
Distraction
  in first adolescence, 246
  in toddlerhood, 204
Divorce, 22
  children after, 339–42
  vs. death, 347
  see also Father without custody; Mother with custody
Divorced fathers, 336
Doctor
  for croup, 428
  for diarrhea, 161
  for ear problems, 435–38
  for eye problems, 433–35
  and fever, 405, 406, 407
  for gastro-intestinal problems, 442–445
  for musculoskeletal problems, 457
  for nose problems, 439
  for pneumonia, 427
  and sick child, 376
  and skin problems, 449–53, 455–56
  for URI, 426
  for urinary tract problems, 446–49
  visit to, 370–71
Doctor kits, 381
Dodson, Dr. Fitzhugh, 153, 212
Dogs, 172–73, 423

diseases of, 392
Dolls, 211
Doll's eye reflex, 40
Double-diapering, 164
Double vision, 55
Down Syndrome (DS), 85, 417–18
DPT shot, 364–65, 405
  for diphtheria, 364
  for pertussis (whooping cough), 365
  for tetanus (lockjaw), 365
Drawing, in toddlerhood, 212
Dream sleep, 55
Dresser drawer, 127
Dressing
  dawdling while, 317–18
  for outdoors, 123–24
  in toddlerhood, 191–92
  and undressing, 121–22
Dress-up clothes, 211
Dried fruits, 197
Driving car, 50
Drouillard, Richard, 420
Drowning, 325, 369, 465
Drugs, 442
  and breast feeding, 74–75
DS, *see* Down Syndrome
Duct, plugged, 79–80
Durkin, Dr. Dolores, 29–30, 308, 309
Dust, and allergic rhinitis, 390
Dysplasia, hip, 456

Earache, 435–37
Ear discharges, 437–38
Eardrum, perforation of, 437–38
Ear infections, 397
Early readers, mothers of, 30, 308–9
Ear problems, 435–38
  earache, 435–37
  ear discharges, 437–38
  hearing impairment, 417, 438
Ears
  in first adolescence, 235
  first aid for, 465
  foreign body in, 465
  in infancy, 149–50
  of newborn, 38
  of preschooler, 275
  of sick child, 375
  at three to six months, 153
  in toddlerhood, 184
Earwax, 437
Easy baby, 116
"Easy child," 105
Eating with family, in toddlerhood, 200–201
  see also Food; Nutrition
Eating style
  in infancy, 143
  in toddlerhood, 194–95

Echolalia, 414
Eczema, 387, 389–90, 454
Edema, 36
Eggs, 139, 196
Electrical appliances, 368
Electrical cords, 174
Electrical outlets, 368
Electric shock, first aid for, 465–66
Elizabeth (Ulrich), 420
Emergencies, in toddlerhood, 230
Emergency numbers, 372
Emotional adjustments, and stepparents, 346–47
Emotional changes, in mothers, 50
Emotional readiness, for toilet learning, 261
Employment agencies, 47
Encephalitis, 366, 397, 399, 431, 432
Encopresis, 443
Endocrine system, in infancy, 56
Engorgement, 79
Enuresis, *see* Bed-wetting
Environment, labeling, 156
Environmental changes
    in first adolescence, 268
    in infancy, 171–72
    and preschooler, 324–25
    in toddlerhood, 227–28
Environmental control
    and breath holding, 393
    in first adolescence, 246
    and sibling rivalry, 225
    and temper tantrums, 190, 217
    in toddlerhood, 203
Ephedrine, 75
Epiglottis, 428
Epiglottis (floppy) syndrome, 41
Epilepsy (seizure disorder), 393, 416–17
Epilepsy Foundation of America, 417
Episiotomy, 50
Equipment (basic), for daily care, 105–10
Erythema infectiosum, *see* Fifth disease
Ethical conduct, and preschooler, 298–99
Eustachian tube, 184
Exceptional Parent, The, 412
"Excited ineffectives," 70
Exercise, 366–67
    and asthma, 388
Expressing feelings, 357
    in first adolescence, 250–52
    during hospitalization, 383
    and preschooler, 289
External cardiac massage, 461
External otitis, *see* Swimmer's ear
Extremities (arms, legs, hands, feet), first aid for, 466–67

Eye color, and skin color, 37
Eye medication, 37, 43–44, 67
Eye movements, 55
    see also Abnormal movements
Eyes, 432–35
    and allergic rhinitis, 391
    blocked tear duct, 432
    chemical injury, 466
    conjunctivitis, 432–34
    first aid for, 466
    in first adolescence, 235
    foreign body in, 466
    in infancy, 55, 147–49
    injuries to, 434, 466
    of newborn, 37
    of preschooler, 275
    of sick child, 375
    stye, 434
    swollen eyes, 434
    at three to six months, 153
    in toddlerhood, 184
    trauma, 466
    vision impairment, 419–20
    vision problems, 434–35

Face
    cleaning, 125
    in first adolescence, 235
    of preschooler, 275
    in toddlerhood, 184
Fainting, 467
Falling asleep, 128–29
Families (Patterson), 414
Family
    changing, 22
    and diabetes mellitus, 402
    eating with, 200–201
    and sick child, 379
    typical American, 22
    see also Blended family
Family council, and stepfamily, 349–350
Family day care (small group day care), 332, 334
Family interaction
    in first adolescence, 238
    and preschooler, 279–81
Family practitioner, 361
Family romance, 348
    and preschooler, 290
Family support groups, 394
Fantasies, at four years to six years, 379–80
    see also Magical thinking
Fantz, Dr. R. L., 147–48
Fast-food restaurants, 201, 293
Fat, in breast milk, 75
Father
    and breast feeding, 65

    as caretaker, 102–3
    and chronically ill or impaired child, 385
    and personality traits, 31
    see also Divorced fathers
Father without custody, 343–44
Father surrogate, 342, 345
Fats, 132, 133
Fat-soluble vitamins, 196
Fears
    in first adolescence, 258–59
    of preschooler, 313–14
    in toddlerhood, 222–23
Febrile convulsion, *see* Febrile fit
Febrile fit (febrile convulsion, fever fit), 405
Feedback technique, 251, 283, 348, 349
Feeding
    in infancy, 51–52, 122
    sick child, 378
    in toddlerhood, 199
    see also Bottle feeding; Breast feeding
Feeding developments, in infancy, 134–35
    head and trunk control, 134
    self feeding, 134–35
    teeth, 134
    tongue and mouth control, 134
Feeding equipment, in infancy, 135–137
    bibs and coveralls, 137
    clip-on baby chair, 136
    cup, 136
    feeding table, 136
    high chair, 135
    plastic plates, 136–37
    utensils, 136
Feeding equipment, in toddlerhood, 195–96
Feeding table, 136
Feed Me, I'm Yours (Lansky), 199, 295
Feelings
    vs. behavior, 357
    at three to six months, 151–52
    see also Expressing feelings
Feet, of newborn, 39
    see also Extremities; Flat feet
Feingold, Dr., 413
Feingold diet, 413
Female achievements, and toddlerhood, 182
Femoral torsion, 457, 458
Fever, 404–7, 426
    and body temperature, 404, 405–6
    clothing for, 407
    and doctor, 405, 406, 407
    home treatment for, 406–7

and immunizations, 405
medications for, 406, 407
sponging for, 406–7
Fever blisters, 440
Fever fit, see Febrile fit
Fifth disease (Erythema Infectiosum), 399
Finger feeding, 142
Fingernail (torn), first aid for, 467
Fingers, first aid for, 466–67
Finnie, Nancy, 415
Fire (fear of), 368
and preschooler, 314, 325
Firearms, 368
First adolescence, 233–40, 395
caregiver for, 334
developmental milestones in, 236–240
explosive nature in, 233–34
language development in, 237
learning self-care in, 239–40
mental development in, 237–38
motor development in, 236–37
physical growth in, 234–36
social development in, 238–39, 263–64
see also Discipline, in first adolescence; Intellectual stimulation, in first adolescence; Nutrition, in first adolescence
First adolescence, special situations in, 257–69
accident prevention in, 268–69
baby-sitters in, 267
comfort habits in, 257
environmental changes in, 268
fears and phobias in, 258–59
peer interaction in, 266–67
pets in, 268
practice outings in, 264–66
sibling rivalry in, 259
social development in, 263–64
temper tantrums in, 257–58
time out in, 265
toilet learning in, 259–63
First aid, 461–70
and abdominal injury, 461
for amputation, 461
for bites and stings, 462–63
for bleeding, severe, 463
for bones: fractures/dislocations, 463
for burns, 464
for chest injury, 464
for choking, 464–65
for cold exposure, 465
for coma, 465
for convulsions, 465
for drowning, 465
for ear, 465

for electric shock or lightning, 465–66
for extremities, 466–67
for eye injury, 466
for fainting, 467
for genitals, 467
for head injury, 467–68
for heat reactions, 468
and initial assessment, 461
for mouth injuries, 468
for nose, 468
for poisoning, 468–69
for shock, 469
for skin injury, 469–70
for teeth, 470
First-aid supplies, 372–73
First Twelve Months of Life, The (Caplan), 63
Fish bite, first aid for, 462
Fishhook injury, first aid for, 469
Fits, see Convulsions
Fitting-together toys, 211
Five-year-old, 274, 278, 279, 280, 283, 298
Flabby breasts, 82
Flat feet, 456
Flat nipples, 81
Fleas, 173
Floors, accident prevention on, 368
Floppy epiglottis syndrome, 41
Fluids
and bed-wetting, 448
for croup, 428
and fever, 407
and vomiting, 445
see also Liquids
Fluoride, and dental care, 369–70
Fluoride supplement, 76
Fontanelles, 36
Food
during breast feeding, 74
choice of, in toddlerhood, 200
dangerous, 140
hard-to-digest, 140
new, 142, 244
see also Eating style; Nutrition; Solid foods
Food allergies, 76
Foreign body
in ear, 465
in eye, 466
in genitals, 467
in nose, 468
in skin, 469
see also Swallowed foreign body
Foreskin, of penis, 44–45, 448
Formula, for bottle feeding, 91–93
choosing, 91–92
preparing, 92–93
Fossler, Joan, 416

Four to six months to three years, hospitalization at, 379
Four-year-old, 274, 278, 279, 280, 282
Four years to six years, hospitalization at, 379–80
Fractures, first aid for, 463
Frailberg, Selma, 419
Freud, Sigmund, 52
Frostbite, 465
Fruits, 139, 197, 443
Functional murmur, of heart, 363
Funerals, 409–10
Fungal infection, 450–51
Fussy baby, and breast feeding, 83

Gag reflex, 58
Game playing
in first adolescence, 246
in toddlerhood, 191
Games Babies Play (Hagstrom/Morrill), 151
Garage, and accident prevention, 368
Garments, for dressing and undressing baby, 121–22
Gastrocolic reflex, 158
Gastroenteritis, 441, 442, 444
Gastro-intestinal functions, in infancy, 158–62
bowel movements, 158–59
constipation, 159–60
diarrhea, 160–61
indigestion, 161
vomiting, 162
Gastro-intestinal (GI) system, 441–445
abdominal pain, 441–42
constipation, 159–60, 442–43
discoloration of stool, 445
in first adolescence, 236
in infancy, 56
nausea, 445
and preschooler, 276
in toddlerhood, 185
see also Diarrhea; Vomiting
Gender identity, and preschooler, 290
see also Positive gender raising
Genitals
of baby, 126
first aid for, 467
foreign body in, 467
injury to, 467
of newborn, 39
Genitourinary system, 445–49
in first adolescence, 236
in infancy, 163–64
penis, 39, 44–45, 126, 448
and preschooler, 276
swelling and tenderness, 448
in toddlerhood, 185

Genitourinary system (*cont.*)
  urinary tract problems, 445–48
  vagina, 448–49, 467
German measles, 397–98
  see also Rubella
Gesell, Dr. Arnold, 274, 279
Getting home, after baby-sitter, 227
Get a Wiggle On; Move it!!! (Drouillard/Raynor), 420
GI system, *see* Gastro-intestinal system
Give Your Child a Head Start in Reading (Dodson), 153, 212
Glass, and accident prevention, 175, 268
Glass bottles, 91
Glomerulonephritis, 400, 447
Goat's milk, 92, 387
Goiter, 441
Gonococcal infection, preventing, 43–44
Gordon, Dr. Ira, 151
"Gourmets," 70
Grandmother, 47
Grandmother's First Law, 104
Grandparents, 47, 385
Grasp reflex, 40
Grief, at death, 409
Grollman, Earl, 410
Grooming, in toddlerhood, 192
Growing Up Reading (Lamme), 153
Growth and development, problems of, 408–21
  behavioral concerns, 408–11
  developmental concerns, 411
  developmental disabilities, 411–21
Gruenberg, Sidonie, 302
Guide for Helping the Child with Spina Bifida, A (Myers), 419

Haas, Barbara, 381
Hagstrom, Julie, 151
Hair
  of newborn, 36
  of preschooler, 275
Hair loss, *see* Alopecia
Hair plucking, 411
Handedness, 279
Hand expression, *see* Manual expression
Handling the Young Cerebral Palsy Child at Home (Finnie), 415–16
Hands
  cleaning, 125
  at three to six months, 151–52
  see also Extremities
Hard candy, 426
Harlow, Dr. Harry, 52
Harvard Preschool Project, 202

Hatred, *see* Sibling rivalry
Hay fever, *see* Allergic rhinitis
Head
  in first adolescence, 235
  first aid for, 467–68
  injuries to, 431, 467–68
  laceration, severe, or mild injuries, 467–68
  of newborn, 36–37
  of preschooler, 275
  problems, 431–32
  of sick child, 375
  in toddlerhood, 184
Head, neck, and chest problems, 423–41
  ear problems, 435–38
  eye problems, 432–35
  head problems, 431–32
  heart defects, 441
  mouth problems, 439–41
  neck problems, 441
  nose problems, 438–39
  respiratory infections, 425–31
  respiratory tract symptoms, 423–25
Headache, 431
Head banging, 411
  in toddlerhood, 215–16
Head control, 58, 134
Health care, *see* Routine health care
Health concerns, 386–458
  gastro-intestinal system, 441–45
  general, 386–423
  genitourinary system, 445–49
  growth and development, problems of, 408–21
  head, neck, and chest problems, 423–41
  musculoskeletal system, 456–58
  shoe problems, 458
  skin, 449–56
Health problems, 375–458
  chronic illness or impairment, 384–86
  convalescence after hospitalization, 383–84
  health concerns, 386–458
  hospitalization, 379–84
  sick child, 375–79
Health record, birth to six years, 370
Hearing impairment, 417, 438
Heart defects, 441
Heart disease, congenital, 363
Heart rate, of sick child, 376
Heaters, and allergic rhinitis, 390
Heat exhaustion, 367, 468
Heat reactions, 468
Heatstroke (sunburn), 468
Heimlich Maneuver, 464–65
Hemorrhoids, 50
Hepatitis, 404, 441

Hernia, umbilical (navel), 39, 448
  see also Umbilical hernia
Heroin, 75
Herpes simplex, 433, 440
Herpes zoster, *see* Shingles
He's My Brother (Lasker), 418
Hiccups, 123
High chair, 135
High-top shoes, 458
Hip dysplasia, 456
Hips
  dislocation of, 363
  of newborn, 39
Histamine, 454
Hives (urticaria), 387, 391, 454–55
Hoarseness, 424
Holding baby, 110–11, 116
Home chores, and mother working outside home, 336–37
Home environment, during hospitalization, 382–83
Home-prepared baby food, 139
Home-prepared formula, 92
Home University, 29
Honey, 139
Hooked foot, *see* Metatarsus adductus
Hook-together toys, 211
Hookworm, 392, 423
Hormonal changes, in mother, 50
Hornet stings, first aid for, 462
Hospital, early discharge from, 46–47
Hospital Book, The (Haas), 381
Hospitalization, 379–84
  calm reactions to, 382–83
  for cancer, 394
  convalescence after, 383–84
  for croup, 428
  for cystic fibrosis, 402
  expressing feelings during, 383
  four to six months to three years, 379
  four years to six years, 379–80
  for heart defects, 441
  home environment during, 382–83
  newborn to four to six months, 379
  and parents, 381–82, 383
  preparation for, 380–81
  regression during, 382
  for Reye's syndrome, 421
  and self-esteem, 382, 383
  and visitation, 382
Hospital procedures, and newborn, 43–44
Hospital Story, The (Stein), 381
Hot tubs, 325
Household play, 211
Howie Helps Himself (Fossler), 416
Hugging, *see* Physical affection
Humidifiers, 427, 428, 429
  and allergic rhinitis, 390

Hunger
vs. appetite, 132
decreased, 395
see also Feeding
Husband, role of, 47
Hydrocele, 448
Hydrocephalus, 363, 418
Hygiene, general, 124–25
see also Dental care; Dental health
Hyperactive Child and the Family,
The (Taylor), 414
Hyperactivity, and sugar, 198
see also ADD
Hyperglycemia, 402
Hyperresponsive baby, 105, 114, 122
Hyporesponsive baby, 105
Hyposensitization, and allergic
rhinitis, 390, 391
Hypothermia, 465
Hypothyroidism, 424

Ice, 454
Ice chips, 445
Ilg, Dr., 279
Ill-child care, 362
see also Health problems
Illness
frequent, 407–8
mother's, and breast feeding, 84
preparation for, 371–74
resulting in rashes, 454
see also Chronic illness or impairment; Health problems; Sick
child
Imagination, see Right-hemisphere
thinking
Imitating baby, 150
Imitation, 154
Immune system
in first adolescence, 235
in infancy, 57
and preschooler, 275
in toddlerhood, 184–85
Immunization, 364–66
and breast feeding, 85
DPT shot, 364–65, 405
for influenza, 428–29
and measles, 85, 365–66, 405
and mumps, 85, 366
and polio vaccines, 85, 365
and rubella, 85, 366
and whooping cough (pertussis),
365, 400–401
see also Vaccination
Impetigo, 451–52, 455
Impulse control system, and preschooler, 289
Incontinence, bowel or bladder, 410–
411

Independence
in first adolescence, 238
and nutrition, 142
and preschooler, 287
in toddlerhood, 189–91
Indigestion, 161
Infancy, 51–63
behavior in, 55, 104–5
birth to three months, 58–59
and breast feeding, 82–83
cardiovascular system in, 57
caregiver in, 334
endocrine system in, 56
and feeding, 51–52
gastro-intestinal system in, 56
general development in, 57–63
immune system in, 57
memory in, 55
nervous system in, 54
nine to twelve months, 62–63
and philosophy of life, 51–54
physical growth in, 54
physiological changes in, 54–57
respiratory system in, 56
senses in, 55
six to nine months, 60–62
skin in, 56–57
sleep in, 55
stimulation in, 53–54
three to six months, 59–60
touching in, 52
Twin Peaks view of, 51
vision in, 55
see also Babies; Baby; Bonding;
Daily care; Discipline, in infancy; Intellectual stimulation,
in infancy; Newborn; Nutrition,
in infancy
Infancy, special situations in, 158–75
accident prevention, 173–75
bathtime problems, 168
central nervous system immaturity,
166
colic, 83, 167–68, 394, 441
environmental changes, 171–72
gastro-intestinal functions, 158–62
genitourinary system, 163–64
pets, 172–73
separation anxiety, 169–71
skin disorders, 164–66
stranger anxiety, 169–71
teething, 162–63
Infant carrier, 108, 149
Infant seat, 107–8, 125
Infections, 408
bladder, 446
boils, 450
breast, 80
fungal, 450–51
impetigo, 451–52, 455

pinworm, 422–23, 446
ringworm, 392, 450–51
of skin, 450–52
urinary tract, 446
see also Immune system; Respira-
tory infections
Infectious diseases, 403–4
see also Contagious diseases
Influenza, 428–29
Influenza A, 428, 429
Influenza B, 428
Information, vs. intelligence, 28
Information and Referral Service for
Autistic and Autistic-Like
Persons, 414
Ingested poisoning, first aid for,
468–69
Ingrown toenail, 456–57
Inhaled poisoning, first aid for, 469
Injected polio vaccine, 365
Injured-child care, 362
see also Health problems
Injury, preparation for, 371–74
see also First aid
Insect bites, 452–54
chiggers, 452
lice, 452–53
scabies, 453–54
Insights from the Blind (Fraiberg),
419
Insulin, and diabetes mellitus, 402–3
Intellectual development
at birth to three months, 58–59,
147–51
at nine to twelve months, 63
at six to nine months, 61
at three to six months, 60
Intellectual stimulation, in first adolescence, 253–56
concepts, 255–56
music, 256
outings, 254–55
pets, 256
questions, 255
stories, 253–54
television, 253
Intellectual stimulation, in infancy,
147–57
at birth to three months, 147–51
and discipline, 146
sensory and motor stimulation,
147
at six to twelve months, 154–57
at three to six months, 151–53
Intellectual stimulation, and preschooler, 291–92, 308–12
language development, 309–11
mathematics, 311–12
and school, 30
thinking, 310–11

Intellectual stimulation, in toddler-
    hood, 209–14
  body, 214
  outside world, 213–14
  play, 211, 212–13
  playthings, 209–13
Intelligence, 28–30
Intensity of response, 104
Interaction with baby, 116–17
International Association of Parents
    of the Deaf, 417
International Childbirth Education
    Association, 90
Interview technique, and preschooler,
    299
Intestinal blockage, 445
Intoeing, see Pigeon-toes
Intrauterine growth retardation, of
    newborns, 48–49
Inverted nipples, 66
Iron, 76
  in toddlerhood, 196
Iron deficiency anemia, 391
Irrationality, in parenting, 28
Itching, 454
  and allergic rhinitis, 391
I Wish I Had a Computer That
    Makes Waffles (Dodson), 153,
    212, 254, 255
I Wish I Was Sick, Too (Branden-
    burg), 379

James, William, 23, 147
Jaundice, 44, 49
Jealousy, in blended family, 346–47
  see also Sibling rivalry
Johnson, Ann, 299
Johnson, Spencer, 299
Johnson, Virginia, 301
Joints, see Musculoskeletal system;
    Sprain
Junk food, in toddlerhood, 198–99

Kastein, S., 420
Kegels perineal exercises, 50
Kicking, 59
Kidneys, 185
Kitchen, accident prevention in, 367
Knife wound, first aid for, 461, 464
Knock-knees, 456

Labeling environment, 156
Labia, condition of, 39
Laceration, first aid for, 467
Lact-Aid Nursing Supplementer, 84–
    85
Lactation, 73
La Leche League International, Inc.,
    66, 89

Lamme, Linda, 153
Language development
  of babies, 29
  at birth to three months, 58
  in first adolescence, 237
  at nine to twelve months, 62
  and preschooler, 277–78, 309–11
  of pretoddlers, 156
  at six to nine months, 61
  at three to six months, 60
  in toddlerhood, 187–88
Lansky, Vicki, 199, 295
Large-group day care, 332–33, 334
Laryngitis, 424, 425
Lasker, Joe, 418
Laundering cloth diapers, 119–20
Laundry room, accident prevention
    in, 368
Lawrence, Dr. Ruth, 81
Law of the soggy potato chip, 247
Laxatives, 443
Layette, 105–6
Learning disability, see ADD
Learning Games for the First Three
    Years (Sparling/Lewis), 151
Learning process, parenting as, 356
Learning self-care
  in first adolescence, 239–40
  and preschooler, 284–85
  in toddlerhood, 191–93
Left-hemisphere thinking, 310
Leg fracture/dislocation, first aid
    for, 463
Legs, of newborn, 39
  see also Extremities
Lesions, see Sores
Let-down reflex, in breast feeding,
    70–71
Let's Go to the Doctor's Office
    (Pope), 371
Level of sensory threshold, 104
Levy, Dr. Janine, 151
Lewis, Isabelle, 151
Lice, 452–53
Lightning, first aid for, 465–66
Like Me (Brightman), 418
Limp, 457
Lip, cleft, 439
Liquids, 139
  and breast feeding, 73, 74
  see also Fluids
Liver-maturation process, 49
Living room, accident prevention
    in, 367–68
Living with Children (Patterson),
    414
Lochia discharge, 49
Lockjaw, see Tetanus
Logical thinking, see Left-hemi-
    sphere thinking

Long trips, and baby-sitters, 227
  see also Airplane trips
Lotions, 454
Love, in infancy, 52
Lying, and preschooler, 317
Lymph nodes, 441

McCollom, Audrey T., 386
Magazines, 298–99, 303
Magical thinking, of preschooler,
    278–79, 409
  see also Fantasies
Maid service, bonded, 47
Mange, 392
Manual (hand) expression, in breast
    feeding, 72
March of Dimes Birth Defects
    Foundation, 412
Marine animals, 462
Marriage, and vacations, 27
Masters, William, 301
Mastitis, 80
Matches, 325
Mathematics, and preschooler, 311–
    312
MBD (minimal brain dysfunction),
    413
Mealtime
  dawdling at, 318
  and preschooler, 285–86, 318
  in toddlerhood, 199–200
Measles (rubeola), 397, 403–4
  immunization vs., 85, 365–66, 405
Meats, 139
Medical care, for newborn, 44
Medications, 175
  for ADD, 413
  for asthma, 75, 388
  for bites and stings, 462
  for conjunctivitis, 433
  for epilepsy, 416
  for fever, 406, 407
  for hives, 455
  for sick child, 376–78
  for URI, 426
  see also Eye medication
Megacolon, 160
Memory, in infancy, 55
Men, changing roles of, 22–23
Meningitis, 431, 432
Meningo-encephalitis, 431, 432
Mental development
  in first adolescence, 237–38
  and preschooler, 278–79
  in toddlerhood, 188
Mental retardation, 417–18
Metal cars and trucks, 210
Metatarsus adductus (hooked foot),
    457
Middle of the night earache, 437

Milk, 139, 140, 141, 196, 426, 443, 444
  in breast feeding, 75–76, 77
  see also Cow's milk
Milk substitutes, 92, 141, 196
  and allergies, 387
Minerals, 132, 196
Miniature world of people and animals, 211
Minimal brain dysfunction, see MBD
Mirrors, 149
Misbehavior, avoiding as preschooler, 304–7
Mites
  and allergic rhinitis, 390
  and scabies, 453–54
MMR vaccine, 366
Mobiles, 148–49
Molding, 36
Montessori, Maria, 322
Montessori schools, 322
Mood, general, 104
Moro reflex, see Startle reflex
Morrill, Joan, 151
Mother
  and breast feeding, 66, 84
  as caretaker, 102–3
  and chronically ill or impaired child, 385
  early discharge from hospital, 46–47
  and early readers, 30, 308–9
  emotional changes in, 50
  as most important teacher, 358
  nutrition as, 73
  physical changes in, 49–50
  and sick child, 378–79
  in work force, 22
Mother with custody, 339–42
Mother Goose rhymes, 153, 212, 254
Mother working outside home, 329–338
  and caregiver, 330–34
  and home chores, 336–37
  and parent-child bond, 335–36
  preparation for starting work, 334–35
  and quality parenting, 338
  and transitions, 337–38
  when to return to work, 330
Motion sickness, see Travel sickness
Motor development
  at birth to three months, 58
  in first adolescence, 236–37
  at nine to twelve months, 62
  and preschooler, 276–77
  at six to nine months, 61
  at three to six months, 59–60
  in toddlerhood, 186–87
Motor stimulation, for infant, 147

Mouth
  control of, 134
  in first adolescence, 235
  first aid for, 468
  injuries to, 468
  of newborn, 38
  of preschooler, 275
  at three to six months, 152
  in toddlerhood, 184
"Mouthers," 70
Mouth-to-mouth resuscitation, 461, 465
Mouth problems, 439–41
  bad breath, 439
  cleft lip, 439
  cleft palate, 439
  sores, 439–40
  toothache, 440–41
Moving
  in infancy, 172
  in toddlerhood, 228
Mowing grass, and accident prevention, 369
  see also Power mower
"Mr. Rogers" (TV show), 337, 371
Mucus, vaginal, 39
Mud, playing with, 210
Multiple births, and breast feeding, 86
Multivitamin preparation, 196
Mumps, 396
  immunization vs., 85, 366
Murmur, functional (heart), 363
Muscles, see Musculoskeletal system; Strain
Muscular dystrophy, 415
Musculoskeletal system (bone, joints, muscles), 456–58
  bowlegs and knock-knees, 456
  in first adolescence, 236
  flat feet, 456
  hip dysplasia, 456
  ingrown toenail, 456–57
  limp, 457
  pain and swelling in, 457
  pigeon-toes, 457–58
  and preschooler, 276
  in toddlerhood, 185–86
Music
  in first adolescence, 256
  in toddlerhood, 212
Musical instruments, 150
Mutual problem solving, and preschooler, 306–7
Myalgia, 457
My Dentist (Rockwell), 371
Myelomeningocele, see Spina bifida
Myers, E. J., 419
My Friend the Dentist (Watson), 371
My Friend the Doctor (Watson), 371

Nanny, see Baby-sitters
Naps, 72
  in toddlerhood, 219
Nasal decongestants, 426
Nasal-spray products, and allergic rhinitis, 391
National Association for Down Syndrome, 418
National Cystic Fibrosis Foundation, 402
National Easter Seal Society, 415
National Federation of the Blind, 420
National Foundation for SIDS, Inc., 422
"Natural materials," for playthings, 209–10
Nausea, 445
Navel care, 120–21
  see also Hernia
Nearsightedness, 435
Neck, of newborn, 38
Neck injury, first aid for, 461, 463
Neck problems (swelling), 441
Negative attention, 247–48
"Negative" baby, 114–15
Nerve damage, and hearing loss, 438
Nervous system, in infancy, 54
Neural tube defect, see Spina bifida
Neurological system
  in first adolescence, 236
  and preschooler, 276
  in toddlerhood, 186
Neurosis, 25
Newborn, 35–50
  abdomen of, 39
  abilities of, 42
  blood tests for, 45
  breast of, 38
  breathing of, 40–41
  characteristics of, 35–42
  chest of, 38
  circumcision of, 44–45
  contact with, 43
  crying of, 41
  ears of, 38
  eye medication for, 43–44
  eyes of, 37
  feet of, 39
  genitals of, 39
  getting close to, 43
  going home with, 50
  hair of, 36
  head of, 36–37
  hips of, 39
  and hospital procedures, 43–44
  intrauterine growth retardation of, 48–49
  jaundice of, 49
  legs of, 39

Newborn (cont.)
    medical care for, 44
    mouth of, 38
    neck of, 38
    nose of, 38
    postmature babies, 48
    premature babies, 43, 47–48, 84–85
    rashes of, 455
    reflexes of, 40
    and rooming-in, 45–46
    senses of, 42
    and siblings, 46
    skin of, 35–36
    sleeping of, 42
    and special situations, 47–49
    teeth of, 38
    temperament of, 41–42
Newborn to four to six months, hospitalization of, 379
Newborn to three months, medications for, 377
New child, in blended family, 350–51
Newspapers, 298–99, 303
Newsweek, 303
Nicotine, 74
Nightmares, 286–87
Night terrors, 286
Night waking, 131, 394
    and bottle-in-bed habit, 98–99
    in toddlerhood, 221–22
Nine to twelve months, 62–63
    intellectual development at, 63
    language development at, 62
    motor development at, 62
    social development at, 63
Nipples
    for bottle feeding, 91, 97
    for breast feeding, 66–67
    cracked, 81
    flat, 81
    sore, 80–81
Nits, and lice, 453
Noise, 41
Nonsexist child raising, 180–81
Normal Parental Blooper, see N.P.B.
Nose
    in first adolescence, 235
    first aid for, 468
    foreign body in, 468
    injury, 468
    of newborn, 38
    and preschooler, 275
    in toddlerhood, 184
    see also Runny nose; Stuffy nose
Nosebleed, 468
Nose drops
    for sinusitis, 429
    water vs. decongestant, 438–39
Nose problems, 438–39

N.P.B. (Normal Parental Blooper), 25
Nudity, 291
Nursemaid elbow injury, 457
Nursery school, and preschooler, 319–22
    readiness for, 319
    selecting, 319–21
    types of, 321–22
Nursing, and nutrition, 142
    see also Breast feeding
Nursing bottle syndrome, 98, 197
Nursing patterns, for breast feeding, 69–70
Nursing positions, for breast feeding, 67–68
Nursing in public, and breast feeding, 87
Nursing styles, of babies, 70
Nursing support groups, 84, 89–90
Nutrition, 367
    and breast feeding, 73
Nutrition, in first adolescence, 241–45
    how, 243–44
    how much, 245
    what, 242–43
    where, 244
Nutrition, in infancy, 132–43
    basics of, 132–33
    and behavior problems, 141
    and cup, 143
    and eating patterns, 143
    feeding development, 134–35
    feeding equipment, 135–37
    finger feeding, 142
    how, 141
    and independence, 142
    and new foods, 142
    and nursing, 142
    parental influence on, 133–34
    setting stage for, 132
    solid foods, 137–41
    what, 138–41
    and thin vs. fat babies, 133
    when, 137–38
Nutrition, and preschooler, 293–95
    how, 294–95
    what, 294
Nutrition, in toddlerhood, 194–201
    calcium, 197
    choice of foods, 200
    eating with family, 200–201
    eating style, 194–95
    feeding equipment, 195–96
    feeding techniques, 199
    iron, 196
    junk food, 198–99
    mealtime, 199–200
    minerals, 196
    sweets, 197–98

    vitamins, 196
Nuts, 140

Obesity, 133
    see also Overweight
Oil glands, 56
Oils, and eczema, 389
One to three years, medications for, 377
Operating intelligence, 28
Oral contraceptives, 75
Oral polio vaccine, 365
Oral thermometer, 373
Orphanages, 52, 53
Otitis media, forms of, 435
    see also Swimmer's ear
Outdoor climbing equipment, 212
Outdoors
    dressing for, 123–24
    and preschooler, 287
Outings, in first adolescence, 254–55
    see also Practice outings
Outside world
    temper tantrums in, 218–19
    in toddlerhood, 213–14
Overdressing, 124
Overweight, 420–21
    see also Obesity

Pad, for bed-wetting, 448
Panic, and croup, 428
Pants, see Training pants
Parent-child bond, and mother working outside home, 335–36
Parent-child relationship, 299
    in toddlerhood, 189
Parent group, 395
Parenting, 24–25
    and child's intelligence, 28–30
    and child's personality, 30–31
    inconsistency in, 28
    irrationality in, 28
    as learning process, 356
    quality vs. quantity, 338
    rules for, 356, 357
    vacations from, 27
    see also Single parent
Parents
    anger of, 27–28
    as caretakers, 102–3
    and child abuse, 394–95
    and chronically ill or impaired child, 385–86
    of early readers, 30, 308–9
    and hospitalization, 381–82, 383
    mistakes of, 24–25
    and nutrition, 133–34
    responsibility of, 25–27
    rights of, 358
    Ten Commandments for, 355–58

Parents Anonymous, 395
Parent support groups, 385–86, 412
Parents Without Partners, 340
Parmalee, Dr. Arthur, 127
Parroting, see Echolalia
Party shoes, 458
Passing out, and breath holding, 393
Patterson, Gerald, 414
Pediatrician, 361
Pedodontists, 370
Peer interaction
    in first adolescence, 238–39,
        266–67
    and preschooler, 281–84, 288–89,
        318–19
    in toddlerhood, 191
Penis, 39
    foreskin of, 44–45, 126, 448
    see also Circumcision
Peripheral engorgement, 79
Peripheral (side) vision, 55
Personality
    baby as, 104–5
    of children, 31, 356–57
Personality traits, 31
Personal-social interaction, poor, 410
Pertussis, immunization vs., 365
    see also Whooping cough
Pet, 387
    death of, 410
    diseases of, 392
    in first adolescence, 256, 268
    in infancy, 108, 172–73
    and preschooler, 324
    and strep throat, 400
    in toddlerhood, 228–29
Pharyngitis, 430
    see also Sore throat
Phenobarbital, 75
Phenylketonuria, 45
Philosophy of life, and infancy, 51–54
Phobias
    in first adolescence, 258–59
    and preschooler, 313–14
    in toddlerhood, 222, 223
Physical abnormalities, and breast
        feeding, 82
Physical affection, and preschooler,
        299–300
Physical changes, in mother, 49–50
Physical development, in toddler-
        hood, 183–86
    cardiovascular system, 185
    ears, 184
    eyes, 184
    gastro-intestinal system, 185
    genitourinary system, 185
    head and face, 184
    immune system, 184–85
    musculoskeletal system, 185–86

neurological system, 186
nose, mouth, teeth, 184
respiratory system, 185
skin, 183–84
sleep, 183
Physical examination, 362–63
Physical growth, in first adolescence,
        234–36
    cardiovascular system, 235
    ears, 235
    eyes, 235
    gastro-intestinal system, 236
    genitourinary system, 236
    head and face, 235
    immune system, 235
    musculoskeletal system, 236
    neurological system, 236
    nose, mouth, teeth, 235
    respiratory system, 235
    skin, 235
Physical growth, in infancy, 54
Physical growth, and preschooler,
        274–76
    cardiovascular system, 276
    ears, 275
    eyes, 275
    gastro-intestinal system, 276
    genitourinary system, 276
    head and face, 275
    immune system, 275
    musculoskeletal system, 276
    neurological system, 276
    nose, mouth, teeth, 275
    respiratory system, 276
    skin and hair, 275
Physical play
    with baby, 117
    in toddlerhood, 212
Physiological changes, in infancy,
        54–57
Piaget, Jean, 147
Picking up baby, 110–11
Pigeon-toes (intoeing), 457–58
"Pig meal," 295
Pigmentation, 36
Pimples, 36
Pinkeye, see Conjunctivitis
Pinworm infection, 422–23, 446
Plants, 175, 268, 409
Plastic bags, 174
Plastic bottles, 91
Plastic containers, 210
Plastic pants, and diapering, 119
Plastic plates, 136–37
Play
    of pretoddlers, 155–56
    self-expression through, 383
    in toddlerhood, 180, 211, 212–13
    see also Household play; Physical
        play

Playground, accident prevention in,
        369
Playground equipment, 268
Playing "baby," 101
Playpen, 108–9, 153
Playthings, in toddlerhood, 209–13
Plugged duct, 79–80
Pneumonia, 397, 424, 427
Poison, 174, 175, 268, 442
    first aid for, 461, 468–69
    ingested or inhaled, 468–69
Poison ivy, 455–56
Poison oak, 455
Polio immunization, 85, 365
Pollen
    and allergic rhinitis, 390
    and asthma, 388
Pope, Billy, 371
Popsicles, 426, 445
Positive gender raising
    and preschooler, 290
    in toddlerhood, 180–82
Positive reward system, 357
    and courtesy, 297–98
    and dental care, 370
    in first adolescence, 246, 250
    and preschooler, 297–98, 303, 318,
        336
    in toddlerhood, 204–6
    and weaning from bottle feeding,
        100–101
Postmature babies, 48
Postpartum depression, 50
Potential intelligence, 28
Potty chair, 261–62, 443
Power mower, and accident preven-
        tion, 268
    see also Mowing grass
Practice outings, in first adolescence,
        264–66
Pregnancy
    and breast feeding, 86
    and lactation, 73
    and rubella, 397–98
Premature baby, 43, 47–48
    and breast feeding, 84–85
Preschooler, 273–92
    and biological needs, 287–88
    caregiver for, 334
    and death, 409, 410
    and developmental milestones,
        276–87
    and developmental tasks, 287–92
    and expressing feelings, 289
    and family romance, 290
    five-year-old, 274, 278, 279, 280,
        283, 298
    four-year-old, 274, 278, 279, 280,
        282
    and gender identity, 290

Preschooler (*cont.*)
 and home chores, 336
 and impulse control system, 289
 and language development, 277–278, 309–11
 magical thinking of, 278–79, 409
 and mental development, 278–79
 and motor development, 276–77
 and peer interaction, 281–84, 288–89
 physical growth of, 274–76
 and separation from mother, 288
 and sex education, 290–91
 and sleep, 286–87
 and social development, 279–87
 three-year-old, 273, 277–78, 279, 280, 281–82, 296–97
Preschooler, special situations of, 313–25
 and accident prevention, 325
 and adoption, 315
 annoying behavior of, 316
 and baby-sitters, 324
 comfort habits of, 313
 and dawdling, 317–18
 and environmental changes, 324–325
 fears and phobias of, 313–14
 and lying, 317
 and nursery school, 319–22
 and peer interaction, 318–19
 and pets, 324
 and preparation for school, 322–24
 and sibling rivalry, 314
 and social development, 315–16
 and stealing, 317
 and strangers, 316
 temper tantrums of, 313
 whining of, 316–17
 see also Discipline, and preschooler; Intellectual stimulation, and preschooler; Nutrition, and preschooler
Pretoddlers, 154–57
 books for, 156–57
 labeling environment with, 156
 language development of, 156
 play of, 155–56
 toys for, 155
Prickly heat, 36, 165, 456
Private nursery school, 321–22
Problem solving, *see* Mutual problem solving
"Procrastinators," 70
Proteins, 132–33
Psychiatrist, 411
Psychological growth, *see* Mental development
Psychologist, 50, 411
Public library, 303

Pulse, and first aid, 461
Puncture wound, first aid for, 469
Punishment, 247–48
 vs. discipline, 357
 hospitalization as, 380
Pyelonephritis, 446

Quality parenting, vs. quantity parenting, 338
Quarreling, in toddlerhood, 225–26
Questions, in first adolescence, 255
Quiet intellectual play, in toddlerhood, 212
Quiet sleep, 126–27

Rabies, 392
Radioactive materials, 75
Raising the Young Blind Child (Kastein/Spaulding/Scharf), 420
Rapid-eye movement sleep, *see* REM sleep
Rapport, and discipline, 144–45
Rashes, 35–36, 454–56
 diaper rash, 119–20, 164–65, 443, 454
 eczema, 387, 389–90, 454
 hives, 387, 391, 454–55
 illnesses resulting in, 454
 of newborn, 455
 poison ivy, 455–56
 poison oak, 455
 prickly heat, 36, 165, 456
Rat bite fever, 392
Raynor, Sherry, 420
Reactions to new situations, 104
Reading, 153
 early skills, 29–30
 and preschooler, 300, 303
 in toddlerhood, 182
 see also Books
"Reasonable visitation," for father without custody, 343
Rebellion, in first adolescence, 249–250
Records, 150, 153
Rectal thermometer, 373
Red bug, *see* Chiggers
Red Cross, 372
Red measles, *see* Measles
Reflex
 gastrocolic, 158
 in infancy, 58
 of newborn, 40
Refrigerator, bottles out of, 97
Regression, during hospitalization, 382
Regularity, 104
Reinforcement, of behavior, 358

Rejection fears, at four years to six years, 380
Relatives, 47, 331, 334
Relaxation methods, 388
REM (rapid-eye movement) sleep, 126–27, 130, 131
 see also Active sleep
Remarriage, 22
Renoir, Pierre Auguste, 48
Repetition, in infancy, 154
Resources in Human Nurturing International, 84, 90
Respiratory infections, 425–31
 bronchitis, 424, 427
 croup, 427–28
 influenza, 428–29
 pharyngitis (sore throat), 424–25, 430
 pneumonia, 397, 424, 427
 sinusitis, 429–30
 tonsillectomy and adenoidectomy, 430–31
 URI, 424, 425–26
Respiratory rate, of sick child, 376
Respiratory system
 in first adolescence, 235
 in infancy, 56
 and preschooler, 276
 in toddlerhood, 185
Respiratory tract symptoms, 423–25
 cough, 424
 hoarseness, 424
 runny or stuffy nose, 425
 sore throat, 424–25, 430
Response, *see* Intensity of response
Restaurants, 264, 293
 see also Fast-food restaurants
"Resters," 70
Resuscitation, mouth-to-mouth, 461, 465
Retardation, *see* Intrauterine growth retardation; Mental retardation
Retarded baby, and breast feeding, 85
Retention, 447
Reverse time out, in toddlerhood, 206–7
Reward, for toilet learning, 262
 see also Positive reward system
Rey, H. A., 381
Rey, Margaret, 381
Reyes syndrome, 398, 421, 429, 445
Rheumatic fever, 400, 441
Rh factor, 49
Rhinitis, *see* Allergic rhinitis
Rib injury, 464
Rickets, 75, 456
Right-hemisphere thinking, 310, 311
Ringworm infection, 392, 450–51
Ritualism, 169

Rocking, 411
in toddlerhood, 215–16
Rocks, 209–10
Rockwell, Harlow, 371
Rocky mountain spotted fever, 462
Role modeling, in toddlerhood, 182
Role playing, of preschooler, 283, 297–98
Role taking, of preschooler, 283
Room, see Child's room
Rooming-in, 45–46, 84
Rooting response, 40
Roseola, 399
Roundworm, 392, 423
Routine health care, 361–74
dental care, 124, 369–70
doctor visit, 370–71
emergency numbers, 372
exercise, 366–67
first-aid supplies, 372–73
health record, 370
observations and concerns, 364
physical examination, 362–63
preparation for illness or injury, 371–74
screening, 366
temperature taking, 372, 373–74
see also Accident prevention; Immunization; Nutrition
Rubella, immunization vs., 85, 366
see also German measles
Rubeola, see Measles
Rugs, 175
see also Carpets
Runny nose, 425, 439

Sabin, Albert, 365
Safety rules, see Accident prevention
Saliva, 56
Salk, Jonas, 365
Salmonella germ, 392
Sand, playing with, 210
Scabies, 453–54
Scarlet fever, 400, 425
Scarry, Richard, 212
Scharf, B., 420
Schmitt, Dr. Barton, 394
School
and early intellectual stimulation, 30
preschooler preparation for, 322–24
Scorpion bite, first aid for, 462
Scrape or abrasion, first aid for, 469–470
Scratch, first aid for, 469
Screening, 366
Scrotum, 39
Seborrheic diaper rash, 165
Second adolescence, 233

Secret of Childhood, The (Montessori), 322
Seizure disorder, see Epilepsy
Seizures, see Convulsions
Self-assertion, and preschooler, 300
see also Independence
Self-care, see Learning self-care
Self-confidence, and toddlerhood, 179–80
"Self-demand," 52
Self-esteem
and hospitalization, 382, 383
before hospitalization, 381
Self-expression, through play, 383
Self feeding, 134–35
Self-stimulation behavior, 411
Senses
in infancy, 55
of newborn, 42
Sensorimotor stimulation, in infancy, 147, 150–51, 152–53
Sensory threshold, level of, 104
Separation, for baby-sitters, 227
Separation anxiety, 335, 394
and death, 409
at four to six months to three years, 379
in infancy, 169–71
and preschooler, 288
Serous otitis media, 435
"Sesame Street" (TV show), 253, 337
Sex, and breast feeding, 87
Sex education, and preschooler, 290–291, 300–302
Sexual abuse, 396
Sexual stereotypes, 181–82
Shelves, value of, 336
Shields, for breast feeding, 66–67
Shingles (herpes zoster), 398
Shock, first aid for, 461, 469
see also Electric shock
Shoe problems, 458
Shoes, 449
Shoulder fracture/dislocation, first aid for, 463
Showers, 168
Shyness, in first adolescence, 266–67
Sibling rivalry, 23
in first adolescence, 259
and preschooler, 314
and sick child, 379
in toddlerhood, 223–26
Siblings, 108
and breast feeding, 86–87
and chronic illness or impairment, 385
and newborn, 46
Sick baby, and breast feeding, 85
Sick child, 375–79
caring for, 376–79

and doctor, 376
and family needs, 379
feeding, 378
medications for, 376–78
and mother, 378–79
signs and symptoms, 375–76
Sickle cell anemia, 391–92
SIDS (sudden infant death syndrome), 421–22
Sierra Club, 340
Single-bottle method, for bottle feeding, 94–95
Single parent, 24–25, 339–45
father without custody, 343–44
mother with custody, 339–42
widowed single parent, 344–45
Single parent homes, 22
Sinusitis, 429–30
Six to nine months, 60–62
intellectual development at, 61
language development at, 61
motor development at, 61
social development at, 61–62
Six to twelve months
daily care for, 117
intellectual stimulation at, 154–57
Skim milk, 133
Skin
in first adolescence, 235
in infancy, 56–57
of newborn, 35–36
and preschooler, 275
of sick child, 375
in toddlerhood, 183–84
Skin care, and eczema, 389
Skin color, and eye color, 37
Skin disorders, in infancy, 164–66
cradle cap, 56–57, 165–66
diaper rash, 119–20, 164–65, 443, 454
prickly heat, 36, 165, 456
thrush, 166, 440
Skin injury, first aid for, 469–70
bruises, 469
cut or scratch, 469
foreign body, 469
puncture wound, 469
scrape or abrasion, 469–70
see also Amputation; Bites and stings; Burns
Skin problems, 449–56
blisters, 449, 452
burns, 175, 368, 449–50, 464
infections, 450–52
insect bites, 452–54
sunburn, 124, 449–50, 464
wound, 452, 461
see also Rashes
Sleep
bladder control during, 263

Sleep (*cont.*)
  and death, 409
  of newborn, 42
  and preschooler, 286–87
Sleep, of babies, 55, 126–31
  amount of, 127
  bed for, 127
  bedtime blues, 130–31
  falling asleep, 128–29
  through night, 129–30
  night wakers, 131
  patterns of, 129–30
  positions for, 128
  types of, 126–27
Sleep, in toddlerhood, 183, 219–22
  bedtime resistance, 219–20
  crib climber, 220
  naps, 219
  night waking, 221–22
  and staying with child, 221
Sleepy baby, 115
Sliver, first aid for, 469
"Slow to warm up child," 105, 116, 169
Small group day care, *see* Family day care
Smallpox vaccination, 85
Smiling, 42, 59
Smoking, 71, 74
Snacks, 244
Snakebite (nonpoisonous and poisonous), first aid for, 462–63
Snugli Cottage Industries, 108
Soap
  and eczema, 389
  and impetigo, 451
Social development
  at birth to three months, 59
  at nine to twelve months, 63
  at six to nine months, 61–62
  at three to six months, 60
Social development, in first adolescence, 238–39, 263–64
  family interaction, 238
  independence, 238
  peer interaction, 238–39
Social development, of preschooler, 279–87, 315–16
  family interaction, 279–81
  independence, 287
  learning self-care, 284–85
  mealtime, 285–86
  outdoors, 287
  peer interaction, 281–84
  sleep, 286–87
Social development, in toddlerhood, 188–93
  independence, 189–91
  learning self-care, 191–93
  parent/child interaction, 189

peer interaction, 191
Soggy potato chip, law of, 247
"Soiling," 443
Solid foods, and allergies, 387
Solid foods, for baby, 137–41
  conditions for, 141
  time for, 137–38
  types of, 138–41
Soothing baby, 117
Sore nipples, 80–81
Sores (lesions), 439–40
Sore throat, 424–25
  see also Pharyngitis
Souffle, uterine, 42
Soup, 195
Sousa marches, 256
Spanking, 395
  in first adolescence, 247–48
  in infancy, 145–46
  in toddlerhood, 207
Sparling, Joseph, 151
Spas, 325
Spaulding, J., 420
Spider, *see* Black-widow spider; Brown recluse spider
Spina bifida (neural tube defect, myelomeningocele), 418–19
Spina Bifida Association of America, 419
Spitting up, 123, 162
Sponging, for fever, 406–7
Spradley, James, 417
Spradley, Thomas, 417
Sprain (bruising, pain, and swelling of tissues around joint), first aid for, 467
Squint, *see* Strabismus
Stacking toys, 211
Stair guards, 174
Stairways, 368
Startle reflex, 40
Stealing, and preschooler, 317
Steam, for croup, 428
Stein, Sarah Bonnett, 381, 385, 410
Stenosis, *see* Anal stenosis
Stepchildren
  and adoption, 350
  visiting, 351
Stepfamily, larger, 349–50
Stepparents, 23, 346–51
  and emotional adjustments, 346–347
  and larger stepfamily, 349–50
  with no previous children, 346
  questions for, 350–51
  role of, 347–49
Stepping reflex, 40
Stepsiblings, 349
Stimulation, in infancy, 53–54
Stings, *see* Bites and stings

Stool, discoloration of, 445
Store-bought playthings, 210–11
Stories, in first adolescence, 253–54
Strabismus (squint), 275, 434
Straight ahead vision, *see* Central vision
Strain (pain from pulled muscle), first aid for, 467
Stranger anxiety, in infancy, 169–71
Strangers, and preschooler, 316
Street, accident prevention in, 369
Strep throat, 400, 425
Streptococcus germ, 392
Stress, 446
Strollers, 109
Stuffed animals, 152, 387
Stuffy nose, 425
Stuttering, 278
Stye, 434
Substitute care, *see* Caregiver
Sucking, 99
  poor, 82
Sucking reflex, 40
Suckling, 77
Sudden infant death syndrome, *see* SIDS
Sugar, and hyperactivity, 198
Sunbathing, 66
Sunburn, 124, 449–50
  first aid for, 464
  see also Heatstroke
Sunshine, 49, 75
Supplemental bottles, and breast feeding, 88
Supporting response, 40
Support systems, and chronically ill or impaired child, 385–86
Surrogate mother, for breast feeding, 89
Swaddling, *see* Wrapping baby
Swallowables, 174, 175
Swallowed foreign body, 442
  first aid for, 461
Swallowing, as reflexive action, 56
Sweat, 367
Sweat glands, 57
Sweets, in toddlerhood, 197–98
Swelling, and rashes, 454–56
Swimmer's ear (external otitis), 436
Swimming, 369
  and eczema, 389
Swimming pools, 369
Swinging toys, 212
Swings, 108
Swollen eyes, 434
Swollen glands, 441

Tables, 174
  see also Changing table

Talking About Death: A Dialogue Between Parent and Child (Grollman), 410
Talking to baby, 149–50
Taming the Candy Monster (Lansky), 199
Tapes, 150, 153
Taylor, John F., 414
Teacher, 323
Tear duct, *see* Blocked tear duct
Tear glands, 55
Teeth
    in first adolescence, 235
    first aid for, 470
    in infancy, 134
    of newborn, 38
    and preschooler, 275
    in toddlerhood, 184
Teething
    and breast feeding, 89
    in infancy, 162–63
Television (TV)
    in first adolescence, 253
    violence on, 284, 408
Temperament
    of abused child, 394
    of newborn, 41–42
Temperature
    and eczema, 389
    extremes in, 367, 389
    taking, 372, 373–74
    see also Body temperature
Temper tantrums
    and breath holding, 393
    in first adolescence, 257–58
    and preschooler, 313
    in toddlerhood, 190, 216–19
Ten Commandments, for parents, 355–58
Tense baby, 115–16
Tenth Good Thing About Barney, The (Viorst), 410
Terminal heating method, for bottle feeding, 93
"Terrible twos," *see* First adolescence
Testicular torsion, 448
Tetanus (lockjaw), 403
    immunization vs., 365
Thank-you note, 297
Thermal burns, first aid for, 464
Thermometer, reading, 372, 373–74
Thinking, and preschooler, 310–11
Thomas, Dr. Alexander, 25, 104, 105
Three-day measles, *see also* German measles
Three to six months, 59–60
    daily care at, 116–17
    intellectual development at, 60
    intellectual stimulation at, 151–53
    language development at, 60

motor development at, 59–60
    social development at, 60
Three to six years, medications for, 377–78
Three to twelve months, medications for, 377
Three-year-old, 273, 277–78, 279, 280, 281–82
    courtesy for, 296–97
Throwing and catching toys, 212
Thrush, 166, 440
Thumb sucking, 411
Thyroid function, 45
Thyroid gland, 441
Tibial torsion, 457–58
Tick, 173, 462
Time magazine, 303
Time out, 358
    in first adolescence, 248–49, 265
    and preschooler, 285–86, 316–17
    in toddlerhood, 206, 207
    see also Reverse time out
Timing, and separation anxiety, 169–170
Tin cans, playing with, 210
Toddlerhood, 179–93
    caregiver in, 334
    developmental milestones in, 186–193
    exploration in, 394
    joys of, 193
    language development in, 187–88
    mental development in, 188
    motor development in, 186–87
    physical development in, 183–86
    and play, 180
    positive gender raising in, 180–82
    and self-confidence, 179–80
    social development in, 188–93
    see also Discipline, in toddlerhood; Intellectual stimulation, in toddlerhood; Nutrition, in toddlerhood; Sleep, in toddlerhood
Toddlerhood, special situations in, 215–30
    accident prevention in, 229–30
    and baby-sitters, 226–27
    environmental changes in, 227–28
    moving in, 228
    pets in, 228–29
    phobias in, 222, 223
    quarreling in, 225–26
    sibling rivalry in, 223–26
    traveling in, 228
Toe, first aid for, 466–67
Toenail (torn), first aid for, 467
    see also Ingrown toenail
Toilet learning, in first adolescence, 259–63
Toilet teaching, 395

in toddlerhood, 192–93
Token breast feeding, 68
Tongue, of newborn, 38
Tongue control, in infancy, 134
Tonsillectomy, 430–31
Toothache, 440–41
Tooth decay, and sweets, 197–98
Toothpicks, 243
Torn nail, first aid for, 467
Touching, 52
    at three to six months, 151–52
Toxemia, and breast feeding, 84
Toxoplasmosis, 392
Toys, 325
    for pretoddler, 155
    in toddlerhood, 182, 211, 212
Tracheitis, 424
Training pants, 262
Traumatizing child, 25
Traveling
    in infancy, 171–72
    in toddlerhood, 228
Travel sickness (motion sickness), 422
Trench mouth, 440
Trial visits, of baby-sitters, 227
Triplets, 86
Trips, *see* Airplane trips; Long trips; Outings
Trunk control, 134
Tuberculin skin test, 366
Tuberculosis, 403
Tubs, *see* Hot tubs
TV, *see* Television
Twenty-One Balloons, The, 311
Twin Peaks view of infancy, 51
Twins, 86
Two-year-old, *see* First adolescence

Ulcers, 442
Ulrich, Sharon, 420
Ultraviolet light, 49
Umbilical cord, 39
Umbilical hernia, 120–21
    see also Hernia
Umbrella stroller, 109
Unconsciousness, and breath holding, 393
    see also Right-hemisphere thinking
Underarm temperature, 373
Underweight, 420
Undesirable behavior, 358
    in first adolescence, 247–48
Undressing, and dressing, 121–22
United Cerebral Palsy Association, 415
University of California at Berkeley study, 308
University of Rochester study, 84

University of Washington rating
    scale, 339
Upper respiratory infection, see URI
Urethral irritation, 446
URI (upper respiratory infection),
    424, 425–26
Urinary stream, 446
Urinary tract infection (cystitis), 446
Urinary tract problems, 445–48
    bed-wetting, 447–48
    pain and frequency, 446
    retention, 447
    urinary stream, 446
    urine color and odor change, 447
Urination, 185
    and fever, 407
Urine, of sick child, 376
Urine color, and odor change, 447
Urticaria, see Hives
Utensils, in infancy, 136
Uterine souffle, 42
Utility room, accident prevention in,
    368

Vacations, from parenting, 27
Vaccination
    and breast feeding, 85
    for influenza, 428–29
    see also Immunization
Vagina, 448–49, 467
Vaginal mucus, 39
Value system, and preschooler, 298–
    299
Value Tales (Johnson/Johnson), 299
Vaporizer, 426
    and allergic rhinitis, 390
Varicella, see Chicken pox
Vasomotor rhinitis, 425
Vegetables, 139, 140, 443
Venous bleeding (severe), first aid
    for, 463
Very wakeful baby, 115

Veterinarian, 324
Vinegar treatment, for swimmer's
    ear, 436
Violence, and preschooler, 283–84
Viorst, Judith, 410
Viral conjunctivitis, 433
Viral illnesses, 408
Vision, in infancy, 55
Vision impairment, 419–20
Vision problems, 434–35
Visitation, and hospitalization, 382
    see also "Reasonable visitation";
    Trial visits
Vitamin A, 70, 196
Vitamin B_{12}, 74
    see also B vitamins
Vitamin C, 74, 196
Vitamin D, 75, 140, 196, 456
Vitamin E, 70, 196
Vitamin K, 44, 196
Vitamins, 132
    in toddlerhood, 196
Vitamin supplements, and breast
    feeding, 74
Vomiting, 56, 133, 162, 445
    of sick child, 375

Waking, see Night waking
Waking bladder control, 262–63
Walkers, baby, 110
Walleyed, 434
Washing, and impetigo, 451
Wasp sting, first aid for, 462
Wastebaskets, 175
Water
    and accident prevention, 369
    in milk, 75
    playing with, 154, 210
Water nose drops, 438–39
Water-soluble vitamins, 196
Water toys, 211
Watson, Jane, 371
Weaning, 88–89

from bottle feeding, 99, 100–101
    and positive reward technique,
    100–101
Weather, see Cold weather; Tempera-
    ture
Weight loss, and bottle feeding vs.
    breast feeding, 78
Weight problems, 420–21
Well-child care, see Routine health
    care
What's Inside of Me?, 303
Whining, of preschooler, 316–17
White, E. B., 410
Whooping cough, 400–401, 404
    see also Pertussis
Widowed single parent, 344–45
Wing, Lorna, 415
Winnie the Pooh, 311
Wise, Margaret, 410
Women, changing roles of, 22–23
Women's movement, 22
Wonderful Story of How You Were
    Born, The (Gruenberg), 302
Wooden blocks, 210
Wood scraps, 209
Wool, and eczema, 389
Work, and breast feeding, 87–88
    see also Mother working outside
    home
Workshop, accident prevention in,
    368
Worms, 422–23
Wound, 452
    first aid for abdominal, 461
Wrapping baby, 111–12
Writing, and preschooler, 300

Xiphoid bone, 38

Yellow jacket sting, first aid for, 462

Zorba the Greek, 233